ALLSTATE MOTOR CLUB

NATIONAL PARK
GUIDE

Michael Frome

Prentice Hall
New York

Editor-in-Chief
Catherine Fay

Associate Editor
Karen Katz

Production Manager
Diane C. Rote

Advertising Manager
Donna Cleppe

Advertising Production
Lynn Katz

Designer
Danielle Sacripante

PHOTO CREDITS
Cover: Galen Rowell (Olympic NP), Jerry Ellis/Ellis Wildlife Collection (gray wolves). x: Jeff Gnass. 6: Ric Ergenbright. 8: Canada Environment-Parks/B. Olsen (top), Canada Environment-Parks/A. Guindon (middle), Canada Environment-Parks/W. Wyett (bottom). 9: Jeff Gnass (top), Larry Ulrich (bottom). 10: Martin Price (left), Canada Environment-Parks/J. Poirel (right). 14, 17: David Muench. 18: Utah Travel Council. 22: Jeff Gnass. 25: David Muench. 27: Richard Frear for the National Park Service. 28: Jeff Gnass. 30, 32-33: David Muench. 36: Utah Travel Council. 38: David Muench. 42: Richard Frear for the National Park Service. 44: Dennis Halliman for FPG. 46: National Park Service. 50-51: David Muench. 54-55: R. Mason. 57: Tom Bean. 58, 62-63: Jeff Gnass. 68: Pat O'Hara. 73: Jeff Gnass. 75: Tom Algire. 79: Jack Zehrt. 81: Jeff Gnass. 84: Robert Wenkham. 87: David Muench. 89: Richard Frear for the National Park Service. 91: Johnny Johnson/AlaskaPhoto. 93: Charles Krebs/AlaskaPhoto. 95: National Park Service. 97: David Muench. 100: Kentucky Travel Division. 102, 106-107, 110: David Muench. 114: Jeff Gnass. 118: David Muench. 122: Ray Atkeson. 125: Jeff Gnass. 130: Tom Algire. 136-137: Jack Zehrt. 139: Jeff Gnass. 140-141: Fritz Henle. 144, 147: David Muench. 149: National Park Service. 151: Tom Algire. 158-159: Jack Zehrt. 162: David Muench. 166: W.R. Wilson/Alpha. 167: Leila G. Hendron/Starwood. 169: Washington Convention and Visitors Association. 171: United Air Lines. 173: Dick Kent. 174: New Mexico Department of Development (top), American Airlines (bottom). 177: Richard Frear for the National Park Service. 180: Virginia State Travel Service. 187: A.A. Rockefeller Folk Art Museum. 190: Carol Bates. 214: David Muench. 216: Ray Atkeson. 225: M. Woodbridge Williams for the National Park Service. 226: National Park Service. 227: M. Woodbridge Williams for the National Park Service. 248: Toby Ansel Cooper.

Published by Prentice Hall
A division of Simon & Schuster, Inc.
15 Columbus Circle
New York, NY 10023

ISBN 0-13-025412-6

Manufactured in the United States of America.

ABOUT THIS BOOK

Michael Frome's *Allstate Motor Club National Park Guide* is your own personal tour guide—before, during and after your visits to the national parks.

Michael Frome, called "the voice of the wilderness," *knows* the national parks. He has explored them through the years as a camper, backpacker, canoer and horseman. He skillfully guides you through these 49 national parks—each brought to life with vivid portraits that reveal the park's history, geology and unique points of interest, as well as Frome's personal observations of the parks.

A Practical Guide to each park gives vital information on park access, visitor centers, park activities (including birdwatching, hiking, bicycling, fishing), accommodations, climate, weather and recommended reading. Full-color, detailed maps add yet another dimension to the guide's planning aids.

In addition to this wealth of information on the individual parks, the guide explores the many other areas administered by the National Park Service. These include the parks and monuments found in and around Washington, DC, and historical archaeological ruins throughout the country. In addition, the country's national historical parks, military sites, battlefields, memorials and cemeteries are explored.

This year, new national monuments, historic sites, historical parks and more have been added to the *National Park Guide*. See the Additional National Park Service Areas section for these newly added areas: Charles Pinckney National Historic Site, San Francisco Maritime National Historical Park, Mississippi National River and Recreation Area, Hagerman Fossil Beds National Monument, City of Rocks National Reserve, Zuni-Cibola National Historical Park, Steamtown National Historic Site, Poverty Point National Monument, National Park of American Samoa, Kalaupapa National Historical Park and Jimmy Carter National Historical Site.

Lastly, our nation's national treasures, the natural and recreational areas—parkways, seashores, lakeshores, riverways and more—are colorfully described.

This guide also devotes separate chapters to treasures of Canada's national parks and to Alaskan monuments, preserves and historical parks. To help you plan your stay, a handy guide to lodgings is offered.

Michael Frome has provided us with a thoughtful update on Yellowstone National Park. He reminds us that there is more to the fires of 1988 than the charred forest. Fire, he tells us, marks a rebirth, and a continuation of life that visitors to the park can observe, absorb and appreciate. Yellowstone visitors have the opportunity to examine the greatest example of a Yellowstone fire in 300 years, to look, listen and learn, to express their views and to help.

We are confident that you will enjoy your national parks visits with the aid of your personal tour guide to the national parks.

CONTENTS

THE NATIONAL PARKS

ADDITIONAL NATIONAL PARK SERVICE AREAS

LIST OF MAPS

The 1990 Volkswagen Camper.

It only makes sense that a camper this versatile would be engineered by Volkswagen. After all, we pioneered our first Camper over 35 years ago. And since then, hundreds of thousands of Campers have carried the Volkswagen logo. So it should come as no surprise that Volkswagen

has developed a camper that's both a great recreational vehicle and a mini-van you can drive every day.

You won't believe the space. Look inside the Camper and your first reaction will be: How did the Volkswagen engineers do it? Design a fully-equipped kitchen in a vehicle this size? And still give you so much room to live. The Camper is a study in the efficient use of space. It has a refrigerator, a two-burner stove, a stainless steel sink with running water, two fold-out tables, two separate sleeping compartments (with double beds)—all in a vehicle that's shorter than any midsize station wagon.

Then there's the unique Volkswagen pop-top. This distinctive feature really sets Camper apart. Pop it up and you get eight feet of interior headroom. Plus a second story window that lets in light and fresh air. And best of all, our one-of-a-kind pop-top opens and closes in seconds. So you'll spend less time setting up and breaking down your camp and more time camping.

And you'll love the Camper's storage space. There are eight separate storage areas, including a hanging closet, a large storage area under the rear seat and another one behind the rear seat. So Camper has enough room to keep your camping supplies stored away—on board—all the time.

It's the camper you can drive every day.

You won't believe the versatility. Unlike many RV's, the Volkswagen Camper is a mini-van you'll enjoy driving every day. It's the perfect vehicle for your daily commute. Camper has rack-and-pinion steering, 4-wheel independent suspension and a 2.1 liter fuel-injected engine. For a car-like ride that's unmistakably Volkswagen. Camper's wheelbase is shorter than every domestic mini-van on the market, too. So it's easy to maneuver in traffic and easy to park.

And how many RV's can fit easily into a standard garage?*

Think of the Camper as part mini-van, part limousine, part pick-up truck and part recreational vehicle and you'll understand what we mean by versatile. Plus Camper is available in 4-wheel drive!

You won't believe the price. Volkswagen is the only carmaker today that combines European design and performance with an affordable price. And Camper is no exception. This year's model comes with a base price of only $20,990.** And that includes a long list of standard features—even air conditioning. Camper hasn't been this affordable in years.

Compare the price of our Camper with other fully-equipped RV's and you'll see why it's time to think about Volkswagen again.

For more details, call **1-800-444-VWUS**.
*Garage door heights may vary.
**M.S.R.P. does not include options, tax, registration, destination charges or dealer prep. Model shown has optional alloy wheels.

It's time to think about Volkswagen again.

PREFACE TO THE TWENTY-FOURTH EDITION

From time to time I am asked to name my favorite national park or parks, and I always try to respond, but it's like asking a parent to pick a favorite child; the only answer can be, "I love them all, equally." The truth is that I never met a national park I did not like or would not recommend.

Nevertheless, at this particular moment I recall the satisfaction and pleasure derived from a recent visit to Harry S Truman National Historic Site, at Independence, Missouri, a few miles east of Kansas City. Theodore Roosevelt once called the Grand Canyon "the one great site every American should see." Well, maybe the Truman home is that kind of place, too. It has grandeur in its simplicity, reflecting the lifestyle of "a most uncommon common man," and a lesson for all of us in his ways and words, such as "I tried never to forget who I was and where I'd come from and where I was going back to."

The Truman home is very well maintained. Harry's coat, distinctive hat, and cane hang in the hall as though waiting for him to take his usual early morning walk. The dining room table is set with Bess's own china as if for a family dinner. And so on throughout the house, which receives the care and attention it deserves from the National Park Service. This includes a limitation on the number of people admitted to visit the home every day, not to dent access, but rather to protect the property and to enhance the quality of the visit as an intimate experience.

I think of other homes of presidents administered by the National Park Service and cite them, too, as favorites. I like the Herbert Hoover National Historic Site, at West Branch, Iowa, showing the humble beginning of the 31st president, the first president born west of the Mississippi River. The birthplace cottage itself, amazingly, is only 14 feet by 20 feet. Along the walking trail, it's easy to spend hours looking at buildings and exhibits, and at the parcel of restored prairie, a part of the mid-continent landscape that has virtually disappeared elsewhere.

Another choice national historic site, overlooking the Hudson River at Hyde Park, New York, memorializes the president who succeeded Hoover, Franklin D. Roosevelt. He himself, though physically disabled, loved the outdoors and was an ardent conservationist, as plainly evident in the woods and gardens of the historic site. Theodore Roosevelt was also a conservation leader, and anyone interested in his life can trace it from its very beginning at Theodore Roosevelt Birthplace National Historic Site, in downtown New York City, to Theodore Roosevelt National Park, in North Dakota, where he came as a young adventurer to hunt buffalo and learn about life, to Theodore Roosevelt Inaugural National Historic Site, at Buffalo, where he took the oath of office in 1901, to Sagamore Hill National Historic Site, his summer White House at Oyster Bay, Long Island, where he retired and lived out his years.

Much of Abraham Lincoln's life is also chronicled in national parks, from the Abraham Lincoln Birthplace National Historic Site in Kentucky, through the Lincoln Boyhood National Memorial in Indiana, the Lincoln Home National Historic Site (the only house he ever owned), the scene of his memorable address at Gettysburg National Military Park in Pennsylvania, Ford's Theatre National Historic Site (where he was fatally shot), and the Lincoln Memorial, that classic structure of dignity and beauty bordering the Potomac River in Washington, DC.

All of these and other presidential homes and shrines are part of the National Park System. Some, however, are not. Mount Vernon, George Washington's home in Virginia, was rescued privately by concerned citizens long before national parks were conceived (although George Washington Birthplace National Monument, near Fredricksburg, Virginia, later became one of the first historic areas administered by the National Park Service). Monticello, Thomas Jefferson's home at Charlottesville, Virginia, also is administered by a private, nonprofit group. I should mention also the home of Calvin Coolidge, at Plymouth, Vermont, which I visited last year and found a pleasant, rewarding lesson in history, another example of citizen initiative and responsibility.

We need these places as sources of learning and pride in where we have been as a people. We need them in this age of accelerated change to help choose the future heading. I feel privileged to show through the pages of the *National Park Guide* where they are located, and how to enjoy and benefit from these special places.

Michael Frome

ENJOY YOUR VISIT TO THE PARKS

The key to getting full enjoyment out of the national parks is simple. Take it easy. Slow down. Plan your itinerary. Prepare for what you're going to see and do.

Those who try to see the maximum number of parks in the least time miss the message. They make it through the parks, touching only the centers, with little chance to explore. They are part of the crowds and congestion, ending at home in need of a break.

But you can use this book as your planning guide and return home refreshed and uplifted. Follow the slower pace to expand the dimensions of time. It isn't a question of how extensively or expensively one travels, but how intensively and perceptively. Visiting fewer parks, staying longer at each one, leads to better appreciation and more enjoyment.

Start with outlook and attitude, a willingness to adopt an unhurried approach. It's not simply a matter of where but of how—*how* to look at national parks, *how* to absorb the wonders of nature, *how* to reorient patterns of travel and thinking.

National parks are places where young and old can find inspiration. Major parks are crowded, that is true, but mostly at core areas where people congregate because they are used to urban ways. Only a short distance away lie solitude and discovery, with respite from sights, sounds, smells and pressures of civilization.

Proper planning. Preparing to explore the parks can be almost as important as the trip itself. Ask yourself these questions (using a notebook to record the answers will help):

In the given amount of travel time, how much distance will I cover?

How much time will I spend in each national park I intend to visit?

Which principal sights will I see in each park and along the way? In which activities (such as hikes and float trips) will I participate?

Do I have at least a rough idea of accommodations and/or campgrounds on the itinerary? Do I have a reservation for the first night? Am I planning to arrive at a decent hour so that I can be sure of finding a place before dark?

Do I have the proper equipment—for hiking, camping, boating? Have I fully considered climate and weather?

Am I leaving home with enough money to get me there and back? Or, perhaps, should I shorten the trip, or cover less distance, to eliminate the chance of running out of funds?

Have I left word with family and friends on how to reach me in an emergency?

Figure out the answers before you leave and you won't have to worry about them later.

Choose the season. If you must travel in summer, try to go early or late to avoid the mid-season peak. In the parks of the northern Rockies, the best time for a wilderness trip is between July 15 and September 15. In the southwestern mountains, conditions are usually favorable from mid-June to early October.

Although summer has been accepted for years as virtually the only period to visit the national parks, more national parks are open throughout the year than most people realize. Autumn is superb. In the eastern national parks, autumn is an outstanding time for backcountry hiking. The leaves turn color; skies are clear; the sun is bright. Even in the northern parks, roads and some overnight lodgings are open until late October. The desert wilderness shows its spectacular blossoms in late winter and early spring. Best of all, the scene is natural. The animals are relatively undisturbed, the way all visitors hope to see them.

Winter in the parks. One way or another, winter's magic touches almost all national parks. At Mount Rainier, rangers conduct snowshoe walks, for which the Park Service furnishes snowshoes free of charge. The park publishes its own winter tabloid, *The Snowdrift*, full of news about weather, winter activities, accommodations and safety hints. At Yosemite, the Natural History Association conducts winter environmental education programs, including bird watching, field ecology and a seven-day trans-Sierra environmental ski tour.

Such programs are given all across the country. Even urban national parks take on lively winter personalities. In the National Capital Region, at Washington, D.C., you can ice skate near the Lincoln Memorial (when conditions are right), take winter bird walks, learn about winter botany at the Kenilworth Aquatic Gardens, or spend a winter afternoon at Fort Washington Park on the Maryland shore of the Potomac River. Take advantage of these activities. Parks are usually less crowded in winter.

Campground reservations. The National Park Service operates a computerized reservations system for major campgrounds in certain popular parks. Ticketron receives and processes the reservations for these park areas: Acadia, Maine; Cape Hatteras, North Carolina; Grand Canyon, Arizona; Great Smoky Mountains, Tennessee-North Carolina; Rocky Mountain, Colorado; Sequoia-Kings Canyon, California; Shenandoah, Virginia; Yellowstone, Idaho-Montana-Wyoming; and Yosemite, California. You can make reservations in person at many Ticketron outlets. Otherwise, to request a mail-in reservation brochure, write to Dept. R, 401 Hackensack Avenue, Hackensack, New Jersey 07601.

Other park areas accepting mail reservations (but not on the Ticketron system) include Dinosaur National Monument, Colorado-Utah; Cumberland Island National Seashore, Georgia; Ozark National Scenic Riverways, Missouri; and Virgin Islands National Park. Specify desired dates when you write, but do not send the reservation fee until receiving written confirmation.

The remainder of the campgrounds operate on a first-come, first-served basis. Plan to arrive early to get a better site; most open at 8 a.m.

Entrance fees. In 1987, entry fees were raised at many parks and were instituted for the first time at other parks, monuments and historic sites where admission formerly was free. Where does the money go? Until now, rarely did the fees collected directly benefit the parks you paid to visit. But Congress has directed that each park's budget will reflect the amount of money collected; thus, you are helping to pay for park programs and maintenance. If you plan to visit several park areas in one year, or stay a while in any one, take advantage of a Golden Eagle Pass, a Golden Age Passport, or a Golden Access Passport, which you can obtain at any national park or national forest area where fees are charged.

The Golden Eagle Pass allows the bearer, plus all those accompanying him in a private vehicle, to enter all federal recreational fee areas. It costs $25, and covers the entrance fee only, not overnight camping fees.

The Golden Age Passport is for senior citizens, 62 years of age or older. The Golden Access Passport is for residents of the United States who are permanently disabled, blind, or otherwise eligible for federal disability benefits. Both are free of charge and provide a 50% reduction on overnight camping fees at most federal camping areas. Golden Age and Golden Access Passports are readily granted to all those eligible, but applications must be made in person.

Tune in to a park. When driving through a number of national parks, you can listen to more than music on your car radio—and get some excellent information. Stations operated by the Park Service are 10-watt units usually broadcasting at 1610 on your dial.

Bird watching. "Birding" is one of the best activities to bring you in tune with nature. Stop at the Visitor Center for a copy of the park checklist so you can keep notes on the birds you see. Carry along a good bird guide and binoculars. Birding is rewarding in all seasons, usually best in early morning and evening.

Join a group. A novice does well to join an outdoor or hiking club, in which he or she can benefit from trips in association with experts. Chances are there is such a club in your community or at a nearby college, sponsoring low-cost trips to national parks and other attractive areas. The American Wilderness Alliance (7600 East Arahapoe Road, Englewood, Colorado 80112) offers an extensive series of guided trips throughout the West. The American Hiking Society sends teams of volunteers (in good physical condition, between the ages of 16 and 70) to work on projects ranging from trail maintenance in Maine to log cabin construction in Alaska. For information, send a self-addressed, stamped business envelope to AHS Volunteer Vacations, Box 86, North Scituate, Massachusetts 02060.

National forests and other areas. National forests, administered by the Department of Agriculture, have thousands of campsites in their recreation areas. The Bureau of Land Management, a sister agency of the National Park Service in the Department of the Interior, has campsites and recreation areas in western states and Alaska. The Indian people have done the same on their reservations.

Consider also the facilities in state parks, recreational areas administered by the U.S. Army Corps of Engineers at major public reservoirs, and private campgrounds.

More fun without a car. Alternatives to private transportation—such as buses and trams—have proved successful in a number of parks. They help protect the park environment from heavy auto traffic, noise and pollution. When operated by the government, transportation services often are free. When run by concessionaires, there usually is a charge.

Seasonal shuttles are operating at Grand Canyon, Arizona; Grand Teton, Wyoming; Mesa Verde, Colorado; Denali, Alaska; North Cascades, Washington; Zion and Bryce, Utah; Dinosaur National Monument, Colorado-Utah; Carl Sandburg Home National Historic Site, North Carolina; and Kennesaw Mountain National Battlefield Park, Georgia.

Some national parks have developed bike routes, with rentals available. In Yosemite, 150 miles of road are available for cycling, with 20 miles of level road in the valley. Grand Teton has white-striped 25 miles of four-foot-wide paved shoulders in rolling terrain between Jenny Lake and Jackson Lake Lodge for the use of cyclists and pedestrians. You can also bike at Mesa Verde, Glacier and Grand Canyon. The new off-road touring bikes enlarge opportunities, but create problems in resource protection. Check park regulations and live up to them.

Bike routes are installed at some national parks in the East also. You'll find them at Cape Cod National Seashore, Massachusetts; Fire Island National Seashore, New York; and the Chesapeake & Ohio Canal National Historical Park, which extends 185 miles from Washington, D.C., to Cumberland, Maryland. In the Washington, D.C., area, bike paths are extremely popular with visitors and residents alike. Ask for a copy of the *Bike Guide to Washington Area National Parks*, which shows bike routes and rental locations.

For long-distance biking between the parks, consult Bikecentennial, Box 8308, Missoula, Montana 59807. It offers conducted tours as well as a set of cycling maps that cover the country. Of special value are Great Parks North Bicycle Route, Great Parks South Bicycle Route and Southwest America Bicycle Trail.

When cycling in the parks, please comply with regulations and use common sense. Treat bicycling in the parks as a tour, never as a race.

Getting there on public transportation. It can be done, often inexpensively. Bus companies offer low per-mile fares to large and small towns across the continent, as well as discount plans that allow unlimited riding for a week to a month. Air fares are a bargain on high-volume, competitive routes, such as New York-Miami, New York-San Francisco, Chicago-Los Angeles, but they are expensive when flying to small towns, including national park gateways. Amtrak rail fares generally are more expensive than motor coach for the same distance, but less than regular air fares. Watch them all for discounts and excursions.

Most intercity bus lines, trains and airlines have facilities for handling backpacks and skis. However, aluminum frame backpacks are apt to receive harsh treatment on the planes. You can haul more gear with less strain on a bus or train.

For people with physical disabilities. National parks are intended for the use and enjoyment of all people. Federal regulations require elimination of physical barriers to people with physical disabilities wherever government funding is involved. This means that provisions for people who are deaf, blind and confined to wheelchairs must be made in the design of all buildings and facilities of the national parks. A booklet titled *Access National Parks: A Guide for Handicapped Visitors* is available from the Superintendent of Documents. The price is $6.50. See address below under "Publications."

Photography. Plan to bring back a picture record of your travels, but don't let picture taking get in the way of personal observation. The best wildlife picture is one of an animal in its natural habitat—feeding, resting or whatever—and unaware of the photographer. Don't crowd animals; allow them to act naturally by using a long telephoto lens. Be patient; be safe. Good photographs are the product of time.

Use a tripod whenever possible; a steady camera improves photo sharpness. Have plenty of film to allow bracketing and to catch combinations of action and scenery.

Publications. Other helpful booklets issued by the National Park Service include: *National Parks: Camping Guide*, which specifies the camping seasons, duration of stay permitted, fees and facilities available (the price is $3.50). This can be ordered from the Superintendent of Documents, U.S. Government Printing Office, Washington, D.C. 20402. Make checks or money orders payable to the Superintendent of Documents.

Many park Visitor Centers also sell publications that help the visitor understand the history, geology, plants and wildlife of the area.

Pets. Your dog or cat is welcome to join you in visiting the national parks, but it must be kept in your car, on a leash, or caged at all times. Animals are not permitted in public buildings or on trails—with the exception of guide dogs for persons who are blind or deaf. Remember not to leave a pet in a car on a hot day—it may suffer heat stroke, even with the windows open.

Backcountry use permits. These are now required at about 45 major areas. Six areas require permits for white-water float trips on rivers flowing through their boundaries.

Both permits and reservations are free. They generally cover specified trail or boat access camping areas in remote portions of the parks.

For additional information on backcountry permits and reservations, address Backcountry Information at the park you plan to visit. For white-water permits, write River Trips at the park of your choice.

Equipment and clothing. Your choice of equipment and clothes can mean the difference between an enjoyable trip and an ordeal. Learn the temperature range in the part of the country you're visiting and dress accordingly. Use the "layer system," wearing extra garments as you need them, then peeling them off as the weather moderates. Wear a pair of good boots (broken in) and heavy socks to prevent blistering. Have confidence in your sleeping bag to keep you warm in the weather you're facing or change your plans. A tent protects you in bad weather, but its added weight and bulk must be considered. Because open fires are forbidden in some areas, a stove may be necessary.

Develop your own equipment check list. Make sure it includes the following:

Underwear	Eyewear
Outerwear	Tent
Footgear	Ground cloth, insulated pad
Gloves	Sleeping bag
Headgear	Stove and eating gear
Backpack	Flashlight and lantern

Make sure you're prepared for whatever the weather may offer. Such items as wool shirt, heavy sweater, down vest, parka shell and rain pants will come in handy at one point or another. Don't cut corners. Purchase good quality equipment—you're investing in comfort and safety.

Park roads. The routes in a park are not expressways, so take it easy and concentrate on driving. Enjoy the view from overlooks and parking areas. Then make caution your constant companion when leaving the car.

Lyme disease alert. It's something new, caused by tick bites. You'll see warning signs posted in parks where the disease has been found. Best prevention is protection against ticks: use tick repellant; wear long pants; undress and check for ticks. Lyme disease is treatable with antibiotics.

Value your valuables. And they will always be yours. Of all your fellow park visitors, 99 percent are as honorable and trustworthy as you. But watch out for that other 1 percent! Thieves visit national parks, and look for easy prey.

When away from your car, lock everything of value in the trunk, or put it out of sight. Lock all doors and windows. Wherever you stay, keep your radios and cameras out of sight. Thieves look for easy pickings along main park roads where people congregate. You can help the rangers by advising them of suspicious persons in campgrounds and parking areas. Vacationers in the outdoors are in a relaxed frame of mind. Keep your guard up, practice precautions, and you won't be sorry later.

Some words of caution. National parks are governed by rules and regulations; they must be, considering the heavy volume of visitors and the need to protect their resources. But rules involve simple courtesy and common sense. They add to your safety and enjoyment. Use only the designated campgrounds, which are developed for your convenience. Please maintain quiet from 10 p.m. to 6 a.m. Build a fire only in a campground fireplace and extinguish it completely when you leave. Do not smoke on the trail. If you feel you must, stop in a cleared area. Carry out all burned matches, ashes and butts. When driving, use your ashtray. Report fires immediately to a park ranger.

Tread softly, tread lightly. National park use has risen dramatically. Backpackers and day hikers number at least 30 million and are growing by 10 percent annually. Wilderness use in the Grand Canyon alone has increased more than 300 percent in a decade. This kind of growth can't help but have an adverse impact on fragile nature. Try for minimum impact. It costs you nothing. It takes only common sense. The following few tips may help.

Stay on the trails. They lead to your destination via the best route and are marked and designated for your protection. Cutting across switchbacks looks easier, but it can prove dangerous and contributes to erosion.

Use designated campsites where provided, or sites previously used, or sites least damaging to vegetation. Choose a location a reasonable distance away from water to prevent pollution and to allow access for wildlife. Avoid making "improvements," like trenching around tents.

Eliminate need of fires. Campfires are likely to kill vegetation at the site, change soil chemistry and alter ecosystems. Use lightweight backpack stoves. In the hot summertime, it's a good idea to carry meals that require no cooking.

Wash—yourself, dishes, clothes—away from streams and lakes. Carry water to your campsites for these jobs. Use biodegradable soaps (such as Ivory or castile products). Dispose of wastewater away from water sources.

Use toilets where provided. Otherwise, when nature calls, choose a spot away from trails, campsites and water sources—preferably in rich soil. Dig a hole about 6 inches deep; when through, cover it with soil removed. Natural decomposition will do the rest.

Refuse to leave refuse. Pack out what you packed in, crushing cans for compactness. Use emptied food containers for leftovers or messy liquid garbage. If you find somebody else's litter, pack it out, too. We know Indians by their arrowheads—should we be known by our beer cans?

Tread safely. Going alone is officially and properly discouraged, but absolutely meant for some people, at certain times. Keep within the range of your physical capability. Allow about one hour for each 2 miles covered, plus an additional hour for each 1,000 feet of altitude gained. Let someone know your plans.

Guard against giardia, a protozoa that causes "backpacker's diarrhea." Boil water on the trail for one minute or use commercial treatment tablets. And guard against hypothermia, the number one killer of outdoor recreationists. Dress properly to stay dry and warm. Avoid challenging stormy weather. Take along and nibble on high-energy foods.

When lost, try to retrace your steps to where you left the trail. If that fails, don't panic! Find shelter; mark your location (make a large "X" on the ground with clothes and gear so it can be seen from the air). Stay in one place—you'll be found more quickly.

Children on an outing are eager to explore new surroundings, so keep an eye on them. A child can become confused only a few yards from a trail or camp and can easily be lost. Don't let them play near mountain streams unattended at any time, especially during spring runoff.

Fill out the trail registers. This safety measure pinpoints your location, and helps park personnel learn from your answers how better to care for the backcountry. Before you go, study park maps and plan your itinerary carefully. Discuss your trip with park personnel at a visitor center or ranger station. Ask about weather and trail conditions.

Treat all animals as wild. Park regulations that prohibit feeding of bear or deer and the mol-esting of any animal are enforced on your behalf, as well as the animals'. Remember that national parks are meant for wild animals to roam free in *their* native habitat. Some knowledge of wildlife habitats will help you find the animals, and so will a good pair of binoculars. The best approach is to rise with the sun and to hike through forest and meadows. By 8 or 9 a.m., many animals are in seclusion, not seen again till dusk.

Respect the bears. If one approaches your car, stay in it with windows closed until the bear goes on its way. Even though bears appear tame, they may turn impulsively and inflict serious injury. Do not feed, tease, or frighten them in any way. When camping, avoid the use of odorous foods and suspend your food between trees high off the ground. Cook away from your sleeping area, where possible, and keep your possessions clean.

Keep a record of what you see and where; take pictures and pleasant memories to your home. Leave only your footsteps for your family to retrace another day.

Bouquets and brickbats. Take a few minutes when you return home to dispatch letters of praise or complaint. These are *your* national parks and you're entitled to the last word. The best single individual to write to is your congressman or congresswoman. He or she should welcome your views. Write a letter to the editor of your hometown newspaper, too. Let everyone know how you found the parks and how you feel about them.

CANADA'S NATIONAL PARKS

More Treasures to Explore

IN THE SUMMER of 1986 I was traveling with a friend around Lake Superior, the largest and maybe the loveliest, certainly the least spoiled, of all the Great Lakes. We were visiting national park areas on the U.S. side (Grand Portage National Monument in Minnesota, Apostle Islands National Lakeshore in Wisconsin, Pictured Rocks National Lakeshore in Michigan, and Isle Royale National Park, a part of Michigan but the largest island in the lake) and seeing what the Canadians had on their side. When we reached Pukaskwa (pronounced *Pukasah*) National Park, on the northeast Ontario shore of Superior, I was astonished at the wild beauty of its ridges, cliffs, rock-rimmed lakes, streams, and forests.

I realized that here was an area fully worthy, by any standards, of the designation "national park." It was not only appealing, but readily accessible. And so it is with most of Canada's national parks. There are now more than 30 of them, at least one in every province and territory. They aren't all as convenient as Pukaskwa, but the remote Canadian parks challenge the adventurer and show what all the continent was like when life was new and fresh.

Canadian national parks are almost as old as ours. Yellowstone was established in 1872 and Banff, in the Canadian Rockies, in 1885. Work crews were building the railroad, opening frontiers, when someone had the bright idea that a part of the great land should be set aside, free of development and exploitation. Canada, one of the most beautiful countries on earth, thus wisely chose a course to preserve examples of its varied landscapes, along with untamed plant life and wildlife, forests and streams.

Actions were taken in 1987 to establish two outstanding new national parks:

BRUCE PENINSULA, Ontario. A national marine park, protecting shoreline, lake bottom, and nearby islands, as well as spectacular limestone cliffs, caves, and grottoes along the edge of Georgian Bay at the northern end of the Niagara escarpment. It is Ontario's fifth national park, only a four-hour drive from metro Toronto.

SOUTH MORESBY, British Columbia. One of the southernmost islands of the Queen Charlotte chain in the northern Pacific, long the sacred home of Haida Indians, the park now preserves ancient rain forest, islands, lakes, coastline, and cultural heritage. The south end of Moresby is about 120 miles from the north end of Vancouver Island, accessible by B.C. ferry from Vancouver and Prince Rupert.

Best way to obtain details on these and other national parks is to write Parks Canada, Ottawa, Ontario, Canada K1A 1G2. Write also to Canadian Government Office of Tourism, 235 Queen Street, Ottawa, Ontario, Canada K1A 0H6. Ask for addresses of provincial departments of tourism, excellent sources of travel guidance. In addition to national parks, look for Canadian national historic parks and provincial parks to explore and enjoy.

Following, to get you started, are thumbnail sketches of the national parks, listed by province or territory.

Newfoundland

TERRA NOVA. Board a summer cruise boat to see whales and icebergs in Bonavista Bay. Canoe and fish freshwater streams and sheltered saltwater inlets. Hike the Atlantic coastline.

GROS MORNE. Climb the James Callaghan Trail to the summit of Gros Morne Mountain (seven hours round trip) for magnificent vistas of mountains, lakes, fjords, and the Gulf of St. Lawrence. Take the fjord cruise of Western Brook Pond.

Nova Scotia

CAPE BRETON HIGHLANDS. The historic Cabot Trail, now a paved highway, runs along three sides of the park, with shoreline vistas. Hike the trails, swim from sand beaches, or play golf on one of Canada's finest courses.

KEJIMKUJIK. Canoe and hike the rolling wilderness landscape of lakes and rivers in the footsteps of Micmac Indians. The gateway to the park is about 100 miles southwest of Halifax.

South Moresby National Park

Cape Breton Highlands National Park

Pukaskwa National Park

Prince Edward Island

PRINCE EDWARD ISLAND. Along the northern coast of Prince Edward Island, explore 25 miles of sand dunes and red sandstone cliffs. Visit fishing villages and swim from saltwater beaches.

New Brunswick

FUNDY. Observe the famed high tides rise and fall twice daily. Then walk the tidal flats during low tide to see barnacles, anemones, and periwinkles under the rocks. Rent a rowboat or canoe at Bennett Lake.

KOUCHIBOUGUAC. Swim from sand beaches along Northumberland Strait, sheltered from the sea by sand dunes. Rent a kayak, or bring your own, to explore rivers and lagoons.

Quebec

MINGAN ARCHIPELAGO. Bring your binoculars to view Atlantic puffins on rocky islands near the north shore of the Gulf of St. Lawrence—and bring a plant guide, too, to identify rare plants and flowers.

FORILLON. See the eastern tip of the Gaspé Peninsula on a naturalist-guided walk. Watch for whales, seals, and sea birds. Swim from pebble beaches or the sandy beach at Penouille.

LA MAURICIE. Follow scenic drives over the rolling hills. Or take to the trails on foot or bicycle, the water trails by canoe. Winter campground and lodge invite cross-country skiing and snowshoeing.

Ontario

ST. LAWRENCE ISLANDS. Take a commercial water taxi to the 17 islands and 80 rocky islets in the Thousand Islands to see the wildflowers or to camp at primitive sites accessible only by boat.

POINT PELEE. Come spring or fall to walk the boardwalk winding through the marshland to watch thousands of migrating birds. Point Pelee, southeast of Windsor, is the southern tip of Canada.

GEORGIAN BAY ISLANDS. Take a water taxi to 77 islands off the Georgian Bay coast. Camp at one of the primitive sites, then swim, snorkel, scuba dive, or fish. Walk the trails on Beausoleil, the largest island.

BRUCE PENINSULA. For description, see page 7.

PUKASKWA. Here in the Canadian Shield wilderness the Coastal Hiking Trail winds through boreal forest and over volcanic rock. The White and Pukaskwa rivers offer white-water adventure. Look for arctic plants and heron rookeries.

Manitoba

RIDING MOUNTAIN. At this park rising out of a sea of farmland, you'll find both development, with hotels, motels, and cottages, and green wilderness with lakes and streams, foot and horse trails.

Saskatchewan

PRINCE ALBERT. Make a pilgrimage by foot or canoe to the cabin and grave of Grey Owl on the shore of Ajawaan Lake, where the celebrated conservationist worked to protect this choice wilderness and wild country everywhere.

GRASSLANDS. At the Val Marie–Killdeer area, turn back the clock to see a remnant of original short-grass prairie, complete with prairie dog, antelope, falcon, and grouse. Compare the Killdeer Badlands with the Dakotas.

Alberta

WOOD BUFFALO. The park provides summer nesting for the fabled whooping crane. Don't expect to see the flock here. The numbers are still low; as a rare and endangered species, the whoopers need their privacy in nesting. You *can* get a good idea of the habitat, however. Then in winter visit the Texas Gulf Coast for a boat cruise alongside the Aransas National Wildlife Refuge to see the whoopers in their glory.

Banff National Park

Yoho National Park

ELK ISLAND. It's only a half-hour drive from Edmonton, but amid the park's forests and meadows you'll see herds of elk and bison, other mammals, and 200 species of birds. Climb the birding tower, hike, and canoe.

WATERTON LAKES. It's the Canadian section of Waterton–Glacier International Peace Park. You'll see a difference: the Canadians have golf and tennis—but wilderness trails, too.

BANFF and JASPER. See one, see them both in the heart of the majestic Canadian Rockies. They share mountain ranges, icefields, and scenic Icefields Parkway. You can drive it in a day (it's only 145 miles), but give yourself several days with time for day hikes into quiet valleys and alpine meadows. While at Banff, take in the August festival at the School of Fine Arts. Keep autumn in mind, lovely and less crowded.

British Columbia

KOOTENAY. Take the Banff-Windermere Highway, Route 93, running the full length of Kootenay (about 70 miles) north-south, to see spectacles on the west slope of the Continental Divide. Take the trails, then bathe at Radium Hot Springs.

YOHO. Yoho, though lesser known than Banff and Jasper, is a beauty spot in its own right. It's on the Trans-Canadian Highway, Canada Route 1, and once you see the waterfalls, lakes, and meadows, you can judge for yourself. Make sure to visit the natural rock bridge at Kicking Horse River.

GLACIER. More than 400 glaciers comprise only part of the park's attraction. Hike the trails in the Columbia Mountains to wildflower-carpeted meadows and breathtaking forest vistas.

NATIONAL PARKS OF CANADA

Auyuittuq, Northwest Terr.
Banff, Alberta
Bruce Peninsula, Ont.
Cape Breton Highlands,
   Nova Scotia
Elk Island, Alberta
Forillon, Quebec
Fundy, New Brunswick
Georgian Bay Islands, Ont.
Glacier, B.C.
Grasslands, Saskatchewan
Gros Morne, Newfoundland
Jasper, Alberta
Kejimkujik, Nova Scotia
Kluane, Yukon Terr.
Kootenay, B.C.
Kouchibouguac, New Brunswick
La Mauricie, Quebec

Mingan Archipelago, Quebec
Mt. Revelstoke, B.C.
Nahanni, Northwest Terr.
Northern Yukon, Yukon Terr.
Pacific Rim, B.C.
Point Pelee, Ont.
Prince Albert, Saskatchewan
Prince Edward Island,
   Prince Edward Island
Pukaskwa, Ont.
Riding Mountain, Manitoba
St. Lawrence Islands, Ont.
South Moresby, B.C.
Terra Nova, Newfoundland
Waterton Lakes, Alberta
Wood Buffalo, Alberta
Yoho, B.C.

Mount Revelstoke National Park
Nahanni National Park

MOUNT REVELSTOKE. Follow the scenic road to the summit of Revelstoke to overlook the peaks and steep valleys of the Selkirk Mountains. Then choose your trail through forest, alpine meadow, or tundra.

PACIFIC RIM. It's Canada's first national park on the Pacific, composed of three separate units on Vancouver Island. Drive 180 miles north of Victoria to the most accessible part. Go for birdwatching, whale watching, and beachcombing.

SOUTH MORESBY. For description, see page 7.

Northwest Territories

AUYUITTUQ. Fly to Baffin Island, then take a freighter canoe to the park entrance. Summer is short and cool. But it's the Arctic, a preserved portion of the wonderland near the top of the continent.

NAHANNI. Canoeists come for white-water adventure, but you'll also find falls twice the height of Niagara and sulfur hot springs. Reach Nahanni by plane or boat only.

Yukon Territory

NORTHERN YUKON. It's one of the last great wildlife sanctuaries, protecting migration routes of barren-ground caribou, North America's three bear species (grizzly, black, and polar), plus waterfowl on their summer turf.

KLUANE. Together with bordering Wrangell–St. Elias National Park, in Alaska, it comprises a preserve of more than 20 million acres, a complex of massive mountains, glaciers, and tundra, favored by caribou and many other wildlife species. Kluane's mountain peaks are known by hikers worldwide.

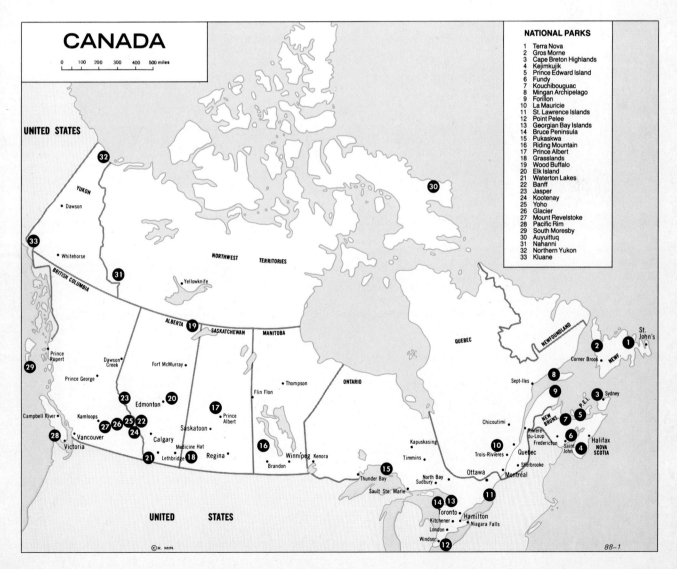

CANADA

0 100 200 300 400 500 miles

NATIONAL PARKS

1 Terra Nova
2 Gros Morne
3 Cape Breton Highlands
4 Kejimkujik
5 Prince Edward Island
6 Fundy
7 Kouchibouguac
8 Mingan Archipelago
9 Forillon
10 La Mauricie
11 St. Lawrence Islands
12 Point Pelee
13 Georgian Bay Islands
14 Bruce Peninsula
15 Pukaskwa
16 Riding Mountain
17 Prince Albert
18 Grasslands
19 Wood Buffalo
20 Elk Island
21 Waterton Lakes
22 Banff
23 Jasper
24 Kootenay
25 Yoho
26 Glacier
27 Mount Revelstoke
28 Pacific Rim
29 South Moresby
30 Auyuittuq
31 Nahanni
32 Northern Yukon
33 Kluane

88–1

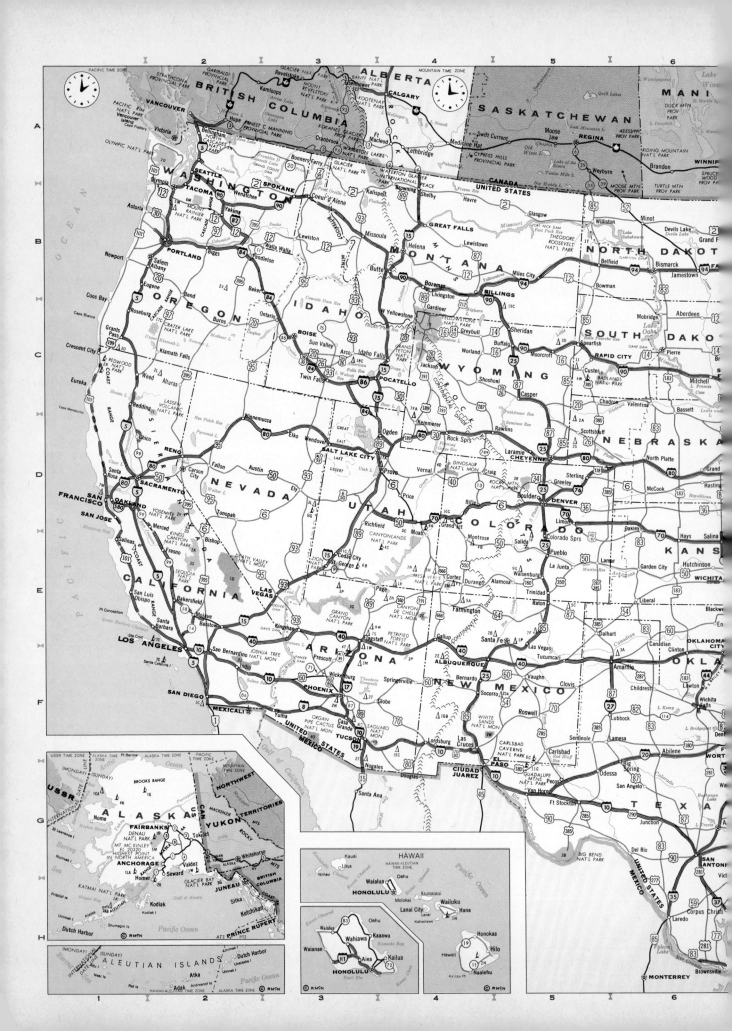

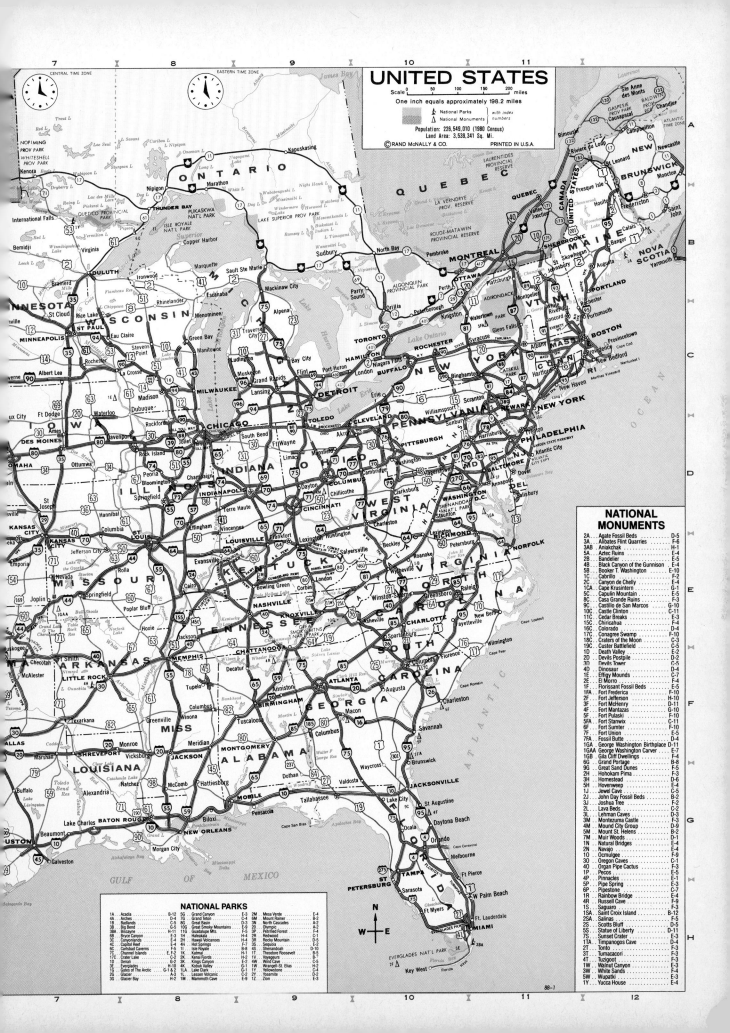

UNITED STATES

Scale
One inch equals approximately 198.2 miles

National Parks } with index
National Monuments } numbers

Population: 226,549,010 (1980 Census)
Land Area: 3,539,341 Sq. Mi.

© RAND McNALLY & CO.   PRINTED IN U.S.A.

NATIONAL MONUMENTS

2A	Agate Fossil Beds	D-5
3A	Alibates Flint Quarries	F-6
3AB	Aniakchak	H-1
5A	Aztec Ruins	E-4
2B	Bandelier	E-5
4B	Black Canyon of the Gunnison	E-4
5B	Booker T. Washington	E-10
1C	Cabrillo	F-2
2C	Canyon de Chelly	F-4
1CA	Cape Krusintern	G-1
5C	Capulin Mountain	E-5
8C	Casa Grande Ruins	F-3
9C	Castillo de San Marcos	G-10
10C	Castle Clinton	C-11
11C	Cedar Breaks	E-3
13C	Chiricahua	F-4
16C	Colorado	D-4
17C	Conagree Swamp	F-10
18C	Craters of the Moon	C-3
19C	Custer Battlefield	C-5
1D	Death Valley	D-2
2D	Devils Postpile	D-2
3D	Devils Tower	C-5
4D	Dinosaur	D-4
1E	Effigy Mounds	C-7
2E	El Morro	E-4
3E	Florissant Fossil Beds	E-5
1FA	Fort Frederica	F-10
2F	Fort Jefferson	H-10
3F	Fort McHenry	D-11
4F	Fort Mantazas	G-10
5FA	Fort Pulaski	F-10
5F	Fort Stanwix	C-11
6F	Fort Sumter	F-10
7F	Fort Union	E-5
7FA	Fossil Butte	D-4
1GA	George Washington Birthplace	D-11
1GAA	George Washington Carver	E-7
1GB	Gila Cliff Dwellings	F-4
6G	Grand Portage	B-8
9G	Great Sand Dunes	E-5
2H	Hohokam Pima	F-3
3H	Homestead	D-6
5H	Hovenweep	E-4
2J	Jewel Cave	D-5
2J	John Day Fossil Beds	B-2
3J	Joshua Tree	F-2
2L	Lava Beds	C-2
3L	Lehman Caves	D-3
3M	Montezuma Castle	E-3
5M	Mound City Group	D-9
6M	Mount St. Helens	B-2
7M	Muir Woods	D-1
1N	Natural Bridges	E-4
2N	Navajo	E-4
3O	Ocmulgee	F-9
3O	Oregon Caves	C-1
4O	Organ Pipe Cactus	F-3
1P	Pecos	E-5
4P	Pinnacles	E-1
5P	Pipe Spring	E-3
6P	Pipestone	C-7
1R	Rainbow Bridge	E-4
4R	Russell Cave	F-4
1S	Saguaro	F-3
1SA	Saint Croix Island	B-12
2SA	Salinas	E-5
3S	Scotts Bluff	D-5
5S	Statue of Liberty	D-11
6S	Sunset Crater	E-3
1TA	Timpanogos Cave	D-4
2T	Tonto	F-3
3T	Tumacacori	F-3
4T	Tuzigoot	E-3
1W	Walnut Canyon	E-3
3W	White Sands	F-5
5W	Wupatki	E-3
1Y	Yucca House	E-4

NATIONAL PARKS

1A	Acadia	B-12
4A	Arches	D-4
1B	Badlands	C-5
3B	Big Bend	G-5
3BA	Biscayne	H-11
6B	Bryce Canyon	E-3
4C	Canyonlands	E-4
4C	Capitol Reef	E-4
6C	Carlsbad Caverns	F-5
7C	Channel Islands	E-2
17C	Crater Lake	C-2
1D	Denali	H-10
3E	Everglades	H-10
1G	Gates of The Arctic	G-1 & 2
1G	Glacier	A-3
3G	Glacier Bay	H-2
5G	Grand Canyon	E-3
7G	Grand Teton	C-3
8G	Great Basin	D-3
10G	Great Smoky Mountains	E-9
11G	Guadalupe Mts.	F-5
1H	Haleakala	H-4
2H	Hawaii Volcanoes	H-4
4H	Hot Springs	F-7
5I	Isle Royale	B-8
2K	Katmai	H-1
2K	Kenai Fjords	H-1
3K	Kings Canyon	D-2
4K	Kobuk Valley	G-1
1LA	Lake Clark	H-1
2L	Lassen Volcanic	C-2
1M	Mammoth Cave	E-9
2M	Mesa Verde	E-4
6M	Mount Rainer	B-2
3N	North Cascades	A-2
3O	Olympic	A-2
5P	Petrified Forest	F-4
3R	Redwood	C-1
4R	Rocky Mountain	D-5
3S	Sequoia	E-2
4S	Shenandoah	D-10
1T	Theodore Roosevelt	B-5
6V	Voyageurs	B-7
4W	Wind Cave	C-5
1W	Wrangell-St. Elias	G-1
1Y	Yellowstone	C-4
2Y	Yosemite	D-2
1Z	Zion	E-3

88-1

ACADIA NATIONAL PARK

Maine

Established 1919

IN TRAVELING the New England coast, I found the finest surviving fragment of unspoiled nature on Mount Desert Island, far north in Maine. We are lucky to have it preserved and protected, a treasure in a thousand and one ways, with surf-splashed cliffs rising to the highest point along the Atlantic and crowned with cool mountain forests.

The beauty of Acadia has long been recognized by artists and writers and by wealthy families in the choice of their summer retreats. I find it fascinating to read how individuals with vision worked to make it a national park. Thanks largely to the efforts of George B. Dorr, a man of means and conscience, a portion of the area was proclaimed Sieur de Monts National Monument in 1916. It was changed to Lafayette National Park in 1919 and, enhanced with bequests of land from John D. Rockefeller, Jr., to Acadia National Park in 1929.

Acadia, 47 miles from Bangor, Maine, is the only national park in the northeastern United States. It is small as national parks go, fewer than 40,000 acres, but with unending variety.

Watching cormorants and gulls as they congregate on a rocky shoal reminds me of the importance of islets, islands, and undisturbed seacoast as nesting grounds for sea birds. The Maine coast, centered in Acadia and Mount Desert Island, has some of the most vital sites for a large variety of North Atlantic sea birds. More than 275 species of birds inhabit the park during the course of a year.

Here I can understand that ours is a nation born of the sea, bred on salt spray, and nurtured with adventures of the deep. The waters of bays and harbors around Acadia are speckled in summer with sails of pleasure yachts, and in every direction the sea roars against the rocks. Champlain sailed this way on his 1604 exploration of the French province of Acadia, and the Jesuits established a short-lived settlement. In time, schooners and brigs were built in every cove, while offshore great fishing fleets would rendezvous and whiten the horizon with hundreds of sails.

In the interior, the landscape of deep-blue lakes shielded by steep slopes tells the story of ancient glacial action. Massive sheets of ice moved down from the frozen north, piling rock, gouging lakes, and shaving peaks to bare granite. Now this land remains under snow each year until April, when the delicate trailing arbutus signals the beginning of spring, first in a procession of 500 varieties of wildflowers. In the low wetlands ducks nest, persistent beavers build their dams, and migratory wading birds, like the magnificent great blue heron, poke their bills underwater searching ceaselessly for fish, frogs, or tadpoles.

A month-long fire in 1947 destroyed 10,000 acres, including prime forest and homes of the age of opulence. But natural fire, like glaciers and the sea, plays its part in the cycles of nature. It's fascinating to return periodically to witness the process of plant succession and emergence of a new virgin forest. Once the fire stopped, small plants took hold, building soil texture and nutrients. They were succeeded by berries, then by birch, aspen, and sumac, pioneering the new forest, and ultimately replaced by spruce and firs, a pleasure to behold.

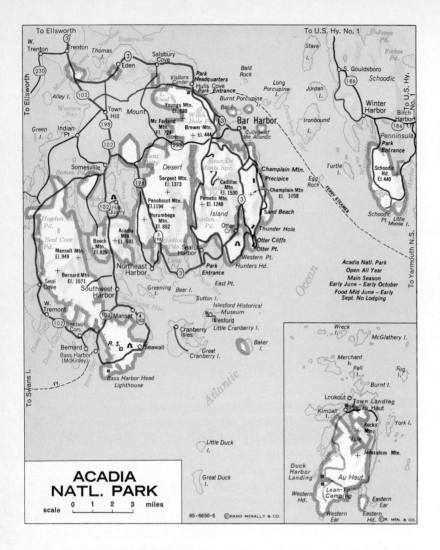

ACADIA
NATL. PARK

scale 0 1 2 3 miles

85-6650-6   ©RAND McNALLY & CO.

THE PRACTICAL GUIDE

The heart of the park is on **Mount Desert Island,** easily reached from the mainland via the Thompson Island Causeway, but there are two other important sections: rocky little **Isle au Haut,** affording a distinctive, simple island experience, and the **Schoodic Peninsula,** the only portion of the park on the mainland. The best way to approach Acadia is on Route 3 from Bangor.

BACKGROUND. After passing through Ellsworth, the mainland town closest to the park, stop at the **Hulls Cove Visitor Center.** On reaching Mount Desert Island, the **Thompson Island Information Center** will be helpful too. You'll find other sources of guidance at Bar Harbor, the largest resort community on Mount Desert.

By car (bus and taxi tours available from nearby towns) follow the 27-mile **Park Loop Road** for the sound and smell of the sea and the lick of the waves, and to view **Great Head,** a promontory above the surf.

Allow plenty of time to stop at scenic overlooks and to walk the trails. Observe

where waves at work have tunneled 85 feet into granite cliffs. Pools glisten from a profusion of rockweed, algae, kelp, flowering anemone, and that brightly colored sea snail called dog whelk.

At **Otter Point,** a trail winds through spruce and fir to the shore, where wild roses meet salt spray. Many arctic plants grow in the cool ocean fringe. Offshore, cormorants and gulls congregate on a rocky shoal, while small lobster boats are seen hauling in their pots—a reminder that in America the delectable lobster grows only in the cold waters off northern New England. When you reach the windswept summit of **Cadillac Mountain,** 1,530 feet, magnificent vistas unfold, from the open sea to Mount Katahdin far inland.

Somesville, the site of Mount Desert Island's first permanent settlement (1761), lies on the loop road at the head of a steep-sided fjord called Somes Sound. **Beech Cliff,** several miles south, is reached on a five-minute walk through a spruce-fir forest. It overlooks Echo Lake. Stop for the breath-

taking view of water, beach, mountains, and fir forests.

Nature walks are conducted by members of the park staff from July 1 to Labor Day. Approximately 150 miles of footpaths reach every mountain summit and transverse every valley; they are designed for all types of walkers and hikers. The **Nature Center** at Sieur de Monts Spring contains displays on nature and history; the adjacent **Abbe Museum** houses Indian Stone Age relics. Evening campfire programs are held in summer.

Naturalist sea cruises are conducted among the islands of Frenchman Bay to Baker Island. Check into the wide variety of trips available—sailing, whale watching, birdwatching, sea-bird watching, and lobster fishing.

Isle au Haut, the least-known part of Acadia, takes planning and preparation to reach but is well worth it for camping, hiking, and birding. The island is reached from Stonington, on the mainland, via a 45-minute ferry trip. Write park headquarters for details. (See address under "For Further Information.")

Schoodic Peninsula, the only mainland section of the park (about an hour and a half by car from Bar Harbor), offers a good day-long side trip. A one-way road leads around the peninsula, and a gravel road leads to the top of Schoodic Mountain.

ACTIVITIES. Acadia offers other activities besides nature walks and sea cruises. **Bicycling** gives an interesting view of the park. Pick up a free copy of the *Bicycle Guide to Acadia National Park* and follow the old carriage trails. Rentals are available in Bar Harbor.

Swimming is popular from Sand Beach (with those who like their ocean water cold) and inland at Echo Lake Beach and Lakewood. **Fishing** is permitted inside the park, both freshwater (state license required) and saltwater from the rocks.

A network of carriage paths, affording scenic views of mountains, lakes, and sea, has been set aside for **ski touring** and **snowshoeing.** Several shops in Bar Harbor rent equipment. Prepare for the sound of snowmobiles; Acadia is one of the few national parks where these machines are allowed.

Maine's windjammers are a delightful way of getting around. These handcrafted schooners accommodate 12 to 25 guests on summer trips that leave Monday morning and return Saturday noon. Most are family owned and operated. They visit fascinating places like Isle au Haut, Frenchboro, and Matinicus, which cannot be reached by car. These trips are great for birdwatching. For information, write Maine Windjammer Association, Box 317B, Rockport, Maine 04856.

ACCOMMODATIONS. Motor courts and guest houses are available at once exclusive Bar Harbor, Northeast Harbor, Southwest Harbor, and Winter Harbor. Reservations are advisable during July and August.

Jordan Pond House was destroyed by fire in June 1979; happily, the venerable restaurant and teahouse were reconstructed and dedicated anew in June 1982. Commanding a view of mountains and forests, the new two-story structure sits on a crest rising gently from the shore of the pond.

CAMPGROUNDS. Two campgrounds inside the park, **Blackwoods** and **Seawall,** are usually filled by noon in July and August. These are supplemented by private campgrounds in the towns.

You can be sure of a site at Blackwoods by making a reservation through Ticketron. Seawall continues to operate on a first-come, first-served basis. Maximum stays are 14 days between May 15 and October 15 at Seawall, all year at Blackwoods.

Lamoine State Park lies less than 15 miles away, with screened sites, a small beach, and boat landing.

SEASONS. Most visitors come in summer, although campgrounds, picnic areas, and other facilities are open from about May 10 to October 15. June is a good month for fishing, birdwatching, and nature walks. It's also the best month to see land birds in the spruce-fir and hardwood forests. Shore birds and pelagic species are most numerous in the outer islands in late July and August. September is marked by mild weather, fall colors, and crisp air. Snow and ice keep the park road system closed December through April. Be sure to bring warm clothing and a raincoat; evenings are cool even in summer, and rainy days occur in any season.

NEARBY. Bar Harbor is the starting point of the international motor ferry operating daily to **Yarmouth, Nova Scotia,** so that can well figure in your trip planning. The trip takes about six hours. Reservations are recommended in summer.

Bar Harbor and other towns offer deep-sea fishing trips and boat rentals. These places still retain the flavor of old fishing days around their docks, attractive to painters and photographers. Shop for hand-carved birds on driftwood bases at **Southwest Harbor,** one of the old fishing settlements from the days when schooners and brigs were built in every cave. **Bass Harbor,** at the southernmost tip of the island, also recalls the tiny down-east boating villages. It is the setting of a photogenic white lighthouse.

RECOMMENDED READING. *The Story of Mount Desert Island,* by Samuel Eliot Morison (Boston: Little, Brown & Co.).

FOR FURTHER INFORMATION. Write Superintendent, Acadia National Park, Box 177, Bar Harbor, Maine 04609.

ARCHES NATIONAL PARK

Utah

Established 1971

EARLY COWBOYS had their own name for it—Schoolmarm's Bloomers. But to me the official name, Delicate Arch, seemed right. There it was, the most famous landmark in the park, balanced precariously atop its base.

Then I realized it was the setting that counted even more, the wind-swept mesa at the edge of the precipitous red cliffs and massive domes of slickrock, a great natural theater more dramatic than any players walking across its stage.

Erosion and weathering have produced more giant stone arches, windows, pinnacles, and pedestals in the red rock here than in any other section of the nation. More than 200 arches have been discovered, with Delicate Arch alone vaulting to a height greater than that of a seven-story building.

Exactly what forces, I wondered, fashioned these formations and the spectacular towers, sweeping coves, balanced rocks, and the figures resembling humans and animals in the red-rock country? Geologists say the earth's crust first warped upward to form an anticline, an arch of stratified rock some 30 miles in length. Then the crest of the huge fold sank in, forming what are now known as Salt Valley and Cache Valley. Water entering cracks in the rock dissolved some of the cementing material, then running water and wind removed the loose sand, forming thin fins of soft sandstone. More rapid weathering of areas in vertical walls resulted in undercutting, while carving by water and frost continue to our day and will beyond it.

Arches is part of a large area, one of the most awesome on earth. The park should never be viewed, or considered, alone, but always within the context of the colorful canyonlands of southern Utah and the upper Colorado River region, where the erosion of nature over aeons has dissected the anatomy of the earth and left it exposed.

I like to compare the stone archways and fins of Arches with the unique formations of nearby Canyonlands National Park. At Arches, the rock was deposited as sand about 150 million years ago, during the Jurassic period. This 300-foot layer, called the Entrada sandstone, lends itself to a cycle of erosion that results in a graceful, smoothly contoured natural arch. Canyonlands has some great arches, too, such as Druid Arch and Angel Arch, but they are found mostly in the Cutler Formation, which tends more toward the development of standing rocks (for which Canyonlands is famous) and apparently lacks the arch-forming capability of the Entrada.

Some arches, such as Delicate Arch, have been left isolated by erosion of surrounding fins. In due course, the continued thinning by weather will result in their collapse. The visitor can observe all stages in the process of development and decay.

Soil, grasses, and trees are scant in this setting. The sparse pinyon-juniper ecosystem prevails, though the land is by no means barren. The desert has a beauty all its own. If I slow down and stay put, I can see a variety of birds as well as ground squirrels, rabbits, kangaroo rats, and other rodents. Deer, coyote, and foxes are present, too, but are most active at night.

Arches was proclaimed a national monument in 1929 in order to preserve its great scenic and scientific values. It was enlarged and boundaries were changed several times until the park was established in 1971. The park now has a total of 73,379 acres. I wish it could be enlarged again to embrace additional adjacent areas of geologic significance.

THE PRACTICAL GUIDE

The park lies only 5 miles from Moab, a logical base of operations for both Arches and Canyonlands. Arches is divided into six distinct sections, with roads and hiking trails twisting through each area. You can't do justice to it by road, so try to allow at least one day for a good hike to see some of the most impressive features in each section.

BACKGROUND. The **Visitor Center** is just off US 191, and you'll find excellent pictures, displays, and explanations of the landscape. Even if you're driving through and have only an hour, it is worth a stop. The main park road starts from here. It winds to the top of the slickrock plateau, then to **Courthouse Towers** for exciting views over the outlying mountains. Take the 1-mile hike from the parking area through **Park Avenue,** a narrow corridor where sandstone walls rise vertically 150 to 300 feet.

Continue over the paved road to **The Windows,** where you can see and photograph eight immense arches, as well as many smaller formations. After another 2½ miles northeast you come to a junction with a graded road leading to viewpoints of **Delicate Arch,** the "Crown Jewel of Arches National Park." Geologists have calculated that it took at least 70,000 years for combined forces of frost, wind, and rain to fashion the trimly tapered freestanding arch. Take the 1½-mile foot trail to the arch itself, for the view of the Colorado River gorge and the snow-peaked La Sal Mountains.

There is history here, too, as you'll discover on the trail to the **Wolfe Ranch,** settled in 1888 by a Civil War veteran, John Wesley Wolfe. He tested himself and the elements for more than 20 years before recognizing the land was too tough. But the corral, root cellar, and cabin of 1906 endure to tell the story of Wolfe and his family.

Then drive past **Fiery Furnace,** a series of parallel fins that provide an interesting excursion for hikers. But this area can be a nightmare of passageways—only ranger-conducted tours are allowed. These leave each morning at hours noted at the Visitor Center. At **Devils Garden,** 9 miles north of Balanced Rock, the road ends. A 2-mile trail leads to beautifully sculptured arches—

Pine Tree, Partition, Double O, and Dark Angel. **Landscape Arch,** the longest known natural stone arch in the world, is also along this trail. By turning off on the graded road at **Skyline Arch** and driving 8 miles across Salt Valley, you reach the **Klondike Bluffs,** a rugged section with a 1-mile hiking trail to **Tower Arch.** Before attempting to explore the bluffs, or any section of the backcountry, notify a park ranger. The ranger will furnish latest road information plus briefing on backcountry travel.

BIRDWATCHING. About 130 species of birds have been recorded in Arches. Although essentially a desert area with relatively little vegetation, the three habitats, or life-communities—desert scrub; pinyon-juniper, or pygmy, forest; and riparian woodland—reveal much of interest to the birder. **Courthouse Wash,** in the riparian woodland, is the most productive birding area, especially during spring and fall migrations, when species the birder doesn't expect to see bathe and rest in washes beneath cottonwood, tamarisk, and willow. **Devils Garden** is the best breeding area in the pygmy forest for birds such as ash-throated flycatcher, hairy woodpecker, gray viero, titmouse, jay, and black-throated gray warbler. During warmer months, the black-throated sparrow is the typical bird of the desert scrub.

TOUR OPERATORS. Outfitters at Moab feature a variety of trips, including the following: for river-running and day river trips on a paddlewheel riverboat, **Tex's Tour Center** (Box 67); for jeep tours, **Tag-a-Long Tours** (Box 1206); for horseback trips, **Bob's Trail Riders** (435 North Main). The zip code for Moab, Utah, is 84532.

ACCOMMODATIONS. A modern campground for tents and trailers is located at **Devils Garden,** an excellent base in the park interior. Campfire talks are given nightly during summer. There are no other services within the park, but good motels and restaurants are quite handy at Moab.

SEASONS. It's dry desert here. (See reference to weather under "Seasons" in Canyonlands section.) Spring and fall are the best times to visit. Summer is hot. From May to August, except in abnormally dry years, you can expect colorful displays of wildflowers in the moist places, particularly in Salt Valley. Winter is cold but comfortable.

NEARBY. The companion piece to Arches is **Canyonlands National Park,** a fantasy of red-rock gorges, canyons, and sheer cliffs. This is the "standing up country," an explorer's delight on foot, horse, or jeep. **Behind the Rocks,** the red-rock escarpment on the northern boundary of Moab, has only been penetrated in the past decade but is becoming a high point for jeep tours.

Twenty-five miles southeast of Arches, **Fisher Towers,** a tall group of pinnacles, guard the entrance to **Castle Valley,** a beautiful area of meadows and pastures banked on one side by red rock and on the other by 12,000-foot peaks of the La Sal Mountains.

FOR FURTHER INFORMATION. Write Superintendent, Arches National Park, 125 W. 200 South, Moab, Utah 84532.

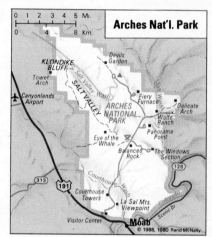

BADLANDS NATIONAL PARK

South Dakota

Established 1978

ON VISITING the Badlands in 1986, I thought about the name and whether it was well applied. To the Sioux this strange, arid, contorted fragment of fantasy in southwestern South Dakota was *mako sica,* or "bad land." Early French traders and trappers agreed, calling it *les mauvaises terres a traverser.* I could understand why in their day it was "bad land to cross." But I saw something different in the varicolored formations resembling spires, towers, and pinnacles in the ridges, low hills, and cliffs between the White and Cheyenne rivers.

I saw the evidence of incredibly abundant fossils that scientists have been studying for more than a century and relatively undisturbed prairie plants that are scarce elsewhere. I saw a bison herd and pictured what life was like when they were plentiful across the plains. And I saw too the great historic sites of the Oglala Sioux. So I perceived the Badlands as good lands, rich in natural and cultural heritage.

The land of White River, as I learned, at one time was part of a shallow inland sea. Then, about 60 million years ago, the Rockies and Black Hills pushed up through the earth's crust, leaving the sea bottom a plain of mud. Streams cut downward, meandering and widening their floodplains. Unceasing wind, rain, water, and frost removed and rearranged the soft fragments of rock. The process still continues—few landmarks long remain in the same form or dimension.

While still a marshy plain, the region was inhabited by forms of wildlife now unknown. With the discovery of fossils unearthed from tombs of mud and clay, paleontologists have identified remains of the three-toed horse, saber-toothed cat, oreodont, and early ancestors of the hog, camel, and rhinoceros. The Badlands are widely known today as a rich repository of fossils of the Oligocene epoch.

Along with change in geology over millions of years, the climate changed, too. With dry winds from the north and diminishing rain, grasslands replaced swamps and silted marshes. Today the annual precipitation is about 16 inches and prairies persist. The mixed-grass prairie with its many species of plant life is one of the most fascinating (though overlooked) aspects of the Badlands. In spring the ground is bright with wildflowers. Early summer finds a covering of big bluestem, needle-and-thread, little bluestem, blue gamma, and buffalo grasses, all bending and dancing in the wind.

The first people to see this region were the native Arikara Indians, who were displaced by the Sioux in the late 1700s. The national park, in fact, is deep in modern Sioux heartland. In the winter of 1890, the fateful year of the Wounded Knee Massacre, a band of more than a thousand Indians fled to the Badlands for refuge, dancing the Ghost Dance atop the Stronghold Table, hoping to invoke the spirits to restore their freedom to roam. But it was not to be.

Then came the homesteaders and ranchers, striving to contend with a harsh natural environment of dry alkaline soil, where droughts are common and where winter lasts half a year and summer temperatures are in the 90s or higher. In 1929 Congress authorized establishment of Badlands National Monument and, with the Dust Bowl days of the 1930s, many homesteaders and ranchers were glad to sell their land for this new federal venture and to move. The monument was officially proclaimed in 1939. With the addition in 1976 of 133,300 acres (formerly used as an air force gunnery range), the monument was more than doubled in size to its present 243,500 acres. Then in 1978 Congress voted to redesignate the area a national park.

That major 1976 park addition, known as the South Unit, lies within the Pine Ridge Indian Reservation. It assures that the spiritual sites of the Sioux are respected. I find it a moving experience to visit the spectacular overlooks and ponder the words of Red Cloud: "Riches would do us no good. We could not take them with us to the other world. We do not want riches, we want peace and love. I never want to leave this country; all my relatives are lying here in the ground and when I fall to pieces I am going to fall here."

THE PRACTICAL GUIDE

The national park is easily reached from I-90. Turn off the interstate on South Dakota 240, which makes an arc through the park, between the towns of Cactus Flat and Wall. You can get an introduction to the Badlands in this 40-mile scenic loop.

BACKGROUND. The center of activity is **Cedar Pass Visitor Center,** near Interior, where naturalists will help you get oriented and answer questions. See the orientation slide program, the museum collection of fossils and Indian artifacts, and the ''touch room.''

The **White River Visitor Center,** located in the South Unit, is south of the town of Scenic. It features Indian cultural exhibits and a videotape program on the history of the Oglala Sioux.

Nature walks and talks are given daily during summer months at the Cedar Pass area, particularly during early morning, late afternoon, and at night, the best times to observe plants and wildlife.

TRAIL ADVENTURES. You can walk anywhere you like in the Badlands (but be careful on the edge of the crumbly formations). Trails are best, however, if only because of the excellent markers that interpret nature at work. **Fossil Exhibit Trail,** for instance, is a ¼-mile walk that shows fossil replicas, like those embedded in soft rock for 35 million years. **Door Trail** is an easy ¾-mile walk starting from the north end of the Windows parking area and leading through a natural doorway into the Bad-

lands formation. You can backpack anywhere in the park and be out of sight just over the ridge crest from the road, but the best long trail in primitive country is **Castle.** The rolling prairie, with grassy hills and wooded draws interspersed with badlands, is a place to see pronghorn antelope, bison, badgers, and prairie dogs and to hear the song of the coyote at night.

There is no permit required for backcountry camping but plan on carrying drinking water (at least one gallon per person per day). Best hiking hours in summer are in early morning and evening to escape midday heat.

Be sure to wear proper footgear. Sturdy boots or shoes in summer will help ward off injury from cactus spines and prairie rattlesnakes. Warm, sturdy, waterproof gear in winter will help reduce exposure to the weather.

Always apply common sense when navigating slopes, since soils can be slippery, especially in rainy weather.

CAMPING. You can camp year-round at Cedar Pass, with 110 campsites and developed facilities, and at Sage Creek if you're prepared to rough it. Reservations are required for groups. Bring cookstoves for hot meals, since fires are prohibited throughout the park.

BIRDWATCHING. Plenty of distinctive birds frequent the Badlands. The prairie horned lark is one of the first to nest in the spring. The western meadowlark arrives

early in March and lingers until a severe autumn storm drives it southward. Look for the western nighthawk (just before sunset, especially in fall migration), marsh hawk, sparrow hawk, and the little western burrowing owl. Pick up a copy of the bird checklist at a visitor center.

ACCOMMODATIONS. Operated by the Oglala Sioux, **Cedar Pass Lodge** consists of rustic, comfortable cabins on spacious grounds, open May 1 to mid-October.

SEASONS. Though summer is most popular, the park is open all year. Spring has generally clear, cool days, with occasional snows in April. Summer can be extremely hot. Fall, with a long Indian summer, is enjoyable. A visit in winter, when peaks are mantled in snow, can also be rewarding, though blizzards may temporarily block roads.

In whatever season you plan to visit, be ready for sudden, drastic weather changes. Summer storms frequently bring lightning, hail, and high winds. Be on guard against heat exhaustion in the summer and exposure in the winter.

NEARBY. A visit to the Badlands is easily linked with a trip to **Wind Cave, Jewel Cave,** and **Mount Rushmore,** all units of the National Park system. In Rapid City, visit the **Museum of Geology** and **Sioux Museum.**

FOR FURTHER INFORMATION. Write Superintendent, Badlands National Park, Box 6, Interior, South Dakota 57750.

BIG BEND NATIONAL PARK

Texas

Authorized 1935

TEXANS CAN CLAIM almost anything about the mighty Big Bend and will be speaking modestly. This wilderness park presents an opportunity for a desert experience unequaled in its region and perhaps in the nation.

The heart of the 740,118-acre park lies 410 miles west of San Antonio and 300 miles southeast of El Paso but is worth all efforts to reach it, if only for the majesty of its vastness and the opportunity to absorb the adventurous, lonely frontier above the Rio Grande.

In driving from the nearest towns, Alpine and Marathon, each more than 70 miles away, I thought there must be a greater population of jackrabbits and deer than people in between. The approach through vast ranch country provides a fitting foreground to this masterpiece of Southwest desert landscape, dominated by the upthrust of the massive Chisos Mountains. The Chisos may be snowless, but their crags, canyons, and rocky spires present a different color tone from every angle and at every hour, from the clear brightness of a sun-filled morning to the purple of twilight setting over the immense, varied wilderness.

I marvel at the geologic history of the park. Millions of years ago an inland sea covered the Big Bend. Sediments of mud, sand, and lime on the floor of the sea later hardened into rock; traces of shells and fossils are still found embedded over the area. During a later period dinosaurs and giant crocodiles (possibly 50 feet long) roamed through dark marshes and tropical forests. Then came volcanic activity and mountain building, followed by millions of years of erosion, and castles and cathedrals were carved in rock.

The waters of the Rio Grande have played their part in the carving process. The river extends for 118 miles along the boundary of the park—which also is the boundary between the United States and Mexico—on its great U-shaped bend. Three times on its course the river cuts through massive, dramatic canyons: Santa Elena, Mariscal, and Boquillas, which provide sightseeing adventures for every visitor.

In 1975, in *Science* magazine, two scientists reported the discovery in Big Bend National Park of bones of the largest flying creature ever known. Douglas Lawson, a doctoral candidate at the University of California, and Dr. Wann Langston, director of the Vertebrate Paleontology Laboratory, University of Texas, said the bones were those of the pterosaur (sometimes called the pterodactyl), a flying reptile with a wingspan of 38 feet. The pterosaur became extinct about 60 million years ago.

Human history is part of the treasure of the Big Bend. Bandits took refuge behind its rocky barricades. Comanche warriors passed through on their way into Mexico. Mexican revolutionaries invaded the United States into the Big Bend in 1916. Before the park was established, large livestock herds grazed where visitors now may enjoy wilderness camping.

I enjoy Big Bend as a place to absorb the richness of the awesome desert. The park contains more than a thousand different plants, including rare species that grow only here.

The beginning and end of the day are the best times to see the park's wide range of animals. Among them are the coyote, ringtail, and possibly the rare kit fox in Tornillo Flats—sometimes the sleek pronghorn will be seen here, too. Mule deer and collared peccary, or javelina, are apt to be in the Grapevine Hills. Lizards and snakes are not uncommon, but they are anxious to give humans a wide berth. Once I saw a tarantula on the hiking trail, but this giant spider was not unfriendly. I looked him over respectfully, from a distance, and then we each went our separate ways. It is wise to travel with a good bird guide, for nearly 400 species of birds have been seen in the park. These include the rare, lyric-voiced Colima warbler, whose only known nesting places are here and in Mexico.

THE PRACTICAL GUIDE

Allow at least three full days to explore the Big Bend, though a full week will occupy any visitor's time usefully, exploring by car, raft, afoot, and on horseback.

Approached from the west, El Paso lies 328 miles from Big Bend. You can reach the park by driving to Van Horn and Marfa, then south to Presidio and the Maverick entrance—it's the long but scenic route, including the River Road along the Rio Grande. You can also head due east from Marfa to Alpine, then south to the Maverick entrance. Or from Alpine continue to Marathon, then south to the Persimmon Gap entrance—the distance is longer but it takes less time. If traveling from and to the west, try to make a loop trip. From the east, Big Bend lies 405 miles from San Antonio, 251 miles from Del Rio, via Persimmon Gap.

BACKGROUND. From the entrance to the park at Persimmon Gap, 39 miles south of Marathon, it is 29 miles to park headquarters at Panther Junction in the foothills of the Chisos. Use the giant relief map at the **Visitor Center** there to chart your course, and ask for current information on river and road conditions.

Principal roads in the park are paved. Improved dirt roads normally are in good condition except following rainstorms.

Get out of your car and hike the trails. You have more than 350 miles of them.

Allow the better part of a day for the trip to **Santa Elena Canyon,** a massive boxlike gorge carved through limestone cliffs. It lies 45 miles from the center of things at Chisos Basin. From the picnic area at the river shore, a footpath leads along a rocky ledge into the heart of the canyon. On the way there or back, stop at **Castolon,** where adobe houses reflect pioneer settlement by Mexican farmers, the U.S. Cavalry, and rugged cattlemen. You can purchase items of food or clothing at the historic Castolon Store, which has been in business since 1919. Nearby, the river is so narrow that you can cross by rowboat to the Mexican village of **Santa Elena.**

Spend part of another day at **Boquillas Canyon,** the longest of Big Bend's famous gorges, where the floodplain of willows and cottonwoods is frequented by many birds, particularly spectacular with late afternoon sun on the canyon walls. It lies 35 miles from Chisos Basin. Be sure to take in the nature trail at Rio Grande Village, to learn about this life-community and enjoy the views above the river. Then visit a village out of yesterday, **Boquillas,** across the "border without barricades." You will pay to ride across the river in a skiff, then on a burro for 1 mile to the village, but the modest fee is well worth it.

If you are in good physical condition (not necessarily an expert rider), the daylong horseback trip to the **South Rim** is one of the finest experiences available in any national park. It reveals the full sweep of the nature community, upward through pinyon, oak, and juniper, through an "island forest in the sky" more like the North woods than Southwest desert. The greatest reward is the view from the crest, more than 7,200 feet high, of the silvery Rio Grande, the tawny desert, and rugged Mexican Sierra del Carmen extending to the horizon. A shorter trip leads to the **Window,** a great gap in the mountains, ideal for picture taking.

Lost Mine Trail from Panther Pass is the most popular hiking route; it takes three to four hours to make the 5-mile round trip to Lost Mine Peak.

Old Ore Road, running north from Rio Grande Village to the yucca forest on Dagger Flats, is an interesting off-the-beaten-path primitive route. It parallels the old stage road to Boquillas across desert flats and arroyos. Hikers can use it to reach the Telephone Canyon trailhead, intersecting the Strawhouse and Marufo Vega trails, the major network on the east side of the park. Almost all dirt roads in the park are primitive.

HIKING GEAR. Wear hiking shoes or boots, not sneakers, in this country to avoid painful contact with thorny mesquite, prickly pear, and catclaw. Wide-brimmed hats are most practical. Don't plan any longer hike across the harsh desert lowlands than you feel sure you can make. Carry plenty of water.

BOATING. This a choice experience on the Rio Grande—for experts. Inflatable rubber rafts are recommended for float trips. Some portaging may be necessary due to shallow water. If the river is above the 5-foot level, no trips are permitted. Water conditions are difficult to predict. From October through March the level is low but stable, and the weather is pleasant. The summers are definitely hot on the river. No boats or accessory equipment is available for rent or loan inside the park. A permit must be obtained at park headquarters or a ranger station.

Rubber-raft trips are offered by private outfitters headquartered at Terlingua and other nearby towns. Check at park headquarters or any ranger station for information. Two-day raft trips include a chance to camp overnight on a sandbar in Boquillas Canyon or Santa Elena Canyon. Mariscal Canyon is a good one-day trip. The Lower Canyons trip lasts six days, covering rugged, isolated country with major rapids and natural hot springs. Experts call it one of the nation's most exciting river runs. Contact Far Flung Adventures, Box 31, Terlingua 79852; Outback Expeditions, Study Butte 79852; Big Bend River Tours, Lajitas 79852;

Rough Run Outfitters, Marathon 79842; or Whitewater Experience, 3835 Farnham, Houston 77098.

PHOTOGRAPHY. Early morning is best at Santa Elena Canyon; by noon there is little or no sunlight on the walls. Boquillas Canyon, in shadow until noon, improves in the afternoon. Sunset through the Window makes a colorful study from almost any point.

BIRDWATCHING. Big Bend is one of the finest of all birding parks. It furnishes habitat for many Mexican birds found nowhere else in the United States. Most celebrated are Colima warblers, rare sparrow-sized songsters that divide their seasons between south-central Mexico and the Chisos Mountains. Here also is the greatest concentration of breeding peregrine falcons remaining anywhere in the United States. Pick up a copy of *Naturalist's Big Bend,* a handbook by Roland H. Wauer, which features a significant chapter on birds. It is published by Texas A & M Press, College Station, Texas, and is available at the Visitor Center. Following wet summers, lowland flats along the Rio Grande are apt to contain vast arrays of wintering sparrows.

ACCOMMODATIONS. The **Chisos Basin,** at a 5,400-foot elevation, is the center of activity most of the year, with a campground, dining room, supply store, and very limited motel-type accommodations. Reservations for lodgings are essential throughout the year. No reservations are accepted for camping. Write National Park Concessions, Inc., Big Bend National Park, Texas 79834. You may want to stay at **Study Butte** or outside the western boundary of the park. **Lajitas,** on the Rio Grande (address: Box 400, Terlingua 79852), is designed to accommodate everything from school groups on field trips to business conferences.

CAMPING. Big Bend provides a variety of opportunity. The two major campgrounds are at **Chisos Basin** (62 sites) and **Rio Grande Village** (99 sites). Chisos is most popular Easter through Thanksgiving, but when it grows cool at the basin it is still shirt-sleeve weather in the desert around Rio Grande Village. Facilities there include a trailer park, large campground, and supply store. There is also a smaller campground at **Cottonwood,** near Castolon, with less-developed facilities. Primitive camping is available along backcountry roads, with a permit obtained from any ranger station. Carry plenty of water and be sure to prepare for potential emergencies.

SEASONS. Sunshine is abundant all year. Snow is light and rare in the mountains. Winter is nippy at higher elevations but pleasant in the lowlands (70 and 80 degrees Fahrenheit even in January), and an ideal season here. Spring arrives early. The desert blooms from late February through April, when Dagger Flats, in the northeast part of the park, presents a rare spectacle of thousands of giant dagger yucca (Yucca carnerosana) unfolding massive clusters of creamy blossoms. Summer is hot (100 degrees) in desert and river valley, but pleasant at Chisos Basin and the best time of year for the mountains.

A good time to walk the desert is at twilight, the witching hour when deer feed on open hillsides and coyotes begin their nocturnal serenade. Be on the lookout for rattlesnakes out to feed on rodents. They won't strike if you keep your distance, so avoid sitting on rocks or logs they're likely to shelter under, and keep your eyes open. Don't worry about giant tarantulas you may meet; they're relatively harmless.

NEARBY. The **Black Gap Wildlife Management Area,** near the Persimmon Gap entrance, covers 100,000 acres, with fishing opportunities on a 20-mile stretch of the Rio Grande. **Fort Davis National Historic Site,** on the road down from Carlsbad Caverns, New Mexico, is a restoration of the most impressive old frontier fort in the Southwest. It adjoins **Davis Mountains State Park,** a combination of scenic peaks and canyons, with modern overnight lodge accommodations and recreation facilities. Motels are located in the towns of Alpine and Marathon, between Fort Davis and Big Bend. At Alpine, visit the fascinating **Museum of the Big Bend** on the campus of Sul Ross State University. You'll learn about the history and settlement of the country. County Route 170, the scenic **Camino del Rio,** leads northwest from the park through the mining ghost towns of Study Butte and Terlingua, noted as the scene of the annual International Chili Cookoff in early November, and on to Presidio, a gateway into Mexico via Ojinaga and Chihuahua.

RECOMMENDED READING. *The North American Deserts,* by Edmund C. Jaeger (Stanford, Calif.: Stanford University Press) and *The Big Bend Country: Facts, Stories & Legends,* by Ross Maxwell (Big Bend, Tex.: Big Bend Natural History Association).

FOR FURTHER INFORMATION. Write Superintendent, Big Bend National Park, Texas 79834.

BISCAYNE NATIONAL PARK

Florida

Established 1980

I COULD hardly imagine so much beauty and variety of life being crowded into so small an area as I found in the coral reef community. The reef was alive with various types of corals, sponges, sea grasses, shellfish, crabs, starfish, and various types of reef fish. It surprised me that I could see all of this while snorkeling in sheltered shallow waters just below Miami.

The only living coral reefs in the continental United States are located here along the scimitar-shaped arc of the Florida Keys. Over the years I've seen most of them destroyed by onrushing civilization. The same might have happened here too.

Submarginal land at the edge of Biscayne Bay in south Florida was rezoned in 1962 in order to allow Daniel K. Ludwig, the shipping and oil magnate, to construct a refinery. Until then the area largely had been overlooked. Although the bay's northern half, bordering Miami and Miami Beach, was already developed (if not overdeveloped), the southern half still remained a rich breeding ground for corals, sponges, shellfish, and fish.

Biologists, engineers, sportsmen, and conservationists rallied to defend the bay. They warned that it is an enclosed body where prevailing winds blow onshore and that industrial wastes could turn the whole bay into a stagnant, oily pool, damaging parks, yacht clubs, homes, and hotels. They had little idea of exactly how to save the bay, but studied one legal and legislative potential after another and established Safe Progress, a broad-based civic organization.

In the midst of their effort on one front, Elliott Key, the major island of the Upper Florida Keys, was subdivided and lots were sold. As the controversy heightened, the developers showed their defiance by bulldozing a path the entire length of the island, barely missing a stand of rare palm trees. But public support for preservation was growing. Secretary of the Interior Stewart L. Udall gave personal encouragement, which led to establishment in 1968 of Biscayne National Monument.

People began to sit up and take notice of this jewel of nature. They found the islands and islets, numbering about 30, support stands of rare mahogany and lignum vitae and species of ferns and palms that had been thought extinct. The tropical forests shelter migratory birds.

As a result, in 1980 the monument was significantly enlarged to cover approximately 175,000 acres and reclassified as a national park. The additions include islands and mainland mangroves that serve as nurseries for marine life. The national park is enhanced by the nearby Key Largo Coral Reef National Marine Sanctuary, which has 100 square miles of underwater life.

The national park today is a haven for boaters, birdwatchers, fishermen, snorkelers, and scuba divers, and an amazing lesson in what people can do. Thanks to those who cared, Floridians and visitors can still experience and enjoy the coral reef.

THE PRACTICAL GUIDE

A small but interesting **Visitor Center** is located at Homestead Bayfront Park, on Biscayne Bay east of Homestead. It's quite easy to reach by car from anywhere in the metro Miami area—and makes a worthwhile stop en route to the Everglades or the Keys. There is a boat-launching ramp at Convoy Point, near headquarters. You will also find access to this underwater park from one of the many marinas along the mainland, as well as in the Upper Florida Keys, where boat rentals are available.

If you don't have your own boat, there is a tour boat to Elliott Key and the reefs for snorkeling. For tour boat information and reservations, contact Aqua-Center in Homestead (phone 305-247-2400).

Elliott Key is easily reached across the Intracoastal Waterway. Here you'll find a harbor with designated slips, a primitive campground, rest rooms, and showers. The Visitor Center has only a few displays, but a ranger is stationed here who will furnish helpful guidance.

SNORKEL AND SCUBA. Much of the area is so shallow you can see abundant tropical fish, corals, and sponges simply with mask, snorkel, and fins. On the eastern edge of the shelf, however, the outer reef drops to depths of greater than 100 feet. Behind the outer reef, in sheltered lagoon-like waters, small patch reefs rise to the surface, affording novice and intermediate divers an opportunity to become acquainted with Florida's coral reefs. While at park headquarters, pick up a copy of the skin diver's guide to four marked patch reefs. You can reach these by boat proceeding via Caesar's Creek, 2 to 3 miles east of Old Rhodes and Elliott keys. At one reef you'll be able to see schools of grunt, porkfish, wrasse, and angelfish flitting in and out of an old schooner wreck. Be sure to display a dive flag and tie to a buoy to prevent damaging the reef with your anchor.

FISHING. In the reefs, fishing for grouper and snapper is popular; you can try your luck for the big ones—marlin, kingfish, dolphin, and sailfish. Bear in mind that Florida law prevails. The bay and creeks are closed to lobstering.

SPECIAL NOTE. Possession, disturbance, or removal of corals, sea fans, sea feathers, tropical fish, shells, historical artifacts, and natural features is prohibited. These are all best left in place for others to enjoy.

NEARBY. Accommodations of all kinds are available in Homestead and neighboring communities. **John Pennekamp Coral Reef State Park,** first undersea park in the continental United States, lies directly south. Onshore the park includes a campground and a marina. **Everglades National Park** is 30 minutes west.

FOR FURTHER INFORMATION. Write Superintendent, Biscayne National Park, Box 1369, Homestead, Florida 33030.

BRYCE CANYON NATIONAL PARK

Utah

Authorized 1924

ALL OF SOUTHERN UTAH —the "Color Country"— might qualify as a national park. Perhaps it all can't be one, but there is no doubt about Bryce Canyon. It is not very large, only 37,102 acres, but it includes some of the most colorful and unusual erosional forms on earth.

The heart of the park is but a short, narrow strip along the jagged edge of the Paunsaugunt Plateau, one of the seven great "tables" dominating southern Utah. Below the plateau rim stand cathedrals, palaces, chessmen awaiting the next move, and entire miniature sculptured cities. Many formations are named, such as Thor's Hammer, Queen's Castle, Gulliver's Castle, Hindu Temples, and Wall Street, but you will find plenty that may suggest names of your own.

These are colored variously pink, iron-red, and orange, blended with white, gold, and cream, and here and there striped with lavender and blue. All of this spreads out from the amphitheaterlike rim as far as the eye can see until, far in the distance, it blends into the expansive Utah-Arizona landscape of plateaus dark with evergreen forests.

Only a few, if any, places in the world provide better opportunity to realize the power and persistence of forces that have shaped the earth's surface than Bryce Canyon. Geology of the last 60 million years began with layers of sediment being deposited by inland lakes, followed by mountain building caused by powerful pressures coming from within the earth. Huge blocks were broken off and raised higher until they formed distinct plateaus, or tablelands. Then over the centuries rain, frost and thaw, running water, plant roots forcing themselves deeper into the cracks, and chemicals in the air have exercised their influences through alternate layers of harder and softer rock.

This country was known to Indians and favored by the Paiutes, who described the formations as "red rocks standing like men in a bowl-shaped canyon." It was they who named the Paunsaugunt Plateau, which means "home of the beaver"; a reminder that many species of wildlife dwell on this high, cool plateau.

Adventurous trappers and prospectors may have visited the area during the period from 1830 to 1850, and Mormon scouts searching for fields and pastures may have reached the south base of the Paunsaugunt Plateau between 1850 and 1866. It was the intrepid Major John Wesley Powell who initiated the scientific investigation of the valleys and plateaus of southern and central Utah, in 1871. His route began at Kanab, ascended Johnson Canyon, then crossed the many deeply trenched streams rising in the plateau walls of what is now the national park. One early settler, Ebenezer Bryce, pushed farther upstream than the others and tried raising cattle, but gave it up and departed, leaving only his name.

J. W. Humphrey, forest supervisor of the Sevier Forest, headquartered at Panguitch, was largely responsible for making the exquisitely scenic area of Bryce Canyon available to the public. He not only publicized its attractions in the local newspaper but pressed for the development of primitive roads.

The Bryce fever caught hold. In 1919, the Utah legislature memorialized Congress, urging the establishment of a national monument to be called Temple of the Gods. The effort was rewarded in 1923 when Bryce Canyon National Monument was designated by presidential proclamation, then was given even greater recognition the following year when Congress raised the status of the area, naming it Utah National Park. In subsequent years the park was enlarged, its name changed once again.

Bryce Canyon was advertised far and wide during the halcyon days of trail travel to the national parks. Those days have long ended and other national parks have been established in southern Utah, but Bryce Canyon remains a jewel among them.

THE PRACTICAL GUIDE

The park is small enough so that you can cover the full drive along the high rim and back, a distance of 34 miles, in less than three hours, but plan to stay much longer. Scenic overlooks provide broad perspective before seeing the formations at close range from hiking and riding trails.

The approach roads to Bryce are deceptive: 4,000 feet in elevation are gained in the last 60 miles. This is high country, ranging from 8,000 to 9,000 feet above sea level, and it demands a leisurely pace, particularly for anyone with a heart condition. Allow extra time for everything, including eating and hiking.

WITHOUT A CAR. Color Country Tours provide transportation by motor coach three times weekly from Cedar City. This is designed primarily as a one-day tour with stops at Zion Canyon–Overlook, **Cedar Breaks National Monument,** and Navajo Lake before reaching the park Visitor Center. However, one-way transportation is offered, including pickups at Cedar City Airport (served by Sky West from Salt Lake City). You can also reach Cedar City via Greyhound or Trailways.

BACKGROUND. Located at the park's entrance, the **Visitor Center** contains orientation exhibits on geology, biology, and archaeology. Illustrated talks are presented daily in summer. For an introduction to the park, take a van trip from Bryce Canyon Lodge to Bryce Point, Inspiration Point, and Paria View. Then prepare to walk.

Main Bryce Amphitheater, between **Boat Mesa** and **Bryce Point,** a distance of 4 airline miles, contains a concentration of sights. In this compact area are 21 miles of trail and spectacular vistas. You can see how the vegetation changes with elevation. Sagebrush claims the valley floors below. The slopes up to 7,000 feet are covered with pinyons, junipers, and Gambel oaks. Above and below the rim, between 7,000 and 8,500 feet, are ponderosa, limber, and bristlecone pines, and Douglas fir.

Navajo Loop, most popular hike (about 1½ miles and 1½ hours), starts from the inspiring setting of **Sunset Point.** It begins with a gradual 521-foot descent into the canyon, then winds among an outstanding array of formations, with time for rest and picture taking en route. The last lap is an amazing series of stairlike switchbacks. Guided walks are given daily.

Under-the-Rim Trail, completed in 1965, offers 23 miles of hiking into quite wild country, with opportunities for solitude and exploration. Yet it parallels the main park road, so it can be taken conveniently in sections; you can reach it from three spur trails. Extending from Bryce Point to the south boundary at **Rainbow Point,** this trail opens the heart of the Pink Cliffs scenery.

The traveler who is concerned with preserving park features for the future will stay on the trails. The traveler who is concerned with his or her children's safety will be sure they do the same.

HORSEBACK RIDES. These afford the least strenuous way of probing the canyon trails, on a morning or an afternoon trip from Bryce Canyon Lodge. There is a lot of variety to enjoy, riding through cool and shadowed canyons, over switchbacks and ridgetops, and along the base of cliffs.

PHOTOGRAPHY. Opportunities are limitless. Use your imagination to bring home more than a visual record of where you have been; shoot your own interpretation of what you have seen. In Bryce Canyon you can experiment with sidelighting and backlighting, using the brilliant landscape to your advantage. Be careful to shade your lens when shooting toward the sun. The deeper the blue of the sky, the more intense will be the coloring of the rocks. Telephoto and wide-angle lenses are helpful but not essen-

30

tial. **Yovimpa Point** is the best place to catch the setting sun's rays on the Pink Cliffs; it is unsurpassed for beauty.

BIRDWATCHING. Three distinct habitats support varied birdlife. Good birding is found in the pinyon pine–juniper–Gambel oak areas of Jolley Hollow, the Mossy Cave area, and along the trail from Sunset Point to the town of Tropic. You're likely to find scrub and pinyon jays, black-throated gray warblers, and Cassin's kingbirds. In the ponderosa pine–sage areas, best bets are in the meadows around the Visitor Center and around Sunrise and Sunset viewpoints; you're likely to see bluebirds, tanagers, warblers, olive-sided flycatchers, and Townsend's solitaires. Then in the Douglas fir and white fir forest, observe closely at Rainbow Point, where you may see Williamson's sapsuckers, hermit thrushes, and ruby-crowned kinglets. Naturalist-led bird walks are given occasionally and an evening program on birds about every two weeks.

ACCOMMODATIONS. A 70-unit motel is available in the park. **Bryce Canyon Lodge** has 40 newly renovated western cabins and is listed on the National Register of Historic Places. The lodge has a dining room and snack bar. For reservations, write TW Services, Inc., Box 400, Cedar City, Utah 84720. Outside the park is **Ruby's Inn,** the **Pink Cliffs Motel,** and **Bryce Canyon Pines.** Motels are located also in Panguitch, Hatch, and along US 89 and Utah 12.

CAMPING. Two campgrounds are located inside the park near the Visitor Center; a grocery store is available with limited supplies. The camping limit is 14 days. This area requires permits for backcountry use.

SEASONS. If you come in late spring or summer, wildflowers alone will make your trip worthwhile, including paintbrush, columbine, yarrow, and penstemon. Temperature, like vegetation, varies with altitude.

Between April and October, days are warm, with occasional thundershowers, followed by cool evenings.

The lodge is open from mid-May to the end of September only; all park roads are kept open during winter, when white snow contrasts with the brilliant colors of the Pink Cliffs. Skies are deep blue and haze free.

NEARBY. The **Dixie National Forest** encircles the park. The nearest recreation area, at Pine Lake, elevation 8,200 feet, has fishing, boating, camping. **Red Canyon** campground is located midway between Bryce and Panguitch, off Utah 12. **Panguitch Lake,** in addition to forest camping, has boat rentals, cabins, and fishing. Panguitch, 27 miles west of Bryce, is an interesting ranching community. **Escalante Petrified Forest State Reserve,** 50 miles east of Bryce Canyon on Utah 12, has self-guiding nature trails and a campground. To hike the spectacular Escalante Canyons along the Escalante River, stop at the Bureau of Land Management office in Escalante to obtain a backcountry permit.

If you are coming from the direction of Salt Lake City, consider a side trip to **Capitol Reef National Park,** a 20-mile uplift of sandstone cliffs, near Torrey. East of Cedar City, a short side trip will take you to **Cedar Breaks National Monument,** a natural amphitheater in the Pink Wasatch Cliffs.

Bryce Canyon, Zion, and **Grand Canyon** national parks are intimately related geologically. A visit to all three of these parks is like a tour through gigantic galleries of 600 million years of the geologic past—a magnificent opportunity that is unmatched anywhere else.

FOR FURTHER INFORMATION. Write Superintendent, Bryce Canyon National Park, Bryce Canyon, Utah 84717.

BRYCE CANYON NATL. PARK

scale 0 1 2 miles

CANYONLANDS NATIONAL PARK

Utah

Established 1964

IN THE FALL of 1985 I went camping and hiking with friends in the section of Canyonlands called the Needles, so named for its thousands of red-and-white rounded pillars, spires, and balanced rocks, some rising as high as 30-story buildings. One day we hiked to the confluence of the Green and Colorado rivers, entrenched in their deep, winding gorges, from which benches of land spread outward to meet cliffs of orange-red sandstone. It was a dramatic, wild setting, out of the fictional pages of Zane Grey and the real-life pages of John Wesley Powell, who explored the full length of the Colorado River.

Days were warm, though not uncomfortable. Nights were cool to chilly. We were alone most of the time but did encounter a few parties on the trail. They were composed of older people, cheerful hikers traveling with pocket guides and binoculars. They did not want things to be easy in the wilderness.

Until recent years the Canyonlands region was little known outside of southern Utah. A few dirt roads penetrated the edges, but most of it was inaccessible. Since 1964, when it became a national park, the world has been learning of the flaming color and rocky landscape.

Here the Colorado and Green rivers sliced through layers of rock and stripped them back to raveled ancient edges. Tributary streams, rain, and frost then carved the details. The puzzles of how and when these events happened are part of the enchantment.

The elevations in the park range from 3,600 feet in low-lying basinlands to plateaus and mesas of almost 7,000 feet, with unending variety in landscape.

Though portions of the 337,570-acre national park are still unexplored, evidences of prehistoric humans have been located in ruined villages and in petroglyphs chipped nearly a thousand years ago.

Native plants and animals are typical of the arid pinyon-and-juniper community, except for the cottonwoods and water-loving plants around the seeps and springs. Deer, coyotes, and foxes are among those present but rarely observed. A local native population of desert bighorn inhabits a portion of the park. From May to August, except in extra dry years, wildflowers carpet the moist locations.

33

THE PRACTICAL GUIDE

Most roads are unpaved. Portions of the backcountry can be seen only by four-wheel-drive vehicle, boat, horseback, or afoot. Yet visitors can get a generous sampling of the area with time and patience.

BACKGROUND. Two approaches are available by passenger car to the Canyonlands frontier. The northern gateway is the old pioneer Mormon town of **Moab,** where Zane Grey set many of his novels—in the days before uranium, oil, and potash. A graded, dry-weather road off Utah 313 leads to the **Island in the Sky** section of the park. Dominating the land between the two rivers, the tip of this mesa, **Grandview Point,** affords a spectacular rimrock view of the park with its red-hued cliffs, buttes, and mesas. At the end of a short hiking trail, **Upheaval Dome,** a mysterious fragment of geology, is a deep, vertical-walled crater with a cream-colored mass of stone upthrust through surrounding red-tinged sandstone.

From the southeast gateway, **Monticello,** at the foot of the Abajo Mountains, US 191 travels north 15 miles to Church Rock. Paved Utah 211 leads first to the landmark known as **Newspaper Rock,** in Newspaper Rock State Park, where a series of petroglyphs were chipped into the cliffside by prehistoric and historic Indians. The ranger station just inside the park is a good place to learn about park programs and facilities. Passenger cars find it passable to **Squaw Spring** and Squaw Flat Campground, about 3 miles beyond the ranger station. But a four-wheel-drive vehicle is essential to reach **Elephant Hill,** at the brink of the spectacular **Needles** area.

Four-wheel-drive vehicles afford opportunities to explore more of the park. A challenging jeep trail heads west from Squaw Flat into the Needles and **Chesler Park** along **Devil's Lane** to the confluence of the Green and Colorado rivers.

TOUR OPERATORS. Jeep tours are conducted by local experts into the Needles and also deeper into the backcountry to see such features as **Angel Arch,** a sandstone span guarded by an angellike figure. Angel Arch and surroundings were first discovered and named as recently as 1955. Outfitters also run guided pack trips for hikers and horseback riders. A list of the outfitters is available by mail from the park.

Adventures are offered by the **Canyonlands Field Institute** during spring, summer, and fall "for those who wish to understand, not just to see." These include guided trips, seminars, photo workshops, and programs for children. Write Canyonlands Field Institute, Box 68, Moab, Utah 84532.

BOATING. Access to portions of the park is feasible from two directions. One is from the town of **Green River,** which is the starting point of the annual 196-mile Friendship Cruise and Motorboat Marathon to Moab every May and June. The other direction is from **Moab** on the Colorado River to the confluence of the two rivers. Boat tours are run frequently, giving a new dimension to the Canyonlands experience. Wild **Cataract Canyon,** below the junction, is known as "the explorer's nightmare and modern river runner's challenge." Commercial river trips with proper boats and expert rivermen are the best way to view these rapids.

In big-water rapids like Cataract Canyon small boats are often lashed together, side by side, to form a "G-rig," named for Georgie White, the woman who invented this kind of arrangement for floating the once-mighty waters of the Colorado River in Grand Canyon.

If you are capable of going on your own, you must apply for authorization and a required permit. However you go, count on viewing abundant and varied birdlife, from ouzels along the rocks to high-flying golden eagles. Be sure to plan your trip with a copy of *Canyon Country Paddles,* by Verne Huser (Salt Lake City: Wasatch Publishers, Inc.).

ACCOMMODATIONS. The park has no overnight lodgings, food, or gasoline facilities. Motels are located in Moab, Monticello, and Green River. Camping supplies are available in these towns.

CAMPING. Inside the park, campgrounds at **Squaw Flat** and **Willow Flat** are equipped with tables, fireplaces, and pit toilets; there is a 14-day limit. Firewood is not available, so bring your own fuel as well as water. This area requires permits for backcountry use. Primitive camping is permitted at designated locations in the **Island in the Sky** section and in the backcountry. Plan to carry extra water at all times. State park campgrounds are located at **Indian Creek,** near the Needles area, and at **Dead**

Horse Point, south of Moab. Good campgrounds are located in timbered **Manti-La Sal National Forest,** one section of which is just south of the park; another, east of Moab.

SEASONS. This is desert country, where daily, as well as seasonal, temperature changes can be extreme: hot days in summer get up to a maximum of 110 degrees Fahrenheit, cooling rapidly after sundown to a low shortly before sunup, then rising rapidly again. The average annual temperature is from 50 to 55 degrees Fahrenheit, but there are lows of 20 below zero. Some snow falls on the rims during winter. Spring and autumn are mild and pleasant. The average annual precipitation is 5 to 9 inches, much of the moisture coming in late-summer thundershowers.

NEARBY. The companion piece to Canyonlands, **Arches National Park,** outside of Moab, contains an overwhelming concentration of red-rock arches, immense windows, and pinnacles.

Within 25 miles of the heart of Canyonlands, the Monticello and Moab districts of **Manti-La Sal National Forest** provide the contrast—high cool woodlands rising to summits of the La Sal and Abajo mountains, more than 11,000 and 12,000 feet, with fishing, camping, and scenic drives. Downstream on the Colorado lies **Glen Canyon National Recreation Area,** where Lake Powell, a major watersports center, is formed behind the third highest dam in the world. Near Blanding and Bluff, **Natural Bridges National Monument** contains three huge sandstone bridges, magnificent canyons, and ancient Indian ruins. **Hovenweep National Monument** embraces a chain of well-preserved but isolated prehistoric Indian towers in the famed Four Corners region of the Southwest, near the point where the boundary lines of Colorado, Utah, Arizona, and New Mexico converge.

Southwest of Bluff, the town of **Mexican Hat** is gateway to fantastic **Monument Valley,** a land of buttes and mesas, where the Navajo Indians are developing visitor facilities astride the once-remote Utah-Arizona desert boundary.

FOR FURTHER INFORMATION. Write Superintendent, Canyonlands National Park, 446 South Main Street, Moab, Utah 84532.

CAPITOL REEF NATIONAL PARK

Utah

Established 1971

FOR A WHILE I looked away from the scenery of tilted cliffs and rainbow rock layers in south-central Utah, a strange and still little-known land, to read an excerpt of the 1880 description of it by Clarence E. Dutton, a pioneering geologist. The year was 1880. "The colors are such as no pigments can portray," he wrote. "They are deep, rich and variegated; and so luminous are they that light seems to flow or shine out of the rock rather than to be reflected from it."

His words are still valid. Here I explored the Waterpocket Fold, a strip of colorful rock layers almost 100 miles long (72 miles within the national park), formed from a buckling or wrinkling of the earth's crust. At Cathedral Valley, in the northern end of the park, I saw spectacular monoliths 400 to 700 feet high, of reddish brown sandstone capped with grayish yellow strata—many freestanding on the valley floor.

Capitol Reef itself, a segment of the Waterpocket Fold, is a 20-mile-long uplift rising 1,000 feet above the Fremont River (roughly midway between Canyonlands and Bryce Canyon national parks), embracing the beauty Mr. Dutton described; but this is only a portion of the new park. It now includes nearly all of the most spectacular, readily understood monocline in the United States. Exposed and eroded rock layers laid down more than 125 million years ago stand on edge like pages of a gigantic geology book.

Due to its isolation and difficulty of access, the Capitol Reef country actually was undiscovered by whites and unexplored until comparatively recent times. The earliest inhabitants apparently were pre-historic Indians who arrived during the Basket Maker III period, dating back to about A.D. 700, and who remained until not later than 1275 (when the great 25-year drought began). These people left reminders of their occupancy in the form of large, distinctive petroglyphs, some of which are found near Fruita and on Pleasant Creek.

The first white people of record to see any part of this area were members of the William Wolfskill party of 1829. On his celebrated voyage down the Colorado River in 1869, John Wesley Powell discovered the Dirty Devil River, which he later renamed the Fremont and revisited on his expedition of 1871.

Soon afterward, Professor A. H. Thompson, Powell's geologist, explored and mapped the area, applying names to various features, which are still in use. Other geologists followed, including C. E. Dutton, who looked down on Capitol Reef and described the Waterpocket Fold.

At the Grand Wash I observed another kind of history. Climbing a steep and strenuous trail to the high cliffs, I came to Cassidy Arch, named for Butch Cassidy, the outlaw, who may have used the area as a hiding place. If so, he certainly knew how to pick his out-of-the-way spots.

In 1937, a scenic spur of this huge monocline was proclaimed Capitol Reef National Monument. Later enlarged to 241,865 acres that take in the entire Waterpocket Fold running north to south and striking downward west to east, the area was made a national park in 1971. It presents a complete geological story, enhanced by its isolation.

THE PRACTICAL GUIDE

The main access to the park is via Utah 24, an all-weather road connecting with I-70 on the northeast (near Green River), on the northwest with US 89 (near Salina). Though the road cuts through the northern portion of the park, this area is most enjoyed by hikers and backpackers.

BACKGROUND. Before taking to the trails, see a ''new'' side of the park at the one-room **Old Fruita School House,** the first building restored (in 1984) under a Park Service program for preserving this area's unusual history. Fruita, settled in the 1870s and 1880s, was a farming outpost at the edge of dry desert. Miners, cowboys, outlaws, and explorers found it a welcome oasis in their travels. Park headquarters now occupies the former townsite. Besides the schoolhouse, the restoration program features part of the original orchards, a pioneer dwelling, barn, and smokehouse.

A number of trails, ranging from easy to strenuous, provide opportunities for everyone. Serious distance hikers need to recognize possible problems of lack of water or too much of it. The arid climate makes the park susceptible to long droughts that dry up seeps, springs, and water pockets. Then, a sudden shower may send tons of water hurtling down a narrow canyon. Always check with park rangers on water and weather conditions.

The road entering from the west passes a series of scenic viewpoints—**Chimney Rock, Panorama Point,** and **Goosenecks**—opening on footpaths of varying lengths. Goosenecks Overlooks face the deep zigzag canyon carved by Sulphur Creek. You'll find others en route east, nota-

bly **Hickman Bridge** and **Behunin's Cabin.**

Six miles from the park's west boundary, the modern **Visitor Center** features displays of the area's first inhabitants, pre-Columbian Indians of the Basket Maker period, and of the 19th-century Mormon settlers. The orientation program will help prepare you to tour the park's roads and hiking trails. Observe Park Service precautions about flash floods: never park in a shallow lowland area or enter a gorge while it's raining.

On this route **Grand Wash** affords a fairly easy hike of 2¼ miles along the bottom of the wash. You'll pass between sheer canyon walls displaying unusual rock formations. There is another trail, more strenuous, climbing steeply to the high cliffs and **Cassidy Arch.** Four miles south a spur road leads to **Capitol Gorge,** passing thousands of "solution pockets" (or potholes) carved by wind and water, and the start of a hiking trail to the base of the **Golden Throne,** a massive butte providing spectacular views over the entire canyon. Inside the gorge you'll find Indian petroglyphs, names of pioneers carved into the rock, and enormous natural water tanks.

For years Grand Wash and Capitol Gorge were the most popular attractions of the national monument, but there are many more accessible now, particularly for those with four-wheel-drive or high-clearance vehicles. **Cathedral Valley** is one such section, a good day's trip from the Visitor Center. Rock formations bear such names as Temple of the Sun, Temple of the Moon, Gypsum Sinkhole, and Glass Mountain. Going north into Cathedral Valley, it is first necessary to pass through the **Valley of Decision,** a narrow gap where a driver must choose whether to proceed or, in the face of clouds and threatening skies, turn back. The roads into Cathedral Valley are unpaved, and travel can be difficult, or impossible, if rain does occur. But it may well be worth it for the chance to see and photograph the sandstone buttes against the background of towering Thousand Lake

Mountain. Check at the Visitor Center for latest information on road conditions.

The **Waterpocket Fold** derives the first part of its name from the shallow depressions that sometimes collect rainwater and hold it for long periods as a boon to human and animal alike. **Burr Trail,** an old cattle-drive route, is the only way to go east-west across the fold in the southern end of the park; other routes through the fold are through Fremont River canyon, Capitol Gorge, Pleasant Creek, and Oak Creek. From the west, approach through the town of Boulder, expecting switchbacks and steep grades on a road usually suitable for auto traffic but not recommended for heavy trailers. Before entering the park, you'll pass through a 30-mile stretch of public domain land and find plenty of spectacular sandstone country, everything from near-white buff to deep red. From the top of Burr Trail, you come to the junction with **Muley Twist Canyon,** running north and south. North are several arches, accessible by jeep or foot traffic, while to the south you will find choice wilderness backpacking country.

ACCOMMODATIONS. A park campground is located 1 mile south of the Visitor Center near the Fremont River. Evening programs are conducted during the summer by park naturalists.

Rim Rock Ranch is located 2 miles west of the park boundary near Torrey; it offers jeep trips through portions of the park. Motels are available at Bicknell, about 20 miles west. Closest accommodations on the east are 37 miles from the Visitor Center at Hanksville.

CAMPING. Capitol Reef's campground is a mile south of Utah 24. It has campsites, water, and toilets, plus pump station, and is open all year for 14-day stays.

SEASONS. Summer daytime temperatures at the Visitor Center (elevation 5,418 feet) are in the 80s and 90s; nights are generally cool. Spring and autumn are mild, with cold weather lasting from mid-December through February. An abundance of insects and birds brings new life to spring.

In the lowlands of Cathedral Valley, desert plants turn glorious shades of red and gold in autumn.

NEARBY. At Boulder, on the site of an Indian ruin dating back nearly 1,000 years, **Anasazi State Park** gives an introduction to the Anasazi—the Ancient Ones—who roamed the Southwest. **Calf Creek Recreation Area,** between Boulder and Escalante, run by the Bureau of Land Management, provides good camping facilities and a 5½-mile round-trip scenic trail to Calf Creek Falls. **Escalante Canyon,** portions of which are accessible by car or jeep, is explored best on backpack trips of two to four days. Escalante country, wild and beautiful, combines deep, narrow canyons, river-cut cliffs, natural bridges, hanging gardens, and waterfalls—one of the finest unprotected wilderness areas in America. Best months for hiking the canyons are April, May, September, and October. In the **Henry Mountains,** rising to more than 11,000 feet on the east side of the Waterpocket Fold, the Bureau of Land Management has developed four recreation sites with access to hiking.

FOR FURTHER INFORMATION. Write Superintendent, Capitol Reef National Park, Torrey, Utah 84775.

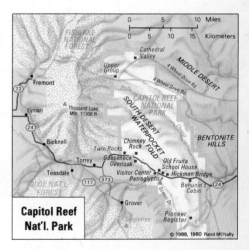

CARLSBAD CAVERNS NATIONAL PARK

New Mexico

Established 1930

I WOULD NEVER have expected (if I hadn't known what was coming) to find such a display beneath the foothills of the tawny Guadalupe Mountains in southern New Mexico, a few miles north of the Texas border. Aboveground, desertlike flatlands and mountains swept away to remote horizons. Below, however, a whole new world would unfold.

Although other cave systems are known to be deeper and a few have more miles of surveyed passageway, none surpasses Carlsbad in the immensity of its chambers. The famous Big Room is considered the largest underground room in the world.

I found that immensity is not Carlsbad's only distinguishing quality. The formations of limestone are of endless variety and beauty. Some of the inverted spires known as stalactites are shaped like fragile chandeliers. Stalagmites grow from the floor like massive domes or frozen waterfalls of stone. In some cases, stalagmites and stalactites are joined, forming monumental columns and pillars. Yet alongside may be densely clustered growths called helictites, phenomenal for their delicate appearance.

The limestones in the caverns are very old. They formed about 200 million years ago, during the Permian period, from a reef bordering an inland sea. In a process that began less than 60 million years ago, these caverns were hollowed out by underground water slowly dissolving its way through cracks in the earth. In more recent times, the inside water has drained away and another stage of formation has begun. Slowly and carefully, nature builds anew on drops of rain and snow seeping down from the surface. Each drop carries a tiny amount of dissolved limestone. The water passes on, leaving its cargo of minute increments to cavern formations.

During the 1880s ranchers and settlers of New Mexico referred to the cavern as Bat Cave. They were content to let the bats have it as their special place. Soon after, however, the deposits of bat guano attracted attention. Within a few years thousands of tons were extracted by a mining company. Early in this century a local boy, James Larkin White, went exploring, armed only with a kerosene lamp. His reports on the marvels found in the cave attracted the interest of others, notably Robert Holley of the General Land Office and Dr. Willis T. Lee of the United States Geological Survey. On October 25, 1923, President Calvin Coolidge proclaimed Carlsbad Cave a national monument, embracing 719 acres.

With national publicity, Carlsbad became famous. Visitors thronged to this remote attraction, even though (in those pre-elevator days) entrance to it was via a miner's bucket lowered by windlass almost 200 feet to the cavern floor. Carlsbad remained a national monument for only seven years. In 1930, a bill to make it a national park passed Congress without opposition and was approved by President Herbert Hoover.

More than 70 caverns lie within the 46,753-acre park, but development has been limited to the largest and most easily accessible of these, the mighty Carlsbad Cavern, in which the famous Big Room has a ceiling as high as a 60-story building and a floor space large enough for 14 football fields.

THE PRACTICAL GUIDE

You can stop off to view the cave and the aboveground environment in half a day with ease. During most of the year, you may enter at any time during operating hours to spend as long, or as short, a period as you wish on self-guided trips underground. Rangers are around to answer questions and provide assistance. A nominal fee is charged for entry into the cavern.

Two traditional trips are available. The long one requires approximately three hours with 3 miles of walking, starting with a relatively steep descent down switchback trails to a depth of 829 feet. The shorter tour requires about one hour and covers 1¼ miles of mostly level trail in the Big Room, 750 feet below. It begins at the Visitor Center; descent is by elevator. Visitors in wheelchairs can travel into the Big Room.

From early June through Labor Day, the caverns are open 7:30 a.m. to 6 p.m. During the rest of the year hours are from 8:30 a.m. to 3:30 p.m.

Guided trips are conducted four times daily during portions of December, January, and February.

BACKGROUND. The **Visitor Center** lies at the end of the 7-mile drive from the park entrance. Stop here first to see the displays on the history of the caverns. You'll find a restaurant at the Visitor Center; lunches and refreshments are also available when you reach the Big Room underground.

The **cave walk** begins at the natural entrance, through an arch 90 feet wide and 40 feet high in its greatest dimensions. National Park Service rangers are in charge. The caverns' temperature remains at 56 degrees Fahrenheit throughout the year; carry a sweater or wrap. The trail extends a mile downward through the main corridor, with high ceilings and large passages, through the **Green Lake Room,** named for a small green pool, into the **King's Palace,** which many visitors consider the most ornate of all chambers. Electric illumination reveals the circular form of the palace and its curtains of glittering cave onyx. The trail leads through a series of brilliantly scenic rooms. The **Queen's Chamber** is adorned with formations so translucent that a light placed behind them brings out faint tints of pink and rose.

The **Papoose Room** is a beautiful little chamber, its low ceiling gleaming with stalactites. All of these are only a prelude to the **Big Room.** After a luncheon stop and rest, the walk continues to the vast chamber where the ceiling arches 255 feet overhead. One formation poised over the path is aptly named Sword of Damocles. It is followed by totem poles, snowbanked forests, the celebrated Rock of Ages in a dark central alcove, and the Giant Dome. All trips end with a welcome elevator ride to the Visitor Center at the surface.

New Cave, a cave in another area of the park, was opened to the public in 1974. Guided lantern tours, limited to 25 persons, are conducted through this large, undeveloped cave. Reservations are required for the challenging New Cave trips, scheduled daily during summer and weekends only in winter. New Cave is accessible only by walking up a steep ½-mile primitive trail from the mouth of Slaughter Canyon. The cave was discovered in 1937 by a goat herder, Tom Tucker, searching for lost animals. It was used in 1950 as the setting for the film *King Solomon's Mines.*

Bat flights can be observed every evening from May through October, as bats spiral outward for their nightlong feeding on insects in the surrounding valleys. Despite age-old superstitions, the bats of Carlsbad Caverns reveal themselves to be fascinating creatures: alert, great divers and fliers, and useful to people by feeding on destructive insects. Once numbering 7 to 8 million but now only about half a million, they spend the day hanging head downward in dense clusters from the walls and ceilings. At night they zoom out, 5,000 a minute, on the trail of moths and other insects. A park naturalist explains the bat flight each evening at the cave entrance, just before the flight begins at sunset.

Aboveground the surface of the national park conserves an attractive display of semiarid vegetation and wildlife. Mule deer are frequently seen from the park road in the morning and evening. Fawns of the mule deer arrive into the world in late June and early July. Lizards of many kinds perch on top of rocks while sunning themselves and watching for food or enemies. Stroll along the self-guiding nature trails, if only to learn the identifying names of cacti and other plants that clothe the desert of the Southwest.

Guided nature walks are conducted over the **Oak Springs Trail.** An observation tower atop the Visitor Center provides the best view of the vast Delaware Basin. On a clear day you can see Guadalupe Peak, highest point in Texas.

Off-trail hiking and backpacking opportunities are plentiful. Elevations range from 3,600 feet to 6,300 feet atop Guadalupe Ridge at the park's western boundary. If you want to hike the backcountry, register first at the Visitor Center. Trails are poorly defined but can be followed with a topographic map. There is no water available in the backcountry, so don't plan a trip without adequate preparation.

PHOTOGRAPHY. You will probably do most of your shooting in the Big Room. It will be helpful to learn in advance the equipment and exposures to use below; also to identify the principal features, such as Hall of the Giants, Giant Dome, Temple of the Sun, and Rock of Ages. Don't overlook the four scenic rooms on the first part of the long trip. Photos may be taken at will, the only restriction being that visitors are not permitted to leave the paved trails.

WITHOUT A CAR. T.N.M. & O. coaches make a round trip daily to Whites City, at the park entrance, from El Paso, Texas, and from Carlsbad, New Mexico. Bus service is available from Whites City to the park Visitor Center four times daily.

ACCOMMODATIONS. Families traveling with pets will be pleased to find kennels available at the park. There also is a nursery for children too young to undertake the cavern tour. However, there are no overnight facilities in the park. Motels, hotels, and campgrounds are located in Carlsbad, 27 miles from the park, and at Whites City near the park entrance.

SEASONS. The park is open every day of the year except Christmas Day. Winter temperatures are mild, snow and ice rare. Spring and fall are excellent times to visit, when desert flowers bloom. Summer days are hot, but the cool caverns provide welcome relief, and during the evening temperatures drop.

NEARBY. Tie in a visit to **Guadalupe Mountains National Park** in Texas for good hiking and surprising mountain vistas.

FOR FURTHER INFORMATION. Write Superintendent, Carlsbad Caverns National Park, 3225 National Parks Highway, Carlsbad, New Mexico 88220.

CHANNEL ISLANDS NATIONAL PARK

California

Established 1980

I'VE BEEN to the Channel Islands twice, marveling every minute at this natural wonderland so close to the Southern California megalopolis. The rocky beaches and outcrops provide important breeding and resting areas for sea birds. The islands are a stronghold for seals and sea lions, including the only breeding colony of northern fur seals south of Alaska. Waters around the islands are on major migration routes of whale species—including not only the familiar gray whale, but the blue whale, the world's largest mammal.

It didn't take me long on arrival to determine why the Channel Islands have been left largely to their own. Wind and fog are common, storms likely. But weather creates a mood to match the raucous cries of the sea lions and landscape of untamed seas.

Between Point Conception and the Mexican border, off the coast of California, the eight Channel Islands lie in two groups, 10 to 70 miles from the mainland. The park consists of five of them, plus 125,000 acres of surrounding submerged land and water. The northern quartet of islands, all in the park, was once an extension of the Santa Monica Mountains, broken away by the sea in geologic history. The islands were discovered by the intrepid Juan Rodriguez Cabrillo in 1542, when they were still inhabited by the seafaring Chumash Indians.

Rocky beaches teemed with fur seals, sea lions, and elephant seals, and the offshore kelp beds with sea otters. The cliffs and beaches were dense with birds, including colonies of auklets, cormorants, murrelets, and pelicans. Then the Spanish began taking eggs and seal meat. They were followed by the Russians in their massive quest for fur, and ultimately by the Americans, who came to exploit whatever fur sources remained and to introduce cattle, sheep, and hogs.

Of the southern Channel Islands, offshore between Los Angeles and San Diego, San Nicolas and San Clemente have been administered by the U.S. Navy as bombing-range and missile-tracking stations. Santa Catalina, privately owned, is developed as a well-known resort and ranch, presently accessible to the public through the Santa Catalina Island Conservancy and Los Angeles County Department of Parks and Recreation.

Since 1938 two of the islands, Anacapa and Santa Barbara, with their cliffs, beaches, mountains, and canyons, have been protected as a national monument. With the 1969 oil spill off the coast of Santa Barbara, concern arose for these and the other islands and the waters around them. Consequently San Miguel, the westernmost island (administered by the navy), was added to the monument in 1976. And in 1980 the new national park was established, with provisions for acquiring Santa Rosa and a portion of Santa Cruz.

The islands continue to become more accessible and their special values better known and understood. Geologists are intrigued by the earthquake faults, freshwater springs, mountain ranges and valleys, as well as the varieties of rock. It is also a treasure of flora, with more than 600 plant species, including some that grow nowhere else in the world.

Archaeological values are high on all the islands. Midden and village sites of the Chumash people on Santa Rosa and San Miguel are especially significant because of their antiquity and abundance. Charred remains of dwarf mammoth associated with island sites have tentatively been dated at about 40,000 years old, indicating one of the earliest evidences of people in North America.

I came away with a delightful memento purchased at the park Visitor Center, an "audio postcard," a tape with the sounds of birds and gulls, of pinnipeds, and of waves in the intertidal zone. Not as good as the real thing, but it helps to remember a choice place in the sea around us.

THE PRACTICAL GUIDE

A stop at the park Visitor Center is worthwhile. Follow the signs to the end of the harbor in Ventura. Exhibits and slide shows furnish an introduction to the islands. Island Packers (1867 Spinnaker Drive, Ventura, California 93001; phone 805-642-1393), located adjacent to park headquarters, provides tours to Anacapa Island and transportation to Santa Barbara Island, most frequently June to September, with special whale-watching trips in winter. Two weekends a month Island Packers dispatches a 35-passenger boat for a daylong trip to the century-old Scorpion Ranch at the east end of Santa Cruz Island, 23 miles off the coast. Bring your own lunch and drinking water and dress warmly.

Transportation, on an irregular basis and by charter, is available from other ports. For those traveling in personal boats, be warned that Santa Barbara Channel is subject to afternoon rising sea and high wind. Anchoring at either Santa Barbara or Anacapa can be hazardous, and you need a skiff or small boat to go ashore. Only expert boaters should try to make it to San Miguel Island, which is usually subject to rough conditions. You are well advised to first visit

park headquarters, at the Ventura Marina.

BACKGROUND. Closest to the mainland (about 11 miles south of Oxnard) and most accessible is **Anacapa Island,** really composed of three separate islets covering a total of 700 acres. Best anchorages include East Fish Camp and Frenchy's Cove (the latter named for "Frenchy" LeDreau, who lived peaceably in a shack on the island from 1928 to 1956). The National Park Service utilizes a cluster of old Coast Guard buildings, where personnel were stationed until 1969 to operate the lighthouse and horn. East Island Campground has fireplaces and tables, but you must bring your own water and fuel. Campground reservations are required; they may be obtained by writing park headquarters (or call 805-644-8262). Though beaches on the island are few, cliffs rise 250 feet above the sea. You'll see many birds, including Brandt's cormorants, double-creasted cormorants, gulls, and oystercatchers. West Anacapa has been set aside as a sanctuary for brown pelicans, a species rebounding from the brink of extinction—landings are prohibited. Following the 1½-mile nature trail on East Island, you will pass unusual

plants and animals as well as spectacular scenery, 150 feet above the waterline. On land, the giant coreopsis, a striking treelike sunflower, grows in dense stands.

Santa Barbara, the smallest island, lies 38 miles west of San Pedro Harbor in Los Angeles. It takes a steep climb of more than 100 feet from Landing Cove to the small primitive camping area. Though vegetation has suffered due to past grazing, because of Santa Barbara's isolation sea mammals abound.

San Miguel, westernmost island, and little **Prince Island** cover a little less than 10,000 acres. Fog and wind are common. In fact, wind-driven sand covers much of the island, with caliche forests in the dunes. There are more species of pinnipeds found on San Miguel than in any other single location in the world. Mating, giving birth, and/or hauling out are California sea lions, northern elephant seals, Steller sea lions, harbor seals, northern fur seals, and Guadalupe fur seals. These furred mammals once were found in great numbers along the mainland coast, but today breed and pup almost exclusively in the Channel Islands. Access to San Miguel is by permit only; check at park headquarters.

Santa Cruz, the largest island, covers 60,500 acres with peaks over 2,000 feet, rugged slopes, and steep shoreline. A large part of the island is administered by the Nature Conservancy, which welcomes a certain degree of public use. Check with them at 213 Stearns Wharf, Santa Barbara, California 93101, about naturalist-led day trips to Pelican Bay. Island Packers can arrange for stays at refurbished but simple Smuggler's Cove Ranch at the east end of Santa Cruz. **Santa Rosa,** covering 53,000 acres, is still private property and is worked as a cattle ranch.

DIVING AND FISHING. With caves, coves, and shipwrecks, the Channel Islands offer some of the best diving off the West Coast. Divers also like to bring back abalone, lobster, and scallops. Rockfish, perch, and sheepshead are among major targets for anglers. Special restrictions do apply. Check with park headquarters.

NEARBY. For camping near park headquarters, try **Emma Wood State Beach,** 3 miles north of Ventura on US 101, and **McGrath State Beach,** 3 miles south on Harbor Boulevard. You can learn a lot about the Channel Islands at the **Santa Barbara Museum of Natural History,** which displays a replica of a Chumash dugout canoe and charred dwarf mammoth taken from Santa Rosa.

FOR FURTHER INFORMATION. Write Superintendent, Channel Islands National Park, 1901 Spinnaker Drive, Ventura, California 93001.

CRATER LAKE NATIONAL PARK

Oregon

Established 1902

I HAD HIKED the 2½ miles on fairly gentle grade to the fire tower at the summit of Mount Scott. It was the highest point in the park, 8,926 feet, almost 2,800 feet above Crater Lake, the jewel of southern Oregon. The color of the lake was the deepest, most brilliant blue—resulting from the reflection of sunlight on waters more than 1,900 feet deep. I was struck also by the setting, the green Cascadian forest of pines, fir, and hemlock, fitting to the jewel.

It was a clear day, and to the south, 100 miles distant, I saw the great snowy cone of Mount Shasta, 14,000 feet high. It made me think of what Crater Lake was like—in the time before the lake.

It was only yesterday, as time beyond our own time is measured, 10,000 years ago, when Mount Mazama, a 12,000-foot volcanic peak, rose above the green crest of the Cascades, along with her neighbors, Mounts Shasta, Adams, Hood, St. Helens, Rainier, and Baker—all mighty sentinels of the Northwest range. Then about 6,840 years ago Mazama erupted with violence.

The mountaintop collapsed, forming an immense crater 20 square miles in area, surrounded by towering walls. This masterpiece of nature's creation is known as a caldera. Now I could take in the entire lake, cradled in the extinct volcano, at one time from the rim of lava cliffs, a spectacle hard to match.

This scenic wonder apparently was discovered in 1853 by John Wesley Hillman, one of a party of miners searching for the Lost Cabin Mine near the headwaters of the Rogue River. He and his friends voted to name it Deep Blue Lake, but the discovery was not made public for 31 years. The first official exploration was conducted in 1883 by Dr. J. S. Diller, a geologist, who conducted a sounding of the lake and recorded its depth at 2,008 feet.

William Gladstone Steel, a transplanted Kansan, who first saw Crater Lake in 1885, is credited as "Father of the Park." His determined crusade began with a petition to President Grover Cleveland that all lands around Crater Lake be withdrawn from homesteading and other claims; this was granted February 1, 1886. From then on he fought an uphill battle until Congress voted to establish the national park, with an act which President Theodore Roosevelt approved on May 22, 1902. Steel was appointed the second superintendent in 1913.

Crater is the deepest lake in the United States. In the Western Hemisphere only Great Slave Lake in Canada is deeper. While the lake is the focal point, the 183,180 acres of green meadows and forests inside the park serve as a sanctuary for species of wildlife under harsh attack elsewhere. The badger, coyote, bobcat, and mountain lion are rare but do exist; more common is the beautiful red fox. The yellow-bellied marmot usually can be found in the rockslides. Golden-mantled ground squirrels make their appearance at every parking turnout. I saw California gulls frequently over the lake, even bald eagles and a high-flying golden eagle. Jays and nutcrackers were common along the rim, experts in poaching the tourist circuit. Juncos, chickadees, and nuthatches made good companions on the hiking trails. Each traveler becomes conscious of his or her own favorites.

THE PRACTICAL GUIDE

Plan enough time at Crater Lake to be there at sunrise, when the calm, mirrorlike water reflects the high peaks with sharp clarity. Late afternoon is a choice time, too, especially to see deer in the meadows.

Approaching from Klamath Falls (57 miles away) via the south entrance, or from Medford (69 miles) via the west entrance, note the action of Annie Creek, Castle Creek, and other streams carving their vertical-wall canyons ever deeper in the channels where glaciers once flowed.

BACKGROUND. The **Visitor Center** is conveniently located at Rim Village, between the cafeteria and Crater Lake Lodge. Interpretive displays will answer many questions, and rangers will help to start you right. The broad terrace of **Sinnott Memorial,** outside the exhibit building, is an excellent orientation point, where talks on the geologic origin of the lake are given several times daily.

From the Visitor Center at Rim Village begin **Rim Drive,** a 33.4-mile trip around the lake. At Cleetwood Cove, halfway around the lake, the road merges into one way. From this point all vehicular traffic must travel in a clockwise direction. Buses operate from Klamath Falls in summer, and scenic bus tours around the drive are scheduled daily. **Cloudcap,** among the snowbanks and whitebark pines, provides a sweeping vista that complements the one at Sinnott Memorial. Hikers may want to follow the 2½-mile trail to the fire tower at the summit of Mount Scott. **The Pinnacles,** 6 miles off Rim Drive (from Kerr Notch), are spires and fluted columns formed when loose volcanic fragments solidified around gas and steam vents.

A number of trails lead from the drive to other views. The end of **Discovery Point Trail** is near the spot where the young miner Hillman and his friends first spotted the incredible sight of what he called Deep Blue Lake. **Garfield Peak** is one of the best vantage points, with a clear view of **Wizard Island,** actually a small volcanic cone produced by seething fire within the caldera after destruction of Mount Mazama.

Pumice Desert, produced by ancient volcanic action, lies along the north entrance road leading to Diamond Lake (4 miles north) and Bend (92 miles north). The lodgepole pine has gained a precarious foothold on the desert floor in nature's mission of clothing old devastation with a new forest.

TOUR OPERATOR. A 2½-hour launch trip around the lake, accompanied by a park naturalist, from the boat landing at the foot of Cleetwood Trail will afford an intimate perspective of the inside of a volcano and its multicolored lava cliffs. The concession-operated launches run from late June through Labor Day, 9 a.m. to 3 p.m. The trail is the only access to the water. It is only 1.1 miles, but allow plenty of time; carry water and limit gear to essentials. It is steep going down, steeper on the return. It is well worth the effort to observe the vistas of Wizard Island and Phantom Ship.

HIKING TRAILS. The varied types of trails provide the chance for exercise and intimate contact with nature. More than 100 miles of trail through evergreen forests are open to hikers. The leisurely trail through **Castle Crest Wildflower Garden** presents orchids, violets, columbine, asters, and a host of others, identified by plant labels. A 2½-mile trail from Rim Drive leads to the fire tower at the summit of **Mount Scott,** above Cloudcap. For serious backcountry travel, buy a trail guide at park headquarters or the Visitor Center. Permits (free) are required for overnight stays.

CAMPFIRE PROGRAMS. These are held every evening at Mazama Campground. Indoor campfire programs are conducted in Rim Center building.

BICYCLING. Riding is feasible but challenging, with long, steep grades. Rim Drive is narrow, without shoulders, half of it is open to one-way traffic only in a clockwise direction from Cleetwood Cove. Be sure to carry water; Rim Village is the only source along the rim.

ACCOMMODATIONS. The **Crater Lake Lodge** and cabins at **Rim Village** offer plain accommodations. Reservations are advisable. Write Crater Lake Lodge, Inc., Crater Lake, Oregon 97604. Many motels are located in Klamath Falls, Medford, and other nearby communities.

CAMPING. Two campgrounds in the park operate first-come, first-served. **Lost Creek,** on The Pinnacles spur road from East Rim Drive, has 12 sites for tents only; no fees are charged. It opens in late July. **Mazama Campground,** operated by the park concession (fee charged), has no hookups, but provides fresh water, flush toilets, and dump station. Other campgrounds are in surrounding national forests.

SEASONS. Lodge and cabins are open from about June 15 to September 10, and campgrounds from July through September. Weather during the short two-month summer is unpredictable, with warm days and chilly nights. The north entrance is usually closed by snow until late June, and Rim Drive till late July; but the south and west entrances are open all year. From late October through May heavy snowfalls create a glistening attraction, with reflections of high peaks in the mirrorlike water.

NEARBY. The **Cascade Mountains** surrounding Crater Lake comprise one of the finest recreation areas of the Northwest. Four miles north of the park, **Diamond Lake** lies within **Umpqua National Forest,** with campgrounds on the east shore and miles of forest trails to **Mount Bailey, Mount Thielsen,** and along the Pacific Crest Trail. **Lake of the Woods** is one of the most attractive areas of Winema National Forest, with good fishing for rainbow trout and camping near the base of Mount McLoughlin. The **Ashland Loop Drive** passes through stands of Douglas fir and ponderosa pine within **Rogue River National Forest.** So does the **Pacific Crest Trail,** running from Washington to the California border. **Ashland** is the scene of the Oregon Shakespearean Festival, mid-July to early September. If driving up from the west coast of California, be sure to stop at **Redwood National Park,** between Orick and Crescent City, California, and at **Oregon Caves National Monument,** a limestone and marble cavern with formations of unusual beauty. If coming from the south, visit **Lava Beds National Monument,** California, a scene of ancient volcanic activity that became a battleground in the Modoc Indian War of 1873.

FOR FURTHER INFORMATION. Write Superintendent, Crater Lake National Park, Box 7, Crater Lake, Oregon 97604.

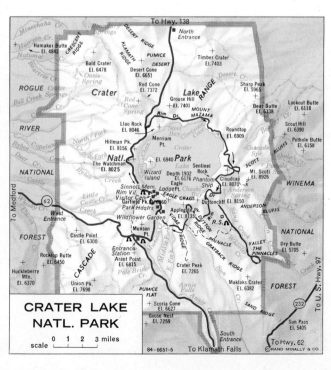

CRATER LAKE
NATL. PARK

scale 0 1 2 3 miles

84-6651-5   ©Rand McNally & Co.

DENALI NATIONAL PARK

Alaska

Established 1917

EARLY ALEUT INDIANS knew Mount McKinley as *Denali,* "the high one." To others it is simply *the* mountain. However you look at it, Mount McKinley constitutes a massive monument to the forces of nature.

The overpowering feeling is one of largeness and naturalness, which is Alaska's special gift to the nation. "Can one describe such a scene and such an environment to wander about in?" once wrote the master of wilderness, Olaus J. Murie. He could find no words, except to add that for him this region comprised the greatest scenic experience on the North American continent.

When I come to Denali I wish that I had more time to wander in this wonderful national park and preserve of 6 million acres, an immense sanctuary of glaciers, forests, tundra, blue lakes, and wildlife roaming free. But time seems in short supply, despite all the conveniences of the age. I realize the need to concentrate on perception in order to understand and fully appreciate Denali. In early territorial days this was rough, untracked country, testing the skills of sourdough prospectors, hunters, geologists, and naturalists. Those people had the time to take it all in. Even after establishment of the national park in 1917 as a great wilderness reserve, it remained inaccessible. But since 1957, with completion of the Denali Highway, the park is easy to reach from Anchorage and Fairbanks. So easy that the wilderness would be overrun without some measure of control. Instead of allowing private vehicles, the park provides free bus transportation—and that's a blessing.

In 1980 Congress voted to enlarge the park to almost 4,700,000 acres, bordered by a new national preserve of 1,330,000 acres. The addition includes the southern half of the mountain and spectacular peaks of the Kichatna Mountains. Congress also voted to change the name to Denali—from Mount McKinley—

National Park, adopting the ancient Indian name for the mountain.

The park terrain rises from about 1,400 feet to 20,320 feet, the highest point on the continent, at the summit of Mount McKinley. There are other major peaks, like Mount Foraker, or "Denali's Wife" (called Sultana by early Indians), at 17,400 feet also taller than anything in the "lower forty-eight"; Mount Silverthrone, 13,220 feet; and Mount Russell, 11,670 feet. Many glaciers, up to 30 and 40 miles long, are still active on these and other mountains inside the park. One of them, Muldrow Glacier, the largest northward-flowing glacier in Alaska, stretches from the summit of Mount McKinley's twin peaks to within a mile of the park road. The whole landscape is influenced by glaciation of the past and present, with broad, U-shaped valleys, small kettle lakes, old and new moraines.

White and black spruce are the chief evergreens growing in the park, with cottonwood and willow along the streambeds, dwarf birch on the lower mountain slopes, quaking aspen and Alaska birch interspersed with the spruce. Most of the park, however, lies above timberline, which varies from 2,500 to 3,000 feet. The vegetation becomes alpine tundra—lichens, mosses, tough grasses, sedges—a variety of dwarfed, matlike plants capable of surviving in severe climate and also of producing a surprising display of delicate blossoms.

Lichen proves useful in this setting, maybe not immediately to humankind, but as a food source to the wildlife community that humankind protects. Caribou, the most numerous large animal in the park, feeds on such humble plants during its annual stay here, but the concentration of caribou in great herds has not been evident in recent years.

With binoculars, or even the naked eye, the Dall sheep, a species of bighorn, looks like a white speck on the higher slopes, as it safeguards itself by climbing to crags beyond the reach of predators like the wolf. It is fascinating to watch the Dall's short, springy, and muscular jumps when running over the flats. The Dall is obviously unsuited to level terrain, in contrast to its efficiency on the cliffs.

Since the "1910 Sourdough Expedition," Mount McKinley has been successfully climbed by mountaineers from all over the world. Despite technological advances in equipment and conditioning of modern climbers, McKinley remains a difficult challenge. The weather is unpredictable and severe. The mountain has claimed its share of casualties.

Mount McKinley rises nearly 17,000 feet above the surrounding country, and all above 7,000 feet is enveloped by snow and ice—tough for climbers, spectacular for scenic enjoyment. The mountain has two peaks: South Peak, the upper portion, 20,320 feet, and North Peak, 19,470 feet, two miles away. It is so brilliant a landmark that it can be seen on clear days from Anchorage and Fairbanks, when not obscured by low-hanging clouds.

THE PRACTICAL GUIDE

You'll have 16 to 20 hours of daylight during summer; use them all. Some of the best weather is in early morning, about 3 a.m. Many visitors spend one night as part of an Alaska tour and then depart the next day. However, this great park is worthy of at least two or three days in order to really catch the flavor of the arctic wilderness, wander over the tundra, the vast river bars, and through the spruce forests. Binoculars are essential to observe animals. Insect repellent is advised for anyone planning a hike.

ACCESS BY CAR. Arrive via George Parks Highway and Denali Highway, Route 3, extending from Paxson (at Milepost 185.5 on Richardson Highway) to Cantwell (Milepost 209.9 on Parks Highway). The park road extends 90 miles from its connection with Denali Highway, but during summer months private vehicles beyond Savage River check station (Milepost 12.0) are restricted to those people with camping reservations. Once at designated campsites they, and others, must use the free shuttle-bus system. The gravel, curving park road does not lend itself to a heavy volume of traffic, and protection of the environment is an even more important factor. Restricting auto traffic enables visitors to view wildlife, which otherwise would be driven away. Shuttle-bus service begins at the Riley Creek Campground and runs all the way to Wonder Lake. During the summer season, shuttle buses operate outbound from Riley Creek from 6 a.m. to 5 p.m. and inbound from Wonder Lake from 8:30 a.m. to 6:20 p.m. Buses drop off and pick up visitors at many points along the highway. Carry your food with you; there is no service beyond the entrance area.

TRAINS, PLANES, BUSES. The Alaska Railroad provides daily service in summer from Fairbanks (four hours) and Anchorage (eight hours). In 1985 Tour Alaska introduced the Midnight Sun Express, restored superdome cars. These are the last two cars of the express train, with a dining room beneath the dome lounge. During summer, planes fly regularly, at least twice weekly, connecting Anchorage and Fairbanks with the park airstrip. Buses run on daily schedules and on sightseeing tours.

BACKGROUND. Eielson Visitor Center, 65 miles west of the entrance, is at an elevation of 3,730 feet. Glass-enclosed exhibit rooms face Muldrow Glacier and the towering twin peaks. The displays interpret glacial geology and the mountain-climbing history of the park. The first climbers were sourdoughs impelled by the urge to see the top.

McKinley Park Station, gateway to the park, includes a service station, store, campground, hotel, and park headquarters. The mountain becomes visible, on clear days, about 8 miles farther on.

Teklanika River, 27 miles from the entrance, typifies glacial rivers flowing north from the Alaska Range over numerous channels and wide gravel bars, creating a braided course. The milky cast derives from glacier-ground rock flour.

Igloo Canyon is an excellent locale for animals, particularly Dall sheep. Learn to spot animals by looking for contrasts of color and form in the landscape.

Sable Pass, elevation 3,900 feet, is the best place to observe grizzly bears browsing on lush grass or ripping tundra for its succulent roots. Though most common here, bears may be seen anywhere in the park, roaming the spruce forests, the aspen thickets, the bare mountain slopes. A feeding grizzly is not impressive looking, seemingly slow moving, but it can run faster than a horse and demonstrates pride in being called *Ursus arctos*. He's powerful—stay away. The best place to see moose is in the **Savage River area,** though they may appear anywhere along the road. They spend a great deal of time in lakes and ponds searching for summer food and should not be approached closely, either.

At **Highway Pass,** the most breathtaking view of the mountain bursts upon the motorist coming over the rise. The full sweep hits your eye, to the snow plume of the **South Peak.** For the rest of the way you are almost constantly in view of the peaks, always changing, but always dominating the landscape. Caribou are common from this pass westward.

Wildflowers spread across the fields of **Stony Hill Overlook** in June and early July—which here means springtime. These include the state flower, forget-me-not, as well as arctic poppy, densely carpeted white dryas, white and pink pyrolas, and heather. Take time for at least a short walk from the overlook parking lot. Many birds nest on the surrounding tundra. A search with binoculars may reveal a wildlife spectacle: grizzlies on nearby hillsides, caribou feeding on the lowlands, a wolf on a hunting trail.

You can photograph and dream over reflections of the mountain at **Wonder Lake.** It was near here that Olaus Murie, while exploring with another distinguished biologist, his brother, Adolph, discovered his "greatest scene." He wrote: "We looked before us, across the wide valley to the white Denali and the snowy Alaska Range rising high on the horizon. To be on that ridgetop, to look at what was before us!"

The southern side of the 1980 **park addition** is generally accessible from Parks Highway, which runs between Fairbanks and Anchorage. Scattered motel and commercial campground accommodations are located along the way, with a fine campground available at Byers Lake in **Denali State Park.** Access to the northern portion is possible by charter flights to **Lake Minchumina.** Backpacking and wilderness camping opportunities are plentiful for those who can take care of themselves. Be sure to get a backcountry-use permit.

TO SEE THE MOUNTAIN. The view of Mount McKinley is one of the world's truly spectacular sights, but thick clouds frequently obscure it from visitors. The mountain can be seen clearly fairly often in the early morning and late evening hours, but seldom at noon. Studies over a two-year period indicate that the view is best during the morning hours, and that August is by far the best month.

HIKING AND BACKPACKING. Register at the Riley Creek Information Center and obtain a backcountry-use permit for off-highway camping. No fires permitted; use gas stoves. Always check with the information center or with a ranger for current information on wilderness travel. Certain areas may be restricted due to critical wildlife habitat. Cross-country travel is complicated by heavy patches of brush, tundra, marshes, and streams.

FISHING. Licenses are not required. Despite the wide renown of Alaska's fishing streams, fishing in the park is poor because most rivers are silty and ponds are shallow. Count on far better luck at the Brooks Camp in Katmai National Park.

MOUNTAINEERING. Mount McKinley is climbed by many parties each summer. Most attempts are made from the south side of the mountain with Talkeetna as the jump-off. Park personnel will assist in briefing all mountaineering parties wishing to climb McKinley or other peaks within the park; in fact, regulations require advance registration with the superintendent.

Cathedral Spires comprise a fantastic landmark of the new addition, visible from the air. They are a challenge to the most indomitable of mountain climbers. Kichatna Spire, the highest of the Cathedrals (8,985 feet), was first climbed only as recently as 1966. The spires are rated as North America's greatest single stand of vertical rock. Eight major glaciers and other smaller ones radiate from among these granite spikes.

TOUR OPERATORS. The Denali National Park Hotel runs bus tours daily during summer as far as the Toklat River, starting at 4 a.m., 6 a.m., and 3 p.m. A box lunch is furnished. The driver stops briefly for good views of wildlife and accommodates photographers as much as the schedule permits before returning to make connections with the train to Anchorage.

PHOTOGRAPHY. Long hours of day-light provide plenty of time for picture taking. Days are often cloudy, obscuring the mountain, but cloudy days can be excellent for wildflower photography. Try to interpret the three life-communities of the park: northern forest (or taiga), tundra, and perennial snowfield.

Professional wildlife photographers prefer late summer and early fall, when many animals are at their prime in appearance. In summer, large mammals generally wear scruffy, matted coats; moose and caribou have only partially formed antlers.

ACCOMMODATIONS. Near the entrance station, **Denali National Park Hotel** provides overnight lodgings in 100 rooms. The sourdough breakfast of hot-cakes, eggs, and bacon will soften the blow of rising at 2 or 3 a.m. Dinner of king crab or salmon steak will prepare you for another morning at the same hour. Naturalist-guided walks and lectures are given daily at the hotel area. For rates and reservations write ARA Outdoor World, Ltd., McKinley Park Station, Alaska 99755. **Camp Denali,** just north of Wonder Lake, offers one of the finest experiences in Alaska for lovers of nature. This delightful wilderness retreat has rustic chalet cabins with family-style meals in the dining room. Daily guided trips combine hiking and driving to points of interest in the park and historic Kantishna, once a booming mining town. Special sessions are scheduled in wildlife photography and nature lore. Write Camp Denali, McKinley Park Station, Alaska 99755 (September 11 to May 31, Camp Denali, Box 67, McKinley Park Station, Alaska 99755). New accommodations are emerging outside the park on George Parks Highway. Close to the entrance these include **McKinley Chalets** and **McKinley Village.** Accommodations also are available at Cantwell and Healy. A recreation-vehicle campground in Healy offers full facilities, including groceries, showers, coin laundry.

CAMPING. Six campgrounds are well spaced along the park road; one is off the highway by trail. The closest to the McKinley railroad station is **Morino** (1/8 mile by trail), then **Riley Creek** (1 1/2 miles), **Savage River** (12 miles), **Sanctuary River** (22 miles), **Teklanika** (29 miles), **Igloo** (33 miles), and **Wonder Lake** (84 miles). Motorists may drive in their own vehicles without a permit to Riley Creek (100 sites) and to Savage River (29 sites). The controlled-access areas are beyond the Savage River Bridge: Sanctuary River (7 sites), Teklanika (50 sites), Igloo (7 tent sites), and Wonder Lake (20 tent sites).

Permits to camp beyond the Savage River Bridge are available at the Riley Creek Information Center. All stays are limited to 14 days. The park requires permits for backcountry use.

Warm clothing, waterproof shelter, and mosquito repellent are important. Firewood can be purchased in the park.

SEASONS. Spring arrives late, in June and early July, with wildflowers, nesting birds, 24 hours of daylight—and mosquitoes. After August 15, you have a share of two seasons. The atmosphere is crisp and clear; animals appear in their glossy winter coats, and mosquitoes are gone. Leaves of the very few hardwood trees turn gold and orange, while the alpine tundra turns into a vast Persian carpet of gold, red-orange, purple, brown, and green. Nights at this season are dark and invariably chilly. Summers are moderately warm, wet, cloudy. Come prepared with clothing for temperatures from freezing to 80 degrees Fahrenheit. For comfort, dress in layers.

The park road and public facilities are usually open from mid-May to mid-September. Morino and Riley Creek campgrounds are open all year.

Though most public facilities are closed in winter, the park is open to dog mushing, ski touring, and snowshoeing. Trails are established through much of the park, but check at headquarters for weather and trail conditions.

RECOMMENDED READING. *Two in the Far North,* by Margaret Murie (Edmunds, Wash.: Alaska Northwest) and *Denali: The Story Behind the Scenery,* by Steve Buskirk (Las Vegas: KC Publications).

FOR FURTHER INFORMATION. Write Superintendent, Denali National Park, Box 9, McKinley Park Station, Alaska 99755.

EVERGLADES NATIONAL PARK

Florida

Authorized 1934

THE EVERGLADES comprise a park of wonderful watery boulevards, avenues, alleys, and lanes. So it seemed to me while canoeing with a friend through overgrown passageways of red mangrove on the Hells Bay Trail. I was struck also by the diversity of water habitats in the park, producing a limitless variety of aquatic life. Salt waters extend from the clear depths of the Gulf of Mexico on the west to the supersaline shallows of most of Florida Bay. Clear fresh waters of the glades and brown-stained waters of the mangrove rivers produce microscopic life that serves as food for fish, which in turn feed the rich birdlife.

We paddled for the better part of a day, but we might have gone for a week, following the hundreds of miles of winding mangrove rivers. Primitive camp-sites, as I learned, are located along most trails. The route to the first campsite on the Hells Bay Trail was marked with white floats. It was only four miles from the starting point (just off the main road), or three hours travel time, and we went to inspect it. The Park Service had constructed six shelters, or "chickees," in the native Indian style—elevated roof platforms of wood, without walls—and equipped them with grill and table. It was a facility well suited to the environment.

I recalled while we glided through the water that proposals to safeguard this unusual country were first advanced early in this century, when Theodore Roosevelt was president. "It has its place among the country's native wonders, like the Mammoth Cave

and Niagara Falls," wrote Edwin A. Dix and John M. McGonigle in an article in *Century Magazine* of February 1905. "After all, it is rather a good thing to have a little of wonderland left."

It took many years to achieve the goal, but certainly all Americans have benefited from saving this bit of wonderland at the southern tip of the Florida peninsula. The park today is an expanse of tall, swaying grasses; tropical plants and trees; and dozens of low islands, or keys, rising from the sheltered waters of Florida Bay. This is what the word *Everglades* means to me, all this plus a refuge for beautiful tropical birdlife found hardly anywhere else on earth.

The Everglades constitute a refuge for humans, too—a place at booming Miami's doorstep to find

inspiration from the unimproved works of nature. The Everglades themselves, and some of the birds, reptiles, and mammals, are either rare or cannot be seen elsewhere in the nation. Here are the storks (the only ones in the United States) called wood ibis, huge birds whose pure white feathers contrast with their jet-black wing tips. Along the palm-fringed shoreline, brown pelicans may be seen gliding or flapping their wings while flying in formation to a distant rendezvous. Over the mangrove swamp inland, yellow-crowned and black-crowned night herons soar over the trees. Elsewhere are the roseate spoonbills, big pink birds with crimson splashes, and the great white herons spreading their immense wings seven feet from tip to tip.

These birds and others, colored blue, green, black, yellow, red, and several shades in between, gather by the thousands to build their nests and bring their young into the world. Their refuge in the Everglades, covering 1,400,533 acres, is larger than the state of Delaware.

Long before the European explorers arrived aboriginal Indians, the Calusa and Tequesta, were attracted to this region by its abundant resources—the great beds of conchs, oysters, and clams. They made their homes on the islands or on the riverbanks and hammocks nearby, utilizing the fish, game, and plant foods around them. The modern Indians—Miccosukees and Seminoles—arrived in Spanish Florida after the American Revolution. Many Creeks of Georgia and Alabama, crowded by the invading white settlers, fled to the Florida peninsula. They were forced continually southward, finally retreating to the Everglades, where deer, fish, and fruit were plentiful. They traded alligator hides, otter skins, and egret plumes with the white settlers. The white men were few, primarily hunters and fishermen, though some came to cut cypress and mahogany trees, to use royal palms to beautify budding urban communities, or to farm on the limited land available.

At the turn of this century the Everglades area was known as the home of many varieties of birds of striking beauty; some, like the egrets, were prized for plumes on women's hats. They were shot on a large scale and even then threatened with extinction. The National Committee of Audubon Societies raised funds in 1902 to engage a warden, Guy Bradley, but he was murdered in 1905. It was a tragedy that gave impetus to both the bird conservation movement and to the preservation of the area.

Sparked by the Florida Federation of Women's Clubs, Royal Palm State Park was established in 1916. Five years later, in 1923, Stephen T. Mather, director of the National Park Service, declared in a report, "There should be an untouched example of the Everglades of Florida established as a national park." The Tropical Everglades National Park Association, headed by Dr. Harold Bailey and Ernest F. Coe, was founded to lead the citizen movement to achieve that goal.

Through their efforts, Congress in 1929 authorized a study on the desirability of a national park. Action, however, was slow, even though in 1934 Congress voted to establish an Everglades National Park, for opponents in the House tacked on a provision that no money be appropriated to purchase land for five years.

Fortunately, Governor Spessard Holland worked with citizen groups to get the money for Florida's share of the land purchase. In 1946 the state legislature provided $2 million for the purchase of private lands in the area, clearing the way for the park's establishment. Everglades National Park was dedicated December 6, 1947, by President Harry S Truman. Leaders in the effort, besides Coe and Bailey, had been Spessard Holland, who had gone from the governor's chair to the United States Senate, and John D. Pennekamp of the *Miami Herald*. Another writer, Marjory Stoneman Douglas, helped the cause further with her powerful book *The Everglades: River of Grass.*

Unfortunately, since 1948 dikes and drainage canals constructed around the park to divert water for the benefit of large-scale agriculture and real estate have severely disturbed the natural balance. The decreased water flow has reduced the aquatic life and, in turn, the tropical birdlife for which the park is noted. The establishment of Big Cypress National Preserve helped safeguard the remaining natural flow of fresh water.

The true everglades were called by the Indians *Pahay-Okee,* the "grassy waters," or "river of grass," but the park is a many-sided spectacle of unusual plant communities and wildlife. Clusters of trees and dense vegetation in the open glades form islands called hammocks, with hardwood trees that are common in the West Indies, including the mahogany, strangler fig, and coppery-barked gumbo-limbo. In other sections are bald cypress and pine forests of the southern swamps. Hundreds of interesting plants grow from the edge of Florida Bay and the Gulf of Mexico into the wilderness: from graceful, towering royal palms to delicate lilies and ferns.

The Everglades teem with life—from fish, crustaceans, and shellfish to snakes, deer, raccoons, and possums. The park is the last major sanctuary of the Florida panther. The lagoons provide a pasture for Florida's strange, air-breathing, vegetarian sea cow, the manatee. The most celebrated swamp dwellers are the blunt-nosed alligator, who sticks to fresh water, and the rare long-snouted crocodile, who prefers its water salty. The crocodile once ranged as far north as Jacksonville but now is rarely found anywhere but in Florida Bay and the national park.

THE PRACTICAL GUIDE

It is possible to get a peek of the Everglades even in a few hours. If you are driving down to Key West, or vacationing in Miami, go through Homestead into the park for at least a little while.

This is a park of wonderful watery boulevards and byroads for boaters. In fact, the Western Water Gateway at Everglades, southeast of Naples, provides access *only* by boat. Visitors traveling by boat are well advised to obtain a set of navigational charts.

BACKGROUND. Approaching from Homestead, the **Visitor Center** on Florida 27 features an excellent slide program. (Other Visitor Centers are at Royal Palm, Flamingo, and Everglades City.) Two miles beyond, the **Royal Palm Area** presents a good Everglades cross section. Here the **Anhinga Trail,** an elevated boardwalk across the slough, features a dependable

wildlife show, with alligators, water snakes, and a variety of wading birds. The **Gumbo-Limbo Trail,** an easy 1/3-mile loop, will introduce you to much of the flora of the area, including air plants, ferns, orchids, and tropical hardwood trees.

Flamingo, 38 miles from the park entrance, at the subtropical tip of the mainland, is the main center, converted from an old fishing village. This is your base for exploratory trips into the wilderness of Whitewater Bay and hundreds of miles of winding mangrove rivers, the channels and keys of Florida Bay, the Gulf area, the mangrove coast, and tropical beaches of Cape Sable. Flamingo features a concession-operated motel, dining room, screened-in pool, housekeeping cabins, and lounge. The Visitor Center provides a graphic history of the park and serves as a springboard for sightseeing and exploration. Facilities at

Flamingo include a 57-slip marina with diesel and gas fuel, tackle, live bait, and general store; canoes and 14-foot skiffs are available for rental. Guides and charter boats are on hand for sportfishing, birdwatching, and photography trips.

Canoe trails vary in length, so you can paddle for any length of time from an hour to a week. The five trails are Noble Hammock, Hells Bay, West Lake, Bear Lake, and, longest of all, the Wilderness Waterway. Primitive campsites are located on most trails; be sure to get a campfire permit. The Wilderness Waterway is a well-marked 100-mile route between Everglades City and Flamingo through creeks, rivers, and open bays. Backcountry campsites are available along the way, but there is no water.

Study *Guide to the Wilderness Waterway of the Everglades National Park*, by William G. Truesdell (University of Miami Press);

before you begin your trip.

Cape Sable (named for the sable palm) is tucked away on the southernmost point of the continental United States. Experienced canoeists, traveling inland waters, can reach it in four to six hours from Flamingo; motorboats take about 45 minutes. The Cape has beautiful white beaches and desertlike vegetation—yucca, century plants, prickly pear cactus. Obtain a permit and camp at one of the primitive sites.

TOUR OPERATORS. Boat tours are offered from Everglades City by a national park concessioner, Sammy Hamilton, a native of the area. His trips are among the finest anywhere in the national parks. From Flamingo the one-hour sunset cruise affords a spectacular view of roosting grounds of thousands of birds in the shallow waters of Florida Bay. The Whitewater Bay cruise, conducted three times daily, is a two-hour excursion among mangroves, with plenty of chances to view birds and wildlife.

The park also offers naturalist-led canoe excursions and overnight backpacking hikes into remote areas. These are reservations-only activities, operating from late November to early April. Canoeists can rent craft or bring their own; you need to provide your own life jackets, food, and water—bring cameras, too, for excellent photo opportunities. Hikers may expect to wade through saw-grass prairies.

TRAM TOURS. Departing from **Flamingo,** these are designed to interpret plant and birdlife of the wilderness area. Early in this century, egrets and spoonbills were slain and whole rookeries destroyed in hunting for plumes for women's hats; at one period these beautiful birds almost disappeared, but now they display their plumage for admiration, not exploitation.

Shark Valley open-air tram bus tours provide a different opportunity to see an abundance of wildlife. The tours originate at a parking area just inside the park entrance, 30 miles west of Miami on the south side of the Tamiami Trail. The trip parallels a canal to the Shark Valley Observation Tower, which affords an excellent view. The two-hour tram tours generally leave every hour on the hour during the winter season and at two-hour intervals during the summer season. Tram service is usually discontinued during September and October, although high water in the area may extend the closure. A fee is charged. For reservations call 305-221-8455.

NATURALIST PROGRAMS. Included are daily talks and walks during the winter season. The Visitor Centers at Flamingo and Parachute Key house displays on natural and human history, from the era of the ancient Indian Mound Builders to the age of the modern bird conservers. Evening campfire programs offered during the winter season at Flamingo and Long Pine Key campgrounds include slide programs, demonstrations, or living-history presentations.

FISHING. The waters offshore are famous for sea trout, tarpon, redfish, snapper, and other fish. Fully equipped charter boats run from Flamingo and Everglades. Freshwater fishing with rod and reel requires a Florida fishing license; however, none is needed for saltwater fishing.

ACCOMMODATIONS. The **Flamingo Inn** offers modern motel-type rooms, dining room, and cafeteria. Housekeeping cottages are suited for family use. A swimming pool is available for lodge and cottage guests. Rates are lower between April 15 and December 15 than during the winter peak. For reservations phone 813-695-3101. Motel accommodations are available in nearby Homestead, the Keys, and many resorts of south Florida. The Barron River provides access to prime fishing waters, with boats and guides available.

CAMPING. Campgrounds are located at Long Pine Key (6 miles from park entrance) and Flamingo. Stays are limited to 14 days between November 1 and May 1, to 30 days the rest of the year.

Camping is permitted in the backcountry if you first obtain a permit at park headquarters or a ranger station. Camping facilities near the park are located at Collier-Seminole State Park, 19 miles north of Everglades, on the Tamiami Trail, and at private campgrounds north of Homestead.

SEASONS. Winter and early spring are ideal for watching birds and wildlife—because animals concentrate around the few remaining water areas. The weather is usually mild enough for shirt-sleeves. Mosquitoes can be a problem in late spring and are likely to become fierce by summer, when conditions are apt to range from uncomfortable to unbearable. From June until August giant loggerhead turtles crawl onto the beaches at Cape Sable to lay their eggs.

NEARBY. Two outstanding companion areas are **Big Cypress National Preserve** and **Biscayne National Park** (see separate listing). Showpiece of the Seminole country is the **Dania Indian Reservation** at Hollywood, north of Miami, with an outstanding arts and crafts center and display of Seminole life. The **Seminole campground,** open to the public year-round (fee charged), is a base for airboat and swamp-buggy tours.

For a naturalist's tour south of Miami, start with the beautiful **Fairchild Tropical Garden** in Coral Gables, displaying palms, cycads, an amazing rain forest, and desert forest. Include a stop at **Redland Fruit and Spice Park,** a center of tropical plant culture, north of Homestead. Coming down the west side of Florida, start at the **Thomas A. Edison Botanical Gardens and Laboratory,** where the wizard of electricity maintained his winter home amid 14 acres of rare trees, ferns, and flowers. The **Everglades Nursery,** 6 miles southwest, one of the largest nurseries for palms and tropical plants, presents a bougainvillea exhibit every February. On the way south, **Everglades Wonder Gardens,** at Bonita Springs, display over 2,000 specimens of native wildlife. In Naples, the **Caribbean Gardens** contain an outstanding collection of orchids, bromeliads, and air plants—plus a large assortment of waterfowl—on its 30 subtropical and tropical acres. From mid-January to May 1, you can take an all-day combination tour of the gardens and the National Audubon Society's **Corkscrew Swamp Sanctuary.** Corkscrew, a wildlife sanctuary of 6,000 acres, is truly the companion piece to the Everglades. Containing our country's largest remaining stand of virgin bald cypress, many towering 130 feet, it is 35 miles from Naples and is reached on station-wagon tours.

South of the park on the sparkling overwater road to Key West, **John Pennekamp Coral Reef State Park,** in the Atlantic Ocean off Key Largo, is the first undersea park in the continental United States—a fantasyland of coral beauty, protected as the breeding ground of fish, shellfish, and turtles. You can explore the park by glass-bottomed boat and see brilliantly colored fish swimming among old wrecks caught in the reef. Onshore the park has a campground, nature trail, wading area, and marina (rental boats and diving gear available). Another state park, **Bahia Honda,** south of Marathon, has facilities for fishing, picnicking, boating, camping, and an excellent beach for swimming.

In Key West, a visit to the **Audubon House** is appropriate, for it is restored to its appearance of 1832, when it was occupied by America's greatest nature painter; it was he who discovered the great white heron that now finds its refuge in the national park.

Finally, the land runs out, but 70 miles west of Key West lies **Fort Jefferson National Monument,** a 19th-century coastal fort in the reef islands called the Dry Tortugas, famous for their rich bird, plant, and undersea life.

RECOMMENDED READING. *The Everglades: River of Grass,* by Marjory Stoneman Douglas (St. Simons Island, Ga.: Mockingbird Books).

FOR FURTHER INFORMATION. Write Superintendent, Everglades National Park, Box 279, Homestead, Florida 33030.

GATES OF THE ARCTIC NATIONAL PARK

Alaska

Established 1980

FLYING INTO THE BROOKS RANGE from Fairbanks and Bettles, I was struck by the dramatic scene, larger than life, of granite peaks and knifelike ridges intersected by long valleys, many highlighted by sparkling lakes and rivers. The immensity of the country was overwhelming.

The entire national park lies above the Arctic Circle, about 200 miles northwest of Fairbanks. It embraces 7,952,000 acres on Alaska's North Slope. To give an idea of its dimensions: Gates of the Arctic park is almost four times the size of Yellowstone National Park, in the Rockies. It is, in fact, the second largest national park in the world, exceeded in size only by Wrangell–St. Elias National Park, in southeastern Alaska. Its river courses flow through some of the largest untouched basins in America.

This region has long been regarded as worthy of protection. From 1929 to 1939 Robert Marshall, scientist, explorer, and conservationist, conducted research around the headwaters of the Koyukuk River. Tracking up the North Fork, he observed two facing peaks, which he named Frigid Crags and Boreal, collectively, Gates of the Arctic. It was Marshall who suggested that the 600-mile-long Brooks Range, from the Yukon to the Arctic Sea, be designated a wilderness area.

As Eskimo tribes, the "Inuit" people of the North, have known for centuries, the Brooks Range is richly endowed with wildlife. Here I saw a portion of the great Western Arctic caribou herd that migrates hundreds of miles each year, pouring back and forth through the passes between northern calving and feeding grounds to the winter range south of the mountains, feeding on moss and lichens of the tundra. Many species find their niches: black bear in spruce lowlands of the south; Dall sheep on windswept mountainsides; moose among the willows; wolverines, wolves, lynx, grizzly, eagles, falcons, and many migratory birds.

THE PRACTICAL GUIDE

A number of guides lead trips into the Brooks Range in summer. Outfitters can supply all the necessary equipment—though visitors in this terrain should be experienced hikers and campers and be trained in survival skills. Be sure you and your equipment are up for it. Fairbanks has a complete range of merchandise and services. Bettles, about 50 miles south of the park, is reached on scheduled airline service and is the jump-off for small-plane charter flights into the park.

WHERE TO STAY. There are no established campgrounds within the park and preserve, but campsites are available—with lots of elbow room. Bettles is the site of a lodge and store, as well as headquarters for guides and outfitters.

HIKING AND BACKPACKING. The best plan is to be dropped off and picked up by chartered aircraft. Be sure to pick a com-

petent, experienced bush pilot: these pilots can land on lakes, rivers, or river bars, as well as airstrips. Higher elevations provide excellent hiking, usually combining open tundra, sparse shrubs, and occasional woodland.

FLOATING AND FISHING. Among the rivers, the pristine **Noatak** rises in the central Brooks Range and then flows for almost 450 miles to Kotzebue Sound, on the Arctic Ocean. A large part of its journey is through the new Noatak National Preserve. Other key rivers are the **Alatna, John, North Fork** (of the Koyukuk River), **Nigu-Itivilik,** and **Kobuk.** Fishing is good within the park. **Walker Lake,** a 13-mile-long jewel, and other lakes and rivers within the park contain grayling; you will also find lake trout and char. **Anaktuvuk Pass,** a village within the park, is the home of a Nunamiut Eskimo group noted for the ceremonial masks

made of animal skin (usually caribou) and fur trim they make and sell here.

SEASONS. Midsummer temperatures along south slopes occasionally reach the 80s and, once in a long while, the 90s during the day. Highlands are generally cooler, with freezing temperatures at night on the north slopes by mid-August or early September. Weather can change abruptly at any time during the summer, so pack rain gear. Prepare for insects: first mosquitoes, then gnats later in the summer, especially on the vegetated west lowlands.

RECOMMENDED READING. *Alaska Wilderness: Exploring the Central Brooks Range,* by Robert Marshall (Berkeley: University of California Press).

FOR FURTHER INFORMATION. Write Superintendent, Gates of the Arctic National Park, Box 74680, Fairbanks, Alaska 99707.

GLACIER BAY NATIONAL PARK

Alaska

Established 1980

S KIES WERE OVERCAST and a light rain fell, typical southeast Alaska weather, but virtually all of us passengers on the *Glacier Bay Explorer* were on deck with our binoculars. The waters of Glacier Bay were flecked with icebergs and dotted with islands and rocks teeming with birds—cormorants, guillemots, horned and tufted puffins, gulls, and eagles. At least half a dozen humpback whales made their presence known, breaking the surface, blowing, then diving out of view. We saw hundreds of seals, a black bear with cub along the beach, and mountain goats on the high crags. All told, a superlative wildlife show.

The changing coastline, visible from the *Explorer,* was forested by vegetation ranging from spruce-hemlock rain forests to small pioneer plants claiming a foothold in recently exposed glacial slopes. Glaciers were in every stage of development, from actively moving ice masses to those nearly stagnant; I recalled that as recent as 250 years ago the entire bay was covered with an ice sheet 3,000 feet thick. At narrow, fjordlike inlets we approached ice cliffs up to 200 feet high and observed icy blocks "calving," crashing into the sea and causing huge waves.

John Muir publicized Glacier Bay and made his way into the heart of that distant, dazzling glacial world. Muir went near the end of October 1879 when, as he wrote, "young ice was beginning to form in the branch inlets occupied by the glaciers, and the mountains were mantled with fresh snow all the way down from the highest peaks and ridges of the Fairweather Range nearly to the level of the sea."

Why had Glacier Bay not been found earlier, since its surroundings in southeast Alaska were known? The answer is uncomplicated: when Captain George Vancouver sailed through the waters of Icy Strait, in 1794, Glacier Bay was little more than a dent in the shoreline. A towering wall of ice completely filled the broad, deep basin. That wall actually was the seaward outlet of an immense glacier.

By Muir's time the ice front had retreated 48 miles. A tall spruce-hemlock forest had begun to take its place, while tidewaters had invaded the basin and filled the deep, narrow fjords. Based on what he saw and learned, the great naturalist produced some of his finest writing. For example: "Here one learns that the world, though made, is yet being made; that this is still the morning of creation; that mountains long conceived are being born, channels traced for coming rivers, basins hollowed for lakes; that moraine soil is being ground and spread for coming plants . . . on predestined landscapes, to be followed by still others in endless rhythm and beauty."

The glaciers kept receding. By 1916, Tarr Inlet was free of ice, and the terminus of Grand Pacific Glacier stood 65 miles from the mouth of Glacier Bay. Nowhere else on earth have glaciers receded at such a rapid rate.

Glacier Bay was set aside as a national monument in 1925. Congress voted in 1980 to declare it a national park, with considerable enlargement. The park covers a little more than 3,220,000 acres, bordered by a national preserve of approximately 55,000 acres and a wilderness area of more than 2 million acres.

THE PRACTICAL GUIDE

By plane, you can fly from Anchorage or Juneau via Alaska Airlines or from Juneau via LAB, a commuter line. Flight time from Juneau is about 30 minutes. Planes land at Gustavus Airport, about 10 miles from Bartlett Cove, center of activity in the park, reached by bus. Cruise liners traveling the Inside Passage from Vancouver and Seattle visit Glacier Bay, but their time is limited. Yacht trips or combination fly/cruise tours from Juneau and Gustavus to Glacier Bay are available, with overnight accommodations on land or aboard ship. There is no ferry service, but the *Glacier Express*, a high-speed catamaran, operates daily from Juneau. The one-way trip takes about three hours. Large windows enable viewing of wilderness islands.

CRUISING THE BAY. From the center of activity at Glacier Bay Lodge, the concession-operated cruise boats depart up the bay. The *Thunder Bay* makes an all-day excursion, while the *Glacier Bay Explorer,* a mini-class cruise liner (with 32 double staterooms, dining room, and lounge with picture windows) travels deep into the bay to overnight at the base of active glaciers. A National Park Service naturalist travels aboard each of the boats.

ACCOMMODATIONS. The **Glacier Bay Lodge,** in a rain forest at Bartlett Cove, near the head of the bay, has a restaurant and 55 rooms with baths. In 1987, 2 rooms were set aside for dormitory use (one each for men and women). Each room sleeps up to eight persons. It serves as an excellent base for fishing, with panoramic views of Lower Glacier Bay, the Beardslee Islands, and the Fairweather Range, which culminates in 15,300-foot Mount Fairweather. You can get a tour package, including air transportation, hotel, and cruise, through a travel agent or by phoning toll free, 800-426-0600. The Glacier Bay Lodge address during summer is Gustavus, Alaska 99826; the rest of the year, Metropolitan Park Building, Seattle, Washington 98101. **Gustavus Inn,** a small family-run inn outside the park, features charter fishing and kayaking. The address is Gustavus Inn, Gustavus, Alaska 99826.

CAMPING AND KAYAKING. A campground at **Bartlett Cove** is open May to September. **Sandy Cove,** about 20 miles up the bay, is a popular anchorage (bear activity may close it to camping); wilderness camping is available throughout the park. The cruise boat will drop off and pick up hikers at points en route for an additional fee. Kayaking is increasingly popular. The cruise vessel is equipped to carry kayaks. Rentals and guided trips are available; make arrangements in advance. You can make a pleasant one-day trip from Bartlett Cove out among the Beardslee Islands; pack a picnic lunch and insect repellent.

SEASONS. At Bartlett Cove summer temperatures range from 55 to 75 degrees Fahrenheit. Prepare for periods of mist and moisture, interspersed with clear and warm days. Remember that summer days in Alaska are long, with only brief darkness.

FOR FURTHER INFORMATION. Write Superintendent, Glacier Bay National Park, Bartlett Cove, Gustavus, Alaska 99826.

GLACIER NATIONAL PARK

Montana

Established 1910

FROM AVALANCHE CAMPGROUND I followed the two-mile trail to Avalanche Lake, an easy walk that anyone could enjoy. The trail ran along a stream scoured by stones swirling in the torrent of milky glacial water from Sperry Glacier. It led me to thinking of how glaciers and streams had shaped the peaks and valleys, gouged out the lakes, and sculpted rich land formations of the northern Rockies.

I looked up to see a great natural amphitheater, a glacial cirque; a thin knife-edge of rock, an arête; and a towerlike sentinel gouged by two or more glaciers, a horn. But I saw much more: the telltale signs of grizzly droppings on the trail and claw marks on the trees; a red-tailed hawk wheeling overhead, and a slate-gray water ouzel, shaped like a chunky wren with short tail, bathing in the stream. As a wilderness sanctuary of 1,013,598 acres, Glacier is one of the last strongholds of the grizzly, along with bighorn sheep, mountain goats, mules, deer, moose, and elk—at least 57 species of mammals and 210 species of birds.

Feeling that hardly any area of its size concentrates as much rugged mountain splendor as Glacier National Park, I came ultimately to Avalanche Basin, where waterfalls plunge over 2,000-foot-high rock walls.

The scenery of its thousand waterfalls tumbling from glacial snow masses into sparkling lakes and streams, surrounded by primitive forests, is over-whelming to everyone who comes this way. Yet the experience here is intimate, for the visitor can walk in the company of wildflowers up to the frozen rivers themselves and spend a cool summer's night in a chalet within easy walking distance of a glacier.

This mighty place is more than one nation's park. Its proper name is Waterton–Glacier International Peace Park, a reminder that it not only lies astride the Continental Divide but spills over the Montana border of the United States into the southwest part of Alberta, Canada. Through a sanctuary of nature two countries commemorate the spirit of good will.

Few areas in the West produce a more comprehensive show of trees, plants, and wildflowers. Glacier is a rendezvous of a thousand species of the South, East, West, and even the Arctic. In the valleys on the east side are stands of Engelmann spruce, subalpine fir, and lodgepole pine, but across the western slopes, where moisture is heavier, the forests are more luxuriant with groves of ponderosa pine, Douglas fir, larch, hemlock, and western red cedar. Beneath these trees and across the open meadows a colorful display of wildflowers stands out everywhere as one of the park's major attractions. The showiest one to me is bear grass, a misnamed member of the lily family, while other flowering plants include the glacier lily along the edge of snowbanks, Indian paintbrush, fireweed, gentians, and asters.

THE PRACTICAL GUIDE

Seven days, or even 14, are not too many to spend in this park with its superb 700-mile network of hiking and riding trails.

If you are on a Northwest tour, Glacier deserves three full days and two nights. If you're traveling by Amtrak's Empire Builder, arrange to stop over and tour the park. The Empire Builder stops daily at both Belton (West Glacier) and East Glacier (late April through late October) or Browning (the rest of the year).

You can reach the park by bus as well. Rocky Mountain Stage makes six trips weekly from Great Falls to East Glacier from May 1 to October 1. Shelby, Kalispell, and Great Falls are served by Intermountain Transportation, which connects with Greyhound and Trailways.

BACKGROUND. A full range of exhibits, information, and introductory programs is available at the major **Visitor Centers** at Apgar, St. Mary, and Logan Pass.

The **naturalist program** includes accompanied boat and trail trips, evening campground programs, and slide talks in the hotels. **Glacier Institute** offers outdoor courses of two to five days for credit or noncredit. Courses include color photography, alpine ecology, grizzly ways. The institute's address is Box 527, West Glacier, Montana 59936; phone 406-888-5215.

Going-to-the-Sun Road, the 50-mile link between St. Mary Lake on the east side and Lake McDonald on the west side of the park, crosses the Continental Divide at Logan Pass (elevation 6,664 feet), where springtime prevails and alpine flowers reach their height of bloom as late as August. One of the outstanding scenic routes in the world, open from mid-June until mid-October, Going-to-the-Sun climbs gently above treeline while it unfolds vistas of lakes, waterfalls, and high cliffs. Portions of the Going-to-the-Sun Road are closed to bikes 11 a.m. to 4 p.m., June 15 through Labor Day, due to heavy motor traffic.

Vehicles (and vehicles with trailers) more than 30 feet long are not allowed on the road during July and August; during the rest of the year when the park is open, the limit is 35 feet. Width is limited to 8 feet, including mirrors or extensions. **Chief Mountain International Road** is an outstanding park-to-park highway on the eastern flank of the mountains, through the Blackfeet Indian Reservation and around the base of Chief Mountain, with a view of the Great Plains bending eastward, then through a beautiful spruce and fir forest. It crosses the Canadian border with a clear view of Mount Cleveland, Glacier's highest peak (elevation 10,448 feet). **Waterton Lakes National Park,** on the Canadian side, receives half as many visitors as Glacier, but is a jewel in its own right. When going to Canada you need to pass through customs.

TOUR OPERATORS. All-expense tours ranging from one to ten days may be arranged by travelers arriving by bus or train with Glacier Park, Inc., the principal concessioner.

TRAIL RIDES. Saddle horses are available at Apgar Corral, Lake McDonald Lodge, and Many Glacier Hotel. A popular all-day trip leads from **Many Glacier Valley** over Swiftcurrent Pass, one of the most scenic, to Granite Park Chalet. Other trips range from two-hour and half-day tours for novices to longer climbs for experts.

HIKING TRAILS. The trails fan out in all directions from hotels, chalets, and campgrounds. From Logan Pass on the Going-to-the-Sun Road, take the **Alpine Meadow**

Walk through a lush garden bordered by massive mountains with endless vistas of wilderness. The wooden walkway enables visitors to see and enjoy the scenery while protecting fragile tundra vegetation. Another popular easy walk, the **Avalanche Lake Trail,** leads from Avalanche Campground, off the Going-to-the-Sun Road, to Avalanche Basin, a good route on which to carry a picnic lunch and fishing gear.

For serious overnight hiking, obtain topographic or hiking maps and guidebooks available at Visitor Centers. Park officials advise against trying to cover too much country in a day, or crossing glaciers, which can be treacherous. Hikers must register at a ranger station and obtain a free, but required, backcountry permit for overnight trips. Mountain climbing is ill advised because of fragile rock, unpredictable weather, and hidden glacial crevices. **Sperry Chalet** affords the opportunity to make an intriguing overnight hike without being burdened with camping gear. Cooking is done for you when you arrive and servings are plentiful; box lunches are available. The chalet, reached only by trail from Lake McDonald or Sun Point, is in a high mountain cirque near the Continental Divide, with opportunity for exploring Sperry Glacier and for fishing in nearby lakes. Mountain goats are often seen climbing the sheer rock walls. **Granite Park Chalet** is located in one of the best hiking regions of the park and makes an excellent target for the long-distance hiker on the trek south from Waterton or north from Logan Pass. Reservations are necessary.

BEAR FACTS. Bears wander, covering a lot of territory in search of food. A bear will claim any it finds; so keep a clean camp, store your food suspended high in a tree, and sleep well away from it. A considerate camper and good conservationist will dispose of garbage in a bearproof garbage can or pack it out of the backcountry—and never bury it. Though normally shy, grizzly bears can be a problem in the backcountry when approached without warning. Hikers do well to carry a bear bell, or rocks in a can, to make their presence known on the trail.

At Avalanche Campgrounds and Many Glacier, the Park Service allows camping only in hard-sided vehicles. You may elect to stay in the park's protected camping area, or "bear cage"—a link fence, barbed-wire enclosure, accommodating 12 campers at a time.

LAUNCH TRIPS. These are operated on Lake McDonald, the largest lake in the park, on the west side; Two Medicine Lake, in the southeast corner; St. Mary Lake, surrounded by soaring peaks, waterfalls, and primitive forest; and on Swiftcurrent and Josephine lakes, in the Many Glacier

region, to view spectacular glacier-carved scenery. Photo trips on launches are offered. Small boats and fishing tackle are available for rental.

FISHING. The season extends from the third Saturday in May through November 30. Be sure to obtain your permit (no fee). Seasonal migrations of native cutthroat, bull trout, and Kokanee on the west side provide much speculation, but mackinaw, or lake trout, are taken in the larger lakes. The pygmy whitefish is the most unusual, but rare, found only in a few widely scattered localities in North America. Fly casting with artificial fly is generally practiced; using live or dead fish for bait is not permitted.

BIRDWATCHING. Of special interest to birders is the high-altitude alpine environment from mid-June to early September. Watch especially for white-tailed ptarmigan, golden eagle, blue grouse, water pipit, Clark's nutcracker, mountain bluebird, and gray-crowned rosy finch. Each fall Kokanee salmon and bald eagles migrate to Lower McDonald Creek, where they produce an unforgettable wildlife spectacle (best viewed from the Apgar Bridge). While the salmon spawn, the eagles feed on the salmon. The peak usually comes around mid-November. The eagles begin to feed each day about 30 minutes before sunrise, continuing for two hours. Then many spend the rest of the day perching in large trees, as many as 30 or more eagles per tree.

BICYCLING. The Going-to-the-Sun Road is challenging but popular. During peak hours of motor traffic the road is closed to bikers. Specially designated campsites are available at Sprague Creek Campground. You can rent a bike at Village Inn, Apgar.

RAFT TRIPS. West Glacier outfitters conduct raft trips daily during summer on the Middle Fork of the Flathead River, scenic, splashy, and safe. They take half day or full day (with lunch included).

SKIING. This sport is growing in popularity. Get a copy of the *Ski Trails* brochure published by the Glacier Natural History Association, outlining 14 marked trails in the park, rated beginner, intermediate, and advanced. Trails are designated with orange metal markers. Izaak Walton Inn, at Essex, features 30 miles of groomed trail just outside the park.

ACCOMMODATIONS. The best concentration of attractions is in the Many Glacier region, the setting of **Many Glacier Hotel,** where bighorn sheep sometimes are seen on the lawn; the modern **Swiftcurrent Motor Inn;** and economy (cold water) **Swiftcurrent Cabins. Rising Sun Cabins** and modern **Rising Sun Motor Inn** are located inside the park near the Sherburne entrance. **Glacier Park Lodge** is at the southeast corner of the park. Across the park is **Lake McDonald Lodge,** originally built about 1914. All the above, plus the modern **Village Inn,** at the foot of Lake McDonald in Apgar (a tourist settlement inside the park), and **Prince of Wales Hotel** at Waterton Lake, are operated by Glacier Park, Inc., East Glacier Park, Montana 59434 (from October 16 through May 31, Greyhound Tower, Station 5185, Phoenix, Arizona 85077). **Sperry and Granite Park chalets** are run by Belton Chalets, Inc., Box 188, West Glacier, Montana 59936. Reservations are necessary. **Izaak Walton Inn,** at Essex, midway between West Glacier and East Glacier on Route 2, is an unusual and historic small hotel just outside the park, especially attractive to rail fans (and reachable by Amtrak). The address is Box 653, Essex, Montana 59916. Motels and cabins on the west side are located in Apgar and outside the park on US 2 in West Glacier, Hungry Horse, Whitefish, and Kalispell; on the east side, on US 2 around East Glacier Park, and along US 89 in the vicinity of Browning and St. Mary. **Rocky Mountain Youth Hostel** is at Kalispell, 35 miles southwest of the park.

CAMPING. Major campgrounds are located around St. Mary, Rising Sun, Apgar, and Two Medicine. Smaller, less developed facilities should not be overlooked. **Kintla Lake** campground, for instance, is an isolated beauty spot in the North Fork Valley near the Canadian border, with wonderful hiking along the lake. Attractive campsites can be found along the North Fork of the Flathead River in **Flathead National Forest** and southeast of the park in **Lewis and Clark National Forest.** Canadian campgrounds are different from those in the United States, being equipped with community kitchen shelters. **Glacier** requires permits for all backcountry use. There are 70 backcountry camps. Camping permits for these particular camps cannot be obtained more than 24 hours before starting your trip, for a maximum of six days, with no more than three consecutive nights in any one campground.

SEASONS. Going-to-the-Sun Road is usually closed by snow from mid-October until early June. Naturalist-conducted activities run from about June 15 to Labor Day. Accommodations inside the park are open mid-June to mid-September. Still, early June has its special appeal, with light crowds, freshness of spring, and wealth of flowers. So has September (even the end of the month). With the coming of autumn, scarlet berries and yellow and orange leaves make the park a colorful panorama. The golden-yellow needles of the larch, a strangely behaved conifer, stand out in

bright contrast against a background of its green neighbors. During summer, days are warm, evenings chilly. Warm clothing is essential for hiking in the high country; so is a raincoat to cope with thundershowers.

SHOPPING. In Apgar village, **Montana House** is a showcase of arts, crafts, and handmade clothing of the entire state. The **Northern Plains Indian Crafts Association** has a trading center at St. Mary, just outside the park. Shops at Waterton sell English woolens, Eskimo sealskin slippers, and wildlife prints.

NEARBY. Close to the western entrance to the park, **Kalispell** and **Whitefish** provide motel accommodations and access to camping, fishing, boating, and hiking in **Flathead National Forest** and state parks. At Kalispell, visit the restored **Con-rad Mansion,** an authentic example of luxurious living and architecture in the Northwest at the turn of the century. **Flathead Lake,** south of Kalispell, is the largest natural freshwater lake west of the Mississippi (28 miles long, 10 miles wide), bordered by the mighty Mission Mountains and the forested foothills of the Salish Mountains. At Browning, 12 miles from East Glacier Park, the **Museum of the Plains Indian,** near the center of the million-acre Blackfeet Reservation, interprets the ancient customs of the Indians of the Great Plains. The excellent exhibits and displays of early wood carvings and frescoes make the visit worthwhile.

FOR FURTHER INFORMATION. Write Superintendent, Glacier National Park, West Glacier, Montana 59936.

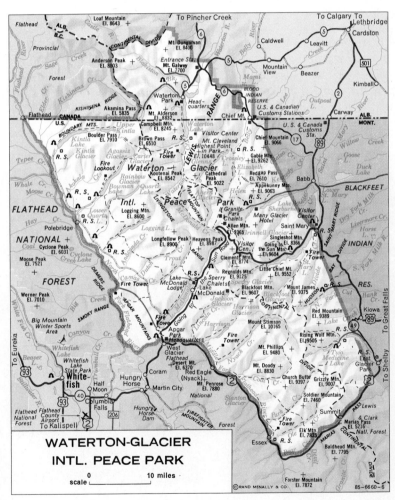

WATERTON-GLACIER INTL. PEACE PARK

0 scale 10 miles

GRAND CANYON NATIONAL PARK

Arizona

Established 1919

AFTER HIS FIRST TRIP to the Grand Canyon in 1903, President Theodore Roosevelt advised, "Do nothing to mar its grandeur. Keep it for your children," he urged, "and your children's children, and all who come after you, as the one great sight which every American should see."

On every visit I make to the Grand Canyon, I can understand why he said that. The first sight of it excited my appetite to see more, the first answers to my questions stimulated my curiosity to ask a thousand more questions. I recall being at the rim before daybreak to watch the first rays of the sun illuminate the walls, and then again at dusk to watch darkness reclaim the scene. I felt humbled, cleansed of self-interest, swept up by the spirit of what John Burroughs called "the world's most wonderful spectacle, ever changing, alive with a million moods."

One winter I came to spend Christmas at the Grand Canyon. It was a very different place, uncrowded, peaceful, the white of snow softening the reds of ancient rock. My friend and I enjoyed our Christmas dinner at El Tovar, the great old hotel at the canyon rim. A Christmas to remember.

Another time, in summer, I went down the Colorado River in a wooden dory, plunging through the great rapids, camping on the sand beaches, and thinking of John Wesley Powell. In 1869, he made the first daring voyage through the canyons of the Green and Colorado rivers in just such a dory, a modern odyssey of a thousand miles, worthy of the ages. Motor trips in

big rubber rafts cover the 277 miles of Colorado River through the Grand Canyon in 7 to 12 days. The dory trip took 18 days, without a single moment of boredom.

In form, size, glowing color, or geological significance, nothing approaches the Grand Canyon of the Colorado River. President Theodore Roosevelt recognized its value to the nation by proclaiming Grand Canyon National Monument in 1908. It became a national park in 1919. Congress nearly doubled the size in an act signed by President Gerald Ford on January 3, 1975. The expansion increased the park acreage from 783,561 acres to 1,218,375.

The park now extends from the mouth of the Paria River to the Grand Wash Cliffs. The Marble Canyon

absorption adds the upstream 50 miles of the Grand Canyon, with rapids and 3,000-foot canyon walls. This addition completes protection of the 285-mile water route extending from historic Lees Ferry, where river runners start downstream, to the Grand Wash Cliffs, overlooking Lake Mead.

From rim to rim, the canyon varies in width from .1 mile in Marble Canyon to 18 miles farther downstream. Measured from the North Rim developed area, which is 1,200 feet higher than Grand Canyon Village on the South Rim, it is 5,800 feet deep—substantially more than 1 mile straight down.

The North and South rims are only 9 miles apart (214 miles by road), but they are distinctly different—two of many worlds within the universe of the Grand Canyon. The North Rim extends into the Canadian zone of climate and plant life and, at 9,000 feet, into the subarctic Hudsonian zone. The famous blue spruce on the heavily forested North Rim are not seen at all on the other side of the canyon, which is more typical of the arid Southwest. Nor is the white-tailed, black-bodied Kaibab squirrel. On the other hand, the Abert squirrel, grizzled gray of body and tail, with white underparts, is strictly a South Rim dweller. The two color phases of the tassel-eared squirrel never meet.

How old is the Grand Canyon and how, actually, was it formed? Century after century, the walls have weathered, crumbled, tumbled their shreds of sand, gravel, mud, and rock into the water and have given the river tools for scouring and gouging. The canyon widens and changes constantly. Its appearance varies with the hour of the day.

The rock layers exposed to view are pages in the textbook of earth's history, spanning 2 billion years. The uppermost strata, the Kaibab and Toroweap formations of Permian age, were formed approximately 250 million years ago. Below them lies the Coconino sandstone, the solidified remains of sand dunes, in which fossilized footprints indicate a lizard type of life. Next are the Hermit shale and the Supai shale and sandstone, with traces of amphibians and fossil ferns. The course of history can be traced through one layer to another to the tilted layers of late Precambrian rocks, perhaps a billion years old. The rocks at the bottom of the Inner Gorge are among the oldest exposed rocks on earth, the hard black rocks of the early Precambrian age.

The down-cutting process began somewhere between 6 and 25 million years ago. At first, geologists thought that the ancestral Colorado River meandered over a broad plain until a general rising of the land caused it to flow more swiftly. Instead of being displaced, it cut downward. According to the traditional theory, the slow rise was concurrent with the lifting of the Rocky Mountains, which gave the river greater runoff and consequently more carrying and cutting power. As the Colorado deepened its course, the canyon walls grew steadily higher. A recent theory, endorsed by many experts on the Colorado Plateau geology, declares that the Colorado River once drained eastward and was separated by the Kaibab Plateau from another drainage to the west. Then the land uplift near the present Arizona–New Mexico border blocked the flow of the Colorado, forming a large lake. When the western drainage eroded toward its source, it tapped the waters of the lake, and the period of canyon cutting began.

Any theory must account for water flowing through a hill, rather than around it. Water runs downhill. Why didn't it flow around the hill instead of through it? Or was the river here first? And did it continue to cut down as the hill was uplifted? Or did a stream flowing off the top of the hill cut down through the hill and capture an ancestral Colorado River ponded to the east? Or is the story even more complex, involving several periods of uplift and possible damming of the Colorado River to the east of the canyon?

We may never know all the answers. Certainly human knowledge and human affairs are dwarfed by these older natural forces. We can, however, trace Indian occupation of the canyon back 4,000 years. The record of Europeans dates only to 1540, when the Spaniard Don Lopez de Cardenas was led by Hopi Indians to the great gorge. Essentially it was John Wesley Powell, geologist, explorer, and chronicler of the arid West, who made Americans aware of it.

A few entrepreneurs, who felt the Grand Canyon should be exploited for its resources, endeavored to block establishment of the national park. Others have wanted to control a tourist toll road on Bright Angel Trail, or to string a cable car into the canyon. To this day proposals are advanced to mine the region and to dam the Colorado River. But most people support Roosevelt's idea: to do nothing to mar its grandeur.

THE PRACTICAL GUIDE: SOUTH RIM

This side is easier to reach, more heavily visited. Stay at least two days here, if only to watch the magic change between dawn and dusk. Do the usual things if this is your first visit, but then go on to the *unusual* opportunities available to explore Grand Canyon. **Main gateways to the South Rim** are Williams and Flagstaff, less than two hours by car. Bus lines run limited schedules from these two cities; Amtrak arrives at Flagstaff and connects with bus service to the canyon. Airlines serve Grand Canyon directly by means of an airport 10 miles south of the park; each flight is met by a bus from Grand Canyon Village.

BACKGROUND. The **Visitor Center,** at the east end of the village, is an important stop for orientation exhibits and dioramas. For times and places of all interpretive programs, check the free park newspaper, the Grand Canyon *Guide.* **South Rim drives** from Grand Canyon Village give the introduction, covering 33 miles with excellent views and linking the main focal points. The West Rim is closed to private cars from Memorial Day to Labor Day. However, the free Canyon Shuttle minibuses operate at frequent intervals, with stops at the key points along the 8-mile route from the Bright Angel Lodge to Hermits Rest. Visitors are encouraged to get off the shuttle buses in order to listen to interpretive talks and gain different views. The West Rim Shuttle operates from 7:30 a.m. to sunset, Memorial Day through Labor Day. The West Rim Drive leads 8 miles to **Hermits Rest,** passing excellent lookouts and the head of Bright Angel Trail.

The Main Village Shuttle provides regular service from early morning through late evening, spring through fall, between the Bright Angel Lodge and Maswik Lodge area, Mather Center (bank, general store, post office, and Yavapai Lodge office), Yavapai Museum, the Visitor Center, El Tovar Hotel, and back to the starting point.

Yavapai Museum is ½ mile east of the Visitor Center. The museum displays interesting exhibits on the geology of the canyon. Farther east, the East Rim Drive leads to **Tusayan Ruin,** a small prehistoric pueblo with a museum, which tells the story of Pueblo people who inhabited and left Grand Canyon before the white people came; **Lipan Point,** with a view of the winding river and the San Francisco Peaks to the south; and the **Watchtower** at Desert View, perched on the brink of the canyon, 25 miles from the village, with telescope views of the Painted Desert, Kaibab National Forest, and the surrounding Indian country.

DAY HIKES. Even short in duration, day hikes can be rewarding and revealing, giving a feeling for the immensity and natural beauty of the canyon. Hiking here is the reverse of mountain climbing. The downhill part comes first, then the upward climb, which takes more time—and more energy. So decide in advance how many hours you wish to hike. When one-third of your time has elapsed, turn around and start back. The two best trails for day hikes, particularly for hikers new to the canyon, are South Kaibab and Bright Angel. Limiting yourself to walks along the rim is a good idea until you become used to the thin air at this elevation.

On the steep **South Kaibab Trail,** the hike to Cedar Ridge—which offers magnificent scenery—covers 1½ miles each way. It takes about 2½ hours round trip. On the **Bright Angel Trail** (originally used by Havasupai Indians to gain access to Indian Gardens), you can descend from the South Rim just west of Bright Angel Lodge and head for Mile and a Half Resthouse or Three Mile Resthouse (water in summer). The trip to **Indian Gardens** covers 4½ miles each way, or at least 9 miles round trip. This oasis lies 3,060 feet below the rim. Allow ample time to return before dark.

Permits are not required for day hikes, but

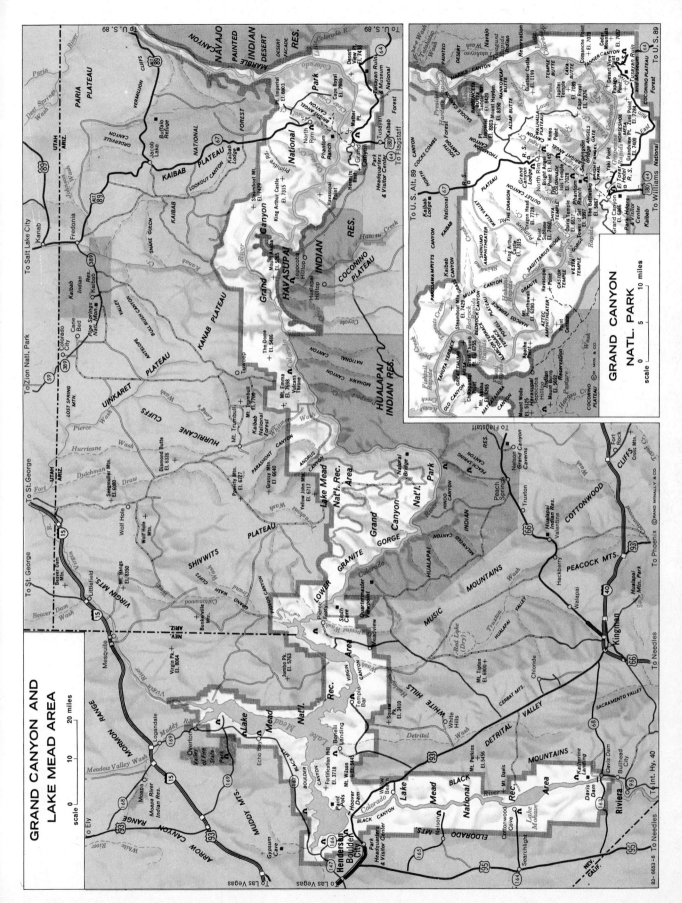

GRAND CANYON AND
LAKE MEAD AREA

GRAND CANYON
NATL. PARK

it is always a good idea to discuss your plans with a ranger.

ACCOMMODATIONS. Lodgings at the South Rim cover a wide range, including rustic **Bright Angel Lodge** and cabins, **El Tovar Hotel,** modern **Yavapai, Thunderbird, Kachina Lodges,** and **Maswik Lodge.** For reservations write Grand Canyon National Park Lodges, Box 699, Grand Canyon, Arizona 86023. Grand Canyon International Hostel provides simple dormitory facilities at a convenient site in the park. Write Arizona Council, AYH, Box 270, Grand Canyon, Arizona 86023.

EATING—SOUTH RIM. There are many beautiful viewpoints for sunrise and sunset picnics, but be sure to carry out trash. Food and picnic supplies are available in the park and in the surrounding area, but you may want to shop for them in Flagstaff. **El Tovar,** built in 1905 to celebrate the railroad bonanza, has a lovely dining room overlooking the South Rim. Arrive early to get a table near the window. The **Arizona Room,** adjoining Bright Angel Lodge, is a cheery modern steak house. **Bright Angel Restaurant,** near the rim, and **Moqui Lodge,** outside the park, offer casual dining. **Yavapai** and **Maswik** Lodge cafeterias have fast-food service.

SEASONS. Facilities on the South Rim are open all year. While the summer is crowded and reservations are imperative, during the winter the park is congestion free. Temperatures drop well below freezing at night but are warmer during the day.

NEARBY. A trip outside Grand Canyon National Park to the **Havasupai Indian Reservation** is a separate excursion from the generally visited South Rim area. This is an attraction unique in the United States, a desert oasis with the turquoise-blue waters of Havasu Creek cascading in spectacular waterfalls. It is a 190-mile drive from the South Rim Visitor Center to the end of the road at Hualapai Hilltop, the point of entry.

Access from there to the town of Supai, 2,000 feet below, is over a precipitous trail. The 11 miles must be covered on horseback or on foot. Havasu Canyon is of special interest to geology students, botanists, birdwatchers, and anthropologists. All campers are required to call the campground reservation office in Supai, Arizona, 602-448-2121, to make or confirm reservations before leaving the rim at Hualapai Hilltop. Reservations must be made through the Havasupai Tourist Enterprise, Supai, Arizona 86435. The Tribal Council assesses an entry fee, payable at the Tourist Office. There is a seven-day limit and an additional charge for camping.

There are two tourist lodges with kitchen facilities in the village. The Havasupai operate a village cafe; you can also purchase groceries in the tribal store. Arrangements for horses and lodging also must be made in advance, by telephoning or writing Havasupai Tourist Enterprise.

THE PRACTICAL GUIDE: INNER CANYON

The Inner Canyon may be reached by foot, muleback, or boat. Summer heat is brutal. Winter temperature extremes between rim and canyon floor are severe. Spring and fall are ideal times to descend into the Grand Canyon's desert. Some of North America's wildest scenery makes effort and discomfort worthwhile.

CAMPING. Camping below the rims is a rewarding experience, if planned with plenty of time. Hikers can be accommodated at **Phantom Ranch** or at numerous primitive campsites (reservations are required). Going on foot is challenging to those in excellent physical condition. On the **Bright Angel Trail,** water is available in summer at two points between the South Rim and Indian Garden; from there to the river, the hottest part of the trip, none is available. From Bright Angel Lodge it's 9½ miles to Phantom Ranch. The serpentine trail descends 4,600 feet, passing layers of sedimentary rock.

On the steeper **South Kaibab Trail,** 6½ miles to the river from the rim at Yaki Point, no water is available. Summer temperatures in the canyon are extremely high. Study preventive measures and treatment of heatstroke and exhaustion. Plan to carry an adequate water supply, a gallon a day per person. And drink it! The toughest part comes at the end with the uphill climb. If you have the stamina, consider the cross-canyon hike from Phantom Ranch to the North Rim on the **North Kaibab Trail** (approximately 14 miles).

Hikers planning to camp in the Inner Canyon must obtain a permit or reservation at the Backcountry Reservations Office or the North Rim Ranger Station. To be assured of campsites, consider it mandatory to make reservations. You can't count on finding one of the campsites below the rim open when you want it.

The backpack trip from the North Rim to Phantom Ranch is filled with superb scenery, passing aptly named **Ribbon Falls,** 4,560 feet below the North Kaibab Trailhead. The last 5 miles are the hottest, but under partial shade following the course of Bright Angel Creek.

Phantom Ranch consists of 11 cabins and 4 dormitories capable of sleeping 92. Each cabin has four beds, a good desk with light, a heater, toilet, and key to the bathhouse where you can get a hot shower. **Bright Angel Campground,** adjacent to Phantom Ranch and Bright Angel Creek, requires a backcountry permit. Reservations are required: contact Grand Canyon National Park Lodges, Box 699, Grand Canyon, Arizona 86023.

WHITE-WATER ADVENTURE. There are many ways to see the Grand Canyon, but perhaps none as thrilling as from a rubber raft or wooden boat, navigating the turbulent Colorado River. Campsites are usually on white-sand beaches.

Twenty concessioners are licensed by the National Park Service; write the Park Superintendent for a complete list (see address under "For Further Information"). Write several of them for literature and check them out to be sure you get the trip you want. A motor-powered raft will get you through faster, but that's not how John Wesley Powell did it.

Lees Ferry, at Page, Arizona—just below Glen Canyon Dam—is the usual launching site for Grand Canyon river trips. You can travel the river for about 277 miles, running 160 recognized rapids, all the way to Lake Mead; though most parties end at Mile 225 at Diamond Creek. Motor trips take 7 to 12 days; oar-powered rafts 10 to 12 days; and wooden dories 18 days. Options are available for partial trips of 3 to 8 days, beginning or ending at Phantom Ranch.

Boaters wishing to raft the Colorado on their own must apply long in advance for a permit. Address inquiries and applications to the Park Superintendent (address under "For Further Information").

SEASONS. Temperatures in the canyon in summer commonly rise as high as 110 degrees Fahrenheit. Heat exhaustion is a real possibility. Hiking conditions are best in spring and autumn when weather is mild on the rims and within the canyon.

TOUR OPERATORS. Going by muleback to Plateau Point is a one-day trip that provides a popular way of viewing the canyon from the ground up. The trip from the South Rim begins on the celebrated twisting **Bright Angel Trail** at the west end of Grand Canyon Village and goes to the Tonto Plateau and Plateau Point.

Even more adventuresome is the two-day trip into the Inner Gorge, stopping overnight at the small guest facility, Phantom Ranch, alongside Bright Angel Creek. The ride down over switchbacks cut into the sheer cliffs seems forbidding, but the surefooted mules haven't lost a rider yet in more than 50 years. Riders must be over 4 feet 7 inches tall, weigh under 200 pounds, and be conversant in English. After lunch at Indian Gardens, a cottonwood oasis, the trail reaches the level of the roaring Colorado, crosses the narrow Kaibab Suspension Bridge, and continues a mile farther to the ranch. The schedule includes a period of relaxation before dinner. The temperature is 20 degrees warmer here than on the South Rim, 4,600 feet above. The next morning, you start the return trip by the **South Kaibab Trail,** equally colorful but a little shorter, reaching the South Rim at Yaki Point, 3½ miles east of the village, in time for lunch.

Confirmed reservations for muleback trips are necessary. Write Grand Canyon National Park Lodges, Box 699, Grand Canyon, Arizona 86023. If you do not have a reservation, make it your first point of business on arrival in the park.

The **North Rim muleback trip** into the canyon is a one-day outing on the North Kaibab Trail, cut from solid rock, to **Roaring Springs.** For reservations, write to Trail Rides, Box 1638, Cedar City, Utah 84720.

THE PRACTICAL GUIDE: NORTH RIM

Being less accessible, this side is not often congested. It affords different views and a different feeling. The vistas are spectacular, and the cool Kaibab Plateau is covered with beautiful forest, where families of deer roam late in the day and flowers of mountain and field meet.

BACKGROUND. The **Gateway to the North Rim** is Jacob Lake, Arizona, where a 44-mile paved road leaves US 89A taking visitors to the Grand Lodge on Bright Angel Point.

Cape Royal Drive from Grand Canyon Lodge extends 20 miles to **Cape Royal,** with choice stopping places en route. **Point Imperial,** 3 miles off the main road, is the highest point of the entire canyon rim, at 8,803 feet, with excellent views over the Painted Desert, Marble Canyon, and the Little Colorado River. Along the last part of the drive, the roadway is bordered with fragrant locust. A graded road, no less scenic, leads through the Kaibab Plateau forest to

Point Sublime, 17 miles west of the entrance highway; there the Inner Gorge is closer than at any other spot along the North Rim.

Bright Angel Point is the tip of the promontory jutting a mile into the canyon, flanked by Roaring Springs Canyon and the Transept. A self-guiding nature trail from Grand Canyon Lodge is an easy walk of ½ mile.

NATURALIST PROGRAMS. The daily schedule includes geology talks at Cape Royal, evening campfire programs at the campground on Bright Angel Point, and other programs. For a complete schedule check at the information desk in the lobby of the lodge.

TUWEEP. The western portion of the national park is the area formerly included in Grand Canyon National Monument, which contains remote portions of the Grand Canyon and is an ideal target for the rugged traveler.

The most outstanding location is at **Toroweap Point,** 2,800 feet above the snakelike Colorado River, on a sheer, vertical wall. It is reached by driving 9 miles west from Fredonia, Arizona, into the Kaibab Indian Reservation, then turning south onto a 50-mile graded road to Tuweep, and then an additional 5 miles on an unimproved road. A small campground is on Toroweap Point, but there is no water or gasoline, and the last food available is at Fredonia.

ACCOMMODATIONS. The **Grand Canyon Lodge** provides modest facilities.

CAMPING. A campground (with showers) is located near the ranger station. Stays are limited to seven days.

SEASONS. The North Rim is open mid-May to early November if weather permits. Evenings are cool even during the summer. During winter, heavy snows close the access roads. From September until mid-October, days are mild and clear, and golden-leaved aspen mantle the hillsides.

THE PRACTICAL GUIDE: GRAND CANYON

Adjacent to both North and South Rim are units of the **Kaibab National Forest,** with many recreation areas. The North Kaibab contains an abundant and famous herd of mule deer.

Bryce Canyon and **Zion** national parks are related geologically to the Grand Canyon and are linked by highway with the North Rim. Phases of the Colorado River story unfold upstream at **Glen Canyon National Recreation Area,** on the Utah-Arizona border, and downstream at **Lake Mead National Recreation Area,** where Arizona, Nevada, and California come together. Driving south on US 89, the traveler can visit **Wupatki National Monument,** preserving prehistoric Indian pueblos, and **Sunset Crater National Monument,** a volcanic crater active as recently as A.D. 1065.

Flagstaff, at the foot of the San Francisco Peaks, is a growing, changing city of the West. The **Museum of Northern Arizona** is a companion piece to the Grand Canyon, the one physical and visual, the other devoted to arts, anthropology, and the study of natural sciences. Flagstaff is also gateway to the **Navajo** and **Hopi reservations** that border the Grand Canyon to the east.

Lowell Observatory, where U.S. moon astronauts trained, offers guided tours at 1:30 p.m. weekdays, holidays excepted. During summer months, visitors can obtain tickets from the Flagstaff Chamber of Commerce to peer through the powerful Lowell telescope on Friday evenings.

VISITING THE RESERVATIONS. Full guest accommodations are available at Cameron, Tuba City, Kayenta, and the Hopi Cultural Center at Second Mesa—a good place to buy Hopi arts and crafts.

RECOMMENDED READING. *Exploration of the Colorado River and Its Canyons,* by John W. Powell (New York: Dover Publications); *Grand Canyon,* by Joseph Wood Krutch (New York: William Morrow & Co.); and *A Field Guide to the Grand Canyon,* by Stephen Whitney (New York: William Morrow & Co.).

FOR FURTHER INFORMATION. Write Superintendent, Grand Canyon National Park, Box 129, Grand Canyon, Arizona 86023.

GRAND TETON NATIONAL PARK

Wyoming

Established 1929

THE GUIDE SAID that he normally was an English teacher in Jackson, but he most certainly was an expert in piloting the rubber raft down the Snake River and pointing out the highlights along the way. We drifted silently past wildlife—coyotes, elk, ducks, herons, bald eagles feeding their young in a high nest—with plenty of chances for photography. The boatman reminded us in a pleasant way always to give wildlife a break, wherever we might be, by keeping a respectable distance. He felt a responsibility, which he clearly wanted to share.

It was a leisurely trip. The Snake was mostly calm and quiet, providing the opportunity to shift my attention to the 40-mile-long cluster of huge peaks dominating the landscape. Some mountain ranges are taller and more massive, but the Tetons rise, without foothills, boldly and abruptly from the earth. From the west side, in Idaho, I had seen them like towering spires parading against the sky. From their bases within the park they spread their images across large, forest-bordered lakes. On the mountain trails along their flanks, they become a network of rock gardens filled with glaciers, waterfalls, and wildflowers.

We stopped for lunch at a beautiful picnic area on Deadman's Bar. The boatman and I talked a while. His name was Vern Huser and we became friends. It was a long time ago, and Vern since then has gone on to write books about running rivers all over the country. So it's not only the places that make the national parks, but the people you meet in them.

The frontispiece of the sheer, jagged peaks, the high basin known as Jackson Hole, is part of the treasure of the 310,418-acre national park. John Colter, who in 1806 left the Lewis and Clark expedition to trap beaver and explore the country, may possibly have been the first white man to come this way, where only Indians had passed before to hunt elk. Then followed the mountain men, the traders, trappers, and the cattlemen. In the 1880s the homesteaders arrived, but they learned the country was too high, cold, and barren for successful farming.

The valley, about 50 miles long, varying in width from 6 to 12 miles, is rimmed by mountains—the high plateaus of Yellowstone National Park on the north, and the Mount Leidy Highlands and Gros Ventre Range on the east and south. It is bisected by the Snake River flowing through Jackson Lake, then through sagebrush meadow and finally through forest and between steep bluffs.

Moose, the largest and least wary member of the deer family, are often seen. Antelope, bison, elk, and mule deer—the wildlife for which Jackson Hole has been famous since the era of the mountain men—are as large as life.

Streams and lakes abound in fish and waterfowl. The trumpeter swan, largest of all swans, once reduced to near extinction, has made a healthy comeback, thanks to its sanctuary in the Tetons.

The story of the park is hardly complete without reference to the late John D. Rockefeller, Jr. He first came to visit this country in 1926. Encouraged by Horace M. Albright, then superintendent of Yellowstone National Park, Mr. Rockefeller in years that followed purchased more than 30,000 acres of the Jackson Hole Basin and presented them to the government for preservation. In the face of extensive local opposition to the park, it wasn't easy. But I can't imagine anyone regretting it today.

THE PRACTICAL GUIDE

You can see the mountains on a breezy drive-through, but you can do the same from the pages of a picture book with less effort. Give yourself a chance to really appreciate this park; even on a short tour, plan to spend at least one full day. **Signal Mountain Overlook,** accessible by automobile, provides the best orientation to the mountains. Turnouts along the way up offer picture-taking vistas. The summit commands a panoramic view over the Snake River valley. It lies off the **Teton Park Road,** which leads to campgrounds, fishing sites, and most mountain trails. The **Rockefeller Parkway,** parallel to the Snake River, is one of America's most scenic roads, with wayside turnoffs and displays; it is part of the valley motor loop.

NATURALIST PROGRAMS. The Tetons are filled with the widest range of activities, whatever your interest may be. These will contribute to the enjoyment and appreciation of the park. Illustrated talks are presented in the campgrounds each evening during the summer and three times weekly at Jackson Lake Lodge. Guided nature walks are conducted every day, and all-day hikes, two days a week. The two Visitor Centers complement each other in telling the story of the Tetons: **Moose,** the fur-trading era (open year-round); **Colter Bay,** Indian Arts Museum, displaying the varied art forms of the American Indian from the David T. Vernon collection, including intricately carved pipes, masks, and weavings (open mid-May to mid-October). Pick up a printed copy of the naturalist programs in the park newspaper.

At Jackson Lake Lodge, square dance programs are held every Wednesday during summer.

SUMMER SEMINARS. Most are five days long, conducted in the park by the Teton Science School. Subjects covered include geology, photography, wildlife, and techniques of wilderness living. Participants are free to stay in group campgrounds or hotels. For information write Teton Science School, Box 68, Kelly, Wyoming 83011.

HIKING TRAILS. The trails are the means to fully exploring and appreciating the Tetons. Short hikes of half-day or all-day duration are rewarding and worthwhile. A good get-acquainted hike will take you to **Hidden Falls.** It can begin and end with a boat trip across beautiful **Jenny Lake,** at the foot of the Cathedral group, to Cascade Canyon. Overnight trips permit leisurely viewing of mountain flora, varied wildlife, and expansive mountain vistas. The well-conditioned person has no difficulty hiking from the 6,500-foot valley floor to the **Teton Crest Trail,** about 4,000 feet higher, where it becomes possible to make a loop trip

completely encircling the Grand, Middle, and South Tetons and adjacent high peaks. The **Paintbrush Canyon Trail** climbs from the south end of Leigh Lake to the upper end of Paintbrush Canyon, bordered with paintbrush and other wildflowers, and with fine views of the lakes beyond the mouth of the canyon. More than 200 miles of trail furnish a wide variety of hiking—through the valley to high mountain lakes and craggy passes above timberline. Watch for sparrow hawks, prairie falcons, and golden eagles, soaring and wheeling on rising air currents above the cliffs and peaks. One part of the Teton Range, from **Leigh Canyon to Berry Creek,** is wilderness in the truest sense, being almost devoid of trails. Expert hikers who want to test their skill in this area can obtain helpful advice from the Colter Bay or Jenny Lake ranger stations. Be sure to obtain a backcountry camping permit—it is required. Warm clothing, comfortable hiking shoes, and a good sleeping bag are all essential for overnight hikes; water-repellent clothing and equipment are useful in the event of sudden summer squalls.

HORSEBACK RIDING. Opportunities are available at various levels of ability. Children can enjoy an hour or two on a saddle-horse trip around the lakes, starting from the park concession corrals at Colter Bay, Jenny Lake, or Jackson Lake Lodge. Better riders can spend a full day on the high trails or arrange pack trips through the concessioner or guest ranches in the valley.

MOUNTAINEERING. Mountain climbing begins where trail hiking leaves off. The Exum Mountain Guide Service (Box 56, Moose, Wyoming 83012), headquartered at Jenny Lake, and Jackson Hole Mountain Guides (Box 547, Teton, Wyoming 83025) offer training for beginners. Even on the first day you practice crawling upward like a spider and swinging from a clifftop in a 20-foot rappel. Two days of instruction are required to go on the guided overnight climb of Mount Owen, Mount Moran, or the Grand. In a single year about 2,000 climbers make the ascent of the Grand, over at least 16 basic routes, ranging from relatively easy (with guides) to some of the finest rock-climbing in the nation. Mountaineering, however, can never be taken lightly. All climbers are required to register in person at the Jenny Lake Ranger Station. The summer climbing season usually extends from June 15 to September 15, the brief summer season at high elevations between snows and storms.

FISHING. In wild streams and lakes, fishing is typical of recreational angling in the northern Rockies. Cutthroat and native trout may be taken with an artificial fly during most of the summer and autumn, but

mackinaw trout in Jackson and Jenny lakes can best be caught by trolling with heavy tackle. A Wyoming license can be obtained at tackle shops for the season or a five-day period.

PHOTOGRAPHY. Wildlife shooting—with camera. One of the great sports in the Tetons is observing animals in their natural state. These creatures are part of the rich legacy of the West, and pictures of them are among the best possible souvenirs. It will help to have a telephoto lens. For safety's sake, keep your young photo fans (and grown-ups) a considerable distance from all animals. More than 100 species of birds inhabit the park. Look for the huge trumpeter swans in flight over the lakes or building their mounded nests, sometimes over the lodges of muskrat and beaver.

Near the south entrance to the park is the **National Elk Refuge,** which is maintained primarily for the winter care of the Jackson Hole elk herd. Most of the flock of this handsome native deer, second largest to the moose, spend the summer grazing in the high range beyond view. Moose can be seen at any season in the early morning and at dusk along river bottoms and in fragrant meadows. There aren't many mule deer in the park, but hikers may see them, or their tracks, along the trails. The sleek pronghorn sometimes appear in small bands on Antelope Flats. A herd of bison runs free in the park. One of the great prizes of the bird watcher and photographer is the shy and rare trumpeter swan, sometimes seen in the elk refuge and other times on Christian Pond east of Jackson Lake Lodge.

FLOAT TRIPS. Snake River trips give a sample of adventure on a western stream. Rubber rafts, piloted by expert guides, make a four-hour trip from Pacific Creek every day during the summer, with a stop for lunch at Deadman's Bar. Two-hour trips are also available. You can put a canoe into the water at **String Lake** and be immersed in solitude, free of outboard motors. Canoe rentals are available at Pelican Bay Marina, Colter Bay Village, and Signal Mountain Marina.

Scenic boat rides are operated on **Jackson Lake,** the valley's largest and deepest body of water, to the far shore, where you look deep into wilderness country. Regularly scheduled, narrated scenic cruises, conducted by Grand Teton Lodge Company, include the Fire Cruise, which provides insight into the "Let-the-fire-burn" policy successfully practiced in various national parks. The Sunday evening "Steak Fry Cruise" leaves in late afternoon from Colter Bay Village in a 50-passenger cruiser for Elk Island. Visitors often observe sandhill cranes at close range. Steaks are barbecued and served around sunset. You can also rent rowboats and canoes on the lake. And on Jenny Lake, rental boats are also available. If you bring your own boat, you must obtain a permit at park headquarters; motor-propelled craft are allowed only on Jackson, Jenny, and Phelps lakes. For strictly boating recreation, larger and better bodies of water are located within driving distance, outside the national park.

Menor's Ferry, near park headquarters, is a reconstruction of the pioneer vessel that began operating across the Snake River in 1892. Exhibits tell about the settlers and their early transportation. When water level of the river permits, ranger-naturalists conduct demonstration rides.

ACCOMMODATIONS. In a shaded setting, **Jenny Lake Lodge** consists of splendid one- and two-room log cabins for the higher-priced trade. The Sunday buffet is one of the dining treats of Wyoming (reservations advisable). **Jackson Lake Lodge,** in the center of activities, is a large, modern motel-type facility with swimming pool. Dining room and coffee shop are open to all park visitors. Its Stockade Bar is a welcome rendezvous for relaxation at sunset. **Colter Bay Village** has two singular types of accommodations designed for family use: tent-cabins, a combination of log and canvas, with stove, grill, screen window, and bunks (camping gear for rent, or bring your own); and rustic log cabins, originals of pioneer settlement days, assembled in one area and furnished with appropriate but modern facilities. The above are operated by the principal concessioner, Grand Teton Lodge Company, Box 240, Moran, Wyoming 83013; reservations are advisable, particularly during July and August.

Other facilities in the park include **Dornan's Moose Enterprises,** east of Jenny Lake near the south entrance, with kitchen-equipped cottages (Box 39, Moose, Wyoming 83012); **Flagg Ranch Village,** on the Rockefeller Parkway between the Tetons and Yellowstone, with motel, cabins, RV park and campgrounds (Box 187, Moran, Wyoming 83013); **Signal Mountain Lodge,** 25 miles north of Jackson, with cabins, lodge units, and marina (Box 50, Moran, Wyoming 83013); and **Triangle X Ranch,** with log cabins and central dining, and guided trail riding (Box 120, Moose, Wyoming 83102). Hotels and motels offering facilities in a wide range are located in and near Jackson.

CAMPING. Five public campgrounds are maintained by the Park Service: **Colter Bay** (largest and most developed, with coin laundry, general store, restaurant), **Lizard Creek, Signal Mountain, Jenny Lake,** and **Gros Ventre.** In addition the concessioner-operated **Colter Bay Trailer Village** has trailer sites with power, water, and sewer connections. Limit of stay at all campgrounds is 14 days, except at Jenny Lake, where the limit is 10 days. This park requires permits for backcountry use and accepts reservations for backcountry camping. Twelve developed campgrounds in adjacent **Teton National Forest** are part of the total camping complex.

TRANSPORTATION. Most visitors arrive by car, but there are other ways, too. Greyhound operates bus service to Idaho Falls, Idaho, with connections to Jackson by Star Valley Stage. Air service on Trans Western and Western airlines reach Jackson from Idaho Falls, Idaho, and Salt Lake City, Utah, all year. Buses run by the Grand Teton Lodge Company meet each flight and connect with Jackson Lodge, Colter Bay Village, and Jenny Lake Lodge. Cars are not essential inside the park. Daily guided tours cover the most important scenic areas (and also include Yellowstone National Park on separate schedules). There is convenient interpark service to hiking and fishing trail heads, and bicycles are now available for rental.

SEASONS. Most activities are concentrated in the months of July and August, although the naturalist program begins in early June. Jackson Lake Lodge is open mid-June to mid-September and is least crowded before July 4 and after Labor Day. Colter Bay has a longer season, late May to October 1. Flower months are June and July in Jackson Hole, July and August in the high country. Fishing is best in September, when days are sunny and clear, though snows may swirl around the summits. In autumn, elk are most easily observed and most exciting to watch. At this time of year, when golden aspens glitter on the hillsides, the mature bulls round up their harems of cows. The area about Signal Mountain and Burnt Ridge is the best part of the park from which to watch their activity and to hear the challenging bugle of the bull elk. This alone is worth the visit.

Winter is a season of majesty, un-dreamed of by the nearly 4 million visitors who come this way in summer. Roads are open from Jackson through the park and over Togwotee Pass, affording vistas of the mighty Tetons rising stark and white between the snow flats and a clear sky. In early winter, depending on snow and weather, large bands of elk move across the open flats to their wintering area south of the park. During a severe winter as many as 11,000 elk have concentrated in the refuge, part of an old migration route, which is now critically blocked from further southward movement by the settlement of man. To winter visitors, the spectacle of this mass of wild animals, many still bearing enormous racks, is the thrill of a lifetime. The public is invited to ride horse-drawn sleds (small fee) into the midst of the herd to see and photograph the animals.

SKI TOURING. This sport is increasingly popular, and the eastern part of the park has four marked trails. Each is about 8 to 10 miles long. Park concessioners offer rental equipment and instructions.

NEARBY. The national park is part of an immense western outdoor recreation region. It includes Yellowstone National Park; John D. Rockefeller, Jr. Memorial Parkway; Bridger-Teton, Shoshone, and Targhee national forests. The closest, the Bridger-Teton National Forest, encompasses three sides of Jackson Hole, with elevations up to 12,165 feet, plus the headwaters of the Yellowstone River and the South Fork of the Snake. Swimming is available at **Granite** and **Astoria Hot Springs,** both south of Jackson. **Jackson** itself, a historic western supply point, still has its wooden boardwalks leading to restaurants, saloons, and craft shops. This is a year-round vacation crossroads for dude ranchers, fishermen, campers, and for hunters and skiers. Don't overlook **Driggs, Idaho,** 40 miles from the south entrance to the park. It's the Targhee side of the Tetons, with choice hiking, backpacking, and skiing, as well as motels and resort lodgings.

RECOMMENDED READING. *One Day at Teton Marsh,* by Sally Carrighar (Lincoln: University of Nebraska Press); *Across the Wide Missouri,* by Bernard De Voto (New York: AMS Press); and *Teton Trails,* the park trail guides.

FOR FURTHER INFORMATION. Write Superintendent, Grand Teton National Park, Box 170, Moose, Wyoming 83012.

GREAT BASIN NATIONAL PARK

Nevada

Established 1986

THE GREAT BASIN is one of the most lightly populated and least-known parts of our country, but no less worthy than any other part. So I found myself thinking while driving almost 500 miles from Salt Lake City west across the open frontier. It was June 1987, only a few months following action by Congress to establish our newest national park, the first one in Nevada.

The region called Great Basin has been derided as a desert, but not as I saw it. It extends from the Wasatch Mountains in Utah to the Sierra Nevada in California, and from Idaho south to Arizona, landlocked, with no outlet to the sea. It is dry and arid, blocked from moist Pacific winds by the high Sierra peaks, but is never dull. I stopped again and again to admire the hardy vegetation, sagebrush, rabbit brush, grass saltbush, pinyon, juniper, grasses, and sedges, that survive and thrive in a harsh environment, and mountain peaks rising like sentinels here and there above them. Flowers, including primroses, buttercups, phlox, paintbrush, and beautiful coral mallow, flash in springtime. The Great Basin is marked by the remnants of Pleistocene lakes, like Lake Bonneville, an ancient inland sea in northwest Utah, and Great Salt Lake.

It's a long way between post offices in the Great Basin. I'm glad there still are such regions, where this generation can envision the openness of times past. To locate the new park properly, it lies on the eastern edge of Nevada, near the small town of Baker a few miles south of US 50. It is 70 miles east of Ely, on the route to Reno, and 290 miles north of Las Vegas (via US 93).

The park embraces 76,800 acres, a relatively small parcel considering the grandeur of the country. The highlights are Lehman Cave, one of the largest limestone caverns in the West (formerly protected as a national monument), and Wheeler Peak, 13,063 feet, one of the highest points of the Great Basin. Between cave and summit, the park embraces everything from sagebrush to alpine meadows, glacial lakes, aspen forests, and stands of venerable bristlecone pines, 4,000 years old, among the oldest living things on earth.

The park is new, but the idea of a national park dates from early in the century. Mining and ranching influences blocked it, but conservationists never quit. In the 1950s, Weldon Heald, a well-known Arizona writer, championed the concept. In the sixties, Darwin Lambert, then a newspaper editor in Ely, organized the Great Basin National Park Association, enrolling members in many states. They spread the gospel, leading ultimately to the park's designation in 1986.

THE PRACTICAL GUIDE

You will undoubtedly have traveled a long distance to reach Great Basin National Park, so consider it an important destination and allow ample time to do it right. If you're camping, you can spend two or three days or longer to advantage. If driving on a timetable, plan at least the better part of a day here.

BACKGROUND. The **Visitor Center** is the first structure on entering the park. It was built to serve the former Lehman Caves National Monument and is well established, with wall maps, introductory film, historic displays, and literature. Spend an hour at the center. Talk with the ranger on duty; he or she will suggest the best ways to spend your time and will help with travel informa-

tion. Don't miss the chance to learn about history: of how Jedediah Smith explored the Great Basin, to be followed by early adventurers, surveyors, and gold seekers; and of how Wheeler Peak was named for Lieutenant George Wheeler, who led a survey party in 1869 and again in 1879.

LEHMAN CAVES. Take the naturalist-led tour starting from the Visitor Center. (A fee is charged.) It takes about 1½hours to walk two-thirds of a mile underground. You'll see huge fluted columns, curtains of stone, color-splashed ceilings, twisting helictites, and other unusual formations found in few other caves. Compare the formations you see here with those in other western national parks and monuments

(such as Wind Cave, South Dakota; Carlsbad, New Mexico; Timpanogos, Utah; and Oregon Caves, Oregon), and Lehman will rank high by any standard. Temperature in the cave averages about 50 degrees Fahrenheit, so *wear warm clothing*. The ticket for the tour carries a minimap showing the **Gothic Palace, Lodge Room, West Room, Grand Palace,** and **Talus Room**—ask the naturalist to sign and date it and you have a neat memento.

WHEELER PEAK SCENIC DRIVE. This extends 12 miles on a winding gentle grade to the 10,000-foot level. Stop along the way for unfolding vistas of the Great Basin. You'll see **Baker Creek** and **Lehman Creek** flowing out of the glaciated canyons of snowy Wheeler Peak. The road ends at Wheeler Peak Campground, where further adventure begins, now on foot.

HIKING TRAILS. Well developed and attractive, the trails lead through aspen groves and along bubbling high mountain creeks. In spring and summer many kinds of wildflowers—lupine, yellow aster, larkspur, columbine, and others—bloom along the trail, advancing higher up the mountain with the season. With good luck you may catch sight of wildlife—mule deer, bobcats, bighorn sheep, or a mountain lion. But don't be surprised to see cattle grazing, since Congress chose to allow it here, unlike in other national parks.

Take one of the easy trails to **Stella Lake** or **Teresa Lake.** If the snow has melted, leave the loop trail near Teresa Lake for the 1-mile side trip to the forest of bristlecone pine, embracing some of the oldest trees in the world. They have made it through many centuries on these quartzite ridges, gnarled and wind bent, each tree a living lesson in survival. With time and planning and condition, hike up the talus ridges to the windy summit of **Mount Wheeler,** 13,063 feet, the highest mountain peak entirely in Nevada. But be sure to carry water wherever you hike, and protect yourself against the possible stomach upset of giardia from drinking untreated water.

SEASONS. For half the year the slopes are covered with snow. Lehman Cave is open all year, but the upper trails may not be accessible until late June or July.

ACCOMMODATIONS. The park has five **campgrounds (Baker Creek, Lower Lehman, Upper Lehman, Snake Creek, Wheeler Peak),** all with trailer spaces and access to good hikes. The little town of Baker, 5 miles from the park, has two small motels, likely with more to come, while Ely, 70 miles west, has a full range of overnight and eating facilities.

While the park itself offers camping only, the concession-operated **Lehman Caves Cafe and Gift Shop** at the Visitor Center merits a special word for its old-fashioned fountain, homemade soup, and Native American crafts.

FOR FURTHER INFORMATION. Write Superintendent, Great Basin National Park, Baker, Nevada 89311.

GREAT SMOKY MOUNTAINS NATIONAL PARK

North Carolina—Tennessee

Authorized 1926

I T WAS an adventure I'll never forget. I expected spring in late March, but it was strictly winter in the Smokies. Where wildflowers should have been bursting with color, the ground was mantled with snow, and, in places, with ice. Consequently, it took a while to get organized with the right gear for the weather, and it was after midday before we started up the trail to Mount LeConte, one of the favored vista points in the park, especially for sunset watching.

I confess that my friend, Mack Prichard, who works for the Tennessee Department of Conservation, carried the heavy pack. We followed a stream thickly bordered by laurel and rhododendron. The sky was generally clear, though scattered clouds, typical of the Smokies, hung low about the mountaintops and in the valleys. We saw forests dusted white with snow extending in rolling waves—it was reminiscent of a picturebook scene of Bavaria or the Black Forest. The higher we climbed, the colder it became. As we passed under the rocky outcrop of Alum Cave Bluff, the tree limbs were weighted with glistening icicles, which now and then broke loose with thundering pops. We made it to the mountaintop and huddled all night in the old stone shelter, built for summer use and downright breezy in winter. Looking back, I realize it was well worth the effort.

Astride the common border of North Carolina and Tennessee, unbroken for a distance of 70 miles except for one transmountain road, the Smokies stand as the masterwork of the Appalachian highlands. Fed by the fertile land and nourished by rain and rushing streams, plant life is luxuriant and varied, with more kinds of trees than in all of Europe. Most of it was logged before the coming of the park, but not LeConte, whose great trees we saw covered with snow.

The park covers 517,014 acres, embracing some of the oldest mountains on earth. Their foundations were laid on the floor of a shallow sea over 500 million years ago. The loftiness of the mountains was produced during a long period of earth upheavals called the Appalachian Revolution, about 200 million years ago. The Smokies escaped the icy tongue of glaciers and gave sanctuary to many plant species fleeing the frigid North. As a result, it is today the meeting ground of northern and southern types of forests.

I find the history of the region as fascinating as its natural endowments. For hundreds of years, the Smokies were part of the mountain empire of the Cherokee Indians, which at its height extended from Virginia south to Georgia and Alabama. They lived in harmony with nature in small communities along the streams, but once the advancing colonists—moving in one direction inland from Charleston, South Carolina, and in another down from Virginia and Pennsylvania—pressed their settlements into the hills the Indians were doomed.

At first, settlers took up the generous valleys and coves. On the North Carolina side, John Jacob Mingus settled in the Oconaluftee Valley in 1792. He may have been the first white man to live in what is now the national park. Others followed in the 1800s, living in isolation, moving into the subvalleys, along creek branches and up the steep hillsides to scrabble for a hard living. They grew almost everything they ate and made almost everything they wore.

The national park was a long time in coming to the Great Smoky Mountains. The idea was first advanced by Dr. Chase Ambler of Asheville, North Carolina, who organized the Appalachian National Park Association in 1899. It was renewed in 1923 by Mr. and Mrs. Willis P. Davis of Knoxville, Tennessee. But establishing a national park in the southern Appalachians, or anywhere in the East, demanded a different approach than in the West. Essentially, western parks were carved out of land already owned by the federal government as part of the vast public domain. But in the Smokies, 85 percent of the total acreage was owned by 18 timber and pulpwood companies, while the remaining 15 percent was divided among a multitude of 6,000 small farmers and owners of summer homesites.

In 1924, however, the Secretary of the Interior appointed a special committee to survey the entire mountain region for the best location for a national park. Finally the committee reported that: "The Great Smoky Mountains easily stand first because of the height of the mountains, depth of valleys, ruggedness of the area and the unexampled variety of trees,

shrubs and plants." In 1926 legislation was enacted by Congress to establish three national parks: Shenandoah, Smoky Mountains and Mammoth Cave National Parks.

The Smokies lie about one hour's drive from Asheville, North Carolina, or from Knoxville, Tennessee. They are within a day's driving time of almost all the large cities of the East and Middle West. Hikers may follow approximately 900 miles of winding trails along clear streams and waterfalls. The Appalachian

Trail follows the mountain crest the full 70-mile length of the park, with a chain of overnight trailside shelters. I've also enjoyed short trails passing forest giants hundreds of years old, and valleys alive with spring wildflowers and blooming summer plants. Road viewpoints unfold the vista of wilderness—the peaks rising above 6,000 feet and extending to the horizon like green waves, and the valleys screened by bluish or smokelike mist, from which the mountains derive their name.

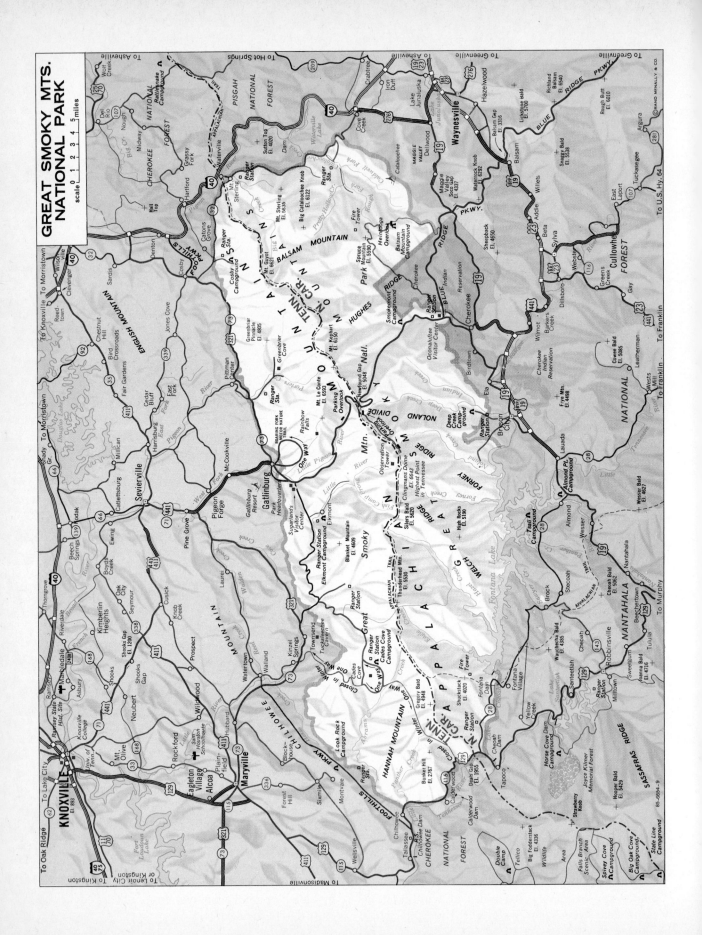

GREAT SMOKY MTS. NATIONAL PARK

scale 0 1 2 3 4 5 miles

THE PRACTICAL GUIDE

Plan for at least two days, or take to the trails for a longer stay. Avoid the mistake of trying to "see" the Smokies only by driving over the transmountain road (US 441) on your way to another destination.

BACKGROUND. When approaching from Tennessee, through Gatlinburg or Townsend, stop first at Sugarlands Visitor Center near park headquarters. On the North Carolina side, stop at the **Oconaluftee Visitor Center** to obtain information and to see the 19th century farmstead. Nearby **Mingus Mill** presents a water-powered, turbine-driven gristmill as another page out of the past. Along US 441, a major viewpoint is at **Newfound Gap**.

Cades Cove is one of the choicest spots of any national park. Drive the 11-mile loop road past fields, frame churches and pioneer homesteads. May through October, the miller grinds corn at the Cable Mill and you can purchase a bag at Cades Cove Visitor Center.

ACTIVITIES. Hiking. A number of trails begin from US 441. From Alum Cave parking area, you can hike to **Alum Cave Bluffs** (five miles round trip), where rose-purple rhododendron bloom in mid-June. The stronger hiker may climb the **Chimney Tops** (four miles and three hours round trip), a high, rocky perch. The **Cove Hardwoods Trail** is an easy one. It passes through an area where settlers once cultivated the land; then plunges through virgin forest. From Newfound Gap, you can sample the Appalachian Trail.

Many visitors enjoy hiking short distances on the **Appalachian Trail**, either from Davenport Gap at the eastern boundary; Fontana Dam, the southwest terminus; or from Clingman's Dome. The full distance takes six to eight days, with shelters spaced about a day's journey apart; each shelter provides bunks for at least 12 persons and is normally restricted to one night's use. Be sure to pick up a backcountry permit at any Visitor Center or Ranger Station.

Bicycling. Though much of the park terrain is too steep, the 11-mile loop through Cades Cove is ideal for cycling, and bicycles are available for rent at the Cades Cove Campground Store. Check with rangers for other routes suitable for cycling.

Bird watching. More than 200 species have been recorded in the park. Spring migration and summer nesting season are generally the best times for bird observation. While hiking the trails, watch hardwood forests and rhododendron thickets for nesting sites. Pick up a copy of *Notes on the Birds of Great Smoky Mountains National Park*, by Arthur Stupka.

Naturalist Programs. These are conducted by park personnel during the summer season. For more serious activity, the National Park Service and the University of Tennessee conduct a series of summer workshops under the heading of Smoky Mountain Field School. In these minicourses of two to five days, you will study birds, plants, photography, geology, backpacking and conservation issues. Camper College is conducted weekends from late June through August in cooperation with Western Carolina University. Classes usually meet Friday and Saturday from 9 a.m. to 4 p.m. Subjects include Appalachian plants, music, folklife, dancing, Indian basket weaving, backpacking and kayaking. For information write Division of Continuing Education, Western Carolina University, Cullowhee, North Carolina 28723.

Fishing. Fishing is permitted year-round in open waters. Some 600 miles of streams flow through the park, many offering opportunities for rainbow and brown trout. The possession of any brook trout is prohibited. Certain streams are closed to fishing, as protection for the brook trout. A Tennessee or North Carolina fishing license is required. Inquire at the Ranger Stations or Visitor Centers for a free copy of park fishing rules and regulations.

ACCOMMODATIONS. Overnight lodgings for noncampers are found at two locations inside the park. Secluded **LeConte Lodge**, atop Mount LeConte, is reached by foot or horse trail. Popular from spring through autumn, it provides a genuine national park experience. For reservations, write LeConte Lodge, Gatlinburg, Tennessee 37738. **Wonderland Hotel** at Elkmont is small (27 rooms). It was here as a private club long before the park came into being and now operates as a public facility. It is open Memorial Day to November 1; reservations essential. Write Wonderland Hotel, Elkmont, Gatlinburg, Tennessee 37738. **Fontana Village**, near the southwestern edge of the park, is a unique family resort center.

More lodgings are listed in the last chapter of this book, "A Guide to Lodgings."

CAMPING. During summer months, the three major campgrounds (Elkmont, Smokemont and Cades Cove) are on a computer reservation system operated by Ticketron. Mail reservations should be received by Ticketron at least two weeks in advance; at walk-in outlets no later than the day before the reservation begins. You must have your reservation ticket when you arrive, and then you are assigned a specific site. This area requires permits for backcountry use and accepts backcountry camping reservations. Campgrounds are also located in communities near the park.

SEASONS. Spring weather can begin as early as January or as late as March. Hikers and campers should bring warm clothing for cool weather until May. Wildflowers usually are outstanding for the Spring Wildflower Pilgrimage, held annually at Gatlinburg the last weekend of April, with wildflower and botany lectures, photography seminar, bird walks and field trips in the park. The lowlands in summer are warm; the summits are always cooler. Rainfall and thundershowers are likely, making raingear a must. For a rewarding experience, hike to Gregory's Bald in late June, when spectacular masses of wild azaleas bloom along the edges of this hillside meadow. During the last weekend of September and the first weekend of October, sorghum making is demonstrated alternately at Cades Cove and Oconuluftee Farm Homestead in the manner handed down from generation to generation.

NEARBY. Just outside the park, in North Carolina, the **Oconaluftee Village** and **Qualla Crafts Shop** display the handicrafts and history of the Cherokee people. They serve as a fitting prelude to an evening performance of the outdoor drama, "Unto These Hills." The **Blue Ridge Parkway** provides motoring adventure and picnic areas at high, cool elevations, with expansive vistas of the Smokies and other ranges. **Pisgah National Forest** includes 80 miles of the Appalachian Trail and the site of the historic "Cradle of Forestry in America" at the Pink Beds south of Asheville. **Nantahala National Forest**, the Cherokee "land of the noonday sun," has facilities for fishing, camping, hunting and the beautiful Joyce Kilmer Memorial Forest, with towering giants 500 and 600 years old. **Fontana Lake** is the largest of a network of TVA and other reservoirs providing water sports. On the Tennessee side, the **Cherokee National Forest** has many camping sites, plus nature trails and scenic drives. Enthusiasts of handicrafts will want to attend the **Craftsman's Fairs**, held at Asheville in July and at Gatlinburg in October.

RECOMMENDED READING. *Strangers in High Places* by Michael Frome, *Our Southern Highlanders* by Horace Kephart and *Hiker's Guide to the Smokies* by Dick Murlless and Constance Stallings.

FOR FURTHER INFORMATION. Write Superintendent, Great Smoky Mountains National Park, Gatlinburg, Tennessee 37738.

GUADALUPE MOUNTAINS NATIONAL PARK

Texas

Authorized 1966

I VISITED the Guadalupe Mountains before they were designated as a national park, in the company of J.C. Hunter, Jr., who made the national park possible. "I hold title to the land," he said, "but how can anyone consider himself owner of this magnificent country, when these mountains have stood alone here for millions of years?"

Actually, the first proposal for a park of some kind was made by his father, Judge J.C. Hunter, of Culberson County, Texas in 1925.

Judge Hunter purchased one section of land in remote West Texas and had prospects of donation of an additional 6,000 to 8,000 acres from other owners for park purposes, but that initial project fell through. He continued to acquire land during the 1930s and '40s. The judge and his son used this territory west of the Pecos as a ranch for angora goats to produce mohair wool, but were careful to avoid overgrazing the land, in anticipation of it one day becoming part of a national park. Even after the death of the judge in 1945, his son continued to expand the "Hunter Lands" in the Guadalupe Mountains.

New impetus was given in 1958 when Wallace E. Pratt offered to donate his ranch lands, which included the mouth and north fork of McKittrick Canyon, an area rich in natural values. Pratt had been associated with Humble Oil Company as chief geologist and vice president until his retirement in 1945. His donation of 5,632 acres was completed in 1961. Then J. C. Hunter, Jr., moved to offer 72,000 acres around McKittrick Canyon at a price of $1.5 million. When Congress, spurred by Senator Ralph Yarborough of Texas, authorized establishment of the park in 1966, it picked up one of the greatest land bargains in history—a national park at $21 per acre. Following acquisition of mineral rights from the State of Texas and other sources, the park was formally established and dedicated on September 30, 1972.

I rode a mule, surefooted and determined, rather than stubborn, up the rugged, brushy slopes. The foot of the mountains I found landscaped with agaves and cacti, but with rising elevation the vegetation changed to pines, alligator juniper, even Douglas fir in favorable settings. I learned that on the highest peaks, some spots show decidedly alpine characteristics.

The Guadalupe Mountains stand like an island in the desert, 110 miles from El Paso and barely below the border that Texas shares with New Mexico. The most prominent feature of the 76,293-acre national park is El Capitan, a sheer, thousand-foot, whitish-colored cliff. Directly north of it, Guadalupe Peak, 8,749 feet, is the highest point of the Lone Star State.

Geologically speaking, they are a spectacular exposure of one of the world's most extensive and significant fossil reefs. They date from the Permian period, between 230 and 280 million years ago, when a vast saltwater basin occupied a large part of present Texas and New Mexico. In the shallower water, marine organisms and waterborne minerals formed a limestone reef similar to the one that shelters the coastland of Queensland, Australia, today. Also of major geological interest is the tremendous earth fault on the abrupt west side of the park.

Prehistoric Americans evidently occupied these canyons as early as 12,000 years ago. Many pictographs are found in caves and rock shelters.

Roasting pits found at all elevations indicate that early inhabitants followed the ripening of native plants from the valley floor in spring to the highest ridges in autumn. The first references in history were written by the Spanish conquistadors in the course of their journeys north from Mexico. They found Mescalero Apaches living in the area.

I saw hawks, hummingbirds, vireos and warblers, among the 200-plus species of birds found in the canyons and over clifftops. I wish that I had caught a glimpse of a mountain lion, bear or wild turkey. With luck, you might succeed where I failed.

THE PRACTICAL GUIDE

Roads cross only limited portions of the park, but more than 80 miles of rugged, scenic hiking trails provide broader access. Several scenic sites, including the remains of a stage station on the Butterfield Stage Line, are accessible by car.

BACKGROUND. Center of activities, the new Visitor Center is located 1 mile east of Pine Springs, Texas, and 55 miles southwest of Carlsbad, New Mexico. It is on US 62/180 and is open 7 a.m. to 6 p.m. in the summer and 8 a.m. to 4:30 p.m. in the winter. Be sure to see the slide show in the auditorium; it concentrates on the park wilderness. A self-guided, 2-mile hike to Smith and Manzanita Springs can be made at any time. Another self-guided walk is available near the McKittrick Canyon contact station.

A paved road leads to the **McKittrick Canyon** contact station, at the mouth of McKittrick Canyon. Allow time to see the exhibits and self-starting slide program. This area is open for day use only; the road is closed each evening. You will see rare plant communities on the lower floor of the canyon. The walls reveal the Capitan Reef and fore-reef and back-reef marine deposits. The trail covers 3½ miles. The upper portion of the canyon may be closed from May to mid-June to protect the critical breeding habitat of peregrine falcons;

the aerie is renowned for its long record of successful breeding.

HIKING. Trails are available for both experts and novices. Unless experienced in this type of country, content yourself with one-day hikes. Trails are rocky and often steep. Weather conditions are apt to change rapidly. The hike to **Devil's Hallway** leads up the floor of Pine Canyon; it takes about six hours. Watch for the rare spotted owl, which has been seen on many occasions along trails into the high country.

Hikes in the high country afford spectacular sights of the Chihuahan desert and salt flats spreading out below. The McKittrick Canyon Trail leads 4 miles along the canyon floor, then climbs steeply to Turtle Rock and junction with Lost Peak Trail. You'll see historic sites, including the "Pinery" stage station, Frijole and Williams ranch houses and the Pratt stone cabin.

CAMPING. Pine Springs Campground, a short drive from the information station, is at the entrance to the Pine Springs Canyon. It offers 24 tent sites and space for 17 recreational vehicles, water and modern restroom building. A fee is charged per night per vehicle.

Dog Canyon Campground and trailhead are reached from New Mexico. Dog Canyon lies 70 miles from Carlsbad via US 285

and New Mexico 137 through Lincoln National Forest. The campground, 1 mile inside the park boundary, contains 18 tent sites and five spaces for self-contained vehicles. There is no charge for camping in Dog Canyon. At 6,300 feet elevation, summer is comfortable and pleasant. This is a good place to start either a day hike or backpack, since you don't have the steep climb on the eastern escarpment near Pine Springs. You can have a good hike to Lost Peak, 2½ miles south over a well-marked trail. You can bring private horses to Dog Canyon, but you must have feed and water.

In addition to the campgrounds in the park, several private campgrounds are located at Whites City and in the city of Carlsbad. If you are planning to camp in the backcountry, register at the Information Station, where you can purchase a good topographic map of the high country and obtain a permit for one of the designated camping areas. Be sure you have proper equipment, including sturdy boots, map, head cover and adequate water. Watch out for rattlesnakes, especially during their early morning and evening feeding hours.

FOR FURTHER INFORMATION. Write Superintendent, Guadalupe Mountains National Park, 3225 National Parks Highway, Carlsbad, New Mexico 88220.

HALEAKALA NATIONAL PARK

Hawaii

Authorized 1960

I T WAS one of those typically clear Hawaiian days. From the observatory at the summit of Haleakala crater, I looked across the waters of the Pacific. The Big Island of Hawaii rose boldly against the sky, while in the opposite direction, northwest of where I stood, were the neighboring islands of Lanai, Molokai and Oahu. All of them, I thought, are like children of the sea, raised from the earth's crust by repeated volcanic action.

The Hawaiian islands, with their distinctive birds, plants and Polynesian culture, are as much a part of the United States as any part of the mainland, yet they add extra dimensions to the character of the nation. Where else could I stand in the "House of the Sun," or Haleakala, where the demigod Maui held the sun prisoner in order to give his people more daylight hours? And whether legend or not, I saw where the sun has helped produce unusual native plants among the multicolored cones, cinders, pumice and ash.

Maui, the "Valley Island," on which Haleakala is located, was formed, so they tell us, by two volcanoes rising from the sea. In one million years or so, a small part of the island has been tempered into fertile fields, now growing sugarcane and pineapple, but the mammoth crater of Haleakala bears eloquent witness to the volcanic explosions of the Pacific.

Haleakala was a spiritual and cultural focal point of Hawaiians for perhaps a thousand years before Captain Cook arrived in the islands. In fact, while hiking within the crater, I saw the remains of an ancient hand-laid stone and learned that some archaeologists suspect that Hawaiians have occupied the crater for religious purposes.

Missionaries, seafarers and surveyors visited Haleakala in the 1800s. The most famous American to describe it was Mark Twain, in *Roughing It*. He was so enthusiastic about this site that in 1881 he wrote to Charles Warren Stoddard: "If the house would burn down, we would pack up the cubs and fly to the isles of the blest, and shut ourselves up in the healing solitudes of the crater of Haleakala and get a good rest ..."

It was Lorrin A. Thurston, grandson of missionaries and publisher of the *Pacific Commercial Advertiser*, who led the effort to establish a national park of Hawaii's volcanoes. In 1907, the Hawaii legislature invited no less than 50 members of Congress and their wives to see the proposed park area firsthand. Their visit included a fancy dinner cooked over hot lava vents at the edge of Halemaumau. In 1912, Dr. Thomas Jaggar, lately hired as director of the Hawaiian Volcano Observatory, joined the campaign. He and Thurston were tireless boosters of the park idea. In 1916, with little controversy generated, Congress voted to authorize the new Hawaii National Park, consisting of three separate sections: Kilauea, Mauna Loa and Haleakala. In 1960, Haleakala was established as a park in its own right, giving official sanction to what had been a sacred, unspoiled wilderness for perhaps 1,400 years.

Early in 1969, major portions of Kipahulu Valley became part of the national park. The addition includes the beautiful pools of the 'Ohe'o stream and 54 acres fronting on the ocean. The Kipahulu Valley, on the east slope of Haleakala volcano, provides ancient forests, waterfalls and lava pools.

The park covers 28,665 acres, but when I reached the rim, I realized that most of it is contained within the crater; it is 7½ miles long, 2½ miles wide and 21 miles around. The floor of the crater, the heart of the park with its richly colored cinder cones, lies 3,000 feet below the summit, covering an area of 19 square miles. The last volcanic action on Maui occurred in the 1700s (outside the crater), but earthquake activity is still recorded and felt here.

I marveled at the unusual life of the crater. The plant most characteristic of Haleakala is the rare, yucca-like silversword, which grows as a mass of silvery, saberlike leaves; when full grown its flower stalk produces a hundred or more vivid purplish blooms. As soon as the seeds of this bloom mature, the plant dies.

I caught sight of an io, a high flying Hawaiian hawk, and several honeycreepers. It was not surprising to learn that 70 different birds indigenous to the island are unlike any others in the world, and that a few of them live only in Haleakala.

THE PRACTICAL GUIDE

ACCESS. Passenger planes make several flights daily (20 minutes) from Honolulu to Maui. Arrangements for tours can be made at Kahului Airport or at Maui hotels. Some visitors come by rental car. The park is reached on the highest paved road in the mid-Pacific, often with clear views of the ocean and at other times with flowing mists and cloud banks, creating a variety of Pacific moods. For the full enjoyment of the park, plan two or three days, and stay overnight in the cabins within the crater, which are reached only by hiking or on horseback. Reservations for the cabins must be made in advance.

The real adventure is within the crater itself. There are no roads, but 30 miles of well-marked trails show how plant life increases as you descend and move eastward. Here you find rare birds like the Hawaiian goose, or nēnē. Though it has entirely forsaken the water, its feet retain some webbing. This native bird was reintroduced to the island near Paliku Cabin in 1962, in a cooperative project by the State of Hawaii, the U.S. Fish and Wildlife Service and the National Park Service. To protect rare and endangered species, pets are not allowed in the crater.

BACKGROUND. Park headquarters are located 1 mile beyond the entrance. A ranger can help you plan your visit. Even if your time is limited, he will suggest a drive to the crater rim viewpoints, which rise steadily upward to the summit. **Kalahaku Overlook** contains an area of silversword, enclosed to protect them from troublesome goats roaming loose and from thoughtless visitors, but even here roots have been damaged by overeager amateur photographers. This striking, unusual plant once flourished so abundantly that the crater appeared bathed in moonlight from the glow of its silvery leaves. But by the beginning of this century human vandalism and unchecked livestock grazing brought the silversword to the edge of extinction. Plants are still found on the slopes of cinder cones in the crater. Depending on weather, as many as 100 plants flower in a good season. Each plant flowers but once, a bright yellow and reddish-purple, then dies slowly as seeds mature.

From the Visitor Center near the summit, a trail goes up 380 yards to White Hill, a formation lighter in color than most Hawaiian lava.

ACTIVITIES. Hiking. If you plan to hike any of the crater trails, remember the difference in altitude here; if you are accustomed to the atmosphere at sea level, take things easy and settle for a sample.

Red Hill Overlook, the highest point of the rim (and on the island), affords an excellent vantage for picture taking.

Two hiking trails lead into the crater, **Halemauu** at 8,000 feet and **Sliding Sands** at 10,000 feet. Most persons enter via Sliding Sands and return via Halemauu, and are encouraged to do so. For safety reasons, a permit is required for all overnight trips into the crater.

The hike down Sliding Sands, across the floor and out on Halemauu covers about 12 miles. You can do it in a day. En route you'll see a variety of native shrubs with unusual flowers or berries; Hawaiian snow, a lichen, the first plant to appear after a lava flow in higher altitudes; sandalwood trees; and mountain pili, distinct from the lowland variety once used for grass houses.

Paliku is a lush oasis deep inside the northeast corner of the crater. Clouds moving up the windward slopes and spilling over the rim have furnished the moisture. Here the nēnē feeds upon grasses, leafy plants and berries in open or semi-open areas.

Bottomless Pit lies along the Halemauu Trail. Keep away from the crumbly edges of this old spatter vent, since the bottom is 65 feet down. Nearby are Pele's Paint Pot, a colorful pass between cinder cones and Pele's Pig Pen (reached on a cross trail), a half-buried spatter vent. Near Holua Cabin you'll cross the Silversword Loop Trail.

For comfortable hiking, wear sturdy boots, and carry a canteen. Be sure to have a light raincoat and a sunhat. If you haven't been out in the sun lately, use suntan lotion liberally.

Botany, Bird watching. Hawaii provides habitat for plants and birds found nowhere else in the world, and to many others of the tropics alone. Visit the two national parks, Haleakala and Hawaii Volcanoes, for about a thousand different kinds of flowering plants, ferns and fern allies. Get a copy of *Trailside Plants of Hawaii's National Parks* by Charles H. Lamoureux (professor of Botany at the University of Hawaii) and be on the lookout for species like the ti, a member of the lily family, and the noni, a small tree that is a member of the coffee family, probably introduced by early Polynesian settlers. Both are near the Pools of 'Ohe'o. Among the birds, the parks shelter rare and lovely species like the nukupuu, a honeycreeper long thought extinct, and the brilliant iiwi, with bright scarlet body and black wings and tail. Travel with your own copy of *Hawaii Birds*, published by the Hawaii Audubon Society.

Whale watching. Waters stretching between the islands of Maui, Molokai, Kahoolawe and Lanai are favored courting, birthing and nursing grounds of the magnificent humpback whales. Usually they appear about mid-December through April, bearing and nursing young in comparatively quiet inshore waters. Though humpbacks once numbered about 100,000, their worldwide population is now estimated at 5,000. Besides the playful humpbacks, most graceful of the great whales, you are also likely to see groups of pilot whales, spinner porpoises and bottlenose dolphins.

The **Pools of 'Ohe'o stream and Wailua Cove** are major scenic attractions along an unspoiled section of the Maui coast. A slow, winding road, Hawaii 36, circles east Maui, providing access to several small villages. Driving time from the Wailuku-Kahului area should be between three and four hours, but allow the better part of a day for stops at scenic state parks and freshwater pools where you can take a dip. At Keanae, drive down to the little settlement along the coast to see the century-old church and the surf pounding lava outcrops. There are several resorts and campgrounds in the Hana vicinity to use as a base to visit beautiful beaches, gardens and the national park. Try to hike some of the upper jeep roads and trails that lead to exciting views of several waterfalls. The two-mile hike up Pipiwai Valley passes ancient Hawaiian farmsites and goes through an extensive bamboo forest to Waimoku Falls. Most Saturday mornings at 9 a.m., a guided nature hike leaves the Pools of 'Ohe'o Bridge. It takes about four hours. Swimming in the pools is a pleasant pastime, but the water is usually cool.

TOURS. Saddle tours of one or more days into the crater are provided by private operators with advance arrangements. The Park Service recommends the two-day trip, which includes an overnight stay in the cabin in order to observe native birdlife and have time for photography. For rates and reservations, write park headquarters.

ACCOMMODATIONS. Three cabins located in different sections of the crater floor are maintained by the Park Service for visitors' use at a small charge. The cabins are reached by trail only. Each has 12 bunks, drinkable water, cookstove and firewood. Demand is so great the National Park Service holds a lottery the first day of each month for reservations two months ahead. Send your request at least two weeks before the lottery, stating the number in your party and preferred (also alternate) nights. Maximum stay is two nights in one cabin and three nights on the crater floor. Bring food, canteen with water for hiking, matches, raincoat or poncho and sleeping bag.

CAMPING. One campground is located near the park entrance in the **Hosmer Grove**, surrounded by introduced trees and native shrubs. Backpack camping is allowed at two designated areas—**Holua** and **Paliku**—in the crater, by permit only. You can obtain a permit at park headquarters. Camping is limited to two nights at either site and to a maximum of three nights per month. Hikers are asked to pack out all refuse and to be self-contained, because of the fragile environment of the crater. At **Kipahulu** an undeveloped campground is located in an open pasture southeast of the pools, near the ocean. Neither firewood nor drinking water is available. A camping permit is not required, but camping is limited to three nights per month.

SEASONS. Rarely does temperature on Maui fall below 55 or rise above 90—rarely above 80 in the mountains. Come prepared for cool, windy weather at the high park elevation. Summers usually are clear; winters are more cloudy and rainy. At night, temperatures will drop into the low 40s, or high 30s, even during summer.

NEARBY. Maui has become a bustling resort center with a variety of oceanside hotels, motels and apartments. A few small inns, such as Kula Lodge and Silversword Inn, are located in the high valleys en route to the park. Camping is permitted without charge in public parks, with four-day limit; permits are obtained by writing Superintendent, Maui County Department of Parks, 1580 Kaahumanu Avenue, Wailuku, Maui, Hawaii 96793.

Seven parks are located on beaches along the shoreline, including **Waiehu Beach Park**, with excellent shelling and fishing. The drive between **Hana** and **Wailuku**, on the coast below Haleakala, offers unusual beauty among heavily foliaged gorges, fishing settlements and small villages. You can fly direct to Hana from Honolulu in a little under one hour. Hotel Hana-Maui is one of the finest resorts anywhere in the islands. **Waianapanapa State Park**, just outside "heavenly Hana," offers camping and kitchen-furnished cabins (requiring reservations well in advance). Visit the little Congregational church facing the sea chosen by Charles A. Lindbergh as his final resting place. In a setting of flowering oleander and plumeria the simple burial stone bears this memorable inscription; "... If I take the wings of the morning and dwell in the uttermost parts of the sea."—C.A.L.

FOR FURTHER INFORMATION. Write Superintendent, Haleakala National Park, Box 369, Makawao, Maui, Hawaii 96768.

HAWAII VOLCANOES NATIONAL PARK

Hawaii

Established 1916

I COULD hardly believe that I was climbing to the summit of Mauna Loa, but there I was on the world's largest volcano, a mountain built by layer upon layer of lava, rising from about 20,000 feet below the sea to 13,677 above. It was 1985, though my mind traveled back to the early Hawaiians making their way to the top without shoes, backpacks or freeze-dried food, perhaps without warm clothing, living close to nature as they were meant to.

My companion and I hiked upward through a forest of 'ōhi'a, the pioneer tree of fresh lava flows. "The invincible 'ōhi'a," Mark Twain called it after observing its trunks emerging like spears of grass from volcanic crevasses. Hawaiians of other days fashioned spears, mallets and bowls from its hard wood. Though we hadn't heard many sounds since starting from the trailhead, we suddenly became aware of a whirring of wings and stood very quietly. Joe, my companion, a national park ranger, said it was an apapane, the most common surviving species of Hawaiian honeycreeper, flitting from tree to tree to feed on nectar from 'ōhi'a blossoms. We could not catch sight of this striking bird, but were lucky enough to hear its rambling, rolling song.

Everything natural and native about Hawaii—its birds, insects, plants, ferns and trees—seems so distinct and luxuriant, explaining why native Hawaiians speak of "Aina," the traditional love of land, or reverence for life. Their poetic oli, or chants, and the hula recount traditions that weave humankind into the universe. The summit of Kilauea, for instance, is considered the sacred palace of the goddess Pele. As daughter of Earth Mother and Sky Father, Pele came to Hawaii in flight from her cruel older sister, goddess of the sea. She found her refuge in the volcano, where she has prevailed ever since as goddess of fire.

Our climb took the better part of two days—we spent the night at a shelter cabin conveniently sited at the 10,000-foot level, but I made it to the top of mighty Mauna Loa. Its lava flows occupy more than 2,000 square miles of Hawaii, the "Big Island." Its 1949 eruption continued for almost five months. A year later it spewed one of the most voluminous flows in history, producing about 600 million cubic yards of lava in 23 days.

Mauna Loa then slumbered for 25 years, until July 5, 1975, when it erupted in a six-mile curtain of fire at the Mokuaweoweo Crater and a two-pronged lava flow from Pohaku Hanalei. The eruption wiped out the upper portion of the trail to the summit. Earthquakes were continuing at the rate of one or two a minute five days later. Mauna Loa erupted again on March 25 to April 15, 1984.

Neighboring Kilauea has been more active, erupting 50 times since 1980. Repeated eruptions in 1983 and 1984, continuing into 1985, provided awesome views and extensive property damage along the park's eastern boundary. This eruption created a new cone over 700 feet high. Whenever a new eruption occurs, Hawaii residents rush out to view the magnificent fiery display. Parking lots on the rim are quickly filled and airplanes buzz overhead.

Kilauea and a portion of the flank and summit of Mauna Loa are within the 229,117-acre national park. These young volcanoes, which may have been formed only within the last million years, grow with energy, keeping ahead of the ever-present agents of erosion.

Fortunately, despite their seeming ferocity, Mauna Loa and Kilauea are relatively gentle giants that seldom become dangerously explosive even while liberating tons of molten rock from vents and cracks. I have never, on any of my several visits, seen an eruption in progress, but the signs of geologic upheaval and earthbuilding are everywhere—in hissing fumaroles, smoldering firepits, pungent sulfur banks gleaming against black moonscapes and once-molten lava still showing the patterns in which it was spewed. Climbing to the top and looking over it all proves a superlative national park adventure.

THE PRACTICAL GUIDE

ACCESS. Passenger planes make frequent flights daily from Honolulu to the Big Island. Direct flights also operate to and from Kona and the mainland. The national park is included in the itinerary of guided motorcoach tours. Cars can be rented either at General Lyman Field, Hilo, or at Kailua-Kona.

BACKGROUND. Park headquarters is off Hawaii 11, the Mamalahoa Highway, connecting Kona and Hilo. Allow ample time for the Thomas A. Jaggar Museum, on the volcano's rim. Completed in 1987, it is one of the finest museums in any national park. It contains maps, models and paintings on the story of the park; color films of recent eruptions are shown hourly each day. It is named in memory of Dr. Thomas A. Jaggar, who established the Hawaiian Volcano Observatory in 1912. A Visitor Center is located at Wahaula Heiau near the Kalapana entrance, with exhibits devoted to the story of the early Hawaiian people.

Crater Rim Drive, covering 11.1 miles, provides the best orientation to the park. It leads from park headquarters to the **Thurston Lava Tube**, formed when the outer crust of lava hardened and the inner portion flowed away. You can explore the tunnel-like formation for a distance of about 500 feet. Nearby thrives the glorious **Tree Fern Forest**. Rains average about 100 inches annually, sustaining a growth of many varieties of ferns, overtowered by a dense growth of tropical ʻōhiʻa trees. Whenever the ʻōhiʻa blooms, one finds the ʻapapane, a small nectar-sucking bird as red as the lehua (the feathery ʻōhiʻa blossom), but with black wings and gray belly. Equally abundant in the forests is the ʻamakihi, a small yellow-green insect gatherer, and the ʻelepaio, a perky flycatcher. The road dips into the crater to a parking area at the brink of the **Halemaumau pit**.

Northwest of the Hawaiian Volcano Observatory, in the direction of Mauna Loa, lies **Kipuka Puaulu**, or "Bird Park," a typical "island" of old surface surrounded by young lava flows. A nature trail leads into a forested section, an arboretum of 40 varieties of trees, some peculiar to the island of Hawaii. A few are the only living representatives of their vanishing species. On fresh rock surfaces of the younger lava flows the sturdy ʻōhiʻa, the colorful ʻaʻaliʻi and pūkiawe shrubs pioneer a new forest. Perhaps the final point of interest on Crater Rim Drive is **Devastation Trail** at Kilauea Iki crater overlook, scene of the 1959 eruption. From this viewpoint you can look across the crater and view the cinder cone, part of the main caldera, and, on a clear day, Mauna Loa.

Kau Desert, the leeward slope of Kilauea Crater, also on the rim road, receives very little rain from the trade winds but is soaked occasionally by a heavy general storm. The Southwest Rift is marked by a great crack area.

ERUPTION NEWS. You can get the latest with a phone call. On the Big Island, dial 967-7977. From Oahu and the other islands, dial 1-967-7977.

ACTIVITIES. Hiking. Mauna Loa Trail provides one of the most unusual hikes in the National Park system. The route to the summit, at 13,677 feet, is 18 miles one way.

Allow at least three days and plan very carefully with a copy of Lisa Peterson's excellent *Mauna Loa Trail Guide*, which you purchase at the Visitor Center. From the mountain parkland the trail rises through the fringe of straggling mamanis and railliardias. Above 10,000 feet, it enters the vast expanse of barren lava fields, winding between pumice cones and along lava-splattered cracks. Ice lingers in the cracks most of the year. Hikers can stay overnight at park cabins at Red Hill, 10,000 feet, and on the summit. Another good backcountry trip is the **Halape Coastal Hike**, about 8 miles one way to the coastal section of the park, with camping near a fine white sand beach. Even if you don't go the whole length, drive out to Hilina Pali, reached from a turnoff halfway down the Chain of Craters Road. Then walk out at least a little way for the marvelous views of the untouched and still forming southeast coast. Few visitors take the trouble to visit this point, though they are missing one of the finest ocean views on the island. Actually, the park has over 150 miles of foot trails.

Photography. Park headquarters area receives about 100 inches of rain yearly. This means many days are overcast and dark. Fortunately, a rough pattern is predictable—most early mornings are clear and bright, but by noon the northeast trade winds have blown in a dense cloud cover. If you are fortunate enough to arrive during an eruption, you will find high-speed color film and a telephoto lens useful.

ACCOMMODATIONS. Volcano House, at 4,000 feet elevation on the rim of Kilauea, is a modern, comfortable lodge, a good stop for lunch or overnight. It is located within easy walking distance of park headquarters and the Visitor Center. A sauna bath, supplied by natural volcanic steam vents, is available 24 hours a day. The Volcano House is something of a museum piece in itself, a large part of its character being derived from the personality of the late George Lycurgus, who acquired the earlier Volcano House in 1904 and established it as a "celebrity" inn. He died in 1960, at the age of 101. The original Volcano House, adjacent to the Visitor Center, was built in 1877 and used contin-

uously until 1939. It was refurbished and reopened in 1975 as the new Volcano Art Center, an excellent place for shopping. It is listed on the National Register of Historic Places.

CAMPING. The park concessioner operates 10 tiny, unfurnished A-frame cabins in a koa and eucalyptus forest 3 miles from park headquarters, which places you near the 100-acre Bird Park, a green island amid stark lava flows. Each cabin sleeps four. Community rest rooms have hot and cold water. A modest charge is made, and linens are extra.

The national park itself has two cabins for hikers to the summit of Mauna Loa. One, near 10,000 feet elevation, sleeps nine persons; the other, at 13,250 feet, the southwest edge of the summit caldera, sleeps eleven. Both are free, but expect company of other hikers. You'll find a water catchment and pit toilets. Bring food, flashlight, bedroll, parka, water and gas stove. No reservations are taken; when registering at the Kilauea Visitor Center you'll learn the number of hikers already on the trail.

SEASONS. Seasons are not pronounced in semitropical Hawaii, but the weather can be cool at any time at the high elevations in the park. Rainwear will be essential, as heavy precipitation can be expected frequently.

NEARBY. Five miles from the Kalapana entrance to the park, **Harry K. Brown County Park** provides picnicking and overnight camping. **Puʻuhonua O Honaunau National Historical Park**, (formerly City of Refuge National Historic Park), on the Kona coast, which became part of the national park system in 1961, contains an ancient burial temple of Hawaii's kings and interprets the story of the early Hawaiian settlers. An interesting horticultural area, **Akaka Falls State Park**, distinguished by its varied tropical plants, trees and shrubs, is located north of Hilo near the sugar fields of Honomu.

A visit to Hawaii Volcanoes should be linked with a stop at Maui to see **Haleakala National Park** together these areas formerly constituted Hawaii National Park.

FOR FURTHER INFORMATION. Write Superintendent, Hawaii Volcanoes National Park, Hawaii 96718.

HOT SPRINGS NATIONAL PARK

Arkansas

Established 1921

WALKING down Bathhouse Row in downtown Hot Springs, I let my imagination lead me into the past. I pictured the scene in the 1930s and '40s—the baths filled with pilgrims seeking relief from the aches and pains of arthritis, gout and assorted other diseases. I tried to visualize American life in the age before vaccines and the modern miracle drugs we now take for granted.

Hot Springs is a bit of a ghost of itself. From a million baths in 1946, it's down to about 100,000 baths a year now. Still, it holds a special charm, maybe like the beginning of the hot tub. The Indians had the right ideait was a sacred place for them. Then Hot Springs was discovered by French trappers and explorers in the 1700s. I would like to have been with them when they watched the vapors rising from the valley and felt the healing properties of the springs. Ultimately, the federal government in 1832 established the springs as a federal reservation. I wonder if anyone back then could have envisioned that action as the first step to the national park.

In the 19th century, resorts with medicinal bathing ("spas") were extremely popular. The idea of the bath as a recreational pursuit goes back in history to the ancient days of the Greeks, Romans and Saxons. In fact, Bath, the most famous spa in England, had its beginning when the Romans discovered the healing qualities of the waters; the remains of the luxurious baths are now Britain's most significant Roman relic. From Europe, the spa idea was transplanted to America as a mark of culture.

Virtually all spas were reserved for the wealthy and aristocratic. Establishment of the Hot Springs Reservation on behalf of the people was a fitting action in a growing republic. Nevertheless, the area remained largely in private holdings, with titles in litigation for years. In 1870, Congress set up legal procedure for settling titles and claims to titles. The national park was established in 1921, through the influence of Stephen T. Mather, as a successor to the reservation that had existed previously. It's very different from all other national parks, covering only 4,787 acres. But it tells a particular story told in no other park.

The park's 47 hot springs are along a fault, or ancient break, in the earth's crust. The water from two springs can be seen emerging naturally. The water from the upper springs is collected and released near the Arlington Lawn in a water display to one side of a massive tufa surface. The water from other springs is collected in a 300,000-gallon reservoir for use in the bathhouses.

With so many developments in modern medicine, notably cortisone, antibiotics and painkillers, the demand for therapeutic bathing has declined. Eight historic bathhouses are still preserved along Bathhouse Row, but only two remain open. The full treatment, including hot packs, steam cabinet and needle shower, lasts 90 minutes. Many swear there is nothing more relaxing.

With their marble walls, mosaic floors, polished brass banisters and some stained glass windows, the bathhouses reflect another age. The National Park Service has begun to lease the empty baths for use as shops, restaurants and art galleries.

Because the park is small and nearly surrounded by a busy resort city, the 24-mile network of hiking trails and the undisturbed woodland are a pleasant surprise to those who find them. I like to walk in the dense forest that covers the steep, rocky hills of the park, with wildflowers blooming seasonally. Nearly 150 species of birds have been identified. The altitude of the park varies from 600 feet on the valley floor to 1,400 feet on the summits. It reminds me of how much there is to absorb without covering any great distance.

THE PRACTICAL GUIDE

BACKGROUND. The Visitor Center, at the corner of Central and Reserve Avenues, explains the theories on the origin of the hot springs. **Display Springs** are not sealed and still emerge naturally; they are located adjacent to the **Grand Promenade**, a landscaped, brick-paved walk. These two open springs have been set aside for viewing purposes.

A daily summertime tour, "Hot Prospects among the Thermal Features," includes the underground Indian Spring and other sites associated with the geology of hot water. It starts from the south grounds of Health Services Bathhouse. "Golden Opportunities" visits the elegant (but nonoperating) Fordyce Bathhouse in the center of Bathhouse Row, complete with stained glass, statuary, marble and decorative tile.

The rugged hill country around Hot Springs abounds in hunting, fishing, canoeing and hiking opportunities. Three man-made lakes are in the area, including DeGray Lake, which is the site of the newest state park in Arkansas.

ACCOMMODATIONS. Hotels, motels and tourist homes are abundant in the city. Several of the hotels have their own bathhouse facilities.

CAMPING. The 47-site Gulpha Gorge Campground is set in a beautiful valley 2 miles from the center of Hot Springs, at the foot of Hot Springs Mountain. During summer, there are outdoor evening programs in the amphitheater and guided hikes to the prehistoric quarries on Indian Mountain. The campground is an excellent place for bird watching, especially during winter. Pick up a copy of the park's

bird checklist, which includes nearly 150 species. As you will observe, the park's forest of shortleaf pine, oaks, hickories and gum, along with the dense ground cover, provides choice habitat for a variety of birds.

For another worthwhile attraction, visit the new Hot Springs Mountain Observation Tower.

SEASONS. The season at Hot Springs covers the entire year. Winters are mild, allowing for outdoor activities. Spring and fall offer special features for nature lovers and photographers. Fall colors abound in October, especially along the West Mountain Scenic Road.

FOR FURTHER INFORMATION. Write Superintendent, Hot Springs National Park, Box 1860, Hot Springs, Arkansas 71902.

ISLE ROYALE NATIONAL PARK

Michigan

Authorized 1931

I WAS listening hard to orchids poking up from the underbrush. I mean it was so quiet and alone on the trail that I felt I could have *heard* the orchids if only I would be still and be attentive to them. Then I wandered on toward Mount Franklin. It was not very highonly 1,074 feetbut it provided wonderful vistas of forested wilderness, fjordlike harbors, lakes, rugged waveswept shores, surrounding islets and the waters of Lake Superior extending to the distant horizon in all directions.

Isle Royale National Park, covering 539,280 acres, is the largest island in Lake Superior, the largest and cleanest of the Great Lakes. In the summer of 1986, I drove completely around Lake Superior and learned something of its marvels, like the Apostle Islands off the cost of northern Wisconsin, Pictured Rocks on the Upper Peninsula of Michigan and Pukaskwa National Park in Ontario. Then I went to Isle Royale, out in the heart of Lake Superior, where there are no cars, no roads and the only loud noise was the sound of an outboard motor offshore.

The only way to reach Isle Royale is by boat, but it attracts creatures than can fly, swim or drift across the water barrier.

Beaver, muskrat, mink and weasel are residents. So are the snowshoehare, squirrel and red fox. The bald eagle, osprey, pileated woodpecker, 25 kinds of warblers and, most frequently seen, the herring gull, have made their way across 45 miles of water from the nearest Michigan shore, 18 miles from the Minnesota shore, or 15 miles from Canada. But not so for the deer, bear, porcupine and skunk, unable to bridge the water.

Moose, which I saw along streams and on the shores of inland lakes, were not known on the island before 1900, but when the lake froze in about 1912, a number of them may have ventured over the ice, or they may have swum across. In the winter of 1948-49,

wolves made their way across, arriving at a time when the moose herds had grown overabundant. The wolves have since played their role in the balance of nature. I wish that I had caught sight of a wolf, or heard a wolf howl. The wolves were "out to lunch," but I felt their presence, which heightened the experience of being there. I learned with sorrow that during the 1980s the wolf numbers were low— below two dozen—for reasons scientists could not explain.

Studies of the wolf-moose relationship at Isle Royale have achieved much recognition in the world of biology, reminding me that parks are much more than playgrounds; they are also laboratories of learning.

At various locations in the park, I saw ancient Indian mining pits, and learned that radio carbon tests date these pits back 3,800 years or more. I learned also that copper mined by hammerstone in the prehistoric age was used on the trading trails throughout the Great Lakes.

I came to Isle Royale on the six-hour boat crossing from the Upper Peninsula of Michigan, a prelude-filled anticipation. The promise was wholly fulfilledthe park experience amounts to relaxed isolation, with plenty of healthy exercise. A chain of campgrounds extends almost the full 45-mile length of the island and across its 9-mile width. Attractive and comfortable accommodations are provided at Rock Harbor, with many opportunities for photography, fishing and the study of nature in all its moods.

One thing I learned is that rain on the trail is a strong likelihood. Another lesson, a bit of incidental intelligence, has stood me well in the game of trivia. What is the name of the largest island in the largest lake on the largest island in the largest lake in the world? Isle Royale is the largest island in Lake Superior. Now, find the rest.

THE PRACTICAL GUIDE

About 15,000 visitors make the crossing from mainland Michigan or Minnesota each year during the May-September season. They stay an average four days either at the full-service lodge or the backpacking campsites. By contrast, the average stay in Yellowstone or the Grand Canyon is four hours. At Isle Royale, a week is even better.

ACCESS. The "main highway to the park" is *Ranger III*, the National Park Service motor ship, 165 feet long, which makes two round trips weekly. It sails from Houghton on Michigan's Upper Peninsula, 70 miles away, returning one day later. The crossing aboard this modern 650-ton ship takes about six hours. A Park Service lecture is delivered aboard in both directions, but carry a good book to help pass the time. There is a snack bar, so you won't go hungry. The *Ranger* delivers you to Rock Harbor, the main center of activity. Advance reservations should be made by writing the Park Superintendent.

The park is served by ships other than the *Ranger*. The privately owned *Isle Royale Queen II* makes a round trip daily from Copper Harbor to Rock Harbor. From the west, the *Wenonah*, operated by Sivertson Brothers, makes a round trip daily from Grand Portage to Windigo, a distance of 20 miles, leaving 9:30 a.m. June 20 to Labor Day. This trip gives you the opportunity for a one-day excursion, with time ashore for a hike at Windigo. The 65-foot *Voyageur II* makes a two-day trip from Grand Portage to Windigo and Rock Harbor each Monday, Wednesday and Saturday at 9:30 a.m. The vessel remains overnight at Rock Harbor. Boat operators will transport your small runabout or canoe. Gasoline may be purchased at Rock Harbor and Windigo marinas.

ACTIVITIES. Hiking. The national park is laced with more than 170 miles of foot trails. The **Greenstone Ridge Trail** extends

40 miles from Rock Harbor Lodge to Washington Harbor, following the backbone of the island. The trip should be planned to cover several days.

Even if you don't go all the way, you can get a good sample by hiking to Mount Franklin, then continuing to **Ojibway Lookout**, with a superb view from the tower of the Canadian mainland standing out 15 miles north. There are other fine trails as well. One leads to the mellowed and abandoned **Rock Harbor Lighthouse**, built in 1885 to guide boats into the harbor during the early copper mining days. Another goes to **Monument Rock**, a towering 70-foot pinnacle carved by waves and ice, then continues past ancient beaches and a copper mining site, used by prehistoric Indians, to **Lookout Louise**, for one of the most beautiful views in the park.

Windigo Mine. This ruin of an old copper pit was mined by white men until about 1899. A fine trail leads from Washington Creek along the river to the mine.

Fishing and Boating. Motor launch trips can be arranged at Rock Harbor Lodge. Boats and canoes can be rented. A modern marina for small boats and private cruisers is located at Rock Harbor. About 50 kinds of fish are found on inland streams, bays and lakes and in Lake Superior. No fishing license is required for inland waters of the park. With its numerous lakes, deep bays and offshore islands, Isle Royale provides many miles of waterways for the canoeist and kayaker. Use caution, however, respecting the chance of sudden winds and rough waters. Canoeing here is definitely not recommended for beginners. You can get water taxi service from Rock Harbor to any dock on the northeast half of the island.

Naturalist Program. Naturalist-guided walks are conducted from Rock Harbor and Windigo. Illustrated talks on various topics are conducted each evening at 8:30 at both of these places, and at Daisy Farm Campground twice weekly.

TOURS. A good way to make the round trip over the whole island is to go one way by trail and the other by boat. The *Voyageur*, privately owned, circumnavigates the park three times weekly. You can board it at Rock Harbor Lodge and travel to Windigo, or vice versa; or you can arrange to have it pick you up at lakeside camps. Write Sivertson Brothers Fisheries, Box 754, Duluth, Minnesota 55802.

From Rock Harbor Lodge you can take a half-day sightseeing trip aboard the *Sandy*, operated by the park concessioner. With a park naturalist aboard, the boat vis-

its important landmarks like Lookout Louise, Mott Island, Daisy Farm, Raspberry Island and the historic Rock Harbor Light House.

Field Seminars. Isle Royale Natural History Association (87 N. Ripley, Houghton, Michigan 49931) conducts worthwhile five-day seminars on Isle Royale ecology, folklore and photography, led by professionals. Costs are moderate.

ACCOMMODATIONS. Rock Harbor Lodge has 20 attractive twin-unit housekeeping cabins, suitable for families, plus 60 lodge rooms. Dining room and snack bar are open to the public. It is a well-run operation; the atmosphere is friendly and informal. Reservations should be made at least three weeks in advance. Write National Park Concessions, Inc., Isle Royale National Park, Michigan 49940 (before June 1, c/o Mammoth Cave, Kentucky 42259).

CAMPING. This is a great park for camping, if you plan carefully and come fully prepared. On arrival, register and get a permit. The best type of facility for the first night is one of the three-sided shelters (capacity six persons). Then take off for the tent sites. Keep in mind that long-term campground stays are not available. Camping supplies are sold at Rock Harbor and Windigo, but you'll be wise to bring your own.

SEASONS. The weather is cool and the travel season short—from mid-June until shortly after Labor Day. Fog is common during June and early July. Mosquitoes, blackflies and deer flies can be a problem early and midsummer, although shelters are screened. Temperature during the day seldom rises above 80 degrees, and nights always are cool. Warm clothes are important.

NEARBY. Michigan's Upper Peninsula is the center of an old copper mining industry. The **Museum at the Michigan Technological University** at Houghton contains a large collection of minerals. **Fort Wilkins State Park**, northeast of Copper Harbor, contains restored buildings and historical museum relating to a remote army post established in 1844. Anyone coming from Grand Portage should visit the **Grand Portage National Monument**, on the site of the "great depot" of the fur trading days.

RECOMMENDED READING. *The Wolves of Minong*, by Durward Allen.

FOR FURTHER INFORMATION. Write Superintendent, Isle Royale National Park, 87 N. Ripley Street, Houghton, Michigan 49931.

KATMAI NATIONAL PARK

Alaska

Established 1980

K ATMAI was the scene of a violent eruption in 1912, which turned a nameless green valley on the southern shore of the Alaska Peninsula into the Valley of Ten Thousand Smokes, but I remember it most as the place where I watched an Alaska brown bear, otherwise known as a grizzly, and her two cubs feed on migrating salmon in the Brooks River. Katmai takes some effort to reach, but superlative Alaska wilderness scenery and its abundant wildlife make it an excellent choice on any itinerary. As for the ten thousand smokes, there are no longer active fumaroles in the valley, but the signs of live volcanoes are evident on surrounding mountains.

Katmai was designated a national monument in 1918. In 1980, Congress voted to enlarge the area to 3,669,000 acres and reclassify it as a national park, bordered by a national preserve of 423,000 acres.

Of many lakes, one of cobalt blue color fills the crater of Mount Katmai. Sportsmen know Katmai for some of the best trophy sportfishing in Alaska. Whether catching fish or absorbing lakes, rivers, glaciers and waterfalls, Katmai is the trophy in itself.

THE PRACTICAL GUIDE

ACCESS. Take a scheduled jet from Anchorage on a spectacular 290 mile flight passing over great volcanoes and glaciers to King Salmon on the park's west side, then a commercial flight (June through Labor Day) or air charter to Brooks Lodge.

ACCOMMODATIONS. Brooks River Lodge, operated by Katmailand, Inc. (4700 Aircraft Drive, Anchorage, AK 99502), is quite attractive. It is the starting point of the scenic bus tour to the Valley of Ten Thousand Smokes; it is a handy access spot for trout and salmon fishing in the fabulous Brooks River. Katmailand also operates Kulik Lodge, Grosvenor Camp, Enchanted Lake Lodge and Nonvianuk Camp, small lodges catering mostly to fishermen.

CAMPING. Start by setting up headquarters at the campground on the shore of Naknek Lake near the Brooks River Lodge. Check with the rangers about backcountry travel. With a permit you can camp anywhere, but prepare for the pesky white sox in mid- to late summer.

Canoeing and kayaking on the Grosvenor and Savanoski rivers are worthwhile activities. The country is rough but rewarding. Be wary of the big bears.

SEASONS. The travel season runs from mid-June to mid-September. The temperature is usually mild, but rain is always a possibility, so carry raingear.

FOR FURTHER INFORMATION. Write Superintendent, Katmai National Park, Box 7, King Salmon, Alaska 99613.

KENAI FJORDS NATIONAL PARK

Alaska

Established 1980

I DROVE south from Anchorage to the Kenai Peninsula. Seward, the only town on the east coast of the peninsula and gateway to Kenai Fjords, is only 127 miles from Anchorage. I found the entire trip a delight, like a prelude to the unspoiled natural wonder of the national park. The Seward Highway follows the shore of Turnagain Arm (which Captain Cook mistook for a river leading to the Northwest Passage), through Chugach State Park, one of the largest in the country, and Chugach National Forest, with broad vistas of the Kenai Mountains. The peaks and ice fields form the spine of the peninsula, and I felt as though I was driving across Switzerland—but Alaska, I daresay, is more expansive.

Seward proved a fitting gateway, cradled between mountain ranges, yet a harbor at the edge of the sea. This was only the beginning. A full-day cruise showed what surely must be one of the most beautiful marine environments on earth. This area was little known until establishment of the national park in 1980. Its 580,000 acres embrace rugged cliffs, mist-shrouded fjords and a massive icefield, with mountaintops rising thousands of feet above it.

Harding Icefield, the dominant feature, covers 300 square miles, with its outflowing glaciers about 1,100 square miles. The central ice core is a rare example of Pleistocene ice masses that once covered half of Alaska. It rises above the landscape and seascape, with its mountaintops fittingly called *nunataks*, the Eskimo word for "lonely peaks."

During the course of the cruise, I learned that the fjords of the park were formed when the ancient ice cap flowed down to the sea and then retreated, leaving behind deep inlets—which world travelers will at once compare with the fabled fjords of Norway and New Zealand. One difference here is that throngs of marine mammals inhabit or migrate through the park's coastal waters, including sea otters, Steller's sea lions, dolphins and whales. Icebergs from calving glaciers provide ideal refuge for harbor seals, while the rugged coastline provides habitat for more than 100,000 nesting birds. No less than 4,000 sea lions are said to inhabit these waters. I saw and heard many of them, raucously expressing themselves on sheltered islands and islets.

Back on shore, I drove to Exit Glacier, one of several rivers of ice flowing off the ice field. This retreating, yet active, glacier provides an excellent setting to explore. Newly exposed scoured bedrock, mountain goats and a regime of plant succession from the earliest pioneer plants to the mature forest of Sitka spruce and western hemlock are part of the setting.

Kenai Fjords is certain to become one of the principal highlights of any Alaska itinerary. It is now possible to take the train from Anchorage, which I plan to do next time I'm in Alaska.

THE PRACTICAL GUIDE

ACCESS. The 127 mile Seward Highway is fully paved from Anchorage and marked with mileposts. Train service is available May 27 to September 4 on Friday, Saturday and Sunday, and occasionally during the week, leaving Anchorage at 7 a.m., arriving in Seward at 11 a.m. Scheduled bus service and commuter flights (35 minutes) are available between Seward and Anchorage. The Alaska Marine Highway connects Seward with Homer via Kodiak, and also provides service to Valdez and Cordova.

BACKGROUND. The park **Visitor Center**, on Fourth Avenue, Seward, should be your first stop if you're arriving by car. It is open 8 a.m. to 5 p.m. daily in summer. From here head for the most accessible of the park's glaciers, Exit Glacier. Turn at Milepost S 3.7 on the Seward Highway, then follow Exit Glacier Road for 9 miles. From here you can follow a ½-mile walking trail to the face of the glacier. Allow plenty of time to stop at the Exit Glacier Ranger Station and picnic area a mere ¼-mile from the glacier.

ACTIVITIES. Sightseeing. Daily charter sightseeing cruises of full-day and half-day are offered from Seward. You can arrange an overnight charter for a more extensive trip. Be sure to bring binoculars. Bring warm clothes and raingear. While there are only a few landing sites, you'll see a magnificent vista from the boat: rock rising from sea level thousands of feet to snowy peaks, and rock fins, sea arches, caves and cliffs that are being constantly reshaped by the pounding energy of incoming tides. In **Resurrection Bay**, largest of the fjords, keep a sharp watch for whales, porpoises, harbor seals and sea otters.

Bird watching. Aialik Bay and **Harris Bay** harbor immense concentrations of sea birds—puffins, murres, kittiwakes and auklets. Nearby **Chiswell Island**, part of the Alaska Maritime National Wildlife Refuge, is another great spot for sea birds and marine mammals, which seek out these small islands because the fractured ledges seem to suit their needs.

Sea Kayaking. Bring your own kayak or rent one at Seward. You can join a guided trip even if you haven't had experience. Consider the 3-day, 2-night trip to Holgate Arm, viewing whales, sea lions and sea bird rookeries, with camping on the beaches. Write Alaska Treks n Voyages, Box 625, Seward, Alaska 99631.

Fishing. This is popular along the coastal area. Resurrection Bay is known for silver salmon up to 20 pounds and halibut up to 200 pounds. Other fish include lingcod, a variety of rockfish, as well as chum and pink salmon.

Sailing. This is another top sport. You'll find charter operators able to provide everything you need.

ACCOMMODATIONS. There are no accommodations in the park, but a full range of services is available in Seward, including motels, RV parks and bed and breakfasts.

CAMPING. A 10-site walk-in campground is located at Exit Glacier. Two municipal campgrounds in Seward are open when free of snow, which is usually from about March to November.

SEASONS. Summer temperatures reach into the 50s and 60s. The climate can be very wet, so prepare accordingly. In September begins the wet, steamy fall, the end of the tourist season. Exit Glacier is open to winter visitors.

NEARBY. Take the walking tour of picturesque Seward, nestled between mountain ranges. A number of homes and shops date back to the early 1900s. Visit the small-boat harbor, port to fishing boats, charter boats and sailboats. Make a stop at the Seward Museum, operated by the Resurrection Bay Historical Society. Exhibits and films are on display at the Institute of Marine Science Building. Several Forest Service campgrounds are located along the Seward Highway.

FOR FURTHER INFORMATION. Write Superintendent, Kenai Fjords National Park, Box 1727, Seward, Alaska 99664.

KOBUK VALLEY NATIONAL PARK

Alaska

Established 1980

I WAS 40 miles north of the Arctic Circle with a friend, Bob Belous of the National Park Service. He had spent considerable time in the Arctic and knew the country well. We were on the Kobuk River, an ideal stream for easy canoeing and kayaking. The vegetation was tundratype, the kind that reveals an intimate beauty when examined closely. Bob mentioned that the dry, cold climate supports a remnant flora that once characterized the tundra bridge over which prehistoric men and women crossed from Asia to Alaska. He was especially interested in showing the Great Kobuk Sand Dunes spread over 25 square miles, with rolling dunes rising to heights of 100 feet—a rare spectacle.

In striking contrast is Onion Portage, the site where for thousands of years caribou have crossed the Kobuk River and where Eskimo and their prede-cessors have camped to hunt them. Uncovering lay-ers upon layers of artifacts has brought to light a sequence of cultural development spanning 10,000 years; as my friend mentioned, Onion Portage has been called "the most important archaeological site ever found in the Arctic."

The national park covers 1,710,000 acres, the basin of the broad, gently winding river rimmed by moun-tains. It provides summer breeding habitat for more than 100 species of birds coming from all over North and South America and from lands bordering the Pacific Ocean. Twice yearly, thousands of caribou funnel through passes of the Baird Mountains be-tween northern calving grounds and southern win-tering grounds, foraging while in the Kobuk's tundra plains, in company with grizzly and black bear, wolf and fox.

THE PRACTICAL GUIDE

ACCESS. Regular jet service connects Kotzebue, one of Alaska's oldest and larg-est Eskimo communities, with Anchorage and Nome. Chartered light aircraft and scheduled bush air carriers serve several Eskimo villages, particularly **Kiana** and **Ambler**, strung along the Kobuk River.

ACTIVITIES. Backpacking and Canoe-ing. The Kobuk River is almost 300 miles long, flowing from the south flank of the Brooks Range and picking up the waters of at least 50 tributaries before emptying into Kotzebue Sound and the Chukchi Sea. Within placid Kobuk Valley, about 150 miles inland from Kotzebue, the river seems like a series of lakes to the canoeist. Bring fishing gear; the Kobuk specialty is the Shee fish. You can head out from Ambler or Kiana, which have small stores and simple facilities operated by Eskimos.

Terrain in most areas is good for hiking. You can reach the sand dunes on an easy hike from the river.

Camping. There are no campgrounds. Camp anywhere except in the archaeolog-ical zones or any private property along the river.

ACCOMMODATIONS. Kotzebue has a hotel, not inexpensive, where service is erratic.

SEASONS. Summer temperatures often reach the 80s during the day, then drop sharply at night. June and July are the clearest months, followed by rainy August and September. Mosquitoes reach their peak in June, but you're apt to find gnats and other insects later in the summer.

NEARBY. Kotzebue is the commercial center of Northwestern Alaska, gateway to **Bering Land Bridge National Preserve** and **Cape Krusenstern National Monument**, as well as Kobuk Valley National Park. It is essentially an Eskimo community, where the Fourth of July features traditional native games. During the Arctic Trade Fair, the week following, people from throughout the region trade handicrafts and participate in traditional dances and feasts. There are no sidewalks in Kotzebue and there is only a short stretch of paved street, near the airport.

The **Museum of the Arctic** is the princi-pal attraction, featuring wildlife dioramas, Eskimo dancing for tour groups and dem-onstrations of Eskimo skills. The west end of the building houses the National Park Service information center, open 7 a.m. to 9 p.m.

RECOMMENDED READING. *Coming into the Country,* by John McPhee.

FOR FURTHER INFORMATION. Write Superintendent, Kobuk Valley National Park, Box 287, Kotzebue, Alaska 99752.

LAKE CLARK NATIONAL PARK

Alaska

Established 1980

M Y FRIENDS, Chuck and Sara Hornberger, operate Koksetna Camp, a lovely little lodge at the edge of Lake Clark that scarcely intrudes on the wilderness around them. They exemplify harmony in life, with nature, each other and their guests. Sara grows her own vegetables, no small feat in Alaska, while Chuck guides visitors on intimate excursions through the country he knows and loves.

He can't possibly show it all, of course. The national park and preserve cover a little more than 4,045,320 acres in the heart of the Chigmit Mountains, where the mighty Alaska Range meets the Aleutian Range. Here is a composition of wilderness peaks, glacial valleys, sparkling lakes, waterfalls and streams, plus towering semiactive volcanoes that show how this portion of the earth is still in the process of formation.

Though roadless, the national park lies only 150 miles from Anchorage and is readily accessible by plane. The flight itself gives an inspiring overview. Lake Clark Pass and Merrill Pass, the main routes through the mountains, open up vistas of hanging glaciers lining the valley walls. The coastal region of the park, bordering the western shore of Cook Inlet, is highlighted by the fuming volcanoes, Mount Iliamna and Mount Redoubt, both rising more than 10,000 feet above their bases at sea level.

I've been to Koksetna twice, in summer, but I've listened to Chuck and Sara describe the quiet adventure of winter on Lake Clark. It sounded appealing, a time of peace, when nature rests, which some winter I hope to experience.

THE PRACTICAL GUIDE

ACCESS. Air charters are available from Anchorage and Kenai. It costs less, however, to take a scheduled commercial flight to Iliamna, 35 miles west of the park, and charter from there.

ACCOMMODATIONS. Several small lodges on the shores of Lake Clark provide accommodations, guide service and boat rentals. Most of the resorts fly fishermen in float planes to Turquoise Lake, Twin Lakes and other lakes and streams. One of the lodges, Koksetna, emphasizes bird watching by boat; you're likely to observe eagles, falcons, owls, ducks, and swans.

ACTIVITIES. River-Running and Fish-ing. The Chilikadrotna River offers an excellent whitewater experience for rafters and kayakers. The Chilikadrotna flows out of Twin Lakes in a good steady current, past the Bonanza Hills and through a spruce-hardwood forest. The four-day float to the Mulchatna River takeout provides plenty of opportunity for fishing and hiking. You could also start from Turquoise Lake and float the Mulchatna for two days to the end of Bonanza Hills.

Grayling are easy to catch. Around mid-July rivers and creeks become choked with spawning bright red sockeye salmon. Several species of salmon, as well as trout, northern pike and char, are in the lakes and streams.

SEASONS. Between June and August temperatures in the eastern portion of the park average between 50 and 65 degrees, but the western and interior portions are warmer, reaching as high as 80. Autumn, though cold, is an attractive time. A few lodges stay open year-round for those interested in ice fishing, winter camping and sheer solitude with nature.

FOR FURTHER INFORMATION. Write Superintendent, Lake Clark National Park, 701 C Street, Box 61, Anchorage, Alaska 99513.

LASSEN VOLCANIC NATIONAL PARK

California

Established 1916

I ARRIVED in June (of 1987) and it was barely summer. The nighttime temperature in the campground was still around freezing. No wonder the park was so thoroughly uncrowded. But that's what I like about Lassen. It lies within a day's drive of the San Francisco Bay area, but is lightly used, except for the peak of summer.

It is truly a jewel, though, with much to offer. Lassen Volcanic is the smallest (106,372 acres) of the five national parks on the California mainland, but a beauty spot nonetheless, being in the heavily wooded northeast part of the state where the Sierra Nevada Range meets the Cascades.

One of the most recently active volcanoes in the United States forms the core of this national park where snow sometimes falls lightly in summer on blue lakes and evergreen forests. In January, cross-country skiers take to the high slopes and visit steaming fumaroles, hissing hot springs and boiling mud pots. Thus, visitors can enjoy the park and learn about volcanism in any season.

The towering mass of Lassen Peak, 10,457 feet, is the southernmost of the chain of volcanoes in the Cascades that stretch nearly 700 miles north to British Columbia. Arrayed in stately single-file rank, they form part of the Pacific "Ring of Fire" that arcs from South America to Alaska, Japan and Indonesia and includes three-fourths of the world's active volcanoes.

The violent eruption of Mount St. Helens in 1980 came as a reminder that the Northwest has been the scene of earthly cataclysms over millions of years. St. Helens, most symmetrical of Cascade volcanoes, has seldom gone more than 100 to 150 years without an eruption. Mount Baker, in northwest Washington, came close to erupting in 1975 and Mount Rainier shows steam vents and warm caves along the rim of its crater and has a history of massive mudflows.

At Lassen, the last series of eruptions began in the spring of 1914, after at least 400 years of quiet slumber, and continued over a period of seven years. In 1915, red tongues of lava spilled through a notch in the crater rim, flowed down the western slope 1,000 feet and hardened in place. But on the northeast flank, hot lava melted the deep snowpack, causing a mammoth river of mud to rush downhill carrying 30-ton boulders in its path. Three days later, a column of vapor and dust rose more than five miles in the sky, while a low-angle blast struck the northeast flank again, widening the path of destruction to more than a mile, mowing down trees and all life in its path for a length of five miles. It was these eruptions that drew nationwide attention.

The geology of the volcano had been studied for more than 30 years (notably by J. S. Diller of the U.S. Geological Survey) before establishment of the park. In 1907, President Theodore Roosevelt signed a proclamation setting aside Cinder Cone and Lassen Peak as national monuments. Then, following the eruptions of 1914-16, Lassen Volcanic was established as a national park. The park carries the name of Peter Lassen, a Danish pioneer who, during gold rush days, boarded emigrants and guided them across the mountains, but he had no connection with the purpose of the park or the volcanism for which it is known.

Lassen is now dormant, but scientists believe that future eruptions are possible. In the meantime, it is a pleasure to experience the deep forest, rushing streams and waterfalls, the alpine meadows and the best bubbling mud pots, sulphur springs and other thermal features west of Yellowstone.

THE PRACTICAL GUIDE

BACKGROUND. Many important scenic and volcanic features can be seen from the 30-mile-long Lassen Park Road, which half encircles Lassen Peak, so it can easily be included as a half-day side trip while driving north or south on I-5 (California 99) or US 395. Most of the eastern half of the park is superb for hiking and camping. More than 150 miles of marked trails lead to old volcanoes, thermal features, lakes and other natural features.

Manzanita Lake, near the northwest boundary, is rimmed with firs and pines. At least six types of pines are found in the park: Jeffrey, ponderosa, sugar, western white and lodgepole at lower elevations, plus whitebark pine, which climbs and struggles to survive at 10,000 feet. Willows and thin-leafed alder dip their roots into the clear waters of the lake. For information, stop at Park Headquarters, on California Route 36, near Mineral, *outside* the park (on the road from Red Bluff), or at Manzanita Lake Visitor Center, on the Lassen Park Road.

Chaos Crags and **Jumbles**, along the Park Road. The Crags, like Lassen Peak, are towering, plug-like masses pushed up through vents a few thousand years ago. Violent steam explosions from the base of the Crags caused avalanches, forming the hummocky Jumbles. The small coniferous trees growing around them are known as the Dwarf Forest. You can see a young pine forest taking hold of the soil while you drive 2½ miles through the **Devastated Area**, which was denuded of all vegetation in the volcanic blast of 1915.

ACTIVITIES. Hiking. Lassen Peak Trail starts from near the summit of the Park Road at 8,512 feet elevation. The climb is 2½ miles and takes four to five hours round trip, but the view from the summit is worth the effort. Overlooking craters, blue lakes and forests, this is the high point of a visit to Lassen Volcanic.

The trail from **Kings Creek Meadows** to the falls, 1.3 miles, shows Lassen's wildflowers at their best, including crimson snow plant, leopard lily, paintbrush, lupine, penstemon and bleeding heart.

Bumpass Hell is the destination of a 1.3-mile walk worth taking for the name alone. It leads from the Park Road through an alpine wildflower area to the largest display of hot springs in the park, with bubbling mud pots testifying to underground turbulence. It was named for an early hunter, whose tragic mistake in placing one leg into a boiling pool should be fair warning to stay on trails and skip the shortcuts.

Sulphur Works is 2 miles from the southwest park boundary. A self-guiding trail leads through an area of seething gases and heat emitted from the central vent of Mount Tehama.

Cinder Cone is one of the outstanding volcanic features of the park, which justified its separate establishment as a national monument in 1907. It is believed to be the source of "fires" and "flaring lights" in 1850-51, which were seen as far off as 160 miles. Black in color, bare of vegetation, it lies surrounded by multicolored heaps of volcanic cinder and ash, called the Painted Dunes, and looks as though it was formed yesterday. Cinder Cone is reached by hiking from Summit Lake or from **Butte Lake** in the northeast corner of the park. Fantastic Lava Beds is a mass of lava flows that originated from the base of Cinder Cone.

Winter Sports. Downhill skiing is available at concession-operated Lassen Park Ski Area, just inside the southwest entrance. Facilities include one triple-chair lift and two rope tows, plus day lodge with ski rental. Heavy snow closes the main highway November to June, but the entire park is open to cross-country skiing. Trails starting from Manzanita Lake and Lassen Chalet are marked according to skill levels. The trip between the lake and chalet covers about 30 miles. The park staff conducts snowshoe hikes, winter wildlife programs and winter survival workshops. Call park headquarters at 916/595-4444. Lodgings are available outside the park.

Fishing and Boating. Rowboats and

canoes can be used on most lakes (except Reflection, Emerald, Helen and Boiling Springs). In the spirit of backcountry recreation, motorboats are prohibited on all lakes in the park. Many lakes and streams have an abundance of rainbow, brook and brown trout; remember that a California fishing license is required.

Naturalist Programs. Check the schedule at Manzanita Lake Visitor Center or at any entrance station. Guided walks and hikes are held every day in summer. Start with the Early Bird Watch and end with the Star Watch. Campfire programs are conducted during the summer at Manzanita Lake and Summit Lake.

ACCOMMODATIONS. The only overnight facility in the park is Drakesbad Guest Ranch, in Warner Valley, which operates mid-June to mid-September. Rooms are modest, most without electricity. Horseback riding and pack trips are featured. For rates and reservations write California Guest Services, 2150 North Main, No. 7, Red Bluff, California 96080; in-season, Chester, CA 96020. A number of privately owned resorts are nearby on California 36, 44 and 89. Winter resorts in Tehama County, south of the park, are easily reached from Chico or Red Bluff. They range from luxury to rustic, with shades in between.

CAMPING. Campgrounds below 6,000 feet are generally open mid-May to October; those above 6,000 feet may not open till mid-June. Campgrounds at Manzanita Lake, Crags and Summit Lake on the Lassen Park Road have spaces for trailers and some modern conveniences, but no hookups for electricity, water or sewage. The Southwest campground has modern conveniences also, but you must walk about 100 yards from the parking area to the site. Summit Lake is best for backcountry hiking. Other campgrounds are at Lost Creek, Juniper Lake, Warner Valley and Butte Lake, on dead-end spur roads. Camping is permitted June to October, depending on weather. The camping limit is seven days at Summit Lake and Lost Creek; 14 days at all other sites. This area requires permits for backcountry use.

SEASONS. Summer is the main season. Overnight accommodations in the park are open mid-June to mid-September. Wildflowers burst into bloom in early summer, but the show continues until September. Lassen's annual snowfall is between 400 and 700 inches; winter sports programs are offered at the northwest and southwest entrances.

NEARBY. Many campgrounds and recreation areas lie within the 1,147,000 acres of **Lassen National Forest**. A major campground is located southeast of the park on the west shore of **Lake Almanor** (elevation, 4,550 feet), one of the largest artificial bodies of water in California, noted for its abundant trout. Other camping and picnic areas are conveniently located north of the park along **Hat Creek**. At **McArthur-Burney Falls Memorial State Park**, 11 miles north of Burney, Burney Falls is a cataract of singular beauty.

FOR FURTHER INFORMATION. Write Superintendent, Lassen Volcanic National Park, Mineral, California 96063.

LASSEN VOLCANIC NATL. PARK

scale 0 1 2 3 miles

MAMMOTH CAVE NATIONAL PARK

Kentucky

Authorized 1926

I TRIED to imagine what Mammoth Cave was like 4,000 years ago, when, according to bits of evidence (implements, clothing, several natural mummified bodies), it was first inhabited by primitive people seeking shelter, flint, gypsum and other materials. The national park is relatively new, but the cave is ancient, and I find much of its appeal in history. Electrification began only in the 1920s. On my first visit, in the 1950s, rangers would still demonstrate the old lighting technique: heaving torches of wood or cloth into receptacles, or baskets, high in the cavern chambers.

Discovered by white settlers sometime before 1799, this great cave was destined to become an attraction of wide renown and lasting appeal. Edwin Booth, the Shakespearean actor, once recited from Hamlet's soliloquy in an underground room now called Booth's Amphitheatre. Ole Bull, the celebrated Norwegian violinist, performed here in 1851—the same year Jenny Lind, the Swedish nightingale, shattered the subterranean stillness with her golden voice. Those were thrilling days, when visitors eagerly toted whale-oil lamps, and ladies were advised that "bloomers or Turkish dress" constituted proper attire, and many came from afar to explore "the greatest cave that ever was."

Mammoth Cave still provides a full quota of thrills. Although Carlsbad Caverns National Park in New Mexico contains the largest single chamber, Mammoth Cave is recognized as having the most extensive cave system in the world. It consists of more than 300 miles of charted passageways filled with spectacular rock formations and domes, though nobody knows how large it really is. Several levels have been explored, but many underground streams are still at work, shaping more passages.

The national park, about 90 miles from Louisville and the same distance from Nashville, covers 52,369 acres. It lies near Bowling Green in south central Kentucky, where the limestone terrain is pitted by depressions called sinkholes. Some geologists call the area the Southern Sinkhole Plain, but local people are apt to refer to it as the "Land of 10,000 Sinks." Walking through the portions of the cave open to public view, chambers and passageways bearing such names as "Grand Central Station," "Wright's Rotunda" and "Cleveland Avenue," I marveled at the formations of travertine, or cave onyx, in thousands of intricate and artistic patterns, including stalagmites, stalactites, draperies and cascading flowstone. Mammoth Cave was the first known cave to contain gypsum, restricted to drier portions, where slow leaching of calcium sulfate through porous limestone forces the gypsum crystals outward into the cave.

These subtle processes of nature have been under way for a period longer than humans can imagine. They continue to form new caves, to decorate the older ones and to enhance the visual beauty of the mammoth underground that has delighted visitors since its discovery. For many years, the cave was in private hands; the country is fortunate that it is now protected as a public trust.

There is more to the park than the underground. I particularly enjoy the scenic hills and valleys on the surface. A wide variety of birds and wildflowers enliven the forest of hardwood trees. White-tailed deer, woodchucks, cottontails and squirrels are likely to be encountered.

The Green River, joined by underground streams, winds 25 miles across the park. It is the key to the active circulation of underground and surface waters, assuring that new passages will continue to be formed at the lower levels of Mammoth Cave for a new world of hidden beauty.

THE PRACTICAL GUIDE

You can see the cave on one of the guided tours conducted every day, ranging from one to six hours, and then be on your way. But don't overlook the good overnight accommodations and campgrounds, and the opportunities for hiking, boating and fishing on the Green and Nolin rivers.

Watch the road signs carefully when approaching this park. There are several commercial caves in the area. Don't confuse them with the national park.

BACKGROUND AND TOURS. Tours into the cave are conducted every day of the year except Christmas Day. Reservations for principal cave tours are available through Ticketron outlets. Reservations for all tours are available at the Visitor Center. Only persons accompanied by a National Park Service guide may enter the cave. Most trails are solid and reasonably smooth. The temperature is 54 degrees all year; carry a sweater or jacket. Low-heeled shoes are a must for comfort; do not wear sandals. The pace underground is leisurely, with frequent rest stops, but if you have any doubts about your endurance, settle for one of the shorter trips. A special tour is conducted daily for visitors in wheelchairs.

Frozen Niagara Tour (one half mile, one and a half hours) displays a variety of formations. Among them is Frozen Niagara, the largest travertine formation in the cave, a fine example of flowstone, formed through centuries of deposition from water flowing over rock formations instead of dripping from them. Then you look down at Crystal Lake, a pool formed by a stalagmite dam.

Historic Tour (two miles, two hours) is a conducted tour. Enter through the natural opening near the Visitor Center, then see the **Rotunda**, scene of saltpeter mining during the War of 1812, and Indian artifacts. The trip continues to **Mammoth Dome**, aptly named. The blindfish from underground streams are seen along the route.

The Half-Day Tour (four miles, four and a half hours) takes you to some beautiful gypsum formations. The group stops for lunch 267 feet underground in the **Snowball Room**, with its clusters of gypsum that resemble snowballs on the ceiling. Then it passes through **Frozen Niagara**, the spectacle in travertine.

Lantern Tour (three miles, three hours) is unique. It gives the thrill of times past, before the cave was electrically wired. Trips are scheduled four times daily during the summer and are limited to 40 persons.

Wild Cave Tour (five miles, six hours) is scheduled during summer. This rugged spelunking adventure, which extends through crawlways and unimproved passages, requires the aid of hard hats and headlamps. Participants must be at least 16 years of age. Advance reservations are required: contact park headquarters by mail or phone (502/758-2328).

Tour for people with physical handicaps (one half mile, one and one half hours) is available to persons confined to wheelchairs. Inquire at the Visitor Center for details.

Green River Cruise. The *Miss Green River II*, a twin diesel-powered cruiser, makes several cruises daily. The twilight cruise reveals not only the forests along the riverbanks, but deer, beaver, turtles and a snake or two, all completely at home. Cruises last more than one hour. The ticket office is in the Visitor Center.

Cave Island Nature Trail. It begins and ends near the Historic Cave entrance, winding through the woods for about a mile. In addition, there are more than 7 miles of hiking trails keyed to geology, botany and zoology. Guided walks are conducted daily during the summer.

ACTIVITIES. During the summer months, evening programs are given nightly at either the campground or the amphitheater.

Hiking. If you want to avoid crowds, take to the back country, where you can hike and camp for as long as three days without seeing another person or crossing your own trail. A network of meandering trails leads along high ridges and through steep, scenic valleys.

Fishing is permitted all year with throw lines, pole and line, rod and reel. No license is required. Swimming conditions are unsafe along the river.

Kentucky Craft Shop features outstanding weaving, pottery, metalcrafts, baskets, brooms and wood carvings. Here you can acquire a dulcimer.

ACCOMMODATIONS. Facilities include the Mammoth Cave Hotel and the Sunset Point Motor Lodge at the edge of the forest. There also are cottages and plain cabins. For rates and reservations, write National Park Concessions, Inc., Mammoth Cave, Kentucky 42259. Motels are located in nearby Cave City, Park City and Horse Cave.

CAMPING. The campground of 110 sites, southeast of the Visitor Center, is adjacent to laundry, supply store and showers, which are open during the summer. There is a limit of 14 days all year.

SEASONS. In spring, the hardwood forest is filled with wildflowers. In summer, the coolness of the cave provides visitors with natural air conditioning; nights in the park are cool and comfortable. Autumn is the time of brilliant color changes, when the days are mild and clear and the nights are crisp and chilly.

NEARBY. Ten miles north of the national park, **Nolin Lake Reservoir** formed behind Nolin Dam, completed in 1963, has over 6,000 acres of boating and fishing waters.

North and east of Mammoth Cave lie **Abraham Lincoln Birthplace National Historic Site** and the **Bluegrass** country around Lexington.

FOR FURTHER INFORMATION. Write Superintendent, Mammoth Cave National Park, Mammoth Cave, Kentucky 42259.

MESA VERDE NATIONAL PARK

Colorado

Established 1906

I DROVE across the Four Corners country, coming northeast from the Grand Canyon. It was winter, a few days after Christmas. The weather outside was quite cold and the landscape stark, a combination of mountain and desert, with little vegetation. It was magic in a way, a world of endless horizons, free of cities and modern structures. It was Indian country, settled first two thousand years ago, and still Indian country.

From the main highway, I reached at last the narrow mountain road, with sharp curves and steep grades, leading to Mesa Verde.

The tableland runs 15 miles long and 2,000 feet above the valley to the north. Its rimrocks command the horizon for more than a hundred miles, up through the purple Rockies and down across the stark desert of the Four Corners. On its south side, this table mountain is honeycombed with deep canyons. In long crannies and huge arching caves within these canyons and on the mesa tops stand hundreds of villages. They bespeak a lost world that struggled to survive in a harsh environment, flourished for a time and was abandoned two centuries before Columbus.

Although it was winter, there were plenty of visitors in the park (though nowhere near the crowds of summer). Our fascination with Mesa Verde lies in its mysteries. Enthusiasts sometimes ascribe to these cliff dwellings superlatives such as "the largest," "the earliest" or "the most important." All of these may be true, and none may be true, for the only constant in history, as in nature, is change. From these ruins, archaeologists have given their best interpretation of a creative chapter in the story of prehistoric America, but their evaluations change as they acquire new knowledge.

The park covers 52,036 acres in the southwestern tip of Colorado. The region initially was occupied about the beginning of the first century A.D. by nomadic hunters turning to the land. At first they seem to have ignored the Mesa Verde, choosing instead the stream valleys for their villages. During the sixth century, however, they took up residence among the heavy forests of juniper and pinon on the mesa tops. They found a permanent supply of water, arable soil and shelter. These Indians remained for 800 years, during which they advanced and refined arts, architecture, agriculture and industry. From pithouses and crude pueblos, they progressed to great structures in the sheer rock, to which we have assigned such names as Cliff Palace and Balcony House—towers, terraces, whole towns built in the caves. Toward the end of the 13th century, they left their houses empty in the cliffs, their Temple to the Sun unfinished and wandered away to search for water and to mingle with other tribes in the Southwest. Their bloodlines could well be carried down to many of the modern Pueblo Indians along the Rio Grande in New Mexico and west to the Hopi country in northern Arizona. As to why they deserted their villages, there is no simple answer. The abandonment was gradual, over a long period of time; the precise reasons are part of the puzzle of archaeology and history.

The early period of exploration to unravel the mysteries began in 1859, with a series of geological surveys. In 1874, William H. Jackson, the famous frontier photographer of the Hayden Survey, visited, photographed and named Two Story House in Mancos Canyon, at the southern tip of Moccasin Mesa. B. K. Wetherill and his five sons became intimately familiar, through their cattle-herding activities, with Mesa Verde and its treasures. In 1888, Richard Wetherill and Charles Mason discovered Chapin Mesa. In 1891, Baron Gustavus Nordenskiold, of Sweden, guided by the Wetherills, recorded 22 cliff dwellings and performed major excavations; some of the materials he took to Europe now form part of the collection of the Finland National Museum. Indeed, some of the choicest prehistoric American artifacts are housed in European museums.

As the ruins became known, they were increasingly ravaged by cowboys and adventurers in search of salable artifacts. In protest against the vandalism, scientific and educational institutions urged that protective measures be taken. In 1891, the Colorado legislature memorialized Congress for the establishment of a national park on a part of the Ute Indian Reservation. Legislation to achieve that goal was introduced but continually failed (partly in dispute over whether mining should be permitted) until 1906, the same year that saw passage of the Antiquities Act. Unfortunately, the new park included almost none of the ruins it was supposed to preserve. The most valuable, including Cliff Palace, were on Ute deeded lands. In 1906, the Secretary of the Interior called for an archaeological survey, to be conducted by the Smithsonian Institution, to determine

exactly what ruins situated on Ute lands should be embraced in the park and what the boundaries and acreage should be. But the Utes refused to trade until 1913, when they finally agreed to accept a much larger acreage of their own selection. The boundaries were again changed in 1931, 1932 and as recently as 1963 to insure protection of the mesas and their ruins.

Concerned citizens and scientists prominent in the early history of the park included Mrs. Gilbert McClurg, who organized and promoted the Colorado Cliff Dwelling Association; Dr. J. W. Fewkes, of the Smithsonian Institution, who conducted extensive excavations and repairs over a period of years; and Dr. Jesse Nusbaum, who served as a young photographer on the 1906-07 Smithsonian survey, and who later became superintendent of Mesa Verde National Park.

A great deal has been learned about the changes in the ways of people while they dwelt here. Life at Mesa Verde is divided into four ages. The first is called the Basketmaker Period, when shallow caves furnished shelter and corn and squash were raised in small fields on the mesa top. Basketry, the earliest American craft, characterized this era, and woven baskets, bags, sandals and containers of all sorts were created. Sometime after A.D. 450, their culture advanced into the Modified Basketmaker Period, when their architecture included development of the pithouse, a semi-subterranean room with low walls and a flat roof of mud-covered poles and sticks.

There were all sorts of variations in the shape of the pithouse—circular, D-shaped, square with rounded corners; antechambers with doorways; ventilator tunnels with vertical shafts; and ladders giving access through a smokehole in the rooftop. The Modified Basketmakers replaced some of their baskets with pottery, which enabled them to cook in fireproof vessels.

The Developmental Period, a time of experimentation, saw the emergence of a new type of house, a rectangular structure with vertical side walls and flat roofs. Houses were joined to form compact groups around open courts, where daily activity went on. Instead of pithouses, people built underground pitrooms in the courts, stylized ceremonial rooms called kivas, which are still used by Pueblo Indians. This was a period of expansion, flourishing arts and crafts and the introduction of cotton, along with the use of the true loom. The people of this period built an ingenious chain of ditches to conserve water atop Chapin Mesa and to save the time it took to haul water from springs below.

Then came the climax of Mesa Verde culture, the golden age called the Classic Pueblo Period, from A.D. 1100 to 1300. Nearly all house walls were double, with massive outer walls. It was the sophisticated age of fine craftsmanship, beautiful black-on-white pottery made without the aid of a wheel, turquoise jewelry and woven cloth. In the last phase, the twilight of Mesa Verde, architectural monuments were constructed in the most spectacular locations, on the cliff ledges and in the caves. Walls of houses and kivas occasionally were covered with handsome designs, sometimes colored red, white, yellow and black.

Of hundreds of silent cities in the cliffs, actually few have been scientifically studied. A major archaeological project started in 1958 on Wetherill Mesa, one mile wide and 10 miles long, has finally been completed. It was opened to visitors in 1972—the first new area since the park was established in 1906.

Mesa Verde is the best known archaeological monument in the Southwest, but I like to view it in a context with others, like Canyon de Chelly, Chaco Canyon, Bandelier and Hovenweep. They fit together, unfolding a story, offering a common lesson about the past, and perhaps about the future as well.

THE PRACTICAL GUIDE

BACKGROUND. During summer, since large crowds jam the park, several ruins are open on a first-come, first-served basis, with numbers limited. Stop at the Far View Visitor Center for details and guidance. Park roads, designed as scenic drives with reduced speed limits, will take longer than normal highway driving.

From the park entrance, the center of activities lies 21 miles ahead. This is the place to decide whether to make overnight reservations in the park (if there are vacancies), to head for the campground, or to spend a few hours and travel on.

Park Point Fire Lookout is one of five numbered stops at points of interest along the entrance road. At 8,572 feet above sea level, this is the highest elevation in the park. It opens views into Arizona, Utah, New Mexico and Colorado, the states sharing the Four Corners. The mighty landmark of the desert, Shiprock, on the Navajo Indian Reservation, rises 1,400 feet. Viewed at sunset, it shimmers in the alpenglow, looking more like a ship than a rock.

Park Museum. A series of outstanding dioramas, accompanied by baskets, feather cloaks and jewels found during excavations, reveal the successive cultures of the cliff dwellers. At the museum visitors learn the ground rules for visiting the dwellings, which have been dangerously weakened by time; cliff dwellings are visited only with rangers on guided trips, or when marked "open for visitation" with a ranger posted on duty; mesa top ruins, which are less susceptible to damage, may be visited unaccompanied, 8 a.m. to sunset.

Ruins trip on Chapin Mesa. Check the museum for the daily schedule. This is your chance to enter the inner sanctum of the American Stone Age. The trips are self-guiding in summer, led by a ranger in other seasons. **Spruce Tree House**, best preserved and one of the largest cliff dwellings in the park, contains 114 living rooms, of which 8 are kivas. **Cliff Palace**, the largest and most famous community dwelling, was discovered by Richard Wetherill and Charles Mason in 1888. Built under the protection of a high vaulted alcove roof, it contains more than 200 rooms, of which 23 are kivas. Houses rising in some sections to four stories were home to as many as 200 persons. **Balcony House**, in a high cave on the west wall of Soda Canyon, demonstrates architectural detail and construction skills in a choice defensive setting.

Ruins Road drive. Two self-guiding loops cover 12 miles and provide views of many cliff dwellings with roofs still intact after a thousand years. Ten excavated mesa-top ruins may be visited. They demonstrate the entire range of architectural development in the sequence in which they were constructed, starting with a Modified Basketmaker pithouse of the late 600s. The road passes **Square Tower House** (not open), with a tower rising to a height of four stories, built against the near-perpendicular wall of Navajo Canyon, with the cliff forming its back wall. **Sun Point Pueblo** is interesting because its inhabitants, in the late Classic Pueblo Period, deliberately tore down the roofs and walls and used them to build a cliff dwelling in a nearby canyon. The last stop is **Sun Temple**, a great ceremonial structure also of the late Classic Pueblo Period, built on a promontory over Cliff and Fewkes Canyons. No part of the building was roofed, and only some stone-working tools were found within.

Wetherill Mesa is second only to Chapin Mesa for the impressive concentration of cliff dwellings. Wetherill is spectacular but fragile. At the Far View Visitor Center, you can board a free bus for the 12-mile ride to Wetherill. Then you switch to an open-sided minitrain for a leisurely trip along a narrow path through the pinon-juniper forest to see the impressive ruins dating from the 12th and 13th centuries. Private autos are allowed to visit the site. The road from Far View Visitor Center includes 12 miles of pulloffs with exhibits and spectacular views. Be sure to stop to visit Step House and Long House.

TOURS. Conducted bus trips of two or three hours around the ruins are run by Far View Lodge.

ACTIVITIES. Hiking. This activity is restricted in Mesa Verde because of the fragile nature of the ruins. Petroglyph Point Trail leads from the museum around the base of the cliff on the east side of Spruce Tree and Navajo Canyons, but you must obtain a written permit from the chief ranger's office. Longer trails are located in Morefield Canyon. Hiking is best done in areas outside Mesa Verde, and visitors should acquaint themselves with the Federal Antiquities Act and the Archeological Resource Protection Act, prohibiting "pot-hunting" and vandalism in this and similar areas. Under this act, it is a federal offense to remove, injure, damage or destroy "any historic or prehistoric ruin or monument, or any object of antiquity" situated on federal lands. Children should be advised firmly that every piece of pottery, bone and stone plays a part in telling the story and that regulations are strictly enforced.

Evening campfire programs are presented nightly at the Morefield campground amphitheater, 9 p.m. from June until Labor Day.

Photography. The cliff dwellings are best photographed in the afternoon, for most caves face west-southwest. Large mesa-top ruins are good any time of day. Excellent scenic views are obtained from Mancos and Montezuma Valley Overlooks and Park Point.

ACCOMMODATIONS. Modern motel-type accommodations are located at **Far View Lodge**, a 10-minute drive from park headquarters. **Spruce Tree Terrace** sells snacks and picnic supplies. Write Reservations Manager, Mesa Verde Company, Mancos, Colorado 81328; or phone 303/529-4421 (May to mid-October), 303/533-7731 (rest of the year). Outside the park, accommodations are plentiful at Cortez, 10 miles west; Mancos, 7 miles east; and Durango, 38 miles east.

CAMPING. Morefield Canyon Campground, five miles from the park entrance, at 7,800-feet elevation, has modern campsites, most of which accommodate trailers. The campground runs on first-come, first-served basis, with a 14-day limit. Morefield Village, operated by the park concessioner, includes supply store, coin-operated laundry, showers and carry-out snack shop. Service stations are located at Far View and Morefield Village.

SEASONS. Accommodations are provided about May 15 to October 15 (limited basis after Labor Day), but an interpretive program is presented year-round, with trips scheduled to at least one cliff dwelling, weather permitting. The park is open all year; after October 15 you may visit the museum and drive one loop of the ruins road, viewing cliff dwellings from canyon rims and visiting the mesa-top ruins. Summer days are warm, evenings chilly. Freezing weather arrives early at this high elevation.

Airlines operate daily flights to Durango, where rent-a-car service is available.

NEARBY. For a new, off-beat travel adventure, visit Ute Mountain Tribal Park, covering about 125,000 acres of cliffs, mesas and canyons, with hundreds of ruins in various degrees of stabilization, along a 25-mile stretch of the Mancos River, just south of Mesa Verde National Park. The season opens in May, or possibly June, depending on weather and road conditions.

San Juan National Forest to the north offers excellent fishing, hunting, back-country trails and numerous small campgrounds, all within two hours drive of Mesa Verde. Check for locations at ranger offices in Durango and Marcos.

Durango is the starting point of a ride on the historic **Durango and Silverton Narrow Gauge Railroad**. The train runs daily, except Christmas. From mid-May through October the train makes a round trip each day from Durango to the old mining town of Silverton, a journey through the deep canyons of the Animas River. The rest of the year the trip is from Durango to the Cascade Canyon. From late June through August, reservations are necessary. Phone 303/247-2733 for more information.

Mesa Verde was isolated and hard to reach for many years, but modern paved highways have shortened the driving time to one day from Denver and Salt Lake City. Grand Canyon is a six and one half hour drive, and Santa Fe approximately six hours. Road improvement across Monument Valley, Arizona, links Mesa Verde, via US 160, with spectacular frontier scenery of the Four Corners country.

Mesa Verde will be appreciated more when you visit and compare it with national monuments of the region. A dry climate and the use of stone and adobe by ancient architects have combined to produce extremely well-preserved ruins. Because of the excellent stage of preservation and the impressive structures, more archaeological sites have been incorporated in the National Park system in the Southwest than in any other part of the country. National monuments in the vicinity of the Four Corners are **Aztec Ruins**, New Mexico, a great prehistoric American town of the 12th century; **Chaco Canyon**, New Mexico, representing a high point of the ancient Pueblo civilization; **Hovenweep**, a network of towers and pueblos spread across Colorado and Utah; **Navajo**, Arizona, three of the largest, most elaborate cliff dwellings; and **Canyon de Chelly**, Arizona, fantastic ruins in red cliff and cave country, where modern Navajo Indians have homes and farms.

FOR FURTHER INFORMATION. Write Superintendent, Mesa Verde National Park, Colorado 81330.

MOUNT RAINIER NATIONAL PARK

Washington

Established 1899

I MADE it to Camp Muir, at 10,000 feet, in a little over four hours. I went with a light day pack, starting from Paradise, the center of activity in the park, at 5,450 feet. The forest of Douglas fir at the lower elevation yielded to trim alpine fir and grassy highland meadows flecked with wildflowers. I hiked alone at my own pace, stopping where I wished to watch the wonderful white and green world of the Cascades unfold. At Pebble Creek, the sign said Camp Muir was only 2.4 miles, but it was steep and tedious, virtually all on snow. Above the flower fields, Rainier became a complex of cliffs, ridges, canyons and cascading glaciers, such as long, narrow Nisuqally Glacier bordering the route on the west.

Camp Muir was as far as I went. It was enough for me. I rested and ate my pack lunch at this cluster of stone shelters, the gateway to the summit at 14,410 feet. Climbers start from here as early as 1 a.m., roped together, hoping to reach their goal and back before the sun brings ice fall dangers, returning all the way to Paradise by late afternoon. It is a challenge under the best of conditions, with weather, snow and ice, variable and unpredictable, adding to the mystery and magnetism. As John Muir wrote in 1888, after reaching the site now named for him (then known as Cloud Camp): "The night was like a night in Minnesota in December."

The trip down from Camp Muir was effortless, sheer pleasure; it was almost as easy to roll as to walk. I marveled at the great mountain above me.

About 40 square miles of icy, glacial rivers cap Mount Rainier, the loftiest volcanic peak of the Cascade Range. They flow downward from the 14,410-foot summit of Columbia Crest to timberline, at about 6,500 feet, and contribute to lakes and waterfalls in the midst of flowering meadows. In the valleys around the base of the mountain, heavy precipitation spurs the growth of dark, cathedral-like forests of the mighty and wonderfully proportioned Douglas fir, Western hemlock, Western red cedar, Sitka spruce, Pacific silver fir and other giants of the Northwest.

Rainier is a gleaming landmark visible for hundreds of miles in all directions when the weather is clear. It is the fifth highest peak in the United States south of Alaska, rising higher above its base than any other in the "lower 48." At close range, however, the mountain is a rendezvous for hikers, mountain climbers, wildflower lovers and bird watchers, autotourists, campers and those interested in observing the rivers of ice called glaciers.

The broad dome of Mount Rainier is a kingdom of glaciers. The Emmons Glacier, about 4.3 miles long and 1 mile wide on the northeast flank, is the largest glacier by overall size in the United States south of Alaska, while the Carbon Glacier, on the north face of the mountain, is the longest—6 miles. The glacier system of Rainier, though a mere remnant of its former size, is recognized as the country's most extensive "single peak" glacial system outside of Alaska. It contains a total of 26 named glaciers and 50 small, unnamed glaciers and ice patches.

In this national park, which covers 235,404 acres, the visitor can learn some of the simple truths that are known about glaciers and their behavior. On the Nisqually Glacier, the body of ice has been determined to move from 50 to over 400 feet per year at the 6,000-foot level. Movement varies within each glacier; the masses of ice move downward by virtue of their own weight, faster at the center than along the edges, and are influenced by the steepness of slope. Most glaciers of the world have been receding and growing shorter, as the case had been at Mount Rainier from the late 19th century until recent years. Slowly, vegetation crept into the barren areas. In recent years, however, the major glaciers on Rainier have reversed the trend and expanded, advancing downhill.

I picture Mount Rainier as a glacial laboratory in which I can watch the rivers of ice in action and the effects of their movements. The glacier churns and moves the earth's mantle and pieces of bedrock; it rasps the firm rock in its path, leaving it smooth; it carries away the plowed-off and filed-off debris, plus rock fragments fallen from the mountain slopes. Around the base I can identify glacial moraines, representing the accumulation of earth and rock dust where they are finally deposited. Then I observe how glacial debris, plucked and scoured from the mountain cone, is transported downstream.

Climate is a major influence upon Mount Rainier. It becomes more severe with rise in elevation, so that Longmire, elevation 2,760 feet, receives about one-third as much snow as Paradise, elevation 5,500 feet, which has averaged about 575 inches a year. The snow feeding Mount Rainier's glaciers originates as clouds over the Pacific Ocean. Rising to pass over the mountains, westerly winds are cooled, and the condensing moisture falls as rain and snow.

I find much to enjoy at lower elevations, where heavy moisture produces a luxuriant growth of trees and wildflowers, equally as lovely as the more celebrated flowers of the mountain meadows. The species of the deep woods, such as the three-leaf anemone, long tube twinflower, Pacific trillium, calypso and spring beauty, actually outnumber those typical of the higher elevations. But almost anywhere I go there are blossoms, right up to the edge of the snowbank and sometimes up through the snow. The entire experience is enriched by the sight and sounds of more than 50 species of mammals and 130 species of birds. I look for mountain goats in bands along

the rocky crags between 6,000 and 9,000 feet during summer and for closeups on the trail of the hoary marmot, a large furry rodent, sunning himself on rocky slopes from 5,000 feet to timberline. Elk migrate into the park each spring and remain until late fall.

THE PRACTICAL GUIDE

ACCESS. Mount Rainier National Park is a good one-day automobile trip from Seattle or Tacoma, both about two hours driving distance. Hikers, mountain climbers and campers enjoy longer stays. Each year, more than two million people visit the park, mostly in summer. Snowfields are enjoyed by 35,000 winter visitors—it's a good time to come.

TOURS. One-day bus tours leave Seattle daily before 9 a.m. and return by 6 p.m. They're easy to arrange through most Seattle hotels or by calling the Gray Line office.

BACKGROUND. The four Visitor Centers of the park are at Longmire, Paradise, Sunrise and Ohanapecosh.

ACTIVITIES. Hiking. Mount Rainier is a

107

hiker's park, offering more than 300 miles of trail. You can hike for an hour or a day, or spend two weeks backpacking while absorbing breathtaking views and experiences to remember.

Note especially that the famed Blue Ice Caves have been closed due to excessive melting, which has weakened and collapsed the ceiling of ice.

Try to take at least one of the easy trails, no matter how short your time in the park. In the Longmire area, the **Nisqually River Trail** makes a pleasant two-mile family hike from Cougar Rock Campground down to the Visitor Center. The **Silver Falls Loop**, from Ohanapecosh Campground and Washington 123, is a good low-level destination when storms sweep the high country; the three-mile loop rises only 300 feet through the forests along the Ohanapecosh River. With more time, make a full-day hike to such places as **Panorama Point**, on a four and a half mile loop from Paradise parking lot, with a climb of 1,400 feet, and **Van Trump Park**, a climb of two and a half miles and 1,900 feet from Christine Falls parking lot (10 miles up Paradise Road from Nisqually entrance) to beautiful Comet Falls.

A backcountry use permit is required for all summer overnight camping. If headed for a popular area on a summer weekend, you'll be wise to reserve a campsite in advance. Contact Hikers' Center, Mount Rainier National Park, Ashford, Washington 98304 or call 206/569-2211.

Wonderland Trail offers one of America's top hiking experiences. It completely encircles the mountain, a distance of 93 miles, with campsites spaced about 8 to 12 miles apart. It travels through dense forests, climbs to alpine meadows and passes close to glaciers. It requires preparation and proper gear. It's a long 93 miles, with plenty of steep climbs and descents, so plan for at least 10 days and count on more like 14.

Parts of the trail can be enjoyed a day or two at a time, or even on a half-day hike, being linked with spur trails to the park road system. The 30-mile section between **Paradise** and **Sunrise** passes lakes, waterfalls and the glacial-formed Box Canyon of the Cowlitz River. From Sunrise to **Carbon River**, 1½ miles, hikers enter the deep backcountry to see Winthrop Glacier, Mystic Lake at 5,800 feet and through Moraine Park at the foot of Carbon Glacier. From Carbon River around to **Longmire**, the trail crosses one stream after another while passing the Mowich Glaciers, Golden Lakes and between the fingers of Tahoma Glacier.

Northern Loop Trail, a branch off the Wonderland Trail, winds from Sunrise, at 6,400 feet elevation, through the meadows of Berkeley Park, carpeted with paintbrush, lupine, mountain buttercup and other flowers, across the southern tip of the beautiful Cehnuis Mountain to **Ipsut Creek Campground** on Carbon River, a distance of 17½ miles.

Stevens Canyon Road, completed in 1957 as part of the 117-mile road network in the park, is an outstanding scenic drive of the Northwest. The park has five approaches: via the **Nisqually**, or southwest entrance; **Carbon River**, or northwest entrance; **Ohanapecosh**, or southeast entrance; **Chinook Pass** entrance, on the crest of the Cascade Range at the east boundary; and **White River** entrance, off the beautiful Mather Memorial Highway from the northeast. An attractive route for motorists leads from the Nisqually entrance to **Longmire**, then 13 miles past Cougar Rock campground and Christine Falls to **Paradise Valley**, with subalpine fir, mountain hemlock and fields of wildflowers. Continuing east from Paradise, Stevens Canyon Road passes beautiful Reflection and Louise Lakes, with vistas of the rugged Tatoosh Range and Mount Adams. It intersects the East Side Road north of Ohanapecosh; you can turn north to Tipsoo Lake near Chinook Pass or continue north to the White River entrance, leading into Sunrise, the highest point reached by improved road in the State of Washington, facing Emmons Glacier.

Mountain climbing. This is one of the thrills of this national park, which served as training grounds of the 1963 American Mount Everest expedition. The concession guide service conducts a varied program for both novices and experienced mountaineers. The best is the climb to the summit, a long, strenuous ascent over moderately difficult terrain. It takes serious training and conditioning. Part of the pleasure of the trip is just participating in the snow- and ice-climbing school (one day). The climb takes two days. Climbing gear is available for sale or rent at Paradise. Contact Rainier Mountaineering, Inc., Paradise, Washington 98397; phone 206/569-2227. In the winter, write to 201 St. Helens Avenue, Tacoma, Washington 98402 or phone 206/627-6242. About 4,500 climbers reach the summit each year over several routes. But it takes an expert guide or leader to spot treacherous crevasses and crumbling lava. Routes are officially open all year, but weather is best from late spring to early fall.

Winter Sports. Snows blanket the high country. Paradise is open all winter, for snowshoeing and cross-country skiing, with supervised and prepared tube runs open on weekends. The Visitor Center, in fact, offers guided snowshoe walks and winter interpretive programs. Major ski developments with mechanical lifts are located nearby in the **Snoqualmie National Forest**.

Fishing. All waters are open, except those posted, without a license. Special restrictions exist for several areas in the park. Lakes normally are open July 4 to October 31, but snowpack may delay opening until late July or even early August; stream fishing conforms to the state fishing season. Glacial streams and upland lakes are generally too cold to support much aquatic life, but some remote lakes and clear streams provide fair to good trout fishing. Boats without motors are allowed in most lakes. Swimming conditions are poor.

Naturalist Programs. Guided nature walks and evening illustrated talks are conducted at Paradise, Longmire, Sunrise, Ohanapecosh and Ipsut Creek. The Ecology of Birds of Mount Rainier is the theme of weekend and weekday workshops in July, jointly sponsored by the National Park Service and Central Washington State College at Cispus Environmental Learning Center. Field trips and classes focus on identification, behavior and natural history. Accommodations are in Cispus dormitories. For information write Department of Biology, Central Washington State College, Ellensburg, Washington 98926.

Wildlife Watching. Many, and varied, species of birds frequent the park—because of its environmental diversity. Look for hawks and golden eagles in subalpine meadows, Canada geese and pintail ducks on the lakes, passing through on migration. Almost 150 species have been recorded during one season or another, so carry a good bird guide. Mammals on the park checklist total about 50. Deer are mostly seen in high forests and meadows during summer. They come into lowlands for the winter, and fawns are dropped during May and June. The best place to find elk is on Shriner Peak, reached by trail from Ohanapecosh. Best places for goats are Van Trump Park, Emerald Ridge and the Colonnades and Cowlitz Chimneys. When traveling in high country you won't have to look for marmots—they'll be there. Carry a good pair of binoculars and scan the cliffs as you hike. Avoid feeding wildlife; they become dependent on panhandling and can't make it on their own through rough winters.

ACCOMMODATIONS. Overnight lodgings inside the park are provided in the National Park Inn, at Longmire, open all year, and Paradise Inn, at Paradise, during the summer. For rates and reservations write Rainier Hospitality Service, Star Route, Ashford, Washington 92304, or call 206/569-2706. Motels, restaurants and grocery stores are located on the approach roads to the park. The Lodge Youth Hostel, ¼ mile outside the Nisqually entrance to the park, provides low-cost accommodations in bunkrooms. Address: Box 86, Ashford, Washington 98304; phone 206/569-2312. On the east side, new and improved resorts are found along the Mather Memorial Highway, at White Pass and at Packwood.

CAMPING. The main campgrounds inside the park are at Cougar Rock, Ohanpecosh and White River. Sunrise is a pleasant walk-in campground. For those who want solitude and more primitive conditions, small Class B campgrounds are at Sunshine Point and Ipsut Creek. Limit is 14 days, no trailer utilities. Camping is permitted in remote areas of the park. From June 15 through September 30, a backcountry use permit must be obtained. Other campgrounds are adjacent to the park in Snoqualmie National Forest.

SEASONS. Views of the mountain and glacier are obscured much of the year by clouds and fog, but warm, clear weather may be expected during the height of the summer season from about July 1 to early September. Two wildflower climaxes occur, one in early July and the other during August. Indian summer weather sometimes continues well into October. Most roads, including Stevens Canyon, are closed for the winter after the first heavy snowfall, usually about November 1. The road from the Nisqually entrance is open all year, although snow conditions may cause it to be closed for short periods. In winter, the road deadends at Ohanapecosh and no services are available.

The weather conditions can be uncertain during late winter and early spring. Snowstorms are interspersed with many clear, warm days. Be prepared for a sudden snowstorm. Be sure to carry tire chains.

NEARBY. Named in memory of the first director of the National Park Service, Mather Memorial Highway, a 50-mile scenic drive on Washington 410, starts at the boundary of the Snoqualmie National Forest southeast of Enumclaw, continues through the park to Chinook Pass, then down the American River. **Federa-** tion Forest State Park, 15 miles north of the White River entrance on Washington 410, contains a museum and interpretive center on the natural history of White River Valley. **Crystal Mountain**, a great new ski center and year-round resort, provides one of the finest views of Mount Rainier and the whole Cascades from the top of the chair lift—a vista embracing Mount Baker to the north, Mount Adams and Mount St. Helens to the south in Washington and Mount Hood in Oregon. Paths lead from Crystal Mountain to the **Washington Cascade Crest Trail**.

RECOMMENDED READING. *Exploring Mount Rainier*, by Ruth Kirk, and *50 Hikes in Mount Rainier National Park*, by Ira Spring and Harvey Manning. For climbers: *Cascade Alpine Guide—Columbia River to Stevens Pass*, by Fred Becky, and *The Challenge of Rainier*, by Dee Molenaar.

FOR FURTHER INFORMATION. Write Superintendent, Mount Rainier National Park, Tahoma Woods, Star Route, Ashford, Washington 98304.

MOUNT RAINIER
NATL. PARK

scale 0 1 2 miles

82-6657-5

To Centralia   To Yakima   ©RAND McNALLY & CO.

NORTH CASCADES NATIONAL PARK

Washington

Established 1968

From Bellingham on the coast, my friends John and Rotha Lou and I drove southeast to Sedro Woolley, stopping at the North Cascades Visitor Center (operated jointly by the National Park Service and U.S. Forest Service). We picked up maps, asked a few questions and headed east on State Route 20, the North Cascades Highway, one of the most scenic roads in America. We drove only to Marblemount, forking onto the Cascade River Road to the trailhead at the base of Cascade Pass. It was a brilliant, sunny day in the summer of 1987. I would not say the trail was crowded, but a good number of people were out to stretch their legs and to enjoy a day in the mountains.

The trail was laid out in relatively easy switchbacks that almost anyone could handle. John had been over this route many times. As a hiker, climber, skier and historian, he knew the North Cascades intimately. Now and then, he would cite bits of history and lore, but he was absorbed with the show of wildflowers sprinkling the hillsides and meadows. We hiked leisurely for about two hours to reach Cascade Pass (elevation 5,384 feet), a vantage point for viewing steep rock ridges, glaciers, snowfields and cascading waterfalls, a setting to compare with the most spectacular mountain scenery on earth.

In order to protect it for posterity, Washington's third great national park was established in 1968. The region is often called the "American Alps," and is one of the last of our primeval landscapes. The most prominent structural features of the Cascades—the volcanoes—are considered the largest freestanding objects in the contiguous United States.

This country had long been known to the Indians. The first white men who ventured into the North Cascades undoubtedly were trappers and hunters. In addition to a great variety of furbearers and game animals, they found a breathtaking land of alpine scenery, snow-capped peaks, cascading streams and western foothills covered with dense softwood forests. In 1814, Alexander Ross, backed by fur-trading interests, went over Cascade Pass in search of a short route to the Pacific.

Sometime prior to 1850, gold and other metallic ores—including silver, copper, lead, mercury, iron and chromium—were discovered. Prospectors and fortune-seekers were immediately attracted to the region, although the only profits were made by those selling food and equipment to the miners. The net effect was to stimulate river transportation, trail improvement and settlement by hardy souls. Lucinda Davis, who had mining claims up the Cascade River, moved to Cedar Bar in 1897, near the present town of Diablo, opened an inn and became the first woman to climb Sourdough Mountain and Davis Peak. The harvest of timber from the dense Cascade forests also began around the mid-1800s, but it was decades later that large-scale commercial logging became important.

An abundance of high-quality water, stemming partly from melting snowfields and glaciers, was another resource to be recognized. In 1919, Seattle City Light started its hydroelectric developments, which led eventually to the construction of the towns of Diablo and Newhalem.

In 1899, Mount Rainier National Park was established out of the old Mount Rainier Forest Reserve. During the following years, many proposals were advanced for additional areas of national forests in the North Cascades to be transferred to the National Park Service. The critical need for action did not become obvious, however, until the 1950s. In his classic work, *The Wild Cascades*, Harvey Manning recalls that as recently as 1948, he and other outdoorsmen felt "the wilderness was inexhaustible, and if one valley was logged, or two or three or a dozen, we could always escape to what seemed uncountable virgin valleys remaining." Then the growing infiltration of bulldozers, chain saws and logging trucks changed everything.

The North Cascades Conservation Council, headed by Patrick D. Goldsworthy, and the Sierra Club, led by David Brower, mounted a major national campaign. In January 1963, the Secretaries of Interior and Agriculture (responsible for parks and forests, respectively) agreed to form a study team to review administration of the North Cascades. Despite the political power of the timber industry and resistance of the Forest Service, the study team report of October 1965 recommended establishment of a new North Cascades National Park, though not as large as conservationists had wished and with some key features, such as Mount Baker, omitted. In February 1966, appropriate legislation was introduced in both houses of Congress. Hearings were held in Washington, D.C., and Washington State in 1967 and 1968, and in the latter year, the bill was passed, establishing a national park and two national recreation areas, Ross Lake and Lake Chelan, totaling 674,000 acres.

I marvel at the North Cascades as a range of giant faults and massive overthrusts, a thoroughly complex geology. Formed of weather-resistant rock, the high stretch of the Cascades intercepts some of the continent's wettest prevailing winds. The resulting precipitation has produced a network of hanging glaciers and icefalls, ice aprons and ice caps, hanging valleys and waterfalls. Works of ice make the North Cascades a rough, tall country, and a steep one from valley to summit. Some of the finest mountaineering opportunities in the United States are found here.

Between the moisture-laden west side and the dry east slopes, plant communities show a tremendous variation, ranging from subalpine conifers, green meadow and alpine tundra, back down to pine forests and sunny-dry shrub lands. They combine to form a vast array of unimpaired wilderness life communities; the national park was established to keep them free.

On a backpack trip I made in 1985, hiking to Cascade Pass from Stehekin, on the east side, I saw many deer on the trail. A pair of spotted fawn poked their inquisitive noses into my campsite at Basin Creek, while a hummingbird flitted among the shrubs. I hiked for a time with a young woman, Irene, who knew her plants and gave me a field lesson identifying yarrow, thimbleberry, elderberry, serviceberry and other plants and flowers that flourish during the brief summer.

On another trip, in winter, I floated the Skagit River in a rubber raft from Marblemount to Rockport, a few miles from the edge of the park, counting more than thirty bald eagles roosting in the trees and feeding on salmon in the stream.

Mountain goats, deer and black bear are frequently seen in the wilderness. Other wildlife include the wolverine, marten, fisher, grizzly bear, cougar and moose. White-tailed ptarmigans and a host of smaller birds and mammals make this harsh land their home.

The national park covers 504,780 acres in two units, each with a major wilderness as its core; Ross Lake National Recreation Area separates the two. The northern unit, bordering Canada, includes Mount Shuksan and the Picket Range, composed of glaciers, granite peaks, high lakes and remote valleys. The southern unit includes the "Eldorado high country" and the Stehekin River valley, one of the finest glacier-carved canyons in the Cascades.

The Ross Lake Recreation Area covers 117,574 acres between the Pasayten Wilderness of the Forest Service and the two units of the national park. Lake Chelan National Recreation Area consists of 61,890 acres at the head of the lake and in the lower Stehekin Valley.

THE PRACTICAL GUIDE

ACCESS. The major access to the park is on Washington 20, the North Cascades Highway, a link between Okanogan and US 97 in north central Washington and Mount Vernon on I-5 on the Pacific coast.

Slow down to enjoy the vistas; the road is not meant for speeding. The highway was dedicated in 1972 as "the most scenic mountain drive in Washington." Points of interest include (coming from the east) Early Winters Information Station (operated by Okanogan National Forest and the National Park Service); Washington Pass, the highest point on the highway (with picnic area and scenic overlooks); Rainy Pass, with picnic area and day hikes on the Pacific Crest Trail; and Ross Lake Recreation Area.

Besides the cross-park route, access to the periphery is possible via Washington 542 from Bellingham on the west, Highway 3 in Canada from the north and by boat or float plane service daily from Chelan (north of Wenatchee on US 97) at the southern end of 55-mile-long Lake Chelan. There are almost 360 miles of trails in the park and adjacent recreation areas.

Ross Lake is one of three lakes formed by dams on the Skagit River, which starts in Canada and flows through the Ross Lake National Recreation Area. The lake is 1,600 feet above sea level and extends 1½ miles into Canada, collecting water from a 1,200-square-mile watershed. The reservoir, completed in 1950, is in the center of a region with 150 active glaciers and hundreds of jagged peaks. Drainage from these perpetually snow-covered peaks makes Ross Lake quite cold even in August.

Access to Ross Lake is gained via a 3½-mile trail starting at the Diablo Lake Resort or from the Ross Dam powerhouse at the head of **Diablo Lake** along a 1-mile gravel road. At the Ross Lake Resort you can stock up on gas and ice, or rent boats, motors and cabins. The lake is 24 miles long and 2 miles across at its greatest width. It takes strong paddlers to canoe on Ross Lake. Boaters can't put ashore just anywhere, because of steep canyonlike walls ringing the lake. The gorgelike terrain creates hazardous gusts of wind, which can be counted on to whip up every afternoon and early evening. Large boats should have poles aboard to push them off from shore should they experience power failure in the wind; small-craft owners need to be alert to winds that can blow them onto the rocks.

ACTIVITIES. Backpacking. This is a favorite sport in the Ross Lake country. On the west rise the peaks of the Picket Range; farther north, Little Jackass Mountain and the Canadian peaks beyond the head of the lake. Most of this country can be hiked, but don't try the rugged ridges unless you have a rock-climbing background. From the town of Diablo, a strenuous 7-mile hike leads to Sourdough Mountain, looking up at towering peaks and glaciers. Rangers at Hozomeen, just below the Canadian border, can give directions to smaller lakes overlooking Ross Lake. By all means travel with a good topographical map.

Hiking. About 360 miles of hiking and horse trails exist throughout the four units of the North Cascades complex. North from Diablo Lake you can go up Big Beaver Creek to Whatcom Pass and the high lakes—this trip does not require rock-climbing experience, nor does the hike to Ruby Mountain.

Diablo Lake, which covers 910 acres to the northeast of Newhalem in the Skagit Valley, lies between the north and south units of the park. An impressive trip to the south—not strenuous, but two or three days for most walkers—leads up **Thunder Creek** and over **Park Creek,** then down to **Lake Chelan.** This trip passes close to spectacular glaciers and the lofty peaks of the Eldorado wilderness, such as Eldorado, Forbidden, Buckner and Goode.

An alternative to this route is to drive from the west to Marblemount on the Skagit River, then 22 miles along the Cascade River, stopping 2 miles short of Cascade Pass in the scenic climax of the range. The short hike to the pass takes one through an alpine world of flowering meadows, sheer cliffs and glaciered peaks, and the headwaters of two wild rivers flowing east and west. Cascade Pass is one of the most popular areas.

Lake Chelan furnishes the classic approach to the range. The passenger ferry *Lady of the Lake II* operates daily. Lake Chelan, set in a glacial trough, is 1,642 feet deep and varies from ¼ mile to 2 miles wide, flanked by forested slopes and wilderness peaks.

The trip from Chelan to Stehekin takes about 4½ hours. Do as the locals do: drive to Fields Point, about 15 minutes by car above Chelan, where you can park and leave your car in safety and board the ferry. You will save an hour and still see the best of the lake. You can also fly from Chelan to Stehekin by float plane via either of two local carriers: Chelan Airways, 509/682-5555, or Stehekin Air Service, 509/682-5065. A good idea is to fly one way and take the ferry the other.

Stehekin is gateway to a wilderness wonderland, a delight for backpackers and day hikers. You can camp in the valley or find comfortable bed-and-board if you wish.

Wherever you stay, be sure to go to dinner one evening at Cascade Corrals; it has been operated for many years by the Courtney family.

Then climb aboard the shuttle bus at Stehekin Landing and ride up the road into the park. You can get off at any of a number of trailheads. Between arrival and pickup, a party may walk along forest trails, climb peaks, or fish the rivers and lakes. Take the shuttle 23 miles to the last stop at **Cottonwood Camp** and hike to **Horseshoe Basin,** one of the great spectacles of the Cascades. Or head up the switchbacks to **Cascade Pass,** and down to the Johannesberg parking lot on the Cascade River Road from Marblemount. It takes planning, but it is well worth the trouble.

Field Classes. The North Cascades Institute (2105 Highway 20, Sedro Woolley, Washington 98284) conducts a popular series of two-day and three-day courses on botany, ecology, history, archaeology and history during the summer. Winter seminars cover birding, edible and medicinal plants and weather watching.

Fishing and Hunting. Besides the two big lakes, many small lakes and countless streams tempt the fisherman with rainbow, eastern brook, cutthroat and Dolly Varden. Be mindful of special regulations when fishing Ross Lake. The season usually opens in late June or early July; for exact dates, check with the Washington State Game Department or park rangers. Several areas closed to fishing are well marked. These include spawning grounds at the north end of the lake. Fishing in the Canadian part of Ross Lake and the Skagit River requires a British Columbia license. Lightning Creek, to the south, and Little Beaver, to the north, provide some of the lake's choice fishing. So does the channel alongside Cat Island.

Hunting is permitted within the two recreation areas, in accordance with state laws, but not in the park.

CAMPING. There are several campgrounds in the area: at North Cascades National Park, Lake Chelan National Rec-Area and Ross Lake National Recreation Area. All have 14-day limits. North Cascades requires permits for backcountry use.

SEASONS. At lower elevations and on the big lakes, the season extends from early April to mid-October, at higher elevations from mid-June to mid-September. The western side of the range receives more rain and has more lakes and streams; consequently, days are cooler. On the east side, the combination of more sunshine, warm rock surfaces and sparse vegetation makes for warm days and cool nights.

The North Cascades Highway is generally closed by snow for part of each winter. However, you can still reach Stehekin Valley by ferry (or float plane), and take in cross-country skiing, which is becoming increasingly popular here.

RECOMMENDED READING. *The Wild Cascades*, by Harvey Manning.

FOR FURTHER INFORMATION. Write Superintendent, North Cascades National Park, 800 State Street, Sedro Woolley, Washington 98284.

OLYMPIC NATIONAL PARK

Washington

Established 1938

I WALKED along Shi Shi Beach, just below Neah Bay, and listened to chattering seabirds. The Northwest is endowed with many miles of scenic beaches, of which Oregon's are the best known. Admiring the spectacular rock formation at Shi Shi known as Point of Arches, I felt that Washington's coast may be the most underrated along the entire Pacific. The coastal wilderness certainly adds a great deal to Olympic National Park; I was glad I wasn't taking it for granted. Wild and beautiful Shi Shi has always been there, to be sure, but only in 1976 did Congress vote to include it in the national park, and then it took nine years—until 1985—to complete the transfer of the land from state to federal ownership.

While wading around the Shi Shi tidal pools, I looked up at the Olympic Range. The mountains and the rain forests beneath them are the companion pieces to the ocean strip. They fit together in nature's pattern. The mass of peaks embraces the moisture-filled Pacific winds, wringing from them rain, snow and mist.

From glaciers and snowfields, water flows downward through rushing streams, over forest slopes and outward past a sandy beach, returning to its source and a renewed journey. Along the course of the water cycle, momentous happenings combine to tell the story of 908,720-acre Olympic National Park.

The finest results of heavy precipitation are represented in the valleys along the Pacific, the Bogachiel, Hoh, Queets and Quinault, the serene botanical gardens called rain forests, comprising the entire sweep of plant progression from fungi, mosses and lichens to immense trees 300 feet high and a thousand years old. Similar forests parallel the ocean from Alaska to California, but no forests are more luxuriant than those here.

The Olympic Peninsula, the "upper left-hand" corner of the West, lies in semi-isolation, bordered by the waters of the Pacific, the Strait of Juan de Fuca, the clustered cosmos of Puget Sound and the Hood Canal. It presents a marvelous geological story, with about 60 living glaciers in the high country. Six major glaciers, some blue, some white, are on 7,965-foot Mount Olympus alone. It gets the greatest precipitation of any spot in conterminous United States, perhaps 200 inches, most of it in the form of snow. I've learned never to visit the Olympics without raingear.

Below the glaciers, the alpine meadowlands on the northern side of the park, a mile above the sea, are especially rich in mountain wildflowers, including glacier and avalanche lilies, lupine, white buckwheat, columbine, asters, Indian paintbrush and others. According to the experts, eight species of herbaceous flowering plants are found in these high mountains and nowhere else.

Growing conditions in the moderate climate have been so favorable since the last glacial age that the Olympic Peninsula, below the meadows, has bloomed into a forest of evergreen giants. Within the national park are record-making trees, or near-record-making trees, of the "big four" Olympic species. Western red cedar, growing largely in moist valley bottoms, reaches heights of 175 feet. It has a cinnamon-red, fibrous bark and flat, lacy sprays of almost fernlike leaves. Western hemlock, a little smaller, grows at elevations up to 3,000 feet, a tree of dark russet-brown bark, showing abundant, very short cones at the end of its branches. Then, in the rain forests, the energetic, lordly Sitka spruce towering over most other trees is easily recognized by its sharp, silvery-green needles. The mightiest of the big four is the Douglas fir, exceeded only by the redwood and giant sequoia in size of all trees on the continent. This stately, wonderfully proportioned tree grows to heights of 250 feet and sometimes 300 feet. In age, the larger trees may be from 400 to 1,000 years old. The Douglas fir was discovered by Dr. Archibald Menzies, in 1791, on the west coast of Vancouver island, but was named for David Douglas, the roving Scottish botanist who brought a specimen back to England. The big trees of the Olympic Peninsula have been the source of controversy for many years. Only a few of the great stands are protected in the national park, while heavy logging of old-growth forests continues on private timberlands and on areas administered by the U.S. Forest Service.

The Olympic area first received national recognition because of its wildlife, particularly the Roosevelt, or Olympic, elk. These large members of the deer family grow as heavy as 900 to 1,000 pounds. Between 4,000 and 5,000 live in the park, mostly on the west side, constituting the largest remaining herd of their kind anywhere in the world. Though many of them migrate in summer to the high country, I noted in the forest much evidence of their presence—footprints in the hardened mud and telltale elk pellets scattered in clusters over the ground.

Of more than 50 different species of wild mammals, black-tailed deer are frequently seen in the lowlands as well as in mountain meadows. Birds include the rare spotted owl.

I saw wildlife of another sort along the 50-mile-long coastal portion of the park called the Pacific Coast Area. Four species of seals, sea lions and whales, the flippered animals, frolic in the offshore waters or on the rocks. Thousands of marine birds nest on small islands, and the strip lies within one of the major flyways of migrating birds. I watched persistent waves and the encroaching sea continue the endless process of sculpture—carving seascapes on tree-studded islands, rocky arches and crescent beaches.

THE PRACTICAL GUIDE

Spend at least two days seeing the highlights of the park as part of a tour of the Olympic Peninsula. You can combine it with ferry cruises across Puget Sound and to Victoria, British Columbia. Check with Washington State Ferries (206/464-6400).

BACKGROUND. Principal Visitor Centers are at the **Pioneer Memorial Visitor Center and Museum** located at the southern edge of Port Angeles, gateway to the most accessible portions that lie along the north side, and at the **Hoh Rain Forest** on the west side. From Port Angeles, start the **Heart O' the Hills Road,** leading to **Hurricane Ridge Road,** 18 miles of paved road from sea level to 5,229 feet. Trailers should not try to make it beyond the campground, 5.4 miles from US 101. Halfway up, at **Lookout Rock,** vistas unfold across the Strait of Juan de Fuca; on a clear day you can see the snowy mass of Mount Baker in the northern Cascades.

ACCESS. Without a car, from Port Angeles take the Clallam Transit System to Lake Crescent Lodge, Fairholm Campground and Sol Duc Hot Springs Resort (daily during the summer). Reach Port Angeles by Greyhound from Seattle. Or, from Olympia take Washington Coast Lines to Lake Quinault, southwest entrance to the park.

TOURS. Scheduled and charter tours are offered during the summer by Gray Line of Port Angeles and Evergreen Trailways, Seattle.

ACTIVITIES. Hurricane Ridge is the upper terminal of the main road. Superb views of the Olympic Mountains are framed through the windows of Hurricane Ridge Lodge. The **Big Meadow Nature Trail** is a leisurely walk that anyone can take and enjoy. Or, drive 8 miles more on a narrow, unpaved road (open during summer only) to **Obstruction Point,** elevation 6,450 feet, which places you at the threshold of the heart of the high country, with the best view of mighty Mount Olympus available by road. This is the starting point of fine hiking trails, including one to **Deer Park Campground,** passing wildflower meadows—with a good chance to observe Columbian black-tailed deer and Olympic marmot. Fifteen roads enter the park like the spokes of a wheel, but none is permitted to penetrate the core of wilderness. "Where the roads end," according to park enthusiasts, "trails begin." Over 600 miles of trail thread the park, permitting short, easy trips of a day or less and more difficult hikes of a week and more. Trailside shelters are now few and far between, so bring your own tent or shelter material—and be sure to carry rain clothing.

Lake Crescent, the largest lake in the park, is nestled between the forested slopes of Pyramid and Mount Storm King. US 101, west of Port Angeles, follows the shore of the lake for 10 miles. From the western end of the lake, a road follows the Soleduck River to **Soleduck Campground,** the beginning of trails to **Seven Lakes Basin,** in the subalpine zone, and other high country of exceptional beauty.

Rain Forest Nature Trails are at the end of Hoh River Road on the west side of the park. The river is often swollen with "milky" silt from the glaciers on Mount Olympus, but it is only one feature of the forest, where precipitation averages 140 inches yearly. This forest is a complex community of many living things. The forest litter contains a thriving population of mice, shrews, salamanders and insects. Sitka spruce is the most characteristic large tree of the rain forests, and here it reaches its greatest size; one of the largest anywhere (though the record holder is outside the park), 41 feet, 8 inches in circumference, is located about 3½ miles up the trail from the Hoh Rain Forest Visitor Center. At least 70 kinds of mosses are present, some covering rocks, others growing like air plants from the limbs of trees, draped in fragile beauty like mysterious poetry of the forest. Roosevelt elk are sometimes seen in the vicinity of the Visitor Center and along the trails.

Kalaloch borders Washington 101 at the southern end of the park's coastal strip. Seven short trails lead from the highway to the beach, where ocean waves have worn back the land. In this laboratory of life between the tides, colorful hydroids, sea urchins and anemones thrive in pools where the shore is rocky and protected from strong waves. Densely clustered mussels and barnacles cling to rocks near shore, while crabs scurry for shelter beneath them. Other creatures prefer the sandy beaches. On a weekend in clam season, when the tide is low, Kalaloch Beach becomes pockmarked with holes and bumpy with piles from the "guns" (spades with long, narrow blades) of clam diggers in quest of Pacific razor clams (Siliqua patula), a delectable, meaty shellfish that grows from California's Pismo Beach to the Aleutians. On a hike along the shore, a bald eagle might be seen flying from a nest in the top of a tall snag; other birds are always present, including gulls, crows, oyster catchers and cormorants.

Three Indian villages are encompassed by the Pacific Coast Area, while a fourth abuts it on the south. A few of their fishermen still use dugout canoes hewn in traditional fashion from single cedar logs. The $2 million Makah Cultural and Research Center, opened in 1979, traces five centuries of Makah cultural history. The museum was built after tidal erosion exposed the ruins of an ancient Indian settlement near Lake Ozette. The exhibit hall includes a replica of a traditional Makah longhouse.

HIKING. Ozette is about 68 miles west of Port Angeles. Two routes lead to North Wilderness Beach: the 3⅓-mile Indian Village Trail to Cape Alava and 3-mile Sand Point Trail to the beach south of Alava. You can hire an outfitter at Lake Ozette Resort to boat you and gear to either the Ericson Bay Trail or Allens Bay route. You can also reach North Wilderness Beach via La Push. From just south of La Push, several trails reach out to secluded beaches, often heavily used in summertime. To the north of La Push, Rialto Beach is a popular day-hike area, and a jumpoff spot for the 3-day hike up the coast to Cape Alava. Another route to the Pacific beaches is from Neah Bay south.

Bring a tide table. If you miscalculate, you're apt to be trapped by incoming tides. Pick up a wilderness permit to camp on the beach, but prepare for rain at any time with durable tent and rain gear.

Naturalist Programs. The three Visitor Centers (Pioneer Memorial Visitor Center and Museum in Port Angeles, Kalaloch and Hoh Rain Forest) offer an important introduction to the park—enhancing one's understanding as well as enjoyment. July 1 through Labor Day, terrace talks and short walks are conducted daily by naturalists, most often at Hurricane Ridge, the Hoh Rain Forest and along the coastal beach. Excellent evening programs, illustrated with slides or movies, are given at the eight major campgrounds after sunset.

Fishing. The extensive streams and lakes contain rainbow, brook, cutthroat and the anadromous steelhead trout. No license is required, but check regulations.

Field Seminars. For those interested in studying botany, photography, wildlife, anthropology and geology, field seminars are offered at modest fees throughout the year. Write Olympic Field Seminars, 600 East Park Avenue, Port Angeles, Washington 98362-6798.

Bird watching. With its great coastal and inland features—from glaciers and snowfields to lush rain forests—Olympic is outstanding for birders in the Northwest. Seabirds nest on offshore rocky islands, and migratory birds make this a rest stop along the Pacific flyway.

ACCOMMODATIONS. A variety of motel-type lodges and housekeeping cabins are available at several localities inside the park. The largest are Lake Crescent Lodge, at the foot of Mount Storm King, with access to fishing, boating and hiking; and Kalaloch Beach. Other facilities are found at La Push in the coast area, Sol Duc Hot Springs Resort and Log Cabin Resort at Lake Crescent. For information, write the Superintendent. In addition, there are hotels, motels and resorts in Port Angeles and elsewhere on the peninsula outside the park. For information, write the Resort and Hotel Association, Seattle Ferry Terminal, Seattle, Washington 98104.

CAMPING. Campgrounds are maintained near the end of, or adjacent to, nearly all the entrance roads in the park. Most have complete camping facilities during the summer. All major park campgrounds have sanitary dump stations, but they lack hookups. Camping near the beaches of the Pacific Coast Area is pleasant during dry weather. Other campgrounds can be found on the peninsula in state parks, the Olympic National Forest and on private lands.

SEASONS. This park has special features to admire in every season of the year, even though snow covers high country roads and trails from late fall to early spring. Port Angeles and the northern side of the peninsula are served by bus throughout the year from Seattle; San Juan Airlines operates daily flights during the summer; rental cars are available; and ferry service is maintained across Puget Sound. Winter is best for spotting elk, and for quiet walks along the ocean beach (where lodgings are open all year). Hurricane Ridge is open weekends for skiing (with the aid of two rope tows and Poma-lift). Naturalists conduct snowshoe walks (snowshoes provided), cross-country ski tours, demonstrations of winter skills and informal fireside talks. Most popular snowshoe and ski route on Hurricane Ridge is the 1.5-mile Hurricane Hill Road. You can also ski from Hurricane Ridge down to Port Angeles, a distance of 3 miles. Hurricane Ridge Road is open daily as far as conditions permit. Weekends and holidays the road opens at 9 a.m., then closes to uphill traffic at 4 p.m. For current weather and trail information call the Port Angeles Visitor Center (206/452-9235).

Come prepared with proper clothing and repair equipment for skis and snowshoes. By late May all accommodations and most of the developed campgrounds are open, and by June wildflowers start marching up the mountains.

Summer is mostly cool and sunny, though rainproof garments are a must for hikers and campers. September and October are often delightful, with Indian summer; in early fall spawning salmon may be seen in many rivers, performing the grand and final act of their lives. In this normally misty land, mid-autumn is often clear and cloudless for days on end.

NEARBY. US 101, the broad Olympic Highway, nearly encircles the peninsula. It begins at the southern tip of Puget Sound, in **Olympia**, where the state capitol is handsomely landscaped and restaurants are famous for oyster dinners. Along the way campgrounds and scenic areas in **Olympic National Forest** unfortunately are interspersed with heavy logging. In the southwest corner of the national forest, along the shore of Lake Quinault, are three campgrounds, summer homes and the Lake Quinault Lodge, with fishing, boating and swimming enhanced by the surrounding dark forests. Within walking distance is the rain forest of the Quinault Natural Area, including the famous "Big Acre," the greatest known stand of Douglas fir in the United States. **Port Angeles**, Washington, fishing center and northern crossroads of the peninsula, is linked by ferry with **Victoria**, British Columbia, a city with gardens that are almost as lovely as Olympic's botanic splendors.

RECOMMENDED READING. *Exploring the Olympic Peninsula*, by Ruth Kirk.

FOR FURTHER INFORMATION. Write Superintendent, Olympic National Park, 600 East Park Avenue, Port Angeles, Washington 98362.

PETRIFIED FOREST NATIONAL PARK

Arizona

Established 1962

Driving across the high plateaus of northeastern Arizona, it was hard for me to believe that once a forest grew here. Yet, dense beds of ferns, mosses and trees thrived in marshlands and along streams. Conifers once flourished in scattered groves on hills and ridges above the water.

That was about 200 million years ago, in the Triassic period, when this region was a low-lying swamp basin. The scene has changed since then. The land now receives less than ten inches of moisture yearly. Most plants I saw were small and inconspicuous (though many have delicate, beautiful flowers), with only occasional junipers and cottonwoods.

This was, however, the Painted Desert, a wide arid land of plateaus, buttes and low mesas—low in water and plant growth, but lavish in displaying many hues in bands of sandstones, shales and clays. Logs of petrified wood are often brilliant and vivid, leaving little doubt about the ancient forest.

Indian ruins and petroglyphs show that ancient man dwelled in these environs. The Anasazi, prehistoric farmers who inhabited the area from about the time of Christ until A.D. 1450, shaped the petrified wood into tools and weapons and used the brilliantly colored pieces as trade items.

Curiously, Spanish explorers showed no interest in the petrified wood, probably because it lacked valuable minerals. Early traders and fur trappers repeatedly crossed the area, but they also showed no interest in the fossil wood. The first written reports of note apparently were made by American military and railroad surveys following the Mexican War. Still, the area remained almost unknown until the coming of the railroad and settlers late in the last century. Then began a rush for riches by souvenir hunters, gem collectors and commercial jewelers that might have destroyed in two or three decades the treasures that nature had taken millions of years to create. Large quantities of wood were either dynamited for gems or freighted to stations at Adamana and Billings (Bibo) for shipment to the East. The erection of a stamp mill to crush the logs into abrasives stirred public opinion into demanding federal regulations to protect these fossil deposits.

Though Arizona was not yet a state, its territorial legislature petitioned Washington in 1895 to have Chalcedony Park, as the Petrified Forest was then called, set aside as a national preserve. President Theodore Roosevelt responded to the plea by declaring the area a monument. In 1962, private land holdings within the boundaries were acquired and Petrified Forest was made a national park.

The national park of 93,493 acres consists of six separate "forests," with great logs of agate and jasper lying on the ground, many of them broken into fragments. It is believed the trees were transported by flooding streams from the surrounding highlands and buried under mud and sand, then covered over by layers of silica-rich volcanic ash. Traces of iron, manganese and carbon stained the silica to form the present rainbow colors.

That life once thrived in this arid, isolated land seems difficult to accept. Yet, occasionally, the bones of giant amphibians and reptiles are washed from their burial places in the soft rock. Thus, in June 1985, a 1500-pound block containing the world's oldest known dinosaur skeleton was airlifted from the Painted Desert for removal to the Museum of Paleontology at Berkeley. The skeleton of the dinosaur, named "Gertie," is considered 225 million years old. Gertie was taken to Berkeley for study and preparation before return to Petrified Forest for display.

THE PRACTICAL GUIDE

ACCESS. Main points of interest lie along a 28-mile road running north-south through the park between I-40 (US 66) and US 180. Short drives to several places back from the main road may increase the distance of the complete trip to about 34 miles. You can see the main features and wayside exhibits within one and a half to three hours. If you are driving west, there is no need to double back, for the town of Holbrook lies 26 miles from the north entrance and 19 miles from the south entrance. Eastbound parties should simply reverse the order, leaving I-40 (US 66) at Holbrook and proceeding to the south end of the park via US 180. After driving north through the park, rejoin US 66 from the north boundary. Gallup, New Mexico, lies 70 miles east.

ACTIVITIES. Rainbow Forest Museum. Exhibits at the museum include outstanding specimens of polished petrified wood, fossils, minerals and diagrams explaining how wood becomes petrified. A spur road to the **Long Logs** reveals the "logjam" character of deposits, with logs piled helter-skelter upon one another. A partially restored pueblo, the **Agate House**, built centuries ago of petrified wood chunks, overlooks the Rainbow Forest at the end of a foot trail.

Rainbow Forest is near the south entrance. Many trunks exceed 100 feet in length; the ground is strewn with chips of onyx, agate, carnelian and jasper.

Jasper Forest was named for the opaque colors of some of the petrified wood here. A parking viewpoint located on a ridgetop faces great masses of log sections strewn on the valley floor. Nearby **Agate Bridge** is a mammoth single log, with over 100 feet exposed and both ends encased in sandstone. A deep ravine has gradually been carved into the sandstone, leaving the log looking like a natural bridge. North along the park road lies the beautiful **Blue Mesa**. Colorful banded buttes, mesas and cones clearly reveal the ancient layers of marsh. Erosion nibbling at the soft earth has left some petrified logs stranded in unusual postures on slender pedestals.

Newspaper Rock, a massive sandstone block, is filled with picture writings of prehistoric Indians. The signs and symbols have never been interpreted, but probably represent clan symbols, religious symbols and simple doodling. Nearby lies the **Puerco Indian Ruin**, the remains of a pueblo occupied in the 14th century. The pueblo consisted of about 75 rooms which surrounded a large courtyard. The 6-mile **Rim Drive** along the desert rim has nine overlooks that offer spectacular views and photographic opportunities. The most amazing property of the Painted Desert is the ever changing quality of its colors. Minute quantities of iron oxide have stained the layers of land many shades, ranging from harshly gaudy red to softly soothing blue. Colors are most vivid after a rain in early morning or late evening. **Pilot Rock**, 6,235 feet, the highest point in the park, lies to the northwest. **Black Forest**, a concentrated deposit of dark petrified wood, is not accessible except by hiking— try it only if you are conditioned to the desert, and first notify a ranger of your plans.

Stop at the old **Painted Desert Inn Museum**. The inn was built as a hip-roofed stone trading post. Between 1936 and 1940 workers of the Civilian Conservation Corps added the fine beam ceilings, hand-carved corbels, buttresses and other features. In 1948, when the building was a Fred Harvey inn and restaurant, Fred Kabotie, noted Hopi artist, installed the murals. The Inn Museum, 2 miles north of the Visitor Center just off I-40, is open June through August.

Be sure to stop at the Administration Building, near the north entrance, to see the displays.

Souvenirs for sale. Samples of polished petrified wood, found on private land *outside* the park, may be purchased at the Painted Desert Oasis and Rainbow Forest Lodge. These establishments, about 26 miles apart, are located near the park entrances. Both are open every day of the year (except Christmas Day) to sell souvenirs and refreshments. The Painted Desert Oasis also offers lunches and gasoline. Children should be restrained from attempting to pick up loose petrified wood in the park; if each youngster took one piece, there would be little left in 20 years for *their* children to see and enjoy. Though commercial exploitation has been halted, theft by park visitors poses a threat just as dangerous. For this very reason, federal law prohibits removal of any petrified wood from the park, no matter how small the piece. Obey the numerous warning signs; don't run the risk of being arrested, with a possible fine or jail sentence.

Photography. Colors are most vivid to record after a rain. Early or late in the day are the best times for pictures, because shadows provide contrast, and the warmer light intensifies the red colors of the soil.

SEASONS. This is high country, ranging from 5,300 to 6,200 feet in elevation. During the winter, be alert for icy spots on the highway. During spring, the showy blossoms of yucca, cactus and mariposa lily will be on display, followed by blooms of paintbrush, aster and other plants during summer.

NEARBY. There are no overnight facilities inside the park, and backpacking camping is available in wilderness areas only (permit required). Campgrounds are in the **Sitgreaves National Forest**, over 50 miles south; **Coconino National Forest**, nearly 100 miles to the west; and in the Indian lands to the north. Motels and restaurants are located at Holbrook and other nearby communities. The closest to the park, coming from the east, is at Navajo, 15 miles away. Ask a park ranger about road conditions and facilities on Arizona 63 to **Ganado** and **Chinle** in the heart of the Navajo Reservation. **Canyon de Chelly National Monument**, near Chinle, is one of the fantastically beautiful areas of the Southwest. Inquire also about conditions on Arizona 77 across the Five Buttes into **Keams Canyon Campground** on the Hopi Reservation. About 100 miles due south of the park, **Hawley Lake** on the Fort Apache Reservation provides motel facilities, fishing and recreation.

FOR FURTHER INFORMATION. Write Superintendent, Petrified Forest National Park, Arizona 86028.

REDWOOD NATIONAL PARK

California

Established 1968

With friends I walked the Tall Trees Trail, winding down to Redwood Creek and then alongside it. The setting was misty and moody, a world of rich alluvial soil and deep shadows among giants. It was mid-February 1986 and raining steadily, which only added to the mystery of the scene. I stood beneath the tallest tree, 367.4 feet, a monument in itself, a testament to life, yet helpless and dependent.

The Redwood Empire is a shrunken kingdom as compared with a century, or even a quarter century, ago. Establishment of Redwood National Park in 1968 gave national recognition and protection at last to one of the natural wonders of the United States and the world. It assured the preservation of an area representative of the finest remaining virgin growth of redwoods, with the incomparable scenery of the tallest trees on earth.

The coastal redwoods constitute a special province. In early geological times, these trees were widely spread across North America. Today, they are found only in a narrow band along the moisture-rich northern coast of California. As a living tribe, the redwoods are remnants of the age of dinosaurs; as individual creatures, some have been growing a thousand years or more.

The redwood is the earth's tallest living tree, commonly growing more than 200 feet high, occasionally more than 300 feet. Trunks are 15 to 20 feet in diameter, with exceptional specimens up to 25 feet.

The first successful redwood preservation effort came in 1902 with establishment of Big Basin Redwoods State Park in the southern redwood belt near Santa Cruz. The establishment of Muir Woods, just north of San Francisco, followed in 1908 as a gift of land from Congressman William Kent to the federal government in honor of John Muir.

In 1918, the Save-the-Redwoods League was formed. In half a century, with matching funds provided by the State of California, it placed large acreages of primeval redwood forest in the California State Park System. Three of these parks—Jedediah Smith, Del Norte Coast Redwoods, and Prairie Creek Redwoods—form the core of what is now the park.

In 1963 and 1964, the National Park Service made a survey of the redwood region. Of the original growth forest of almost two million acres, only 15 percent remained. Of this volume, only two and one-half percent, or approximately 50,000 acres, was protected in state parks. At the annual rate of redwood logging, it was estimated that virtually all old growth redwoods not protected in parks would be gone within 20 or 30 years.

Although the national park was established in 1968, critical problems remained unsolved. Logging practices of large timber companies around the borders of the park threatened erosion of the famous Redwood Creek watershed, site of the world's tallest trees. As a consequence of erosion, streambeds rose and great old trees were literally drowned. In 1978 Congress expanded the park by an additional 48,000 acres, bringing the total size to 106,000 acres.

The expansion area is composed mostly of cutover lands—with 200 miles of logging roads, 3,000 miles of skid trails, and thousands upon thousands of burnt stumps of what were once magnificent redwood trees. I visited this area during my 1986 trip and saw a major rehabilitation effort: seeding logging roads, reshaping contours to cope with gullies and landslides, and planting young forests. I see it as an expression of faith in the future. One day giant redwoods may grow here again.

On another day, my friends and I hiked in the rain on trails in Prairie Creek Redwood State Park. There were towering, overpowering redwoods, but also the thick understory produced by abundant winter rain: rhododendrons 40 feet tall, red-barked madrone, alder, oak, maple, azalea, and skunk cabbage. One friend, Lucille Vinyard, spoke of the springtime beauty of the redwood forest, but I was absorbed with the ferns, waist-high around me: lady ferns, large and delicate; sword ferns, with leaflets resembling miniature swords complete with hilts; giant horsetail, so named for the tufts growing from the main stem; and the five-fingered fern, whose black stems the Indians favor to create designs in basketry. Ferns are among the most ancient living creatures; where others evolve, ferns survive. Painters, photographers, and poets, I thought, come to the forest to transpose nature into art; what they find is art in nature.

THE PRACTICAL GUIDE

BACKGROUND. Of the national park's 106,000 acres, about 40,000 acres are considered "old growth," with trees of 400 years and older. Some of the finest stands are in three California state parks which lie within the national park and which eventually will be transferred to the federal government.

These three parks provide camping for tenters and small trailers. During the summer the campgrounds fill early. Fees are charged and sites may be reserved, either through any Ticketron outlet or by writing Reservations Office, Department of Parks and Recreation, Box 2390, Sacramento, CA 95811.

National Park information offices are located at Orick and Crescent City. At these sites, learn where and how to join interpretive programs which during summer range from guided tide pool walks to recreations of pioneer history. Allow time to learn the differences between the coastal redwood and its cousin, the giant sequoia (see Sequoia National Park and Yosemite National Park chapters for references to the latter). At the Orick center, on the west side of Highway 101 near the mouth of Redwood Creek, buy a ticket for the shuttle service operating during summer to within a mile of the Tall Trees Grove on Redwood Creek.

VISITOR CENTER. Stop at the Newton B. Drury Center, headquarters of the National Park at Crescent City (24 miles south of the Oregon border). Evening programs are scheduled during the summer months.

ACTIVITIES. Field seminars on birds, photography, and park ecosystems are conducted summer weekends; a small fee is charged (write College of the Redwoods, 401 Highway 101 North, Crescent City, CA 95531). Most participants camp in a group, but motels are available.

Orick, a small town close to the Pacific Ocean and 330 miles north of San Francisco (or about 40 miles north of Eureka), is the southern gateway to the park. About ½ mile north, turn onto Bald Hills Road, which passes through a towering stand of redwoods. Park your car 2 miles up and start to walk the **Lady Bird Johnson Grove Trail.** The loop is a mile in length and takes an hour to walk, passing the site where the park was dedicated on November 25, 1968.

The Tall Trees Grove, containing some of the tallest trees on earth, is accessible via shuttle service during summer. The 16-mile ride takes about 30 minutes. The walk from the trailhead to Redwood Creek is mostly downhill, so allow twice the time to hike back. You may want to hike the entire trail, which is one of several backpacking opportunities in the park. The trail is flat and easy, running mostly along Redwood Creek. You can make the round trip in a long day, but

you'll get more out of it in two days, with time to look up to treetops more than 300 feet high. Camping is allowed in the streambed. The trail crosses the creek at several points on footbridges in place during summer months only. Obtain a backcountry permit at the trailhead.

Continuing north, **Prairie Creek State Park** presents a superb botanical garden combining great coastal redwoods, Douglas fir, western hemlock, and Sitka spruce knit together with broad-leafed trees and many flowering plants. Visit the lovely grove dedicated in June 1979 to the memory of Newton and Aubrey Drury, the two brothers who worked tirelessly in the campaign to save the redwoods. The park is almost a rain forest, with up to 100 inches of rain falling mostly in the winter months. More than 20 hiking trails wind among the redwoods here. At least half begin at the trail map at park headquarters. Two campgrounds, Elk Prairie and Gold Bluffs Beach, provide a total of 100 sites (reservations through a Ticketron outlet).

The 1,100-acre Madison Grant Forest lies within the park boundaries. Here about 200 Roosevelt elk roam free. They make excellent picture subjects, but avoid getting too close—for your own good.

The park ranges in elevation from 1,500 feet to sea level. The western slopes drop off abruptly at the **Gold Bluffs,** fronting the Pacific, an area of sand flecked with gold, rugged promontories, and huge waves breaking over the smooth sand beaches. When visiting the ocean section of the national park, always respect the tide, the heavy undertow, and the rocky shoals that make the beach one for watching rather than swimming and surfing. In summer a naturalist program is presented at Prairie Creek.

Driving north on US 101, the Redwood Highway passes through many miles of redwoods. Klamath, midway between Orick and Crescent City, is famous for its steelhead and salmon runs on the Klamath River. Look for the start of the **Coastal Trail** at Lagoon Creek. The trail winds south along the bluffs, through spruce forests, ending high on Requa Hill overlooking the mouth of the Klamath River. This is a choice route for birdwatching, so carry binoculars. You're likely to see cormorants, oystercatchers, several species of gulls, possibly a great blue heron, and little birds called turnstones.

Klamath Beach Road, 11 miles long, covers some spectacular scenery. Fishermen can also try their luck in the numerous streams of **Del Norte Coast Redwoods State Park,** 8 miles south of Crescent City. Del Norte contains four groves of red-

woods, with steep slopes bearing the trees almost to the ocean shore. It is one of the rare places where the natural ecological transition from virgin redwood growth down to a wild ocean shoreline remains essentially undisturbed. Follow Damnation Creek Trail to see this at its best. The park is noted also for the profusion of rhododendron blooming in May and June, in areas easily reached by foot trails. Del Norte has excellent camping facilities at Mill Creek Campground, 1 mile east of US 101. Reservations can be made through Ticketron. Mill Creek, running through the campground, is pleasant for swimming, wading, and trout fishing in season.

A number of small beaches are unsafe for swimming, although the rocky coast, marked by heavy surf, does not discourage surf casters.

The northern boundary of the national park lies on the beautiful Smith River above Crescent City. In **Jedediah Smith State Park** is an outstanding dense forest of redwoods along Mill Creek. Because of its location at the northern edge of the coast redwood belt, this park contains an interesting array of coastal and inland trees, including ponderosa pine, with a lush underbrush of rhododendron, azalea, fern oxalis, salal, and huckleberry. The entire park is laced with trails. **Stout Memorial Grove** has the largest trees in the park, including the 340-foot Stout Tree, which is a giant among giants.

The Smith River in Jedediah Smith State Park has a very long sandy beach for bathing, with a picnic area nearby. To get campsites in the park during summer, arrive early.

Fishing is good for rainbow trout and cutthroats in spring and summer, then for large steelhead and salmon running from October to the end of March.

Bicycling. Avenue of the Giants is the most popular route for cyclists, a scenic alternative to US 101. It extends 28 miles from the Phillipsville exit of US 101 in the south to Pepperwood in the north.

SEASONS. Campgrounds in Prairie Creek State Park usually are filled in summer; a choice time to visit is from Labor Day through early November, when the deciduous trees change color. Birdwatchers should bear in mind that the redwoods lie in the Pacific Flyway, attracting migrants to stop off during spring and autumn migrations. Winter has a special appeal; the moisture-drenched redwoods seem most natural.

FOR FURTHER INFORMATION. Write Superintendent, Redwood National Park, Drawer N, 1111 Second St., Crescent City, CA 95531.

ROCKY MOUNTAIN NATIONAL PARK

Colorado

Established 1915

I LIKE to travel in Rocky Mountain National Park with Enos Mills as my guide. He was more responsible for the park's establishment in 1915 than any other person. He knew and loved the park. He was "the John Muir of the Rockies," spreading national park sentiment everywhere in the country. At the ceremony dedicating the park (September 4, 1915), which Mills organized and supervised, notables and nature enthusiasts were abundant. The event, according to the *Rocky Mountain News*, inspired a rendition of the national anthem "probably never given by so many voices at so high an altitude before."

Two years later, in 1917, Mills published his guidebook, *Your National Parks*. "Magnificent mountains in the sky, peak after peak along the horizon—an inspiring skyline—such is the setting of Rocky Mountain National Park," he wrote. "From one hundred miles distant, out on the plains of Colorado or Wyoming, these snowy, rugged mountain-tops give one a thrill as they appear to join with the clouds and form a horizon that seems to be a part of the scenery of the sky."

The scenery of the sky still prevails. The park embraces the untamed portion of the Front Range, one of the highest regions of the country—rough, spectacular, and noble, deriving its name as the first wave of the Rockies to rise from the central Great Plains.

The valleys are about 8,000 feet above sea level, but within the park are 59 peaks 12,000 feet in elevation or higher. Perpetual snows mantle the highest summits and valley walls, while small glaciers still decorate the heads of some of the high mountain canyons. Highest of all towers Longs Peak, 14,255 feet. A variety of trails make this a "climbing and hiking park." And when you drive to the summit on Trail Ridge Road, in the section between Lava Cliffs and Fall River Pass, you are at a lofty 12,183 feet, as high as a motorist can go anywhere in the national parks.

The park covers 265,193 acres, although Mills wanted it to be much larger. I marvel, on each visit, at the geologic story. One hundred million years ago a great sea covered much of this area, with subtropical forests lining the shores. Gigantic forces within the earth caused an uplifting of the land under the sea. During a long period of upheaval and erosion, another series of uplifts, 40 to 60 million years ago, raised the mountain range still higher, giving the streams vigor to carve deep, sharp valleys. Then, about a million years ago, the Ice Age began and glaciers carved their characteristic U-shaped valleys. They left enormous moraines—deposits of loose rock material—and other evidence of their work. As Mills noted, nowhere in America are glacial records of such prominence more numerous, accessible, and easily read.

At least a thousand years ago Indians passed through, leaving arrow points, hand hammers, and even fragments of crude pottery. Within the past two centuries the park was the haunt of the Utes, then of the Arapahoes, who left their mark in trails still in use.

After the United States acquired the region through the Louisiana Purchase, explorers and adventurers passed near the park. The intrepid John C. Frémont made two expeditions, in 1843 and 1844, and Francis Parkman was there in 1846. In 1859, during the Colorado Gold Rush, Joel Estes visited the area and the following year settled his family in the grassy meadow now known as Estes Park. An Irish nobleman, the Earl of Dunraven, fell in love with this magnificent country in 1872 and resolved to build a great estate and game preserve. Through his feudal regime, many beauty spots were preserved. He publicized the region and entertained Albert Bierstadt, the celebrated artist of classic Rocky Mountain landscapes. During the 1880s a mining boom occurred in the area that is now the west side of the park; prospectors filed claims and operated out of little settlements like Lulu City, Dutchtown, and Teller, but they found little pay dirt, and the boom soon collapsed.

Forests and wildflowers on the mountain flanks reflect the story of the struggle of earth forces and the adjustment to varied environments. At the summits, tiny dwarf plants of the alpine tundra, like those of the arctic tundra in Siberia and northern Alaska, cluster densely together and carry the banners of life high above tree line. Far below, pines, blue spruce, and aspen thrive in the sheltered valleys.

Between the two extremes, some 750 kinds of plants are spread over the wide range of elevations, soils, and exposures to the sun and moisture.

The lofty rocks are the natural home of bighorn, or mountain, sheep—powerful, agile animals that symbolize Rocky Mountain National Park. You may also see elk, beaver, golden eagles, and hawks, depending on where you are and how perceptively you look. Bear in mind that the mountains are still their dwelling place and humans the outsiders.

I enjoy looking for different species of birds in different sites and different seasons. The rose-finch and ptarmigan live year-round near the snow line above the limits of tree growth. During flower-filled, sun-flooded days of June, while evening shadows cross the openings, the beautiful silvery notes of the hermit thrush mingle with the wild surroundings. In

June, too, the cheerful water ouzel carols intensely by its chosen home along the mountain streams. It's wise to carry a bird guide, considering that about 150 species dwell in, or visit, the park.

And there are butterflies, too. On a recent summer while coming down a trail in the tundra, hikers were excited by a number of "black butterflies." It proved to be a swarm of Magdalena Alpine, *Erebia magdalena*, the only pure, velvety black butterfly in North America, known to frequent high, precarious rockslides above timberline (usually over 10,000 feet) in a few western states. Collectors and watchers travel many miles, sometimes risking their lives while treading treacherous scree, to encounter these black beauties. While *Erebia magdalena* is normally a rare sight, denied to all but the agile, here was a swarm flitting from rock to rock within 10 feet of a parking lot.

THE PRACTICAL GUIDE

BACKGROUND. Stay three or four days to sample the highlights, longer for a mountain vacation, at one of the campgrounds or resorts in the area. However, if you are in Denver (65 miles away) with time to spare, take a bus tour (or rent a car) and head for the gateway of Estes Park and the Trail Ridge Road.

Gear your pace to change in elevation. At high altitudes the atmosphere is thinner than at sea level, increasing the work of heart and lungs. Motoring and normal sightseeing cause little problem, but strenuous hiking and climbing can, unless you are in prime condition. If you have a heart condition, do not overexert. Even climbers should start slowly, acclimating to 7,500 and 8,500 feet before heading for 12,000.

Trail Ridge Road climbs 5,000 feet on its winding course from Estes Park, at the east entrance, to the crest of the Front Range, then descends 4,000 feet to Grand Lake at the west entrance; yet this modern, high 44-mile road, following an ancient Indian trail over the Continental Divide, is comfortable and safe all the way. Dress warmly; while the air is light and dry, you are entering a cold-climate zone. Allow a minimum of three hours for the drive.

However you travel, whether by car, foot, or horseback, take note of changes in plant life from the valleys to the high peaks. At lower elevations the climate is relatively warm and dry. Open stands of ponderosa pine and juniper grow on slopes facing the sun, while on the cooler north slopes Douglas fir is mixed with them. Along the streamsides you'll see blue spruce. On drier sites you'll see dense stands of lodgepole pine. Look for the lovely groves of aspen, with leaves that tremble in the wind and turn a golden yellow in autumn. Allow plenty of

time to walk trails in meadows and glades where wildflowers carpet the ground, among them Rocky Mountain iris, pasqueflower, and penstemon.

Above 9,000 feet or so, cool dark forests of Engelmann spruce, subalpine fir, and limber pine dominate the scene, while luxuriant wildflower gardens spread over the forest floor. The beautiful blue Colorado columbine is particularly abundant in this subalpine zone, especially on rockslides (although found in all zones of the park). Unfortunately, the columbine has become scarce in many areas of the state through thoughtless picking and digging, which is now prohibited by law. As you near timberline, where cold winds constantly blow, note how the trees became twisted, bending with the wind and hugging the ground.

Presently trees give way to alpine tundra, open expanses of grasses, mosses, and lichens characteristic of the Arctic. These plants grow close to the ground, their way of surviving the desiccating winds. They flower brightly and produce seeds quickly during the brief summer, then take on autumnal colors of choice beauty. Trail Ridge Road takes you through 11 miles of the tundra world above tree line.

VISITOR CENTERS. Approaching from Estes Park, the **park headquarters**, a beautiful low building of reddish-pink stone, houses an audio-visual program and relief model of the park. If coming from the west, start at the **Public Information Building** or the **Kawuneeche Visitor Center** near the Grand Lake entrance. These are both open all year. Two others (Moraine Park Museum on Bear Lake Road and Alpine Visitor Center on Trail Ridge Road) are open summers only.

ACTIVITIES. Sightseeing. From park

headquarters you may decide to go up the old **Fall River Road,** narrow, winding, and completely safe if you stick to the 15-mile speed limit; it is intended for sightseeing and picture-taking at a leisurely pace. It joins the main road at Fall River Pass (so you can make a loop tour from Estes Park). If you go the main route, from Many Parks Curve you see the whole central and eastern portions, dominated by Longs Peak. From **Rainbow Curve,** the Mummy Range is visible to the north and the Great Plains to the east. Soon you rise above timberline where fir, pine, and spruce covering yield to rock and tundra, and reach the 4-mile section above 12,000 feet—one of the world's unforgettable motoring experiences. From **Rock Cut,** you get superlative views of glacial-carved peaks along the Continental Divide. From the lower end of the parking area, take the one-hour round trip by trail to the **Toll Memorial,** in the center of tundra meadowlands.

Continuing on the western side, at **Milner Pass,** 10,759 feet, you cross the Continental Divide, the backbone of North America. From Kawuneeche Valley, the road follows the Colorado River to **Grand Lake,** largest natural lake in Colorado.

Living history. In 1974 the nationally famous Never Summer Ranch, one of Colorado's first dude ranches, became the first living history exhibit in the park. At the end of 1973, John G. Holzwarth, Jr., the popular proprietor, closed the 800-acre ranch and sold it to the government for a modest price, rather than make an easy fortune from developers. The ranch lies 9,000 feet high in the Kawuneeche Valley between the Continental Divide and Never Summer Mountains. When you visit the homestead you'll be walking 50 years into the past. Another worthwhile site, the **Old MacGregor Ranch,** is on a scenic easement to the park, at the edge of Estes Park. Lurilla MacGregor willed, when she died in 1970, that the ranch continue raising cattle as "an educational and charitable institution." Here visitors can see a vignette of the past, while black angus cattle graze in a mountain meadow.

Hiking and climbing. Over 300 miles of trail thread the park to the famous and lesser-known scenic points. Some are designed for a half-hour's leisurely walk, others for strenuous exploring.

The **Five Senses Trail,** built by the Youth Conservation Corps at the edge of Sprague Lake, makes a lovely scene accessible to the handicapped; it also encourages sensitivity and observation by everyone.

The energetic hiker who wants to become a climber does well to take a few lessons from the Colorado Mountain School, an approved park concession (351 Moraine Avenue, Estes Park, CO 80517). For any hike to the summit of Longs Peak (8 miles from Longs Peak Campground), check first at the Longs Peak ranger station and be sure to sign out and in on the trail register. A bivouac permit must be obtained at park headquarters or the ranger station by all planning overnight climbs. Severe storms come quickly in the mountains, surprising climbers unused to the Rockies. Rangers require that you never climb alone, always attempt routes within your ability, and turn back when adverse weather or exhaustion threatens. Following this advice

assures that you will climb again.

Five small glaciers still exist in the park as a result of strong winter winds from the west, which drift dry, powdery snow into the heads of canyons on the east slope, where they accumulate. These drift glaciers are different from the large alpine glaciers of Mount Rainier, Olympic, and North Cascades National Parks in Washington State, where the snowfall is heavy; but they do move at the rate of about three feet a year and develop crevasses late in summer.

Andrews Glacier can be reached by a fairly strenuous hike of about 4 miles; Andrews Tarn, at the foot of the glacier, is milky in appearance because of the pulverized rock carried by meltwater. The other glaciers can't be reached by trail, but take

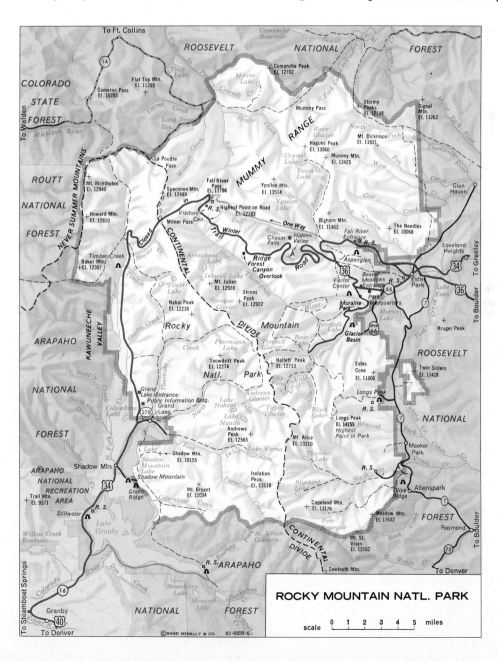

ROCKY MOUNTAIN NATL. PARK

scale 0 1 2 3 4 5 miles

the 5-mile hike from Bear Lake to Flattop Mountain to view Tyndall Glacier, which lies between Hallett Peak and Flattop.

Trail riding. Most trails in the park can be traveled on horseback, including the **Flattop Trail,** a good day's ride across the Continental Divide between Estes Park and Grand Lake. A number of livery stables adjacent to the park have horses and guides available for pack trips in the high country. Horses may also be rented from a livery concession at Glacier Basin and Moraine Park within the park.

Naturalist program. To really know the fascinating natural history of these mountains, join one or more of the many hikes led by ranger-naturalists. These trips range from two hours to all day and open a new world of understanding. The naturalist will show where and how to look for beavers building dams, will help identify some of the birds of the park, and will try to bring you within sight of mule deer grazing at the edge of forest or on the tundra. Campfire programs, usually illustrated with slides or film, are held at the main campgrounds and park headquarters. Moraine Park and Alpine Visitor Centers have interpretive museums. The building at Moraine Park is worthy of attention in its own right. Dating from 1923, it was part of a popular summer resort, one of a number scattered over the mountains that have been acquired by the national park.

Summer seminars. Sessions of a weekend and one week in ecology, geology, botany, photography, archaeology, and biology are conducted in cooperation with Colorado State University and the University of Northern Colorado. These are professionally taught and offered for college credit (Rocky Mountain Nature Association, Inc., Rocky Mountain National Park, Estes Park, CO 80517).

Birdwatching. Conducted bird walks, talks, and evening programs for beginning birdwatchers are scheduled regularly three or four times weekly on the east and west sides of the park. Take advantage of these opportunities. June is a choice month to watch birds, since they are breeding and establishing territories. Pick up a copy of *Birds of Rocky Mountain National Park,* by Allegra Collister.

Bicycling. Three routes are open from the end of May to mid-October: Bear Lake Road (8 miles); Trail Ridge Road (18 miles); and Horseshoe Park/Estes Park Loop (16 miles). Trail Ridge is the toughest, but all have steep uphill climbs. Auto exhaust fumes can be a problem, especially in late afternoon. Keen cyclists will find challenge and reward.

Fishing. Fishing season is open year-round, except as posted. A Colorado fishing license is required, but special fishing regulations apply in the park. Familiarize yourself with these before you fish.

Photography. The most spectacular scenery of snow-crowned mountains faces the east, so morning light is best at most locations. The west side is good for pictures of streams, lakes, and ranches.

TOURS. Circle bus trips are conducted from Denver during the summer travel season by Estes Park Bus Company. The most popular is the 240-mile, two-day loop to Estes Park, over Trail Ridge Road to Grand Lake (overnight stop), then returning to Denver over Berthoud Pass, twice crossing the Continental Divide. This company also makes connections at Denver with airlines, railroads, and buses for service to the park area. Sightseeing trips in the park are scheduled daily during summer by the Estes Park Bus Company and the Rocky Mountain Park Company.

ACCOMMODATIONS. The two principal tourist centers are the villages of Estes Park and Grand Lake, which provide a full range of hotels, motels, and cottages. If you want to try the informal ways of the Rockies, you may want a dude ranch vacation. For a list of ranches near the park, write Colorado Dude and Guest Ranch Association, Box 6440, Cherry Creek Station, Denver, CO 80206. Families should consider the Estes Park Center, YMCA of the Rockies (Estes Park, CO 80511-2800), covering 1,400 acres and bordered on three sides by the national park. It includes 220 rustic but modernized rental cabins and lodges, plus varied recreation facilities and activities.

CAMPING. Campgrounds have seven-day limits, except Longs Peak, where the limit is three days. No electric or shower facilities are available. The largest and most developed are at Glacier Basin, Aspenglen, and Moraine Park on Bear Lake Road. Timber Creek Campground, on the western slope, has similar facilities (fireplaces, flush-type comfort stations, running water, picnic tables). Longs Peak is popular with those who plan to ascend the mountain. Trailers are permitted in all but Longs Peak, which is for tent camping only. There are numerous trail camps. Permits are required for backcountry camping and bivouac climbs.

Glacier Basin campsites are available for summer use, through Ticketron outlets.

SEASONS. Spring reaches the lower altitudes in late April and advances upward in ensuing weeks. The scheduled official opening of Trail Ridge Road is Memorial Day. Sometimes it opens earlier, sometimes on that day, but then may be closed for a week by snow. Summer is the peak season, the time to enjoy the high country with its brilliant skies, warm sun, and sparkling streams. The state flower, Colorado columbine, is found in bloom June through August, depending on location, amidst a myriad of other wildflowers. September is a superb month in the Rockies, a time of clear, crisp days when aspens glitter golden on the hills. With good fortune you may hear a bull elk bugling and catch a glimpse of one on a hilltop with his handsome rack sharply outlined against a blue sky. Reduced rates are offered during autumn at many ranches. Winter activities (mid-December to mid-April) are centered at Hidden Valley, 10 miles west of Estes Park. The area is open every day. Activities include skiing, ice skating, platter sliding, and snowshoeing.

Ski touring. The three most popular areas are Bear Lake, the glacier basin of Sprague Lake, and Wild Basin. Detailed maps are available from park rangers or in Estes Park. Ski rentals, instruction, and guide service are provided by Colorado Mountain School (351 Moraine Avenue), Rocky Mountain Ski Tours (156 Elkhorn Avenue), and elsewhere in Estes Park and other communities.

NEARBY. Bordering the park on the east, northeast, and south, **Arapaho-Roosevelt National Forest** comprises almost 800,000 acres, with good campgrounds, choice lake and stream fishing, and active glaciers accessible by trail. Unique off-the-highway tours operate from Estes Park in four-wheel-drive vehicles to the forest observation tower at Panorama Peak, overlooking the Great Plains and mountain ranges extending from Wyoming to New Mexico. Big Thompson Canyon lies on US 34, the main road from Estes Park to Loveland; for 16 miles the road is flanked by a foaming, roaring stream and rugged rock walls. Across the Divide, bordering the southwest corner of the park, **Arapaho National Recreation Area** complements majestic natural beauty with a scenic lake and mountain playground. Formerly known as Shadow Mountain National Recreation Area, it was administered by the national park until 1979. It is now a unit of Arapaho-Roosevelt National Forest.

Man-made reservoirs, Lake Granby and Shadow Mountain Lake are linked by channel to Grand Lake to form the "Great Lakes" of Colorado. This area offers camping, riding, swimming, fishing, boating, and sightseeing boat cruises. Guided tours at the **Granby Pumping Plant** on Lake Granby unfold the story of the Colorado/Big Thompson Project, which diverts water via 13 miles of tunnel from the western slope under the great peaks of the park for irrigation and hydroelectric power in eastern Colorado; power lines and terminals of the tunnel were kept outside the park.

FOR FURTHER INFORMATION. Write Superintendent, Rocky Mountain National Park, Estes Park, CO 80517.

SEQUOIA and KINGS CANYON NATIONAL PARKS

California

Established 1890 and 1940

MY FRIEND Marvin Jensen and I headed by car for the trailhead at Mineral King. It was only 25 miles from Three Rivers, but a long drive, winding and climbing along the East Fork of the Kaweah River, on a road built by miners over a century ago. We stopped for lunch at Silver City, a little settlement at 6,900 feet, a gateway to the high valley that recalled the early days. For a few short years in the late 1870s Mineral King promised to become another Comstock Lode, a mountain of rich silver ore. Prospectors scrambled over the peaks and staked their claims, without finding much metal.

But I found what I was looking for—a thoroughly challenging and stimulating national park experience, hiking and backpacking in an area only recently added to Sequoia National Park. A little strange, perhaps, considering that Sequoia, the second oldest national park (second only to Yellowstone), was established in 1890. Both Sequoia and adjacent Kings Canyon were set aside to preserve groves of giant sequoia trees, the largest of living things, remnants of once widespread forests that covered a great portion of the northern hemisphere. The two parks, which are administered as one, do much more. Stretching 65 miles from north to south, they protect an unbroken wilderness of granite peaks, gorges, rockbound glacial lakes, flowering alpine meadows, and virgin forests. The parks comprise, for me, the heart of the Sierra Nevada, the country's highest mountain range this side of Alaska, a jagged crest extending from the Cascades southward for some 400 miles, with elevations from 7,000 to 14,000 feet.

In 1978 Congress added Mineral King Valley to Sequoia National Park. The beautiful alpine valley's high peaks, lakes, and clear streams are protected and preserved; so are its rare wildlife species, including peregrine falcon, bighorn sheep, spotted owl, and pine marten.

It was now June 1985. A few years before, I traveled with my friend Marv down the Colorado River through Grand Canyon National Park, when he was stationed there. He was strong, agile, and tireless. Once we took off from the Mineral King trailhead at 7,500 feet, the steep climb, high elevation, and loaded pack meant nothing to him. There was no easy route to the alpine lakes basin, but he chose the toughest unmaintained trail leading to the Mosquito Lakes. We reached the first lake, surrounded by a red fir forest, and kept climbing the chaparral slopes flecked with wildflowers, finally stopping to camp on the rocks overlooking the middle lake, the second of three.

Next morning Marv proposed climbing the trailless flank of the high ridge between the Mosquito Lakes Basin and the Eagle Lake Range. It was a forbidding challenge that I would never attempt on my own; with a patient guide and friend, however, I dared to meet the challenge. Besides, the country was irresistible—with granite peaks, gorges, canyons, and meadows, expansive and wild. Once on top, we dropped our packs and advanced up the rocky, knife-edged ridge. Marv indeed knew where we were going, for presently we intercepted the trail to Eagle Lake, at about 11,000 feet. Descending from the ridge on the Eagle Lake side, after picking up our packs, should have been easier, but the slope was steep and rocky, with narrow ledges and loose, sliding material. Yet there was chaparral in the rock, abundant with blooming wildflowers, including rein orchis, Indian paintbrush, shooting stars, and leopard lily.

During our pilgrimage of two nights and three days, we saw few people. Perhaps that's how it should be. That country needs to be used lightly to be understood and loved, to impart the feeling of freedom, and the confidence and control that I shared with my friend on the trail.

I spent another day on my own, revisiting well-established portions of the park. Before walking the easy trails in Giant Forest, I read a few pages of John Muir's *Summering in the Sierra*. It recounted his adventures of 1875, when he studied the sequoia belt. Muir faced hard mountaineering before the winter storms, but was confident. "I will make a way, and love of King Sequoia will make all labor light." With Muir as guide and companion, the mind becomes receptive to more than the eyes can see. At Giant Forest, I recalled Muir's description of "giants grouped in pure temple groves." These trees grow naturally in about 75 separate locations along the western Sierra

slope, but Giant Forest is the largest of them all, enhanced by mild winters and gentle terrain. The giant sequoia (*Sequoiadendron giganteum*) and its relative the coastal redwood (*Sequoia sempervirens*) are the last surviving species of a large genus of ancient times. The redwood, growing near the Pacific Ocean in a more or less continuous belt 450 miles long, is the world's tallest tree, with a relatively slender trunk, while the giant sequoia is the world's largest tree in *volume*, with an immense trunk and very slight taper. In fact, the entrance to the finest part of Giant Forest is guarded by the General Sherman Tree, the world's largest living creature, at least 2,500 to 3,000 years old, 272 feet tall, and at least 32 feet in diameter at the base.

Beneath the giant sequoia, the forest floor is often covered with lupine, dogwood, hazelnut, chinquapin, and willow, creating a contrast of color in dark groves. Magnificent stands of sugar pine, sometimes attaining a base diameter of 11 feet with finely tapered trunk rising more than 200 feet, ponderosa and Jeffrey pine, white and shasta fir, and incense cedar also thrive here. But the sequoias, massive and vigorous, tower above all as patriarchs of the forest community. They can be seen now as John Muir found them here.

The high country constitutes a vast region of unbroken wilderness, providing one of the outstanding experiences of the National Park System. Motorists can glimpse the wild country from overlooks, but by foot or horse trail you put yourself into the midst of canyons, rivers, lakes, and meadows, as well as high on the Sierra Crest, ranging in elevation from 11,000 feet to the 14,495-foot summit of Mount Whitney. The hiker's principal boulevard is the John Muir Trail, which runs 218 miles from Yosemite Valley down through two national parks and three national forests. These areas preserve the feeling of the original California, the country where Indians roamed and fished, and where the Spaniards gazed on the plunging waters of the Kings River and named it *Rio de los Santos Reyes*—River of the Holy Kings.

THE PRACTICAL GUIDE

BACKGROUND. One can hike or ride for days on end without retracing his course. However, Sequoia and Kings Canyon offer choice opportunities to get started in wilderness backpacking on weekends. Even if you're not going to the backcountry, allow at least two or three days.

Note the four key centers of activity and plan activities at and from them: **Giant Forest/Lodgepole,** in Sequoia National Park; **Grant Grove,** preserving the General Grant Grove of sequoias in Kings Canyon National Park; **Cedar Grove,** where the South Fork of the Kings River flows between massive granite walls, also in Kings Canyon National Park; and **Mineral King,** at the end of a long, winding road in Sequoia National Park, definitely for the backcountry traveler.

ACCESS. From mid-May to late October, Guest Services provides bus transportation from Fresno airport, rail, and bus depots. Stops in the park are at Grant Grove, Lodgepole, and Giant Forest (phone 209/ 565-3373).

VISITOR CENTERS. If you must approach via the Ash Mountain entrance, the first center is one mile east, a good spot to get your bearings. During your stay, allow time to visit the Grant Grove and Lodgepole Visitor Centers and absorb the displays on the story of the trees and the geology of the parks. Make the most of guided walks and talks.

BACKGROUND. Giant Forest embraces all phases of the giant sequoias within a small area, from tiny saplings to giants which have lived their lives and now, toppled by some wintry blast, lie with roots uptorn. The growth is dense: eight sequoias can be counted within a radius of 50 feet, and four others, perhaps four feet in diameter, within a radius of 25 feet.

General Sherman Tree, the largest of living trees, is in Giant Forest near the Generals Highway. It is approximately 275 feet tall and 102.6 feet in circumference; there are taller trees, but none of such bulk. To protect the tree, the Park Service has built a wooden fence around it, a gentle reminder that damage possibly can occur from heavy human impact. Actually, the beauty of the tree is best appreciated when viewed from a point where the visitor's eye can encompass its great size. Trees such as this continue to reproduce themselves, and thousands of young sequoias grow in favorable localities throughout the park, their lovely cone-shaped forms seeming like a mass of Christmas trees.

Within easy driving or walking distance of Giant Forest are a number of notable sights. **Moro Rock,** 2 miles by road or trail, is one of the great monoliths of the Sierra Nevada. From its top, or even its slopes, you can see both the ridges of the Sierra's backbone at the horizon and the silvery Kaweah River, 4,000 feet below and almost straight down. Not far away, in **Crescent Meadow,** an easy trail leads to **Tharp's Log,** headquarters of the pioneer white man of Giant Forest, Hale Tharp, who had been guided up the mountains by Indians. He built a cabin in a fallen sequoia log, which Muir called a "noble den." Make it to **Beetle Rock** and **Sunset Rock** at sunset for views to remember. If you don't mind a ½-mile downhill hike from the parking area, and back up again, you can visit **Crystal Cave,** a small but beautiful marble cavern, open during the summer. Tours are provided.

Generals Highway, a scenic drive worthy of the superb country, connects the two parks, running 47 miles from California 198 at Ash Mountain in Sequoia to California 180 at Grant Grove in Kings Canyon. It is open all year.

General Grant Tree, from which Grant Grove takes its name, is second in size to the General Sherman, measuring 267 feet tall with a circumference of 107.6 feet. The **Robert E. Lee Tree** in the same grove is almost as large. A few minutes' drive leads to **Big Stump Basin,** filled with ghostly reminders of early logging. The **Hart Tree** (277.9 feet tall), stands in the **Redwood Mountain Grove,** west of the Generals Highway.

Cedar Grove, center of activity in Kings Canyon, is reached from General Grant Grove, on California 180, on a 28-mile drive through Sequoia National Forest and along the South Fork of the Kings River. The road descends through open country and past hillsides, then into the river canyon. From an overlook you can watch the brawling waters of the South and Middle Forks form their junction. Beyond, one canyon vista succeeds another until the highway crosses the river at Boyden's Cave; then the route closely follows the foaming river. Six miles past Cedar Grove Ranger Station, the road ends at Copper Creek, or Roads End, beneath solid granite walls, one of the take-off points for the great expanse of high mountain country, which makes up more than four-fifths of the area of these two parks.

ACTIVITIES. Hiking. Trips of a single day and outstanding character can be made from Giant Forest, Crescent Meadow, Lodgepole Campground, Dorst Campground, and Roads End. **Twin Lakes,** reached from Lodgepole, are famous for their unsurpassed setting at an elevation of 9,500 feet; if you have the time, Silliman Pass is worth the extra climb.

Bearpaw Meadow, elevation 7,800 feet, is the destination of a choice overnight trip from Giant Forest, a distance of 11 miles over the **High Sierra Trail,** a close rival of the John Muir Trail for outstanding scenery. Travel light and rent a tent cabin with meals provided (advance reservations), or pitch your own tent. The High Sierra Trail joins the John Muir Trail at Wallace Creek, 37 miles east of Bearpaw, offering many possibilities for side trips into the Great Western Divide country—Big Arroyo, Kern Canyon, and Mount Whitney.

Mineral King Valley is 25 miles east of Three Rivers. Facilities are rustic and limited; trails rise sharply from the valley floor—already 7,500 feet above sea level. Its timberline peaks, sub-alpine meadows, and surrounding lake reward you with astonishing beauty.

Backcountry is accessible over about 800 miles of trail, via 28 trail entrances. Travel leisurely; relax, fish, and enjoy nature along the way. By so doing you avoid overexertion in the rugged terrain and high altitude. Most backcountry trails are snow-covered until late May. Wilderness permits are required for overnight camping and some trails have limited access. Plan your trip and make reservations at least two weeks in advance. Before starting out, check with a ranger so that someone knows where you are and when to expect you back.

Horseback trips over the hundreds of miles of pack trails are popular. Saddle horses are for rent in Giant Forest, General Grant Grove, Cedar Grove, Owens Valley, and Mineral King.

Many people enter the high country from Owens Valley, east of the Sierra. From Lone Pine, a road leads to **Whitney Portal,** elevation 8,367 feet, closest point by road to Mount Whitney, and the location of a pack

station. The trail up is considered fairly easy, but it is a long trip. The Mount Whitney Trail is limited to 75 persons a day; reserve space in advance (Mount Whitney Ranger District, U.S. Forest Service, Box 8, Lone Pine, CA 93545; 619/876-5542). Many other mountains in the two parks are popular with climbers, too, but consult with a park ranger before starting; hikers can become injured, or get seriously ill from altitude sickness.

Fishing. There are 800 miles of stream and 500 lakes, many with rainbow and eastern brook trout. The headwaters of the Kern are the native habitat of the highly prized California golden. Buy a state fishing license at stores.

Streams are usually very cold, swift, and powerful, and surrounding rocks are slippery; therefore, **swimming** can be dangerous. Be especially careful of children, who tend to underestimate the power of moving water.

Skiing. Giant Forest Village and Grant Grove Village are the main centers of cross-country ski activity. The Wolverton ski bowl is a great spot for family fun. A favorite trail for skiers and snowshoers follows an unplowed road from Giant Forest Village to sequoias in Crescent Meadow, with a stop at Moro Rock on the way. Temperatures are just above freezing during the day. Ski shops have rental equipment.

ACCOMMODATIONS. Facilities inside the park cover a wide range, not including luxury. Giant Forest Lodge has cottages and tent cabins. Nearby Camp Kaweah has a motel, cottages, and housekeeping cabins with and without bath. Grant Grove Lodge has cottages and tent cabins; Bearpaw Meadow Camp has tent cabins and family style meals. Reservations at all sites are recommended (Sequoia and Kings Canyon Guest Services, Sequoia National Park, CA 93262; 209/565-3373). You can also stay at one of the several motels at Three Rivers, western gateway to the park. M Bar J Guest Ranch features trail riding (into the park), square dancing, and meals cooked with local foods (Box 121-G, Badger, CA 93603).

CAMPING. Campgrounds at Lodgepole, Dorst Creek, Grant Grove, and Cedar Grove are well developed. Lodgepole is best suited to trailers, though it has no electric or sewer connections. Occupancy is limited to 14 days, and in summer it operates on a strict reservation basis. Reservations are

available through Ticketron for Lodgepole; all others operate on a first-come, first-served basis.

SEASONS. Most accommodations in the park are open mid-May to mid-September and some until late October. Limited facilities are open at Giant Forest and Grant Grove all year. Entrances to the high mountain passes are seldom open before July 1, but the General Grant Grove section and Giant Forest area are open all year, and roads generally are kept clear in winter. In winter the giant sequoias are draped with snowlike candelabra and express a liveliness that contrasts with their somber summers. Though most visitors come during the summer, an equally good time to visit is in April and May, when the foothills are covered with flowering redbud, buckeye, and laurel. However, spring weather is very changeable. Storms can bring fresh snow in mid-May. If heading for the high country, prepare for everything from sunshine to blizzard. During autumn, dogwood, aspen, and oak enliven the landscape with their brilliant foliage.

NEARBY. More than 50 camping and picnic sites are located in **Sequoia National Forest,** which lies adjacent to the two national parks on the west. **Hume Lake,** on CA 180 north of General Grant Village, offers recreational facilities, including swimming. **Stony Creek Campground,** lodge, and service station are convenient to Kings Canyon National Park, south of Grant Grove on the Generals Highway. High mountain lakes and streams noted for golden trout enhance the forest's beauty. On the east side of the park, **Inyo National Forest** has nearly 900 natural lakes set among granite peaks towering from 12,000 to 14,000 feet. From **Big Pine** a road leads west to Palisades Glaciers, a mass of living ice flush against Bishop Pass in Kings Canyon. In contrast to this high, cool country, only 80 miles to the east of Mount Whitney is the lowest point in the Western Hemisphere, Bad Water, in **Death Valley National Monument** astride the California—Nevada boundary.

RECOMMENDED READING. *Summering in the Sierra,* by John Muir. *Starr's Guide to the John Muir Trail* and *Backpacking in the Sierra Nevada. Discovering Sierra Trees,* by Stephen F. Arno.

FOR FURTHER INFORMATION. Write Superintendent, Sequoia and Kings Canyon National Parks, Three Rivers, CA 93271.

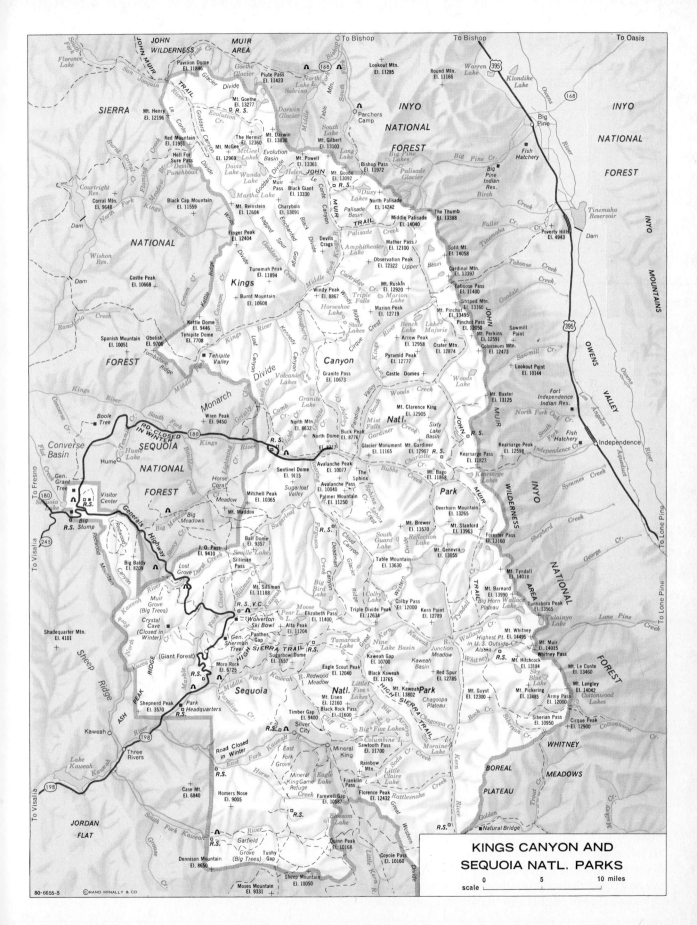

KINGS CANYON AND
SEQUOIA NATL. PARKS

0   5   10 miles
scale

80-6655-5   ©Rand McNally & Co.

133

SHENANDOAH NATIONAL PARK

Virginia

Authorized 1926

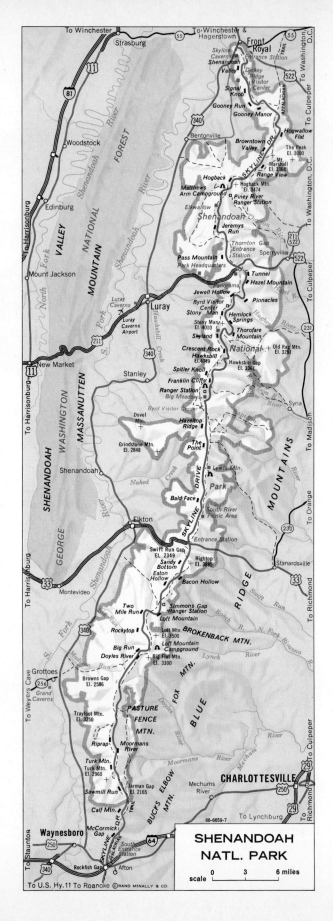

I WAS overnighting at Skyland, once a private resort and now part of the concession operation in the national park, and I thought of how particular individuals had influenced the park. That afternoon, I had stopped at the Harry F. Byrd, Sr. Visitor Center, named for the prominent Virginia governor and U.S. senator who knew Shenandoah National Park intimately. Byrd was a self-avowed mountain lover. He climbed every peak in the park, and his favorite peak, Old Rag, once a year. "In the tragedies and other strains of our modern world," he wrote, "generations to come will receive a peace of mind and new hopes in lifting their eyes to the peaks and canyons of the Shenandoah National Park."

That prophecy has already come true. Shenandoah National Park is a natural refuge of hills of hardwood and pine forests, and open meadows, with vistas of gentle valleys and mountains beyond them. Though deep in the Blue Ridge Mountains of Virginia, the park lies but 75 miles from the nation's capital, and less than one day's drive from New York, Cleveland, or Charleston, SC. To the populated East, it provides the chance to find peace of mind and inspiration.

Sixty mountain peaks, ranging from 2,000 to over 4,000 feet, reach up to blend their gentle summits with the billows of bluish haze that give the mountains their name.

While at Skyland, I thought of the alliance between Byrd and George Freeman Pollock, the colorful owner of this mountaintop resort. Pollock, a born naturalist, had come to the Blue Ridge from Washington, DC, in the 1890s, starting with a tent camp, then log cottages. Byrd first came to Skyland in 1907, when it could only be reached by horseback or buckboard. His father owned a cottage there, which he gave the future governor as a wedding present. Without the love and concern for the mountains of these two men, the national park might never have come into being.

134

When Pollock Knob was dedicated in October 1951, the *Washington Evening Star* editorialized: "Mr. Pollock loved the Appalachians and it was his vision of their permanent value to successive generations that finally led to the Shenandoah Park's being set aside as a permanent recreational property of the whole Federal commonwealth."

The highlands of Shenandoah (meaning "Daughter of the Stars" in an Indian tongue) are part of the same Appalachian range that stretches to the Acadian hills of the Northeast. Skyline Drive is a lofty vantage point for viewing the panoramas of the Shenandoah Valley, or Valley of Virginia, to the west, and the rolling hills of the Piedmont Plateau to the east. For a distance of 105 miles, this scenic route stretches like a ribbon down a bright tapestry, crossing and recrossing the ridgetop. In precolonial times, game and Indian trails ran along this crest, and by the time of the Revolution, the beauty of the Shenandoah area in the Blue Ridge was known to Americans. The nine years of labor that went into construction of the drive forged the first link of a longer mountaintop boulevard that continues southward for almost 500 miles over the Blue Ridge Parkway to the Smokies.

Though the land is ancient, establishment of the national park is fairly recent. Shenandoah was first approved by Congress in 1926, when Acadia was the only national park east of the Mississippi. But complete acceptance depended upon the people of Virginia acquiring the land and deeding it to the federal government. Unlike the western parks, these were not public lands, but privately owned, mostly by struggling mountain folk. It took almost ten years, but individuals like Pollock sparked enthusiasm and energy to make this beautiful highland a gift to the nation. Even a president's personal landholding—Herbert Hoover's fishing camp on the Rapidan—became part of the park.

I like to hike to Camp Hoover from Big Meadows wayside (a little more than six miles round trip, but easy and scenic all the way). The camp is surprisingly simple, but it served Hoover's purpose. He enjoyed the region, where he could fish the quiet pools and riffles in the streams. Today the park is a hiker's paradise, with 500 miles of trails, including part of the Appalachian Trail. It is a delight for birdwatchers, who can find more than 200 species at one time or another during the year, and for wildflower enthusiasts, who may identify as many as 80 flowering plants in a day's walk.

THE PRACTICAL GUIDE

BACKGROUND. You could easily cover the full length of Skyline Drive in a day, but you would miss the meaning of it. Stay at least one or two nights at a lodge, motel, or campground. Drive within the speed limit (35 mph) for both touring enjoyment and safety. Allow time to stop at overlooks and to sample the trails.

ACCESS. Four main entrances lead to the park and Skyline Drive, including the north entrance at Front Royal; Thornton Gap, between Luray and Sperryville; Swift Run Gap, between Stanardsville and Elkton; and the south entrance, the link with the Blue Ridge Parkway, at Rockfish Gap, between Charlottesville and Waynesboro. Seventy-five parking overlooks give plenty of opportunity to observe the mountain slopes and surroundings in all their moods. From **Hogback Overlook,** on a clear day, you can count 11 bends in the Shenandoah River.

VISITOR CENTERS. If you enter from the north, stop at **Dickey Ridge Visitor Center,** where exhibits describe park attractions and facilities. Also visit the **Byrd Visitor**

Center at Big Meadows. It interprets the culture of the colorful, hardy mountaineers who lived in the park area.

ACTIVITIES. Trail trips. A variety of short trail trips enables intimate contact with park features. From Skyland, you can hike the 1½-mile round trip **Stony Man Nature Trail.** This leisurely path leads through a cross section of the nearly 100 species of trees in the park. It ascends the slopes of Stony Man Mountain to its craggy 4,010-foot summit. The 5-mile hike (allow half a day) to **Whiteoak Canyon** begins just south of Skyland, taking visitors through an ancient hemlock forest into a wild, water-splashed garden of rock, vines, and shrubs. Five miles farther south, the **Hawksbill Mountain Trail** (2 miles round trip) leads to the highest point in the park, 4,049 feet above sea level, clothed in remnants of a spruce-fir forest. From Big Meadows, trails lead to waterfalls and other points of interest. The trail to **Old Rag Mountain** leads to the most spectacular, fascinating peak in the park. It lies east of the main Blue Ridge chain, an imposing mass of granite, with a rocky, boulder-

strewn ridgecrest nearly 5 miles long. Hikers love it because of unique Ridge Trail, which winds around massive boulders for more than a mile, and even through a cave, before reaching the summit with expansive views in all directions. The 7.7-mile circuit hike is tough and takes a full day. The starting point for the hike, at the little town of Nethers (near Sperryville), is a drive of 30 miles from Skyland, 40 miles from Big Meadows. To reach **Hoover Camp** on the Rapidan River, where the president's old lodge and a caretaker's cabin have been restored, start at Big Meadows wayside, just past milepost 51. The circuit hike, a little over 6 miles long, is easy and scenic.

The Appalachian Trail follows the mountain crest for 94 miles through the park, with numerous spur trails. It is possible to take the trail in large or small measure. Park your car at a picnic area, overlook, or parking area on Skyline Drive and you can hike for an hour or a half-day. For overnighting in the backcountry or designated wilderness areas, secure a free camping permit at a ranger station. Five locked cabins are furnished with mattresses, blankets, stove, cooking utensils, and dishes (for reservations, write the Potomac Appalachian Trail Club, 1718 N Street, N.W., Washington, DC 20036).

Riding and cycling. Horses can be rented at Skyland for an hour, half-day, or all day. Heading to Whiteoak Canyon will give the taste of a wilderness trail ride, but the horses are gentle enough for children. Overnight pack trips can be arranged. Bicycling is welcomed on Skyline Drive and the public roads in developed areas.

Fishing for native brook trout is good in a number of beautiful mountain streams, April to mid-October. A Virginia license is required (three-day nonresident trout license is available at all major concession facilities). Rapidan and Staunton Rivers and their tributaries are "fishing-for-fun" streams.

Naturalist program. Guided hikes are conducted daily, mid-June to Labor Day, to major points of interest. Campfire programs are given at Skyland, Loft Mountain, Big Meadows, Mathews Arm, and Lewis Mountain campgrounds.

Birdwatching. At the height of spring migration you are likely to spot 100 different species (though the park is visited by twice that number during the year). Woods are filled with songbirds—listen for wrens, warblers, thrashers, and tanagers. With good fortune, especially in the northern part of the park, you are apt to spot a wild turkey. Common ravens, uncommon in the eastern United States, are residents of Shenandoah. Look up and you'll see the soaring birds—hawks, vultures, and ravens—riding air currents over mountaintops and valleys.

Events. The Ol' Time Festival and Fair Days in June and Mountain Heritage Days in July feature arts and crafts, music, food, and mountain dancing. Hoover Days, held the weekend closest to Hoover's birthday, August 10, include programs and exhibits at the Byrd Visitor Center and guided tours of Camp Hoover.

TOURS. Motorcoach tours run through the park, spending at least one night at Skyland or Big Meadows. Itineraries usually include other highlights of Virginia, such as the Caverns of Luray, Charlottesville, and Staunton. The tours are available from most major cities in the East.

ACCOMMODATIONS. Splendid overnight lodges and dining rooms (specializing in Virginia foods) are located at Big Meadows and Skyland, with views of Shenandoah Valley and mountain ranges beyond. Most units are modern motel-type, but some experienced travelers prefer the rustic cottages. Lewis Mountain has the southernmost accommodations, with housekeeping cabins for 24 persons. Advance reservations are desirable, early April

through October (write ARA Virginia Sky-Line Company, Inc., Box 727, Luray, VA 22835). Restaurant facilities also are available along the Skyline Drive at Elkwallow, Panorama, and Loft Mountain. Picnickers, hikers, and fishermen can pick up box lunches at Skyland and Big Meadows. Since the national park is long but very narrow, facilities outside its borders are easily reached. Front Royal, at the northern entrance, and Waynesboro, at the southern entrance, offer many motels, restaurants, and campgrounds; so does Luray, on US 211 just west of the park. Winchester, Harrisonburg, Charlottesville, Staunton, and Lexington are within driving range and have plenty of tourist facilities.

CAMPING. Campgrounds in the park are located at Big Meadows, Lewis Mountain, Loft Mountain, and Mathews Arm near Elkwallow in the north district. Most operate on a first-come, first-served basis, with a 14-day limit. Big Meadows and Loft Mountain have supply stores, pay showers, coin laundries, ice, and wood. Campers who fail to keep food (including ice chests) locked in car trunks may expect company—black bears. There are no utility connections for trailers, but sewage disposal stations are located at Big Meadows, Mathews Arm, and Loft Mountain.

Shenandoah requires backcountry use permits and accepts reservations for backcountry camping. Big Meadows campsites can be reserved through Ticketron.

SEASONS. Skyland opens in late March, Big Meadows Lodge opens in May, and both remain open till late October or early November. Big Meadows Wayside and campground are open March through December; the other campgrounds are open from mid-April or May to November. The park itself is open all year, except when severe ice or snow storms close Skyline Drive for short periods. The beauty of winter in the highlands is a special treat. Ski touring is often practical, especially on old roads. Rangers will suggest the best areas. On cold, crisp days evergreens stand out boldly against the snowy white mountain background. Icicles cascade over the cliffs, presenting opportunities for unusual photography. Winter walkers should stay on the designated trails, wear adequate clothing, and not push their physical endurance while walking through snow. Motorists should carry a good set of chains and have adequate ventilation while the car motor is running. The park remains cool until June, though spring flowers and budding trees—hepatica, red maple, and bloodroot—begin their show in late March. In mid-April the magenta flush of redbud floods the valleys, followed by the creamy white of dogwood. In succession come azalea and black locust, then the pink and white mountain

laurel—a profusion of flowers during most of June. In summer, temperatures are a comfortable 15 degrees lower than in the valley below. You can usually count on mid-70s by day, mid-40s at night. This is the peak period for visitors, though crowds are fairly light in midweek. By mid-September, foliage begins its autumn color change, gradually flowing downward from the mountain tops to coves and hollows. There

are several color peaks; the most luxurious displays among non-oak species usually occur between October 10 and 20. Yet there is still new blossoming of yarrow, asters, and witch hazel. In spring and fall, naturalists present illustrated evening talks at the Byrd Visitor Center at Big Meadows.

NEARBY. Both the Piedmont and Shenandoah Valley are rich in Civil War battle sites. **Lexington,** in particular, is associated with Robert E. Lee, who served as president of Washington and Lee University, and Stonewall Jackson, who left for the war from the faculty of Virginia Military Institute (VMI). **New Market Battlefield Park,** a surprising and outstanding area, depicts Jackson's valley campaign and the role of VMI cadets. The national park is flanked by **George Washington National Forest.** Its largest recreation area, **Sherando Lake,** 14 miles south of Waynesboro, provides a campground, sand beach, bathhouse, and naturalist program. An unusually interesting area, **Elizabeth Furnace,** in the Massanutten Mountains near Front Royal, has camping and a nature trail winding through an old iron furnace community.

FOR FURTHER INFORMATION. Write Superintendent, Shenandoah National Park, Luray, VA 22835.

THEODORE ROOSEVELT NATIONAL PARK

North Dakota

Established 1978

THE Badlands, I felt sure, looked much to me as when Theodore Roosevelt first saw them more than a century ago—wild, untamed, composed of what he called a "curious, fantastic beauty." My hunch is the Badlands remain wild today because the pioneers couldn't subdue them. The climate is severe in both winter and summer, and the soil resists cultivation. I studied the contrasting bands of light and dark in the buttes and bluffs, the mesas, washes, and sharply eroded valleys—all reminders of the ancient past, when broad rivers deposited thick layers of sediment on a plain. At Scoria Point, I saw massive bluffs capped with red scoria, where a vein of lignite burned and baked sand and clay into natural brick. Doubtless there is some commercial value to it, but this country is better admired than exploited.

Theodore Roosevelt learned that lesson the hard way. He first came to the Badlands in the fall of 1883 to hunt buffalo. Though still in his early 20s, he was already a Harvard graduate, deeply interested in history, adventure, and the outdoors. In this primitive frontier country, a strange region of buttes, gorges, and canyons carved by the Little Missouri River, Roosevelt found a "postgraduate course" in life itself.

On that first trip, he and his guide camped beneath the stars or found shelter, on occasion, with friendly ranchers. He was so impressed that he bought a share in his first cattle ranch. From then until the end of the century, he made a career of ranching, full-time in some years, part-time in others. "There are few sensations I prefer," he wrote in this period, "to that of galloping over these rolling limitless prairies, rifle in hand, or winding my way among the barren, fantastic and grimly picturesque deserts of the so-called Bad Lands." As a result of a bitter winter, Roosevelt lost more money than he made in ranching, but he learned the need for protecting natural resources from indiscriminate use and later became the "con-servationist president."

Roosevelt, like many others, was fascinated by the weird erosional patterns carved by the restless Little Missouri. Where a huge section of the bluff has slipped to the valley floor, bands of color once horizontal are now perched at almost any angle. "Viewed in the distance at sunset it looked exactly like the ruins of an ancient city," wrote General Alfred Sully after viewing the Badlands in 1864.

In that year Sully led 2,000 men into western Dakota Territory on a military expedition against the Sioux, the nomadic native people who ranged over a vast domain in the heartland of the continent. Sully's troops pushed west across the Little Missouri and routed the Sioux near Square Butte, 7 miles from the present site of Medora. Though he withdrew and the Sioux regained control of the area, their independence was short-lived. By 1880 all organized Indian resistance on the northern plains was broken.

Then came cattlemen after free rangeland and hunters after abundant game. The great buffalo herds were eradicated from the plains and their place was taken by livestock. Before long, the grasslands were overstocked and overgrazed. Ranchers suffered crippling losses when cattle perished by thousands during harsh winters. Following the turn of the century, small farms and ranches dominated the scene, but they fared little better. Hard times in the 1930s forced many residents to pull up stakes and let their submarginal holdings of land revert to the government.

The idea of setting aside a portion of the Badlands in honor of Theodore Roosevelt was first advanced by local friends soon after he died, in 1919. A national memorial park, the only one of its kind, was established by Congress in 1947 to cover 70,000 acres. It was reclassified in 1978 as a national park, to serve as a natural sanctuary linking humanity to all things of past and present.

THE PRACTICAL GUIDE

ACCESS. The park is located in western North Dakota, with its headquarters at Medora, 17 miles west of Belfield (138 miles west of Bismarck) and 62 miles east of Glendive, MT. It can be reached easily via I-94, which runs east-west. Coming from the south, US 85 intersects I-94 at Belfield.

Medora is the gateway to the South Unit of the park. The North Unit is reached by continuing north on US 85, which provides direct access to it. A third unit, the site of Roosevelt's Elkhorn Ranch, is difficult to reach; for directions, check at park headquarters.

South Unit. Start at the Visitor Center to see exhibits covering Roosevelt's early life and the cattle industry, as well as the natural history of the Badlands. Visit the restored

Maltese Cross Cabin directly adjacent. This was Roosevelt's first home in the Badlands, moved here from its original site 7 miles away; though it may seem simple now, it was luxurious in its day.

While in the South Unit, drive the scenic loop road to **Wind Canyon,** probably the best example of Badlands erosion accelerated by the force of wind. It affords a spectacular vista of weird and brilliantly colored tablelands, buttes, and other formations. **Buck Hill Overlook,** the highest formation in the Painted Canyon, gives the broadest panoramic view. **Petrified Forest,** an area of ancient conifer stumps (which may have been a species of Giant Sequoia), with diameters of 6 and 8 feet, can be reached on foot or horseback—it's a round trip of 16 miles.

North Unit. Take the drive of about 13 miles for breathtaking views of bluish bentonitic clay and the weird erosional patterns carved by the meandering Little Missouri. Note that cottonwoods are first to grow in newly deposited sediment along the river's edge, stabilizing the soil and providing shade. This creates an environment for less hardy trees like ash and juniper, which eventually supplant the cottonwoods.

ACTIVITIES. Hiking. Opportunities are extensive and varied. Both units have short, self-guiding nature trails readily accessible and longer routes for those who want to get off the beaten path. Pick up a copy of the free *Backcountry Guide.* Hikers are not restricted to existing trails, but exercise caution by picking areas with good footing; soil can be slippery when wet and crumble under you when dry. Wear a cap to protect you from the sun and a pair of good hiking boots. Talk to the rangers about precautions for rattlesnakes and bison.

Horseback riding is popular in the vicinity, and you'll find a number of opportunities to join trail rides. A horseback riding concession is located at **Peaceful Valley Ranch** in the South Unit; other trail rides operate outside both units.

Floating. Canoeing on the Little Missouri affords an ideal way to explore the Badlands. You can put in at the South Unit of the park (at old US 10), journey through remote country, pass the site of Roosevelt's Elkhorn Ranch, camp in cottonwood groves, and take out at the North Unit about four days later. Actually, you could travel much farther, since the Little Missouri State Scenic River covers 274 miles from the southwest corner of the state (near Marmath) to Lost Bridge on North Dakota 22, close to the state park at Little Missouri Bay.

Birdwatching is a choice experience. Among more spectacular birds are the golden eagle, the great horned owl, and the sandhill crane. The park is frequented by ducks, geese, and other migratory species traveling the Missouri River flyway.

ACCOMMODATIONS. In Medora, there are modern motels and the refurnished, century-old Rough Riders Hotel, where Teddy Roosevelt stayed. Other motels are located at Watford City, 15 miles from the entrance to the North Unit, and Dickinson, 38 miles east of Medora.

CAMPING. Two excellent campgrounds are located in the park (limit 14 days). Sites cannot be reserved, but arrive by early afternoon and you will probably find an attractive location. If you plan to camp in the backcountry, check with a park ranger for tips on camping spots—and be sure to register. There are campgrounds in **Custer National Forest,** which surrounds the national park. **Sully's Creek State Park,** located south of Medora, provides primitive camping along a tributary of the Little Missouri.

SEASONS. Summer is the most popular time, though the park is scarcely overrun with visitors. Summer greens soften tones of the stark Badlands. In autumn, too, trees and shrubs cover the river bottom with harvest hues. The first snows of late September signal the coming of winter. The park is kept open all year, and the South Unit road from the Visitor Center to Wind Canyon is plowed in winter. In the North Unit, the road is plowed from the entrance to the Caprock Coulee trailhead.

NEARBY. The little town of Medora is linked intimately with the park. The **Chateau de Mores,** a lavish two-story mansion, was built by the founder of Medora, the Marquis de Mores, a contemporary of Roosevelt. The **Museum of the Badlands,** located just outside the park entrance, houses an outstanding collection of relics of early frontier life.

FOR FURTHER INFORMATION. Write Superintendent, Theodore Roosevelt National Park, Box 7, Medora, ND 58645.

VIRGIN ISLANDS NATIONAL PARK

Virgin Islands

Authorized 1956

S NORKELING in the clear, sunlit waters of Leinster Bay, I felt as though I was traveling in some other world. Coral of many hues rose like trees, mountains, and spires in the underground forest, while schools of brilliantly colored fish rested lazily on stony branches or glided in and out among rocks and plants. Lacy purple sea fans swayed in the gentle current, and delicate anemones carpeted the reef like flowering shrubbery in full aquatic bloom.

On each visit to the Virgin Islands, I realize anew that here is one of the smallest, yet most beautiful, national parks. It covers just over half of the island of St. John, which itself is only nine miles long and five miles wide. The park occupies 12,900 acres, including 5,600 acres of offshore water and reefs. Yellowstone, by contrast, occupies more than 2.2 million acres.

This doesn't make our little park in the Caribbean any less appealing or less of a treasure, for coral reefs are to the Virgin Islands what geysers are to Yellowstone and granite domes are to Yosemite. Few areas span so wide a range of life, from the underwater coral to sea grape shading the strand of white sands along indented bays, and from tropical flora clothing the valleys to green mountaintops opening vistas of neighboring islands and the distant sea.

The park was established in 1956; none too soon, considering that the past few years have seen the unending discovery and commercial development of one "unspoiled" West Indies beach after another. In time, St. John may be one of the few areas left to show sparkling beaches, tropical forest, Danish ruins, and coral reefs in their untouched state.

The course of its history began more than 100 million years ago, when volcanoes erupted deep in the ocean and the buckling crust of the earth raised rock islands above the surface of the sea. Ever since, the beaches of St. John have been a zone of arriving life, with ocean currents and each new tide delivering animals and plants, insects, eggs, seeds, and seedlings to form new colonies here. Meanwhile, the coral reefs have formed a world of flowers that are not plants but tiny animals of the subtropic seas. The coral gardens derive their varied and vivid colors from the myriad tiny organisms living within them.

While hiking the island trails, I found the pattern of life changing upward from the sea. The pale strand is shaded here and there by a seagrape tree, its large leaves tinged with red, and with small purple fruit. Heading to the rainy mountaintops, I observed a swift transition in vegetation, and was glad to have a tropical plant guide in my pocket.

Humans have lived in the Virgin Islands for several thousand years. Among the earliest were the Arawaks and the Caribs, who left petroglyphs be-hind. Christopher Columbus touched St. Croix, the largest island, on his second voyage, in 1493 (the beginning of European contact), but it was the Dutch and the Danes who shaped the colonial culture. Denmark acquired the Virgin Islands in the 1700s; its nationals established sugar plantations, imported slaves, and built their estate houses on high, breezy hills. They prospered until the mid-19th century, when sugar prices fell, the slaves were freed, and the old plantations were left to become shadowy ruins of history. The United States bought the islands in 1917. The other islands, St. Croix and St. Thomas, developed much more rapidly, happily for St. John.

THE PRACTICAL GUIDE

ACCESS. The Virgin Islands are only four hours from New York, and less from Miami. Flights go to St. Thomas, the capital. Take a taxi from the airport to Red Hook, for the ferry ride across Pillsbury Sound to Cruz Bay, the main community on St. John. You can also take a ferry from downtown Charlotte Amalie (on St. Thomas); it's a longer trip, but very pleasant, and you will avoid the congested traffic to Red Hook. Another possibility is to fly to San Juan, PR, then go directly to St. John via flying boat.

If you plan to stay on St. Thomas, take one of several excellent one-day package tours to the park, which include the ferry trip, guided shuttle tours, swimming and snorkeling, and lunch. If you come over independently on the ferry to the park entrance at Cruz Bay, taxis with guides offer worthwhile tours. You can rent a jeep, but it's not really necessary, since open-air vans run around the island frequently.

Dress casually and comfortably, but respect local customs—for example, refrain from strolling through town in a bathing suit. Bring walking shoes, cool clothing, swimsuit and snorkel, sunscreen, and insect repellant.

VISITOR CENTER. Start early at the park visitor center at Cruz Bay for information, maps, and exhibits of the park's many features. Check here for the schedule of naturalist-conducted historic and nature walks and the evening programs at Maho Bay, Caneel Bay Plantation, and Cinnamon Bay.

ACTIVITIES. Sightseeing. Centerline Road, the main road of St. John, climbs over the heights to the harbor of Coral Bay on the east. The road winds up past buildings of the 1700s, including the Moravian Bethany Church. From a distance, the wooded hills resemble the New England countryside, but there are fruit trees like the soursop and mango; little plants and vines bearing local botanical names such as clashie melashi, eye bright, and better man better; and exotic trees like the gnarled, strangely shaped silk cotton, which produces kapok in its seed pod. Avoid eating strange wild fruits—some are poisonous. From the overlook near **Mamey Peak**, elevation 1,147 feet, islands of the American and British Virgin Islands spread over the brilliant blue sea around Coral Bay.

Reef Bay Trail is of special interest to the visitor who wants to hike or find subjects for sketching and/or photography. From the top of Centerline Road, the 2½-mile trail winds down (a descent of about 800 feet) on an old Danish carriage road, through a moist, then dry, forest. A short side trip leads to undeciphered petroglyphs dating from Arawak and Carib days at the base of a waterfall. Another side trail leads to the Reef Bay estate house, once the center of a flourishing plantation. The trail ends on the sand beach. A park naturalist leads a scheduled trip this way, returning to Cruz Bay by boat (a fee is charged).

Snorkeling. Anybody who can swim can snorkel, and equipment can be rented at the Cinnamon Bay Dive Shop and Trunk Bay Snack Bar, or at St. Thomas. If you're a beginner, join the guided snorkel tour at Cinnamon Bay. It starts with the basics of snorkeling. Never snorkel alone. Test the snorkel gear in shallow water. If it leaks, don't use it. Respect submerged features—leave them for others to enjoy.

Trunk Bay Beach leads to the **underwater self-guiding trail**, which reaches a depth of only 10 feet. Most visitors can read the labels etched on submerged glass plates.

Swimming, with or without a snorkel, is one of the pleasures of the park, but the safest places to swim are where lifeguards are on duty.

Boating and fishing. Sailboats and other boats are available for rent on St. Thomas and St. John. On your first experience, it pays to engage a skipper. Bear in mind that dropping anchor in the reefs damages the coral, so avoid it. Saltwater fishing is equally good in all seasons. Three bonefish flats are near St. John. Tackle may be rented from Cinnamon Bay Camp, while charter boats are available in Cinnamon Bay, Cruz Bay, and St. Thomas for offshore marlin, tuna, sailfish, wahoo, and others. Spearfishing in waters of the park is prohibited.

Annaberg Ruins. A self-guiding trail helps recapture the story of the sugar estates at these ruins on the North Shore, which the Park Service has stabilized as a protection against further weathering. Cane grown on the hillsides was carried by mules, donkeys, or oxen to be crushed in the windmill or on the grinding platform.

ACCOMMODATIONS. Maho Bay is a complex of attractive tent-cottages of three rooms each, located on private land within the national park. Essentially, it provides a camping experience with a measure of comfort. There is a moderately priced restaurant at hand, but you can pick up groceries and incidentals at the camp store and do your own cooking (for reservations, write Maho Bay Camps, 17 East 73rd Street, New York, NY 10021 or Box 113, Cruz Bay, St. John, VI 00830; phone 800/392-9004).

The largest guest facility on St. John outside the park is **Caneel Bay Plantation**, one of the finest resorts in the Caribbean, with excellent beach facilities, though it is high-priced during the winter peak. **Virgin Grand**, near Cruz Bay, is another luxury resort. **Gallows Point** is an apartment complex at Cruz Bay. There are also smaller facilities on St. John offering apartments and cottages (for the complete list, write Virgin Islands Division of Tourism, Box 6400, St. Thomas, VI 00801).

CAMPING. Cinnamon Bay Campground facilities include bare sites for tent camping; prepared sites with tents; and modest beach cottages with cots, bedding, linen, and cooking utensils. All are in great demand, so write far in advance for rates and reservations (Cinnamon Bay Campground, Box 120, Cruz Bay, St. John, VI 00830). The camping limit is 14 days. There are no ticks or chiggers, but mosquitoes and sandflies are present year-round. The camp sells groceries and supplies. More varied foods and laundry facilities are available at Cruz Bay.

SEASONS. Peak periods of use for campsites and beach cottages are November to March and June to August. Peak popularity of the Virgin Islands in general, as a refuge from winter cold, extends from December to March. April and May are very attractive months. The climate is equable year-round, with an average annual temperature of 79 degrees. The lowest recorded temperature is 61 degrees; the highest is 98 degrees. The water temperature is delightful for swimming.

NEARBY. Both St. Thomas and St. Croix are popular Caribbean resorts, landscaped with bright hibiscus, oleander, and bougainvillaea. At Charlotte Amalie, the capital city, visited by many cruise liners, the 25 shops between Queen's Street and Waterfront Promenade feature merchandise from all over the world—because St. Thomas is a duty-free port. St. Croix, 40 miles south, clings to its Danish colonial architecture and history. **Christiansted National Historic Site**, along three waterfront blocks of the main city, encompasses an old fort and public buildings. **Buck Island Reef National Monument**, a mile and a half off the coast of St. Croix, is regarded as one of the finest marine gardens in the Caribbean; it is visited on boat cruises from St. Croix and provides snorkelers with an underwater nature trail.

FOR FURTHER INFORMATION. Write Superintendent, Virgin Islands National Park, Box 806, St. Thomas, VI 00801.

VOYAGEURS NATIONAL PARK

Minnesota

Authorized 1971

I SPENT a day following foot trails on the Kabetogama Peninsula in Voyageurs National Park and that day was all too short. The park includes large lakes—some of the largest in the upper Midwest—on which motorboating is allowed, but once away from the powerboat lanes, I found the Kabetogama filled with fresh, sparkling, and intimate scenes. The boreal forest, though broken here and there by bogs, surprising palisades, and sand beaches, for the most part reached to the water's edge. Wild rice grew in shallow bays and streams. I saw part of a chain of internal lakes well suited for canoeing.

On the trail into Agnes Lake, I heard a rustling in the brush. At first it sounded like the wind, but the air was calm. It proved to be a bear cub that I had disturbed, scampering up a tree. The beaver ponds I saw were habitat for aquatic plants, which fed insects, which in turn fed fish and birds. Across the water, I observed a loon scanning the scene, then diving for lower depths as suddenly as it had appeared.

Minnesota's national park embraces a choice portion of the forested lake country on the northern border, once the setting of an epic chapter in American history. For a century and a half, French-Canadian voyageurs plied this network of lakes and streams in sturdy canoes, transported trade goods, explorers, missionaries, and soldiers to the West, and returned to Montreal with vast quantities of furs.

Sentiment for preserving this area had been felt and expressed in Minnesota for many years. In 1962, Governor Elmer L. Andersen and state officials toured the area with major landowners and representatives of the National Park Service; they issued a joint memorandum recommending field studies as soon as possible. In 1965, Andersen's successor, Karl Rolvaag, and 5,000 fellow Minnesotans signed a petition at the State Fair urging establishment of Voyageurs National Park. And in 1967, a third governor, Harold LeVander, committed the "full force" of his administration to establishment of the park. During the same year, the National Park Service reaffirmed its choice of Kabetogama as "the outstanding remaining opportunity for a national park in the northern lake country of the United States." The entire Minnesota delegation, led by Representative John Blatnik and Senator Walter Mondale, then introduced legislation in Congress, which acted favorably. The bill authorizing the new park was signed in January 1971.

Sigurd Olson—author, naturalist, and a living Minnesota legend—played a major role in the park movement, making countless presentations in his home state and Washington. Voyageurs National Park Association, headed first by Judge Edwin P. Chapman, labored toward making Minnesota's first national park a reality.

Although the log forts and other physical traces of the *coureurs du bois* and voyageurs have long since vanished, it is still possible to capture a sense of solitude and challenge. The park has all the wildness and immense scale associated with the northern shield region—a surface shaped by continental glaciation into an endless system of internal waterways. Of the park's 217,300 total acres, 87,500 acres are water. Nature is still at work here, revealing its handiwork of times past while constantly changing it. The landscape is marked by more than 100 lakes and a tangle of streams. Smooth, polished, and grooved rock surfaces are visible on many islands—they are the tops of rocky crags the glacial ice failed to remove.

It requires no scientific analysis, however, to enjoy or appreciate the Voyageurs country of today. Stands of fir, spruce, pine, aspen, and birch reach to the water's edge, broken here and there by bogs, cliffs, and sand beaches. Wildlife species such as deer, moose, and black bear remain. This is one of the few places in the country outside of Alaska with a pack of timber wolves. Beavers thrive among the aspen. Throngs of birds indigenous to the area and numerous varieties of waterfowl make their nests and feed in the peninsula's many bays and lagoons.

I found a choice bit of cultural history here, too, at the Kettle Falls Hotel, at the extreme east end of Rainy Lake. Built in 1913, the hotel served trappers, traders, fishermen, and lumberjacks. It reopened in 1988 after a $2.5 million restoration. It's a treasure to enjoy, worthy of the north woods around it.

THE PRACTICAL GUIDE

BACKGROUND. Lying east of International Falls, the park is irregular in shape, measuring about 40 miles from east to west and varying in width from 3 to 15 miles. It includes numerous islands and more than 100 lakes. The main body of land, Kabetogama Peninsula, covers 75,000 heavily forested acres, relatively undeveloped and accessible principally by water. Surrounding the peninsula are waters ranging from narrows less than 100 feet wide to lakes several miles across, dotted with islands accented with rocky points. Four lakes dominate the area within the park: **Namakan**, **Kabetogama**, **Rainy**, and **Sand Point**. Rainy Lake, the largest, covers 350 square miles.

ACCESS. The primary access to the park is via US 53, extending from Virginia, MN, north to International Falls. County and state roads lead from US 53 to Crane Lake, at the eastern end of the park; the south shore of Lake Kabetogama; the Ash River and Rainy Lake's Black Bay. There are no roads into the interior of the park.

Crane Lake Gorge, lying just to the west of the park, is one of the spectacular scenic wonders of Crane Lake, where the Vermillion River tumbles through a narrow chasm between vertical rock walls before it flows into the lake. There are trails on both sides of the canyon and many plants and mosses on the moist forest floor. Wild rice grows in shallow bays and streams, and cranberry bogs are common.

TOURS. Tour boats are an important part of the interpretive program. Visitors are able to drive to the visitor centers at the park edges, but access to the interior is by boat. Tour boats feature interesting narration by a park naturalist or boat operator. The *Pride of Rainy Lake*, departing from the Rainy Lake Visitor Center, is the largest jet-powered passenger boat in Minnesota, carrying 49 passengers. Voyageurs National Park Boat Tours offers rides from the new Kabetogama Lake Visitor Center. The *Locator Lake Adventure* combines a two-mile naturalist hike and canoeing on Locator Lake with the boat trip. Another option is the three-hour dinner cruise.

Historic values are high. Underwater archaeologists have recovered parts of voyageur canoes, muzzle-loading rifles, beads intended for Indian trade, and other artifacts. An existing link to a more recent era is the **Kettle Falls Hotel**, "Minnesota's most remote resort," a choice spot for a meal, even if you can't stay over. There was a brief gold rush in the early 1890's at **Rainy Lake City** following discovery of the Little America Island vein, but little evidence remains.

ACTIVITIES. Boating and canoeing. State regulations apply. Boaters not familiar with these waters should obtain the services of a guide (through a local resort or hotel) or obtain charts. Large lakes are formidable and can become suddenly rough. Small boats and canoes should prepare to wait out rough water; better yet, plan a course that avoids wide expanses. Canoeists can put in at several points and paddle for a day, week, or all summer, and never run out of new vistas. Local outfitters rent full equipment.

Fishing. The four large border lakes—Rainy, Sand Point, Namakan, and Kabetogama—are popular with walleye anglers; they are also rich in northern pike and smallmouth bass. Shoepack Lake on the peninsula is known for its muskellunge, while trout can often be found in some of the smaller lakes and streams.

ACCOMMODATIONS. Clustered mostly at Crane Lake, Kabetogama Lake, Ash River, and Rainy Lake, 60 resorts lie near the park. They offer everything from housekeeping cabins, hotel rooms, and houseboat rentals to guide services and charter trips by boat or floatplane.

CAMPING. National Park Service island campsites are available without charge. The state of Minnesota and the U.S. Forest Service provide camping spots near the park. Along both the north and the south shores of Kabetogama Peninsula are many places with smooth, glaciated rock that are well suited for camping and picnicking. The peninsula's interior holds a number of lovely lakes that can be reached only by foot.

The park has small campgrounds at King Williams Narrows and Mukooda Lake, accessible only by boat.

Private campgrounds are located in the vicinities of International Falls and Lake Kabetogama.

SEASONS. Summers are cool. Warm clothes and insect repellent are important. September, when aspen and birch change colors, can be a beautiful month.

NEARBY. East of the park lies the renowned **Boundary Waters Canoe Area**, which includes portions of the **Superior National Forest** and **Quetico Provincial Park** across the border in Ontario. Main gateways are at Grand Marais, Ely, and Crane Lake. **Fort Frances**, Ontario, linked by bridge with International Falls, was the site of Fort St. Pierre, built by Pierre de la Verendrye, the explorer, in 1731.

RECOMMENDED READING. *The Singing Wilderness*, by Sigurd Olson; *Rainy River Country*, by Grace Lee Nute; and *Voyageur Country*, by Robert Treuer.

FOR FURTHER INFORMATION. Write Superintendent, Voyageurs National Park, US 53, International Falls, MN 56649.

WIND CAVE NATIONAL PARK

South Dakota

Established 1903

I WATCHED two prairie dogs, standing upright like furry little men or women. They advanced toward each other, embraced in greeting like family or friends, then went their separate ways. One of them scooted into its hole, and I wished that I might have peeked into that underground house, which is said to be the most complex, elaborate dwelling constructed by a North American mammal.

The colonies of prairie dogs at Wind Cave comprise, for me, one of the treasures of the National Park System. For one thing, they typify the prairie, or what remains of it. At one time, prairie dogs numbered in the millions. Their "towns" were surprisingly huge—one, in Texas, was estimated in 1900 to cover 25,000 square miles and to contain 400 million animals. Now they are found only in a few places, mostly in sanctuaries like Wind Cave.

I enjoy this national park as a prairie vignette. I watch the seas of grass ripple in the wind, short and medium grasses sprinkled with wildflowers. The sleek pronghorn, alone or with a mate, roves across the hillsides. Small herds of huge, shaggy bison lumber slowly, following ancient pathways. The animals are remnants of great herds that once covered the mid-continent. I wish there were more—more animals and more prairie saved—but at least there is this much to yield the feel and flavor of original America.

The park contains 28,059 acres, a relatively small area. Yet it includes not only a prime example of mixed-grass prairie, but a meeting ground of eastern and western flora. Here I can see the stately American elm and burr oak from the east merging with ponderosa pines of the western mountain forests and with yucca, cactus, and cottonwood from the arid Southwest.

Below the surface, the Wind Cave was formed in one of the thick limestone formations which underlie a large part of the Black Hills. It derives its name from strong currents of air that blow alternately in and out, believed to be caused by changes in atmospheric pressure outside.

Development of the cave began in the 1890s with the "Wonderful Wind Cave Improvement Company." Passages were opened and stairways built, leading to galleries decorated with unusual crystal formations. These were formed when cracks in the ancient limestone were filled with calcium carbonate deposits.

In 1902, legislation was introduced to set aside Wind Cave as a national park. It was enacted that year and signed by President Theodore Roosevelt on January 9, 1903. Wind Cave thus became the first cave park to be established in the National Park system.

I still favor the park above ground, where I observe dominant grasses of both the true prairie and short-grass plains. In spring and summer, I look for pasqueflower (South Dakota's state flower), scarlet globemallow, prairie coneflower, mariposa lily, and prickly poppy. I watch elk, buffalo, and pronghorn. And prairie dogs, of course. They're not really dogs, but burrowing ground squirrels that rely on keen hearing, excellent eyesight, and a community warning system for protection. Like all wild creatures threatened by the advance of civilization, they have not had an easy time of it, yet they enrich the landscape by being part of it.

146

THE PRACTICAL GUIDE

BACKGROUND. Wind Cave is a lightly visited national park, thus increasing its charm to the visitor who prefers elbow room. It makes for a very pleasant natural interlude amidst the Black Hills. Conducted tours of the cave, requiring one to one and a half hours, are given year-round.

VISITOR CENTER. Open daily except Thanksgiving Day, Christmas, and New Year's. Travel information and educational publications are available. A concession-operated lunchroom is located here; food service is available late spring, summer, and fall.

ACTIVITIES. Cave trips are led by uniformed guides of the National Park Service, using either the walk-in entrance or elevator. Trails are hard-surfaced. Low-heeled, rubber-soled walking shoes are best for comfort and safety. Temperature year-round is approximately 53 degrees; wear a light sweater or jacket. Besides the regular trips, **candlelight tours,** reminiscent of the turn of the century, are held several times daily during summer (limit 10 persons per party). **Spelunking tours** are conducted daily in summer, with spacecrawling into a primitive section of the cave (limit 10 persons).

Rankin Ridge Nature Trail leads to the highest point in the park (elevation 5,016 feet). The trail is 1¼ miles long and takes about an hour. Binoculars are useful in getting a panoramic view of the Black Hills from the observation tower.

Wildlife is wonderful to watch and photograph, from a respectable distance. Do not approach bison on foot; even a young bison may inflict serious injury. Early morning and evening are good hours for viewing elk and deer. Cliff swallows, golden eagles, bald eagles, and several varieties of woodpecker are often spotted here. The white-winged junco can be seen only in the Black Hills.

Naturalist program. Activities will keep you on the go from morning till after dark. Campfire programs are held each evening on many subjects, and naturalist-led activities will acquaint visitors with other aspects of the park.

CAMPING. One-half mile north of the headquarters area, **Elk Mountain Campground** provides camping and trailer sites from mid-May through mid-September, but electric, water, and sewer hookups are not available. There are numerous private and public campgrounds in the area.

SEASONS. Cave tours are conducted year-round, except major wintertime holidays. Tourist centers in the Black Hills are jammed in midsummer. Early summer wildflowers and autumn foliage make these attractive seasons. In May, prairie dog pups emerge from their holes for the first time. You can see the "booming," or courtship dance of the sharptailed grouse. In June, bison and elk calves, deer fawns, and pronghorn kids are first seen, while spring flowers are abundant. September and October are excellent months for wildlife watching, with elk and deer mating and pronghorns grouping together.

NEARBY. Within easy range are **Mount Rushmore National Memorial** and **Jewel Cave National Monument,** a series of chambers and limestone galleries with sparkling crystal-lined walls. **Custer State Park,** adjacent to the national park, contains a very large bison herd.

Campgrounds are located in **Black Hills National Forest** and **Custer State Park.** The state park contains several overnight lodgings, including **State Game Lodge,** once the summer residence of President Calvin Coolidge. The lodge is a good place to have a sizzling buffalo steak, or "buffalo burger."

A word of caution: the Black Hills contain a heavy concentration of commercial tourist attractions advertising "fun for the entire family" and "education" for your youngsters. Choose carefully, particularly if you are on a close budget.

FOR FURTHER INFORMATION. Write Superintendent, Wind Cave National Park, Hot Springs, SD 57747.

WRANGELL-ST. ELIAS NATIONAL PARK

Alaska

Established 1980

I CHECKED the map as my friend Paul and I drove east from Anchorage. The country all around us looked as though it would easily qualify as national park land. It was expansive, natural, and free of settlement. We stopped for lunch at Glennallen, the hub of the Copper River frontier and gateway to the Wrangells. While the countryside was relatively flat, with small lakes and streams, I could see clearly the great peaks ahead—Sanford, Drum, Wrangell, and Blackburn—that make the Wrangells a special place.

North America's "mountain kingdom" embraces the greatest concentration of high peaks on the continent, including Mount St. Elias, at 18,008 feet the second highest (after Mount McKinley), plus several others rising above 14,500 feet. Covering 12,318,000 acres, Wrangell-St. Elias is the largest park in the National Park system, yet larger still when considered together with bordering Kluane National Park in the Yukon Territory of Canada. Together they have been placed on the United Nations' World Heritage List of outstanding natural areas.

Glaciers and snowfields of these massive mountains dominate the landscape. More than 100 major glaciers constitute the largest ice field in the world below the polar region. One glacier alone, the celebrated Malespina, is larger than the entire state of Rhode Island.

Paul and I spent our time exploring the Chitina Valley, the heart of the park, drained by the Chitina River, one of a dozen major rivers flowing down from the rugged mountain. We saw Dall sheep abundant on the rocky ledges and signs of grizzly along the trails. The park also includes coastal beaches on the Gulf of Alaska, which I hope to visit soon.

We also found human signs, at the old mining towns of McCarthy and Kennicott, focal points of activity within the Chitina Valley portion of the park. These towns were born in the early 1900s, when the Kennecott Copper Company began mining and milling one of the world's richest copper deposits. In its heyday, McCarthy had more than 1,000 residents, compared with the handful there today who relish its isolation. With this setting, I could hardly blame them.

THE PRACTICAL GUIDE

ACCESS. The easiest way to arrive is flying by charter service direct from Anchorage, or from Glennallen or Chitina. The flight affords spectacular views of glaciers, mountains, and roaring rivers. It is also feasible to go by car. Allow a full day from either Anchorage or Fairbanks. Drive to Glennallen and then south on the Richardson Highway to the Edgerton Highway into Chitina, at the confluence of the Copper and Chitina Rivers. From there the 63-mile "McCarthy Road" follows the roadbed of the Copper River and Northwestern Railway. The scenery is spectacular, but can be enjoyed only if you take your time. A four-wheel drive vehicle is highly desirable.

ACTIVITIES. There are lots of opportunities for hiking and backpacking, with routes including those on the Hanagita Valley, Nikolai Pass, Jacksina Creek drainage, and the demanding Chitistone Canyon. Mount Drum and Mount Sanford, in the Wrangells, and Mount St. Elias are among the most challenging peaks known to climbers. The

148

Bremner, Chitina, and Copper Rivers offer excellent rafting with all classes of water. For a thrilling four-day trip, put in on the Kennicott River, near the glacier, and float down through the Nizina River Canyon and into the Chitina, which joins the mighty Copper River at the town of Chitina.

ACCOMMODATIONS. The colorful and comfortable **McCarthy Lodge** (outside plumbing) is open from late May to early September. Three miles northeast stands the old company town of Kennicott. Dominated by a 14-foot processing plant, it con-

sisted of 50 buildings, all painted red with white trim. From McCarthy or Kennicott, you can hike on the Kennicott Glacier or explore the old mines. During summer, wildflowers and berries cover the countryside. Dall sheep, caribou, and moose are likely to be seen crossing the hills; occasionally black and brown bear can be seen as well.

Backcountry travelers will find accommodations at guide cabins and fish camps located at **Tanada Lake** and **Copper Lake** in the northern part of the park, **Ptarmigan**

Lake and **Rock Lake** in the northeast, and **Tebay Lake** and **Hanagita Lake** in the south-central portion.

SEASONS. July generally has the best weather, with clear, warm days. Otherwise, the Wrangells can be cool, cloudy, and wet. Autumn is an attractive time, mosquito-free. Winter is also pleasant, with plenty of opportunity for cross-country skiing in dazzling settings.

FOR FURTHER INFORMATION. Write Superintendent, Wrangell-St. Elias National Park, Box 29, Glennallen, AK 99588.

YELLOWSTONE NATIONAL PARK

Wyoming—Montana—Idaho

Established 1872

SOON after the great Yellowstone fires of 1988, I met my friend Russell E. Dickenson, a former Director of the National Park Service (from 1980 to 1985), at a conference in Washington State. "The Yellowstone you and I knew for those many years," he said rather ruefully, "will never be the same." That is true. Visitors now see a new and different Yellowstone. But the more I consider it and discuss it with experts, the more convinced I become that Yellowstone emerges better than ever.

I revisited Yellowstone in June 1989, and found life after fire, a rebirth, the continuation of a life-cycle that visitors can observe, absorb, and appreciate. The damage of 1988, unquestionably extensive, in a sense was more commercial than ecological. Concession-operated accommodations in the park were evacuated for a time, then closed earlier than normal. Tourist trade in nearby communities was affected. But there is more to fire than the charred forest, hotel evacuation, and commercial loss. And in a national park, above all other places, there should be more.

Prepare to see evidence of the Big Burn. It will be extensive, but not solid. Some areas remain untouched. About 45 percent of the park was affected to some degree, although the flames skirted many popular scenic vistas. Within the burns, large sections remain unaffected. The heaviest fires were in stands of aging lodgepole pine, waiting to be ignited to make way for new growth. Wildlife, in the long run, benefits. Plants, insects, fish, and wildlife find new food sources. Visitors have the chance to examine the greatest example of Yellowstone fire in 300 years; to look, listen, and learn.

Covering 2,221,773 acres, Yellowstone embraces vast distance without factory fumes or firearms. Its spaciousness is a stronghold for wildlife—the grizzly bear, elk, bighorn, and bison, noble creatures that must have roaming room to live and perpetuate their species; so too for majestic winged animals of the wilderness: the bald eagle, trumpeter swan, raven, and great gray owl. Its spaciousness is a stronghold for people—where city dwellers can stretch their legs beneath a clear sky and parents can show their kids one tremendous unspoiled section reminiscent of what the continent was like.

Old Faithful, spouting hot water jets, and more than 10,000 other geysers, hot springs, and bubbling mud volcanoes make it the most extensive thermal area in the world—but they are only the beginning of the park's wonders. Here are the Grand Canyon of the Yellowstone River, where brawling waters rush through twisting rock walls, and Yellowstone Lake, famed for its scenic beauty and its fighting cutthroat trout, and as a gateway to backcountry canoeing. Here are innumerable plants, trees, and wildflowers of stream and lake, sagebrush desert, open meadow, and high forest.

Millions of years ago, this region was submerged beneath an inland sea. During a period of internal upheaval, the earth pushed its crust upward and the water receded. Then followed a sequence of volcanic explosions and lava flows over the Yellowstone plateau. The earth's crust fractured, great faults developed, and mountain ranges arose. In time came falling temperatures and the age of the glaciers.

Glaciers modified the hot-spring basins, which are remnants of volcanism—an expressive link between the ancient age and our own. Cold ground water, trickling downward, strikes vapors rising from seething super-hot magmas perhaps a mile down. The water boils upward, emerging at the surface as steam, causing caverns in soft rock below and terraces above.

Geyser activity varies greatly. During 1978, Steamboat Geyser, which had been bubbling quietly for almost a decade, blew its stack twice, raising spectacular columns of water 350 to 400 feet high. It thus became "the largest active geyser in the world," dwarfing Old Faithful, which rises to an average of 130 feet. However, while Steamboat is irregular and unpredictable, Old Faithful erupts with some regularity. The interval between eruptions lengthened following large earthquakes in and near Yellowstone in 1959 and 1975. Old Faithful's average interval since the 1983 earthquake at Mt. Borah, ID, has increased from about 69 to 78 minutes. Nearby geysers are erupting with greater frequency. Another major geyser, Giant Geyser, located near Old Faithful, exploded in 1978 for the first time since 1955. The park is home to over 300 geysers.

John Colter, who took leave of the Lewis and Clark expedition in 1806 to do some independent exploring, is believed to have been the first white man to see and report on this wondrous place. Among trappers and explorers who followed, Jim Bridger ("Old Gabe") added, with some exaggeration, his version—which became known as "Jim Bridger's lies." In 1859, Bridger guided the first government expedition into the area—the Army Corps of Topographical Engineers, with F. V. Hayden as geologist. Other expeditions followed, recording the wonders of Yellowstone.

One group that came to verify the frontier stories was the Washburn-Langford-Doane expedition of 1870, a party of 19 organized by several influential Montana citizens. It was named for Henry D. Washburn, Surveyor-General of Montana; Nathaniel P. Langford; and Lieutenant Gustavus C. Doane, who commanded the small military escort. They spent almost four weeks investigating the area and naming many features, including Old Faithful. Most important, they sat around a campfire one evening to discuss the future of the fantastic place they had explored. According to H. M. Chittenden, the noted historian of Yellowstone, it was Judge Cornelius Hedges who insisted that no part of the region should ever be privately owned, but that it ought to be held by the government for the use of the people. The others agreed and charted the campaign to make Yellowstone a national park.

The writing and lecturing done by members of this expedition resulted in an official exploration in 1871 by the U.S. Geological Survey. The enthusiastic endorsement of F. V. Hayden, the leader, was buttressed by a superb set of photographs taken by

William H. Jackson. From that came a recognition of the superlative nature of the Yellowstone "wonders." Representative William Horace Clagett, of Montana, introduced his famous Park Bill in 1871; it succeeded after one of the most formidable public-interest lobbying campaigns in history.

President Ulysses S. Grant signed the bill into law on March 1, 1872, placing—for the very first time—a parcel of the public domain under protection of the federal government as "a public park or pleasuring ground for the benefit and enjoyment of the people."

Fire has been part of Yellowstone since long before the park was established and long before the first explorer saw it. Fire swept through periodically, releasing the nutrients—such as nitrogen, calcium, phosphorus and potassium—that come from burned wood. They mixed into the soil to act as a fertilizer. Fire also opened the cones of lodgepole pines, raining seeds on the ground. Most fire did not kill all the trees within a burn; those it left, free of competition for nutrients, light, and water, grew stronger and healthier.

Many Indian tribes considered fire a friend, just as primitive peoples in various parts of the world set fire to "green up the grass" and stimulate new growth. But as a consequence of wildfires devastating to val-uable commercial timber forests, American public policy for the past century has been designed to suppress all fires. So the national parks were managed until 1972, when "natural regulation," or "let burn," became the policy, allowing natural fires, such as those caused by lightning, to run their course, except when threatening human life or property.

Research has shown the vast majority of wildfires die on their own, seldom burning more than 100 acres. In the 16 years before 1988, for example, 140 natural fires in Yellowstone burned an average of 240 acres.

Then came June of 1988. Lightning danced in the sky and sparked in the trees. A severe drought had turned trees into tinder. Dead litter on the forest floor, untouched during the years of fire suppression, made it worse. A carelessly tossed cigarette butt set off a new massive blaze in July.

In early September, when I was in the Grand Tetons, 50 miles south, I saw the first snow fall on Wyoming. It helped extinguish the fires, which involved about 400,000 acres. When I visited the national park the following summer, I found that more than half of Yellowstone remained untouched. The landscape indeed has changed, stimulating a new perception of our first national park and of the natural forest at work in it.

THE PRACTICAL GUIDE

BACKGROUND. A trip to Yellowstone deserves forethought and preparation. Pick your time carefully. Some 70 percent of the park's visitors come during July and August, when concessions and park facilities are hard-pressed; if you come during these months have a good idea of where you will stay. Study a map of the area. Major park campgrounds could be full, and no overflow camping is allowed. U.S. Forest Service campgrounds, reasonably convenient to major park features, are an alternative.

Allow three to five days to tour the highlights, not simply the one and a half days to do the Grand Loop. The park has five entrances: Gardiner, MT (north); West Yellowstone, MT (west); via Grand Teton National Park and Jackson, WY (south); via Cody, WY (east); and Cooke City, MT (northeast).

Principal park roads normally are open from early May through October, depending on weather conditions. Early and late snowstorms can close the roads at any time. In winter, the only road open to automobiles is from the North Entrance at Gardiner, MT, to Mammoth Hot Springs and on to Cooke City, MT, near the Northeast Entrance.

ACCESS. During the summer, you can reach West Yellowstone by Greyhound and several airlines. TW Services, the park concessioner, operates buses daily during the summer from Bozeman, Livingston, and West Yellowstone, MT; and Cody and Jackson, WY, to Canyon Village in the park. (The Bozeman bus operates once weekly in the off season as far as West Yellowstone.) Bozeman and Livingston are both served by Greyhound.

VISITOR CENTERS. Each of the five Visitor Centers interprets a different phase of the Yellowstone story. **Grant Village** features fire ecology, with video shows, three-dimensional displays, and relief models depicting the fires of 1988. **Mammoth** contains exhibits on Indians, early park history, and wildlife. **Fishing Bridge** describes birdlife, fish, and geology of the Yellowstone Lake area. **Old Faithful** explains hot spring and geyser activity, with probable erupting times of Old Faithful posted prominently. The other is at **Canyon Village.**

Wildlife. Not many visitors see a grizzly, for the bears are few in number. Though normally shy, grizzly bears can be a problem in the backcountry. Observe from a distance! Don't test your luck! Park officials have announced intention to close recreational facilities near Fishing Bridge—prime bear habitat—placing the facilities at Grant Village and elsewhere. Check with rangers for restricted or closed areas.

You will increase your chances of seeing wildlife if you fit your schedule to theirs: the early and late hours of the day are best. Many a meadow is dotted with elk in those periods, especially around Norris, but empty when the sun beats down and insects grow active. Best chances of finding moose are in Hayden Valley, near Fishing Bridge, Yellowstone Lake Lodge area, and Pelican Creek; bighorn sheep on Mount Washburn or near Soda Butte; bison along Nez Perce Creek south of Madison Junction; pronghorn near the north entrance; and coyote in both Lamor and Hayden Valley.

TOURS. TW Services, Inc. conducts tours of varying lengths. Package tours lasting two and three days start from Yellowstone and Grand Teton, featuring both national parks.

ACTIVITIES. Sightseeing. Grand Loop links the best-known park features on a 145-mile drive. Before you start, decide how much time you have available and which points interest you the most.

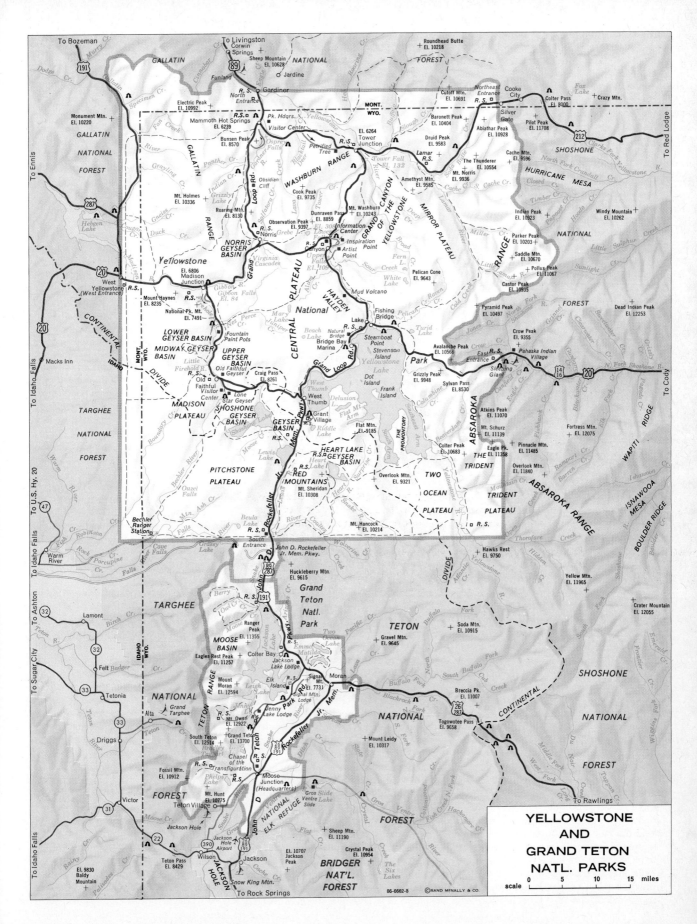

YELLOWSTONE
AND
GRAND TETON
NATL. PARKS

scale 0 5 10 15 miles

Starting from the north entrance (Gardiner), and going counterclockwise around the Grand Loop, the main features begin at **Mammoth Hot Springs**, near park headquarters. Well-marked trails enable close-range views of the brimming, terrace-like formations created by limestone deposits. **Norris Geyser Basin**, 21 miles south, is filled with exciting geysers and bubbling springs, including Steamboat, the most powerful geyser in the park. See where crown fires roared through in 1988, charring trees on the Black Basin loop trail. **Madison Junction** is within view of National Park Mountain, at the foot of which the pioneering 1870 expedition camped. Drive along Firehole River, a stream warmed by the springs in its bed. **Old Faithful** is located in an area extensively burned during the 1988 fires, but it still erupts on schedule. Each of the three basins—Upper, Midway, and Lower—should be explored, for each has its own claim to fame. Some of the most beautifully colored pools are found at **Black Sand Basin**, where vivid orange and yellow colors trace colonies of algae, water plants growing at the limits of life in the hot springs. **Geyser Hill Nature Trail** leads through a wonderland of scalding water and superheated steam. Old Faithful, the emblem of the park, has never missed an eruption during more than 80 years of observation, at intervals averaging about 70 minutes.

At **West Thumb**, after the Grand Loop twice crosses the Continental Divide, the gaudy mudpots operate against the backdrop of sparkling **Yellowstone Lake**. The road winds around the northwest shore of the lake, the largest body of water in North America at so high an elevation (7,733 feet). Its blue waters, 320 feet at its deepest, are fed by snow stored in forests above its 100-mile shoreline. Allow time for a stop at the museum, built in the early 1930s of logs and stone, restored and refurbished in the early 1980s. It contains mounted fish, birds, and mammals. Benches behind the museum overlook Yellowstone Lake, a choice spot to rest and observe. From the famous **Fishing Bridge** (no fishing allowed) at the outlet of the lake, you may see a variety of birds on the water, including white pelicans, gulls, mallards, and geese. North of Fishing Bridge, the road follows the **Grand Canyon of the Yellowstone**, 1,200 feet deep, a breathtaking spectacle from any vantage point along its twisting, 24-mile course. The dominant color of the walls is yellow, ranging in shade from pale lemon to brilliant orange. The most exciting way to see and hear the thundering **Lower Falls**, twice as high as Niagara, is to go by trail down to the brink, a rather strenuous walk. The **Upper Falls** are spectacular, too, and can be viewed without a climb. **Tower Fall**, named by the men of the 1870 expedition, is best

seen from the observation platform. Along the canyon walls, one of the most interesting rock formations of basalt, a dark lava, looks as though it had been pressed into columns.

Side roads. Take a pleasant detour off the main loop by traveling a secondary road. The **Virginia Cascade Drive**, between Norris and Canyon, provides a spectacular waterfall view. **Fountain Flats Drive**, from Madison Junction to Old Faithful, offers a dramatic view of Midway Geyser Basin and Grand Prismatic Spring.

Naturalist programs. Plan your trip to include campfire programs, which are given each evening during the summer at the main areas. There is no television or commercial movie theater in the park, but these illustrated programs by park naturalists are much better, dealing with the wonders you came to enjoy.

Field seminars of five and six days are conducted each summer by the nonprofit Yellowstone Institute, combining scientific study, nature appreciation, and recreation. Subjects include fire ecology, wildlife, wildflowers, photography, and backpacking. The Institute also offers a series of courses in the winter of four and five days on winter camping, photography, and ecology, with field travel on skis (for information, write Yellowstone Institute, Box 515, Yellowstone National Park, WY 81290).

Hiking. Yellowstone has more than 1,000 miles of well-marked, safe, backcountry trails. Some of the finest are explored on rewarding naturalist-conducted hikes. If you have but two hours to spend, try the easy **Storm Point Walk**, any morning from Fishing Bridge, to observe birds and plants along the shore of Yellowstone Lake. The **Clear Lake Walk**, afternoons from the Grand Canyon, explores the life of forest and meadow on the way to picturesque Clear Lake, a leisurely introduction to the wild country. If you're interested in seeing mudpots off the beaten path, join the three-hour hike to Pocket Basin, which leaves three mornings a week from Midway Geyser Basin.

An excellent, not-too-strenuous, all-day hike of 7.2 miles round trip leads through forest and flowering alpine meadows on the slopes of Mount Washburn to the snowy 10,243-foot summit, an adventure capped by the breathtaking view of the whole park from the lookout tower. This trip is held three mornings weekly from Canyon Village as soon after July 1 as snow conditions permit. A rewarding, but rigorous, naturalist hike leaves three times weekly from Lamar River Bridge, on the northeast entrance road, to **Specimen Ridge**, the setting of the many-layered fossil forest. The **Avalanche Peak Hike** takes you above the timberline to lofty summits; it leaves Fishing

Bridge four times weekly, beginning July 1, or as soon as snow conditions permit.

Backpacking. Trails open the way to hot springs, choice fishing streams, and wildlife summering in the high country. From the Bechler Ranger Station, in the southwest corner of the park (reached by car from Ashton, ID), the **Bechler Trail** leads past one waterfall after another. Sandhill cranes, rare trumpeter swans, ducks, and shore birds find an ideal home in meadows and swamps. Diagonally across the park, **Hellroaring Creek Trail** starts three miles west of the Tower Fall Ranger Station, leading down along Elk Creek and across the Yellowstone River on a high, narrow suspension bridge. Deer, elk, and moose are commonly seen here. Fishermen consider this a choice area. Careful study of a U.S. Geological Survey topographic map and a talk with a ranger will reveal the wide variety of trips to appeal to your own interest. Notify the ranger of your backcountry itinerary when you obtain a permit. All areas require permits for backcountry use.

Riding. You can take good one-day guided trips from Mammoth Hot Springs, Canyon, and Roosevelt Lodge near Tower Junction. Top outfitters are conveniently located around the park in Montana, Idaho, and Wyoming; they can arrange trips that last a week or a whole summer, during which you never cross a motor road or retrace your own tracks.

Boating and fishing. For good fishing and nature enjoyment, take a trip to the South Arm or the Southeast Arm of Yellowstone Lake, where no roads reach and no power boats are permitted, but where a series of camps lines the shore. Though canoes are not rented, you can hire a good rowboat. Gear, equipment, and a boat can be hauled or towed by boat taxi from Bridge Bay to (and from) Plover Point, the gateway to the South Arm. Deep in the Southeast Arm, the Molly Islands are nesting grounds for white pelican, gull, cormorant, and tern. Around Peale Island in the South Arm, the trout fishing is celebrated. Abundant moose may be observed—from a safe distance—munching aquatic plants.

Another outstanding experience is the trip from **Lewis Lake** to **Shoshone Lake**, 7 miles in length but well worth the effort (average time about three hours), especially for backcountry camping. Travel here is restricted to hand-propelled craft. Shoshone, a sanctuary for animal and bird life, abounds in fish, with a geyser basin at the southwest corner. Canoeists and rowboaters must bear in mind that Yellowstone waters are icy cold, and that sudden winds can whip up a violent surf within minutes. Craft 16 feet or less in length and all canoes are well advised to stay within ¼ mile of shore. A boat permit is required for all boats used on park waters. Boats longer than 40 feet are not allowed in the park.

Fishing and Yellowstone are synonymous, though the best waters are in the backcountry. Heart, Grebe, and Shoshone Lakes are recommended for combined hiking, camping, and fishing trips. Firehole River is a choice dry-fly trout stream, due to abundant aquatic insect life and the tempering influence of warm springs. Consider engaging a guide at one of the popular tackle shops near the park. You are required to obtain a fishing permit (free) to show you understand the regulations. Opening dates and catch limits vary throughout the park. "Fishing-for-fun" is encouraged.

To maintain native species despite a steady increase in fishing, many rivers and streams within park boundaries are on "catch-and-release" regulations. Fishing is no longer allowed on the famous Fishing Bridge near the outlet of Yellowstone Lake. Instead, fish-viewing—of trout coming to spawn on nearby gravel beds—has become popular.

Photography. Use fast shutter speed to photograph geysers. Hot pools are best on warm days, when steam does not obscure the subjects. Clean your camera lens with a soft, lintless cloth after leaving each area, since silica residues stick to the surface once they dry.

Birdwatching. Yellowstone's checklist is a long one. The trumpeter swan, the park's largest bird (rescued from near extinction), stretches snow-white wings seven feet and squawks its low-pitched "beep" while gliding gracefully over streams, such as the Madison River, in search of food. Yellowstone Lake and its islands provide breeding grounds for the white pelican, gulls, double-crested cormorants, and terns.

ACCOMMODATIONS. Three concession-operated hotels, built many years ago, are located along the Grand Loop: Mammoth Hot Springs Hotel, Old Faithful Inn, and Lake Hotel. A fourth unit is the motel-type Canyon Village Lodge. Old Faithful Inn, a classic log structure built early in the century, underwent major rehabilitation in 1981. Lake Hotel rooms and lobby were completely refurbished and restored for the 1988 season, and landscaping was completed in 1989. Unrenovated cabins offer rustic comfort at lower rates. The hotel marks its centennial in 1990, along with the State of Wyoming.

Roosevelt Lodge, in the Tower Fall area, has the flavor of the Old West, with rustic cabins at modest prices. For a complete guide to park accommodations, including rates, write TW Services, Inc., Yellowstone National Park, WY 82190.

Accommodations also are available outside the park at Cooke City, Gardiner, and West Yellowstone, MT; along US 191, the Island Park section of Idaho; and Cody and Jackson, WY; some visitors use facilities in Grand Teton as their base for touring both parks.

CAMPING. Consider staying in smaller campsites in or outside the park. During the summer peak, you may expect to find major campgrounds filled to capacity. Before leaving home, check Ticketron for site reservations at Bridge Bay, initiated on a trial basis. Ask a ranger for suggestions about less crowded sites. Trailers are permitted, but there are no electrical or plumbing hookups. Scenic Forest Service campgrounds around the park perimeter include **Snake River**, near the south entrance; **Pahaska** and **Three Mile**, east entrance; **Chief Joseph** and **Colter**, near Cooke City; and **Bakers Hole** and **South Fork**, west entrance.

SEASONS. Lodgings and stores gradually start to open in May; all are in business from about June 20 to mid-September; some remain open through October, and two facilities are open in winter. Accommodations are always available in nearby communities. The northern portion of the park is open all year through the Gardiner entrance.

Flowers are in full bloom in the lowlands around Mammoth Hot Springs in late May, when much of the park is still snowbound. Flowers appear on Mount Washburn in mid-July. The best periods to see animals and birds are May through June and September through October. In summer, animals spread over the high country range, while some birds move north and others become secretive around their nests. In autumn, snows on high ridges nudge animals to sites nearer the roads, and birds start moving south. The most memorable hour of any September visit involves the sound (and sometimes sight) of bull elk bugling their challenge. Flies and mosquitos can be troublesome in June. Summer temperatures average in the 70s, though nights are cool, with temperatures dropping to the 30s before sunrise. September is frequently as pleasant, though a little cooler.

Winter is a newly popular visitor season. The road from Gardiner at the north entrance through Mammoth Hot Springs to Cooke City at the northeast is open all winter, affording an excellent opportunity to see wildlife. Private snowmobiles are restricted to unplowed roads in the park. Snowcoaches leave from the west entrance, from Mammoth and from Flagg Ranch on the south side of the park, to Old Faithful, where winter accommodations are available. Old Faithful Visitor Center is the starting point of ski and snowshoe treks and of naturalist-led hikes around Geyser Hill Loop. All unplowed roads and trails are open to cross-country skiing and snowshoeing. Mammoth also remains open all year.

NEARBY. Due east through Sylvan Pass, the Buffalo Bill Highway (US 14/20) leads through **Shoshone National Forest**, the country's oldest forest reserve, a scenic region of lakes, glaciers, and camping areas, to Cody, location of the outstanding **Whitney Gallery of Western Art**. Northeast, through Silvergate and Cooke City, the Beartooth Highway (US 212) winds around snow-clad Granite Peak, the highest point in Montana (12,850 feet), and through Red Lodge to spectacular Beartooth Pass in **Custer National Forest** en route to Billings. **Madison River Canyon Earthquake Area**, north of West Yellowstone, scene of the 1959 earthquake, is interpreted in displays and by personnel of the **Gallatin National Forest**. South of West Yellowstone, the **Island Park** region of **Targhee National Forest** in Idaho offers streams and reservoirs for boating and fishing. Due south of Yellowstone National Park lie the mighty **Grand Tetons**, a worthy companion park to Yellowstone.

RECOMMENDED READING. Write to Yellowstone Library and Museum Association, Yellowstone National Park, WY 82190, for its complete literature list. Recommended are: *U.S. Geological Survey Topographic Map of Yellowstone; Exploring Yellowstone*, by Ruth Kirk; and the Sierra Club Totebook, *Hiking the Yellowstone Backcountry*.

FOR FURTHER INFORMATION. Write Superintendent, Yellowstone National Park, WY 82190.

YOSEMITE NATIONAL PARK

California

Established 1890

THE idea that in 1990 Yosemite National Park turns 100 years old made me think of it as history. Even though they are designed to preserve nature, national parks embody history as well, perhaps none more so than Yosemite. Whenever I come to the park, I picture it as it once was, and the people who walked the trails before me and who interpreted its purpose.

Indians dwelled and traveled through the Yosemite country, giving many of the place names we use today. They, alas, were doomed by the gold rush that began in 1849. The Mariposa Battalion, dispatched by the governor of California in 1851, chased the Indians from Yosemite Valley, and subsequently spread the word of marvels to be seen: massive El Capitan, Half Dome, Bridalveil Falls, Yosemite Falls, the Merced River flowing through meadows and pines, and giant sequoias in the Mariposa Grove of Big Trees. Horace Greeley visited in 1859, gathering material for his book *Overland Journey to San Francisco,* and proclaimed, "I know of no single wonder of Nature on earth which can claim a superiority over the Yosemite."

Presently, the valley was well established as a tourist attraction, with trails and hotels. The concerns of a thoughtful few led Congress in 1864 to turn Yosemite Valley over to the state of California "to be held inalienable for all time," not the entire park as we know it now, but only the valley and the Mariposa Big Tree Grove. Frederick Law Olmsted, a pioneer of park principles, was one of Yosemite's early champions. He saw preservation of natural scenes as beneficial to the human spirit. So did John Muir, who made his first trip to Yosemite in 1868, the start of his 40 years of adventure, exploring, interpreting, and defending the country. He launched the campaign that led to the establishment of Yosemite as a national park.

I think of Muir while hiking and camping in Yosemite. He is the guide who is always there with his words illuminating the surrounding natural treasures. I listen to what he called "the most songful streams in the world"; and rejoice at the sight of "the noblest forests, the loftiest granite domes, the deepest ice-sculptured canyons, and snowy mountains soaring into the sky."

Yosemite is the embodiment of grandeur in nature, and also of its gracefulness. The towering waterfalls sound at close range like roaring volcanoes, but from a distance appear like strands of silver. The granite spires and domes rising massively from the floor of Yosemite Valley are softened by subtle shadows and the conifers growing beneath them. The giant sequoias are impressive as towering monarchs, but I can observe one closely and appreciate its intimate beauty.

Few areas of this size (760,917 acres) have a wider variety of native plants and animals. From the warm foothills, at 2,000 feet above sea level, to the windy summit of 13,114-foot Mount Lyell, five of the seven continental life zones are represented. They range from the Upper Sonoran, where trees begin to crowd out brushy chaparral at Arch Rock, to the Arctic-Alpine above treeline at Mount Lyell. Between these two limits, bear, deer, and about 75 other species of mammal make their homes. Observers have noted about 220 kinds of birds, 25 kinds of reptiles, and nine kinds of amphibians. There are more than 1,200 species of flowering plants and many species of trees, including magnificent stands of pine and fir and enormous incense-cedars, whose red bark leads some visitors to mistake them for giant sequoias.

The natural history of Yosemite spans many millions of years, starting from the ancient age when a warm, shallow sea spread across what is now the Sierra Nevada and Great Valley of California. The first of at least three glaciers extended down the Merced River canyon as far as El Portal, while the last left a moraine of rock debris damming the Merced back into Yosemite Valley. Sediments that subsequently filled the lake form the level valley floor of today. Glacial action rounded and polished domes like Liberty Cap in Little Yosemite Valley and Lembert Dome in Tuolumne Meadows. Other domes, however, like Sentinel and Half Dome, are the result of a geologic process called *exfoliation,* a steady weathering, chipping, and crumbling of rock layers that shape angular monoliths into rounded contours on their way toward ultimate dissolution.

Muir studied the glaciers and proved their influence in shaping Yosemite. In 1892, he organized the Sierra Club, now an influential national organization, to aid in the effort to secure federal administration of the entire Yosemite region. In 1905, California receded the Valley and the Grove to the federal government and Congress formally accepted jurisdiction of the area in 1906.

In 1903 President Theodore Roosevelt spent three days in the park with Muir. The first night they bedded down in fir boughs among giant trunks of the sequoias, listening to the hermit thrush and the waterfalls tumbling down the sheer cliffs. "It was like lying in a great solemn cathedral," wrote the president, "far vaster and more beautiful than any built by the hand of man."

That feeling still prevails, I'm sure not for me alone. "Here are worlds of experience beyond the world of aggressive man, beyond history, beyond science," wrote Ansel Adams, the celebrated photographer of Yosemite. Yosemite continues to stimulate such profound ideas and ideals.

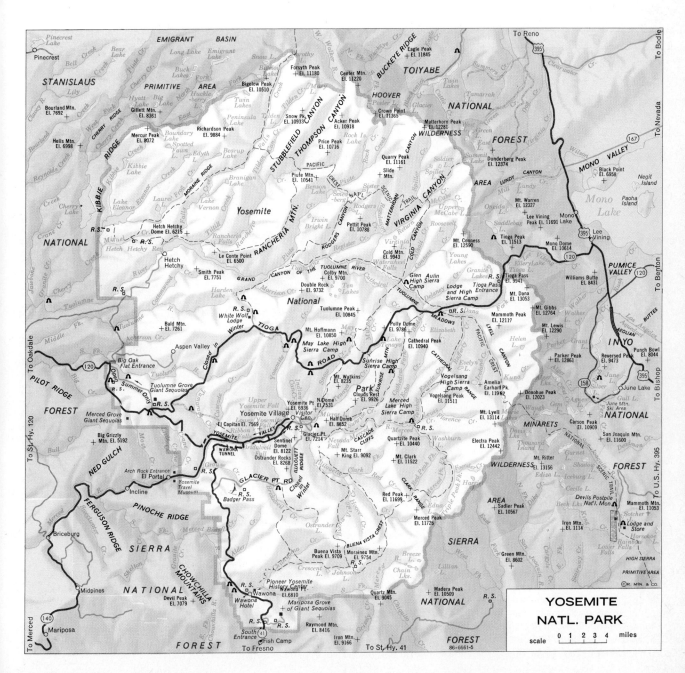

YOSEMITE NATL. PARK

scale 0 1 2 3 4 miles

THE PRACTICAL GUIDE

BACKGROUND. Though some people mistakenly regard Yosemite Valley as the whole park, the valley actually occupies only 7 of the total 1,189 square miles. Plan two days here if you're on a tour of the West; allow one week for a good backcountry trip.

ACCESS. The park has four entrances. Three are open all year: Arch Rock Entrance (67 miles from Merced via El Portal); South Entrance (59 miles from Fresno), connecting with Wawona Road; and North Entrance on Big Oak Flat Road (71 miles from Oakdale). The Tioga Road, which

offers the only entrance from the east via Tioga Pass, traverses the park from the high country to a junction with Big Oak Flat Road, but is open only from about Memorial Day weekend to early November.

Airlines, AMTRAK, and bus lines from Los Angeles and San Francisco serve Merced and Fresno, where rental cars are available. California Yosemite Tours offers daily bus service—by reservation only—between Merced AMTRAK Station and Yosemite Lodge; also between Fresno Air Terminal and Yosemite Valley. The Yose-

mite Transportation System (a unit of Yosemite Park and Curry Company) operates daily during summer from both cities (and from Merced all year) to Yosemite Valley; the company also runs bus service from Lee Vining via Tioga Pass in summer. In the park, free shuttle buses travel between lodgings, campgrounds, and visitor facilities in Yosemite Valley. The buses usually run from 9 a.m. to 10 p.m., though frequency varies from season to season. Bicycles can be rented in Yosemite Valley.

VISITOR CENTER. Yosemite Valley Vis-

old structures and conveyances associated with the early days of the area. Illustrated evening naturalist programs are conducted year-round in Yosemite Valley and during the summer campfire talks are offered at many of the campgrounds. Field seminars, sponsored by the Yosemite Natural History Association, complement the interpretive program. Subjects covered in seminars of two to seven days include geology, ecology, backpacking, photography, and art (for information, write Yosemite Natural History Association, Box 545, Yosemite National Park, CA 95389).

Sightseeing. Yosemite Valley. Filled with inspirational sights, the mile-wide valley is flanked with granite walls, domes, and peaks rising as high as 4,892 feet, and lovely waterfalls streaming down to feed the Merced River. Instead of driving, try the shuttle bus system that moves visitors on a loop in the eastern half of the valley—you'll enjoy the park more, ease congestion, and help lessen pollution. At the head of the valley from the west, the massive buttress of **El Capitan**, a geological wonder, has scarcely a fracture in its entire perpendicular wall. Other imposing formations are the **Three Brothers** (named for sons of Chief Tenaya, whose tribe lived in the mountains), **Sentinel Rock**, **Cathedral Spires**, and, at the end of the valley, mighty **Half Dome**. The famed waterfalls include **Upper Yosemite Fall**, dropping 1,430 feet, a height equal to nine Niagaras, and **Lower Yosemite Fall**, immediately below, dropping another 320 feet, as well as celebrated **Bridalveil**, **Ribbon**, **Vernal**, **Nevada**, and **Illilouette**.

From the stone lookout at **Glacier Point**, get a sweeping bird's-eye panorama from the crest of the Sierra Nevada down into Yosemite Valley. Hiking trails start here, including Four Mile Trail, leading to the valley 3,254 feet below.

Yosemite has three groves of giant sequoias *(Sequoiadendron giganteum)*, a relative of the coastal redwood, *Sequoia sempervirens*. The largest stand in the park, the **Mariposa Grove** near the South Entrance, contains 200 trees exceeding 10 feet in diameter, and 500 mature sequoias, overall. The oldest, the Grizzly Giant, is estimated to be near 3,000 years of age and stands 209 feet tall. Park in a designated area at the edge of the Mariposa Grove and ride through Muir's "Columns of Heaven" on an open-air shuttle tram, subject to modest fee. Trams operate from mid-May until mid-October. Better yet, combine a walking and riding tour through the grove. The **Tuolumne Grove**, a group of 25 fine specimens, covers about 20 acres east of the Big Oak Flat entrance. Four miles south, the **Merced Grove** contains 20 large trees. In this same region is the "**Rockefeller Tract**," one of the finest stands of sugar

itor Center has outstanding exhibits about the valley. During summer, demonstrations of Indian basketry and cooking are presented outdoors. Naturalists provide information on more than 750 miles of trails and answer a thousand questions a day about wildflowers in bloom and guided hikes, and still enjoy their work.

The **Indian Cultural Museum**, in the building west of the Visitor Center, is a recent major addition to the Yosemite scene. The collections include rare, unique objects loaned from museums throughout the country. They depict the cultural history of the Miwok and Paiute people from early times to the present.

ACTIVITIES. A focal point of the **naturalist program**, which began in 1920 as the first in any national park, is the Happy Isles Nature Center at the upper end of Yosemite Valley, with exhibits on plants and animals. Here also children 8 to 12 are invited to participate in the unique summer Junior Rangers Program. Interpretive facilities vary throughout the park. At Wawona the Pioneer Yosemite History Center displays pine in the world, whose purchase price was contributed by John D. Rockefeller, Jr.

Tuolumne Meadows is the park's major wilderness threshold, an ideal camping place and starting point for fishing, hiking, and climbing trips across meadows flecked with wildflowers, tumbling streams, and along blue lakes in the shadow of glacial cliffs. It is the only one of the six permanent trail camps accessible by automobile. From this favorite region of John Muir, the **John Muir Trail** starts at Happy Isles, traverses Tuolumne, then winds its spectacular way along the Sierra Crest to Mount Whitney, 188 miles southeast, in Sequoia National Park.

Trips may be taken on foot or horseback to aptly named Waterwheel Falls, as well as to Glen Aulin, Muir Gorge, Tenaya Lake, and Soda Springs. During the summer months the park conducts a naturalist program, including nature walks and hikes.

High Sierra by muleback. Saddle trips of six days start twice a week from Tuolumne Meadows, making a loop into the mountains. Overnight stops are made at the permanent trail camps, each set in an area of scenic beauty 7 to 10 miles apart. For instance, **Glen Aulin** is located at the foot of the White Cascade of the Tuolumne River, in the outer fringe of one of the finest stands of graceful mountain hemlock. Nearby is the spectacular series of falls made by the river in its drop to the Grand Canyon of the Tuolumne. **Merced Lake Camp**, at the head of one of the largest lakes bordering the western Sierra slopes, lies 13 miles from Yosemite Valley over a thrilling stretch of trail. The camps provide hot showers, dormitory-style tent accommodations, and wholesome food served family style. Mules are really not stubborn, just surefooted and mountain-wise. Besides the group trips, you can arrange for a guided saddle-horse-pack trip, or hire a pack burro to haul your gear while you hike. For information, write Yosemite Park and Curry Company, Yosemite National Park, CA 95389.

Hiking the loop. The Yosemite Natural History Association also conducts seven-day trips afoot, beginning each Monday and Wednesday from early July through early September from Tuolumne Meadows. A naturalist leads the way for a maximum 20 persons in a party so that everyone gets a good understanding of trailside flora, fauna, and geology. Backpacking is also popular in Yosemite. Use of the park's backcountry is regulated year-round with a limit of 4,000 visitors in the area at any one time. Permits

are required for overnight backcountry use; reservations for backcountry camping are accepted from February through May; otherwise, permits are issued on a first-come, first-served basis.

Fishing and boating. The Tuolumne and Merced Rivers, and tributary streams and lakes, all remarkably clear, offer many possibilities for dry fly and a variety of lures. A California fishing license with stamps is required. Boats (without motors) are permitted on only a few lakes.

ACCOMMODATIONS. The most celebrated and expensive lodging is the **Ahwahnee Hotel**, a classic of historic architecture, not quite gone out of style. Even if you don't stay there, stop by for a drink in the El Dorado Room and a meal in the splendid dining room (dinner reservations required all year). Vastly renovated and improved is **Yosemite Lodge**, with motel-type units among the pines near the foot of Yosemite Falls. The largest facility, **Curry Village**, consists of 600 units in wood and tent cabins. **Curry Housekeeping Camp** along the Merced River consists of tent cabins rented unfurnished except for cots and stove; either bring or rent as much gear as needed. Besides these facilities in Yosemite Valley, the **Wawona Hotel** lies 4 miles inside the south (Fresno) gateway to the park. It is the oldest hotel in continuous service in the National Park system, dating from 1879. The gingerbread wooden structures are within an easy walk of the Pioneer Yosemite History Center, a complex of early buildings assembled here from various parts of the park. Among other lodgings are the tented **Tuolumne Meadows Lodge**, **White Wolf Lodge**, and **High Sierra Camps**. For rates and reservations (advisable in all seasons), write Yosemite Park and Curry Company, Yosemite National Park, CA 95389.

CAMPING. The 330-site **Tuolumne Meadows Campground** is the largest, most popular of eight Tioga Road campgrounds, a good base for hikes to 13,000-foot Mount Lyell. Half of the Tuolumne campground is on the Ticketron system, and half is held aside for same-day arrivals—which means get there early. Narrow roads lead to more secluded campgrounds, including **Tamarack Flat** and **Yosemite Creek**. The 50-site **Tenaya Lake Campground** is for hike-in traffic only. For information, reservations, and campground data, call 209/372-0302.

SEASONS. Yosemite Lodge and Curry Village are open all year. The Ahwahnee closes only briefly in late autumn. The Wawona Hotel runs mid-May to mid-Octo-

ber. Tuolumne Meadows Lodge and White Wolf Lodge close in early September. Two campgrounds in Yosemite Valley and one at Wawona are open all year, but others in the park open during summer only. Usually in May and early June, when snows are melting, the great falls are at their thunderous best; mariposa lilies and other wildflowers spread carpets of color across the lower meadows. By July, the upper meadows are bright with flowers and the short High Sierra season begins; by late summer, many of the falls practically disappear. To many, autumn is the finest time to see Yosemite Valley, particularly for the vista from Glacier Point, overlooking the coloring of oaks, willows, and cottonwoods. By the end of October, Big Oak Flat and Wawona roads are often in riotous display. In winter the high passes are snowed in, but the towering granite walls shelter the valley. Winter sports facilities include a large outdoor skating rink near Curry Village, ski slopes and school at Badger Pass, 20 miles away, and ski touring trails to the hut at Ostrander Lake. Join a ranger on a daily two-hour snowshoe walk or a five-hour Saturday cross-country ski tour (equipment available). Yosemite Mountaineering School offers daily classes in cross-country skiing and guided trips of two and three days. Yosemite Natural History Association conducts winter environmental programs, including trans-Sierra ski tours and trips to Ostrander Lake.

NEARBY. An interesting approach to the park from the northwest is via California 49 and 120, through the **Mother Lode Country** and old gold mining communities like Amador City, Angels Camp, and Columbia. On the east side of the park, near Lee Vining, **Mono Lake** at 6,400 feet elevation harbors a protected gull rookery, with boat launching and campsites on the shore. **Devils Postpile National Monument**, in a magnificent lake and forest country southeast of the park, features an extraordinary formation of colored basalt columns, some rising more than 60 feet and fitting together like the pipes of a great organ. Flanking the park are four national forests: **Stanislaus**, on the west and northwest; **Toiyabe**, on the northeast; **Inyo**, on the east; and **Sierra**, on the south, all with fishing, swimming, and camping.

RECOMMENDED READING. *Gentle Wilderness—The Sierra Nevada*, text by John Muir, pictures by Richard Kauffman.

FOR FURTHER INFORMATION. Write Superintendent, Box 577, Yosemite National Park, CA 95389.

ZION NATIONAL PARK

Utah

Established 1919

IT TOOK me a little more than half a day to cover the five-mile round trip hike from the trail head on Zion Canyon Road to Angels Landing; parts of it were fairly tough going. It's almost 1,500 feet uphill, and the final stretch involves holding on to handrails along a steep, narrow path, but the time and energy were more than worth it. Every step of the way opened a new vista of the "Land of the Rainbow Canyons" in southern Utah. I traced the vertical walls of red sandstone as they gradually merged upward into white, while beneath them shales of purple, pink, orange, and yellow revealed what surely must be some of the most brilliantly colored rock in the world.

Zion's rich concentration of bold, multicolored features appeals to everyone—the color photographer, landscape artist, geologist (amateur or professional), trail rider, and hiker, with a special challenge awaiting the tested backcountry explorer in the aptly named "Narrows" of the Virgin River.

Through this strange land of high plateaus, deep canyons, and broad mesas, the Virgin River has cut its valley. The rock reveals that at times Zion was covered with water, oceans moving in and out as the region continued to rise, then subside. At other times broad, raging rivers traversed its surface. Most rock was laid as gravel, sand, mud, and limy ooze, which then consolidated and cemented. Across its six geologic epochs were periods of deserts with moving sand dunes, and of tropical lowlands with cycad and tree-fern forests. Embedded in the rock are fossilized seashells, fish, trees, and the bones and tracks of land animals. Thus it is known that immense reptiles and dinosaurs once wallowed in marshes and bayous in this area.

One of the most surprising discoveries was made in 1976 in a small park spring: a relict, or remnant, population of minute snails, believed to have survived for 10 to 15 million years. Totaling 10,000 to 15,000 in number, these snails likely comprise a distinctive species, found nowhere else on earth.

Zion Canyon, central feature of the 147,035 acre park, bespeaks the middle, or Mesozoic, period of geological history. It begins where the ancient record of the Grand Canyon leaves off, and it ends where the later history of Bryce Canyon begins. In these three parks, one can journey through a thousand million years of time, unfolding the story of this continent from one logical sequence to the next. Geologic forces, the water, wind, and ice—even the plants and animals—that shaped this narrow canyon in the Markagunt Plateau are still at play.

During spring runoff and after a sudden summer storm, the Virgin River, an important erosion force, may become a raging torrent, depositing debris at every turn—logs, rock, and other material from many miles distant.

Zion's "hanging gardens" in the cliffs are beautiful during spring and summer, with a cover of columbine, shooting-star, and cardinal flowers. The park's most interesting blossom, however, the sacred datura, grows on the canyon floor, reaching heights of two feet and more; its large, white, trumpet-shaped flowers open in the evening and wilt beneath the morning sun's rays.

In contrast to the desert vegetation and water-loving plants crowding the river bottoms are the deep-green forests of pine, Douglas fir, and white fir along the cool upper ledges and at the rim of the plateau. It takes time to see and appreciate the diverse parts that shape the whole landscape.

Human history in Zion, traced through crumbling ruins, reaches back to the Basketmakers, the earliest inhabitants of the Southwest, followed by the Pueblos, followed by the Paiutes, a peaceful people who claimed this region when the Spaniards arrived at the time of the American Revolution. It was the Mormons of the succeeding century who named it Zion, interpreted as the "heavenly city of God." They gave religious names to natural temples in the canyon, and when I reached the perch of Angels Landing, I felt they had named it well.

THE PRACTICAL GUIDE

BACKGROUND. Many scenic attractions of Zion Canyon are visible from the roadway, but allow at least two days, even more if you want to take wonderful trips into the backcountry on foot or horseback.

Zion-Mt. Carmel Highway, the approach from US 89 and the east gate (elevation 5,725 feet), ranks among the spectacular drives of the country. In descending 11 miles and 1,800 feet from the entrance, the highway passes through mile-long Zion Tunnel, where window-like galleries gouged in the rock enable travelers to view the panorama of the canyon and scenic wonders like East Temple and the Great Arch. Then it zigzags over six huge switchbacks, dropping 800 feet in less than 4 miles. (Stopping is prohibited for safety reasons.) The **Kolob Canyons Road** is a 5.2-mile spur leading into the northeast corner of the park from I-15.

VISITOR CENTERS. The **South Visitor Center**, an attractive, low building near the south entrance station on Utah 9, is an important stop. Besides observing the museum displays, check the schedule of naturalist-guided walks conducted several times each day during the summer. Illustrated evening programs are presented by naturalists nightly at park campgrounds and at Zion Lodge. **Kolob Canyons Visitor Center** is an excellent stop for local and regional information on the Grand Circle of southwest national parks, monuments, and recreation areas. It is conveniently located at the I-15 exit into the northwest section of the park and is open daily all year.

TOURS. From May to October, Color Country Tours provides bus service from Cedar City and from St. George three times weekly. Zion Lodge provides one-hour narrated tram rides along the scenic drive. Horseback trips are conducted by the concessioner every day during the summer travel season from Zion Lodge on the Sand Bench Trail.

ACTIVITIES. Sightseeing. Zion Canyon Scenic Drive, a round trip of 12 miles, provides a constantly changing vista of varicolored cliffs rising above the valley floor. The dominant feature, beyond Twin Brothers, Mountain of the Sun, and Red Arch, is the towering 2,400-foot monolith called **Great White Throne**. The throne ranges in color from deep red at the base up through pale pink and gray to white at the top. North of the throne, the road and river make a wide swing past a splintered crimson formation called the Organ, with Angels Landing rising 1,500 feet behind it. As the canyon steadily narrows, the roadway reaches its end at the **Temple of Sinawava**, a huge natural amphitheater, with two large stone pillars, The Altar and The Pulpit, in the center.

Weeping Rock Trail is one of three easy, self-guiding nature trails. It takes only 45 minutes from the parking area at the foot of Cable Mountain, climbing gradually to the Weeping Rock, with a display of wildflowers along the way. The abundant vegetation is due to water-resistant qualities in the shale; downward percolation from the highlands is interrupted, so the water streams down the rock face and seemingly "weeps." Another self-guiding trail, **Canyon Overlook**, begins at the upper end of Zion Tunnel, following the rock ledges above Pine Creek Canyon through pinyon pine, juniper, yucca, and cactus to a point directly above the Great Arch.

Gateway to the Narrows Trail is the third easy, popular trip (of two hours or less) starting from the Temple of Sinawava and following the Virgin River up the narrow canyon to a point where there is no longer room for both river and trail—only a few feet separate walls one-quarter mile high. This is a naturalist-guided walk, but you may take it on your own. The high cliffs, springs, and seeps offer a cool, moist environment for a large variety of plants and animals. Watch for mule deer along the trail, and for tracks of skunk, bobcat, gray fox, and ringtail. You may see the "blue-bellied lizard" and a few choice snakes, including the rare, beautiful, regal ringneck. Well-maintained trails of approximately 55 miles give access to other impressive features. Going to **Angels Landing** requires a fairly strenuous 5-mile round trip to the top, but you'll be rewarded with beautiful views of the canyon.

Kolob Canyons Road (or Taylor Creek Road) leads to the northwest section of the park near Kanarraville, with overlooks commanding spectacular views. It contains the red sandstone canyons of the Kolob, a deeper red than in Zion Canyon itself. Sheer walls form box canyons 1,500 feet deep. Hurricane Fault represents a displacement of rock caused by splitting of the earth's crust. Layers from the time of the Kaibab formation are clearly exposed by the fault.

Backcountry trails. Among several routes, a choice, accessible one is the **West Rim Trail**, 12.3 miles long, good for two days of backpacking. The West Rim country, formed of deep, beautiful canyons and high, forested plateaus, is rich in wildlife, with a few cougars and such birds as swallows, nuthatches, bluebirds, and warblers. Hawks and golden eagles nest in the higher pinnacles. **LaVerkin Creek Trail** affords an opportunity to view the high, rugged wilderness at its best, with an excellent backpacking and horseback route and good campsites along LaVerkin Creek. The trail can be approached from Lee Pass on the west side, and a topographic map (available at the Visitor Centers) should be part of your equipment. An interesting side trip is **Kolob Arch**, 120 feet thick and 390 feet high, even higher than the famed Rainbow Bridge. The Kolob Canyons constitute some of southern Utah's most scenic country. Routes starting on the headwaters of the Virgin River, north of the park, join the celebrated, unique **Narrows Trip**, which ends at the **Temple of Sinawava** in Zion Canyon. A three-day trip begins on Deep Creek in Dixie National Forest near Cedar Breaks National Monument. The most popular hike, 12 miles on the North Fork, starting from the vicinity of Chamberlain's Ranch, can be done in one day, but may be better in two. Much of the trip is negotiated by wading between sheer, sandstone walls. Sometimes the walls overhang the stream; at other times they widen into amphitheaters of sculptured cliffs where glens are carpeted with grass and wildflowers. Rocky bars and sandy banks in shoal areas provide campsites. Such was the way of travel of the Paiutes and the early explorers like Jedediah Smith, who named the river for a contemporary, Thomas Virgin. Weather conditions govern the trip season. It is dangerous in spring due to snow runoff from the mountains, and even more so during July and August when flash floods rise in the narrow gorge. The best months are June, September, and early October, but even then hiking parties should obtain a Narrows Permit and check for advice at the Visitor Centers. Permits are required for overnight backcountry use.

Birdwatching. Among almost 250 species, you are apt to see birds of the desert, like the roadrunner and spurred towhee, as they dart across canyon lowlands, or the western kingbird perching on a fence ready to pounce on insect prey. In the narrow, moist canyon of the Virgin River you can hear the shrill "cheep" of a canyon wren and catch sight of this lively bird flitting from rock to rock. Zion is known for southern birds at the northern limit of their range; these include the black hawk, gray vireo, and painted redstart. The Kolob Plateau is an excellent place to observe highland species during spring and summer.

Photography possibilities are unlimited with deep shadows and bright cliffs. Along with recording scenery, you can tell the story in pictures of Zion's intriguing geology. Start with the pattern of crossbedded deposits in Checkerboard Mesa near the east entrance. Shoot the East Rim trail for Navajo sandstone, the East Temple for Carmel limestone, the Chocolate Cliffs or Belted Cliffs of Moenkopi, ancient rock exposed to view—before long you'll find new meaning in photographs, and in your travels. During summer, midmorning is best to photograph Zion Canyon; midday is best in winter. Photography in the high country is best during morning and late afternoon.

ACCOMMODATIONS. In the center of Zion Canyon, Zion Lodge comprises hotel, rustic cabins, and dining room. For rates and reservations, write TW Services, Inc., 451 North Main Street, Cedar City, UT 84720, or Bryce-Zion Trail Rides, Tropic, UT 84776.

CAMPING. The park's two large campgrounds are the South and the Watchman, both just inside the South Entrance. Lava Point has a small campground with pit toilets and no water. All have 14-day limits.

SEASONS. The park is open all year, but accommodations are available only from early spring to late fall. The exact dates vary from year to year. Though winter is usually mild and snowfall is light in the canyon, the higher trails can become impassable. Colored cliffs stand out in contrast to snow-covered terraces and slopes. May is the time for violets, orchids, penstemons and, in shady nooks, columbine and monkey flowers. Summers are hot (up to 100 degrees), except in the high country. Late summer is a blooming time, of asters, paintbrush, and cardinal flowers. September and October are excellent months to visit Zion, with clear skies and light crowds.

NEARBY. The North Rim of the **Grand Canyon** lies 125 miles south, while **Bryce Canyon National Park** lies 89 miles northeast—a compact triumvirate of scenic and geological marvels. **Cedar Breaks National Monument**, 86 miles north on the Markagunt Plateau, contains a gigantic, multicolored natural amphitheater, the Pink Cliffs, a part of the Wasatch formation. At elevations as high as 10,700 feet in surrounding **Dixie National Forest**, Navajo Lake is a favored vacation spot with fishing, lodge, and choice campgrounds. **Strawberry Point**, southeast of the lake, affords panoramic views across the Zion Canyon country. **St. George**, just above the state line on the road to Lake Mead and Las Vegas, is the site of the first Mormon temple in Utah. Standing 175 feet high, it was built in 1877 of hand-quarried sandstone. In the center of town, the colonial-style winter home of Brigham Young contrasts with the rough pioneer dwellings of the period. At **Santa Clara**, 5 miles west of St. George, the 1862 house of Jacob Hamlin, Mormon scout and peacemaker among the Indians, still stands. Nearby **Snow Canyon State Park**, with its walls of red and yellow sandstone, has been the setting of numerous western films (and the hideout of early outlaws). Motel accommodations can be found in Springdale and nearby Cedar City, Glendale, Kanab, and St. George.

FOR FURTHER INFORMATION. Write Superintendent, Zion National Park, Springdale, UT 84767.

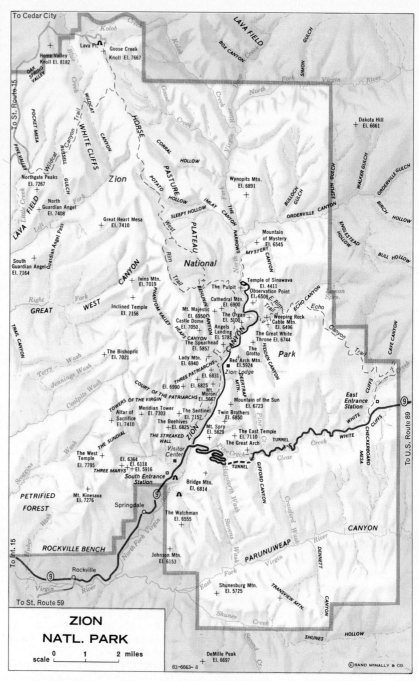

ZION NATL. PARK

164

ADDITIONAL NATIONAL PARK SERVICE AREAS

IN AND AROUND WASHINGTON, DC

Almost all of the major monuments and shrines and nearly everything green in Washington, DC, are administered as part of the National Park System. Activities and facilities range from concerts, nature walks, and picnic areas, to jogging and bicycle trails, and countless scheduled events.

It's impossible to do it all in a weekend, or even in a week. I strongly advise starting with a ride on the concession-operated Tourmobile, which provides interpretive shuttle service to 18 key sites in the heart of Washington, plus Arlington National Cemetery and Mount Vernon in Virginia. You can get on and off all you want at these locations without extra charge on the same day. You can also get guidance from Park Service personnel stationed at information kiosks in the monumental heart of the city.

Make a list of your own special points of interest. If this is your first visit, include the Jefferson and Lincoln Memorials, Washington Monument, Vietnam Veterans Memorial, and the White House. Work with a map to conserve time and energy. You'll do plenty of walking, so choose a few sitting activities, such as a boat trip on the Chesapeake & Ohio Canal or a concert at Wolf Trap Farm Park.

You'll get a new vista of the capital from the open-air observation level of the renovated Old Post Office Building, 12th and Pennsylvania N.W. Free tours are conducted to the clock tower. The Old Post Office is midway between the White House and the Capitol, with a variety of places to shop and eat. Other eating places worth mentioning are: the National Sculpture Garden; the National Gallery of Art; and cafeterias at the Capitol and most government buildings—some serve breakfast; for lunch, get in early.

More than 150 miles of bike path are administered by the National Capital Region. These include compacted gravel and asphalt trails, sidewalks, and side streets in the Mall area, East and West Potomac Parks, the C & O towpath from Georgetown to Great Falls Park, Maryland, and the Virginia bikeway extending all the way to Mount Vernon.

A great deal has been done to make the parks and monuments accessible to physically disabled visitors. Sign language tours can be arranged at almost every National Park Service site, including Ford's Theatre and Frederick Douglass Home.

For daily schedules, special events, entry fees (where they apply) or further information on any of these areas, call Dial-a-Park (426-6975) or National Capital Region (426-6700) or write National Capital Region, National Park Service, 1100 Ohio Drive, S.W., Washington, DC 20242.

Arlington National Cemetery

167

ARLINGTON HOUSE
Virginia

Robert E. Lee married and lived here until he left for the Civil War. The house was occupied by Union troops, and in 1864 the surrounding estate was transformed into a cemetery. The stately mansion, now beautifully restored with original furnishings, faces the national capital as the frontispiece of Arlington National Cemetery, with the grave of John F. Kennedy on the knoll below. You can reach it by car via Memorial Bridge and park at Arlington Cemetery Visitor Center, but you don't really have to drive. Take the Tourmobile, which stops at the Visitor Center (a significant point of interest in itself).

CATOCTIN MOUNTAIN PARK
Maryland

This mountain retreat of 5,700 acres is near Thurmont, 65 miles north of Washington. Park Central, the main park road, begins at the Visitor Center off Maryland 77, winds through the park for 4.6 miles to its junction with the Foxville-Deerfield Road. Twenty-five miles of well-marked trails traverse the park, leading to outstanding views and natural features. The Owens Creek Campground is available from mid-April through October for family camping. Modern rest rooms, tables, and fireplaces are provided. Camping is limited to seven consecutive days and fourteen days per season; a nominal fee is charged. Due to the terrain, trailers more than 22 feet in length are not permitted. A full program of interpretive services, such as guided walks, talks, and campfire programs, is offered; a schedule is available at the Visitor Center, which houses a museum. The two camps you pass along Park Central Road—Greentop and Misty Mount—are now used primarily for Environmental Education. Greentop is available on spring and fall weekends to organized groups; Misty Mount, to the general public from May to the end of October. Camp David, the presidential retreat, is closed to the public.

CHESAPEAKE AND OHIO CANAL
NATIONAL HISTORICAL PARK
District of Columbia-Maryland-West Virginia

Many canals were built in the age of westward movement, but this remains one of the longest and least altered. The canal was begun with enthusiasm in 1828, designed to link Georgetown, in the District of Columbia, with Pittsburgh, on the Ohio River. However, endless difficulty and adversity slowed things down so that by 1850 it extended only as far as Cumberland, in western Maryland, and by then the railroad obviously was becoming the dominant means of transportation. The canal lingered on until 1924, principally as a carrier of coal from Cumberland to the eastern market.

Had it not been for the care and concern of Justice William O. Douglas and other conservationists during the 1950s, the C & O Canal might have become a paved highway. Justice Douglas described the canal as a long stretch of quiet and peace "not yet marred by the roar of wheels and sound of horns." In 1977, Congress dedicated the park to him "in grateful recognition."

Mule-drawn barge trips travel three miles of the canal in 1½ hours. Interpreters in period dress describe daily barge life and perform music of the canal era. There are two barges from which to choose: the *Georgetown*, which leaves from 30th Street in the heart of Georgetown, and *Canal Clipper*, from the historic Great Falls Tavern, now a park museum, in Potomac, Maryland, about 15 miles northwest of Washington.

At its peak, during the 1870s, about 500 boats navigated the 185 miles from Georgetown to Cumberland, loaded with coal, flour, grains, and lumber. Each was pulled by two or three mules and raised and lowered through 75 locks along the way. All told,

almost 500 structures have been left to represent the canal era.

The historic canal was placed under the National Park Service in 1938, then proclaimed a national monument in 1961; through congressional action the park was significantly enlarged in 1971 and given historical park status. In 1972 a hurricane caused severe damage. An extensive repair program was undertaken and now most is restored.

Along the towpath the National Park Service has installed a series of simple campsites, nicknamed "Hiker-Biker Overnighters," 10 miles apart, from Dam 3, opposite Harpers Ferry, to Cumberland. Antietam Creek Campground is the largest one, providing access to the towpath and to fishing (for bass, catfish, and sunfish) in the nearby Potomac.

Attention, birdwatchers. Mark early May as the time to see the famed spring eastern warbler migration from along the towpath. You'll see many other species, including cardinals, bluebirds, and wood ducks, even on the mule-drawn barge trip from Georgetown.

The Kiwanis Youth Hostel near Sandy Hook, Maryland, provides simple, inexpensive accommodations for American Youth Hostel members. Near Harpers Ferry, it is close to mile 58 on the Canal, where the Appalachian Trail crosses the Potomac River.

CLARA BARTON NATIONAL HISTORIC SITE
Maryland

Clara Barton, founder of the American National Red Cross (who lived from 1821 to 1912), built this large house in Glen Echo, Maryland, a suburb of Washington, DC, in the 1890s. The 36 rooms and 38 large closets were designed to accommodate Red Cross workers and their emergency relief supplies. From 1897 to 1904 the house was national Red Cross headquarters. Miss Barton lived here her last twenty years. Reminders of her life and times, including her strong support of women's rights, are displayed throughout the house.

FORD'S THEATRE NATIONAL HISTORIC SITE
District of Columbia

Abraham Lincoln was fatally shot here by John Wilkes Booth on April 14, 1865. It has been authentically restored to its appearance of that period. Plays are presented usually from September through May. Some, but not all, are historic in nature. Prices are high for the average family, though children and groups are favored with special rates. The **Lincoln Museum** in the basement houses valuable exhibits associated with the fallen president's life. The **House Where Lincoln Died**, directly across the street, is restored to its original appearance. Here Secretary of War Stanton uttered his memorable words, "Now he belongs to the ages."

FORT WASHINGTON PARK
Maryland

The fort is across the Potomac River from Mount Vernon. This is an imposing bastion of another age. The first fort was built in 1809, designed by Pierre Charles L'Enfant (who laid out the city of Washington). It was destroyed by the British during the War of 1812, then subsequently rebuilt as an outer defense of the Capital. Open 7:30 a.m. to dark.

FREDERICK DOUGLASS HOME
District of Columbia

The former slave who became a prominent statesman as well as America's leading Negro spokesman lived in this 14-room Victorian home, which he named "Cedar Hill," from 1877 until his death in 1895. This lovely home and its furnishings were saved through the years by organizations until they were added to the National Park system in 1962. The little one-room study he called the "Growlery" was reconstructed in 1981. Open 9 a.m. to 5 p.m. daily.

GEORGE WASHINGTON MEMORIAL PARKWAY
Virginia-Maryland

Landscaped with native plants, the 23-mile completed section of the parkway extends from the Capital Beltway (I-495) on the Virginia side of the Potomac River to the country's foremost mansion, George Washington's home at Mount Vernon. Since it opened, in 1932, the parkway has become a well-traveled route from the nation's capital to the shrine. Many walk the paths along the Potomac, some fish, others watch birds. Picnic tables are popular.

The parkway includes important shrines and recreation areas. **Great Falls** offers spectacular views of the Potomac River gorge and falls on both sides of the river. On the Virginia side are picnic areas and remnants of an old canal started by George Washington; on the Maryland side, the old Great Falls Tavern, C & O Canal locks, and conducted walks during summer months.

At the U.S. Marine Corps War Memorial, popularly called the **Iwo Jima Memorial**, the American flag flies 24 hours a day; weekly sunset reviews are given by Marines during the summer. Nearby, the **Netherlands Carillon** represents an expression of appreciation from a small nation for help during World War II; carillon concerts are given Saturdays spring to fall, and on holidays. **Arlington House** (formerly Custis-Lee Mansion) is the frontispiece of Arlington Cemetery (see page 168) facing Washington. **Theodore Roosevelt Island**, reached by footbridge, is an 88-acre preserve in the Potomac River with forest and swamp trails (see page 170).

At the south end of the parkway the great reward is to stroll the grounds of Mount Vernon (administered by the Mount Vernon Ladies Association) and gaze over the Potomac to the opposite shore, where some parts are preserved today much as they looked years ago. Nearby points of interest associated with Washington's family and friends include Woodlawn Plantation, Gunston Hall, and Pohick Church.

GREENBELT PARK
Maryland

This 1,078-acre woodland park is 12 miles northeast of Washington on the Baltimore-Washington Parkway. It has 12 miles of marked trails, abundant wildlife, and facilities for hiking and camping. The 178 campsites are available for 5-day stays from June to Labor Day, 14 days the rest of the year.

JOHN F. KENNEDY CENTER FOR THE PERFORMING ARTS
District of Columbia

The Concert Hall, Opera Hall, Eisenhower Theater, Film Institute, and other facilities comprise a national cultural center in this overpowering structure on the banks of the Potomac River between Key and Memorial Bridges. It opened in September 1971. The Park Service is responsible principally for maintenance and protection. It is one of the most heavily visited buildings in Washington, handsomely furnished with gifts of other nations. Regular tours are conducted daily 10 a.m. to 1:15 p.m.

KENILWORTH AQUATIC GARDENS
District of Columbia

Located in Anacostia Park, reached via Kenilworth Avenue, N. E., the gardens were started by a government employee as a hobby 80 years ago. Now they contain more than 100,000 water plants,

169

including rare exotic species with immense leaves up to six feet in diameter. Best time to visit is mid-June, when thousands of plants are in bloom. In late July and August the tropical water lilies open. Many flowers close in the heat of day, so visit in the mornings. Open year-round.

LINCOLN MEMORIAL
District of Columbia
The classical structure of dignity and beauty at the approach to Arlington Memorial Bridge is bordered by 36 columns, one for each state in the Union at the time of Lincoln's death. Within the chamber, the 19-foot marble statue of the emancipator, by Daniel Chester French, occupies the place of honor, while on flanking walls the Gettysburg Address and Second Inaugural Address are inscribed. On the wall behind the statue are these words: "In this temple as in the hearts of the people for whom he saved the Union, the memory of Abraham Lincoln is enshrined forever." The memorial is very impressive at night when the lights come on.

Ask about reservations for the guided tour called "Looking Under Lincoln," which is given periodically. It's the only spelunker's tour in Washington, going 45 feet below the surface into the memorial's cave-like foundation. You'll find stalagmites and stalactites, as in a natural cave, formed by water percolating through cracks in the memorial's limestone foundation.

LINCOLN MUSEUM. See Ford's Theatre, page 168.

LYNDON BAINES JOHNSON MEMORIAL GROVE ON THE POTOMAC
Virginia
A grove of 500 white pine trees forms a living memorial to the late president. The 15-acre site, in Lady Bird Johnson Park, on the west bank of the Potomac River commands an imposing vista of the national capital. The park includes a mile of walking trails. A towering slab of Texas pink granite has been engraved with some of President Johnson's more significant statements.

MARY McLEOD BETHUNE COUNCIL HOUSE NATIONAL HISTORIC SITE
District of Columbia
The 4-story Victorian townhouse on Logan Circle was the home of the famed educator from 1943 until her death in 1955. Born to slave parents in South Carolina, she was founder and president of Bethune-Cochran College in Florida, as well as an advisor to four presidents starting with Calvin Coolidge. The house contains the National Archives for Black Women's History and a memorial museum.

NATIONAL MALL
District of Columbia
The original 1790 plan of French architect Pierre de L'Enfant for the new capital city called for a formal park, the Mall, from the Capitol to the present Washington Monument. Now extended to the Lincoln Memorial, the Mall contains 145 acres of lawns, reflecting pools, hiking trails, and wooded glades. Units of the Smithsonian Institution and the National Gallery of Art are located on the Mall.

OXON HILL FARM
Maryland
The farm, which overlooks the Potomac River a few miles south of Washington, includes pens and pastures with common farm animals. Hay barn, feed room, equipment shed, and workroom are open; machinery and equipment are displayed and demonstrated. Open daily 8 a.m. to 5 p.m.

PISCATAWAY PARK
Maryland
Seven miles of riverfront across the Potomac River from Mount Vernon preserve the scenic view from Washington's home. The historic landscape of marshes, streams, forests, and open fields enhance fishing and picnicking. The **National Colonial Farm**, operated by the Accokeek Foundation, showcases agricultural techniques of the 1700s. Staple crops are raised without the use of insecticides. Tilling and planting are done by hand. Livestock include Devon cattle and Dorset sheep, types prevalent during colonial times, as an integral part of the farm. Each spring and fall the farm conducts sales of its goods and reenacts colonial life.

PRINCE WILLIAM FOREST PARK
Virginia
The forested parkland is located at Triangle, about 35 miles south of Washington, DC. It is an excellent place to camp on a visit to the Washington area. Approximately 35 miles of trails and fire roads afford access to the wilder regions of the park. Parking areas along park roads provide convenient starting points for many hikes. Self-guiding nature trails begin and end at each picnic area and campground. There are also bike trails in the park and rental bicycles available. Oak Ridge Campground has 113 family sites, each with a paved slip, available on a first-come, first-served basis. Turkey Run Ridge Campground has 12 group tent sites, for which reservations are required. Travel Trailer Village, operated by a concessioner, has 98 all-year sites for 7-day stays.

ROCK CREEK PARK
District of Columbia
James Bryce, the British statesman, said there is "nothing comparable" in Europe's capitals to Rock Creek Park. John Burroughs said "Rock Creek has ... not only pleasing but wild and rugged scenery." This natural woodland in northwest Washington, some 4 miles long and a mile wide, is one of the country's larger urban parks, favored by hikers, bicyclists, and horseback riders. Its 1,754 acres contain: historic Pierce Mill; the Joaquin Miller Cabin; a superb nature center and planetarium; outdoor activity facilities; and the Carter Barron Amphitheater—an outdoor setting for musical and variety programs.

SEWALL-BELMONT HOUSE NATIONAL HISTORIC SITE
District of Columbia
The 2½-story red brick house is reputed to be one of the oldest on Capitol Hill. It stands as a memorial to the dedication of Alice Paul and her associates, who were leaders in the woman's suffrage battle and founded the Congressional Union, later called the National Women's Party.

THEODORE ROOSEVELT ISLAND
District of Columbia
This island of plants and animals in a wild state is a living memorial to Theodore Roosevelt, who, while in the White House (1901-09), did more than any other president to preserve the nation's natural resources through establishment of the national forests and wildlife refuges. Even in Washington he loved to explore the outdoors. Roosevelt Island, one mile long and a half mile wide, lies south of Key Bridge in the Potomac. The woods and waters provide the habitat for raccoons, muskrats, and other small animals; you may see or hear a variety of birds from kingfishers to woodpeckers and wood thrushes. Interpretive programs are given frequently. The island is now accessible by footbridge from the Virginia shore. A highway crossing the southern tip of the island was constructed in the 1960s. There is no access to the park from that highway.

THOMAS JEFFERSON MEMORIAL
District of Columbia

Reflections of the circular colonnaded structure in the waters of Washington's Tidal Basin enhance its beauty, especially in early spring when Japanese cherry trees are in blossom. Jefferson's words, "I have sworn upon the altar of God eternal hostility against every form of tyranny over the mind of man," are inscribed above the 19-foot bronze statue of the man who wrote the Declaration of Independence and served as third president of the United States. Open daily, 8 a.m. to midnight.

VIETNAM VETERANS MEMORIAL
District of Columbia

This striking, simple monument evokes strong memories of those who lost their lives in America's most controversial war. Its simple geometric form, two gleaming walls of polished black marble in a landscaped setting, pointing to the nearby Lincoln Memorial and to the Washington Monument, makes it one of the most significant places of pilgrimage in Washington, DC. A bronze life-sized sculpture of three servicemen faces the wall, as though looking for their own names. Almost every day visitors leave behind a single rose, a wreath, a religious object, or a small American flag. Park Service personnel are stationed at the memorial to assist in finding names. Some visitors decline the help, preferring to be alone. "A lot of the people I help," noted one Park Service aide, "are here to take pictures of the names, or do rubbings they can take home to somebody who lost a son or brother in Vietnam. They cry, and we cry with them."

WASHINGTON MONUMENT
District of Columbia

Construction began in 1848 but proceeded slowly, with delays and changes in design over the years. By 1884, the monument,

a classic obelisk, was completed. It was the tallest structure in the world.

A fitting monument to the father of his country, the granite shaft rises 555 feet from ground to apex. The elevator ride to the 500-foot-high observation room takes one minute. The observation windows afford the finest orientation view of the capital—on a clear day you can see everything within 20 miles. Open 9 to 5; summer, 8 a.m. to midnight. Prepare for long waiting lines in spring and summer.

WHITE HOUSE
District of Columbia

The grounds of the nation's foremost residence and office are administered by the National Park Service. Many of the trees are of historic interest; every president from James Madison through Ronald Reagan has planted a tree on the grounds. Mrs. Reagan planted a Magnolia Alba. The White House is open to visitors Tuesday through Saturday from 10 a.m. to 12:45 p.m. in summer; 10 a.m. to noon in winter. Summer tours are organized; free tickets are issued, starting at 8 a.m. Tickets are available the day of the tour only. Check with the office of your Congressman or Senator for tickets to "Congressional Tours," given 8:15 a.m. Tuesday through Saturday.

WOLF TRAP FARM PARK FOR THE PERFORMING ARTS
Virginia

The park, located near Vienna, about 14 miles from Washington, is a showcase for opera, jazz, modern dance, ballet, and symphony concerts. You can sit under cover in the 6,900-seat Filene Center, or bring a blanket and picnic and enjoy the lawn beyond it.

ARCHAEOLOGICAL AREAS

MANY of the archaeological ruins of the Southwest were observed by the early Spanish explorers. Father Kino is believed to have discovered the Casa Grande ruin, in the Gila River Valley of Arizona, as early as 1694. Escalante, the Franciscan missionary, reported on finding extensive cliff dwellings and pueblos along his route. In 1805 the Spaniards massacred Navajos in Canyon del Muerto, a part of what is now Canyon de Chelly National Monument.

For the most part, the ruins were left as they had been lived in long before the dawn of recorded history on this continent. The aboriginal Indians had abandoned their dwellings in good condition, presumably driven out by a long period of drought in the 13th century. The Spaniards saw no promise of gold in these cities in the rock and caused little disturbance to them.

By the end of the 19th century, however, it was another story. The surge of migration East into the Southwest brought with it a wave of uncontrolled vandalism. Wholesale commercial looting was conducted by "pot hunters" to meet increasing demands for artifacts. Probably no cliff dwelling in the Southwest was more thoroughly dug over in search of pottery and other objects for commercial purposes than Cliff Palace, in what is now Mesa Verde National Park. Parties of "curio seekers" camped on the ruins for several winters. Some of the treasures they carried out are now in museums, others are lost forever to science. Perhaps even worse, in the process of digging they thoughtlessly blew out walls with powder, mutilated the buried kivas and used beams for firewood so that not a single roof was left.

In 1906, at last, Congress adopted the Act for the Preservation of American Antiquities, or the Antiquities Act, which made it a federal offense to injure, damage, or destroy antiquities on federal lands. It also provided for the establishment of national monuments by presidential proclamation. National monuments now can be established either by such proclamation or by congressional action, so long as they have national significance worth preserving—scientific, historic, or natural. All but one of the archaeological areas are national monuments.

Despite best intentions and legislation, the protection of antiquities remains a challenge. When you visit one of the archaeological areas, ask a ranger to bring you up to date.

ALIBATES FLINT QUARRIES
Texas
On this site, 35 miles northeast of Amarillo, the Alibates mines were found and used by ancient man more than 12,000 years ago—7,000 years before the pyramids were built in Egypt. The brightly colored flint was quarried for making tools and weapons. Use of Alibates flint continued into the modern period by the Plains Indians, until metal was obtained from the white man. Tours are conducted by a historian during the summer. The monument is reached by driving northeast of Amarillo on Texas 136, 35 miles to Alibates Road (7½ miles southwest of Fritch), then 5 miles to the Bates contact station. Guided tours are conducted twice daily (10 a.m. and 2 p.m.) from Memorial Day to Labor day; off-season tours by reservation. The tours cover about 1 mile, round trip, including a walk up steep inclines to the Alibates site and a demonstration of shaping flint into weapons. Collecting samples is not permitted at the historic site, though one handful of flint is permitted from the Lake Meridith area.

Traces of pre-Pueblo culture have also been found at Palo Duro Canyon State Park (noted especially for the exposure of 200 million years of geological formations). The Panhandle-Plains Historical Museum, at Canyon, presents the panorama of life in the area from ancient to frontier times. Address: c/o Lake Meredith National Recreation Area, Box 1438, Fritch, Texas 79036.

AZTEC RUINS
New Mexico
Near Farmington and the Navajo Reservation in the Four Corners country, the monument preserves the stabilized ruins of a major prehistoric Indian town built of masonry and timber in the 12th century. The name is misleading, since the Aztecs of Mexico never lived in the area. The people here shared cultures of those at Chaco Canyon National Monument, 65 miles south, and Mesa Verde National Park, 100 miles northwest. Follow the self-guided trail through the west pueblo, site of the restored Great Kiva, to the Hubbard Ruin. Pottery, weapons and jewelry are on display at the Visitor Center. Address: Box 640, Aztec, New Mexico 87410.

BANDELIER
New Mexico
This beautiful canyon country 46 miles west of Santa Fe contains many cliff and open-pueblo ruins of the late prehistoric period. The most accessible features are the ruins in Frijoles Canyon, houses of masonry one to three stories high with many cave rooms gouged out of the soft volcanic ash of the cliff. The Frijoles inhabitants grew corn, beans and squash in their oasis in the dry country. They wove cotton cloth on a floor loom; they made black-on-gray, decorated pottery. The story of these people, where they came from and where they went, is gradually

being brought to light through research. The monument was named to honor Adolph F. A. Bandelier, who carried on an extensive survey of prehistoric ruins and Pueblo Indians in the 1880s.

The monument has an excellent museum in the Visitor Center. A self-guiding walking tour of the principal ruins takes about an hour. The park staff conducts daily activities, including evening campfire programs in summer. Approximately 90 percent of its 32,737 acres is backcountry, accessible by 70 miles of trail leading through forests and steep-walled gorges. These trails unfold the geologic, as well as archaeological, interest in the Pajarito Plateau. During the spring Frijoles Canyon, with its abundant birdlife, holds special appeal.

The monument is open all year except Christmas Day. Weather is favorable and relative humidity generally low. A curio shop and snack bar operate all year. A campground is situated on the mesa above the canyon. Areas of interest nearby include: Los Alamos, the atomic city; Indian pueblos along the Rio Grande; Spanish-American settlements in the Sangre de Cristo Mountains; and the cultural centers of Sante Fe and Taos. Write Superintendent, Bandelier National Monument, Los Alamos, New Mexico 87544.

CANYON DE CHELLY
Arizona

About 300 Navajos have their summer homes on the floor of the canyons, while they pasture cattle between sheer red sandstone walls rising about 40 feet at the mouth and up to 1,000 feet at Spider Rock. Canyon de Chelly itself is joined by Canyon del Muerto, 35 miles long. Pictographs and petroglyphs on walls of cliffs and caves date to early prehistoric occupation. Cliff-dweller ruins and natural formations like 800-foot Spider Rock make Canyon de Chelly one of the finest adventures in the Southwest. All inner-canyon visitors must be accompanied by a park ranger or authorized guide, except for those hiking the self-guiding trail from White House Overlook to the White House ruin.

Thunderbird Lodge operates jeep tours up the canyon floor daily from mid-April to November 1, depending on weather conditions. Navajo guides are available. The Visitor Center is open daily from 8 a.m. to 5 p.m., late fall to late spring, and 8 a.m. to 6 p.m. during the summer months. Thunderbird Lodge (Chinle, Arizona 86503) provides hotel accommodations and a cafeteria; it and the adjacent campground are open year-round, but winter can be very cold.

The 83,840-acre monument lies one mile east of Chinle Community and is reached either north from Gallup, New Mexico, or Holbrook, Arizona (near Petrified Forest), or south from Farmington, New Mexico. Combine your visit here with a stop at Hubbell Trading Post National Historic Site, a few miles south. Address: Box 588, Chinle, Arizona 86503.

CASA GRANDE RUINS
Arizona

In 1694 the Spanish missionary, Father Kino, discovered the ruins, a classic of Indian construction, and described them as "a four-story building as large as a castle." Self-guiding trail, ranger talks of 30 to 45 minutes; museum devoted to archaeology and ethnology. The ruins are on Arizona 87/287 at Coolidge, near the Coolidge exit of I-10. Address: Box 518, Coolidge, Arizona 85228.

CHACO CULTURE NATIONAL HISTORICAL PARK
New Mexico

Because Chaco Canyon embraces some of the most significant ruins in America, Congress in 1980 enlarged the former national monument and redesignated it as Chaco Culture National Historical Park. It also identified 33 outlying sites as Chaco Culture Archaeological Protection Sites, in light of extensive development of energy resources in the San Juan Basin. These sites constitute part of the 80 known prehistoric communities in the highly organized and far-reaching Pueblo culture centered at Chaco Canyon. To reach the park, located in northwestern part of the state, take unpaved New Mexico 57 at Blanco Trading Post (which is 27 miles southeast of Bloomfield on New Mexico 44). From the trading post it is 30 miles to the Visitor Center. Or take New Mexico 57 from Thoreau on I-40 (near Gallup). From here it is 60 miles to the Visitor Center, the last 20 miles of which are unpaved road. Visitor Center hours are 8 a.m. to 5 p.m. A campground is maintained; but there is no gas, food, or lodging available in the park. Address: Chaco Culture National Historical Park, SR #4, Box 6500, Bloomfield, New Mexico 87413.

EFFIGY MOUNDS
Iowa

Effigy Mounds is a hidden gem of timber, trails and prehistory, along the edge of sheer cliffs plunging to the Mississippi River. The park has been called "Iowa's Yellowstone." The 191 known mounds, most in the forms of bears and birds, were sculpted in the earth thousands of years ago by native Americans. The North Unit, reached by easy trail from the Visitor Center, offers

Bandelier National Monument

MOUND CITY GROUP
Ohio
In the Scioto Valley of southern Ohio, the prehistoric Hopewell Indians reached their cultural zenith from about 200 B.C. to A.D. 500. They are best known for artistic achievements and for erecting burial mounds. From the extraordinary wealth of ornaments, pottery and other items found in the mounds, archaeologists have learned a great deal about these people. An observation deck and marked trails provide a close view of the group of 23 mounds; the Visitor Center displays the fine Hopewell handiwork. Lodging and camping facilities in Chillicothe, 3 miles south, and in nearby state parks. Southern Ohio is rich in prehistoric Indian sites, including several state memorials. Address: 16062, State Route 104, Chillicothe, Ohio 45601.

NAVAJO
Arizona
Three of the largest, most elaborate of known cliff dwellings are preserved in rugged country 31 miles west of Kayenta and 63 miles northeast of Tuba City, completely surrounded by the Navajo Reservation. The most accessible, 700-year-old Betatakin, or "Ledge House," once had almost 135 rooms. During the main summer season, guided tours to Betatakin are given three times daily; they accommodate up to 24 people on a first-come, first-served basis. Write for information about and reservations for the hike or horseback adventure to Keel Seel cliff dwelling (16 miles round trip). Displays and a slide show at the Visitor Center provide a helpful introduction to the Anasazi. Campgrounds are located in the monument. Address: Tonalea, Arizona 86044.

OCMULGEE
Georgia
Circular earthlodge and mounds at the east edge of Macon stand as monuments to ancestors of the Creek Indians who lived along the Ocmulgee River of the Macon Plateau. The museum displays and artifacts interpret lifeways of early people as they developed pottery and uses of stone and natural fiber. Address: 1207 Emery Highway, Macon, Georgia 31201.

superlative Mississippi vistas. The South Unit contains effigies of birds in flight and the "Marching Bear Unit." Accommodations are available at nearby Marquette, with camping at Yellow River State Forest. Address: Box K, McGregor, Iowa 52157.

GILA CLIFF DWELLINGS
New Mexico
These well-preserved, natural cavities in the face of an overhanging volcanic cliff were occupied more than 700 years ago (approximately 1280 to the early 1300s) by the Mogollon Culture people. The monument is in rugged country of southwestern New Mexico, 44 miles north of Silver City on New Mexico 15. The ruins are open 8 a.m. to 6 p.m. Memorial Day through Labor Day; 9 a.m. to 5 p.m., rest of the year. The Visitor Center is open daily 8 a.m. to 5 p.m. Both facilities are closed January 1 and December 25.

HOVENWEEP
Utah-Colorado
In the Four Corners region west of Mesa Verde National Park, six clusters of prehistoric towers, pueblos and cliff dwellings (four in Colorado, two in Utah) are reached only via dirt and gravel road. They represent the northern, or Mesa Verde, branch of the prehistoric San Juan Anasazi Culture that occupied this arid land 700 years ago. There are camping facilities, but carry wood. Address: c/o Mesa Verde Park, Colorado 81330.

MONTEZUMA CASTLE
Arizona
When driving north from Phoenix to the Grand Canyon, allow time to visit this five-story, 20-room "castle" in the Verde Valley. Built in a limestone cliff during the 12th and 13th centuries, it is still 90-percent intact, one of the best-preserved cliff ruins in the Southwest. It lies almost immediately accessible off the main highway (I-17), midway between Phoenix and Flagstaff. The self-guiding Sycamore Trail, starting from the Visitor Center, follows Beaver Creek through the heart of the monument. You can walk it easily in about 45 minutes. The castle, set in a cliff 100 feet above the valley floor, is a 19-room apartment house constructed with stone and wooden tools, that has lasted 800 years. It was a perfect natural fortress, reached by ladders from above or below. Follow the full length of the trail to Castle A, where you may climb into some of the caves. The castle area includes a pleasant picnic spot. The monument also includes Montezuma Well, 7 miles northeast, a large limestone sinkhole rimmed with pueblos and cave houses. Address: Box 68, Clarkdale, Arizona 86324.

PECOS
New Mexico

The remains of an ancient Indian pueblo and a large Spanish colonial mission are located 25 miles southeast of Santa Fe off I-25. When the Spaniards arrived in 1540, they found a five-story communal house with 2,000 inhabitants; the following year Coronado left from here on his expedition into the Great Plains. The first mission was established in the early 1600s by the Franciscans. After the pueblo revolt of 1680, a second mission was established, the ruins of which are seen today. The attractive Visitor Center, worthy of the setting, is the gift of film star Greer Garson and her husband. Visit the ruins on a 1¼-mile self-guiding trail. Address: Drawer 11, Pecos, New Mexico 87522.

PIPESTONE
Minnesota

This was a sacred place known to tribesmen of a large part of the continent. "It is not too much to say that the great Pipestone Quarry," wrote John Wesley Powell, founder of the Bureau of American Ethnology, "was the most important single location in aboriginal geography and lore." Walk the Circle Trail to see how the monument now conserves the remainder of the unusual red stone from which the Indians for at least three centuries fashioned their prized calumets, or ceremonial pipes. The material is now called catlinite, in honor of the artist-explorer, George Catlin, who entered the quarries in 1836 and then gave the first published description. The Visitor Center and connected Upper Midwest Indian Cultural Center provide a museum demonstration area for pipe making. Attractive pipes and other stone products made by local Indians are on sale. The monument lies near the town of Pipestone, in southwest Minnesota, near Sioux Falls, South Dakota. Address: Box 727, Pipestone, Minnesota 56164.

RUSSELL CAVE
Alabama

Excavated only as recently as 1953, the cave contained tools, weapons and other evidence showing a record of life from at least 6000 B.C. to about A.D. 1650. It lies near the town of Bridgeport, close to Chattanooga, Tennessee. Visitor Center and archaeology exhibit. Address: Route 1, Box 175, Bridgeport, Alabama 35740.

SALINAS
New Mexico

This unique complex of original Pueblo Indian and Spanish ruins is located in central New Mexico, at the junction of New Mexico 14 and US60. The name *Salinas* derives from the Spanish name for the region which contains salt lagoons, important both prehistorically and historically. Abandoned by Indians and Spaniards alike in the 1670s, the massive masonry ruins survived the centuries remarkably intact. The limestone ruins of Gran Quivira lie 26 miles south of Mountainair; the red sandstone ruins of Abo, 9 miles west; Quarai, 8 miles north. An orientation center is located in Mountainair; Gran Quivira and Quarai have small museums. Open daily all year. Address: Box 496, Mountainair, New Mexico 87036.

TONTO
Arizona

Reached via the thrilling Apache Trail above Roosevelt Lake, the well-preserved Pueblo cliff dwellings were occupied in the 14th and 15th centuries by Indians farming the Salt River Valley. Small museum and trail provide excellent prospectives. Trail closes at 4 p.m. daily. Address: Box 707, Roosevelt, Arizona 85545.

TUZIGOOT
Arizona

In the Verde Valley near Clarkdale, the excavated ruins include a pueblo which housed 200 to 400 persons, with each unit individually designed—an outstanding example of late prehistoric pueblos. It's estimated that the community peaked around A.D. 1250 and disappeared by 1450. Museum has pottery, basketry, stone tools and turquoise jewelry. Address: Box 68, Clarkdale, Arizona 86324.

WALNUT CANYON
Arizona

Cliff dwellings in shallow caves at the edge of Flagstaff were inhabited by Sinagua Indians about 800 years ago. Utilizing projecting limestone ledges as foundations, the houses apparently were built for separate families. Museum, observation building and self-guiding trails. Address: Walnut Creek Road, Flagstaff, Arizona 86001.

WUPATKI
Arizona

Red sandstone prehistoric pueblos about 45 miles northeast of Flagstaff were occupied from about A.D. 1100 to 1225 by farming Indians, from whom the Hopi are believed to be partly descended. After the late 11th century eruption of nearby Sunset Crater made farming productive, this became one of the most densely populated sections of northern Arizona, until winds eventually removed or drifted the water-retaining cover of ash and cinders. Among the most impressive of more than 800 ruins are Wupatki, the "Tall House," and the Citadel, built at the edge of a limestone sinkhold. There are also earth lodges on the mesa tops and isolated field houses of one and two rooms, used by the Indians while tending crops. Self-guiding trail through Wupatki and Citadel ruins. Address: Tuba Star Route, Flagstaff, Arizona 86001.

HISTORICAL AREAS

Mᴏʀᴇ than one-half of all areas of the National Park system relate directly to the aspirations, inspirations, struggles, and achievements of human-kind on the American soil.

These include national historical parks, national military parks, national battlefield parks, national historic sites, national battlefield sites, national memorials, and national cemeteries. The differences in nomenclature have to do more with size and legal origin than with purpose. Most battlefields, for instance, had been administered by the War Department until transferred in 1933 to the National Park Service. Two years later Congress adopted the Historic Sites Act, directing the Park Service "to preserve for public use historic sites, buildings and objects of national significance."

Prepare to find history entwined with nature. You may go to Gettysburg to view the battle scene, but you will also be treated to a rich variety and abundance of birds. Look also for art and architecture, the cultural story unfolding with history.

ABRAHAM LINCOLN BIRTHPLACE NATIONAL HISTORIC SITE
Kentucky

A granite memorial building encloses a log cabin believed to be the one in which Abraham Lincoln was born, at Hodgenville on February 12, 1809. The Lincoln family lived at this location for the first 2½ years of Abraham's life and then moved to another small farm 10 miles away. The grounds include 100 acres of his father's farm. Address: Route 1, Hodgenville, Kentucky 42748. While in Kentucky, visit his father's boyhood home, Lincoln Homestead State Park, at Springfield.

ADAMS NATIONAL HISTORIC SITE
Massachusetts

The home at 135 Adams Street in Quincy of the distinguished Adams family for four generations, beginning with the second president of the United States, is one of the century's finest historic houses. The beautiful garden was started by Mrs. John Adams. The site includes the birthplaces of John Adams, at 133 Franklin Street, and of John Quincy Adams, at 141 Franklin Street. It is easily reached from Boston, only eight miles away. Address: Box 531, Quincy, Massachusetts 02269.

ALLEGHENY PORTAGE RAILROAD NATIONAL HISTORIC SITE and JOHNSTOWN FLOOD NATIONAL MEMORIAL
Pennsylvania

These twin parks interpret periods in the growth of western Pennsylvania. Stop at the Visitor Center in the historic Lemon House, a portal to the canal and railroad system considered a technological marvel in its day. The Portage Railroad, built between 1831 and 1834, crossed a forested mountain divide to link the Eastern Seaboard with the Ohio Valley. Charles Dickens in 1842 found it an exciting trip, yet "not to be dreaded for its dangers." The park preserves remaining buildings, structures, and portions of the Allegheny Portage Railroad and interprets the role the railroad played in the nation's history. Allow time for hiking and picnicking and to see craft demonstrations in summer. The valley town of Johnstown has been hit by three serious floods during the past 100 years. The memorial park commemorates the most severe, which occurred in 1889 with a human death toll of more than 2,200. The park trails are good for bird watching. The Railroaders Memorial Museum in Altoona is a rail fan's must. Address: Box 247, Cresson, Pennsylvania 16630.

AMERICAN MEMORIAL PARK
Saipan

A tribute to those who died in World War II in armed conflict far from home, the park consists of 133 scenic acres along the shoreline of Tanapag Harbor outside of Garapan. It includes a monument and museum, plus picnic facilities along the shoreline and swimming from Micro Beach. Limited boat dock facilities offer glass-bottomed and other boat tours for viewing the coral reef and for access to nearby Managha Island. Address: Box 198 CHRB, Saipan, Commonwealth of the Marianas 96950.

ANDERSONVILLE NATIONAL HISTORIC SITE
Georgia

In the quiet country above Americus, the town of Andersonville recalls how 45,000 Union prisoners were once imprisoned and 12,912 of them died. At the National Cemetery, ½ mile north of the town, Union prisoners are buried among magnolias and hardwoods, resting with men of other wars. Six graves isolated from the rest contain the remains of the Raiders, who were convicted of robbing and murdering fellow prisoners and were sentenced to hanging by the prisoners themselves. The cemetery and prison site are well maintained and interpreted by the National Park Service as a memorial to American prisoners of all wars. Clara Barton, famous Civil War nurse, helped identify and mark the graves of those who died while confined at Andersonville.

The little town of Andersonville is worth exploring in itself. Much of the town has been restored to pre-Civil War appearance. The Visitor Center/Museum will get you started on a self-guiding driving or walking tour. The village and national historic site are on the Andersonville Trail, a 75-mile loop between Perry and Cordele, which includes Georgia's last operating river ferry. Address: Andersonville, Georgia 31711.

ANDREW JOHNSON NATIONAL HISTORIC SITE
Tennessee

The tailor shop where Johnson worked from 1831 until 1843, his last home (1851-1875), and his grave memorialize Lincoln's successor to the presidency. Impeached by the House and acquitted by one vote in the Senate, Johnson was somewhat vindicated with his return to the Senate in 1875. The site is open every day except Christmas; an admission fee is charged at the home. A few miles north of the shop lies Davy Crockett Birthplace. Address; Box 1088, Greenville, Tennessee 37743.

ANTIETAM NATIONAL BATTLEFIELD
Maryland
The scene of the bloody battle on September 17, 1862, between 87,000 Union troops and 41,000 Confederates, that brought to an end Lee's first northern invasion, is marked by monuments, battlefield exhibits, and the Visitor Center. More than 23,000 of both sides were killed or wounded before the day was done; 4,000 men fell in three hours at Bloody Lane. Cannons denote the places where six generals lost their lives. Civil War burials in the National Cemetery number more than 5,000. Address: Box 158, Sharpsburg, Maryland 21782.

APPOMATTOX COURT HOUSE
NATIONAL HISTORICAL PARK
Virginia
The village (20 miles east of Lynchburg) where General Lee surrendered the Confederate Army of Northern Virginia to General Grant on April 9, 1865, bringing the Civil War to an end, has been restored to present a moving and impressive picture of that day. When Grant told Lee, in the McLean House, that Confederate soldiers could keep their horses and mules to work their farms, his old foe replied, "It will be very gratifying and will do much toward conciliating our people." Within the restored village of Appomattox Court House are 27 historic structures, all in easy walking distance from the Visitor Center. Address: Box 218, Appomattox, Virginia 24522.

ARKANSAS POST NATIONAL MEMORIAL
Arkansas
The first European settlement in the lower Mississippi Valley, Arkansas Post was established in 1686 by Henri de Tonty, a French explorer. It is located 7 miles south of Gillett, 18 miles northeast of Dumas. Five different national governments have had jurisdiction over Arkansas Post. In 1819, the territorial capitol was established here, but its existence as community came to an end in January 1863 with the Union victory at Fort Hindman and bombardment of the fort, virtually destroying the town. Address: Route 1, Box 16, Gillett, Arkansas 72055.

ARLINGTON HOUSE. See page 168.

BARTON, CLARA, NATIONAL HISTORIC SITE. See Clara Barton National Historic Site, page 168.

BENJAMIN FRANKLIN NATIONAL MEMORIAL
Pennsylvania
"The American people feel a deep debt of gratitude to Benjamin Franklin for his outstanding services to the Nation as a statesman and for his achievements as a scientist and inventor," Congress declared in designating this memorial in 1972. The Benjamin Franklin Institute has been a leader in scientific progress since its founding in 1824. The main institute building contains James Earle Frazer's 20-foot, 10½-inch marble statue of Franklin. Address: The Franklin Institute, 20th and Benjamin Franklin Parkway, Philadelphia, Pennsylvania 19103.

BENT'S OLD FORT NATIONAL HISTORIC SITE
Colorado
A principal outpost of civilization on the southern plains, this reconstructed fort on the banks of the Arkansas River, 8 miles from La Junta, was a rendezvous for Indians, trappers, traders, and troops. It played a key role in shaping the destiny of the Southwest between 1833 and 1849. Address: 35110 Highway 194 East, La Junta, Colorado 81050.

BIG HOLE NATIONAL BATTLEFIELD
Montana
Remains of shallow, grass-grown trenches and battle-scarred trees in a remote but scenic setting recall the fierce two-day battle in August 1877, when Indian women and children were slain, along with their warriors, by U.S. troops. Led by valiant Chief Joseph, the Nez Perce were making their epic retreat from Idaho when they were trapped here. The Visitor Center occupies a dramatic viewpoint high above the scene. It displays authentic artifacts from the period. Markers tell how, despite defeat in the Big Hole Valley, the Indians pressed on through Yellowstone, only to be captured 40 miles from Canada and freedom. Address: Box 237, Wisdom, Montana 59761.

BOOKER T. WASHINGTON NATIONAL MONUMENT
Virginia
The 224-acre monument, comprising most of the original plantation and replicas of buildings Washington might have known as a boy, is the only one in the park system that interprets life under

Appomattox Court House National Historical Park

slavery. The restored farm embraces buildings, tools, crops, animals, and, at times, people in period dress. A visit to Washington's earliest home demonstrates the challenges he faced to become an eminent educator, presidential advisor, and leader of black Americans. The park, near Burnt Chimney (about 20 miles southwest of Roanoke) is an easy side trip from the Blue Ridge Parkway. Address: Route 1, Box 195, Hardy, Virginia 24101.

BOSTON AFRICAN AMERICAN NATIONAL HISTORIC SITE
Massachusetts
The African Meeting House (1806) on Beacon Hill is the oldest black church building standing in this country. The 1½-mile, easily walkable **Black Heritage Trail** connects the Meeting House with 14 other historic structures significant in the development of Boston's early black community. During peak visitor months, interpretive rangers along the Trail complement the self-guiding trail booklet. Address: 15 State Street, Boston, MA 02109. Telephone: 617/242-5625 for special appointment tours.

BOSTON NATIONAL HISTORICAL PARK
Massachusetts
Eight sites in the heart of Boston, all closely identified with the early history of the United States, are the focal points of this park. All remain under various public and private ownerships, but they are operated and maintained in accord with National Park Service regulations.

Start from the park service **Visitor Center**, 15 State Street, directly across from the Old State House. It is an excellent source of information and literature and is starting point of various guided walking tours. Everyone will want to see the **Charlestown Navy Yard** (also known as the Boston Naval Shipyard). The first operating drydock in the nation was completed here in 1833 and the Navy Yard has built, outfitted, and launched ships for every American war since 1812. Little wonder, with its history and weathered old buildings, it attracts about one million visitors yearly. The most conspicuous sight in the Yard is the USS *Constitution*, or "Old Ironsides," most famous ship in American history, built in 1797 (though it did not see action until the unofficial war with the Barbary pirates at Tripoli in 1803). Visitors may see it as it appeared during its first full-scale sea battle, in the War of 1812, even staffed with sailors in period uniform. Near Old Ironsides is the USS *Cassin Young*, a World War II destroyer and the first and only warship managed by the National Park Service. Other sights in the Navy Yard: Rope Walk, a building almost a quarter-mile long where all the rope for the U.S. Navy was made until 1971; USS *Constitution* Museum, with displays on naval history; the Commandant's House, built in 1803. Also in Charlestown, **Bunker Hill** (or Breed's Hill), surrounded by the 19th century town houses of Monument Square, preserves the battleground of June 17, 1775. On that morning British General Howe advanced up the hill in textbook style with a force of about 3,000 redcoats. The colonials, whose ammunition was low, obeyed Colonel Prescott's famous order not to fire "until you see the whites of their eyes." The 220-foot Bunker Hill Monument now dominates the scene.

Downtown, on Boston's well-marked Freedom Trail, **Faneuil Hall** is the historic marketplace built in 1740-42 that served as a political forum for Revolutionary leaders. By all means climb the stairs to the second-floor chamber where public meetings are still held, thus continuing a tradition over 200 years old. Faneuil Hall Marketplace is one of the liveliest spots in Boston. The centerpiece is Quincy Market, a 500-foot long Greek Revival complex first opened in 1826. It has been restored and revitalized and is occupied by food merchants the way it used to be.

Then follow the Trail to the **Old State House**, built in 1713.

Though engulfed by modern traffic you can still see the circle of cobblestones in front of the building commemorating the Boston Massacre of 1770. Note the balcony where the Declaration of Independence was first read to Bostonians on July 18, 1776. Climb the spiral staircase within to the second-floor Council Chamber, where patriot James Otis argued against the Writs of Assistance, search warrants used by the British to track down smuggled goods. John Adams termed his speech "the first act of opposition to the arbitrary claims of Great Britain."

The **Old South Meeting House** is another venerable structure, built in 1729, then restored in 1783 after the interior had been gutted by the British in 1775. It was here that 5,000 citizens met in protest immediately preceding the Boston Tea Party of December 16, 1773.

At North Square, the **Paul Revere House** stands as the oldest wooden building in Boston—it predates the Revolution by a century. Revere purchased the house in 1770 and lived in it for about thirty years. If you leave North Square by way of Prince Street and walk one block left to Hanover, you will find yourself in a charming Italian neighborhood. This route leads to the Paul Revere Mall, or Prado, and to Christ Church, popularly known as **Old North Church**, the oldest church in Boston, built in 1723. Here the two lanterns (according to tradition) were hung from the belfry by the sexton Robert Newman, on April 18, 1775, to warn the patriots that the British were advancing by sea toward Concord to seize arms stored there. Meanwhile, Paul Revere made his way with muffled oars past British gunboats and began his famous ride.

At **Dorchester Heights** in South Boston a memorial tower and greensward mark the location of American batteries which threatened the British in Boston leading to their evacuation of the city on March 17, 1776. Here the Americans achieved their first real military success in the Revolution. Address: Charlestown Navy Yard, Boston, Massachusetts 02129.

BRICES CROSS ROADS NATIONAL BATTLEFIELD SITE
Mississippi
General Nathan Bedford Forrest led his cavalrymen in a brilliant tactical victory near Baldwyn over a large Union force on June 10, 1864. Sherman was so impressed that he ordered his commander in the field to "go out and follow Forrest to the death, if it costs ten thousand lives and breaks the Treasury." From the high ground of the one-acre site, a large part of the scene of action is within view, identified by marker and maps. Address: c/o Natchez Trace Parkway, Route 1, N.T. 143, Tupelo, Mississippi 38801.

CABRILLO NATIONAL MONUMENT
California
The discovery of the coast of California by Juan Rodriguez Cabrillo in 1542 is commemorated near the scene of his landfall on Point Loma in San Diego Bay. The Cabrillo statue faces the actual landing spot, while the nearby Visitor Center interprets the discovery and subsequent events. Near the southern tip, the famous old lighthouse served from 1855 to 1891. The park is especially popular from mid-December to mid-February as an observation point for watching gray whales offshore heading to Baja California from the Arctic. Also, allow time to walk the nature trail, visiting some of the most scenic tide pools left in southern California. The Bayside Trail starts below the lighthouse as a paved road (once used for military patrol), but presently turns to gravel through coastal scrub and chaparral. Visit the tide pools during a minus tide, and you are apt to see crabs, starfish, and small colorful fish. Address: Box 6670, San Diego, California 92106.

CARL SANDBURG HOME NATIONAL HISTORIC SITE
North Carolina

Connemara, in the highland foothills in Flat Rock, where the noted writer and poet lived the last 22 years of his life, until his death in 1967, is preserved in the 247-acre National Historic Site. The unpretentious, white colonial-style house, with its floor-to-ceiling bookshelves in many rooms, was built in 1838 as a summer residence for Christopher G. Memminger, secretary of the Treasury of the Confederacy. While at Connemara, Sandburg wrote his autobiography, *Always the Young Strangers*. Tours are conducted through the home. Trails lead to the pastures, ponds, and mountain area where Sandburg strolled. *The World of Carl Sandburg*, based on his poetry, humor, folk music, and philosophy, is presented daily during summer by performers of the Flat Rock Playhouse. The actors also present the *Rootabaga Stories*, Sandburg's own tales for children. Address: Box 395, Flat Rock, North Carolina 28731.

CARVER, GEORGE WASHINGTON, NATIONAL MONUMENT.

See George Washington Carver National Monument, page 186.

CASTILLO DE SAN MARCOS NATIONAL MONUMENT
Florida

Since the founding of St. Augustine in 1565, the wooden fortification built there became the northernmost outpost of the vast Spanish New World empire. It strengthened the title to Florida and protected the route of ships returning to Spain. The masonry fort erected in 1672-95 of native shellstone, called coquina, and mortar made from shell lime, continued the original purpose. The buff-plastered walls of the square-shaped, four-bastioned structure were 13 feet thick at the base and 30 feet high—a grim symbol of power and determination. Although it underwent major sieges in 1702 and 1740, it was never conquered. In the 18th century, modernization work gave the Castillo its present appearance, and transformed it into the core of a defense system that reached to the north, south, and west. In 1821 Spain ceded Florida to the United States. The fort's name was changed to Fort Marion and it was used as a military prison, gun battery, and storage. The massive well-preserved structure is the oldest masonry fortification in the country, as well as the most impressive sight of Spanish St. Augustine. Park rangers guide tours and, dressed in 18th century Spanish uniforms, demonstrate the cannon firing on weekends. The fort is open 8:30 a.m. to 5:15 p.m. during the winter; 9:00 a.m. to 5:45 p.m., in the summer. Address: 1 Castillo Drive, St. Augustine, Florida 32084.

CASTLE CLINTON NATIONAL MONUMENT
New York

Built in 1808 as a fort at the tip of Lower Manhattan, it served variously as civic garden festooned with shrubs and flowers; setting of fireworks, gala concerts, and an occasional balloon ascent; receiving depot for more than seven million immigrants following the Civil War; and, from 1896 to 1941, as a fabulous aquarium. It was completely refurbished in 1986 to serve both as a museum and an information center for National Park Service sites in metropolitan New York. Castle Clinton provides a view into military life at a time when the fort was quite new and guarding New York City from possible British invasion.

Stop at the Visitor Center for tickets for the Statue of Liberty Circle Line Ferry, operating between the Battery and Liberty Island. Also ask about the National Park Service program of free guided walking tours of six historic New York City neighborhoods: Brooklyn Heights, Chinatown-Lower East Side-Little Italy, Gramercy Park, Greenwich Village, SoHo, and the Wall Street financial district. These are available to groups by appointment at least two weeks in advance mid-May to mid-October. Phone 212/264-8129. Address: Superintendent, Manhattan Sites, National Park Service, 26 Wall Street, New York, New York 10005.

CHAMIZAL NATIONAL MEMORIAL
Texas

A section of Cordova Island in the Rio Grande at El Paso has been chosen to commemorate friendship between the United States and Mexico and the peaceful settlement of a major boundary dispute. *Chamizal* is the Spanish name for the plants which once covered the area. The national memorial includes a museum, documentary films, and a cultural pavilion, managed by a bilingual staff and designed as a center for the exchange of Mexican and American cultural programs. The 500-seat auditorium and outdoor amphitheater are utilized for musical and dramatic events in both Spanish and English. Performances are scheduled most nights from September through July. Special events include the Border Folk Festival in October and the International Siglo de Oro Drama Festival in March. The Mexicans have constructed a companion park across the Rio Grande in Ciudad Juarez, Mexico. Address: Box 722, El Paso, Texas 79944.

CHARLES PINCKNEY NATIONAL HISTORIC SITE
South Carolina

Located just outside of Charleston, the home and farm of Charles Pinckney, signer of the Declaration of Independence, governor of South Carolina, and member of the U.S. Senate, are now surrounded by housing subdivisions. In 1988 Congress authorized the new historic site to preserve a landmark of national value; facilities will be developed in time. Address: c/o Fort Sumter National Monument, 1214 Middle Street, Sullivans Island, South Carolina 29482.

CHEROKEE STRIP LIVING MUSEUM
Kansas

Located two miles north of the Oklahoma border, at Arkansas City, Kansas, the museum commemorates the famous "Cherokee Strip Run" of September 16, 1863. That was the date when 150,000 settlers lined up at high noon and joined the rush for land in the Oklahoma frontier. The museum displays contemporary newspapers, photographs, and artifacts associated with the Run, as well as Indian and local memorabilia. Address: Box 230, Arkansas City, Kansas 67005.

CHESAPEAKE AND OHIO CANAL. See page 168.

CHICAGO PORTAGE NATIONAL HISTORIC SITE
Illinois

Here is a portion of the famous portage discovered by Marquette and Joliet and used by the pioneers to link the waters of the Great Lakes with the Mississippi. Address: c/o Cook County Forest Preserve, Cummings Square, River Forest, Illinois 60305.

CHICKAMAUGA AND CHATTANOOGA NATIONAL MILITARY PARK
Georgia-Tennessee

These fields and hills, now peaceful, witnessed some of the hardest fighting in the Civil War. The battlefields comprise the oldest and largest national military park in the U.S., and today over 1,400 monuments and markers commemorate the fighting of both North and South, on sites in and around Chattanooga. **Chickamauga Battlefield**, 7 miles south of Chattanooga on US 27, contains more than 5,000 acres over which 120,000 men fought on September 19-20, 1863, for control of Chattanooga. A 7-mile, self-guided tour; slide program; tape tour; and Visitor Center/

Museum display complement a full range of guided tours and demonstrations explaining the events of this major Confederate victory. One of the most complete collections of American shoulder arms is also on display in the Battlefield Visitor Center.

From **Point Park**, in the Lookout Mountain portion of the park, there is a sweeping view of the entire city, and the Moccasin Bend of the Tennessee River below. The Ochs Museum and Point Park Visitor Center interpret the siege and battles for Chattanooga in October and November 1863. Though the focal point of attention is the Civil War, Lookout Mountain is an interesting place to hike on paths through the beautiful hardwood forests.

Civil War buffs should not miss smaller sites that commemorate the battles of Waunatchie and Missionary Ridge, and the site of General Grant's Chattanooga headquarters at Orchard Knob. Directions to these beautifully monumented areas, and further information on the park's varied units, may be obtained from the Point Park and Chickamauga Battlefield Visitor Centers. Both Visitor Centers are open 8 a.m. to 4:45 p.m. all year; later in the summer. Address: P.O. Box 2128, Ft. Oglethorpe, Georgia 30742.

Colonial Militia, Yorktown

CHIMNEY ROCK NATIONAL HISTORIC SITE
Nebraska

Towering 500 feet above the North Platte River Valley, this strange rocky spire of solitary grandeur was a celebrated prairie landmark on the Oregon Trail. Many of the passersby swam the river in order to climb "this great natural curiosity," and also probably to look ahead toward Scotts Bluff, which is 23 miles west. Chimney Rock lies southwest of Bayard, and can be reached in the pioneer style only, afoot. Stop at the interpretive trailer operated by the State of Nebraska on the main highway. Address: c/o Scotts Bluff National Monument, Box 427, Gering, Nebraska 69341.

CHRISTIANSTED NATIONAL HISTORIC SITE
Virgin Islands

Three city blocks on the Christiansted waterfront preserve the colonial aura when "sugar was king" and St. Croix typified Danish plantation society in the New World. In this stimulating environment, Alexander Hamilton spent his youth. Fine architectural taste was reflected in buildings like the Customhouse, Steeple Building, and Government House. In the late 1980s, the site underwent major restoration to its mid-19th century appearance, utilizing methods and material of the past. New exhibits interpret the plantation system, architecture, and military history. Open daily 8 a.m. to 4 p.m. Other key historic points on the island are the Whim Greathouse, a restored sugar plantation; and Fort Frederik, in Frederiksted, dating from 1671, where the Danish governor in 1848 emancipated the slaves. Address: Box 160, Christiansted, Virgin Islands 00820.

CLARK, GEORGE ROGERS, NATIONAL HISTORIC PARK. See
George Rogers Clark National Historical Park, page 186.

COLONIAL NATIONAL HISTORICAL PARK
Virginia

On the Virginia Peninsula, three famous places between the York and James Rivers—Jamestown, Williamsburg, and Yorktown—form a triangle only 14 miles at the base, linked today by the Colonial Parkway. Each has a thrilling story of its own, starting from **Jamestown**, the first permanent English settlement in the New World, established in 1607. Jamestown Island in its entirety is a National Historic Site, jointly administered by the National Park Service and the Association for the Preservation of Virginia Antiquities. From the Visitor Center, a walking tour extends over the town site, along old streets and paths to the site of "James Fort," where Pocahontas was married, and the ruins of early houses, taverns, and shops. Also, visit the glass house, where costumed artisans demonstrate 17th-century glass-making. They sell attractive pieces at reasonable prices. A motor road loops the wildwood section of the island. Though not part of the national historical park, **Williamsburg**, capital of the Virginia colony after the decline of Jamestown, has been restored to its 18th century appearance through the interest of the late John D. Rockefeller, Jr. More than 400 buildings stand in their colonial form; over half are original structures and the rest, faithful reproductions on original sites. From Williamsburg the parkway passes early plantation sites while following the York River to the final battleground of the American Revolution at **Yorktown**. The Siege Line Lookout on the roof deck of the Visitor Center affords a panoramic view over the strategic areas of the famous battle where Washington scored his great victory over Lord Cornwallis in 1781. A self-guided motor drive circles the battlefield, encampment areas, and the old town. Along the tour are the famous redoubts, with cannons in place; the Nelson House, home of a colonial Virginia statesman; the Moore House, where terms of surrender were drawn; and the site of Washington's headquarters. You can rent bicycles at Williamsburg and use the parkway and tour roads at Jamestown and Yorktown. Peak visitor periods are April (gardens in bloom), summer, Thanksgiving, and Christmas through New Year's Day; so, pick another time, or plan early. Address: Box 210, Yorktown, Virginia 23690.

CORONADO NATIONAL MEMORIAL
Arizona
Commemorating the first significant explorations by Europeans into the Southwest, the 4,976-acre memorial lies on the international boundary with Mexico, within sight of the valley through which Francisco Vasquez de Coronado and his expedition entered the present United States in 1540. From the parking area at Montezuma Pass, 30 miles west of Bisbee, a well-marked foot trail leads to Coronado Peak and a view of San Pedro Valley and the stark country through which the bold expedition marched. Another trail, about 3 miles long, follows Smugglers' Ridge to a picnic area. Coronado failed to find the golden cities, but he brought back knowledge of vast lands, paving the way for Spanish colonization. The annual International Borderlands Festival in April combines arts, crafts, music, and dance of Yaqui, Apache, English, and Spanish. Address: Route 1, Box 126, Hereford, Arizona 85615.

COWPENS NATIONAL BATTLEFIELD
South Carolina
General Daniel Morgan, despised and feared by British commanders, won a brilliant victory with backwoods militia and Maryland and Delaware Continentals in January 1781, raising patriot hopes. This engagement, held near the town of Gaffney, served as a step toward the final decision at Yorktown. Address: Box 308, Chesnee, South Carolina 29323.

CUMBERLAND GAP NATIONAL HISTORICAL PARK
Kentucky-Tennessee-Virginia
A park of 20,222 acres in scenic hills where three states meet memorializes the westward adventure of Daniel Boone and his 30 axmen who blazed the "Wilderness Road" into Kentucky, and of pioneers who followed their paths in the trans-Allegheny migration. The Visitor Center, near the Middlesboro, Kentucky, entrance, houses paintings, pioneer tools, and weapons. Naturalist-historians answer questions.

Pinnacle Mountain Overlook, 2,440 feet above sea level, reached on an easy 4-mile scenic drive from the Visitor Center, affords a view of the historic notch in the mountain far below; the Tri-State Peak, where Kentucky, Virginia, and Tennessee meet; and a panorama of forested mountain and valley. **Hensley**, America's "last pioneer settlement," straddling the hilly Kentucky-Virginia line like an Inca fortress, is a restored mountaintop village of 28 buildings. You can see cabins made with hand-hewn logs, stone and wooden hinges, gun racks, plows, bee gums, and possum boards for drying skins. It is a good hike up the Cumberland Mountain to Hensley, but it is worth it.

Some 45 miles of trails lead to many interesting areas, such as **Goose Nest-Sink Sand Cave** (with an entrance 80 feet high), **White Rocks**, and **Hensley Settlement**. The 16-mile Ridge Trail, starting at the Pinnacle, follows the Cumberland crest along the Virginia-Kentucky border with spectacular views of both states. Overnight trails involve fairly steep climbing. Wilderness Road Campground, accessible by car, offers 160 sites and is the starting point for interesting trails, including Woodson Gap Trail and Gibson Gap Trail. Three other campgrounds (Gibson Gap, Martins Fork, and White Rocks) are reached only by foot. A backcountry permit serves as a campsite reservation for backpackers.

Cumberland Iron Furnace, reached on a remaining portion of the Wilderness Trail from the Gap, is one of many coldblast, charcoal-burning furnaces of pre-industrial America. Address: Cumberland Gap National Historical Park, Box 1848, Middlesboro, Kentucky 40965.

CUSTER BATTLEFIELD NATIONAL MONUMENT
Montana
The Sioux and Cheyenne, in the Battle of the Little Bighorn, destroyed the flamboyant Lt. Col. George A. Custer and his troopers of the Seventh Cavalry during two hot days in June, 1876, but it was the final victory in their defense of an independent way of life. The field of "Custer's Last Stand" is in southeastern Montana, near Hardin, on the route between the Black Hills and Yellowstone. Start at the Visitor Center to see maps and dioramas of the battle, then drive the loop road over the frontier ridges. Guided bus tours (modest fee) and interpretive programs are offered daily mid-June through Labor Day. Address: Box 39, Crow Agency, Montana 59022.

DE SOTO NATIONAL MEMORIAL
Florida
On May 30, 1539, Don Hernando de Soto, Knight of Santiago, set foot on the west coast of Florida. The approximate site of the landing on the shore of Tampa Bay is commemorated by a monument marker and the preservation of 25 surrounding breeze-swept acres. The Visitor Center offers exhibits of 16th century arms and armor; also a historical documentary film on De Soto from December through mid-April. A living history camp, complete with costumed conquistadors firing the crossbow and arquebus, gives the visitor an insight into the daily lives of Spanish soldiers. The ½-mile interpretive trail on Shaws Point calls attention to plants and wildlife that De Soto probably encountered. Address: 75th Street, N.W., Bradenton, Florida 33529.

DOUGLASS, FREDERICK, HOME. See Frederick Douglass Home, page 168.

EDGAR ALLAN POE NATIONAL HISTORIC SITE
Pennsylvania
Of the several houses where Poe lived at one time or another during his six years in Philadelphia, only this one—at 532 North Seventh Street—survives. It tells a great deal about the writer and his influence, opening doors to new approaches in mystery, adventure, and science fiction. Address: c/o Independence National Historical Park, 313 Walnut Street, Philadelphia, Pennsylvania 19106.

EDISON NATIONAL HISTORIC SITE
New Jersey
Here are the laboratories where Thomas A. Edison and his co-workers spent 44 years in technological investigation and development. Guided tours (daily, 9 a.m. to 5 p.m.) include his office and library, and the "Black Maria," a reconstruction of Edison's motion picture studio. Here you'll see that classic pioneer film, "The Great Train Robbery," and an early "talkie" newsreel featuring Edison himself. In the visitors' lobby of the lab several hundred photos, models, and artifacts trace the genius of the man.

The site also includes Edison's home, "Glenmont," a 23-room Victorian mansion. The house is decorated with original furnishings, heirlooms, and family portraits. Guided tours are on the hour, 12 noon to 4 p.m., Wednesday through Sunday (except holidays). Make arrangements at the laboratory. Make your reservation as soon as you arrive at the laboratory. You won't be admitted to the residence without a pass and the number per tour is limited. Address: Main Street and Lakeside Avenue, West Orange, New Jersey 07052.

EISENHOWER NATIONAL HISTORIC SITE
Pennsylvania
Dwight D. Eisenhower loved his 230-acre Gettysburg farm adjoining the national military park and often said he wanted to "leave the place better than I found it." But leave it to whom? In 1967, Ike and Mamie made a gift of the property to the people of the United States, reserving the right of lifetime occupancy. He died in 1969, and she ten years later. The house has been open to the public since 1980, furnished much as when the former First Family occupied it—both a home for comfort and a showplace for entertaining. In order to visit the farm, stop early at the park service Visitor Center on Taneytown Road in Gettysburg, where tickets are distributed on a first-come, first-served basis for each day's scheduled tours. Off-season advance reservations can be made for groups only. A shuttle bus takes visitors to the farm and back. Address: c/o Gettysburg National Military Park, Gettysburg, Pennsylvania 17325.

ELEANOR ROOSEVELT NATIONAL HISTORIC SITE
New York
This 180-acre estate of the First Lady includes the Val-Kill, the stone cottage, constructed in the mid-1920s for her by FDR. This site opened to the public on October 11, 1984, on the 100th anniversary of her birth. During the summer and fall tourist seasons, shuttle buses operate from the FDR Home N.H.S. to this site, two miles away. Private auto parking is allowed only during the off-season, except for visitors who are physically impaired. Address: Roosevelt-Vanderbilt National Historic Sites, Bellfield Headquarters, 249 Albany Post Road, Hyde Park, NY 12538.

ELLIS ISLAND. See Statue of Liberty National Monument, page 198.

EL MORRO NATIONAL MONUMENT
New Mexico
Located 56 miles from Gallup and 42 miles from Grants (en route to Zuni Reservation). Principal feature is "Inscription Rock," a sandstone monolith bearing Indian petroglyphs, as well as inscriptions left by Spanish explorers and early western settlers. Trails are self-guiding; small picnic grounds, and campgrounds with water and pit toilets. Campground may be closed during off-season due to weather. Address: Ramah, New Mexico 87321.

EUGENE O'NEILL NATIONAL HISTORIC SITE
California
The genius of modern American tragic drama came to this wooded mountainside overlooking the San Ramon Valley in 1937. Here he wrote his last four great works, from *The Iceman Cometh* to *A Moon for the Misbegotten*. Tours of the home and grounds are regularly scheduled. The site, though in a growing San Francisco suburb, is perched on a remote mountain hideaway. Visitors may not access the site on their own. Tours are on a reservation basis, with transportation provided by Tours Are Us, Inc. For information write: c/o Superintendent, John Muir National Historic Site, 4202 Alhambra Avenue, Martinez, California 94553.

FATHER MARQUETTE NATIONAL MEMORIAL
Michigan
Located in Straits State Park, 2 miles south of St. Ignace on US 2, the memorial pays tribute to the life and work of Father Jacques Marquette, the French Jesuit who came to the area in the 1600s. Address: c/o Parks Division, Department of Natural Resources, Box 30028, Lansing, Michigan 48909.

FEDERAL HALL NATIONAL MEMORIAL
New York
On the corner of Wall and Nassau Streets in downtown Manhattan, site of the present Federal Sub-Treasury Building, momentous events in American history took place. Here stood Federal Hall, where the first Congress met under the Constitution and where George Washington was inaugurated the first president. The stone on which he stood to take the oath of office is preserved in the rotunda, and one exhibit hall is set aside as a memorial to Peter Zenger, whose trial here marked a milestone in freedom of the press. Address: Superintendent, Manhattan Sites, National Park Service, 26 Wall Street, New York, New York 10005.

FORD'S THEATRE. See page 168.

FORT BOWIE NATIONAL HISTORIC SITE
Arizona
Created as a military post in 1862 commanding Apache Pass in the northern foothills of the Chiricahua Mountains, the fort was the center of operations during the bloody campaigns against Cochise and Geronimo, the famed Chiricahua Apache leaders, and the taming of the Southwest. Some of the walls of the fort still stand. The area also includes sections of the Butterfield Overland Stage Route. Address: Box 158, Bowie, Arizona 85605.

FORT CAROLINE NATIONAL MEMORIAL
Florida
East of Jacksonville along the St. Johns River, the reconstructed walls of Fort Caroline and the Visitor Center recall the French colony of 1564. It was the first European colony in North America this side of Mexico. The Spanish-moss-draped trees bordering the entrance road, and the forest surrounding a clearing where the museum is located, inspire a feeling of stillness and isolation.

In 1988, Congress created Timucuan Ecological and Historic Preserve, covering 35,000 acres adjacent to Fort Caroline. The preserve encompasses coastal marshes, islands, mudflats, and meandering tidal creeks of north Jacksonville, facing barrier islands of the Atlantic coast. It provides habitat for rare wildlife species, including spotted turtle, wood stork, marsh mink, manatee, and salt marsh snake. Cultural sites cover a time span from prehistoric Timucuan (tee-MOO-kwon) down to the Spanish-American War. Most of the wetlands and two historic sites, long administered by the State of Florida, are expected to be transferred to the National Park Service. Address: 12713 Fort Caroline Road, Jacksonville, Florida 32225.

FORT CLATSOP NATIONAL MEMORIAL
Oregon
Lewis and Clark enthusiasts will find a replica of the log fort in which the explorers spent the winter of 1805-06, after their epochal journey to the Pacific Coast. Trails from the fort replica corresponding to those used by the explorers, lead to the canoe landing and to the camp spring. Allow time for the living history program. Address: Route 3, Box 604FC, Astoria, Oregon 97103.

FORT DAVIS NATIONAL HISTORIC SITE
Texas
A key post in the defense system of West Texas from 1854 to 1891, Fort Davis guarded immigrants, freighters, and stages from Apaches and Comanches on the San Antonio-El Paso road. The stone and adobe structures, including officers row, barracks, and hospitals, are the most impressive of any Southwestern fort. The

commanding officers' quarters and a kitchen have been furnished in period; in the summer women guides in costume are on duty. During this season a living history program presents officers on duty at the enlisted barracks and commissary. Any day of the year you can enjoy the recording of a sundown dress parade, complete with martial music and the sounds of a mounted review. You may also want to hike a trail to the ridge crest for another perspective of the fort. Adjacent is scenic Davis Mountain State Park (lodge, camping). Address: Box 1456, Fort Davis, Texas 79734.

FORT DONELSON NATIONAL MILITARY PARK
Tennessee
The well-preserved earthen fort, rifle pits, and batteries, along with markers and tablets, trace the course of action near Dover in early 1862, when General U. S. Grant made bold use of the Tennessee River. He moved 17,000 men on transports, then marched them across a watershed between the Tennessee and Cumberland, and attacked. After intensive action Grant's demand for "unconditional surrender" resulted in the capture of some 14,000 Confederate troops and opened a river route into the heart of the Confederacy. Visitor Center contains exhibits and a slide program. Almost 700 Union war dead are buried in the national cemetery. Address: Box F, Dover, Tennessee 37058.

FORT FREDERICA NATIONAL MONUMENT
Georgia
The ruins of the fort on St. Simons Island symbolize Great Britain's struggle to hold southeastern coastal lands against the Spaniards. In its day this was the largest, most costly British fort in America, built of "tabby"—a mixture of oystershell, sand, and lime. In 1742 the Spanish fleet and army attacked, but James Oglethorpe, founder of the Georgia colony, scored a decisive victory in the aptly named Battle of Bloody Marsh fought nearby. Address: Route 4, Box 286-C, St. Simons Island, Georgia 31522.

FORT JEFFERSON NATIONAL MONUMENT
Florida
Work on the largest all-masonry fortification in the Western world began in 1846 in the Dry Tortugas, 70 miles west of Key West, as part of the chain of seacoast defenses strung from Maine to Texas. It was never really finished and never saw action, but served as a Federal military prison during and after the Civil War. The monument is important today as a natural area, with reefs of coral and "forests" of marine plants providing refuge for the myriad forms of animal life in nature's aquarium. Between May and September terns land by the thousands for their nesting season, and white frigate birds glide on thermal drafts above the fort. Camping is allowed at 10 sites, equipped with picnic tables and grills. Transportation to Fort Jefferson is offered from the Keys and the mainland by various charter boats and air-taxi services. Address: c/o Everglades National Park, Box 279, Homestead, Florida 33030.

FORT LARAMIE NATIONAL HISTORIC SITE
Wyoming
Near the confluence of the North Platte and Laramie Rivers, this was a frontier center for trade, diplomacy, and warfare from 1834 to 1890. The fort was associated with Kit Carson, Jim Bridger, Buffalo Bill, Captain John C. Fremont, Red Cloud, and Spotted Tail, and countless wagon trains heading west. Today 11 original structures, including "Old Bedlam" (post headquarters) and the Sutler's Store, have been restored, surrounded by ruins of others. The 1889 commissary storehouse serves as the Visitor Center. Guided one-hour tours are conducted frequently during the day. Many special events are scheduled, including moonlight tours, art exhibits, and old-fashioned July 4th. Visit Chimney Rock and

Scotts Bluff in nearby Nebraska, then come here to picnic in the wooded grove and spend the rest of the day. Address: Fort Laramie, Wyoming 82212.

FORT LARNED NATIONAL HISTORIC SITE
Kansas
As a key frontier post established in 1859, this fort guarded the eastern part of the Santa Fe Trail and served as a base of operations against the Plains Indians. Nine original sandstone buildings frame the quadrangle parade ground with its restored 100-foot flagpole. The Visitor Center (in the enlisted men's barracks) contains a museum and an audiovisual program. Guided tours are available during the summer and on request the rest of the year. Make the most of the living history programs given on summer weekends. Address: Route 3, Larned, Kansas 67550.

FORT McHENRY NATIONAL MONUMENT
Maryland
From a vessel offshore in the Patapsco River, Francis Scott Key, who had gone to secure the release of a friend from the British fleet, witnessed the 25-hour bombardment of this fort at the entrance to Baltimore's inner harbor. A barrage of 1,500 to 1,800 bombs, rockets, and shells was fired until after midnight. In the morning, when he saw the Stars and Stripes still waving, he began to write his immortal lines on the back of a letter. So the National Anthem was born.

The Visitor Center contains various exhibits on the history of the fort and the War of 1812. A weekend summer treat is provided by Fort McHenry Guard volunteers reenacting history in period uniforms. Programs begin at 1 p.m. each Saturday and Sunday. An island of green in the heart of industrial Baltimore, the park is surrounded by water on three sides and is visited by a wide variety of birds during both spring and fall migrations. Address: East Fort Avenue, Baltimore, Maryland 21230.

FORT MATANZAS NATIONAL MONUMENT
Florida
On the southern tip of Anastasia Island in 1565, a Spanish commander put to death two bands of French prisoners and eliminated the threat of continued French settlement in Florida. Later, in 1742, the Spaniards built Fort Matanzas on nearby Rattlesnake Island to protect St. Augustine's south entrance from enemy attempts to reach the city via the inland waterway. The small, historic fort sits on Rattlesnake Island across from the Visitor Center and museum. You can reach it aboard a small free ferry that operates daily 9 a.m. to 4:45 p.m. Address: c/o Castillo de San Marcos National Monument, 1 Castillo Drive, St. Augustine, Florida 32084.

FORT NECESSITY NATIONAL BATTLEFIELD
Pennsylvania
The battlefield surrounding the reconstruction of George Washington's 1754 fort is the park's principal unit and has been reconstructed faithfully. It is 11 miles east of Uniontown on US 40. Here George Washington engaged in his first major battle, signaling the start of the French and Indian War. For 200 years details of the fort were lost (the French burned it). Archaeological research has made possible the present replica of the fort, entrenchments, earthworks, and log cabin.

Include three nearby areas in your visit. Jumonville Glen, about 7½ miles away, was the scene of a wild preliminary skirmish after Washington had led a striking force of 40 men on an all-night march. Braddock's Grave, 1 mile west of the fort, marks the site where Major General Edward Braddock, commander of all British soldiers in the American colonies, was buried, in 1755, after being mortally wounded in the Battle of Monongahela. Note the monument erected to his memory by the Coldstream Guards in 1913. (His aide-de-camp, George Washington, had two horses shot from under him.) Mount Washington Tavern, overlooking Fort Necessity, typifies the sturdy stage stations built during the 1820s on the Old National Pike, when it was a mainstream of travel to the West. It is now a museum of the early pioneer period. Address: The National Pike, Farmington, Pennsylvania 15437.

FORT POINT NATIONAL HISTORIC SITE
California
In the Presidio under the south end of the Golden Gate Bridge is the massive brick fortification built by the Army between 1853 and 1861 to guard the entrance to San Francisco Bay.

The architecture of Fort Point is truly outstanding, incorporating many technical refinements into the masterwork of the Pacific Coast. It was used over a wide span of military history, from the Civil War down through the Indian Wars and the Spanish American War. Address: Box 29333, The Presidio of San Francisco, California 94129.

FORT PULASKI NATIONAL MONUMENT
Georgia
Built in the 19th century with 25 million bricks and walls 11 feet thick, it took 18 years to complete the massive structure on Cockspur Island commanding the mouth of the Savannah River, 17 miles east of Savannah. In the long casemated galleries are examples of some of the finest brickarch masonry in America. Surrounded by a moat, Pulaski was declared impregnable at a time when smoothbore guns would do little damage. And then came the Civil War.

The fort was taken first by the Confederates, but in 1862 Union forces on Tybee Island, a mile distant, unleashed a bombardment with a new weapon, the rifled gun. Within 30 hours the fort surrendered, and the era of the moated medieval fortress was done. Fort Pulaski lies in a natural setting bordered by marsh and woodland; its moat, though a military failure, serves successfully as a rendezvous for semitropical plants and for birds like the heron, crane, and egret.

The best time for Pulaski is spring, and the ideal base is Savannah, a city distinguished by palmetto-shaded squares, small parks, and restored buildings. For further information write Superintendent, Fort Pulaski National Monument, Box 98, Tybee Island, Georgia 31328.

FORT RALEIGH NATIONAL HISTORIC SITE
North Carolina
The restored fort occupies the site of the legendary "Lost Colony," the first attempted English settlement within the bounds of the present United States. The 150 men, women, and children sent by Sir Walter Raleigh arrived at Roanoke Island on the Outer Banks in July 1587. One month later the first child of English parentage in the New World, Virginia Dare, was born. But when Governor John White went to England and then returned to Roanoke Island in August 1590, he found the colony had disappeared. The only clue he found was the word "CROATAN" carved on a palisade post. The mystery of the "Lost Colony" has never been solved. This historic episode is the theme of an outdoor drama presented during summer evenings. Illustrated talks are given in the Visitor Center, which houses excavated artifacts.

The center is the starting place of the scenic Thomas Hariot Trail. Vegetation along the way is like that seen by the first settlers.

The nearby Outer Banks stretch 120 miles along the coast, forming a barrier between the Atlantic Ocean and the interior sounds and constantly undergoing changes caused by wind and wave. Cape Hatteras National Seashore and the Wright

Brothers National Memorial should be visited. Address: c/o Cape Hatteras National Seashore, Route 1, Box 675, Manteo, North Carolina 27954.

FORT SCOTT NATIONAL HISTORIC SITE
Kansas
In 1842 two companies of the First Dragoons began building a fort 90 miles south of Kansas City to be part of a chain of outposts extending from Minnesota to Louisiana marking the boundary between U.S. and Indian lands. Following the Mexican War of 1846, the fort fell into disuse, but soon became a focal point of pre-Civil War conflicts between pro-slavery forces and followers of John Brown, the fabled abolitionist. It was the "Bloody Kansas" period. Then during the war the fort was activated again as a major supply center, with as many as 6,000 troops camped in the area, including two regiments of black soldiers—the First and Second Kansas Colored Volunteer Infantry. After the troops marched out for the last time, in 1873, the fort was forgotten for almost a century. Now the guard house, parade ground, officers quarters, hospital, and other buildings have been restored. Address: Old Fort Boulevard, Fort Scott, Kansas 66701.

FORT SMITH NATIONAL HISTORIC SITE
Arkansas
Although one of the first U.S. military posts in the Louisiana Territory, three decades—from the 1870s through 1890s—represent Fort Smith's period of greatest fame. During that period it sheltered the famous court of Isaac C. Parker, the "Hanging Judge," who sentenced 160 men to the gallows while spreading law to the raw frontier. The site preserves the remains of two forts and Judge Parker's court. The nearby Belle Grove Historic District, covering 22 blocks, protects a variety of notable restored buildings, several of which serve new purposes as shops, restaurants, and apartments. Address: Box 1406, Fort Smith, Arkansas 72902.

FORT STANWIX NATIONAL MONUMENT
New York
The British built this fort in 1758 to protect a major Mohawk River portage in the French and Indian War. The 15-acre site is now in the center of the city of Rome, New York. The fort was completely reconstructed as it was, with logs, barracks, and cannon platform, for the 1976 Bicentennial. This followed archaeological excavation to locate the fort's features so they could be accurately restored. Recovered artifacts also shed light on the garrison life of the time. The original fort was lost through fire and leveling of the site. The fort was the scene in 1768 of the Indian Treaty of Fort Stanwix, in which the Iroquois ceded to the British a vast area east of the Ohio River. When the British attacked the colonies from Canada in August 1777, during the Revolution, the fort withstood a three-week siege. Address: 112 East Park Street, Rome, New York 13440.

FORT SUMTER NATIONAL MONUMENT
South Carolina
The five-sided fort, built on a small island in Charleston harbor as part of the chain of coastal fortifications, gained a place in history on April 12, 1861, when Confederate troops fired the opening shots of the Civil War at the small Federal garrison striving to hold it. For 34 hours the fort was defended until, as the commanding officer reported, "the quarters were entirely burned, the main gates destroyed by fire, the gorge walls seriously injured, the magazines surrounded by flames." After the Confederates occupied the fort, it became a symbol of their new nation. For nearly two years Federal forces were held at bay despite siege and bombardment, until the Confederates made their evacuation in

February 1865. Today the fort is reached on regular two-hour boat tours from the Municipal Yacht Basin in the harbor.

Fort Moultrie, a unit of the national monument accessible by car on Sullivans Island, preserves the scene of one of the first decisive victories of the American Revolution in 1776, and the burial place of the valiant Indian chief Osceola. The fort tells the story of seacoast defense from the Revolution to World War II. Take the multilevel tour through underground powder magazines and installations covering five different time periods. While at the Visitor Center, don't miss the dramatic vistas from the observation deck—in one direction, of the fort with the Atlantic Ocean behind it and in the other direction, of Charleston harbor and the city. Address: 1214 Middle Street, Sullivans Island, South Carolina 29482.

FORT UNION NATIONAL MONUMENT
New Mexico
Located on the route of the Santa Fe Trail, where the mountains meet the plains, this fort was the largest military post guarding the 19th century Southwestern frontier. Kit Carson and General James H. Carleton were two of the lustrous figures who served here. Only adobe walls and chimneys rising starkly from the plains remain today, but a self-guiding trail leads through the ruins. The Visitor Center offers various displays that recall the drama and the adventure of yesterday's Southwest. During its 40 years in operation, the fort guarded the surrounding frontier and received shipments of materials for assignment to other forts in the Southwest. The monument is located 8 miles north of I-25, 26 miles north of Las Vegas, New Mexico. Camping facilities are nearby in Storrie Lake State Park and in the Santa Fe and Carson National Forests. Address: Watrous, New Mexico 87753.

FORT UNION TRADING POST
NATIONAL HISTORIC SITE
North Dakota-Montana
As the principal fur-trading center on the upper Missouri River for four decades, Fort Union became a stopping place for every important trailblazer, trapper, soldier, and traveler, from Jim Bridger to John J. Audubon and George Catlin. The Bourgeois House, once occupied by the fort manager, is the centerpiece of the reconstruction begun in 1986. Other features include the trade house, palisade bastions, and 20-foot-high white wall surrounding the compound. Address: Buford Route, Williston, North Dakota 58801.

FORT VANCOUVER NATIONAL HISTORIC SITE
Washington
Established by the Hudson's Bay Company in 1825 and moved to this site in 1829, Fort Vancouver became the hub of fur trading, political, social, and cultural activity. It was the symbol of Britain's claim to the Northwest when America was still in its expansion period. Much of the fort has been reconstructed. Events during the year include the annual tour by candlelight in October. Address: Vancouver, Washington 98661.

FRANKLIN, BENJAMIN, NATIONAL MEMORIAL. See Benjamin Franklin National Memorial, page 177.

FREDERICK LAW OLMSTED NATIONAL HISTORIC SITE
Massachusetts
Living and working here at "Fairsted" while developing plans for Boston's "Emerald Necklace" of parks, Olmsted was one of the foremost conservationists of the 19th century. His extensive papers are also housed here. Open only Friday through Sunday noon to 4:30 p.m. while restoration is continuing. Address: 99 Warren Street, Brookline, Massachusetts 02146.

FREDERICKSBURG AND SPOTSYLVANIA COUNTY BATTLEFIELDS MEMORIAL NATIONAL MILITARY PARK
Virginia
No other area of comparable size on the American continent has witnessed such heavy and continuous fighting as this setting of four major Civil War battles within a 17-mile radius. The Visitor Centers near the southern edge of Fredericksburg and at Chancellorsville feature dioramas, pictorial displays, and maps, while narrative markers and monuments interpret the field of action with miles of original, well-preserved trench remains and gun pits. Fredericksburg, midway between the two capitals of Washington and Richmond, became the scene of fierce action in December 1862. Chatham Manor, privately occupied for about 200 years, played a key role as an artillery and communications center during the battle at the Rappahannock River. With its restored colonial garden, it is an attractive feature of the park. The site of a federal pontoon bridge that spanned the Rappahannock is nearby. You can see where Longstreet's men fired point-blank from Marye's Heights at charging Federals along the Sunken Road and forced them to retreat over the Rappahannock. In spring 1863 the Confederates won another signal victory at Chancellorsville, but Stonewall Jackson was accidentally wounded by his own men and died at Guiney Station (now Stonewall Jackson Shrine). At battles of the Wilderness and Spotsylvania Court House, in May 1864, a determined Union army under General Grant began the final drive that sealed the Confederacy. More than 15,000 Union soldiers are buried in the National Cemetery here, including 12,000 unidentified. The park also administers Old Salem Church, a 19th century brick structure which was the scene of a sharp battle during the Chancellorsville Campaign. Bicycling is an excellent means to tour the individual battlefields. Address: Box 679, Fredericksburg, Virginia 22401.

FRIENDSHIP HILL NATIONAL HISTORIC SITE
Pennsylvania
This park preserves the country estate of Albert Gallatin, secretary of treasury under Presidents Jefferson and Madison, chief negotiator of the treaty ending the War of 1812, and U.S. envoy to both France and Great Britain. Gallatin built Friendship Hill on the banks of the Monongahela River near New Geneva in 1789. While the house has undergone major restorations, the grounds are open daily, in summer; weekends only, rest of year. Events include wildflower walks on April weekends and Restoration Day in May. Address: c/o Fort Necessity National Battlefield, RD2, Box 528, Farmington, Pennsylvania 15437.

JAMES A. GARFIELD NATIONAL HISTORIC SITE
Ohio
Lawnfield, the home of the twentieth president of the United States, is located on US 20 at Mentor, northeast of Cleveland. The first two floors are furnished with original Garfield possessions. Also on the site are the small building used as headquarters in the 1880 campaign and the log cabin replica of Garfield's birthplace. Address: 1950 Mentor Avenue, Mentor, Ohio 44060.

GENERAL GRANT NATIONAL MEMORIAL
New York
On a bluff overlooking the Hudson River (at Riverside Drive and 122nd Street) in Manhattan, the gray granite memorial to the great soldier who commanded the Union armies contains the sarcophagi of General Grant and his wife. Exhibits depicting the life of General Grant are displayed. Address: Superintendent, Manhattan Sites, National Park Service, 26 Wall Street, New York, New York 10005.

GEORGE ROGERS CLARK NATIONAL HISTORICAL PARK
Indiana

In the oldest city of the state, Vincennes, the imposing circular, columned memorial to George Rogers Clark celebrates his heroism in the winning of the Northwest. The 25 acres of formally landscaped grounds surround the stately memorial on the site of Fort Sackville, with the Wabash River flowing by the western boundary. Start at the Visitor Center to learn the full story from exhibits and motion pictures. As early as 1732 the French built the first fort here, but lost it in time to the English. Within the rotunda a bronze statue of Clark, the fiery young Virginian, is flanked by seven large murals depicting dramatic scenes in his expedition of 1778—79, when his little army swept the British out of the Northwest frontier. Near the memorial other historic structures are well worth visiting. These include: white-spired St. Francis Xavier Church, built in 1826; Grouseland, the home of William Henry Harrison; and the building that served as first capitol of the territory. The annual Spirit of Vincennes Rendezvous Memorial Day weekend at the park features historic reenactments with 300 uniformed members of the North West Territorial Alliance. Address: 401 South Second Street, Vincennes, Indiana 47591.

GEORGE WASHINGTON BIRTHPLACE NATIONAL MONUMENT
Virginia

A pastoral setting on the bank of Pope's Creek, about 38 miles east of Fredericksburg, marks the ancestral plantation where George Washington was born. The original house burned; the present structure, designed to represent a typical planter's quarters, is carefully furnished in the period of Washington's boyhood. Young George spent the first three and one-half years of his life here, until 1735, when his family moved to Little Hunting Creek Plantation, later renamed Mount Vernon. George's half-brother, Augustine, inherited Pope's Creek upon his father's death, in 1743, and young George again spent several of his teen-age years on the plantation, as a companion to Augustine. On the grounds of the estate, the family burial plot contains the remains of his father, grandfather, and greatgrandfather. Important additions have been made in recent years, including a colonial "living farm" and garden. A few miles south along the Potomac is Stratford Hall, the ancestral estate of the Lees of Virginia and birthplace of Robert E. Lee. Address: RR1, Box 717, Virginia 22575.

GEORGE WASHINGTON CARVER NATIONAL MONUMENT
Missouri

Birthplace of a slave who rose to fame as botanist, agronomist, and pioneer conservationist, the monument is located a few miles southeast of Joplin. The Visitor Center traces Carver's career and mighty achievements, including his developing new uses for Alabama clay, peanuts, sweet potatoes, and cotton. A self-guiding trail winds along the stream and through the woods of his youth. Address: Box 38, Diamond, Missouri 64840.

GEORGIA O'KEEFFE NATIONAL HISTORIC SITE
New Mexico

Established in 1980, this area, in Abiquiu, commemorates the career of one of America's foremost artists. Born in Wisconsin and raised in Virginia, O'Keeffe studied art in Chicago and New York. In 1929 she began spending summers in the foothills of the Sangre de Cristo Mountains of northern New Mexico and in 1949 made the area her home, deriving inspiration for her pioneering modernism from the geological fantasia around her. She lived and worked here until her death in 1986. Address: c/o National Park Service, Old Santa Fe Trail, Box 728, Santa Fe, New Mexico 87501.

GETTYSBURG NATIONAL MILITARY PARK
Pennsylvania

Of more than 2,000 land engagements during the Civil War, Gettysburg ranks first in the memory of a nation. On the three days of July 1, 2, and 3, 1863, more men died than in any other battle ever fought on the soil of North America. Under terrible strains and sacrifices, the Confederate Army of 75,000 under Lee reached its high-water mark, but met its match in 97,000 Union troops under Meade and was turned back. Then, four months later, a portion of the battleground was dedicated as a burial ground by President Lincoln in a speech of 272 immortal words.

Gettysburg is one of the world's most monumented battlefields, veritably a museum of commemorative architecture and sculpture, with more than 400 memorials, many impressively large, plus 900 smaller markers. Your starting point should be the **Visitor Center**, which features the famed Electric Map orientation program and houses a large collection of Civil War relics. Within walking distance is the **Cyclorama Center**, where you can view museum exhibits, a 10-minute film, and the mammoth circular Cyclorama painting depicting Pickett's Charge. In the summer, an original copy of the Gettysburg Address is on display. Take your youngsters to the **Campfire Program** at the amphitheater in Pitzer's Woods, nightly at dusk during summer, where a National Park Service ranger conducts a program. At the Granite Farm interpretive site, you will see a typical farm setting of the war period. Note the turkey vultures and black vultures, which, according to legend, first appeared in the Gettysburg area in July 1863. There are several ways of touring the battlefield. The self-guided auto tour is outlined in a free park folder. The park also sponsors the **Licensed Battlefield Guide** program; dispatched from the Visitor Center, the guide provides a two-hour tour in your vehicle for a set fee. Bus tours, tape tours, and bicycles for rent are available at commercial locations near the Visitor Center. (For details on these programs contact the Gettysburg Travel Council, 35 Carlisle Street, Gettysburg, Pennsylvania 17325.) The use of bicycles in the park is encouraged, and suggested routes are outlined in the park folder. Among monuments and memorials you will see are the **High Water Mark**, the climax of Gettysburg, where Pickett's Charge was halted; the **Pennsylvania Monument**, with statues of officers and the names of 35,000 Pennsylvanians who fought in the ranks; the **Virginia Memorial**, surmounted by a statue of General Robert E. Lee on his horse, Traveller; the spirited monuments of other states, possibly including your own; the **Eternal Light Peace Memorial**, dedicated to "peace eternal in a nation united"; and the **National Cemetery**, where Lincoln rose to his full height on November 19, 1863, and transformed the word Gettysburg from memorial to the dead into inspiration for the living.

Winter scene. The Visitor Center, in the heart of the park, is open year-round. Winter has become popular, especially for ski touring. Address: Gettysburg, Pennsylvania 17325.

GOLDEN SPIKE NATIONAL HISTORIC SITE
Utah

The ceremony on May 10, 1869, when the Union Pacific from the East met the Central Pacific from the West, is commemorated annually at the historic site of Promontory. About 1.7 miles of track have been relaid on the original roadbed where the rails were joined, with authentic working replicas of the original locomotives to recreate the emotion and excitement of the ceremony. Address: Box W, Brigham City, Utah 84302.

GRAND PORTAGE NATIONAL MONUMENT
Minnesota

On the site of the old North West Company depot, bordering serene Grand Portage Bay, a newly reconstructed stockade (replacing an earlier one that burned) recalls the adventurous age when voyagers, seeking a treasure in furs, transferred supplies and trade goods from Lake Superior to the border lakes canoe route. The "great depot," established in 1778 near the Canadian boundary, was the first white settlement in Minnesota, a vital link in the 3,000-mile waterway extending from Montreal to Western Canada. Much of the charm of the 710-acre monument today is in the centuries-old trail—the 9-mile portage, with its lichen-covered rocks and reindeer moss. The trail offers an outstanding experience, but wear hiking shoes and expect encounters with mud, mosquitoes, and flies. Excursion boats operate from Grand Portage to Isle Royale National Park, 25 miles away in Lake Superior. If you're driving on the North Shore you'll find that Grand Portage is closely tied in with Old Fort William, the reconstruction of the bustling headquarters of a vast fur-trading empire at Thunder Bay, Ontario, at the western end of the Great Lakes. The old fort is like a living community, and has artisans who make things ranging from clothing to big-freight canoes. Grand Portage Rendezvous Days, in mid-August, revives old ways and traditions of Chippewa Indians and the British Northwest Company. Address: Box 666, Grand Marais, Minnesota 55604.

GRANT-KOHRS RANCH NATIONAL HISTORIC SITE
Montana
Located in the Deer Lodge Valley, north of Yellowstone, the headquarters of a 19th century cattle kingdom—one of the giant "spreads" of the Old West—still preserves early log buildings and the main ranch house. The site commemorates the frontier cattle era of American history. Livestock, together with the ranch collection of saddles, tools, wagons, buggies, and other artifacts, complete the cattleman's saga. Allow time to observe the blacksmith and other artisans at work and the guided tour of the Victorian house. The town of Deer Lodge also has some fascinating public and private buildings, including the Territorial Prison. Address: Box 790, Deer Lodge, Montana 59722.

GUILFORD COURTHOUSE NATIONAL MILITARY PARK
North Carolina
In gentle rolling country near Greensboro, the battle fought here in March 1781 was part of the British campaign to subdue the southern colonies one by one while advancing north. Though the strategy had already backfired at Kings Mountain and Cowpens, Cornwallis won this battle over General Nathanael Greene's poorly equipped colonials. But he lost 25 percent of his troops, and when he advanced into Virginia, it was to the ultimate defeat at Yorktown. Graphic, colorful exhibits at the contemporary-style Visitor Center tell the story of the Southern campaign, while memorials are located at various points on the battlefield. You can follow a one-way tour road by car; better yet, the bicycle trails or footpaths. Address: Box 9806, Greensboro, North Carolina 27429-0806.

HAMILTON GRANGE NATIONAL MEMORIAL
New York
The only home ever owned by Alexander Hamilton, a principal figure in shaping the Republic, and one of the few Federal-period structures surviving in New York City. Eventually the house will be restored to its appearance in Hamilton's time. Present programs are conducted around themes of drama, music, and colonial crafts. Address: Superintendent, Manhattan Sites, National Park Service, 26 Wall Street, New York, New York 10005.

HAMPTON NATIONAL HISTORIC SITE
Maryland
An elaborate Georgian mansion built with formal charm and elegance during the latter part of the 18th century lies on a 60-acre tract near Towson. This once vast agricultural/industrial domain contains 23 separate structures and includes the 14-acre Hampton Farm complex, with overseer's house, slave quarters, granary, and barns. During the Revolution the Hampton ironworks supplied arms and ammunition to the patriots. Charles Ridgely, nephew of the builder, served as governor of Maryland from 1815 to 1818. It was he who developed the Ridgely empire, amassing a great estate that extended as far as the eye could see. The Ridgely family occupied Hampton from 1788 to 1948. Formal gardens and greenhouses still remain with geometric parterres and broad grass ramps. Adjacent to the mansion are the orangery, carriage house, stables, and outstanding trees. Within the mansion, obviously planned for elaborate entertaining, are period furnishings and portraits by such notable early artists as Sully and Peale. Open Monday through Saturday, 11 a.m. to 4:30 p.m., Sunday, 1 p.m. to 4:30 p.m. Address: 535 Hampton Lane, Towson, Maryland 21204.

HARPERS FERRY NATIONAL HISTORICAL PARK
Virginia-West Virginia-Maryland
In the shadow of the Blue Ridge Mountains, where the Shenandoah and Potomac Rivers meet, the hillside town became the scene of John Brown's ill-fated abolitionist raid in 1859, which forced the nation to realize the slavery issue was inescapable. The Visitor Center and museum are located in the paymaster's headquarters of the old arsenal that was the target of Brown's little

Harpers Ferry, an early painting

band in its effort to arm the slaves and establish a free state in the mountains. Gun buffs will appreciate the breech-loading Hall rifles on display. Though Brown's men captured the arsenal, within two days they were driven to refuge in the little engine house known as "John Brown's Fort" and forced to surrender. When the Civil War broke out, two years after Brown's raid, the town was almost a continual battleground and finally was left in ruins. Follow the marked half-mile walking tour (about one hour) past restored old houses, shops, and stores, the "fort" returned to near its original site. Visit the restored blacksmith shop, where craftsmen produce articles for homes and shops of the town with 19th century tools. Then walk to the heights of Jefferson Rock, for a view of the rivers favored by Thomas Jefferson. May and June are especially attractive months in this area, when redbud, dogwood, and wildflowers are in bloom; October coloring on the heights above the river is spectacular. Address: Box 65, Harpers Ferry, West Virginia 25425.

HARRY S TRUMAN NATIONAL HISTORIC SITE
Missouri
This century-old Victorian house was home to President Truman from his marriage, in 1919, until his death, in 1972. It served as the "Summer White House" during his time in office, 1945 to 1953. The first floor was opened to visitors for the Truman Centennial in May 1984. Reservations for guided tours (small fee) are available the day of the tour only, at the Information Center, Truman Road and Main Street. Get there early, then take the free shuttle bus. The neighboring historic district preserves the air of the early 20th century. The Truman Presidential Library is a few blocks away. Address: Box 4139. Independence, Missouri 64050.

HERBERT HOOVER NATIONAL HISTORIC SITE
Iowa
At West Branch, the 31st president of the United States was born August 10, 1874, in a simple two-room cottage that still stands and forms the nucleus of this attractive, landscaped area. A National Park Service employee greets visitors and chats about Herbert Hoover's childhood, while pointing out such family items as the cradle and high chair used by the Hoover children. On the north side of Penn Street, across from the birthplace, the reconstructed blacksmith shop is similar to the one operated by the President's father. During spring and summer blacksmiths demonstrate their crafts. Here, too, are the grave, where Mr. Hoover was buried in 1964 while 75,000 mourners stood in silent tribute, and the limestone Hoover Presidential Library-Museum, a museum full of mementos of a life of humanitarianism and public service. Address: Box 607, West Branch, Iowa 52358.

HOME OF FRANKLIN D. ROOSEVELT NATIONAL HISTORIC SITE
New York
The house at the edge of a gently rolling plateau overlooking the Hudson River where the "Squire of Hyde Park" was born and reared was ample for the large family, but scarcely reflects elegance or opulence. The mood is set by the surrounding woodlands he loved and helped to plant, and by the burial place where he and his wife lie beneath a plain white marble monument within a garden where roses bloom. Oil portraits, gifts of crystal, gold, and brocade, tokens sent by emperors and little people—these are housed with 30,000 volumes and vast correspondence in the adjacent Franklin D. Roosevelt Library, a source of learning for scholars and schoolchildren for generations to come. Visiting hours 9 a.m. to 5 p.m., but crowds are heavy during summer and on weekends, so arrive early. Address: Bellfield Headquarters, 249 Albany Post Road, Hyde Park, New York 12538.

HOMESTEAD NATIONAL MONUMENT
Nebraska
A T-shaped quarter section of prairie and woodland, 160 acres, near Beatrice (due south of Lincoln), is on the site of the claim of one Daniel Freeman, an Illinois farmer, who became one of the first to file for free land under the Homestead Act. This law, signed by Abraham Lincoln in 1862, was an epochal advance in democracy, enabling more than one million citizens to become landholders. The Visitor Center displays trace development of the Homestead movement. The adjacent cabin is furnished to the finest details with remnants of the belongings of the people who once called it home. The restored one-room Freeman School is west of the cabin on Nebraska 4. Displayed behind the center are

farm implements and carriages. History touches everything, even to the 1½-mile-long nature trail. The path winds through native prairie and wooded areas, reaching its high point at the graves of Freeman and his wife, Agnes, high on a hill. More than 130 species of birds have been sighted, showing the richness of the tall-grass prairie. Address: RFD 3, Beatrice, Nebraska 68310.

HOPEWELL VILLAGE NATIONAL HISTORIC SITE
Pennsylvania
The cold blast ironworks symbolize the industrial techniques of the nearly self-sufficient "iron plantations" that were once a way of life. Founded about 1770, Hopewell Village supplied cannon and shot for the Revolutionary War effort and produced cast iron until 1883. Many of the structures beyond the Visitor Center are the originals—the "Big House," or Ironmaster's Mansion, blacksmith shop, charcoal house, furnace, and tenant homes. Others, like the waterwheel, bridge house, barn, and store, have been handsomely restored to complete the walk into America's yesterday. During July and August the village comes "alive" with the costumed interpretation program reflecting the 1820-1840 period. Bird walks are conducted during spring and fall. Hopewell is open daily 9 a.m. to 5 p.m. except December 25 and January 1. French Creek State Park, immediately adjacent, provides facilities for camping, picnicking, and swimming. Address: Route 1, Box 345, Elverson, Pennsylvania 19520.

HORSESHOE BEND NATIONAL MILITARY PARK
Alabama
Near the present site of Dadeville, on March 27, 1814, Major General Andrew Jackson's army of Tennessee soldiers and Indian allies defeated the Creek Indian warriors of Chief Menawa at the Battle of Horseshoe Bend. This battle ended the Creek Indian War. The battle is interpreted at the museum. A free auto tape tour is available at the Visitor Center. Take advantage of the park's picnic area and hiking trails. Address: Route 1, Box 103, Daviston, Alabama 36256.

HUBBELL TRADING POST NATIONAL HISTORIC SITE
Arizona
His name was John Lorenzo Hubbell, but he was known as "Don Lorenzo," champion of Indians, and especially of Indian craftsmen. He established his trading business about 1878. The sprawling adobe home appears as it did at the turn of the century, displaying his valuable collection of paintings and Indian crafts. The trading post is open to all as a living remnant of the old days.

The rug room has been famous for decades. Mr. Hubbell influenced the Navajo women to produce well-made rugs with native patterns and bright red, black, and white colors, products that would find ready acceptance in the east and west coast markets. Today stacks of beautiful rugs are available for inspection and sale. Collections of firearms, books, and other memorabilia further enhance the Southwestern atmosphere of the room.

The Park Service maintains the live atmosphere of the home just as in the operation of the trading post. There are no protective covers on the original furnishings or the Navajo floor rugs—a type of textile that absolutely defies wear. Visitors are not admitted to the home except during conducted tours. At sheep-shearing time visitors may see wool being weighed, purchased, and sacked for shipment to the mills as in Don Lorenzo's day.

The trading post is located 1 mile west of Ganado within the boundaries of the Navajo Reservation, and 55 miles from Gallup, New Mexico. From the east it is on the way to Grand Canyon National Park, Canyon de Chelly National Monument, and the Hopi mesas. Address: Box 150, Ganado, Arizona 86505.

ILLINOIS & MICHIGAN CANAL NATIONAL HERITAGE CORRIDOR
Illinois

This unusual and new type of national park unit was established through legislation signed by President Reagan in Chicago on August 24, 1984. The heritage corridor extends from Chicago south and west for a hundred miles along three parallel canals that cut across the prairie in the valleys of the Des Plaines and Illinois Rivers to the small cities of La Salle and Peru. The common factor tying the region together is the now abandoned Illinois & Michigan Canal, a great feat of manual labor and engineering, which operated from 1848 to 1900 as the first commercial transportation link between the Great Lakes and Great Plains.

The heritage corridor can be reached almost anywhere along I-55 southwest from Chicago to Joliet, then along I-80 to the west. Address: c/o Midwest Region, National Park Service, 1709 Jackson Street, Omaha, Nebraska 68102.

INDEPENDENCE NATIONAL HISTORICAL PARK
Pennsylvania

The principles of self-government by men and self-determination by nations are memorialized in the heart of Philadelphia, in an area properly called "the most historic square mile in America." Here lie the scenes where Congress met during the bitter, trying days of the American Revolution, where the Declaration of Independence and Constitution were conceived and adopted, and where, starting in 1790, Congress and the Supreme Court conducted their affairs for 10 years before moving to the new capital city, Washington.

You will also find this historical park the most extensive and complex restoration ever undertaken by government in the United States, a combined federal, state, and city effort. In block after block, the visitor can see historic and architectural monuments that figured in the flowering of America's independence.

To avoid crowds, try to arrive early. Most buildings are open 9 to 5 daily, but hours are extended at some during summer. From early May to Labor Day, waiting times for tours of Independence Hall range from 15 minutes to an hour. Because of school groups, Thursday and Friday are peak days of April, May, and June, so plan your visit for other weekdays. Picnicking is allowed throughout the park; street vendors provide a wide range of fare. Leave your car elsewhere, even though two Philadelphia Parking Authority garages are located in the park. The park can be easily reached by bus, subway, or taxi.

The place to begin is the **Visitor Center**, at Third and Chestnut Streets, which provides orientation to the park through displays and a film shown in twin 300-seat cinemas. The development of the 20-acre historical park has involved demolishing 100 worn and faded structures, including one 10-story building, and replacing them with 18th century-style plantings and landscape features between historic buildings. This restoration tells a story of Philadelphia as well as the nation. The city stepped in to rescue the hall and square in 1818, when it was proposed to parcel out land for building lots, and it continues to hold title to them.

The main building to visit, of course, is **Independence Hall**. Once, as the capitol of Pennsylvania, it was the most impressive building in the colonies; now it has been pieced together anew after precarious years when ceilings sagged and walls neared collapse. In the interior, the first floor has been returned to its appearance of 1774-87. Toward this end skilled technicians performed patient, minute work and historians examined four million manuscripts in this country and in Great Britain. The Assembly room has been refurnished with authentic period items and originals, and it appears substantially the same as the day when delegates adopted the Declaration of Independence.

Cross Chestnut Street to the **Liberty Bell**, originally ordered in 1751 as a memorial to William Penn's "Charter of Privileges," but which became in time a worldwide symbol of liberty. In the early hours of 1976, the National Park Service moved the 2,000-pound bell from Independence Hall to its new $900,000 pavilion of glass and stone 100 yards away. The bell was moved from a crowded location to permit easier viewing.

Congress Hall next door looks the way John Adams found it for his inauguration, and as Congress knew it at the time that the members formally added the Bill of Rights to the Constitution. Other buildings in this cluster harmonious in style are **Philosophical Hall**, headquarters of America's oldest learned society, founded by Benjamin Franklin; and **Library Hall**, a reconstruction of the original, housing major historical collections.

As one of several major restorations for the Bicentennial, the Park Service opened the unique **Franklin Court** area in 1976. Though Franklin's home is long gone, the site on the south side of Market Street is outlined by a large steel frame, with a ramp leading to an underground museum, featuring sophisticated displays and devices that would have intrigued Old Ben himself. In addition, five bordering row houses on Market Street (three of which he owned) have been restored and adapted to interpret various phases of Franklin's life. At 316 Market Street, a post office now commemorates Franklin's role as the first Postmaster of the United States. Stop in to buy stamps and mail letters—they'll carry the famous postmark: "B. FREE FRANKLIN."

Another major component, the renovated **Second Bank of the United States**, a Greek Revival temple of the 1820s, formerly contained an intriguing gallery of 185 life portraits of leading Americans at the time of the Revolution, but the gallery gave way in 1987 to "Miracle in Philadelphia," a major display marking the 200th anniversary of the Constitution.

Other restored focal points of the Revolutionary era are **Old City Hall**, first meeting place of the Supreme Court; the three-story reconstructed **Graff House**, where Thomas Jefferson stayed while writing the Declaration of Independence and the house once occupied by General Thaddeus Kosciuszko. Plan to have a meal at the reconstructed **City Tavern**, a restaurant serving 18th century fare; it's popular, so you'll need reservations.

Among other notable buildings in the park are: **Christ Church**, where Franklin, Washington, and other statesmen worshiped; Gloria Dei Church, a privately owned National Historic Site and the oldest church in Pennsylvania; and the house where Dolley Todd Madison lived with her first husband. You can walk to **Mikveh Israel Cemetery**, ancient Jewish burial ground, where Haym Salomon, patriot of the Revolution, is interred. Evening makes an ideal time for a walking tour, particularly in summer, when Philadelphia's daytime tends to be humid.

Best of all is the pleasure of browsing along little streets like Delancey, Pine, or Lombard, in the Society Hill section, where the environment of another era pervades. Not all the houses are old, or even simulated antique, but the most modern are in scale. Try not to drive into downtown Philadelphia. If you can't stay at nearby hotels (like the Holiday Inn, or Penn Center Inn), then stay at the outskirts and take public transportation. Address: 313 Walnut Street, Philadelphia, Pennsylvania 19106.

JEAN LAFITTE NATIONAL HISTORICAL PARK
Louisiana

This area, authorized by Congress in 1978, is emerging as an exciting public facility in the Mississippi River Delta. As one of the first steps, a Visitor Contact Station has been opened in historic Jackson Square, in the heart of New Orleans, in order to provide a program of walking tours of the French Quarter and exhibits relating to ethnic cultures.

The former Chalmette National Historical Park is also an administrative unit of the new park. Located 6 miles from New Orleans, it commemorates the last major battle of the War of 1812. The decisive American victory on this site came on January 8, 1815. It shattered British ambitions and led to General Andrew Jackson's rise from the smoke of the battle to national prominence. The Visitor Center and battle museum are in the historic Beauregard House, starting place for touring the battlefield.

Land acquisition of the 8,600-acre Barataria Marsh Unit, 15 miles south of New Orleans, is under way. It comprises freshwater swamp and marsh laced with bayous and canals frequented by Jean Lafitte, the celebrated privateer-smuggler, in bringing contraband into New Orleans. Lafitte led his Baratarians in support of Jackson at the Battle of New Orleans. Kenta Canal runs north from Bayou Barataria through the interior of the park. Bayou des Familles and Bayou Coquille are also parts of a canoe trail completed in 1984. From the Visitor Center you can walk the Bayou Coquille Trail, less than a mile long, bordered by freshwater marsh and cypress-tupelo gum swamp, or the longer Ring Levee Trail. Address: 423 Canal Street, New Orleans, Louisiana 70116.

JEFFERSON MEMORIAL. See Thomas Jefferson Memorial, page 171.

JEFFERSON NATIONAL EXPANSION MEMORIAL
NATIONAL HISTORIC SITE
Missouri-Illinois

Commemorating the territorial growth of the United States, this national historic site covers 91 acres at the "Gateway to the West," the original site of St. Louis. The dominant feature, a 630-foot-high stainless steel arch on the shore of the Mississippi River designed by Eero Saarinen, contains an elevator system—really a

Jefferson National Expansion Memorial

five-passenger train—enabling the visitor to reach a lofty observatory. At the base of the arch, a Museum of Westward Expansion depicts adventures in shaping the western heritage. The Old Courthouse, high above the river, is also part of the memorial. Dating from 1839, it served as setting of the famous Dred Scott case. The Old Cathedral, begun in 1831, has also been preserved and included in the park. In August 1984, President Reagan signed legislation expanding the park to include a portion of the waterfront in East St. Louis, Illinois, opposite the Gateway Arch. A national museum of ethnic culture ultimately may be constructed on the site. Address: 11 North Fourth Street, St. Louis, Missouri 63102.

JIMMY CARTER NATIONAL HISTORICAL SITE
Georgia

In 1975, when Jimmy Carter began his campaign for the presidency, the small south Georgia town he called home became the focus of national attention. Following his election, little Plains overflowed with curiosity seekers, as well as media, Secret Service agents, and government officials. Plains will never be the same again, but the National Historic Site (including the Carter residence, boyhood home, and high school) and the 650-acre preservation district reflect rural southern heritage and culture. The residence is definitely private, protected by the Secret Service, but by all means stop at the railroad depot, in the downtown area, which served as Carter campaign headquarters and is now the park's visitor center. Tie in a visit to Andersonville, the Civil War prison, a few miles north, and Westville, a fascinating restored community in which the Jimmy Carter family has long been interested, outside Lumpkin, a few miles west. Address: c/o Andersonville National Historic Site, Route 1, Box 85, Andersonville, GA 31711.

JOHN FITZGERALD KENNEDY NATIONAL HISTORIC SITE
Massachusetts

At 83 Beals Street, Brookline, the late president of the United States was born on May 29, 1917. The family lived here until 1921. Mrs. Rose Kennedy, the late president's mother, supervised restoration and refurnishing of the two-story house. Address: 83 Beals Street, Brookline, Massachusetts 02146.

JOHN MUIR NATIONAL HISTORIC SITE
California

The apostle of national parks lived in this rambling house in Martinez from 1890 to 1914, while writing some of his most important works. During this period he founded the Sierra Club, a great conservation organization which carries on in his tradition throughout the country. The house actually was built by Muir's father-in-law, Dr. John Strentzel, often called the father of California horticulture. After viewing the interior, walk through the orchard to the historic Martinez Adobe, home of his eldest daughter and her husband. Address: 4202 Alhambra Avenue, Martinez, California 94553.

JOHNSON, ANDREW, NATIONAL HISTORIC SITE. See Andrew Johnson National Historic Site, page 176.

JOHNSON, LYNDON B., NATIONAL HISTORIC SITE. See Lyndon B. Johnson National Historic Site, page 192.

JOHNSTOWN FLOOD NATIONAL MEMORIAL. See Allegheny Portage Railroad, page 176.

KALAUPAPA NATIONAL HISTORICAL PARK
Hawaii

On the north shore of the island of Molokai, at the base of 2,000-foot cliffs, and virtually isolated from the rest of the island, except by plane or muleback, Kalaupapa has long attracted world attention and admiration. Here in 1866 a leprosy colony was established, designed to isolate patients who might spread the disease if left "at large." The work of the legendary Father Damien (from his arrival in 1873 until his death in 1889) in due course focused interest in leprosy, or Hansen's Disease, concern for its victims, and hope for therapy. The establishment of the national park in 1980 marks a landmark in human learning and tolerance, while also safeguarding the settlement and its residents.

Access is limited by geography and regulation. Kalaupapa is jointly managed by the National Park Service and Hawaii State Department of Health. A visitor permit (required to protect privacy and lifestyle of residents rather than for medical reasons) is available through either one of two tour companies locally owned and operated. For details and costs, write Damien Tours or Ike's Scenic Tours, c/o Kalaupapa Settlement, Kalaupapa, Hawaii 96742. The bonus for coming is in observing the spectacular north shore cliffs, rising 3,000 feet from the ocean. Remote areas of the 10,726-acre park include lush rain forests and abundant stone structures and other ancient features that make Kalaupapa a rich archaeological preserve. Address: Kalaupapa, Hawaii 96742.

KALOKO-HONOKOHAU NATIONAL HISTORICAL PARK
Hawaii

Authorized by Congress in 1978, this park on the Kona Coast of the "Big Island" of Hawaii will preserve a complex of structures and sites representing Hawaiian culture before contact with Europeans. At present, all lands remain in private ownership and the area is closed to the public. Contact nearby Pûuhonau Ō Honaunau National Historical Park. Address: c/o Pacific Area Office, National Park Service, Box 50165, Honolulu, Hawaii 96850.

KENNESAW MOUNTAIN NATIONAL BATTLEFIELD PARK
Georgia

A major engagement of the Atlanta campaign of 1864 was fought on the hills northwest of Marietta between the superior invading Union forces of William Tecumseh Sherman and the Confederates under General Joseph E. Johnston. From the top of Big Kennesaw you have a sweeping view of the well-preserved battlefield. After two costly frontal attacks, Sherman outflanked the Confederates, forcing them back toward Atlanta. Exhibits at the Visitor Center interpret the entire campaign; walking tours afford close-up views of the battle lines. Address: Box 1167, Marietta, Georgia 30061.

KINGS MOUNTAIN NATIONAL MILITARY PARK
South Carolina

On a quiet, stony crest in the foothills just below North Carolina, visitors can walk in the footsteps of backcountry men of Appalachia who struck an overwhelming blow against British forces on October 7, 1780, during the darkest period of the Revolutionary War in the South. The 900 men, unsoldierly and roughly dressed, advanced with their long rifles against the steel bayonets and disciplined ranks of Provincial Regulars and Tories who held the mountaintop. They screamed and hooted, charging through tangled brush and wooded ravines, stirring autumn leaves and driving birds to flight. "Face to the hill!" shouted Major William Chronicle when his troops wavered; even as he was struck and killed they moved ahead, destroying the Tory force of 1,100. At the Visitor Center and along the trails lined with memorial stones,

you will learn how the tide was turned at Kings Mountain into the advance toward victory at Yorktown.

Kings Mountain is a beauty spot of the southern highlands in any season. Since the battle occurred during October, autumn is especially appropriate for photography. Address: Box 31, Kings Mountain, North Carolina 28086.

KLONDIKE GOLD RUSH NATIONAL HISTORICAL PARK
Washington

This unit of the park depicts Seattle's historic role as main supply center for stampeders heading north to Alaska and the Klondike gold fields in 1897-98, and complements the unit of Klondike Gold Rush National Historical Park in Skagway, Alaska. Mining exhibits, artifacts, photomurals, and audiovisual programs relate the gold rush drama. History pervades the surrounding Pioneer Square neighborhood. Address: 117 South Main, Seattle, Washington 98104.

KNIFE RIVER INDIAN VILLAGES
NATIONAL HISTORIC SITE
North Dakota

The sites of three Hidatsa and Mandan Indian villages at the confluence of the Knife and Missouri Rivers are rich in history and valuable evidence of the lifestyle of the Plains Indians. Sakajawea, the Indian guide of the Lewis and Clark expedition, lived here.

The site covers about 1,300 acres, recalling the period when the villages were centers of a social order built on buffalo hunting, agriculture, and fur trading. The last village was abandoned in 1845, following decimation of the Hidatsa by smallpox. Address: Box 175, Stanton, North Dakota 58571.

KOSCIUSZKO, THADDEUS, NATIONAL MEMORIAL. See Thaddeus Kosciuszko National Memorial, page 199.

LINCOLN, ABRAHAM, BIRTHPLACE. See Abraham Lincoln Birthplace National Historic Site, page 176.

LINCOLN BOYHOOD NATIONAL MEMORIAL
Indiana

Lincoln's boyhood home and the burial site of his mother, this 200-acre wooded park contains a memorial Visitor Center and museum, built of native limestone connected by a semicircular cloistered walk. At the Lincoln Living Historical Farm, normal farming activities provide visitors the chance to try pioneer skills. Try to use the froe and wooden beatle to rive shingles for the cabin roof the way Abe did. Lake with camping facilities at nearby Lincoln State Park. Address: Lincoln City, Indiana 47552.

LINCOLN HOME NATIONAL HISTORIC SITE
Illinois

To Abraham Lincoln, Springfield was home. Here he moved his family into the only house he ever owned, where he lived from 1844 to 1861. In 1988, following three years of extensive renovation and restoration costing $2.2 million, the house was reopened to the public, returned to its appearance of 1860, with furniture and furnishings of that day. When the Lincolns left for Washington on a rainy Monday in February 1861, the president told a gathered crowd, "Here I have lived a quarter of a century, and have passed from a young to an old man. I now leave, not knowing when, or whether ever, I may return." The historic site covers four city blocks and preserves twelve homes of Lincoln's neighbors. Address: 426 South Seventh Street, Springfield, Illinois 62703.

LINCOLN MEMORIAL. See page 170.

LONGFELLOW NATIONAL HISTORIC SITE
Massachusetts

Henry Wadsworth Longfellow wrote "Evangeline," "Hiawatha," and other literary works here. The mansion at 105 Brattle Street in Cambridge, Massachusetts, was the poet's residence from his appointment as a professor of modern languages at Harvard University in 1837 till his death in 1882. Built in 1759 by a wealthy Royalist, the house is a prime example of Georgian architecture. Starting in mid-July 1775, General George Washington made it his Continental Army headquarters. The property, covering almost two acres, includes a carriage house and formal gardens, all of which have been maintained by the Longfellow House Trust since 1913. Chamber music concerts are given on the lawn on Sunday afternoons during summer. Address: 105 Brattle Street, Cambridge, Massachusetts 02138.

LOWELL NATIONAL HISTORICAL PARK
Massachusetts

Established in 1978, this park commemorates the birth of the industrial revolution in America and what is sometimes called "the first planned community for mass production." The majority of the early work force here was composed of young women from all over New England, attracted by the chance to leave the farm and earn steady wages. In time the textile industry went elsewhere and Lowell suffered decades of decline. The park has sparked its resurgence as one of the liveliest places in New England. The Visitor Center is located in the former Bigelow Carpet Company mill at 171 Merrimack Street. Reservations are required for the free guided tours conducted daily late May through Labor Day. Free tours on turn-of-the-century trolleys run daily late May through mid-October. The two open trolleys are authentic reproductions and serve as a transit system linking Lowell's downtown mills with the park's canal barge network. Address: Box 1098, Lowell, Massachusetts 01853.

LYNDON B. JOHNSON NATIONAL HISTORICAL PARK
Texas

This park is divided into two units located 15 miles apart. The **LBJ Ranch Unit** includes ranch, Texas White House, family cemetery, and reconstructed birthplace. Nearby is Lyndon B. Johnson State Historical Park. A free 90-minute bus tour from the state park features Johnson landmarks. Tours available daily except January 1 and December 25. The **Johnson City Unit** includes Johnson Settlement where the president's grandparents lived and the Visitor Center. Open daily except January 1 and December 25. Reservations available for groups of 15 or more (write, or phone 512/868-7128 or 512/644-2241). Address: Box 329, Johnson City, Texas 78636.

LYNDON BAINES JOHNSON MEMORIAL GROVE ON THE POTOMAC. See page 170.

MAGGIE L. WALKER NATIONAL HISTORIC SITE
Virginia

The residence in Richmond of this pioneer black civic leader became a national park unit through Congressional action in 1978. "Miss Maggie" was the first American woman known to establish and head a bank (in 1903). She was also an early supporter of voter registration for blacks. Most furnishings at the 18-room red brick home at 110½ E. Leigh Street have been left intact. The surrounding area of 19th century row houses is an historic district. Address: c/o Regional Office, National Park Service, 143 South Third Street, Philadelphia, Pennsylvania 19106.

MANASSAS NATIONAL BATTLEFIELD PARK
Virginia

The opening field battle of the Civil War was fought July 21, 1861, about 26 miles southwest of Washington, the first test of strength between two armies. When you reach Henry House Hill, the most significant site within the park, you will be at the location where General Stonewall Jackson arrived at the crucial hour. Another officer striving to rally his disorganized men, pointed to Jackson's line and shouted: "There stands Jackson like a stone wall! Rally behind the Virginians!" Jackson had won his immortal name, and before the day was done, the desperate Confederate defense changed into an attack, routing the Union army back to Washington. The following summer, the Second Battle of Manassas (Bull Run, it was called in the North) was fought between 73,000 Union troops and 55,000 Confederates under Robert E. Lee. After two fierce days the Confederates scored a decisive victory, and Lee prepared to invade Maryland. At the Visitor Center, an electric map traces the troop movements. Two driving tours follow paths of significance throughout the park. In 1980 Congress voted to extend the boundaries of the 3,000-acre national battlefield. Additions include Stone Bridge and the Brawner Farm, where Jackson ordered the charge for the Second Battle. Address: Box 350, Manassas, Virginia 22110.

MARTIN LUTHER KING, JR., NATIONAL HISTORIC SITE
Georgia

Within several blocks of the juncture of Auburn Avenue and Boulevard in Atlanta are the birthplace, boyhood home, church, and memorial grave site of Dr. Martin Luther King, Jr., civil rights leader and advocate of social change through nonviolent action. Guided tours are conducted of the King home; open daily except January 1 and December 25. The national historic site, authorized by Congress in 1980, and surrounding Preservation District include such structures as the 1895 Fire Station; Our Lady of Lourdes Catholic Mission; the King home, Ebenezer Baptist Church; commercial buildings; and the later home of Dr. King. These are among approximately 300 historic structures within 95 acres located several blocks from the heart of Atlanta. Many homes have been owned by the same families since the early 1900s. Address: c/o National Park Service, 522 Auburn Avenue N.E., Atlanta, Georgia 30312.

MARTIN VAN BUREN NATIONAL HISTORIC SITE
New York

The eighth president of the United States lived here at Lindenwald, his estate 25 miles south of Albany, from the time he left the presidency in 1841 till his death in 1862. Born in nearby Kinderhook, in 1782, Van Buren became a leader in the emergence of Jacksonian democracy, served as Andrew Jackson's vice-president, then ran successfully as Jackson's choice to succeed him in 1836. While serving as president, he purchased this house, a 2½-story Federal-style brick structure built in 1797. After his re-election defeat by William Henry Harrison, Van Buren turned his attention to Lindenwald. He installed a ballroom, added a rear wing, a four-story brick tower, and Victorian front porch. The cream-painted house with slate roof appears much as it did in Van Buren's day. Extensive renovations have kept the building closed except for weekends. The 42-acre site includes 13 acres adjacent to the original Lindenwald grounds. Address: Box 545, Route 9H, Kinderhook, New York 12106.

McLOUGHLIN HOUSE NATIONAL HISTORIC SITE
Oregon

One of the few remaining pioneer dwellings in the region once known as the "Oregon Country" was built in 1845-46 by Dr. John McLoughlin, who won enduring fame by aiding American settlers in establishing their homes. Federal, state, and private funds have combined to restore and refurnish the house. Address: Oregon City, Oregon 97045.

MINUTE MAN NATIONAL HISTORICAL PARK
Massachusetts
The celebrated "Battle Road of the Revolution" has been reclaimed from long years of neglect. The park (authorized in 1959 and officially established as a major event of the 1976 Bicentennial) embraces portions of the route in Lexington, Lincoln, and Concord, along which armed citizens declared their right to be free. Original stone walls, boulders, and important landmarks are still in place west of Massachusetts 128 (I-95). About dawn on April 19, 1775, almost 70 militia men faced a force of 700 British soldiers at Lexington Green. Four hours later at Old North Bridge, in Concord, the first British soldier fell and, by Emerson's poetic testimony, "the embattled farmers stood, and fired the shot heard round the world."

Try to start at the **Visitor Center** on Massachusetts 2A, between Lexington and Concord, completed for the 1976 Bicentennial. Then go to Lexington Green. The heroic statue represents minuteman Captain Parker facing the line of British approach. The Revolutionary monument, on the southeast corner, commemorates the eight Americans killed here; they were the first fatalities of the war. The British continued their march—but would return later in the day in defeat.

From the center of Lexington drive to Fiske Hill, start of the preserved 4-mile section of the **Battle Road** on which the famous running battle took place. This was the scene of some of the heaviest fighting. Walk the 1-mile, self-guiding trail to the site of the 18th century Fiske Farm.

Entering **Concord**, you'll want to visit at least a few of the homes of illustrious 19th century literary figures. By all means include the Wayside (associated with the Alcotts, Nathaniel Hawthorne, and Margaret Sidney), which is administered by the National Park Service.

North Bridge, over the Concord River, is a key focal point. On one side of the bridge you'll see the graves of two British soldiers, the first of the king's men to fall in the American Revolution, and on the opposite side the famous Minute Man statue by Daniel Chester French.

Volunteers dressed as minutemen, farm wives, soldiers, and craftsmen often present special programs on summer weekends near the Buttrick Mansion. The first floor of the mansion serves as both information center and exhibit hall.

Visitors with handicaps should note that reservations can be made for "In Touch with the Past," an entire touch-and-feel tour of the Buttrick Mansion (the red-brick 1911 house), complete with spinning wheels, furniture, and tools. Address: Box 160, Concord, Massachusetts 01742.

MONOCACY NATIONAL BATTLEFIELD
Maryland
This park, still under development, is designed to preserve a vital link in efforts of the Union Army to block a Confederate dash into Washington in July 1864. General Jubal Early, one of the boldest rebel leaders, brushed aside outer defenses and was leading his men down the Georgetown Pike near Rockville. On July 9, Union forces slowed Early down in the bloody battle on the Monocacy River, but did not stop him. Meanwhile, hundreds of rugged veterans were rushed by steamboat from the James River and Hampton Roads, in southern Virginia, to the defense of the capital. Early made a brief flurry on July 11, but had lost the edge and retreated. Address: c/o Antietam National Battlefield, Box 158, Sharpsburg, Maryland 21782.

MOORES CREEK NATIONAL BATTLEFIELD
North Carolina
A brief but intensive battle between Loyalists and Revolutionists was fought about 20 miles northwest of Wilmington, North Carolina, in an opening phase of the Revolution—an engagement often called "the Lexington and Concord of the South." It was on February 27, 1776, when 1,600 Loyalist militia attacked a patriot force of about 1,000 entrenched on Moores Creek. The Revolutionists turned back the assault, and captured or dispersed the invaders.

At the Visitor Center, just inside the park entrance, you can learn the full significance of the battle. A trail leads past monuments and to the Negro Head Point Road, where the focal point is the bridge site. As the Loyalists stormed over, they were met by withering musket fire. The victory discouraged the growth of Loyalist sentiment and spurred Revolutionary fervor throughout the colonies. A good time to visit the park is in May, when magnolias and spring wildflowers are in full bloom. Address: Box 69, Currie, North Carolina 28435.

MORRISTOWN NATIONAL HISTORICAL PARK
New Jersey
Barely 30 miles from New York, Americans may experience the richest single source spot of the Revolution. In a little state where over 100 battles and skirmishes were fought, this was the site of Washington's military headquarters and the main encampment of his ragged army during the toughest winters of the war.

The park became federal property in 1933, when the Department of the Interior took it over from the Washington Association of New Jersey, which had operated the Ford Museum since the 1870s. In October 1974, Congress authorized expansion to a 1,677-acre park embracing the Cross estate.

The place to begin is the **Historical Museum**, in the heart of Morristown. It has one of the most extensive collections of military pieces in the country. Exhibits in this modern structure consist of weapons, military equipment, paintings, and old prints. Dioramas depict the Revolutionary events.

Adjacent to the museum, facing Morris Street, the **Ford Mansion** served as Washington's headquarters, where he reorganized his weary and depleted forces almost within sight of British lines in New York. It was here that Lafayette brought the welcome word that a French army was on its way to aid in the struggle. On the inside, much of the furniture now displayed was there when Washington occupied it, while the remaining furnishings date from the Revolutionary period or earlier. Few preserved kitchens of the period are so completely furnished with colonial utensils and cooking equipment.

From the south end of Court Street, a road leads upward into the **Fort Nonsense** area, a key orientation point overlooking Morristown. Jockey Hollow, 4 miles south of Morristown, with rolling woodlands and open fields, closely resembles the setting at the time the main Continental army of 10,000 encamped here during the winter of 1779–80. Many of the campgrounds have remained relatively undisturbed, and physical evidence of army occupation can still be seen. You can photograph reconstructed log huts, chinked with clay and held together with nails and wooden pegs; the originals were built to hold 10 to 12 soldiers each. The **Wick House**, standing along the road to Menham, represents an architectural complement to the **Ford Mansion**, one typifying the elegance of town life, the other the solid qualities of the colonial rural scene. The kitchen garden of the Wick House is a feature in itself, with its herbs and rows of quince, gooseberry, and currant shrubs before the background of fruit trees, the whole ensemble recreating an 18th century scene. Nature, both cultivated and wild, is much a part of this park. More than 100 species of birds, some 20 species of mammals and over 300 species of shrubs, trees, and wildflowers have been identified in Jockey Hollow. A walk over the Primrose Brook Nature Trail affords the opportunity to see many such elements of the park landscape.

Morristown is a park of all seasons. Spring brings dogwood, flowers, and new foliage. Autumn is a blaze of color with brilliant reds and yellows and skies as clear as they can be in the metropolitan area. Winter is the time to see the bare trees and white carpet before the Ford Mansion and the snow nestling in the chinks of the little log huts. Standing there you can feel the same chill breeze that swept over the encampment. Address: Washington Place, Morristown, New Jersey 07960.

MOUNT RUSHMORE NATIONAL MEMORIAL
South Dakota

On the solid granite face of 5,725-foot Mount Rushmore, about 20 miles south from Rapid City in the Black Hills, colossal carved figures represent the heads of four great presidents—Washington, Jefferson, Lincoln, and Theodore Roosevelt. Work began under the direction of Gutzon Borglum in 1927 and was completed in 1941 under the guidance of his son, Lincoln. The giant heads are best seen under morning light; they are also visible by floodlight for a scheduled period each evening. Programs are presented in conjunction with the floodlighting each evening during summer at 9 p.m. in the Memorial Amphitheatre. A similar program is presented at the Visitor Center, at the same time, for persons with handicaps. The avenue leading to a view of the sculptures is lined with flags of each of the 50 states. Food services are provided during the summer by a concessioner. Camp in nearby Black Hills National Forest, Custer State Park, and local communities. Address: Keystone, South Dakota 57751.

NATCHEZ NATIONAL HISTORICAL PARK. See Natchez Trace Parkway, page 218.

NEZ PERCE NATIONAL HISTORICAL PARK
Idaho

Scattered over 12,000 square miles, 24 sites interpreting history and culture of the Nez Percé Indians and the opening of the West are joined together to form a new kind of historical park, a cooperative venture of private organizations, state and federal agencies, and the Nez Percé tribe. The loop tour of the park begins at historic Spalding, near Lewiston, on the Clearwater River. Several campgrounds are located in Clearwater and Nezperce National Forests, which cover more than half this region. The farthest stop is at Lolo Trail and Pass, where Lewis and Clark breached the Bitterroot Range on their way west. It was used again by the Nez Percé Indians in 1877 when they fled the U.S. Army.

An outstanding National Park Service Visitor Center, opened in 1983, is located at Spalding; note the inscribed words of Too-Hool-Hool-Zute: "The earth is part of my body. I belong to the land out of which I came. The earth is my mother." Visit wayside exhibits at Kamiah and White Bird Battlefield. Address: Spalding, Idaho 83551.

NINETY SIX NATIONAL HISTORIC SITE
South Carolina

The site of hard-fought skirmishes and battles during the Revolutionary War, Ninety Six was incorporated into the National Park System by congressional action during the Bicentennial, in 1976. The village of Ninety Six began as a frontier colonial outpost and became a key trading center and seat of justice for much of upcountry South Carolina beyond Charleston. Its curious name derived from the fact that it was located ninety-six miles from the principal Cherokee village of Keowee. A fort was built at Ninety

Six during the bloody Cherokee War of 1759-1760. Like much of the rest of South Carolina, the village was predominantly Tory in sentiment as the Revolution came on. It became the scene of several confrontations between Loyalists and Patriots from the early months of the war until shortly before Cornwallis' surrender at Yorktown. The most notable was a month-long siege conducted by about 1,000 Patriot troops under General Nathanael Greene in May and June, 1781, which ended when Greene was forced to withdraw by the arrival of British reinforcements. Soon after, the British burned the village of Ninety Six, their last important base in the interior, and returned to Charleston. The archaeological remains of the frontier trading post and Indian fort, the colonial courthouse village and its Revolutionary War earthworks, and the post-war rural town form the basis of the new park, where visitors can obtain an understanding of the growth of the southern frontier and this theater of the Revolution. Address: Box 496, Ninety Six, South Carolina 29666.

PALO ALTO BATTLEFIELD NATIONAL HISTORIC SITE
Texas

Designated by the National Parks and Recreation Act of 1978, Palo Alto, north of Brownsville, commemorates the site of one of only two important battles of the Mexican War fought on U.S. soil. It is not yet open to the public. Address: c/o Padre Island National Seashore, 9405 South Padre Island Drive, Corpus Christi, Texas 78418.

PEA RIDGE NATIONAL MILITARY PARK
Arkansas

A hard-fought battle of the Civil War took place 30 miles northeast of Fayetteville (or 10 miles from Rogers) in March 1862. A Confederate force of 16,000 under Major General Earl Van Dorn marched northward planning to sweep across Missouri and capture St. Louis. At the same time, Brigadier General Samuel R. Curtis pushed his 10,500 Union soldiers southward to rid Missouri of enemy secessionists. The two armies collided at Pea Ridge, just south of the Missouri border, and the roar of battle could be heard for miles across the Ozark hills. Casualties were high on both sides. The outcome was of importance, for it secured Missouri for the Union. The events are interpreted at the modern stone Visitor Center beside US 62. For the best overall view of the battlefield, take the scenic 7-mile tour road along the old Telegraph Road (part of the route of the Butterfield Overland Mail Line from St. Louis to San Francisco). Stop along the way at the overlooks atop Pea Ridge and at the restored Elk Horn Tavern. Follow the Headwaters Creek Trail for a fascinating close-up of nature in the Ozarks. Keep a sharp eye for deer, coyote, squirrel, and quail. Address: Pea Ridge, Arkansas 72751.

PERRY'S VICTORY AND
INTERNATIONAL PEACE MEMORIAL
Ohio

"We have met the enemy and they are ours," reported Oliver Hazard Perry after his dramatic victory in the Battle of Lake Erie during the War of 1812. The imposing pink granite memorial, commemorating that victory and the enduring peace between the United States and Canada, is located at Put-in-Bay on South Bass Island, 4 miles from the mainland. It is served during summer by car ferries from Scott Point on Catawba Island and from Port Clinton, and by plane both summer and winter from Port Clinton. From the observation deck (open April to October), near the top of the 352-foot-high memorial, you can see the battle scene between the shorelines of Canada and the United States. Address: Box 78, Put-in-Bay, Ohio 43456.

PETERSBURG NATIONAL BATTLEFIELD
Virginia

Due south of Richmond, Petersburg was the scene of ten months of grim siege and warfare, beginning in the summer of 1864 and ending with the Confederate retreat toward surrender at Appomattox in April 1865. Throughout the siege Grant's huge army continually hammered at Lee's veterans stubbornly protecting their capital and the Petersburg rail center, adding new chapters to the heroism and suffering that was the Civil War. The park's Visitor Center is the start of the one-way, 4-mile auto tour to many points of interest. Battery 5, from which Grant shelled Petersburg with "The Dictator," a 17,000-pound seacoast mortar, is the first stop. Then comes Battery 9, with a trail leading to Meade's Station, which Lincoln visited during the fighting, and Fort Stedman, the site of Lee's "Last Grand Offensive." The most engrossing part of this battlefield surrounds the section called the Crater. Here Union troops from Pennsylvania, who had been coal miners, dug a tunnel under Confederate lines and exploded four tons of gunpowder on July 30, 1864. The explosion killed 278 men and created an immense crater. In fighting that followed, the Confederates recaptured the crater, while the Union Army lost 4,000 men—killed, wounded, or captured. Daily throughout the summer the park's Living History program interprets the lives of a Union regiment in camp, a Confederate gun crew, and other military and civilian happenings during the siege. The park has 6 miles of marked bike trail. It is open year-round from 8 a.m. to dusk; the Visitor Center operates from 8 a.m. to 5 p.m., and 8 a.m. to 7 p.m. in the summer. While in the area, also visit City Point, Grant's headquarters during the siege. It lies at the confluence of the Appomattox and James Rivers, in nearby Hopewell. On the camping grounds of the 50th New York Engineers, you will find Poplar Grove National Cemetery. Address: Box 549, Petersburg, Virginia 23803.

PIPE SPRING NATIONAL MONUMENT
Arizona

The well-preserved Mormon fort, nestled at the base of the colorful vermillion cliffs near Fredonia in northwestern Arizona, was settled by the hardy followers of Brigham Young, who were determined to make their way in a harsh land. Within sturdy high sandstone walls and heavy gates, two houses face each other, sharing the benefits of a spring. Two mirrorlike pools of water and large shade trees enhance the area. A recently developed feature is the "living history ranch," with working cattle branding, baking of cookies, quilting, spinning, and weaving. The Visitor Center has displays interpreting both the Kaibab Paiutes, native Indians of the region, and the Mormon settlers. Gifts and food service are available. Address: Moccasin, Arizona 86022-1099.

PU'UHONUA Ō HONAUNAU NATIONAL HISTORICAL PARK
Hawaii

On the Kona coast of the "Big Island," the ancient place of refuge on a 20-acre lava shelf dipping into the ocean at the village of Honaunau, was a guaranteed sanctuary to vanquished warriors and taboo breakers. Here you can see prehistoric house sites, royal fish ponds, coconut groves, and spectacular shore scenery along the coves, cliffs, and tidal pools. Demonstrations are given in ancient carving and weaving by park personnel. You can also picnic, swim, and snorkel—this is an excellent spot to spend an entire day. The nearby "Painted Church," gable-roofed St. Benedict's, is one of Hawaii's unusual sights, the work of a Belgian priest who wanted to bring his parishioners the splendors of medieval Europe—he painted walls, ceiling, and pillars with copies of religious works in Hawaiian motif. A new unit of the national historical park, Puukohola Heiau National Historic Site,

is located at Kawaihae Bay, on the northwestern shore. Address: Honaunau, Kona, Hawaii 96726.

PUUKOHOLA HEIAU NATIONAL HISTORIC SITE
Hawaii

The fourth unit of the National Park System on the "Big Island" protects the famous temple built by Kamehameha the Great and closely associated with the founding of the Kingdom of Hawaii, as well as remnants of the homesite of John Young, English adviser to the king. Hawaiians constructed the massive platform in 1791 of water-worn lava rocks and boulders, without use of mortar. None of the structures that once stood within the wall now remain. The park is located at Kawaihae Bay, on the beautiful northwestern shore. From the lovely setting here on the Kona Coast, you can see Mauna Kea, Mauna Loa, Hualalai, and the Koala Mountains.

To learn more about Hawaii's fascinating history, be sure to schedule a visit to nearby Lapakahi State Historical Park, which depicts life in an ancient fishing village. Plan to swim (or snorkel) at Spencer Beach Park. Address: c/o Pûuhonua Ō Honaunau National Historical Park, Honaunau, Kona, Hawaii 96726.

RICHMOND NATIONAL BATTLEFIELD PARK
Virginia

Of seven thrusts against the capital of the Confederacy, only two approached success. All attacks were resisted until Grant's siege of Petersburg finally forced abandonment of Richmond. This park links the scenes of battles in defense of the city. Markers, maps, and parts of the fields of combat bring to life the Battle of Seven Pines, the Seven Days' Battles culminating at Malvern Hill and Cold Harbor, which proved to be Lee's last major victory. At Fort Harrison and Gilmer, during the Battle of Chaffin's Bluff, several black Union soldiers earned the Congressional Medal of Honor. Cyclists can cover these units by following the tour route in the park folder. However you travel, start at Park Headquarters in Chimborazo Park. The Watt House and adjacent interpretive trail through a mature oak forest provide a good birding area, especially for warblers in spring. Beginners should enjoy the easily accessible Fort Harrison area for thrushes, woodpeckers, and other birds. Plan to visit other key Civil War sites in Richmond, including the Virginia Capitol, which served as the capitol of the Confederacy; the White House of the Confederacy, where Jefferson Davis lived during the four years of war; and the Robert E. Lee House. More than half the Civil War was fought in Virginia, from the first major battle at Manassas to the surrender at Appomatox Court House. Fields of five major battles are administered by the National Park Service, several others by other agencies. Address: 3215 East Broad Street, Richmond, Virginia 23223.

ROGER WILLIAMS NATIONAL MEMORIAL
Rhode Island

At the site of the old town spring, at North Main and Alamo Lane, in the heart of Providence, this memorial commemorates the contributions of Roger Williams to civil and religious liberty. Displays and an audiovisual presentation at the Visitor Center recall his advocacy of freedom of conscience. One mile north from Market Square on US 1, the North Burial Ground contains the grave of Roger Williams. Address: Box 367 Annex, Providence, Rhode Island 02901.

ROOSEVELT CAMPOBELLO INTERNATIONAL PARK
New Brunswick, Canada

Jointly owned and administered by the United States and Canada, this unique memorial covering 2,600 acres was established in 1964. It lies 80 miles north of Bangor, Maine, just across the Canadian border. The Franklin D. Roosevelt Memorial Bridge links Campobello Island, part of the little archipelago clustered about the mouth of Passamaquoddy Bay, with Lubec, Maine. It was here Franklin D. Roosevelt spent all his summers from age one until stricken with polio in 1921. He described it as a place of "rest, refreshment and freedom from care." The focal point of the park is the 34-room Dutch colonial summer home, the center of a 10½-acre landscaped estate, with its rooms restored and furnished as they were in the 1920s, when FDR lived here. The park is open late May to mid-October seven days a week, 9 a.m. to 5 p.m., to 6 p.m. during July and August. Also on the island (but not in the park) are the Campobello Library and St. Anne's Anglican Church, where Roosevelt prayed. His pew is marked. Campobello Island offers fine beaches and fishing.

Three motels are located on Highway 774 at Wilsons Beach. Camping facilities are at Herring Cove Park. Crossing the Canadian border presents no difficulty, but be sure to carry identifying papers or proof of citizenship, just in case. Address: Box 97, Lubec, Maine 04652.

ROOSEVELT, HOME OF FRANKLIN D. See Home of Franklin D. Roosevelt National Historic Site, page 188.

ROOSEVELT, THEODORE, BIRTHPLACE. See Theodore Roosevelt Birthplace National Historic Site, page 199.

ROOSEVELT, THEODORE, INAUGURAL NATIONAL HISTORIC SITE. See Theodore Roosevelt Inaugural National Historic Site, page 199.

SAGAMORE HILL NATIONAL HISTORIC SITE
New York
The home of Theodore Roosevelt from 1885 until his death in 1919 lies at the end of Cove Neck Road in historic Oyster Bay, Long Island. The rambling Victorian structure, the summer White House for eight years, is furnished with original Roosevelt pieces. Trophies of a crowded life pack the North Room. His gun collection is on the top floor. On every hand are crowded bookshelves, reflecting his wide interests. Also included in the site is the Old Orchard Museum which features exhibits and regularly scheduled documentary films on Teddy Roosevelt. Open all year except Thanksgiving, Christmas, and New Year's Day. Hours: 9 a.m. to 6 p.m. in summer; 9 a.m. to 5 p.m. in winter. Address: Cove Neck Road, Box 304, Oyster Bay, New York 11771.

ST. CROIX ISLAND NATIONAL MONUMENT
Maine
On this island in the St. Croix River, which forms the boundary between Maine and New Brunswick, Canada, the French attempted to found a permanent settlement in 1604; from here Champlain continued his journey to the coast and traveled through the area of present-day Acadia National Park. Address: c/o Acadia National Park, Route 1, Box 1, Bar Harbor, Maine 04609.

SAINT-GAUDENS NATIONAL HISTORIC SITE
New Hampshire
The home (called Aspet), studio, and gardens of the celebrated sculptor Augustus Saint-Gaudens are preserved, with many of his portraits, busts, and casts on view, at Cornish, 18 miles south of Hanover and 2 miles from the Windsor, Vermont, covered bridge. Within the formal garden note especially the copy of the renowned Adams Memorial; the original is in Washington, D.C. Each summer the Saint-Gaudens Memorial sponsors concerts and art exhibitions. Address: Route 2, Box 73, Cornish, New Hampshire 03745.

ST. PAUL'S CHURCH NATIONAL HISTORIC SITE
New York
Nearly a century after Anne Hutchinson settled in this area after fleeing religious tyranny in Massachusetts Bay Colony, St. Paul's became a focal point in the freedom of the press trial of John Peter Zenger. The site includes the restored church, adjacent village green, churchyard, and a Bill of Rights Museum. The grounds are open dawn to dusk. Free tours of the church are offered by appointment Monday through Friday, all year; also special weekend tours. Address: 897 South Columbus Avenue, Mount Vernon, New York 10550.

SALEM MARITIME NATIONAL HISTORIC SITE
Massachusetts
The long Derby Wharf once was the busiest of more than 50 wharves that lined the Salem waterfront. In those early days, when foreign trade was at the heart of the nation's economy, Salem was a gateway to the world (and sixth-largest city in the United States). Most of it is gone, but in nine acres of the waterfront, preserved in the national historic site, you can still walk on the wharves where cargoes were unloaded from around the world. Central Wharf, built in several stages, retains the brick foundation of Capt. Simon Forrester's 1790s warehouse. Derby Wharf, the biggest of all, was crowded with vessels laden with silk from India, tea from China, coffee from Arabia. Just east of the wharf, the brick Derby House, built in 1762, represents the beginning of Salem's tenure as mistress of the seas. It was owned by Elias "King" Derby, the coastal magnate called "America's first millionaire," and contains some of the most elegantly carved woodwork found anywhere. Adjacent to it stands the largest vestige of Salem's seaport glory, the Custom House, erected in 1819, where Nathaniel Hawthorne worked as a bookkeeper in 1846. He described the scene and mood of the wharf, as viewed through his office window, in *The Custom House*. Address: Custom House, Derby Street, Salem, Massachusetts 01970.

SANDBURG, CARL, HOME NATIONAL HISTORIC SITE. See Carl Sandburg Home National Historic Site, page 179.

SAN ANTONIO MISSIONS
NATIONAL HISTORICAL PARK
Texas
Four missions of the century and an historic irrigation system are preserved along a 7-mile section of the San Antonio River at San Antonio. They comprise the greatest concentration of Spanish missions in the United States. The missions still serve active parishes. **Mission Concepcion** originally was established in 1716. After several moves, in 1731 it was located in its present site on the banks of the San Antonio River. The stone church, noted for its twin towers and cupola, has never fallen into ruins and is the oldest unchanged and unrestored edifice of its kind in the United States. **Mission San Jose**, founded in 1720, is admired as "The Queen of the Missions." At one point, it was inhabited by 350 Indians, many proficient in some craft, as evidenced by their carvings on the facade and paintings on the walls of the church. During the 19th century, the mission fell into disuse and the church dome and roof caved in. But in the 1930s it was repaired and, after an absence of more than 100 years, the Franciscan fathers returned.

Mission San Juan was established on the San Antonio River in 1731. The present church, with its walls made of filled-in arches and side-facing bell towers, is believed to be a converted granary used as a temporary church, while the permanent church was under construction. Beginnings of the massive walls and oddly shaped octagon sacristy are still visible.

Mission Espada, founded in 1690 as San Francisco de los Tejas, was the first Spanish mission in Texas. It was moved several times before ending up as the southernmost of the San Antonio missions. Although only the church facade has not been reconstructed, this most rural of the missions demonstrates the most complete Spanish Colonial irrigation system, in continuous use, in the United States.

A fifth San Antonio mission of note, **Mission San Antonio de Valero**, the celebrated Alamo, is not part of the park, but well worth visiting. So is the Spanish governor's palace, an aristocratic mansion of the Southwest frontier. Missions of the park are open daily. Address: 727 East Durango, San Antonio, Texas 78206.

SAN FRANCISCO MARITIME NATIONAL HISTORICAL PARK
California
Board historic ships at the San Francisco waterfront and visit the National Maritime Museum to explore seafaring history. The best way to reach the park is via public transit, including the Powell & Hyde cable car. The oldest of the ships, the *Balclutha*, a square-rigger launched in 1886, is moored at Pier 43, largely restored to her original appearance. Three other ships, also open for boarding, are berthed at Hyde Street Pier. It's a good idea to start at the museum, at the foot of Polk Street, where guided tours are offered daily. Get your bearings, learn the schedule of living history demonstrations, films, and tours of the ships. Allow time to enjoy the vistas of Aquatic Park. Golden Gate Promenade begins here, following the shoreline 3½ miles to Fort Point under the Golden Gate Bridge. Address: Building 201, Fort Mason, San Francisco, California 94123.

SAN JUAN ISLAND NATIONAL HISTORICAL PARK
Washington
Historic sites of American and English camps on San Juan Island, the third largest island in Puget Sound, associated with the Oregon Territory boundary dispute, are protected in this park. Both camps were fortified in the so-called "Pig War" of 1859, but there was no fighting before the final settlement by arbitration in 1872 sustained the American claim to the San Juan, and the last British flag was lowered within territorial United States.

The island is reached by ferry from Anacortes, Washington, or Sidney, British Columbia. Address: Box 429, Friday Harbor, Washington 98250.

SAN JUAN NATIONAL HISTORIC SITE
Puerto Rico
The massive masonry fortifications, the oldest within the territorial limits of the United States, were begun by the Spanish in the 16th century to protect a strategic harbor guarding the sea lanes to the New World. El Morro, at the northwest tip of the city, was enlarged continually between attacks by the English, French, and Dutch. San Cristóbal, the largest castle in the San Juan defensive system, was completed about 1773, to protect the approaches by land.

The fortifications of San Juan have had a colorful history, associated with attacks of Elizabethan Sea Dogs, Dutch merchants, and the contrabandists. In 1595, Sir Francis Drake led an invasion fleet of 23 ships and 3,000 men but was driven off with heavy casualties. Three years later the Earl of Cumberland marched on the city from the land side and captured El Morro, but dysentery forced him to leave. The walls and gun decks were continually enlarged between attacks during the 17th and 18th centuries. Spaniards used El Morro during the war between the United States and Spain in 1898. U.S. armed forces manned the fortifications until the late 1960s, when all of these defenses were transferred to the National Park Service.

The national historic site embraces most of the city walls and the Spanish forts of El Morro, San Cristóbal, and El Cañuelo.

You will also want to examine the city wall, standing around much of the old town, including the harbor front between El Morro and La Fortaleza, and the home of the governor, which dates from 1533. Walking along the old narrow streets, you will find the whitewashed arches and garden patios, the pastel-colored buildings and overhanging balconies with freshly painted grilles. Address: Box 712, San Juan, Puerto Rico 00902.

SARATOGA NATIONAL HISTORICAL PARK
New York
Thirty miles north of Albany, where the Hudson River narrows to flow through wild forest and field, a ragtag rebel army dug in behind fortifications designed by the Polish Volunteer Colonel Thaddeus Kosciuszko. The Crown Forces (British and German) had advanced from Canada, reaching the area within the park in mid-September of 1777. From the Visitor Center and museum on Fraser Hill, you can see most of the battleground, where Burgoyne's "Redcoats" and blue-coated Germans were fought to a standstill by Continental soldiers and American militia from all over New England and New York. This was one of the most decisive series of battles in world history, the victory here earning support for the rebels from France, Holland, and Spain.

The park is extremely well laid out. It is best to enter from New York 32 or US 4, where your first stop is at the Visitor Center and museum, overlooking the battlefield from the highest hill in the park. Battle maps, dioramas, and exhibits tell the story of the two Battles of Saratoga in a first-hand approach.

The combination auto-walking tour route, which begins at the Visitor Center, has 10 marked stops that place you in the heart of the action.

During the summer season park employees, both men and women, in period dress, are stationed at various stops along the tour road. They engage in such 18th century activities as baking waffles and foods of the period, dressmaking, demonstrating the use of muskets and rifles, and playing military music. Special events of various types are held each season, such as lectures by noted scholars on different aspects of the Burgoyne Campaign.

Eight miles north of the park, at Schuylerville (Old Saratoga), New York, the General Philip Schuyler House is a separate portion of the park. The fine country house, the third on the site, was built in late 1777 to replace one the British burned. The 25-acre estate is a gentle reminder of country life in upper New York. Address: RFD 2, Box 33, Stillwater, New York 12170.

SAUGUS IRON WORKS NATIONAL HISTORIC SITE
Massachusetts
A meticulous reconstruction of America's first well-sustained iron works came into being in 1954 as the result of six years of work by historians, architects, archaeologists, and builders financed by the American Iron and Steel Institute. Excavations produced over five tons of artifacts left by the original works, which operated from 1648 to about 1670. The old Ironmaster's House stands complete with 10-foot fireplaces and original hand-hewn beams. The ironworks contain the reconstructed Blast Furnace, Forge, and Rolling and Slitting Mill. The Warehouse and Wharf will help you to imagine the scene when iron and iron products were shipped to colonies along the coast and to overseas customers. A blacksmith demonstrates early methods of iron working, producing nails and other hand-wrought items. Address: 244 Central Street, Saugus, Massachusetts 01906.

SCOTTS BLUFF NATIONAL MONUMENT
Nebraska
The rocky promontory, rising 800 feet above the North Platte Valley, served as landmark and favored camping area for thousands crossing the treeless plains in the westward migrations

between 1843 and 1869 over the Oregon and Mormon Trails. You can easily spend several enjoyable hours here, with Fort Laramie National Historic Site nearby in Wyoming as your next stop en route west. The Oregon Trail Museum tells the story of early fur traders, the wagon trains, and Pony Express, and displays paintings by William Henry Jackson, the pioneer photographer-artist. A paved road and foot trail lead to the summit of the bluff and outstanding views of the North Platte River Valley. Address: Box 427, Gering, Nebraska 69341.

SEWALL-BELMONT HOUSE NATIONAL HISTORIC SITE. See page 170.

SHILOH NATIONAL MILITARY PARK
Tennessee

In the first major battle of the western campaign, General U. S. Grant opened his drive to control the Mississippi River. By victories on the Tennessee River, Grant paved the way for Union advances into Mississippi and Alabama. Federal control of the Mississippi River was completed the following year with the fall of Vicksburg. From the park Visitor Center, where battle relics, exhibits, and maps are displayed, the 10-mile self-guiding auto tour begins. You can also walk the battlefield on foot trails and take advantage of picnic areas. At Pittsburg Landing, Grant's 40,000 troops established their base after steaming up the Tennessee River from Fort Henry and Fort Donelson. At the Reconnoitering Road and Fraley Field, the two-day battle began April 6, 1862, when Confederate armies under General Albert Sidney Johnston attacked the Union forces. The Hornet's Nest was the site of deadly fighting around a natural fortress of dense woods, and at the Bloody Pond soldiers of both sides came to drink and bathe their wounds. About 3,700 war dead are buried at the National Cemetery; virtually all remains of Confederate dead lie in burial trenches throughout the park. Nearby Pickwick Landing State Park offers camping and a modern resort inn. Address: Shiloh, Tennessee 38376.

SPRINGFIELD ARMORY NATIONAL HISTORIC SITE
Massachusetts

The Armory Museum was closed in 1987 for a major renovation due for completion in 1989. When it reopens it will show how for almost two centuries the Springfield Armory produced a stream of military small arms almost legendary in quality and quantity. From its beginning in the American Revolution, the Armory went on to become the small arms center of the world.

The grounds, shared with Springfield Technical Community College, remain open while the museum is closed. Other museums and historic restorations are in downtown Springfield. Address: 1 Armory Square, Springfield, Massachusetts 01105.

STATUE OF LIBERTY NATIONAL MONUMENT
New York-New Jersey

The colossal copper statue on Liberty Island, New York harbor, is a universal symbol of freedom and democracy. "The New Colossus," as Emma Lazarus called it in her celebrated poem, was the work of Frederic Bartholdi, and a gift of the French people in 1884, commemorating the alliance of France and America during the American Revolution.

The "Lady with a Lamp" has lately been restored to her original glory; the refurbished statue was dramatically unveiled on July 4, 1986. The $30-million project included replacement of the original gold leaf torch with a replica plated with gold to make it shine in the sun. During 1985, French craftsmen at the statue's base hammered out copper sheets using the same painstaking technique their countrymen did in building the statue. They pounded two tons of copper into a new torch and flame 21 feet high.

The monument is reached by ferry, a delightful trip starting from the slip at the Battery next to Castle Clinton (every hour on the hour, every half-hour in summer). This trip has been called "the shortest cruise in the world"—it takes 15 minutes. Now you can take another trip into history from the Battery (or from Liberty State Park in Jersey City) to nearby Ellis Island, gateway to the New World for more than 12 million American immigrants.

Liberty State Park, on the New Jersey banks of the Hudson, offers dramatic views of the Statue of Liberty, Ellis Island, and the skyline of lower New York City. At the north end of the park, close to Ellis Island, the Central Railroad passenger station has been reconstructed to reflect the days when it was used by immigrants.

At the Statue of Liberty, an elevator runs to the balcony level, and a spiral stairway leads to the observation platform in the lady's head, affording thrilling views of ships and shoreline. The American Museum of Immigration in the base of the statue has been dedicated as a memorial to the millions who chose to start a new life in this country. Displays, posters, dioramas, photographs—all tell the dramatic story of the life and times of the immigrant, beginning as far back as the arrival of the first Indians.

Ellis Island served as an immigration reception center from 1892 until 1954. In its peak years—1900 to 1914—as many as 5,000 immigrants a day entered the country through this gateway, escaping poverty, persecution, and pogroms. It was opened to the public as a national historic site in 1976. A major museum was due for completion in time for 1990 visitors.

Ellis Island offers an exciting experience. Guided tours are conducted through the historic Main Registry Hall, in which immigrants were processed and inspected before being allowed entry into the United States. Address: Liberty Island, New York, New York 10004.

STEAMTOWN NATIONAL HISTORIC SITE
Pennsylvania

The steam railroad in American history is memorialized appropriately in what once was a major freight yard, roundhouse, and locomotive repair shop of the Delaware, Lackawanna, and Western Railroad. The park was established in 1986, two years after the Steamtown Foundation had moved from Vermont to Scranton, complete with its collection of steam locomotives and rolling stock. Railroad enthusiasts should combine a visit here with a call at Allegheny Portage Railroad National Historic Site, at Johnstown, in western Pennsylvania (see page 176). And keep in mind the Golden Spike National Historic Site, in Utah, which preserves the site of completion of the first transcontinental railroad (see page 186). Address: Box 1280, Scranton, Pennsylvania 18501-1280.

STONES RIVER NATIONAL BATTLEFIELD AND CEMETERY
Tennessee

A stubbornly fought three-day midwinter battle which started December 31, 1862, a short distance from Murfreesboro, began the Federal offensive to split the Confederacy in three parts. The Hazen Brigade Monument, erected in 1863, is the oldest memorial of the Civil War. The decisive turn of events came the second day with a 58-gun concentration of Union artillery roaring out more than 100 rounds a minute on advancing Confederates. In a matter of minutes, 1,800 Confederates fell—killed or wounded. Under the pall of this overwhelming disaster, General Braxton Bragg ordered the withdrawal of his decimated army.

The national cemetery contains approximately 6,400 burials, with about one-third of the bodies unidentified. Address: Route 10, Box 495, Old Nashville Highway, Murfreesboro, Tennessee 37130.

TAFT, WILLIAM HOWARD, NATIONAL HISTORIC SITE. See William Howard Taft National Historic Site, page 200.

THADDEUS KOSCIUSZKO NATIONAL MEMORIAL
Pennsylvania

This small row house at 301 Pine Street, Philadelphia, is the country's only surviving residence of General Thaddeus Kosciuszko, Polish patriot and hero of the American Revolution. While living here in 1797—98, Kosciuszko was visited frequently by Vice President Thomas Jefferson, who asked him to serve as a peace emissary to France. An old friend, Jefferson had described Kosciuszko during the Revolution: "as pure a son of liberty as I have ever known." Kosciuszko wrote his will in this house and gave it to Jefferson, bequeathing his fortune to the cause of freedom of slaves. Kosciuszko volunteered his services to the colonies in 1776. He was appointed chief engineer of the Army in the South, where his logistical planning was instrumental in the campaign's success. Congress bestowed American citizenship on Kosciuszko and commissioned him a brigadier general.

Address: c/o Independence National Historical Park, 313 Walnut Street, Philadelphia, Pennsylvania 19106.

THEODORE ROOSEVELT BIRTHPLACE NATIONAL HISTORIC SITE
New York

In the four-story brownstone at 28 East 20th Street, Manhattan, currently amid an area of commercial building and craft centers near Gramercy Park, the 26th president was born, in 1858. He lived his formative years here—until he was 15—beset by ailments. Furnished in period style, with museum, audiovisual programs, and a guided tour. Address: Superintendent, Manhattan Sites, National Park Service, 26 Wall Street, New York, New York 10005.

THEODORE ROOSEVELT INAUGURAL NATIONAL HISTORIC SITE
New York

Theodore Roosevelt took the oath of office as president of the United States here at the Ansley Wilcox House in Buffalo on September 14, 1901, within hours after the death of President McKinley. Roosevelt had been sidetracked into the vice-presidency by the political bosses, but once he assumed command he became the "Apostle of Energy" in the domestic and foreign policies of the nation. Address: 641 Delaware Avenue, Buffalo, New York 14209.

THOMAS STONE NATIONAL HISTORIC SITE
Maryland

This area, authorized by Congress in 1978, includes the mansion house known as "Habre de Venture" and a 325-acre plantation once owned by Thomas Stone, a signer of the Declaration of Independence, at Port Tobacco, in southern Maryland. The house is being reconstructed and is not yet open to the public. Address: c/o George Washington Birthplace National Monument, Box 717, Washington's Birthplace, Virginia 22575.

TIMUCUAN ECOLOGICAL AND HISTORIC PRESERVE. See Fort Caroline National Memorial, page 182.

TOURO SYNAGOGUE NATIONAL HISTORIC SITE
Rhode Island

The most significant and most exquisitely designed building in Newport is the oldest house of Jewish worship in the United States, founded by 15 families responding to Roger Williams' declaration of religious liberty. The plans were made by Peter Harrison, known as America's first professional architect, who is also responsible for several great Boston churches. Among features of the restored synagogue are Windsor benches, massive bronze candelabra, fine examples of 18th century silversmithing—and the memory of George Washington's appearance in 1790. It continues as the place of worship for Congregation Jeshuat Israel, while the Society of Friends of Touro Synagogue conducts efforts toward fulfilling the 18th century appearance.

From the synagogue it is only a short walk to the old burial ground, a small plot which served as inspiration for Longfellow's poem, *The Jewish Cemetery at Newport*. Address: Touro Synagogue, 85 Touro Street, Newport, Rhode Island 02840.

TUMACACORI NATIONAL MONUMENT
Arizona

San Jose de Tumacacori was a northern outpost of a mission chain built in Spanish Sonora. With the charm of culture planted in the desert, this church was built in 1822, abandoned in 1848. The Park Service has conserved its stately remains, in which you may study interesting structural elements of the neo-classic architecture and the faded but original colors which Indian workmen applied. The museum contains dioramas and artifacts that bring the frontier mission age to life. The visitor can take self-guiding walks about the grounds. Tumacacori is located 43 miles south of Tucson on I-19, just 19 miles north of Nogales and the Mexican border. Open daily, except December 25, from 8 a.m. to 5 p.m. Early each December several thousand visitors gather for the annual fiesta. It features food, entertainment, and booths in which native craftsmen—Apache, Yaqui, and Papago Indians and Mexican-Americans—demonstrate pottery making, woodcarving, basketweaving, and leather tooling. Address: Box 67, Tumacacori, Arizona 85640.

TUPELO NATIONAL BATTLEFIELD
Mississippi

A granite marker serving as a memorial to soldiers of both armies and interpretive maps are within a one-acre tract in the city of Tupelo where Federal forces fought in July 1864, to protect Sherman's supply line while he was moving on Atlanta. Address: c/o Natchez Trace Parkway, Route 1, NT 143, Tupelo, Mississippi 38801.

TUSKEGEE INSTITUTE NATIONAL HISTORIC SITE
Alabama

Founded by Booker T. Washington in 1881, Tuskegee Institute became a major force in launching black Americans into higher education. Students built most of the early structures on the campus. From two or three buildings near Tuskegee, the school has expanded to 161 buildings on 5,000 acres, with 3,500 students. The historic site includes the founder's home, The Oaks, restored to its early 20th century appearance; a museum-laboratory established by George Washington Carver, the famous scientist, in 1938; and Grey Columns, an antebellum mansion, adjacent to the campus. A 50-acre historic district is maintained under agreement with the National Park Service, though retained by the institute. Address: Superintendent, Tuskegee Institute National Historic Site, Box 1246, Tuskegee Institute, Alabama 36088.

U.S.S. *ARIZONA* MEMORIAL
Hawaii

Spanning the width of the sunken battleship *Arizona* is a memorial to the men who lost their lives during the Japanese attack on Pearl Harbor in December 1941, especially those whose bodies are buried with their ship. The memorial, established by the Navy, is now administered by the National Park Service through a cooperative agreement authorized by Congress in 1978. A shore-side Visitor Center provides for visitors. The museum and a film portray the Pacific naval war and the action at Hawaii. A canopied launch, carrying 150 passengers at a time, ferries visitors across the harbor to "battleship row," where the hull of the *Arizona* lies in 38 feet of water. In all, 19 warships were sunk or damaged in the Japanese attack. All but two have been raised by salvage efforts. A large marble wall in the memorial bears the names of 1,177 sailors and Marines who perished with the ship. Address: Pacific Area Office, 300 Ala Moana Boulevard, Honolulu, Hawaii 96850.

VALLEY FORGE NATIONAL HISTORICAL PARK
Pennsylvania
No name in American history conveys more suffering, sacrifice, and triumph than Valley Forge, where 12,000 ragged, hungry men went into camp on December 19, 1777, endured through a harsh winter and emerged in the spring as a trained, disciplined army. General Washington himself had selected this location, named for a small iron forge on Valley Creek, because of its defensive position and his ability to watch the approaches to Philadelphia, 20 miles to the east. You'll find a great deal to see and do at the 2,500-acre park. Among items now on display at the Visitor Center are the original tent used by Washington in the field, probably as combination headquarters and sleeping quarters, and the priceless Neumann collection of muskets, rifles, swords, and other Revolutionary weapons. On leaving the Visitor Center for the tour route, you can see where some 2,000 log huts were raised during the encampment. About 40 have been reconstructed in recent years. Tour other key sites, including the Grand Parade, Artillery Park, and the forts and earthworks thrown up to protect the camp and command nearby roads and rivers. Visit the stone colonial house used by Washington as his headquarters. The National Memorial Arch, a dominant feature of the park, is dedicated to the "incomparable patience and fidelity of the soldiery"—the men who departed here in spring of 1778 as a toughened fighting force. Address: Superintendent, Valley Forge National Historical Park, Valley Forge, Pennsylvania 19481.

VAN BUREN, MARTIN, NATIONAL HISTORIC SITE. See Martin Van Buren National Historic Site, page 192.

VANDERBILT MANSION NATIONAL HISTORIC SITE
New York
The 54-room country home was built at Hyde Park in 1898 by Frederick W. Vanderbilt, grandson of Cornelius Vanderbilt, "the Commodore." This "monument to an era," with Italian marble, Flemish tapestry, a 300-year-old Persian carpet and French Renaissance furniture, is in marked contrast to the stately Victorian home of Franklin D. Roosevelt nearby. Address: Bellfield Headquarters, 249 Albany Post Road, Hyde Park, New York 12538.

VICKSBURG NATIONAL MILITARY PARK
Mississippi
General U.S. Grant, striving to split the Confederacy with daring, large-scale movements across the heartland of America, moved against Vicksburg in the spring of 1863. On May 19, one of Grant's three corps launched an attack. It was repulsed. Three days later his whole army moved. Failure to capture the heavily defended city, despite bloody fighting, compelled Grant to start siege operations, aided by the Union navy, to cut off communications and blast the city from the river. After 47 days of tightening the grip from three sides, Grant took Vicksburg and control of the Mississippi. You can see the main defensive fortifications (along Confederate Avenue) and the main part of the investment line (along Union Avenue) in the semicircular park. About 1,400 monuments, memorials, and tablets have been erected to mark positions of the armies. The equestrian statue of General Grant stands in the area

where the general maintained his headquarters. The national cemetery, at the north end of the park, contains the graves of 17,000 Union soldiers, including many who died in other actions nearby. The Confederate dead are buried in the city cemetery. The Visitor Center, adjacent to the entrance near US 80, contains life-size exhibits. An 18-minute film relates the events of the campaign. In late 1980, the park opened the USS *Cairo* Museum, which houses thousands of artifacts—including bottles, tools, weapons, cooking and eating utensils—recovered from the ill-fated Union gunboat. A Confederate "electric" mine sent the *Cairo* to the bottom of the Yazoo River in 1862, where she lay mired in mud for almost 100 years until discovered by historians. The ship's bell looks almost new, as do thousands of other items brought from the bottom. While in Vicksburg, see the old Court House Museum, with an exhibit of relics from the campaign. Address: 3201 Clay Street, Vicksburg, Mississippi 39180.

WAR IN THE PACIFIC NATIONAL HISTORICAL PARK
Guam
Authorized by Congress in 1978, this park commemorates the bravery and sacrifices of people of all nations involved in the Pacific Theater of World War II. The park provides a center of information of operations involving Japan, Australia, New Zealand, Great Britain, France, Canada, the Netherlands, the Soviet Union, China, the Pacific Islands people, and the United States. The park consists of six separate units. The T. Stell Newman Visitor Information Center houses exhibits on Pacific operations, an audiovisual program, and interpretive information about Guam, the Mariana Islands, and Micronesia. Numerous historic structures are found throughout the park, both on the land and offshore areas. Several trails lead to Japanese pillboxes and gun installations. Sites in park waters protect the remains of the invasion of Guam in July 1944. These areas are accessible to scuba divers. Additional park areas will be opened as they are developed. Address: Box FA, Agana, Guam 96910.

WASHINGTON, BOOKER T., NATIONAL MONUMENT. See Booker T. Washington National Monument, page 177.

WASHINGTON, GEORGE, BIRTHPLACE. See George Washington Birthplace National Monument, page 186.

WASHINGTON MONUMENT. See page 171.

WHITMAN MISSION NATIONAL HISTORIC SITE
Washington
Near Walla Walla, Marcus and Narcissus Whitman, the first family of white settlers to cross the Rocky Mountains, established a mission for the Cayuse Indians and a haven for travelers on the Oregon Trail, which they operated from 1836 until the couple was slain by Indians in 1847.

Start at the Visitor Center to see the orientation film and exhibit on Indian tribes and cultures. Then walk the easy trail past foundation ruins of mission buildings and a trace of the historic Oregon Trail. The Memorial Monument, erected on a high bluff in 1897, overlooks the Walla Walla valley and faces the Blue Mountains to the east. Address: Route 2, Box 247, Walla Walla, Washington 99362.

WILCOX, ANSLEY, HOUSE. See Theodore Roosevelt Inaugural National Historic Site, page 199.

WILLIAM HOWARD TAFT NATIONAL HISTORICAL SITE
Ohio
The 27th president was born in September 1857 in this three-story brick home on Auburn Avenue in Cincinnati. His father had been

Secretary of War and Attorney General under President U.S. Grant, but this did not prevent young William and his four brothers from enjoying a typical boyhood and active neighborhood life, including swimming, skating, and baseball. After studying at Yale, he returned home in 1878 to complete his studies at Cincinnati Law School. Then he began his advance on the national scene, reaching the double pinnacle, as President (1909-1913) and Chief Justice (1921-1930). A major restoration of the house was completed in 1989. The site is open daily 10 a.m. to 6 p.m., Memorial Day through Labor Day; to 4:30 p.m., rest of year. Address: 2038 Auburn Avenue, Cincinnati, Ohio 45219.

WILLIAMS, ROGER, MEMORIAL. See Roger Williams National Memorial, page 195.

WILSON'S CREEK NATIONAL BATTLEFIELD PARK
Missouri
At a site 10 miles southwest of Springfield, Union and Confederate forces engaged in a bitter struggle during the first year of the Civil War (August 10, 1861) for control of Missouri. Though the Southerners won the battle of Wilson's Creek, they were too badly crippled to follow through in pursuit. Thus, Missouri was secured for the Union. Starting from the Visitor Center, wayside exhibits and restored historic structures show the effect of the battle on soldiers and civilians. The Ray House, used as a Confederate field hospital, is the only house of the war period still standing. Address: Drawer C, Republic, Missouri 65738.

WOMEN'S RIGHTS NATIONAL HISTORICAL PARK
New York
On July 9, 1848, five reform-minded women met at a private home near Seneca Falls, New York, planning a strategy that marked the beginning of the women's rights movement. The story of the movement and of its founders is the focus of this park. Tours are conducted from the Visitor Center on Fall Street to significant sites, including the homes and offices of Elizabeth Cady Stanton, Amelia Jenks Bloomer, and other notable early women's rights activists. The park includes the Wesleyan Methodist Chapel, the site of the 1848 Women's Rights Convention. Address: Box 70, Seneca Falls, New York 13148.

WRIGHT BROTHERS NATIONAL MEMORIAL
North Carolina
The site of the first sustained flight by a heavier-than-air machine, made by Wilbur and Orville Wright at Kill Devil Hills in December 1903, is marked by a granite pylon monument in the dunes. The Visitor Center contains a replica of their famous plane, *The Flyer*. Address: Route 1, Box 675, Manteo, North Carolina 27954.

ZUNI-CIBOLA NATIONAL HISTORICAL PARK
New Mexico
South of Gallup, New Mexico, near the Arizona border, the Zuni pueblo has nurtured native American cultures for over 1,700 years. It was visited by Coronado during his gold-searching expedition of 1540, believed to be the first European contact with the people of what is now known as the Southwestern United States. In 1988, Congress moved to cooperate with the Zuni government in preserving and protecting the pueblo's abundant nationally significant resources through this new national historical park. The new park will become operational on completion of a leasehold agreement and management plan designed to protect fragile archaeological sites and the Zuni community from being overrun. The park will feature house ruins, kivas, pictographs, and petroglyphs of prehistoric villages, a mission church, and convents, all registered national historic landmarks. Stop at El Morro National Monument (see page 182) for guidance and latest information. Address: Pueblo of Zuni, Box 339, Zuni, New Mexico 87327.

NATURAL AND RECREATIONAL AREAS

WHETHER they are called national parkways; national seashores, lakeshores, or riverways; national monuments; or national recreation areas—these are all national treasures. All of the natural and recreation areas administered by the National Park Service offer unlimited opportunities for education, recreation, and travel enjoyment.

National monuments are the oldest category in this section. Devils Tower, Wyoming, was established as a national monument by presidential proclamation in 1906. National monuments include prehistoric cliff dwellings, caverns, an underwater marine garden, fortresses, landmarks of early settlement, spectacular canyons and desert wilderness, virgin stands of redwood and cactus. National monuments devoted to nature are described in this section of the guide. (Monuments relating to archaeology are described in Archaeological Areas, pages 172 to 175; monuments of historical significance are included in Historical Areas, pages 176 to 200.)

National seashores, lakeshores, riverways, and wild and scenic rivers, on the other hand, are among the newest categories in the National Park System. All have been established since 1953. The concept of these areas is one of the finest achievements of this recent period. For many years the nation has protected representative portions of other natural environments, such as virgin forest, glacial wilderness, and inland marsh. We have been concerned with rescuing endangered species of wildlife—the alligator, grizzly bear, and whooping crane. Now it can be said that the nation has recognized the value of the native seashores, lakeshores, and rivers.

In this section you will read about some of the largest units of the National Park System (the National Recreation Areas) and the most heavily visited (National Parkways). Parkways are distinctive parks in which the roadway is designed exclusively for pleasure travel by private car, rather than as a means of transportation from one point to another.

The natural and recreation areas offer an infinite variety of outdoor experience; each one of the areas detailed on this and following pages is worth a visit.

AGATE FOSSIL BEDS NATIONAL MONUMENT
Nebraska

The major fossil beds are located in University Hill (named for the University of Nebraska) and Carnegie Hill (for Carnegie Institute), near the end of the eastern monument. Follow the self-guiding foot trail to the two hills to view exposed fossils. You'll see the fossil bones of Miocene mammals where they have been buried for 20 million years. Be on the alert for rattlesnakes, which are present in the area. Though little development has taken place, a temporary Visitor Center museum has excellent exhibits. The terrain of the prairie landscape slopes gradually upward from the Niobrara River, flowing quietly on its journey to the Missouri. The land is covered with bluestem, grama, buffalo, and other grasses. In spring and summer a variety of wildflowers add color to the scene. In May and June creamy white flowers of yucca add particular beauty. Follow Nebraska 29 to the monument, 34 miles north of Mitchell, 22 miles south of Harrison. Address: c/o Scotts Bluff National Monument, Box 427, Gering, Nebraska 69341.

AMISTAD NATIONAL RECREATION AREA
Texas

A joint project of the United States and Mexico, this major international recreational facility in the warm, dry Southwest comprises nearly 63,000 acres of land and water.

Indian pictographs, 8,000 to 10,000 years old, are found along the walls of Lake Amistad; the only way to see them is by boat. One of the most popular sites, Panther Cave, is about 7 miles south of the Pecos River boat landing, just inside Seminole Canyon. The park has provided a boat dock here, where you can tie up and climb the hill to visit the cave. Don't expect to get close enough to touch—a fence has been erected by the Texas Historical Foundation to avert vandalism. There are 9 ramps on Lake Amistad.

Water sports are the main activity through most of the year, but lands bordering the reservoir can be used for camping, backcountry hiking, bird watching, picnicking, and nature study. The tawny desert and scrubby grassland above the Rio Grande have a charm all their own. Mammals in the area include coyote, white-tailed deer, peccary, raccoon, ringtail, squirrel, and jackrabbit.

Many islands at various reservoir levels lend themselves to use by boating parties. The shoreline especially is an angler's delight, with hundreds of pockets, caves, and canyons branching off the main bodies of water. There is no reciprocal license arrangement with Mexico; a license must be obtained before fishing its portion of the lake. One may be purchased in Ciudad Acuna, Del Rio's sister city across the Rio Grande. A Texas license is required for the U.S. side. Hunting is good, particularly for whitetail, mourning dove, and waterfowl. Numerous RV parks and motels are located in Del Rio and along US 90, adjacent to the lake. Address: Box 420367, Del Rio, Texas 78842-03670.

APOSTLE ISLANDS NATIONAL LAKESHORE
Wisconsin

They were thought to number only 12 by the early missionaries who named them, but there are actually 22 islands in the cluster off the Bayfield Peninsula in Lake Superior ranging in size from tiny islets to one of 14,000 acres. Some of the earliest fur traders and French explorers came this way. Established as the core of a new national lakeshore in 1970, the breezy Apostles are among the delights of the Great Lakes region. Some are inhabited only by deer, bear, and birds. Biting insects are common early June to mid-September, so come prepared.

The national lakeshore consists of 68,500 acres, including 21 of the islands and 11 miles of the mainland shore. Start at the Visitor Center in the Old Courthouse Building at Bayfield. See the displays and slide programs and pick up a copy of the weekly schedule of activities. Opportunities include the Raspberry Island Lighthouse Adventure and Historic Hokenson Fishery Tour. Backcountry use permits are issued here.

A mainland unit of the lakeshore adjoins the Red Cliff Indian Reservation, with secluded sand and pebble beaches and vistas of rock cliffs. The Little Sand Bay Information Center provides information and backcountry use permits. Visit ranger stations, open during summer, on Rocky, Stockton, Sand, Devils, Outer, Raspberry, and Michigan Islands; personnel are glad to provide guidance and current information.

Winter beauty draws increasing numbers of visitors for cross-country skiing, snowshoeing, and camping. With heavy snow and temperatures well below freezing, it can be harsh on the unwary and unprepared.

Bayfield, the gateway town, has an attractive boat basin shared by commercial and sport fishermen. From here campers can travel by regular excursion boat to the islands. Then take in interpretive programs and hiking trails, and explore agate beaches, caves, and rock outcrops.

A variety of narrated cruises is offered by the park concessioner from June to early October. The most popular is the "25-Mile Islander Cruise," of 2½ hours, passing sandstone cliffs and forested shores of Basswood and Hermit Islands. "The Sundowner" includes 30 minutes at Manitou with guided naturalist tour and optional whitefish dinner aboard. Cruises also provide scheduled shuttle service for campers. Call Apostle Islands Cruise Service, 715/779-3925.

Madeline Island, the largest of the Apostles (though not included in the National Lakeshore), is reached from Bayfield on a 30-minute ferry ride. At the historical museum opposite the dock you can learn about the activities of John Jacob Astor's American Fur Company. Fifty miles of road lead to small resorts, white beaches, and rock caves. Address: Box 729, Bayfield, Wisconsin 54814.

ASSATEAGUE ISLAND NATIONAL SEASHORE
Maryland-Virginia

Named by Indians, roamed by the legendary Chincoteague ponies, Assateague is a low barrier island, 37 miles, with 19,000 acres of land stretching along the Atlantic Ocean. It is connected by bridges to the mainland at both the northern and southern ends and lies about 90 miles from Norfolk, Virginia. Regular conventional two-wheel drive vehicles can presently travel on the island a distance of 3½ miles from the Maryland Bridge and approximately 4 miles from the Assateague Island Bridge in Virginia. No communities exist on the island, the largest undeveloped seashore between Massachusetts and North Carolina. Assateague and the other national seashores are different in that their purpose is to protect and restore coastal wilderness.

Bird and wildlife watching. Birds flock to the area, which is on the Atlantic flyway, to occupy varying habitats of sea, beach, pine woods and thicket, marsh and bay. More than 275 kinds of birds have been identified, and each season has its own coterie of species. Approximately 11 miles of the southern part of the island form the Chincoteague National Wildlife Refuge, where enormous flocks of shore birds are seen in migration during September and October, and where large flocks of ducks, geese, and swans are at home all winter. To fully enjoy the shore birds, tramp the wild beach from the parking area at the southern end through the wildlife refuge. The Chincoteague ponies, whose ancestors came here centuries ago, roam wild, living off the marsh grass. The last week in July is "Pony Penning Week," time of the annual sale of the Virginia herd's colts following the traditional roundup.

The exotic small Sika deer (released on the island by a Boy Scout troop in 1923) can be glimpsed occasionally, along with foxes, raccoons, muskrats, and otters.

The north end is fascinating with ever-changing sand dunes and washover areas, marsh grasses, pools, nesting terns and skimmers, as well as shore birds. Assateague State Park, directly across the bridge from the mainland, provides a protected beach, bathhouse, food services, and 311 modern campsites on hardtop loop roads. North Beach, inside the national seashore, has lifeguard protection for swimmers, and two primitive family campgrounds. Three hike-in campsites are located behind the primary dune, and four canoe-in campsites are located on the bay side; these backcountry sites are quite primitive, and all water and shelter must be packed in. Four-wheel-drive, over-sand vehicles are permitted to run as far south as the Virginia line. However, the Park Service has imposed a permit system with stringent restrictions on use of the 16 miles of beach open to vehicles.

At the southern tip, called Tom's Cove Hook, the Park Service operates a 5-mile-long day-use recreation area. This area includes bathhouse and lifeguard protection. During summer both the Park Service and Fish and Wildlife Service offer interpretive nature walks and lectures; the wildlife refuge also offers an open bus ride into the refuge and a boat ride into the bay.

Light cartop boats can be launched at mainland ramps and used in most of the shallow bay, though heavier boats are restricted to bay channels or the ocean.

Marinas are available in nearby towns of Chincoteague, Virginia and Ocean City, Maryland. Nearly all of the island beaches can be traversed by foot, providing for excellent beachcombing during winter; summer beachcombing is rarely good except near the two inlets at either end, or after a heavy storm. The shallow bay offers many places to find hardshell clams and blue crabs.

National Park Service Visitor Centers at both ends will help visitors to understand the ecology of a true barrier beach. Address: Route 2, Box 294, Berlin, Maryland 21811.

BIG CYPRESS NATIONAL PRESERVE
Florida

Comprising 570,000 acres of watershed directly north of Everglades National Park, Big Cypress will assure a degree of critical fresh water and ecological integrity to the park. "National preserves" represent a new category of national park area. The act of 1974 establishing Big Cypress specifies the lands shall be administered "in a manner which will assure their natural and ecological integrity in perpetuity." Rare and endangered species here include the Florida panther, manatee, brown pelican, Everglades kite, and roseate spoonbill. Visitors can enjoy primitive camping, hiking, and sightseeing; hunting, fishing, and trapping are authorized in accordance with state law. The interest in the area is primarily natural, but there are historical and cultural values as well. Following the Seminole Wars in Florida, the Big Cypress became the last stronghold of these Indians, and Miccosukee villages still dot the area. Collier-Seminole State Park, 6,423 acres of swampland and uplands, serves as both a recreation area and informal memorial to the Indians and to Barron Collier, who at one time owned the surrounding Collier County. The park entrance lies off US 41, 17 miles south of Naples. This state park includes camping and picnic areas. Fringing the western edge of the state park, a boat basin, ramp, and marina provide access to the Blackwater River. Address: Star Route, Box 110, Ochopee, Florida 33943.

BIG SOUTH FORK NATIONAL RIVER
AND RECREATION AREA
Tennessee-Kentucky

The Big South Fork flows north into Kentucky from its source on the Cumberland Plateau. En route, its gorges and the adjacent ridges provide outstanding scenery and unparalleled opportunities for outdoor recreation. This is a major new territory to explore. Eventually it will cover more than 100,000 acres of rugged terrain north of Crossville, Tennessee, and within 50 miles of two interstate highways, I-40 and I-75. Newly constructed trails and old logging roads are available to hikers, leading to jewels like Honey Creek and Yahoo Falls. More than 80 miles of choice canoe waters range from easy floats to challenging white-water runs through rapids. Get a copy of the river guidebook at park headquarters. Or sign up with an outfitter like Cumberland Outdoor Adventures, Inc., Route 6, Box 372B, Corbin, Kentucky 40701. **Bandy Creek** complex is a major activities center on the Tennessee side, with trailer and tent camping, canoe rental, and access to trails. **Blue Heron**, named for an abandoned mining community in the Kentucky portion, includes a small campground on the bluffs above the Big South Fork, facilities for hiking, swimming, fishing, and canoeing, plus a program on life in the mining town. **Charit Creek Hostel** (formerly Parch Corn Lodge) at the Station Creek area provides simple facilities at low cost. Call 615/879-4289. Be sure to visit historic **Rugby**, on State Route 52, the restoration of a 19th century utopian village. Lodging and meals are available. Primary north-south access routes are I-75 and US 27 and 127. Address: Box 630, Oneida, Tennessee 37841.

BIG THICKET NATIONAL PRESERVE
Texas

As a crossroads of ecological zones, this 84,550-acre preserve in southeast Texas contains an extraordinary diversity of flora, a wealth of animal life, and magnificent specimens of individual tree species. The Big Thicket embraces eight different biological habitats, ranging from savanna to bald-cypress swamp to uplands of beech, magnolia, white oak, and loblolly pine. Included are almost 300 bird species; mammals ranging from foxes and otter to mountain lions, armadillo, and occasional black bear; 3 kinds of insect-eating plants, and 27 species of wild orchids.

The old, primitive Big Thicket stretched roughly from the Sabine River on the east to past Trinity River on the west. Less than one-tenth remains in wilderness today. The 12 units of the preserve are scattered as far as 50 miles apart; they range in size from 25,024 acres in the Lance Rosier Unit to 550 acres in the Loblolly Unit, a pocket of enormous pines glimmering in spongy swamps. Development of public-use facilities is steady but slow.

Visit the **Visitor Information Station** located on FM 420, 2½ miles east of US 69 (about 7½ miles north of Kountze), for orientation and detailed information. Hike the adjacent 1.7-mile loop **Kirby Nature Trail** for a leisurely introduction to the thicket and a view of lovely Village Creek, a favorite canoeing waterway. Or take the 9.2-mile **Turkey Creek Trail**, which is said to contain the greatest concentrated plant diversification in the preserve. The trail winds through pine plateaus, creek bottoms with huge hard-

woods, cathedral-like beech-magnolia-loblolly glades, and fascinating acid bog "baygalls." Ask about them.

Trails are also available in the **Beech Creek Unit**, **Hickory Creek Savannah Unit**, and **Big Sandy Creek Unit**, each offering different views of the diverse Big Thicket.

Big Thicket Museum, at Saratoga, makes a choice starting point of a visit to the area. Operated by the nonprofit Big Thicket Association, the museum features displays on flora, fauna, and history. Canoe explorations are scheduled throughout the year. Big Thicket Day is conducted annually the first Saturday in June. Write Big Thicket Museum, Box 198, Saratoga, Texas 77585.

Accommodations in the Big Thicket region cover a wide spectrum. The Alabama-Coushatta Indians have developed campgrounds with a fishing lake. Chain-O-Lakes Campground, on Daniel Ranch Road, Romayor, covers 175 acres, with many of the trees, plants, flowers, and vines of the area, including wild orchids growing in the swimming pond. The 250 campsites range from full hookups to wilderness sites. The Triple D Guest Ranch is an excellent base for hiking and riding in the Big Thicket. And Double Lake Recreation Area, 5 miles from Coldspring in Sam Houston National Forest, offers boating, swimming, and fishing, as well as camping. State parks provide camping areas in Steinhagen, Sam Rayburn, Livingston, and Toledo Bend Reservoirs. Address: Box 7408, Beaumont, Texas 77706.

BIGHORN CANYON NATIONAL RECREATION AREA
Wyoming-Montana

Flanked by the Pryor Mountains on the west and the Bighorn Mountains on the east, the Bighorn River cuts a chasm between the mountains. The national recreation area was established in 1966 following completion of the 525-foot-high Yellowtail Dam, which produced the 71-mile-long Bighorn Lake.

Bighorn Canyon offers year-round recreation. Pleasure boating, water skiing, and lake fishing on Bighorn Lake and the afterbay, and stream fishing below the dam are summer activities, while the Horseshoe Bend area offers ice fishing in winter. Fishing regulations follow state laws, and fishing in either Montana or Wyoming requires the appropriate fishing license. The recreation area offers more than water-oriented activities. Visit the **Bighorn Canyon Visitor Center** outside Lovell, Wyoming, or the **Fort Smith Visitor Information Station** near Fort Smith, Montana, for orientation through exhibits, films, and brochures.

Camping comes in a variety of environments. The RV and tent campground at Horseshoe Bend and the boat-in/hike-in campground at Medicine Creek are in arid land. Riparian habitat camping can be found at Barry's Land and Afterbay campgrounds; a pine forest, lakeside campsite at the boat-in only campground in Black Canyon.

Hikers experience a diversity of cross-country hiking. Obtain free backcountry permits at either Visitor Center. For the less adventuresome, the Crooked Creek Nature Trail at Horseshoe Bend and the Om-Ne-A Trail at the dam are well marked.

The scenic drive along Ok-A-Beh Road through short-grass prairie is highlighted by wildflowers from May through July. The wildflower display along Bad Pass Road in the south district is somewhat shorter due to drier conditions. Don't miss the magnificent canyon view offered from Devil Canyon Overlook, looking down near-vertical cliffs to the ribbon of a lake 976 feet below. Bad Pass Road from Horseshoe Bend to Barry's Landing passes through a portion of Pryor Mountain Wild Horse Range.

Access to the north end of the recreation area is from Hardin, Montana, on Montana 313. US14A in Wyoming provides access to the south end. The north and south ends of the recreation area are not connected by a direct route. Address: Box 458, Fort Smith, Montana 59035-0458.

BLACK CANYON OF THE GUNNISON NATIONAL MONUMENT
Colorado

Sunlight sparkles on dark-colored ancient rock, opened to view in the narrow gorge cut by the Gunnison River east of Montrose to a maximum depth of 2,700 feet. The narrowest width at the top is 1,100 feet, and at one point in the bottom the river channel narrows to only 40 feet. A backcountry permit is needed for the descent into the canyon, which is arduous and hazardous. On each rim there is a highway that leads to spectacular observation points over the shadowed depths. Campgrounds on both of the rims are open June to October. Address: Box 1648, Montrose, Colorado 81402.

BLUE RIDGE PARKWAY
North Carolina-Virginia

This highly popular area attracts more than 18 million visitors a year. And little wonder. The parkway is the longest scenic drive in the world, providing quiet, leisurely travel, free of commercial congestion, for 469 miles through the forested mountains of Virginia and North Carolina. It is much more than a road: it is a *garden* of flowering trees, shrubs, and herbs; a *park* with nature trails, picnic grounds, and camping; a *museum* of the southern highlands culture, expressed at restored mills, weathered cabins, and farms bordered by split-rail fences; a *wildlife sanctuary* for deer, bear, bobcat, skunk, and possibly 200 species of birds; and a center of beautiful, authentic mountain handicrafts. It is *not* a high-speed freeway.

In some sections the parkway runs along the very crest of the mountains. Breathtaking vistas unfold from overlooks 2,000 to 6,000 feet high. Many miles of excellent hiking trails are available, from short leg-stretchers to steep climbs. The Appalachian Trail roughly parallels the parkway north of Roanoke. High spots in the Virginia portion include: **Humpback Rocks**, near Waynesboro, the northern end of the parkway, where the self-guiding trail weaves among a cluster of log buildings of pioneer days. **James River Overlook**, high above one of America's historic rivers. Exhibits and a restored lock tell the story of the Kanawha Canal, once a waterway to the West. **Peaks of Otter**, near Roanoke, a high valley sheltered by the towering triple peaks, popular as a mountain retreat since Jefferson's day. **Mabry Mill**, where you can see a genuine water-powered gristmill in operation, grinding corn and buckwheat with crude iron gears and shafts.

Across the border in North Carolina: **Brinegar Cabin** offers weaving demonstrations on an old mountain loom. **Linville Falls**, a wilderness beauty spot around a mighty gorge, presented to the park system by John D. Rockefeller, Jr. **Museum of North Carolina Minerals**, near Spruce Pine, a special delight to rockhounds with a display of gemstones and minerals found nearby. **Mount Mitchell** (6,680 feet), in a state park bordering the parkway, the highest mountain in the East. **Craggy Gardens**, north of Asheville, a favorite spot to walk among flowering rhododendrons of late spring. **Devils Courthouse**, a rocky summit affording a 360 degree view across the mountains of the Carolinas, Tennessee, and Georgia.

Shopping Guide. Craft demonstrations at key points and the finest souvenir shops in the entire National Park system help visitors to appreciate native skills and to purchase worthwhile travel mementos. **Northwest Trading Post**, near West Jefferson, North Carolina, features everything from homemade cheeses and jellies to five-string banjos of curly maple. At the **Folk Art Center**, east of Asheville at Milepost 382, members of the Southern Highlands Handicraft Guild are seen making rugs and baskets and weaving. A series of one-week workshops in Appalachian crafts, open to all at modest fees, is conducted here by the guild.

Bird watching. Late September and early October are prime for observing southerly migration of many birds and butterflies from overlooks along the parkway. From Milepost 92, near the Peaks of Otter, in Virginia, hundreds of hawks can often be observed in a single day, gliding on billows of air that rise from the Blue Ridge valleys. Depending on the weather conditions, some birds fly so high that they appear to be mere specks in the sky, whereas spiraling flight patterns of other birds bring them into high level view. The roadside exhibit depicts patterns of various hawks, eagles, ospreys, and vultures.

Seasons and Accommodations. In early spring migrant birds, including many warblers, grace forests and fields. Dogwood and wildflowers open the flowering season late in April. Flame azalea blazes in the hills from mid-May, reaching a peak in the high mountains around Asheville in June. Mountain laurel and snowy-white rhododendron continue the flower show until late July. Autumn brings a new set of colors in the spectacular hardwoods of the eastern forests. The parkway is excellent for cross-country skiing because it receives a dependable amount of snow. Some sections are closed to vehicles much of the winter. The entire parkway is a potential ski-touring trail. Lodges and housekeeping cabins provide accommodations for visitors. Advance reservations are recommended at all facilities. Some parkway campgrounds remain open all year, weather and road conditions permitting. Other campgrounds are in national forests, state parks, and private areas all along the parkway. Historic Hotel Botetourt in Buchanan is now a member of American Youth Hostel's network of low-cost accommodations. So is Blue Ridge Country AYH-Hostel, 100 feet off the parkway, 10 miles east of Galax, "capital of old-time mountain music." From mid-June through Labor Day, naturalists and historians lead guided walks and give evening programs at major visitor use areas. Visitor Centers at Humpback Rocks, Peaks of Otter, Museum of North Carolina Minerals, and Craggy Gardens are open May through October. The parkway is open all year, however some sections are closed in icy or snowy weather. Address: 700 Northwestern Bank Building, Asheville, North Carolina 28801.

BUCK ISLAND REEF NATIONAL MONUMENT
Virgin Islands

Off the northeast coast of St. Croix, the prime attraction of this uninhabited island is the lush coral reef—a marine garden of coral, grottoes, sea fans, gorgonias, and myriad tropical fish. Here the Park Service has established the underwater Buck Island Reef nature trail, complete with informational signs on the ocean floor to guide snorkelers. You can swim the trail—an outstanding snorkeling opportunity—in about 30 minutes. Day trips in small boats are conducted by captains operating from Christiansted, 6 miles away, and they will furnish the snorkel gear. There is also ample time to walk the nature trail through the tropical vegetation covering the island, and while on the trail you may get the chance to see the rookery of pelicans and Caribbean birds. The island is also the habitat of several species of sea turtles. Address: c/o Christiansted National Historic Site, Box 160, Christiansted, St. Croix, Virgin Islands 00820.

BUFFALO NATIONAL RIVER
Arkansas

Massive bluffs and deeply entrenched valleys give the Buffalo River a striking setting as it winds 132 miles through the Ozarks of northwest Arkansas to its mouth on the White River at the hamlet called Buffalo City. The Buffalo is undoubtedly one of America's most beautiful streams, with countless rapids, cliffs, caves, hills, mountains, and scenic side canyons, many with waterfalls and sinkholes, along its course. Bordering lands support 1,500 varieties of plants and many types of small animals. Just over 95

205

percent of the land is in federal ownership at this time. Eventually the park will include 95,730 acres for fishing, hiking, boating, hunting, camping, and nature study. One of the park's highlights, Hemmed-in Hollow (which can be reached only by foot), contains the largest free-leaping waterfall between the southern Appalachians and the Rockies.

Canoeing is the main activity. Except for extreme dry periods, the Lower River (east of Silver Hill) can be floated almost any time. The Upper River, however, is usually too low after June 1. Buffalo Point (formerly Buffalo River State Park) is the principal center. Located 17 miles south of Yellville, via Arkansas 14 and 268, facilities include 106 campsites, 14 housekeeping cottages, dining room, and picnic areas. During summer, park rangers conduct nature walks across wild and beautiful terrain. Lost Valley (formerly Lost Valley State Park) lies in the heart of the most rugged section of the Ozarks, with primitive campsites for those who enjoy roughing it. Steel Creek primitive camp is located just downstream from the Ponca low-water bridge and offers spectacular scenery. It is an excellent put-in point for canoeists when water permits. Both Lost Valley and Steel Creek are reached via Arkansas 43 from Harrison or Arkansas 74 from Jasper. Outfitters outside the park offer canoe rentals and guide service if desired. Along the river, camps are made on innumerable gravel bars edging the stream. Primitive float camps have been established, offering minimal facilities. Canoeists are asked to respect the rights of private landowners when selecting a campsite. Maps and additional information are available at Buffalo Point, Silver Hill, and Pruitt Stations. Address: Box 1173, Harrison, Arkansas 72601.

CANAVERAL NATIONAL SEASHORE
Florida
One of the last major wild areas on Florida's Atlantic coast is preserved in this national seashore and its companion, Merritt Island National Wildlife Refuge. Canaveral was established in 1975 from what had been the northern portion of Kennedy Space Center and a Florida state park; it covers 57,627 acres, including 25 miles of beachfront.

Apollo Beach, at the north end, lies about 10 miles south of New Smyrna on Florida A1A. An unpaved road provides about 6 miles of bumpy access. Playalinda Beach, at the south end, is 12 miles east of Titusville on Florida 402. A partially paved road parallels the ocean for about 5 miles behind the tall dunes. Most of the activity takes place at Playalinda. It's a good place for swimming, surfing, and beach walking. Summer weekends are apt to be crowded and visitors may be turned away when the limited parking spaces are filled.

The central portion of the seashore, measuring about 14 miles along the coast, is managed as a roadless area where nature comes first. Scrub vegetation, including saw palmetto, covers most of the land, with the exception of the marsh. In spring and summer, giant loggerhead and green turtles crawl up on the beach at night to lay their eggs. The seashore is wintering ground for thousands of birds of many species. Bald eagles nest in tall pine trees. Brown pelicans occupy a mangrove rookery island in the heart of the seashore. More than 280 species of birds have been sighted along the shore and in the interior. The Merritt Island National Wildlife Refuge provides special opportunities for birdwatching and wildlife observation. The major attraction in this region, of course, is the Kennedy Space Center, which offers excellent displays for visitors and a guided tour of its installations. There is no camping within the seashore, but state parks and private facilities are nearby. Address: Box 6447, Titusville, Florida 32782.

CAPE COD NATIONAL SEASHORE
Massachusetts
The slender, bent arm of land thrust 70 miles into the ocean from the mainland was settled within two decades after colonists established Plymouth, to be lived on by fishermen, sea captains, and whaling men. For generations it was a remote place of heath, marsh, pine forest, and lakes, and its principal visitors were millions of birds en route between Canada and the South. Then it became vacation country, building slowly, with increasing numbers attracted by the aura of the sea, soft summer weather, and graciousness of the towns.

The national seashore was established in 1961, preserving the old heritage on 44,600 acres. Thus was rescued from development a 40-mile ribbon, where the life-community of the land—plants like milkwort, sandwort, and seaside goldenrod—can still steal to the ocean's edge to meet incoming jellyfish, kelp, clam, and rockweed.

Attention, birdwatchers. The beauty and variety of Cape Cod birds reflect different environments to which they have adapted. Some are fishers of the deep sea, while others are waders, scratchers, wood borers, seed eaters, and scavengers. Try to match birds with habitats as you go along. Join illustrated evening bird talks and other programs.

Nauset Area. Start at the Salt Pond Visitor Center, easily reached just off Route 6 in Eastham. It features spectacular views of Salt Pond and Nauset Marsh, plus a wealth of information about seashore attractions and programs. The museum portion, renovated and expanded in 1989, is a showcase of 19th century and early 20th century Cape Cod artifacts. These include the Clark collection of scrimshaw, one of the largest and most impressive in New England, recalling the age when whaling voyages lasted two years or more and sailors hand carved elaborate designs into scraps of whalebone. One of the finest features in the park is the Buttonbush Trail for the Blind; Fort Hill and Nauset Marsh Trails are also very worthwhile. For swimming, head for Coast Guard Beach and Nauset Light Beach (both have lifeguards); for surf fishing for striped bass, Great Beach. A popular bike trail runs through the area. Birders should take advantage of the excellent observation point at Nauset Beach, where thousands of sea birds and shore birds congregate during summer.

Province Lands. Some of the most spectacular dunes along the Atlantic Coast are at the tip of the Cape in a 4,400-acre area set aside ever since 1670, when the "Plimoth Colony" undertook an early conservation action. Swimming beaches (lifeguards on duty) at Race Point and Herring Cove are open 9 a.m. to 5 p.m. Guided walks are conducted through the beech forest and marshland. Eight miles of bicycle trails run through the dunes. Behind the "hook of the cape," the visitor looks at Provincetown on Cape Cod Bay, where the *Mayflower* made its first landfall in 1620.

Pilgrim Heights. Self-guiding trails lead along heath-covered slopes bordering the Atlantic and to a spring where the Pilgrims may have found their first fresh drinking water after leaving England. Picnic tables, guarded swimming at Head-of-the-Meadow Beach, Truro.

Marconi Station. Overlooking the ocean from high, sandy bluffs near the village of Wellfleet, a shelter house stands near the site of the first wireless station in the United States, and contains a scale model of the original from which Guglielmo Marconi successfully transmitted a message to England in 1903. The views are spectacular, particularly of the Great Beach, which was given its name by Thoreau. ("A man may stand there and put all America behind him," he wrote.) Guided walks. A swimming beach is available at Marconi.

Accommodations and Seasons. Resort accommodations ranging from simple cottages to deluxe hotels and motels are located in towns adjoining the seashore. Privately operated campgrounds are within the authorized boundaries, and several are nearby. For complete listings, write the Cape Cod Chamber of Commerce, Hyannis, Massachusetts 02601. The cape is a popular place; advance reservations, for rooms and campsites, should be made for the summer months. Address: South Wellfleet, Massachusetts 02663.

CAPE HATTERAS NATIONAL SEASHORE
North Carolina
A 70-mile slender strand, only 3 miles at its widest, the Cape Hatteras seashore area lies between foaming ocean surf and broad, shallow sounds. One should not come here anticipating the usual seaside vacation, but rather a *different* experience, where the main activities are apt to be watching thousands of snow geese, or the bottle-nosed dolphin rolling and playing offshore, or vivid sunsets over the sea and sand.

This is the first of the national seashores, established in 1953. It covers 28,500 acres from Nags Head, on Bodie Island, southward to include Hatteras and Ocracoke Islands, now connected by bridge and ferry. An asphalt road leads through villages like Rodanthe, Salvo, and Buxton, which date to colonial days. From parking turnouts visitors can walk to the beach to fish, swim, or explore the wreckage of ships that ran aground in the "Graveyard of the Atlantic."

These storied Outer Banks, where the English first tried to establish colonies in 1585, and where Blackbeard was tracked down and killed, are no longer isolated—but they offer a spirit of isolation.

Bodie Island Visitor Center is the best place to start; exhibits preview the seashore, its attractions and facilities. Other Visitor Centers are at Cape Hatteras and Ocracoke. From mid-June to Labor Day guided walks along the beach and illustrated evening talks are held.

Pea Island National Wildlife Refuge, at the north end of Hatteras Island, is a key way station on the Atlantic flyway, and it helps to make the national seashore a birder's delight. Throngs of snow geese winter here, as do large numbers of whistling swans, Canada geese, and ducks. More than 300 species of birds have been recorded.

Cape Hatteras Lighthouse, the best known of three lighthouses in the area, overlooks the treacherous Diamond Shoals. Built in 1870, it is the tallest lighthouse in the country.

Ocracoke Village is well worth a visit, though it lies at the southern tip of the national seashore. The small fishing fleet at harbor, gnarled live oaks, the oldest lighthouse of the Outer Banks, sandy lanes, and Teach's Hole, where Blackbeard may have met his end, are among its attractions. A tiny cemetery, bordered by a white picket fence, marks the burial place of four British sailors whose bodies washed ashore in 1942 after their ship was sunk by a German submarine southeast of Hatteras. The cemetery, leased by North Carolina to the British government in 1976, is maintained by the U.S. Coast Guard.

Besides the free ferry across Hatteras Inlet, Ocracoke can be reached by the Cedar Island ferry from the mainland (it makes several round trips daily) via the town of Atlantic on North Carolina 70, and from Swan Quarter, off US 264.

Sport fishing is celebrated: surf casting from the ocean beach; trolling from boats in the inland sounds and bays and in the deep waters of the Gulf Stream 20 miles offshore. Best periods for channel bass are April 15 to June 15 and September 20 to November 20; cobia, June and July; blues and mackerels, July and August. However, fish may be caught every month. Charter boats available.

Swimming is best where lifeguard service is provided in summer. Strong currents make swimming at unguarded beaches hazardous. Guarded beaches may be found at Coquina Beach,

Salvo Campground, Cape Point Campground, Frisco Campground, and Ocracoke Campground. Water is too cold for swimming before late May. Surfing is popular but restricted from areas near swimming beaches, hotels, and fishing piers.

Accommodations and Seasons. Hotels, motels, and cottages are found in communities just north of the seashore and in villages within the boundaries, including Hatteras and Ocracoke, and Manteo, on Roanoke Island. For a complete list, write Dare County Tourist Bureau, Manteo, North Carolina 27954. Five campgrounds for tents and trailers (no utility connections) are located in the seashore park, generally on flat, shadeless areas; awnings and long tent stakes are advised. Bring mosquito netting and repellent. Reservations through Ticketron June through Labor Day: limit 14 days. Facilities are crowded in summer. Ocracoke, Oregon Inlet, and Cape Point campgrounds are open mid-April to mid-October. Address: Route 1, Box 675, Manteo, North Carolina 27954.

CAPE LOOKOUT NATIONAL SEASHORE
North Carolina
This National Seashore, established in 1966, encompasses 58 miles of ocean shore on Portsmouth Island, Core Banks, and Shackleford Banks south of Ocracoke Inlet. The combination of Hatteras and Lookout National Seashores gives North Carolina the greatest length of continuous protected shoreline on the U.S. east coast. The area is a wintering ground for loons, mergansers, cormorants, gannets, geese, swans, and, occasionally, Arctic birds. In summer, terns, pelicans, egrets, herons, and various shore birds take over. Large, 20-foot high dunes characterize Cape Lookout Bight and Shackleford Banks, while a forest of live oak, cedar holly, and pine backs up the banks at Shackleford. Present use includes sport fishing and waterfowl hunting. Programs are given daily during summer at the lighthouse, Hampton Museum, and Restoration Grounds. Dolphins are a familiar sight.

Ferry service is available from Harkers Island (reached by road from Beaufort) to the Cape Lookout Bight area and from Davis and Atlantic off US 70 to points on the Core Banks. You can reach Portsmouth Village by charter ferry from Ocracoke, at the southern tip of Cape Hatteras National Seashore; from Ocracoke the Cedar Island ferry connects with US 70 south to Beaufort. There are rustic overnight accommodations at the seashore. If you intend to camp, be sure to bring tents with mosquito netting, suntan lotion, insect repellent, food, and water. Address: Box 690, Beaufort, North Carolina 28516.

CAPULIN MOUNTAIN NATIONAL MONUMENT
New Mexico
Ever wanted to walk into a volcano? You can at Capulin Mountain. A 2-mile road spirals to the summit parking lot. Two self-guiding trails tour the summit: short trail to the vent; 1-mile trail circles the rim. The monument lies near the northeast corner of the state off US 64/87, between Raton and Clayton, New Mexico. The Visitor Center and picnic area are open all year. Address: Capulin, New Mexico 88414.

CATOCTIN MOUNTAIN PARK. See page 168.

CEDAR BREAKS NATIONAL MONUMENT
Utah
A huge natural coliseum, eroded into the Pink Cliffs, lies between Zion and Bryce National Parks. The rim of the amphitheater, whose amazing colors change with the sun's rays, averages over 10,000 feet in elevation. Mule deer often graze meadows and slopes in morning and evening. Campground and Visitor Center; recreation facilities in surrounding Dixie National Forest. Address: Box 749, Cedar City, Utah 84720.

CHATTAHOOCHEE RIVER
NATIONAL RECREATION AREA
Georgia

This area, authorized by Congress in 1978, consists of 14 noncontiguous parcels of land along 48 miles of the Chattahoochee River between Lake Sidney Lanier and Atlanta. The Park Service now manages about 3,500 acres along the river. The most popular activities are picnicking, hiking, fishing, and rafting along gentle stretches of the waterway.

The Chattahoochee derives its name from the Cherokee word for "flowering rock," denoting the many waterfalls tumbling in the Appalachian highlands, the source of the river. Nearby is the Kennesaw Mountain National Battlefield Park. There are campgrounds near Lake Sidney Lanier, north of Atlanta. Address: 1900 Northridge Road, Dunwoody, Georgia 30338.

CHICKASAW NATIONAL RECREATION AREA
Oklahoma

This new area combines the lands of the former Platt National Park and Arbuckle National Recreation Area to form, in the words of Congress, "a fitting memorialization of the Chickasaw Indian Nation." The combined area contains cold mineral springs, freshwater springs, woods, and waterfalls in the Arbuckle Mountains of southern Oklahoma, adjacent to the town of Sulphur, south of Oklahoma City.

The Arbuckle Reservoir provides fishing, boating, and swimming. Stream fishing and hiking are features of Upper Rock Creek. Camping and picnicking are also available. So are nature trails through a woodland of oaks, persimmon, osage-orange, hickory, walnut, cedar, and juniper; and shrubs such as sumac, elder, plum, and redbud.

Students have come from great distances to study the unusual geology of the ancient Arbuckle Mountains, which have been uplifted, deformed, and worn down to their roots. Within a few miles of the reservoir are unusual outcrops, rugged slopes and gorges, an outstanding fossil-bearing site, waterfalls, and a dramatic geologic array (along US 77) known locally as the "gravestones."

Visitor Center. Travertine Nature Center, in the eastern end of the area, contains interpretive displays featuring live snakes, frogs, lizards, insects, plants, and fish native to the area. The center is the main visitor information point and start of several nature trails through the Environmental Study Area, an outdoor classroom. During summer, guided walks, movies, a children's program, and evening talks are given each day. The center is open every day of the year except Christmas and New Year's Day.

Perimeter Road, a 7-mile circuit drive, offers motorists a scenic view of the area. Sixteen miles of trail provide access to all points of interest in the recreation area.

Bromide Hill, a steep, wooded bluff easily reached by road or trail, offers a fine panoramic view.

Mineral spring waters may be used by all visitors, but should not be taken in quantity except on a physician's advice. The mud from some sulfur-water pools is said to help in treating certain skin diseases. In the eastern end of the recreation area, Buffalo and Antelope Springs were named because herds of these animals used to come from the surrounding prairies to drink.

Of the area's six campgrounds, two are open all year. Address: Chickasaw National Recreation Area, Box 201, Sulphur, Oklahoma 73086.

CHIRICAHUA NATIONAL MONUMENT
Arizona

A wilderness of unusual rock shapes, gigantic monoliths eroded by wind and water, with strata telling the story of nearly 30 million years of the earth's forces, lies high in the Chiricahua Mountains,

near the old stronghold of Cochise and his Apache braves. The "wonderland of rocks" lies between Willcox on I-10 and Douglas on the Mexican border. A paved road leads to an overlook, with horseback and foot trails reaching all parts of the monument. Visitor Center and campgrounds. Nearest lodgings are in Willcox.

Chiricahua comprises one of the country's truly choice birding spots. Shady glens in the canyon bottoms provide haven for unique species, including many closely associated with Mexico. The wide range of climate and vegetation attracts a wide spectrum of southwest mountain birds. The bridled titmouse and painted redstart are two of the most unusual. At times the elusive Montezuma quail is fairly common here. Some of the most interesting species are best seen in the canyon near the Visitor Center. Address: Dos Cabezas Route, Box 6500, Willcox, Arizona 85643.

CITY OF ROCKS NATIONAL RESERVE
Idaho

Striking granite spires and sculptured rock formations, almost due south of Burley, Idaho, just north of the Utah border, have long made the City of Rocks a special place, with both geological and historical value. Not until 1988, however, did Congress act, designating 14,320 acres (including City of Rocks State Park) for federal protection. Visitors see ruts of wagon wheels left by settlers heading for Oregon, and something more—inscriptions of the pioneers, many applied with axle grease, still legible on the rocks. Camp Rock provides easy access to some of the old writing, a choice spot to reflect on the environment of glaciated mountains, wild rivers, thundering waterfalls, lakes and streams, grassland prairie, and desert. Take time to hike or climb among the rocks. City of Rocks, in fact, is known as one of the best climbing places in Idaho, rewarding to climbers of all skill levels. However, avoid climbing on rocks bearing old inscriptions or where birds of prey may nest. Address: 2647 Kimberley Road East, Twin Falls, Idaho 83301.

COLORADO NATIONAL MONUMENT
Colorado

Steep canyon walls, towering monoliths, and rounded domes have been eroded from the uplifted sandstones of the Uncompahgre Plateau. Rim Rock Drive follows the canyon rims, and overlooks provide views of the magnificent rock sculpture. Spring and summer wildflowers add color to the pinon-juniper forest of the semiarid desert. Campgrounds; a permit is recommended for backcountry use. Lodgings and private campgrounds in and near Grand Junction. Address: Fruita, Colorado 81521.

CONGAREE SWAMP NATIONAL MONUMENT
South Carolina

This unique flood plain contains a rare remnant of southern river bottomland forest barely 20 miles south of Columbia. It includes deciduous hardwoods, huge loblolly pines, bald cypress, and tupelos. Elsewhere in the Southeast, lumbering has all but wiped out such forest stands. Nine trees (laurel oak, loblolly pine, swamp tupelo, possumhaw, sweetgum, swamp privet, water ash, overcup oak, and American holly) may be the largest of their kind in the nation. Congress approved establishment of the national monument in 1976. Reach to monument via South Carolina 48, southeast from Columbia. Nearby are Manchester State Forest and Poinsett State Park. There is a campground in the state park. Address: Box 11938, Columbia, South Carolina 29206.

COULEE DAM NATIONAL RECREATION AREA
Washington

The area centers on Franklin D. Roosevelt Lake, a reservoir extending 151 miles along the Columbia River from Grand Coulee Dam north to the Canadian border. It offers many outdoor activities: fishing, water skiing, swimming, boating, and camping in quiet coves. In addition, it holds interest in the immense dam, rolling hills, varied plants, and wildlife. On the north and west shores are Indian lands, the dwelling place of a dozen tribes, including the descendants of Chief Joseph's Nez Perce, who made their valiant, futile struggle for freedom in 1877.

The best place to gain an impression of the lake's dimensions is the high **lookout point** at the west end of the dam. The dam was completed in 1941 by the U.S. Bureau of Reclamation to provide irrigation water for the Columbia River Basin. The powerhouse is open to visitors during summer. The lake has 660 miles of shoreline, with 13 developed beaches and 26 recreation areas providing camping, boat launching, picnicking, and bathhouses. Camping sites range from highly organized to primitive.

The travel season extends from May to November. Water in the reservoir reaches maximum level in late June or early July and remains full all summer. Illustrated programs are presented at major campgrounds to interpret the geology and plant and animal life, as well as human history, of the Columbia River Valley. A choice is boating from Coulee Dam to the beautiful Arrow Lakes of Canada, a distance of 300 miles. A popular scenic drive leads from Coulee Dam to Fort Spokane, then to Kettle Falls.

Hunting is permitted within the recreation area subject to state regulations. Upland birds are common, and chukars have been introduced. Address: Box 37, Coulee Dam, Washington 99116.

CRATERS OF THE MOON NATIONAL MONUMENT
Idaho

This is an astonishing landscape of vast lava fields studded with cinder cones. Although the last eruptions occurred about 2,000 years ago, volcanic activity in the area dates back over a million years. The repeated floods of massive rivers of liquid rock destroyed all vegetation in their paths. Barren and sterile, the surface presented a harsh environment which at first only the hardiest plants could invade; but in time 200 species of plants and many animals have successfully established themselves in this seemingly desolate area that resembles the craters on the moon.

The national monument covers 53,545 acres. Many features are readily accessible by car and trail. Start at the **Visitor Center**, which contains exhibits explaining the volcanic formations, plants, animals, and history. Then take the 7-mile loop drive and side trips leading from it. Look for "bombs" scattered about the cinder slopes, curious objects formed from ejected blobs of frothy lava that hardened into globular shape while in the air.

In spring, wildflower displays are spectacular in the cinder gardens. You can see them closely on one of the several trails that range from a 20-minute walk in the formation called **Devils Orchard** to a two-hour hike to the **Tree Molds**. For the veteran explorer, who checks first with a ranger, a vast lava wilderness lies waiting in the southern section. From mid-June to Labor Day illustrated programs are presented in the campground.

The national monument campground provides water, tables, grills, restrooms, but no electrical or sewage hookups. Fee charged; no reservations. It lies 18 miles west of Arco, which provides the nearest facilities for gas or food. For further information write Superintendent, Craters of the Moon National Monument, Box 29, Arco, Idaho 83213.

CUMBERLAND ISLAND NATIONAL SEASHORE
Georgia

This national seashore, with its Spanish moss-draped forests and 18 miles of golden beach, is open to the public for day use and limited overnight camping. The island is reached via a National Park Service ferry that leaves twice a day, five days a week, from St. Marys, Georgia. Reservations are advisable for the tour boat, which holds 140 passengers. Call 912/265-1471. With the installa-tion of a 135-foot floating dock, small boaters are able to tie up at the island. The dock is located on a channel off the Intracoastal Waterway with 8 feet of water alongside (measured at low tide). Large boats are asked to anchor out to avoid taking up most of the space.

No private vehicles are allowed on the island. You are welcome to join naturalist-conducted tours covering key aspects of the island. Then strike out on your own with an official Backcountry Map to discover wonders lying along marked trails. Wear long trousers and broad-brimmed hat. Carry mosquito repellent and snakebite kit; check frequently for ticks.

Camping at the park is limited to a total of 120 persons per night. Sea Camp, accommodating 60, is the only developed camp. Four other camping areas have drinking water only. Reservations are required; specific sites are assigned and backcountry use permits issued on arrival. Campers must carry all equipment and supplies to the campsite on foot. Water and comfort facilities are available for day-use visitors, as well as campers. There is no food service on the island.

The island is the southernmost of the **Golden Isles**, which have been inhabited continuously for 10,000 years. The live oak-palmetto and longleaf slash pine forests add a rare dimension to the National Park system's plant communities, including many species heretofore not represented. Deer, raccoon, numerous birds, and nesting loggerhead turtles dwell on the island. A grant from the Andrew W. Mellon Foundation a few years ago permitted acquisition of 8,250 acres by the National Park Foundation, which then turned the land over to the National Park Service. Reservations may be made by writing or calling the superintendent, Cumberland Island National Seashore, Box 806, St. Mary's, Georgia 31558; telephone 912/882-4335.

CURECANTI NATIONAL RECREATION AREA
Colorado

In the heart of Colorado's western slope—an area of rugged high country, open mesas, and rushing mountain streams—a chain of three dams and reservoirs form the Curecanti Unit of the Colorado River Storage Project. **Blue Mesa Dam**, completed in 1965, backs up the largest body of water in Colorado, 20-mile-long Blue Mesa Lake, the major storage feature of the Curecanti Unit.

Blue Mesa is popular for camping, fishing, boating, sailing, and waterskiing. You'll find launching ramps, marinas with rental boats, equipment, and some grocery items. Three major campgrounds border the lake: Elk Creek (16 miles west of Gunnison on US 50); Lake Fork (near Blue Mesa Dam); and Stevens Creek (4 miles east of Elk Creek). Blue Mesa offers choice fishing for Kokanee salmon, and rainbow, brown, and Mackinaw trout.

Stop at **Elk Creek Visitor Center** for interpretive programs and to see the fishpond. Join summer hikes and bird walks that start here and evening campfire programs at the Campground Amphitheater.

Access for anglers and boaters to **Morrow Point Lake** is provided along the east side over the Pine Creek Trail. Even if you're just sightseeing, take advantage of the 2-hour summer boat tours on the lake, in a deep fjordlike canyon (fees are charged). A 30-passenger boat takes visitors on a two-hour, 18-mile round-trip tour. A park naturalist explains various natural features of geology, botany, and wildlife. Seats are reserved at the Elk Creek Marina or by calling 303/641-0403. At **Cimarron** (20 miles east of Montrose), a narrow-gauge railroad exhibit includes locomotive, coal tender, freight car, and caboose that once ran through the narrow canyon before it was flooded by the reservoir. Beyond the railroad exhibit there is a viewpoint that overlooks Morrow Point Dam.

The surrounding high mountain country at the Gunnison and San Isabel National Forests to the north and east and the San

Juan Mountains to the south and southwest add a greater dimension to the enjoyment of this recreation area. The **Black Canyon of the Gunnison National Monument**, to the west, is one of the scenic highlights of western Colorado. Address: Box 1040, Gunnison, Colorado 81230.

CUYAHOGA VALLEY NATIONAL RECREATION AREA
Ohio

In legislation signed by President Ford on December 27, 1974, Congress authorized this park of 32,400 acres. The early Indians had a word for this river: ka-ih-ogh-ha. It meant crooked, or twisting. Through many variations, explorers in the 18th century settled on Cuyahoga as the spelling for the winding stream which comes from the northeast, drops swiftly through a deep glacial-carved gorge, then meanders northward to its outlet at Lake Erie. Miraculously, a 20-mile stretch of the valley between heavily populated metro areas of Cleveland and Akron remains open meadows and wooded hillsides, with remnants of the Ohio and Erie Canal paralleling the river.

More than 20,000 acres are open and available as public parklands, much of it long protected by Cleveland and Akron. Make the most of your trip by starting at either **Happy Days Visitor Center**, on Ohio 303 near Peninsula, or **Canal Visitor Center**, in Valley View. The centers are open daily.

The **Virginia Kendall Unit**, operated by the park service, has a notable trail network leading to a major geological feature, the Ritchie Ledges. Other areas include Brecksville and Bedford Reservations in Cuyahoga County; and Deep Lock Quarry, Furnace Run, O'Neil Woods, and Hampton Hills in Summit County. Each park has recreation and picnic facilities and its own well-marked hiking trails. From almost the northern extremity to the south, the **Buckeye Trail** follows near the river and canal, often on the old towpath. This is the walking trail extending from Mentor Headlands on Lake Erie to Cincinnati on the Ohio River. Blue blazes mark the route.

Bird watchers, note the varying habitats that attract different species. The overgrown canal is a busy spot for waterfowl and other water birds. The Deep Lock Quarry area is particularly good for viewing warblers during migration. Pick up a bird list at Happy Days Visitor Center, two miles east of Peninsula on Ohio 303, or Canal Visitor Center in Valley View.

Rail fans, the Cuyahoga Valley Line Railroad, utilizing rolling stock of the Midwest Railway Historical Foundation, operates Saturdays June through October. The train leaves from Independence at 10:30 a.m., following the century-old valley route along the Cuyahoga River to Hale Farm, then to Quaker Square in Akron. For more information: 216/468-0797.

The area is rich in historic values. In fact, you can stay overnight at the Inn at Brandywine Falls, a bed-and-breakfast inn formerly the James Wallace Farm, adjoining two other historic properties, leased by the government under the historic property leasing program. On Oak Hill Road, the **Hale Farm and Village** complex stands as one of the outstanding restorations of the rural scene in the Middle West. The village, a venture of the Western Reserve Historical Society, typifies a crossroads of the 19th century, complete with working farm, general store, land survey office, blacksmith shop, gristmill, and homes. Other sites include Peninsula Village, with several restored buildings of the middle 1800s; Twelve Mile Lock and Fourteen Mile Lock on the Ohio and Erie Canal; the Frazee/Hynton House, built as a stagecoach stop in 1806; and Moneyshop, the lair of early counterfeiters. Address: 15610 Vaughn Road, Brecksville, Ohio 44141.

DEATH VALLEY NATIONAL MONUMENT
California-Nevada

The vast desert, covering almost two million acres, is one of the world's most colorful places, a classic area where every geologic age, and most of the periods, are to be found. It also includes the lowest point in the western hemisphere, 282 feet below sea level. Climate is ideal from November through April, when daytime temperatures are mild and only a few winter nights are below freezing. But summers are hot, with little nighttime cooling.

More than 600 different species of plants live in Death Valley, ranging from the pickleweed growing at Badwater, well below sea level, to bristlecone pines thousands of years old on Telescope Peak, above 10,000 feet. No less than 21 species of plants are endemic to the valley, while four, possibly five, species of fish also are found only here—these being relic populations of fish descended from ancestors that lived in lakes that existed in this country during the Pleistocene age. There are innumerable insects and other invertebrate animals, including many not found elsewhere. Among larger mammals, the Desert Bighorn sheep is the most spectacular; small bands make their homes in the mountains surrounding the valley. Deer are also in the higher mountains; cougars, foxes, coyotes, badgers, and other mammals are found in the valley.

Death Valley is one of the driest areas of the country; despite low average rainfall (1.76 inches per year) and high temperatures, some streams run year-round. There are springs large enough to support two large resort areas, a date grove, and an 18-hole golf course. One spring forms a lake and marsh area of more than 15 acres. In these water areas many migratory birds come through and stop for a short time—not desert birds, but Canada geese, snow geese, many kinds of ducks, egrets and other herons, ibis, and sandhill cranes; even a flamingo has been seen. The monument, with its long north-south valley, serves as a funnel for migrating birdlife during both spring and fall. Birders, in fact, will find a great array of species, from desert to mountain.

An unusual site is a 40-acre parcel of hillside, part of the national monument but separated from the main body by almost 20 miles of desert, called **Devils Hole**. The Park Service has erected a sign that reads, "In the small pool at the bottom of this limestone cavern lives the entire population of Cyprinodon diabolis, one type of desert pupfish. These fish live in what is probably the most restricted environment of any animal in the world."

Death Valley is famous in western history. Records of Indians go back thousands of years. It first gained its name as an obstacle to the '49ers in the California gold rush. Roads were built in the 1880s for "Twenty Mule Teams" hauling borax from desert mines, and later "Death Valley Scotty" constructed his celebrated castle at the northern boundary. Take a tour of a Mediterranean style hacienda (fee is charged).

Outstanding views accessible by road include **Titus Canyon**, the **Salt Pools**, **Badwater**, **Dante's View**, **Devil's Golf Course**, and **Zabriskie Point** in the rugged Black Mountains.

Many fine short and long hikes are available in all parts of the monument, but hot weather can make any hike here risky. When temperatures top 90 degrees, stay in the shade till another day. Hiking boots, plenty of water, and topographic maps are essential for all-day or overnight trips. Among the long trips, a 7-mile trail leads to the top of **Telescope Peak** from Mahogany Flat Campground, at the head of Wildrose Canyon (elevation 8,133 feet). Most hikers start in the morning, take six to eight hours to reach the summit and return. The best months for the trip are May and June and September and October. Summer is too hot at low elevations and winter is apt to be hazardous, with snow and ice at high elevations. Besides hiking, bear in mind that bicycles are available for rental at Furnace Creek.

There are accommodations at these resorts: Furnace Creek Inn and Furnace Creek Ranch, both operated by Fred Harvey, Inc. (Death Valley, California 92328; call 800/622-0838 or 619/786-2345). Also, Stovepipe Wells Village has motel-style accommodations and trailer park (Death Valley, California 92328; phone

619/786-2387). Accommodations near the park are at Beatty, Shoshone, and Trona.

Nine campgrounds are located in the monument, ranging in elevation from sea level (Furnace Creek and Texas Spring) to 7,500 feet or higher (Thornike and Mahogany Flat). Address: Death Valley, California 92328.

DELAWARE WATER GAP NATIONAL RECREATION AREA
Pennsylvania-New Jersey

The famous gap—a break in the Kittatinny Range of the Blue Ridge Mountains, threaded by the Delaware River—is a forested canyon and a real beauty spot astride the Pennsylvania-New Jersey border near Stroudsburg, Pennsylvania. Highways I-80 and US 611 now pass through the gap, but it was rather remote until recent years, for all its proximity to the eastern megalopolis. The National Recreation Area was originally conceived as part of the proposed Tocks Island dam and reservoir project. In the face of strong citizen opposition, the dam may never be built.

Points of interest are found throughout the park. Activities range from fishing, swimming, and canoeing, to hiking, hunting, and scenic driving. The area excels for bird watching, especially during spring migration before leaves are on the trees and again during fall migration. Tremendous flocks of blackbirds use the Delaware Valley on their migration route. Spring is colorful, with passing warblers and other perching birds. August marks the beginning of the migration of hawks and eagles. The best vantage points for observing the fall phenomenon are along Kittatinny Mountain.

From the overlook near the **Kittatinny Point Information Station**, between I-80 and the Delaware, you get a wonderful view of the river flowing between the rocky walls of the gap. The Appalachian Trail passes here and leads to glacial Sunfish Pond, a mountain lake atop Kittatinny Ridge on the New Jersey side. It has remained unchanged down through the time of the Indians, who came into the valley 10,000 years ago, and the time of the European settlers.

Slateford Farm, off Pennsylvania 611 near Portland, Pennsylvania, affords a unique opportunity to learn about slate quarrying. In Millbrook, 12 miles from I-80 on New Jersey's Old Mine Road, park personnel give tours and demonstrations of 19th century crafts from mid-June to Labor Day. Another 12 miles north of Millbrook, **Peters Valley Crafts Village**, near Walpack, enables visitors to take contemporary craft courses in blacksmithing, ceramics, fine metals, textiles, and wood. Studios are open daily during the summer, as are the crafts store and gallery.

Grey Towers is the family home of Gifford Pinchot—pioneer forester, conservationist, and two-time governor of Pennsylvania. On a high knoll above Milford, Pennsylvania, this unusual 41-room mansion, styled like a French chateau, overlooks the river and the Delaware Valley. The U.S. Forest Service conducts free tours.

Accommodations of wide variety are found in resort centers such as Stroudsburg, East Stroudsburg, and the Poconos. Public campgrounds are located in Worthington State Forest, Stokes State Forest, and High Point State Park, New Jersey. Old Mine Road Youth Hostel, at Hainesville, New Jersey, provides low-cost lodgings to young people and family groups. Address: Bushkill, Pennsylvania 18324.

DEVILS POSTPILE NATIONAL MONUMENT
California

In the eastern part of the Sierra Nevada, near the resort community of Mammoth Lakes and Yosemite National Park, symmetrical blue-gray columns rise as high as 60 feet, fitting closely together, a remnant of basaltic lava flow. Trails lead to the top and to the Rainbow Fall on the Middle Fork of the San Joaquin River. Situ-

ated at an elevation of 7,600 feet, the monument is open approximately July to October. Campgrounds are at the northern end and in surrounding Inyo National Forest. Address: c/o Superintendent, Sequoia-Kings Canyon National Park, Three Rivers, California 93271.

DEVILS TOWER NATIONAL MONUMENT
Wyoming

The first national monument, established in 1906, encompasses the most conspicuous landmark in northeast Wyoming, an 865-foot tower of columnar rock, the remains of a molten formation born of volcanic activity. The sides are symmetrical, almost perpendicular, while the small top, high above the Belle Fourche River, has a growth of sagebrush and grass. A prairie-dog colony is located near the monument entrance. A marked trail from the Visitor Center encircles the monument; there are nightly summer programs at the campground. The campground, accommodating both trailers and tents, makes it a good stop en route from the Black Hills of South Dakota to Yellowstone National Park, in Wyoming. Address: Devils Tower, Wyoming 82714.

DINOSAUR NATIONAL MONUMENT
Utah-Colorado

This monument contains the world's most concentrated deposit of petrified bones of dinosaurs, crocodiles, and turtles. In addition, the folded and tilted rock layers show the results of tremendous forces of earth movement; weird and fascinating contours of the land tell the story of wind and rain erosion; the deep canyons of the Green and Yampa Rivers have a haunting wilderness beauty about them. Dinosaur is a large area of 211,141 acres; the place to begin is the **Dinosaur Quarry Visitor Center**, 7 miles north of Jensen, Utah. One wall is formed by the quarry face, enabling you to watch workmen with jackhammer and chisel cutting away barren rock to expose fossil bones, more than a thousand of which are embedded here. From the **Headquarters Visitor Center** near Dinosaur, Colorado, a 31-mile paved scenic drive leads to the heart of a spectacular canyon country. At Harpers Corner, above the confluence of the Green and Yampa Rivers, you can watch the stream swirl and plunge, almost 3,000 feet below, around the base of Steamboat Rock and through Whirlpool Canyon. The area called Echo Park became the focus of nationwide attention when reclamation engineers proposed to construct a dam; the resulting controversy reached culmination in the 1950s when Congress upheld the principle of park values. Commercial river outfitters offer float trips of one to six days through the wilderness of cliff-bordered rapids. The one-day trip, designed for those with limited time, travels through Split Mountain Gorge. Longer trips originate at Gates of Lodore, on the Green River, and Deerlodge Park, on the Yampa. Campgrounds are at Split Mountain, Green River, and Echo Park. Visit the Field Museum (open till 9 p.m. in summer) inspired by the late Arthur Nord as a great showcase of "Dinosaurland." Address: Box 210, Dinosaur, Colorado 81610.

EL MALPAIS NATIONAL MONUMENT
New Mexico

Established by Congress early in 1988, El Malpais lies 75 miles west of Albuquerque and south of the city of Grants. It protects nationally significant lava flows, volcanic craters, lava tubes, and cultural resources like the Las Ventanas Culture Archaeological Protection Site adjacent to I-40 and along the west side of NM Route 117. El Malpais (Spanish for "badlands"), once a land of fire, is a land of unusual striking beauty—especially when scarlet blooms of cactus dot the black lava. The legislation provides for two special management units, the 114,000-acre national monument, administered by the National Park Service, and 262,000-

acre conservation area, a protective buffer zone administered by the Bureau of Land Management. It also includes ancient sites sacred to native Americans of Acoma pueblo, which the federal agencies have pledged to protect. Two Visitor Centers are being established; one at Grants next to I-40, and the other near Bandera, on NM Route 53, on the northern edge of El Malpais. The New Mexico Welcome Center at Gallup will be helpful. Address: Box 939, Grants, New Mexico 87020.

FIRE ISLAND NATIONAL SEASHORE
New York
Located within 60 miles of Manhattan, this national seashore protects the largest remaining barrier beach off the south shore of Long Island, extending 32 miles, with a changing tableau of high thickets and forests, salt marshes, grassy wetlands, and rolling swales.

Fishing and wildlife watching. On the ocean side, along the Great South Beach, you can catch striped bass, bluefish, mackerel, weakfish, and fluke; in the shallow bay, bluefish, fluke, winter flounder, and blowfish. From October to March, the sheltered waters are alive with waterfowl. Small populations of ducks and geese remain to breed. Night herons nest in the bayside forests. Deer are best seen along the eastern portion of the national seashore. **Swimming** at protected beaches is available at the Watch Hill recreational site and at Sailor's Haven. Visitor Centers are located at both areas. Nature walks and illustrated talks are given during the summer seasons. You also will find a network of foot and bicycle **trails**—a relief from motorways. One of the highlights of any visit is a walk through the Sunken Forest, adjacent to Sailor's Haven, a secluded woodland with gnarled American holly, sassafras, black gun, and serviceberry. The extensive tidal marshes of East Fire Island provide some of the seashore's best waterfowl habitats and excellent sites for birdwatching. Migrating hawks reach their peak in late September and early October. Limited camping, by reservation only (telephone: 516/377-6455).

Most of the national seashore is roadless. You can reach the island near its eastern end by driving over William Floyd Parkway and Smith Point Bridge to Smith Point County Park. Ferry lines operate from Bayshore, Sayville, and Patchogue to the island. Address: 120 Laurel Street, Patchogue, Long Island, New York 11772.

FLORISSANT FOSSIL BEDS NATIONAL MONUMENT
Colorado
The area contains geologic remains of some 35 million years ago. Within the ancient mudflows are sequoia stumps as large as 14 feet in diameter and 12 feet tall, and well-preserved insect and leaf fossils. These beds have been the subject of scientific study since their discovery, in 1874. A museum containing about 500 specimens is open daily, and there is a nature walk to the petrified sequoia stumps. Address: Box 185, Florissant, Colorado 80816.

FOSSIL BUTTE NATIONAL MONUMENT
Wyoming
Fish that were swimming in western Wyoming waters 50 million years ago are visible in fossil form in this 8,178-acre area set aside by Congress in 1972. Fossil Butte contains some of the world's best known and most significant aquatic fossils of the Eocene epoch. Fossilized freshwater life is rare. "No other fossil-bearing formation in North America," says paleontologist Curtis Julian Hesse, "has produced so many and such characteristic fossils as this great series of lakebeds." Perch, paddlefish, garpike, stingray, and herring which once piled the waters of Fossil Butte are preserved here by the thousands. In no other National Park system area is this important chapter in the history of life represented. The monument also contains outstanding examples of lake, shoreline, and tributary river floodplain deposits. The fine-

bedded layers of the Green River formation make up much of the rugged landscape. The richest fossil deposits are in limestone layers three feet thick and 30 to 300 feet below the butte surface. Plant remains—from fossil palm and fern leaves to pollen—are also numerous. Address: Box 527, Kemmerer, Wyoming 83101.

GATEWAY NATIONAL RECREATION AREA
New York-New Jersey
The 26,000 acres of this area surrounding New York Harbor are divided into four units—**Sandy Hook**, on the New Jersey shore; **Staten Island**, across New York Harbor from Manhattan; **Breezy Point**, on the Rockaway Peninsula in Brooklyn; and **Jamaica Bay**, also in Brooklyn. The Jamaica Bay unit contains a 6,000-acre wildlife refuge, one of the few reserves of its kind accessible by subway and bus. The refuge's white poplars, blooming bayberries, extensive saltwater marsh, and calm waters protect more than 200 species of birds and small animals. Dotting the periphery of the bay are recreational areas—Canarsie Pier; Frank Charles Memorial Park; and Floyd Bennett Field.

Exciting times at Jamaica Bay are spring nesting season and fall migration, when thousands of ducks and geese on the Atlantic flyway stop over on the refuge ponds. Other choice birdwatching areas are Sandy Hook (where the near extinct population of osprey shows signs of coming back), Breezy Point on the Rockaway Peninsula, and Great Kills Park on Staten Island.

Fort Tilden, a major defense unit during World War I (with the largest guns protecting New York harbor), is located in the Breezy Point unit. Park rangers lead visitors on explorations of the site and along bays and beaches with fascinating marine life. A short drive from Fort Tilden is Floyd Bennett Field, New York's first important airport. Amelia Earhart, "Wrong Way" Corrigan, and Wiley Post began their adventures here. Now it is the headquarters of the recreation area and of **Ecology Village**, where thousands of young people camp out and learn about nature.

Sandy Hook, long a military area containing old Fort Hancock, has 7 miles of beach ideal for swimming, surfing, and surf fishing. **Sandy Hook lighthouse**, constructed in 1764 to guide merchant ships into New York harbor, is the oldest lighthouse in the country. Address: Floyd Bennett Field, Building 69, Brooklyn, New York 11234.

GAULEY RIVER NATIONAL RECREATION AREA.
See New River Gorge National River, page 219.

GLEN CANYON NATIONAL RECREATION AREA
Arizona-Utah
This is more than a water playground astride the desert boundary of Arizona and Utah; it is an immense 1,200,000 acres, superlative in beauty. Lake Powell, formed behind Glen Canyon Dam, extends 186 miles, with 1,900 miles of shoreline, including vividly colored fjordlike side canyons.

Glen Canyon Dam, a major engineering achievement built across the Colorado River by the Bureau of Reclamation, rises 710 feet above the riverbed. The graceful **Glen Canyon Steel Arch Bridge**, even higher, supports US 89 as a link between Flagstaff (and the South Rim of the Grand Canyon) and Kanab, southern gateway to Utah's national parks. Adjacent to the dam are many scenic viewpoints, an impressive lakeshore drive and the extensive development at **Wahweap**. Here the National Park Service provides complete camping facilities, concession-operated Wahweap Lodge, and a large marina, offering boat rentals and guided boat tours of the lake. One outstanding destination by water (an all-day tour) is **Rainbow Bridge National Monument**, containing the largest known natural stone arch. Another is Hole-in-the-Rock, the famous and seemingly impossible crossing of the Colorado River used by Mormons in 1879-80. A party of 236 men, women, and children drove several hundred cows, sheep, and 80 wagons to Hole-in-the-Rock, then blasted a gap in the slim, impassable crevice that blocked their path. They lowered the wagons by rope, built a boat on the shore, and crossed the river to what is now called Register Rock. Facilities are also available at **Hite Crossing**, **Halls Crossing**, and **Bullfrog Basin**—good road access to Bullfrog is now available on Utah 95 and Utah 276. The Bullfrog Resort and Marina features a lodge with commanding view, housekeeping units, RV facilities, rental houseboats, and power boats. For reservations, call Del Webb Recreational Properties, Phoenix, 800/528-6154. A ferry, the *John A. Burr*, operates between Bullfrog Basin and Halls Crossing, a 20-minute trip covering 3.1 miles. The distance by road between Bullfrog Basin and Halls Crossing is 130 miles. A boat ride on the river above Lees Ferry is a delightful cruise between towering, rust-colored sandstone walls. The twisting channel, now flowing with cold crystal-clear water, is a trout fisherman's paradise. Access to this area, about 55 miles by road from Wahweap, is from US 89A at Marble Canyon, Arizona.

Fishing for bass rates with the best in the West. Lake Powell is currently undergoing the period of a "blossoming" new reservoir when fish population multiplies. In addition, warm weather of late spring and early fall combines with hot summer weather to produce a long growing period. Choice fishing occurs on the Escalante and San Juan Rivers from late September through October, when fish migrate into canyons and coves in search of shallower layers of water.

Boating and swimming can be enjoyed even in the hottest weather, but anyone in an open boat needs protection from the sun. Between mid-June and early September days are hot, and physical activity for most people is limited, (Temperatures at Wahweap sometimes reach 106 degrees.) Nevertheless, hiking or walking in the early morning or twilight hours can be delightful. Many interesting plants can be studied, including several species of cactus and bayonet-tipped yuccas. Because most desert animals are nocturnal travelers and feeders, footprints and tracks become as intriguing as the sight of animals themselves. Look for rounded pad marks of bobcat, doglike tracks of coyote, sharp-pointed tracks of mule deer at drinking places.

Indian ruins dot the lakeshore in several places to attract the attention of hiker, explorer, and photographer. Two of the most interesting are located in **Iceberg Canyon** and off the **Escalante River**. These dwellings, remnants of the Anasazi people, are protected from the elements by huge cliff overhangs which prevent all but the most direct wind and rain from reaching the ruins. Address: Box 1507, Page, Arizona 86040.

GOLDEN GATE NATIONAL RECREATION AREA
California
Golden Gate and Gateway National Recreation Areas were brought into the National Park System at the same time in 1972. "Gateway West" embraces the 26,000-acre scenic coastline north and south of San Francisco's Golden Gate Bridge. The area extends from Tomales Bay in Marin County southward, paralleling Point Reyes National Seashore, to Bolinas Lagoon, and then approximately 22 miles along the Pacific Ocean to the north end of the Golden Gate Bridge. To the south and across the bridge, it extends from the **National Maritime Museum's Historic Ships**, adjacent to Fisherman's Wharf on the east, to Fort Point on the west and then from Fort Point westward and southward along the Pacific Ocean about 9 miles, including **Fort Funston**. **Sweeney Ridge**, a rugged crest in Pacifica, south of San Francisco, surrounds the site where, in 1796, Spanish explorer Caspar de Portola first saw San Francisco Bay. Don't miss the magnificent panoramic views from the summit. Then there is **Alcatraz Island**, visited by almost a million people a year. Alcatraz rangers, known

as "Alcatroopers," will help you make the most of your time. See the slide show first, then take your choice of cellhouse walks, military history walks, natural history walks, and programs on the cellhouse and correctional officer lives.

People are free to hike, bike, fish, and wade, and many do. For the loop trail at Land's End, park your car at the Palace of the Legion of Honor Museum. The trail is excellent for bird watching, for viewing Miles Rock Lighthouse and the last remains of old shipwrecks along the shore. The 3½-mile stretch between Fort Point, under the bridge, and Aquatic Park, near Fisherman's Wharf, undoubtedly is one of the finest promenades in the country. Tie in visits to Fort Mason, the Maritime Museum, and Historic Ships at Hyde Street, which recall the classic age of sail, as well as to Ghirardelli Square and the Cannery. Plan to lunch at Fisherman's Wharf. Then you'll be set for the ferry, which leaves every 45 minutes (9 to 5) from Pier 41, for a worthwhile guided tour of Alcatraz Island, "the Rock," revealing gloomy cell blocks and ruined fortifications of an earlier day. The trip takes two hours. Reservations are available through Ticketron.

The national recreation area is the site of the Western Regional Folklife Festival, the last weekend in September. Musicians, dancers, and craftsmen perform at Fort Mason's Great Meadow. **Fort Mason Center**, next to Marina Green, is a year-round cultural center, with everything from guitar recitals to Irish country dancing and kung-fu lessons. Here you can have a meal of natural foods at the Zen Center restaurant, Greens, or at Cooks and Company.

Golden Gate Youth Hostel is 4 miles from the north end of Golden Gate Bridge. It provides handy access to facilities of the national recreation area. The San Francisco Hostel at Fort Mason is even more centrally located.

Included within the Golden Gate National Recreation Area are **Fort Point National Historic Site** and **Muir Woods National Monument**, administered as separate entities of the National Park System and managed to complement the interpretive themes and recreational opportunities of the total recreation area. The numerous coastal fortifications throughout the recreation area offer an opportunity to relate the history of coastal defense from 1776, when the Presidio was established, to recent defensive missile installations in the Marin Headlands. Sixty miles of trail in the Marin County unit provide excellent opportunities for hiking and riding. For further information call the headquarters, at 415/556-0560. Address: Building 201, Fort Mason, San Francisco, California 94123.

GREAT SAND DUNES NATIONAL MONUMENT
Colorado
Deposited over thousands of years by southwesterly winds, towering sand dunes rise to heights of over 600 feet on the western slope of the lofty Sangre de Cristo Mountains, 36 miles from Alamosa. Medano Creek flows from the mountains and disappears at the edge of the dunes. There is a campground, and you can obtain supplies 4 miles south or at Alamosa (36 miles). Summer days dawn clear and calm, but best hiking is early and late, since midday sand temperature can reach 140 degrees. A round-trip walk from the picnic area takes about three hours. Keep a sharp eye for interesting hardy plants and small mammals that have adapted to this environment. Address: Mosca, Colorado 81146.

GULF ISLANDS NATIONAL SEASHORE
Florida-Mississippi
President Nixon signed the bill creating the eighth national seashore on January 8, 1971, at a critical time when coastal islands and their marshes were falling more rapidly than any other land

type before the bulldozers of "progress." The seashore includes a series of history-rich offshore islands and keys stretching 150 miles from Gulfport, Mississippi, to Destin, Florida. The outstanding recreation resources consist of 52 miles of sparkling white sand beaches, developed primitive camping areas, and facilities for fishing, swimming, and birdwatching.

The national seashore covers 137,598 acres—79,884 in Mississippi and 66,714 in Florida. In the **Mississippi section**, Ship Island, the key island in the barrier chain, was held at various times by France, Britain, Spain, and the Confederacy. It was later used as a prison for captured Confederate soldiers, and old **Fort Massachusetts** still stands in remarkably good condition. Until Gulfport's harbor was completed, in 1902, the harbor at Ship Island was filled for years with 20 to 30 ships at a time, loading southern lumber for export to all parts of the world, a process requiring four to eight weeks a ship. The old ocean-going supply ships have been replaced with fishing boats that anchor there today. Daily excursions (April to October) are available aboard the *Pan American*, *Island Clipper*, and *Pan American Clipper* from Biloxi and Gulfport. The trip covers 14 miles; snack bars operate on the boats. Lower decks are enclosed, but passengers usually ride on the sun deck above. On arrival, there are ranger-led tours of the

fort, which was built when Jefferson Davis was U.S. Secretary of War. There are beaches and surf for swimmers and tables for picnickers. Lifeguards are on duty June to September.

On the mainland, Davis Bayou offers nature trails, picnic area, and campground at 3500 Park Road, outside Ocean Springs, Mississippi.

The other two Mississippi islands, Horn and Petit Bois, comprise the **Gulf Islands Wilderness**. Their brackish inland ponds, lagoons, and marshes provide ideal habitat for wintering migratory waterfowl and nesting places for permanently residing shore birds. Horn Island is believed to support the largest nesting population of ospreys on the Gulf Coast, as well as a sizable population of alligators and ocean turtles. With its many different habitats, Horn Island supports a variety of wildlife, including nutria, rabbits, raccoons, and various snakes. Wild plants and flowers grow in and around the dune.

Attention, birdwatchers. More than 250 species have been identified in the dunes, marshes, woodland, and open beaches of the Florida section. Large numbers of birds congregate during spring and fall migrations. From late September through October migratory flights of hawks can be seen moving westward across Gulf Breeze Peninsula. Look for bald eagles, successfully reintroduced, flying over the barrier islands after an absence of more than 40 years.

The **Florida section** of the seashore embraces portions of Santa Rosa Island, part of Perdido Key, the old Naval Live Oaks Reservation and the historic forts and lighthouse located at the Pensacola Naval Air Station. History and military buffs will find this section especially appealing. Santa Rosa offers **Fort Pickens**, on which construction was begun in 1829, as well as coastal defense structures of later periods up to World War II. The Live Oaks Reservation was set aside in 1828 to assure the Navy of timber for its sailing vessels—probably the first federal conservation measure. Pensacola's forts include Battery San Antonio, built by the Spanish, and two later American additions, Fort Barrancas and Advanced Redoubt of Fort Barrancas. Campgrounds, picnic areas, and lifeguarded beaches are available at the Fort Pickens area. Beach facilities are available at Perdido Key, Santa Rosa, and Okaloosa areas. Address: Box 100, Gulf Breeze, Florida 32561 or 3500 Park Road, Ocean Springs, Mississippi 39564.

HAGERMAN FOSSIL BEDS NATIONAL MONUMENT
Idaho

For hundreds of miles, the Snake River winds through deep gorges and broad plains of southern Idaho. In the Hagerman Valley, near the town of Hagerman, southeast of Boise, between Mountain Home and Twin Falls, a canyon wall alongside the river reveals the remains of animals and plants of 3½ million years ago, the Pliocene period. These are considered among the largest and best preserved sites of their kind in the world.

The 4,394-acre national monument was established in 1988 to protect 310 registered paleontological sites. Most of the land involved was formerly administered by the Bureau of Land Management. The fossil beds are along a spectacular bluff on the west side of the Snake River. Birdlife of the Hagerman Valley includes golden eagles, songbirds, and waterfowl. Monument displays in due course will interpret species now largely extinct—zebra-like horses, saber-toothed cats, mastodons, and smaller animals—living in the ancient ecosystem of an aquatic lake or marshland. Address: 2647 Kimberley Road East, Twin Falls, Idaho 83301.

ICE AGE NATIONAL SCIENTIFIC RESERVE
Wisconsin

Nowhere in the United States is the effect of glacial action more evident or more impressive than in Wisconsin. This scientific reserve, administered by the state of Wisconsin with development assistance from the National Park Service, is designed to consist of nine units preserving landforms shaped by the last great glacial period. These are being joined by the new **Ice Age National Scenic Trail**. The trail traverses land administered by different public and private interests. Look for Ice Age Trail markers and interpretive displays.

Key units of the reserve include: **Kettle Moraine State Forest**, 50 miles north of Milwaukee, famed for the abundant kettles, formed by the melting of buried blocks of ice, and conical hills called moulin kames. The Kettle Moraine Scenic Highway provides access, and the Glacial Hiking Trail a close-up of significant and unusual features. **Horicon Marsh Wildlife Refuge**, west of Kettle Moraine via Route 28, the Wild Goose Parkway, features an extinct glacial lake and choice wildlife observation. **Devils Lake State Park**, less than 50 miles north of Madison (3 miles from Baraboo), lies in the heart of glacial action that shifted the flow of the Wisconsin River. Guided naturalist hikes focus on geology, birdwatching, plants, and flowers (including remnant species of preglacial days). At **Mill Bluff**, hiking trails wind among towering rocky buttes, affording choice views of the ancient lake bed and driftless area. **Interstate**, the westernmost unit, has ancient lava flows and the gorge of the St. Croix River, once a main glacial

drainage. Address: Department of Natural Resources, Division of Tourism and Information, Box 450, Madison, Wisconsin 53701.

INDIANA DUNES NATIONAL LAKESHORE
Indiana

Along the southern shore of Lake Michigan, between Gary and Michigan City, the clean sandy beaches backed by huge sand dunes have long attracted interest. "The Dunes," Carl Sandburg wrote, "are to the Midwest what the Grand Canyon is to Arizona and Yosemite is to California. They constitute a signature of time and eternity." A national park was proposed here as early as 1916. Authorized 50 years later, through the untiring efforts of the Save the Dunes Council and Senator Paul Douglas of Illinois, the unit preserves remaining dunes, bogs, and marshes and provides recreational opportunities. The national lakeshore was enlarged in 1976 and in 1980. Facilities at **Indiana Dunes State Park** include camping, picnicking, swimming, bathhouse, pavilion, and naturalist tours. Cowles Bog, immediately south of Dune Acres, and Pinhook Bog, six miles south of Michigan City, are of special interest for their variety of plants and animals. This habitat includes the northern range of many birds and plants as well as bogs representative of cooler climates. It provides resting, nesting, or wintering areas for at least 223 species of birds. Miller Woods, a composition of open beach, dunes, and oak forest, provides an ideal setting for the Paul H. Douglas Center for Environmental Education. Other major visitor attractions include West Beach, with a bathhouse and a parking area, the Chellberg Farm, and the restored **Bailly Homestead**, built by a French-Canadian trader who settled near the Calumet River in 1822. Park open all year. Address: 1100 N. Mineral Springs Road, Porter, Indiana 46304.

JEWEL CAVE NATIONAL MONUMENT
South Dakota

This beautiful cave in the Black Hills, 14 miles west of Custer, is particularly noted for its lining of sparkling calcite crystal. In the 1960s and early 1970s, a local couple, Herbert and Jan Conn, explored over 60 miles of passage, a bewildering maze that made Jewel Cave the fourth longest explored cave in the world. Many spectacular cave formations were discovered, including several of a type found in Jewel Cave and nowhere else. In some locations cementations of quartz and calcite—called scintillite—cover walls or floors with deep red encrustation of sparkling jewels. At other locations, hoary gypsum "beards" grow over a foot long from limestone walls, fragile beauty swaying in the cave breeze. Tours of varying lengths are conducted May 1 to September 30, with tickets sold on a first-come, first-served basis. A guide fee is charged. Cave tours are strenuous, not recommended for those with heart or respiratory ailments. Cave temperature is 47 degrees Fahrenheit, so dress accordingly. Visitor Center open all year. Address: Box 351, Custer, South Dakota 57730.

JOHN DAY FOSSIL BEDS NATIONAL MONUMENT
Oregon

At three sites in north central Oregon, both plant and animal fossils reveal a classic panorama of earth history. The Clarno Unit in Wheeler County preserves evidence of subtropical growth. The Painted Hills Unit, near Mitchell, has volcanic ash deposits with leaf remnants of a temperate hardwood forest. At Sheep Rock, near Dayville, fossils show progressively drier and more seasonal climates. Along the trails you'll find unusual exhibits depicting the region as it was 28 to 35 million years ago. Stop at the Cant Ranch bunkhouse, now housing the fascinating Fossil and Fossil Hunters Exhibit. Picnic areas are in all three units. Address: 420 West Main Street, John Day, Oregon 97845.

JOHN D. ROCKEFELLER, JR. MEMORIAL PARKWAY
Wyoming

Named in honor of the philanthropist whose gifts of land and money were instrumental in establishment of several national parks, the parkway extends the full length of Grand Teton National Park to West Thumb in Yellowstone National Park, a distance of 82 miles. It includes a 23,777-acre section between the two parks now administered as a recreation area. Camping facilities are provided at the Snake River campground and at the concession-operated facilities at Flagg Ranch. Address: c/o Grand Teton National Park, Drawer 170, Moose, Wyoming 83012.

JOSHUA TREE NATIONAL MONUMENT
California

A choice parcel of the steadily diminishing Southern California desert, the monument abounds in varieties of flora growing among striking granite formations, and provides refuge to desert wildlife, including bighorn sheep, bobcat, badger, and coyote.

The Joshua tree, *Yucca brevifolia*, is found only in the arid lands of California, western Arizona, Nevada, and southern Utah. Varying in height from 10 to 40 feet, with densely clustered, sharp-pointed leaves, the long greenish-white blossoms of the tree are at their best from March through May. Nearly 40 percent of all visitors come during these three months. The Jumbo Rocks and Hidden Valley areas offer exceptional scenery. From **Key View Point**, you can look down over the panoramic Coachella Valley, including Indio, Palm Springs, and the Salton Sea. This is a large area, covering more than half a million acres. Stop at the **Visitor Center** at Twentynine Palms, and chart your course from here into the northern and western sections, where you'll find the largest stands of Joshua trees and the rock formations of monzonite. Ask about the guided spring walks; evening campfires; Sunday morning campfire coffees; and guided car-caravan tours to Desert Queen Ranch (also called Keys Ranch), a fascinating little-known landmark. Be sure to bring your binoculars to view desert birds. In fact, landlocked Salton Sea, southwest of the monument, is a must for birders; it provides some of the most

Joshua Tree National Monument

unusual bird records in Southern California, including a wide assortment of sea birds at various times of the year. The monument is quite cold from late December to early April. Campgrounds are located in the area; accommodations are plentiful in the nearby communities. Address; 74485 National Monument Drive, Twentynine Palms, California 92277.

LAKE CHELAN NATIONAL RECREATION AREA. See North Cascades National Park, page 113.

LAKE MEAD NATIONAL RECREATION AREA
Arizona-Nevada
Nearly 1,500,000 rugged acres of far-reaching tawny deserts, deep canyons, and lofty plateaus spread across Arizona and Nevada from Grand Canyon National Park almost to the edge of lively Las Vegas and southward past Davis Dam. Within these boundaries, Lake Mead and Lake Mohave, vast reservoirs, provide water sports centers in the midst of cactus country.

Boulder City, Nevada, the main gateway, was established in the early 1930s to house personnel building Hoover Dam, eight miles away. In some ways it still looks like the town of that day. There are no highrises, no gambling. The restored Boulder Dam Hotel, opened in 1932, is the only hotel in town. (Overnighters will find a dozen motels.) The Alan Bible Visitor Center, located midway between town and dam at 601 Nevada Highway, is information headquarters for the national recreation area.

Hoover Dam spans the Colorado River, its crescent top serving as a highway. You can park at either side and join a tour of the power plant in the heart of the dam, descending by elevator 528 feet—the equivalent of a 44-story building. The power plant alone, with its turbines and generators, equals the height of a 20-story building. Nearby Boulder Beach is the most developed of six main recreation centers around **Lake Mead's** 550-mile shoreline. It has a modern lodge, marina, and swimming pool. One-hour boat trips operate daily to Hoover Dam, the colorful Paint Pots and Fortification Hill. Boulder Beach has a swimming beach; all centers have launching ramps, camping facilities, boat rentals, lodgings, restaurants, and trailer courts; Las Vegas Wash, however, does not have lodgings. Evening illustrated programs about the area are presented seasonally at Boulder Beach.

The most developed of three recreation areas on **Lake Mohave**, a long, narrow lake extending 67 miles south from Hoover Dam, is at Katherine, near Davis Dam (35 miles west of Kingman, Arizona). Naturalist programs are given in an amphitheater here, too. Fishing is popular on both lakes all year—rainbow trout and bass are the chief catches in Lake Mohave; bass, striped bass, crappie, and catfish in Lake Mead.

Although water is the focal point for outdoor sports, the region is rich in natural, historical, and archaeological resources which should not be overlooked. About 60 species of mammals have been identified, including wild burros along the lakeshores, desert bighorn, coyotes, cougars, and bobcats. Over 200 miles of secondary road lead into the backcountry, where fossilized bones of mammoths, camels, ground sloths, and giant beavers in soft silt of ancient lake basins are part of the patterns of geology. Two roads are of special interest. One leads from Las Vegas to Callville Bay, Echo Bay, and Overton Beach, on the north shore of Lake Mead, with access to **Valley of Fire State Park**, a fantastic desert area with ancient petroglyphs left by primitive Americans amid brilliant sandstone formations. The other cuts across the desert from US 93 along the Grand Wash Cliffs and through a forest of Joshua trees to Pearce Ferry, at the western edge of the Grand Canyon. Pick up a copy of *Flowering Plants of the Lake Mead Region*, or some other good guidebook, so you can learn to identify the many species growing here and to appreciate the

marvel of natural survival and beauty in a tough environment. Address: 601 Nevada Highway, Boulder City, Nevada 89005.

LAKE MEREDITH NATIONAL RECREATION AREA
Texas
This scenic lake, surrounded by grasslands and steep canyons, answered a long-felt need in the High Plains of the Texas Panhandle near Amarillo. It was created behind **Sanford Dam**, the principal structure in the Canadian River reclamation project, and is bordered by seven developed areas providing boating, fishing, picnicking, semi-improved and primitive campsites, and access to hunting. Fish include bass, crappie, walleye, and catfish. Among the animals and birds of the Canadian River country are deer, pronghorn, coyotes, turkeys, and quail, with throngs of ducks and geese. The uplands vegetation typifies the High Plains, with mixed grasses, mesquite, and yucca, while bottomland trees include cottonwoods, hackberries, and salt cedar (or tamarisk). On the south side of the lake, the Alibates Flint Quarries National Monument contains quarries used by prehistoric man 12,000 years ago. Address: Box 1438, Fritch, Texas 79036.

LAVA BEDS NATIONAL MONUMENT
California
Great cinder cones, deep chasms, and more than 200 caves spreading across rugged terrain below the Oregon border, midway between Crater Lake and Lassen Volcanic National Parks, are the products of a shield volcano which has spewed masses of molten lava for a million years. The monument is pleasantly uncrowded. Interpretive programs are offered Memorial Day through Labor Day when conducted walks and talks are regularly scheduled along with evening programs on caves, volcanos, and more. Rangers encourage a "do it yourself" approach to exploration of the caves. They hand you a flashlight and a map and wish you well. Some caves of the 46,239-acre monument, like Merrill Cave, contain permanent ice. In contrast, some caves are carpeted by ferns and mosses, while others bear Indian pictographs on their walls. In a detached northeast section, petroglyphs are carved on the bluffs near Tule Lake, where the national wildlife refuge attracts throngs of ducks, geese, and other birds during spring and fall migration. The lava beds served as principal theater of the Modoc Indian War of 1872-73, when the Indians entrenched themselves in the natural lava fortifications. Campgrounds near park headquarters; lodgings at Tulelake and in Klamath Falls and Merrill, Oregon. Address: Box 867, Tulelake, California 96134.

LOWER ST. CROIX NATIONAL SCENIC RIVERWAY. See St. Croix National Scenic Riverway, page 222.

MISSISSIPPI NATIONAL RIVER AND RECREATION AREA
Minnesota
Eighty miles of the Mississippi River and about 50,000 acres of shoreline in the Twin Cities metropolitan area were designated by Congress in 1988 for addition to the National Park System. A commission was established to prepare within three years a coordinated federal/state/local plan for managing the corridor, which extends from the mouth of the Crow River at Dayton downstream past Minneapolis and St. Paul to the mouth of the St. Croix River near Hastings. Address: c/o Midwest Region, National Park Service, 1709 Jackson Street, Omaha, Nebraska 68102-2571.

MUIR WOODS NATIONAL MONUMENT
California
In a mountain valley just north of San Francisco, at the foot of Mount Tamalpais, the cathedral-like grove of redwoods was

given in 1908 by Congressman William Kent and his wife, in honor of John Muir.

The area covers less than one square mile near San Francisco along a beautiful forested canyon, where redwoods grow in full splendor. The main trail winds among these giant trees, interspersed with other trees of the western forest—Douglas fir, bigleaf maple, California buckeye, tanbark oak, and madrona. The last named is a beautiful broadleaf evergreen related to eastern rhododendron; its bright orange-colored bark and shiny leaves make it seem, as John Muir wrote, "like some lost wanderer from the magnolia groves in the South." Listen closely along the trails bordering Redwood Creek to hear when the water is full or at low ebb, and also when it's dusk and time to leave (from the sound of the great horned owl, of course). The 553-acre monument is reached easily from San Francisco via the Golden Gate Bridge by car or tour bus. Neither picnicking nor camping is permitted in Muir Woods, but there is a campground in adjacent Mount Tamalpais State Park which is a treat in its own right. The canyons and coastal mountains comprise fabulous hiking country. Loops of almost any length are possible. Climb the ridge crest on the Dipsea Trail overlooking the Pacific, perhaps going all the way to Stinson Beach. Weather is often cool or wet, so carry a jacket. Address: Mill Valley, California 94941.

NATCHEZ TRACE PARKWAY
Tennessee-Alabama-Mississippi

The parkway commemorates the storied Indian and pioneer trail between Nashville and Natchez called the Natchez Trace. Along the roadside, the forest, meadows, and fields present a continually changing landscape, with many flowering plants and lush semitropical vegetation. The route is pleasantly free of commercialism. When complete, it will cover 449 miles through the three states. More than 300 miles are finished and open.

A number of recreation areas and vestiges of the old trace lend interest to the trip. In middle **Tennessee**, near Hohenwald, **Meriwether Lewis Site** marks the spot where the great trailblazer died. Nearby **Metal Ford** and **Napier Mine** offer a look at iron mining and smelting of the early 1800s, when the trace was the most heavily traveled road in the Old Southwest, linking the Union with the remote lower Mississippi Valley.

In **Alabama**, **Colbert Park**, at Pickwick Lake, provides water-oriented activities including swimming, boating, fishing, and waterskiing. The lake is administered by the Tennessee Valley Authority and formed by Pickwick Landing Dam in Tennessee.

In **Mississippi**, stop at the **Visitor Center** at park headquarters north of Tupelo to see the film and exhibits that explain how the ancient trail evolved into a post road and highway. Beginning about 1785, farmers from as far up as the Ohio River floated crops down to Natchez or New Orleans, then hiked homeward along the Trace. It was used by boatmen, bandits, settlers, and soldiers until the steamboat and better-roads era of the 1830s. Markers, trails, and exhibits like those at **Chickasaw Village** and **Bynum Mounds** remind you that this was the land of the Choctaw, Chickasaw, and prehistoric Indians. **Emerald Mound**, an ancient ceremonial earthwork covering eight acres, is among features on the southernmost section leading past Port Gibson to Natchez. Here **Mount Locust** has been restored to its 1820 appearance when it served as one of 50 inns like it along the Old Trace. Crafts and lifestyles of the early 1800s are demonstrated in February and March.

Natchez Trace Historical Park was authorized by Congress in 1988 to preserve and interpret the historic sites of this once powerful and wealthy center of the Cotton Belt. Federal facilities are not yet developed, but Natchez already does much to safeguard and show structures of the plantation period.

Seasons and Accommodations. In spring nature trails are at their best in areas like the Tupelo-Bald Cypress Swamp. Camellias and azaleas bloom in March in parkway communities like Natchez and Vicksburg, where semiannual garden pilgrimages are held. Fall foliage provides the background for the annual two-day Meriweather Lewis Country Fair and Arts Festival near **Hohenwald**, Tennessee, in mid-October. An interesting campground is located on the trace at **Jeff Busby**, a high wooded area near French Camp, Mississippi. Another splendid campground is located at **Rocky Springs**, northeast of Port Gibson. A third campground is located at the **Meriwether Lewis Site** in Tennessee. All operate on a first-come, first-served basis. Address: Route 1, NT 143, Tupelo, Mississippi 38801.

NATIONAL PARK OF AMERICAN SAMOA
American Samoa

This new unit (established by Congress in 1988) on an island trust territory in the South Pacific is not a national park in the usual sense. For one thing, the land involved is not and will not be federally owned. For another, it's comparatively small—only 8,500 acres. But these factors do not deny its significance. The primary feature consists of two undisturbed tropical rain forests (2,800 acres above Pago Pago harbor on the island of Tutuila and 5,400 acres on the nearby island of Ta'u), especially choice at a time when rain forests are being lost the world over. The Samoan rain forests comprise five distinct plant communities with hundreds of different plant species—plus two species of native flying foxes, striking animals with wing spans of up to four feet.

The park also includes beautiful coral beaches, coves, reefs, and islets alive with seabird colonies. Because of Samoan traditions of communal land ownership, park legislation provides for long-term leasing from local villages. Visiting American Samoa National Park will be easier when these agreements are completed. But anyone with patience and respect for Samoan courtesies can enjoy a visit now. The three units of the park are as follows. **Tutuila**, the most accessible, with good examples of the park landscape seen on the paved road from Pago Pago to the village of Vatia. Tutuila has some hotels, restaurants, and rental cars. **Ta'u**, remote and pristine, reached by a 40-minute flight from Tutuila, followed by travel on a dirt road to the village of Fitiuta, and hike along the sea. A small motel has opened at Fitiuta, but rental cars and restaurants don't exist. Plan on patience to hire a guide and arrange a place to stay. **Ofu**, a small unit, mostly beach and reef, is also reached by plane. The park is easily accessible on foot (with permission) from the airstrip. A small motel is located next to the strip. Address: Pacific Area Office, National Park Service, Box 50165, Honolulu, Hawaii 96850.

NATURAL BRIDGES NATIONAL MONUMENT
Utah

In a land of brilliantly colored cliffs, tortuous box canyons, sandstone pinnacles, and arches, the three major natural bridges of this monument are outstanding for both their proportions and height. The largest, Sipapu, rises 220 feet above the stream bed, with a span of 268 feet and width of 31 feet. Owachomo, representing the oldest stage of bridge formation, is only 9 feet thick and has a span of 180 feet. Anasazi Indian people lived in the area some 800 years ago. Facilities have been improved, including an 8-mile paved loop road with viewpoints for the major bridges, a Visitor Center, campground-picnic area, and a museum with historical and geological exhibits. The monument's solar power system is becoming an independent attraction. The monument lies 45 miles west of Blanding and can easily be visited on an itinerary that includes Arches, Canyonlands, Monument Valley, and Glen Canyon. Address: Star Route, Blanding, Utah 84511.

NEW RIVER GORGE NATIONAL RIVER
West Virginia
This unit of the park system, a 50-mile stretch of the winding New River, in the southern part of the state, ensures protection of a spectacular portion of one of the oldest rivers in the world. The steep-walled gorge measures from 700 to 1,300 feet deep and exposes ancient rock dating to the Mesozoic era. It is generally considered one of the finest white-water streams in the East because of challenging rapids in the lower 15-mile section from Thurmond to Fayette Station and because usually reliable waters flow the entire summer season. The 23-mile section from Hinton to Prince offers calmer water for canoeing and leisurely float trips. In 1988, Congress established the Gauley River National Recreation Area, covering 9,400 acres along a 24-mile stretch of the twisting, scenic Gauley River extending from Summersville Dam to the Gauley's confluence with the New River. It also designated a 25-mile segment of the Bluestone as a component of the Wild and Scenic Rivers System. Both areas are administered in conjunction with the New River. Commercial outfitters in the vicinity offer varied services from early April to late October. Pick up details at the Canyon Rim Visitor Center on US 19 near Fayetteville and the New River Gorge Bridge, open all year, or the Visitor Center at Hinton, open seasonally. During two weekends in October the New River Train operates all-day excursions through the gorge; the trip is considered one of the most exciting train rides in America and sells out in advance every year. Call the Collis P. Huntington Railroad Society, 304/526-5745. State parks in the gorge provide lodges and campgrounds. For information, call 800/CALL-WVA. Address: Drawer V, Oak Hill, West Virginia 25901.

OBED NATIONAL SCENIC RIVER
Tennessee
On the Cumberland Plateau, this park area, established in 1976, will preserve scenic river gorges comprising some of the most striking scenery in the Southeast. The Obed, and its principal tributaries, Clear Creek and Daddy Creek, are bordered by bluffs reaching 200 to 500 feet high. These multicolored canyon walls are pockmarked by shallow caves—some deep enough to offer shelter. Rapids alternate with deep, long pools amid huge boulders. The Obed system provides highly technical white-water canoeing during the period from December to April or May. Water flow is usually too low during the remainder of the year for canoeing, but the pools provide opportunities for swimmers and fishermen. This country can't support heavy use; facilities are limited and primitive. Address: Drawer 630, Oneida, Tennessee 37841.

OREGON CAVES NATIONAL MONUMENT
Oregon
Joaquin Miller, celebrated poet of the Sierra, did much to attract attention to this area in the Siskiyou Mountains, 20 miles from Cave Junction, by calling the cave the "Marble Halls of Oregon." Columns, stalactites, and canopies of marble formation line passageways and hang from vaulted domes. Guided tours; nursery for small children. Oregon Caves Chateau and cottages at monument entrance; campgrounds in adjacent Siskiyou National Forest. Address: 19000 Caves Highway, Cave Junction, Oregon 97523.

ORGAN PIPE CACTUS NATIONAL MONUMENT
Arizona
A segment of the Sonoran desert, complete with stark mountains, sweeping *bajadas*, or outwash plains, rocky canyons, flats, and dry washes, is preserved within the 330,688-acre monument in southwestern Arizona at the Mexican border. The desert reveals itself as a fascinating life-community of plants and animals. Some 30 species of cactus have been identified within the monument, notably the organpipe, this country's second largest cactus, which produces a cluster of stems some of which reach a height of 20 feet. Desert ironwood, giant saguaro, palo verde, and ocotillo are among other interesting plants that have solved the problem of survival in an arid region. Animals, too, have adapted to the harsh environment, including the Gila monster—the only poisonous lizard native to the United States—desert bighorn sheep, pronghorn, coyote, and a variety of birds.

The monument presents what is likely the finest display of Sonoran desert birdlife north of Mexico. For some species, such as lark bunting and white-crowned sparrow, this is a winter home; for others, including white-winged dove and nighthawk, it is a summer home. Many species are year-round residents. Quitobaquito, a spring-fed pond near the Mexican border, offers an excellent opportunity to see regular desert species and migrants.

The life of the desert is interpreted at the **Visitor Center**, the starting point for two graded scenic loop drives. The Ajo Mountain loop covers 21 miles (about two hours) and the Puerto Blanco Drive, 51 miles (half a day). Organ Pipe's campground hugs the gentle southeast slope of the Puerto Blanco Mountains. Camping is limited to 14 days mid-January to mid-April; 30-day limit, remainder of year. The popular season extends from November until May, when temperatures are comfortable. Summer daytime temperatures frequently reach 100 degrees Fahrenheit, or higher. Follow a few simple precautions for walking or hiking in this country. Wear clothing suitable for rough terrain and strong sun. Carry fresh drinking water. Watch your step around cactus—spines can be painful. Keep an eye out for rattlesnakes, and let them be. Address: Route 1, Box 100, Ajo, Arizona 85321.

OZARK NATIONAL SCENIC RIVERWAYS
Missouri
In the heart of the steep, wooded hills south of Rolla are preserved about 140 miles of the unpolluted, natural, free-flowing Current River and its tributary, the Jacks Fork, both noted for fine fishing and camping on gravel bars. Canoes are available from local outfitters. The headwaters of the Current are formed at an immense spring in **Montauk State Park**, adjoining the north end of the riverways. Principal campgrounds, picnic areas, and other visitor facilities are found at Big Spring near Van Buren; Alley Spring near Eminence; and Owls Bend. Each center has its own attractions and activities: Alley Spring, a gristmill grinding cornmeal and morning classes at Story's Creek Schoolhouse throughout the summer; Big Spring, johnboat and paddle-making through summer; Owls Bend, working blacksmith shop. Special programs feature Ozark music and canoe demonstrations. At a popular fishing spot on the Current River known as Gooseneck, 27 miles southwest of Van Buren, archaeologists have unearthed the remains of a 1200-year-old Indian village, considered a major find. Summers on the Ozark rivers are hot; spring and fall are ideal seasons. Address: Box 490, Van Buren, Missouri 63965.

PADRE ISLAND NATIONAL SEASHORE
Texas
An offshore barrier dune island paralleling the south Texas coast in the Gulf of Mexico and separated from the mainland by the Laguna Madre. This very shallow body of water is part of the Intracoastal Waterway, a dredged canal system along the Texas Coast.

The 113-mile-long island has an endless sweep of broad beaches, grass-topped dunes, and windswept sand formations. It is developed for several miles at both ends, but the boundaries of the national seashore embrace 69 miles of the middle section (up to 3 miles in width).

There are two approaches from the north; one leads from Corpus Christi over a modern causeway to Padre Island and Nueces County Park; the other leads from Port Aransas, historic and scenic seaport, down Mustang Island via Park Road 53. The south end of the island is reached by causeway from Port Isabel to Cameron County Park.

Padre Island National Seashore is a biological showcase. More than 380 species of plants grow here and more than 300 species of birds are either permanent residents, part-time residents, or pass through on migration. These include the rare peregrine falcon. The national seashore contains the only marine nesting colony of white pelicans on the gulf coast of the United States. Commonly seen birds include herons, egrets, ibis, gulls, terns, and more than 30 species of shorebirds. Ducks and geese are abundant in fall and winter, attracting hunters to Laguna Madre. Coyotes are heard at night and occasionally seen in the daytime, but most mammals spend the daylight hours underground to avoid the hot sun, coming out to forage for food in the cool of evening. A major international effort is now being made to establish a nesting population of the endangered Ridley sea turtle. The plan involves transplanting eggs, imprinted in Padre Island sand, from the turtles' primary nesting site at Rancho Nuevo, Tamaulpais, Mexico.

Shelling is a popular winter pastime. Some beaches abound with marine snails, clams, and other mollusks. The struggle and survival of humble plants and grasses in the dunes are a marvel of their own.

Swimming and surf fishing are year-round activities. Redfish, sea trout, and black drum are the most commonly caught fish. A Texas fishing license is required. Guides and boats for deep-sea fishing are available in Port Aransas.

Seasons and Accommodations. Winters are generally mild; however cold snaps ("northers") sometimes drop temperatures to uncomfortable levels for short periods. Summers can be hot and windy. The humidity is high year-round. There are no overnight accommodations in the national seashore. The closest motels are in the Corpus Christi area, to the north, or the Port Isabel area, to the south.

Malaquite Beach Campground, near the northern entrance of the seashore, has modern restrooms with showers and a dump station. Primitive camping is permitted year-round in the north and south beach areas, with a 14-day limit. Chemical toilets are provided.

Nueces County Parks on North Padre Island and at Port Aransas provide trailer facilities. For information on rates and facilities, write to Nueces County Parks, 10901 South Padre Island Drive, Corpus Christi, Texas 78418. For information on camping on South Padre Island, write to Cameron County Parks, Box 666, Port Isabel, Texas 78578.

National Seashore address: 9405 South Padre Island Drive, Corpus Christi, Texas 78418.

PICTURED ROCKS NATIONAL LAKESHORE
Michigan
The multicolored sandstone cliffs called the pictured rocks, rising perpendicularly to heights of 200 feet, stretch approximately 15 miles along the shore of Lake Superior, the largest freshwater lake in the world. They make the national lakeshore on Michigan's Upper Peninsula a place of beautiful landscapes and vistas. Begin with a boat tour (leaving daily from Munising, June to mid-October) to observe the expanse of forest-topped rocks bearing such names as Miners Castle, Indian Head, and Battleship Rock. Then plan to hike at least a portion of the Lakeshore Trail running along the shore the entire length of the park between Munising

and **Grand Marais**. Stop at the Visitor Center to get a list of interpretive programs, including the historic walks on "Lighthouse and Shipwrecks." Near the Visitor Center, enjoy Munising Falls, which drop nearly 50 feet over the sandstone bluff; walk along the natural cavity *behind* the falls and you won't get wet! New trails and old logging roads provide a variety of hiking opportunities. Don't miss the Grand Sable Dunes and Au Sable Light Station near Grand Marais. The park has three campgrounds—Little Beaver Lake, Twelvemile Beach, and Hurricane River—accessible by car, plus additional sites spaced along the Lakeshore Trail. Overnight lodgings are available at Munising and picturebook Grand Marais. Address: Box 40, Munising, Michigan 49862.

PINELANDS NATIONAL RESERVE
New Jersey
The unit was established to preserve and enhance the distinctive tract of 1,100,000 acres in southern New Jersey composed of pine-oak forest, cedar swamps, and streams. Located within 50 miles of Philadelphia and 100 miles of New York City, it is one of the largest open space areas on the east coast. Congress established this national reserve in 1978. Sphagnum moss, cattails, pinecones, blueberries, and cranberries are among the abundant products of nature. The area is underlain by an important natural aquifer, or watershed. Though there are no National Park Service facilities, Batsto Mansion, part of a former iron-making community, serves as a Visitor Center within Wharton State Forest. Batsto Village is a prime spot, with guided tours of the old gristmill, blacksmith shop, sawmill, and other structures. It makes a good starting point for hiking and canoeing. Wharton State Forest has 400 miles of sand roads, mostly unmarked but well suited for naturalist hikes. The 40-mile Batona Trail starts at the village and runs north through the pinelands to New Lebanon State Forest. Four of south New Jersey's popular canoe streams are located within the state forest. Address: c/o Regional Office, National Park Service, 143 South Third Street, Philadelphia, Pennsylvania 19106 or Pinelands Commission, Box 7, New Lisbon, New Jersey 08064.

PINNACLES NATIONAL MONUMENT
California
Here is a real discovery for the off-beat outdoors explorer. The last remnants of an ancient volcano, carved by erosion into spectacular pinnacles and spires, many over 1,000 feet high, contrast strikingly with the surrounding chaparral of west-central California—a chaparral cover considered the finest in the National Park system. There are two entrances to the park: on the east side, south of Hollister off California 25; on the west, via Soledad, which is on US 101. It is not possible to drive across the monument. Climbers have long been attracted to the Pinnacles, but unstable rock surfaces are hazardous and require specialized gear. Self-guiding trails are outstanding, particularly in spring, when wildflowers carpet the hills. Park headquarters and Visitor Center are on the east side, but sites for tent camping (without utility connections) are available on the west side. Address: Paicines, California 95043.

PISCATAWAY PARK. See page 170.

POINT REYES NATIONAL SEASHORE
California
A peninsula noted for its long beaches, sand dunes, and lagoons, backed by tall cliffs, forested ridges, grassland, and brushy slopes, lies barely 35 miles northwest of San Francisco. It escaped private development, perhaps because most of the peninsula was cattle and dairy ranch land, or because the promontory

experiences more wind and fog than any other part of the California coast.

The national seashore was authorized in 1962. Almost half of its acreage remains in ranching as a pastoral zone. Its newest feature, the imposing $1.5-million **Bear Valley Interpretive Center**, is set among historic barns and ranch buildings of Bear Valley, 1 mile west of Olema on famous California 1, the Coastal Highway. More than 250 exhibits and 140 specimens of native plants and wildlife are on display, including two 25-foot trees (a Douglas fir and a Bishop pine), specially preserved for exhibit. You can also see a working seismograph measuring earth movements along California's San Andreas Fault and elsewhere. Just beyond the center you can walk to a replica of a Miwok Indian Village and the Morgan Horse Ranch.

Hiking trails start from Bear Valley and from the Palomarin Trailhead, near the Point Reyes Bird Observatory, off Mesa Road. The trail system, including old ranch roads, covers more than 140 miles of backcountry, but if you're bicycling, the Bear Valley and Coast trails are the only ones suitable. You can rent bikes at Point Reyes Station. Traveling on foot, you can take the Sky Trail to the summit of Mount Wittenberg (1,407 feet), 5 miles round-trip, or continue on the Ridge Trail to Drake's Bay on the coast. Those with time should take the 11-mile complete loop, with a hike through the Bear Valley area. It cuts through a natural break in the Inverness Ridge covered with Douglas fir. Little pocket beaches at the base of cliffs along Drake's Bay are reached only by trail. Beaches are great for hiking, but not for swimming. Even wading can be dangerous in the surf off Point Reyes and McClure's Beaches. Swimming is safe at Limantour and Drake's Beaches, but water stays at 55 degrees year-round.

Birdwatching and wildlife watching are outstanding, with over 300 species of birds ranging from sea voyagers to dwellers of the dense forest. A 1965 Christmas count listed 186 species. Limantour Estero and its mudflats are famous for concentrations of shore birds. Abbott's Lagoon is an important wintering ground for waterfowl. Point Reyes also provides sanctuary to a living fossil, the mountain beaver.

Sir Francis Drake Highway leads across the pastoral zone of canyons and arroyos, freshwater lakes, and grassy lowlands, with access roads to Pacific beaches. Some views are not unlike those that greeted Sir Francis Drake in 1579, when he presumably stopped here on his global voyage, and the 19th century traders, whalers, and fur hunters who frequented Drake's Bay. Near the end of the highway, visit the century-old lighthouse, once a primary landfall beacon for incoming ships. Built in Paris in 1867, it was first illuminated by a flickering oil lamp and then by electricity. In 1975 an automated light just down the cliff replaced it. You can climb down a steep staircase to the lighthouse at the very tip of Point Reyes and examine its clockwork mechanism.

Point Reyes Beach is a beautiful coastal wilderness, a beachcomber's paradise, but it receives the full brunt of the Pacific—prepare for fog and high wind. **Drake's Beach**, on the sheltered side, has facilities for day use (no camping). **McClure's Beach** is near the north end of the peninsula off Drake Highway.

Seasons and seminars. Each season brings distinctive pleasures. Winter is the time to watch whales in migration between the Bering Sea and Baja California. March and April bring out the wildflowers. Summer means warm weather and autumn clear, fog-free days. Field seminars of one to four days are offered through most of the year in natural history, art, and "biophotography." Participants are welcome to stay at the Environmental Education Center dormitory, youth hostel, motels, or campground. Write Point Reyes Field Seminars, Point Reyes, California 94956.

Camping. Hikes to four backpacking campgrounds along the trail system—Sky, Coast, Glen, and Wildcat—go from 3 to 8 miles.

These are in great demand and should be reserved four weeks in advance for winter weekends, six to eight weeks in advance for summer. Telephone the Visitor Center (415/663-1092) for reservations; there is no charge for use of the site. Olema Ranch Campground, a private facility, is located near the Visitor Center on California 1. Other camping facilities are at Samuel P. Taylor State Park, 6 miles from park headquarters on the road to San Rafael. Laguna Ranch Holiday Hostel (Box 59, Point Reyes, California 94956; phone 415/669-9985) provides year-round low-cost accommodations near the end of Limantour Beach Road, 7 miles from park headquarters. Address: Point Reyes, California 94956.

POVERTY POINT NATIONAL MONUMENT
Louisiana

Established by Congress in 1988, this 900-acre archaeological site in West Carroll Parish, in northeastern Louisiana, preserves the largest and most complex geometrical earthwork in North America, quite possibly by native people dating to 1700 B.C. The site is expected to be transferred from the State of Louisiana to the National Park Service. Address: Box 248, Epps, Louisiana 71237.

PRINCE WILLIAM FOREST PARK. See page 170.

RAINBOW BRIDGE NATIONAL MONUMENT
Utah

In the semidesert just north of the Arizona-Utah border, the monument embraces the greatest known natural bridge in the world. With a 278-foot span, the symmetrical arch of salmon-pink sandstone curves gracefully upward to a height of 309 feet. You can reach it by special boating trips on Lake Powell to the Bridge Canyon landing, then walking about 1 mile, or by horse trail from Rainbow Lodge (14 miles), or Navajo Mountain Trading Post (24 miles). There are no facilities within the monument. The nearest town, Page, Arizona, is 60 miles away. Address: c/o Glen Canyon National Recreation Area, Box 1507, Page, Arizona 86040.

RIO GRANDE WILD AND SCENIC RIVER
Texas

This area will preserve a segment on the U.S. side of the Rio Grande from mile 842.3 above Mariscal Canyon within Big Bend National Park, to river mile 651.1 at the Terrell-Val Verde County Line. No land has been purchased yet on portions of the scenic river lying outside Big Bend National Park. Address: c/o Big Bend National Park, Texas 79834.

ROOSEVELT, THEODORE, ISLAND. See page 170.

ROSS LAKE RECREATION AREA. See North Cascades National Park, page 112.

SAGUARO NATIONAL MONUMENT
Arizona

A forest of giants dominates the Sonoran desert east and west of Tucson. Studding this country are thousands of stately saguaros, *Cereus giganteus*, which may live 200 years and reach heights of 35 feet, occasionally higher. The saguaros produce beautiful creamy-white flowers, most profuse in late May. The plant, unique to southern Arizona and Mexico, serves as a nesting site for flickers, Gila woodpeckers, elf and screech owls, and other birds. Huge picture windows of the **Rincon Mountain Unit Visitor Center** (east of Tucson) face the desert and Santa Catalina Mountains. From the center you can start the 8-mile loop drive, with nature trails along the way. A permit is required for overnight backcountry use in the Rincon Mountain Unit. The Tucson Mountain Unit, west of the city, includes a 9-mile scenic loop drive from the **Red Hills Visitor Center**, nature walks, hiking trails, and choice picnic sites. Address: Route 8, Box 695, Tucson, Arizona 85730.

ST. CROIX NATIONAL SCENIC RIVERWAY
Minnesota-Wisconsin

More than 250 miles of the Namekagon and St. Croix Rivers, flowing through scenic, undeveloped portions of Wisconsin and Minnesota, have been designated as part of the National Wild and Scenic River System through federal legislation of 1968 and 1972. The **upper St. Croix and Namekagon** offer choice canoeing through wilderness-like stretches with rapids, alternating with lake-like stretches, or flowages, formed by dams. The **lower St. Croix** extends 52 miles from St. Croix Falls dam to Prescott, Wisconsin, where it joins the Mississippi River. As the river enters the riverway, it plunges through the spectacular high cliffs of the Dalles, then becomes wider and shallower, with many islands, sloughs, and backwaters, allowing for sailboating and power-boating. Stop at the Riverway Visitor Center located on the river at St. Croix Falls. Then allow time to visit the St. Croix-Taylors Falls area, historical communities atop the high bluffs of the river gorge. The Angel Hill district of Taylors Falls, a touch of 19th century New England, is listed on the National Register of Historic Sites. Information stations open in season near Grantsburg (on the upper St. Croix) and in Trego (on the Namekagon). The two largest picnic areas are in Earl Park, near Trego, and near Osceola (the lower St. Croix). Camping along most of the riverway is limited to primitive sites accessible only by canoe; developed campgrounds, in the nearby Chequamegon National Forest, two Minnesota state parks, and state forests in both Minnesota and Wisconsin. Snowmobiles are permitted to cross the riverway on approved trails; groomed cross-country ski trails are maintained near Trego and Grantsburg, Wisconsin. North Country National Scenic Trail (cross-country hiking) traverses the riverway from Gordon to Danbury, Wisconsin. Address: Box 708, St. Croix Falls, Wisconsin 54024.

SANTA MONICA MOUNTAINS
NATIONAL RECREATION AREA
California

The Santa Monica Mountains stretch almost 50 miles westward from Griffith Park, in downtown Los Angeles, to Point Mugu, on the Pacific Coast. In 1978, following 15 years of effort, this national recreation area was established by Congress as a cooperative project to preserve, protect, and wisely use 150,000 acres of mountains and seashore, a legendary domain utilized by ancient Indians and glamorized in our time by moviemakers who used it as natural stage sets to represent landscapes of the world.

Follow famous **Mulholland Drive** and Highway westward from the Hollywood Freeway. It leads 50 winding miles through the national recreation area to Leo Carrillo State Beach. Visit **Paramount Ranch**, near Mulholland on Cornell Road, open daily, where guided hikes of the ranch and tours of the movie set are conducted weekends. **Diamond X Ranch**, off Mulholland east of Las Virgenes, is an outdoor education center. **Peter Strauss Ranch**, 5 minutes from the Ventura Freeway, offers opportunities for hiking and picnicking in a natural setting.

For hiking, **Castro Crest** (reached from Corral Canyon Road) is part of the Blackbone Trail stretching along the Santa Monica Crest. **Rancho Sierra Vista**, north of Point Mugu State Park, is open for hikes and ranger-led interpretation.

Point Mugu State Park itself includes 70 miles of hiking and riding trails and 5 miles of ocean shoreline. Point Mugu, Malibu Creek and Topanga State Parks, plus 9 state beaches, already are available within the park. Address: 22900 Ventura Boulevard, Woodland Hills, California 91364.

SLEEPING BEAR DUNES NATIONAL LAKESHORE
Michigan

This area protects 31.5 miles of shoreline on Lake Michigan on the northwest section of Michigan's lower peninsula, together with the two Manitou islands, bearing sand dunes, forests, and inland lakes of their own. The most prominent feature of the lakeshore is a towering mass of sand that looks from a distance like the profile of a bear at rest. The dunes are fed by sands from wind-eroded headlands and stretch in a shifting pattern across great plateaus. The mile-long Old Grade Trail passes through marsh, meadow, and woodland habitat, providing interesting birding activity. Bird walks are offered periodically. The Park Service administers campgrounds on the mainland and South Manitou. 35 miles of cross-country ski trails show the dunes in different perspective.

To reach South Manitou take the passenger ferry offering service from Leland during spring and summer. The island, 3 miles across and 12 miles around, is rimmed with long, wide sandy beaches, but Lake Michigan is too chilly for all but hardy swimmers. On the mainland, climbing the dunes is a popular activity. The Pierce Stocking Drive, 7.6 miles through forest and across dunes, provides magnificent views of Glen Lake, Sleeping Bear, and Lake Michigan shoreline. Address: 400 Main Street, Frankfort, Michigan 49635.

SUNSET CRATER NATIONAL MONUMENT
Arizona

About 900 years ago the last of a long series of eruptions occurred amid the peaks of the San Francisco Mountains north of Flagstaff. The massive, 1,000-foot-high volcanic cinder cone of Sunset Crater, whose crater-pocked summit is tinted with reddish-orange hues, probably appears much as it did after the eruption. The trail to the rim was closed in 1973 due to excessive erosion. However, the ½-mile self-guiding Lava Flow Nature Trail is open year-round. Easy to visit while driving north to Grand Canyon (with a stop also at nearby Wupatki National Monument). Only on Christmas and New Year's Day is the Visitor Center closed. Address: Tuba Star Route, Flagstaff, Arizona 86001.

TIMPANOGOS CAVE NATIONAL MONUMENT
Utah

A series of small underground limestone chambers, ornamented with beautiful mineral deposits, is situated on the northern slope of snowcapped Mount Timpanogos, between Salt Lake City and Provo, easily reached along Utah 92. Much of the cave interior is covered by a filigree of pink and white translucent crystals. It is noted especially for its delicate and unusual helictites. Open May 15 to October 15 (weather permitting). Walk the 1.5-mile trail along the forested canyon of the American Fork River. It's steep, but interesting in its own right, with numbered stops along the way. Allow at least three hours for the round trip, including the cave tour. Wear comfortable shoes and take a jacket to wear inside the cave. Address: Route 3, Box 200, American Fork, Utah 84003.

UPPER DELAWARE NATIONAL SCENIC
AND RECREATIONAL RIVER
New York-Pennsylvania

The 75-mile stretch of the Upper Delaware River (northwest of Port Jervis, New York, between Sparrow Bush and Hancock) flows through forested and rolling country, dotted with farms and small towns. Its values appeal to canoeists, fishermen, and swimmers; expert canoeists will find special challenge in the white-water rapids. The area is rich in historic sites, which include vestiges of Indian settlements, remains of the Delaware and Hudson Canal (including the Delaware Aqueduct Bridge) and the house, at Lackawaxen, Pennsylvania, where Zane Grey wrote some of his many adventure novels about the West. In 1987, Congress appropriated $300,000 to purchase and restore the Zane Grey house. Some portions of the Upper Delaware have changed little over the years. The river corridor is one of the few places in eastern United States where you can see eagles, ospreys, herons, and vultures in their natural surroundings.

Summer is the most popular season, but autumn colors compare with New England at its best. Rural communities complement the park. Several private campgrounds and a few resorts are located in the river valley. The National Park Service operates several information centers at key public access sites. For daily reports on river and boating conditions, call the Information Line at 914/252-7100. If you don't bring your own canoe, you can easily arrange to rent one. The degree of difficulty does not exceed Class II under normal conditions, even at Skinner Falls (but don't get hurt by taking foolish chances). Lower stretches, from Narrowsburg south, usually are crowded on weekends. A good full-day canoe trip in little-spoiled surroundings is the 20 miles from Hancock to Hankins. Address: Box C, Narrowsburg, New York 12764.

WHITE SANDS NATIONAL MONUMENT
New Mexico

In the wide Tularosa Basin of south central New Mexico lies the world's largest deposit of gypsum dunes. Displays in the Visitor Center explain the story of sediments deposited by receding prehistoric seas and how these gypsum sediments were concentrated into the lowest portion of the Tularosa Basin. Evaporation left gypsum crystals called selenite, which over thousands of years have weathered into sand-grain size by wind and weather and piled into a dune field nearly 30 miles in length and 10 miles in width. A scenic 16-mile round trip loop drive leads to the heart of the dune field, with the final portion on pure, hard-packed gypsum with many pullouts for your convenience. Daytime hours, all year; evening hours, summer only.

Visitors are welcome to climb the dunes for an exhilarating view and choice picture-taking. Extended summer hours from Memorial Day to Labor Day allow visitors to attend naturalist conducted walks, talks, and illustrated slide programs in the dune field or summertime full-moon programs with guest speakers. Moonlight programs begin at 8:45 p.m. A picnic area in the dunes is available with shelters and rest rooms, but no drinking water. Lodgings and meals are available in nearby Las Cruces, 53 miles southwest, and Alamogordo, 15 miles northeast. Address: Box 458, Alamogordo, New Mexico 88310.

WHISKEYTOWN-SHASTA-TRINITY NATIONAL RECREATION AREA
California

High in the northern mountains, the area is located near Redding, within one day's drive of San Francisco and Sacramento, and Portland, Oregon. It is a three-unit area, with the 42,503-acre Whiskeytown unit being administered by the National Park Service, and the Shasta unit and the Clair Engle-Lewiston unit under the jurisdiction of the Forest Service. Whiskeytown Reservoir, with 5 miles of open water, extensive shoreline, and numerous coves, was formed by the Whiskeytown Dam, dedicated by President John F. Kennedy in 1963 as a part of the Central Valley Project of the Bureau of Reclamation. It is an excellent area for boating, water-skiing, scuba diving, and swimming. The shallows begin to warm by late May or early June, although deeper waters are always cold.

Fishing is permitted all year on the reservoir. Stream fishing opens the last Saturday in April and closes November 15. California regulations apply in the area. The California Department of Fish and Game and the U.S. Fish and Wildlife Service stock the lake with trout, bass, and Kokanee salmon. Hunting is permitted during autumn in compliance with California regulations.

Campgrounds, picnic area, marinas, and boat ramps have been constructed and are available for use.

Shasta Bally, the most prominent landmark within the recreation area, rises 6,029 feet in the midst of rolling woodlands and clear streams. Below Whiskeytown Dam, Clear Creek winds through gorges and rocky hills. Address: Box 188, Whiskeytown, California 96095.

ALASKA MONUMENTS, PRESERVES, AND HISTORICAL PARKS

THE 15 UNITS now administered by the National Park Service in Alaska cover more land than all units—parks, monuments, historic sites, seashores, and rivers—administered by the service in the rest of the nation.

Ten of these parklands were established by the Alaska Lands Act of 1980. You may not find the same kinds of facilities you know in other parks. Remember that the parklands are vast in size and that dangers of the wilds are apt to rise. Consider going with an outfitter, guide, or outdoors group, at least on your first trip or two.

Travel within Alaska is different than elsewhere. There are less than 3,500 miles of public highway, much of it concentrated near population centers like Fairbanks and Anchorage. But scheduled and charter planes fly virtually anywhere. Cruise vessels, state-operated ferries, and the railroad provide fascinating alternatives.

Summer is the favorite time to visit Alaska. Days are long, so you can see and do more. But prepare for mosquitoes, usually at their worst in June, then tapering off in July, and gone by late August or September. May, September, and October can be attractive times. Certainly they are less crowded. Fall starts early, around mid-August, with an alluring panorama of birch and aspen turning to gold, the dwarf forest of the tundra changing to yellow and red, and fresh snow whitening the mountains. Days are sunny and clear.

Climate varies widely and defies prediction. Travel light but carry wool clothing, rubber boots, and rain gear. Prepare to peel off or add on layers of garments.

Besides the National Park Service areas, other public areas are well worth including in your itinerary. Misty Fiords and Admiralty Island, in southeastern Alaska, are two major national monuments administered by the Forest Service. Wood-Tikchik and Kachemak Bay are among the state parks with wide interest and appeal.

Guidebooks worth reading include *The Milepost*, the annually revised highway guide, indispensable for driving the Alaska Highway, and *Alaska—the Complete Travel Book*, by Norma Spring. For general background and spirit of the land, read *Two in the Far North*, by Margaret Murie, and *A Naturalist in Alaska*, by Adolph Murie.

To help visitors get their bearings, Public Lands Information Centers have been opened in Alaska's two largest cities, Anchorage and Fairbanks, and at Tok on the Alaska Highway. Stop in for guidance. By touching the screen of a video monitor, you can tell the computer which part of Alaska you want to visit, the type of recreation you want, and how you're traveling to get there. The computer will respond with a choice of recreational opportunities from state and federal lands.

For details and further information on Alaska's 15 units, write National Park Service, 540 West 5th Avenue, Anchorage, Alaska 99501. Another valuable source is the State Division of Tourism, Pouch E, Juneau, Alaska 99811.

ANIAKCHAK NATIONAL MONUMENT AND PRESERVE
Alaska

Aniakchak encompasses more than 600,000 acres on the Alaska Peninsula, which extends from the mainland of Alaska westward toward the Aleutians between the Pacific Ocean and the Bering Sea. In a land of tundra, lakes, rivers, and volcanic peaks, the focal point of the national monument, Aniakchak Caldera, is one of the largest calderas (or cones with collapsed summits) in the world.

Often shrouded by fog and rain, Aniakchak remained unknown until 1922. Relatively few people have seen it even now, and fewer still have walked across the floor. This requires careful preparation and physical fitness.

Aniakchak lies about 400 miles from Anchorage. The most practical gateway, **King Salmon**, lies about 150 miles from the monument and is reached on scheduled airline service; guides and charter flights are available from that point for a trip into the monument. The caldera is subject to violent windstorms and rain, which can make hiking and camping difficult.

Father Bernard R. Hubbard, the "Glacier Priest," led a party into Aniakchak overland in 1930. They entered during a raging storm, but once the torrents subsided, they found a walled world of lush plant and animal life, including ferns growing in areas moderated by subterranean heat. Walls 2,000 feet high lend a feeling of isolation and enclosure. Vent Mountain rises 2,200 feet as a secondary cone inside the caldera, while ancient lava flows spread out across the floor. The world around the caldera is occupied by brown bear, moose, caribou, numerous smaller mammals and birds—somewhat reminiscent of the famed Ngorongoro Crater in Africa. **Surprise Lake**, the favorite landing place for seaplanes, covers 2½ square miles. The Aniakchak, a challenge to white-water rafters, also is included in the National Wild and Scenic Rivers System. Address: Box 7, King Salmon, Alaska 99613.

BERING LAND BRIDGE NATIONAL PRESERVE
Alaska

Just below the Arctic Circle, the preserve covers 2.7 million acres of the **Seward Peninsula**—the gateway to the New World, where human history of the Americas began. This area contains immense deposits of remains directly related to the Bering Land Bridge, where the prehistoric hunters are believed to have migrated from Asia. These remains include vestiges of mammoths, horses, giant bison, and a few traces of early man as well.

Eskimo villages are scattered across the flat landscape of western Alaska, facing the Bering Sea between Kotzebue and Nome. For thousands of years, ancestors of the villagers have lived off the land and sea. A part of the attraction of the national preserve is to observe Eskimos pursuing subsistence lifestyles, managing reindeer herds, and producing handicrafts and art objects.

This preserve is a delight for the adventurous birdwatcher and wildlife watcher. Waterfowl, shore birds, and songbirds swarm to the Arctic to breed in summer. Clear lakes, streams, and lagoons make choice habitat for water birds and fish.

Travelers coming this way must do so equipped with their own food, shelter, and proper clothing. There are no facilities available, though primitive campgrounds are planned for the future. Insects are most active mid-June to early August, the heart of the short summer. Air travel is the principal means of access to and within Alaska's remote country. Nome and Kotzebue are both served by scheduled jet service, and it's possible to charter light planes from either place into **Serpentine Hot Springs** or to the beaches of the preserve. Address: Box 220, Nome, Alaska 99762.

CAPE KRUSENSTERN NATIONAL MONUMENT
Alaska

Touching the Chukchi Sea above the Arctic Circle, Cape Krusenstern reveals a long and fascinating history of nature at work and of human survival. Here it is possible to trace back to the melting of the Wisconsin glaciers, when the ocean level rose and submerged the Bering Land Bridge that had connected what is now Alaska with the Asian land mass.

The national monument embraces 560,000 acres of Arctic coastal lowland above Kotzebue Sound. Where Cape Krusenstern—about 35 miles from the gateway town of Kotzebue—bends eastward, the gravel driven by west winds accumulates offshore. Every 50 years or so, the winds shift to the southwest in the springtime, when the sea ice is breaking up. Giant ice floes then gouge out the gravel and drive it onshore above tideline, where it forms a new beach. This sequence has occurred repeatedly for 5,000 years, as evidenced by 114 beach ridges from the newest beachline to Ingitkalik Mountain. The mountain, which is located far inland, is known to be the ancient frontier of the Chukchi Sea.

There are no facilities within the monument. The determined visitor, however, will find rewarding adventure. Migratory birds are in abundance throughout the summer months. These include

Aniakchak Caldera, Aniakchak National Monument and Preserve

such species as the yellow wagtail shuttling back and forth from Siberia. Pods of beluga whales and spotted seals are often seen offshore.

Kotzebue, which lies at the end of a one-hour flight from Anchorage (and even less from Fairbanks) may be one of the oldest communities on the continent. Historians estimate it began more than 6,000 years ago as a foothold in the migrations from Asia over the Bering Land Bridge. The population of 2,500 is currently about 80 percent Eskimo. Seals, whales, and walrus are still hunted. Salmon that are caught in summer are hung and dried and then stored to be eaten in winter. In an age of changing traditions, the setting is not picturesque. Kotzebue's showpiece, the **Living Museum of the Arctic**, however, is a most worthy representation of ancient ways and of the new National Park System units in the region: Bering Land Bridge, Cape Krusenstern, Kobuk Valley, and Noatak. Address: Box 287, Kotzebue, Alaska 99752.

KLONDIKE GOLD RUSH NATIONAL HISTORICAL PARK
Alaska
This park, authorized in 1976, memorializes the heyday of the 1897-1898 gold rush, when thousands of miners (adventurers, really) streamed over the trails from Dyea and Skagway, Alaska, to the Yukon Territory in Canada. The 13,271-acre park includes the rugged Chilkoot Trail (extending 33 miles from Dyea, Alaska, to Bennett, British Columbia); the White Pass Trail; and 13 historic buildings in Skagway, which grew in a few months from a wilderness trading post to a brawling city of more than 10,000. Many buildings still retain their original appearance, enhancing Skagway's attraction to visitors aboard cruise ships and Alaska state ferries plying the Inland Passage. The restored railroad station is now a Visitor Center, open daily June to September. Stop in for information and orientation to the park, Chilkoot Trail conditions, films, guided tours of the Skagway Historic District, and evening programs. The Chilkoot Trail is a tough climb of 3-5 days, with the prospect of severe weather on route. Consult the rangers about your gear. Another unit of this park is in Seattle, Washington, jumping-off point for the treasure hunters of 1898. Address: Box 517, Skagway, Alaska 99840.

NOATAK NATIONAL PRESERVE
Alaska
A major portion of the largest untouched river basin in America lies within this 6.5-million acre national preserve above the Arctic Circle. It is bordered on three sides by two national parks and a national monument—Gates of the Arctic, Kobuk Valley, and Cape Krusenstern, respectively—to comprise a vast complex of protected lands.

River travel is easier than walking and the first 300 miles of the Noatak, starting from the headwaters, rank with the finest wild stretches of river anywhere. The chief obstacle to walking is the almost impenetrable brush, mostly various types of willow. Walking is a little easier with higher elevation, but the only reasonable routes of travel are rivers and large streams.

The DeLong and Baird Mountains form the river basin, including the steep-walled stretch known as the Grand Canyon of the Noatak, reminiscent of the American Southwest. Migratory birds by the thousands breed on the river and the lakes that dot the basin. Moose are commonly seen, and there always are chances of spotting bear, Dall sheep, caribou, and wolves.

West of the canyon region, the village of **Noatak** is the only permanent settlement in the basin. It lies 50 miles from Kotzebue. The Igichuk Hills, westernmost edge of the Baird Mountains, are the final gate through which the Noatak flows on its course to the Arctic. It becomes a large river, sometimes half a mile wide, influenced by tides.

There are no public facilities within the preserve, but guide and outfitting services are increasing. At **Kiana**, within easy reach from Kotzebue, arrangements can be made to float and fish the Noatak or the Squirrel, which flows south from the Baird Mountains. Address: Box 287, Kotzebue, Alaska 99752.

SITKA NATIONAL HISTORICAL PARK
Alaska

Adjoining the town of Sitka in southeastern Alaska, the park centers around the site of the battle for Sitka where the Tlingit Indians made their last stand against the Russians in 1804. In a forested setting of spruce and hemlock stand 19 totem poles of the finest native craftsmanship. The Visitor Center here is one of the finest historical showcases in Alaska, housing in one wing the Southeast Alaska Indian Cultural Center. It provides an interpretive program of teaching and demonstration to students and visitors. In late 1978 the rebuilt Saint Michael's Orthodox Cathedral was consecrated in Sitka, more than a decade after the original burned to the ground in 1966. The historic structure had been standing on the site since 1848, when it was built as the first Russian Orthodox cathedral in North America. Sitka residents were able to save most of the icons and other treasured pieces, which had come from Czarist Russia. In a recent and ambitious project, the Russian Bishop's House, on Crescent Harbor, has been restored to its 1852 appearance. After 15 years of work (completed in 1988), the first floor has been converted into an impressive museum of Russian colonial days, while the second floor appears as it did when the Bishop lived here. Climb the stairs and step into the last century. Address: Box 738, Sitka, Alaska 99835.

YUKON-CHARLEY RIVERS NATIONAL PRESERVE
Alaska

In the uplands of interior Alaska, this national preserve of 2.5 million acres preserves a 128-mile-long segment of the corridor of the fabulous Yukon River, the central artery of a vast Canadian-Alaskan frontier, known at times as the "Mississippi of the North,"

and the entire Charley River drainage, a little-disturbed watershed with wilderness atmosphere.

This is one national park area in Alaska with gateways readily accessible by motor vehicle. You can either take the Steese Highway from Fairbanks to Circle, in the northwest area, or the Taylor Highway, which begins at Tetlin Junction (near Tok) on the Alaska Highway, to Eagle, in the southeast area. Both towns are reminiscent of the gold rush, riverboat travel, and military days.

At **Circle** you will be only 50 miles south of the Arctic Circle. Old log cabins and assorted items of yesteryear recall when the only sure way to travel was on the Yukon, which flows 2,000 miles from its source in Canada in a great northwest arc across Alaska to empty in the Bering Sea. Lodgings are available in **Circle**, **Circle Hot Springs**, and **Central**.

Eagle, once the main port of entry from Canada, was the trading center for Klondike miners and prospectors. A post office was established here in 1898; a military post, Fort Egbert, one year later; and Eagle became the first incorporated city of interior Alaska in 1901. You can take a walking tour, conducted by the Eagle Historical Society, of the town and fort, much of which are restored. The **Eagle Museum** features displays on Roald Amundsen, the polar explorer who arrived in Eagle in 1905. Lodging facilities are not highly developed, but a campground is maintained and there are stores that sell provisions. Float trips and guide service can be arranged.

Going downstream from Eagle to Circle, a distance of 160 miles, shows a large portion of the preserve. Drifting with the current and camping on bars and shorelines, you will see wildlife such as golden eagles, falcons, water birds, bear, and moose.

The **Charley River** and its corridor demand experienced wilderness river runners, hikers, and campers. The Charley is ideal for canoeing. It flows between Twin Mountain and Mount Sorenseon, 100 miles from mountain headwaters to its rendezvous with the Yukon, bounded in places by gentle slopes and in others with bluffs. White-water rapids dominate a part of the course. Address: Box 64, Eagle, Alaska 99738.

A Guide to Lodgings

In and Near the National Parks

WHERE TO STAY? HOW MUCH WILL IT COST? Do I really need to make a reservation in advance? These are key questions to the national parks traveler. If you're camping, you have the choice of campgrounds in national parks, adjacent national forests, and commercial facilities on nearby private lands catering particularly to recreation vehicles. But if you're looking for a bed for the night—well, then, this guide is for you.

Listings are representative and selective. They don't cover everything available. Chain hotels and motels are included here and there but not emphasized. But here you will find some of the smaller, distinctive accommodations that could be no place else but where they are, akin to the national parks. In some cases these facilities are remote and seasonal. Make an allowance for such conditions. You can't expect luxury in the backwoods; save that expectation for a resort closer to home.

Facilities on federal land in national parks are operated by private concessioners under contract to the government. My own experience shows that quality varies widely. A few of my favorites—the Ahwahnee in Yosemite, El Tovar at the rim of the Grand Canyon, and Caneel Bay in the Virgin Islands—are like remembrances of elegant times past; they're expensive, maybe best for a meal to celebrate. Alaska national parks are endowed with choice accommodations, some unusual, like Koksetna Camp at Lake Clark, McCarthy Lodge at Wrangell–St. Elias, and Brooks River Lodge at Katmai; Glacier Bay Lodge is a top stop, too, and very popular with visitors. Others that stand out in my mind include Shenandoah Countryside, a bed-and-breakfast facility just outside Shenandoah; Kettle Falls at Voyageurs; Rough Riders, at the edge of Theodore Roosevelt; Izaak Walton Inn, just outside Glacier; Volcano House at Hawaii Volcanoes; and Maho Bay in the Virgin Islands.

A word or two on rates and on how to save. They are always highest "in season," then generally drop 10 to 25 percent during the "off-season." For parks like Yellowstone and Glacier in the cool northern Rockies the peak season runs from late June through August. Anytime after Labor Day is definitely off-season. On the other hand, at Everglades in southern Florida winter and early spring are the in-season.

At times it's highly advisable to make reservations in advance. You're assured a bed for the night and know how much it will cost.

When making reservations at a chain hotel or motel, use the toll-free 800 number. You can obtain it easily by phoning toll-free information, 800/555-1212. Many independent hotels and large motels also have toll-free numbers. It's a good idea when you make your reservation to ask about dining hours or where the nearest restaurant may be.

Remember that owners and managers change. Last year's top hotel occasionally proves to be next year's disappointment. All efforts have been made to make these listings current and reliable.

Rates change, too. Rather than include specific prices, the Guide indicates the range: H, for High; M, for Moderate, and L, for Low. Postal zip code and telephone area code are given with the name of the community. Where street addresses are not shown, you can write a lodging facility by using the community name and zip code only.

One final word. Accommodations in America cover the widest range of any country on earth. Try country inns, B&B (for bed-and-breakfast), and hostels, along with standard lodgings you already know. Even if you're camping, take a breather now and then to sleep indoors and have a luxurious bath. Variety is a pep-up to help you enjoy the national parks all the more.

228

ACADIA NATIONAL PARK
Maine

Zip 04609. Area Code 207.

There is camping in the park, but no lodgings. A wide choice of motor courts, guest houses and inns is available on Mt. Desert Island, principally at the resort of Bar Harbor, with others at Northeast Harbor and Southwest Harbor. Reservations are advisable July and August.

Bar Harbor. Zip 04609.

Atlantic Oakes. The former estate of Sir Harry Oakes, with pool, tennis courts and ocean view. Adjacent to Yarmouth ferry landing. Open year-round. 288-5801. H.

Golden Anchor Inn. Overlooking the harbor, with balconies or patios and pool. Sailboat tours offered. 288-5033. H.

Park Entrance Motel. Located opposite park headquarters, with pool, dock and putting green. Rooms with patios or balconies, a few with kitchenettes. Closed mid-October to mid-May. 288-3306. M.

Cleftstone Manor. A 3-story inn built 1894, with 18 units, 12 with bath. Tennis and lawn games. Closed November 1 to May 1. 288-4951. M to H.

Also these campgrounds:

Barcadia Tent & Trailer Park, Box 255T. 288-3520.

Frenchman's Bay Resort Camp, Bar Harbor Box 193, Trenton, ME 04605. 667-4300.

Hadley's Point Campground, RFD 1, Box 45. 288-4808.

Mt. Desert Narrows Campground, RFD 1, Box 83-A. 288-4782.

Northeast Harbor. Zip 04662.

Kimball Terrace Inn. Overlooking municipal pier, with balconies or patios and pool. Open year-round. 276-3383. M.

Asticou Inn. A renovated country inn built 1902, with rooms in the main house and cottages, with light cooking, tennis and pool. MAP (Modified American Plan, two meals daily) mid-June to mid-September. Closed November to April. 276-3344. H.

Southwest Harbor. Zip 06479.

Harbor Lights. Nine bedrooms, private baths and semi-private baths. Use of refrigerator for guests; children welcome. 244-3835. L. Open all year.

Moorings Motor Sail Inn. Nautical motif in motel rooms and cottages. Rowboats, canoes and sailboats at the beach; bicycles for road use. Closed November 1 to May 1. 244-5523. M.

Also these campgrounds:

Smuggler's Den Campground, Box 787. 244-3944.

White Birches Campground, Box 421. 244-3797.

ARCHES NATIONAL PARK
Utah

Zip 84532. Area Code 801.

There is camping in the park, but no lodgings. Nearest facilities are at Moab, 35 miles away. These are listed under Canyonlands National Park.

BADLANDS NATIONAL PARK
South Dakota

Zip 57750. Area Code 605.

Cedar Pass Lodge. Operated by the Oglala Sioux as a park concession, it offers rustic, comfortable cabins and dining room; open mid-May to mid-October. 433-5460. L to M.

Motels are located at Kadoka, eastern gateway to the Badlands, and at Wall, farm and ranch center widely known for the Wall Drug Store, which sells a little of everything. The town of Interior, two miles southwest of park headquarters, has gas stations, store, cafe, and commercial camping with a few motel units. Note that you can get information on the State of South Dakota by calling toll-free 1-800/843-1930 (1-800/952-2217 in South Dakota).

Kadoka. Zip 57543.

Best Western H&H El Centro. Family rates. 837-2287. M.

Sundowner Motor Inn. Heated pool. 837-2296. M.

West Motel. Family rates. 837-2427. L.

Wall. Zip 57790.

Best Western Plains. Family rates; pool. 279-2145. M.

Kings Inn Motel. Children under 12 free. 279-2178. M.

BIG BEND NATIONAL PARK
Texas

Zip 79834. Area Code 915.

Chisos Mountains Lodge. Motel and stone cottages operated inside the park by National Park Concessions, Inc., along with dining room. Reservations essential year round. 447-2291. M.

National Park Concessions also operates trailer sites (with electricity, water and sewer connections) at Rio Grande Village. Lodgings and private campgrounds outside the park are located at Study Butte and Lajitas, west of the park; at Terlingua, the western boundary; and at Alpine, center of ranching and a college town, where you can visit the Museum of the Big Bend on the campus of Sul Ross University.

Terlingua. Zip 79852.

Cavalry Post Motor Inn and Badlands Motel. Styled as frontier fort and western town, facilities include riding, tennis, swimming, and dining. 371-2471. M.

Chisos Mining Company. At Study Butte, 26 miles west on Texas 118. 371-2254. M.

Alpine. Zip 79830.

Best Western Highland Inn. Opposite Sul Ross University; two-story motel with pool. Under 12 free; senior citizen and family rates. 837-5811. M.

Sunday House Inn. Two-story motel with pool. Under 12 free; senior citizen rates. 837-3363. L to M.

Indian Lodge. State-owned and operated pueblo-style lodge in Davis Mountains State Park, 31 miles northwest of Alpine, with handy access to Fort Davis National Historic Site. (Address Box 786 Fort Davis, TX 79734). Swimming pool and scenic walking trails. Under 12 free. Closed 2 weeks in mid-January. 426-3254. L.

BISCAYNE NATIONAL PARK
Florida

Zip 33030. Area Code 305.

The campground on Elliott Key is available to boaters and via concession-operated tour boat, Biscayne Aqua-Center, Inc., Homestead, FL 33030 (305/247-2400). Accommodations of all kinds are located in Homestead and neighboring communities. Also see listings under Everglades National Park.

BRYCE CANYON NATIONAL PARK
Utah

Zip 84717. Area Code 801.

Bryce Canyon Lodge. A 70-unit motel and refurbished rustic cabins are available; meals, campers' store and laundry, operated as a concession inside the park, mid-May to October 2, by TW Services, Inc. (Address: Box 400, Cedar City, UT 84720). Some cottages are without bath. 586-7686. M.

Facilities are also at Panguitch, Cedar City and other nearby communities. Cedar City is the site of Southern Utah State College and Utah Shakespeare Festival mid-July to late August.

Panguitch. Zip 84759.

Bryce Canyon Pines. Six miles from park entrance. Furnished in early American decor, with nonsmoking area. Indoor swimming pool and horseback tours in summer. 834-5336.

Bryce Village (formerly Pink Cliffs). Conveniently located 2 miles north of park entrance. 834-5303. M.

Best Western Rubys Inn (PO Rubys Inn, UT 84764), 1 mile north of park entrance. Horseback riding, indoor pool, square dancing; winter snowshoeing and cross-country ski trails. Trailer park as well as lodge. 834-5341. M.

Cedar City. Zip 84720.

Best Western El Rey Inn. Motel of 1 and 2 stories, with pool and sauna; location of Sullivan's steak and lobster restaurant. 586-6518. M.

Knell and Knell Annex. Some rooms at the Annex are equipped with refrigerators. 586-6566 (and 9487). L to M.

Meaudeau View Lodge. Distinctive log inn, of 9 rooms and suites, all with private bath, at 8,400 feet in Dixie National Forest; offers trout fishing, cross-country skiing in winter. 648-2495. M to H.

CANYONLANDS NATIONAL PARK
Utah

Zip 84532. Area Code 801.

Equipped and primitive campgrounds are located inside the park. Closest lodgings are at Moab, at the Colorado River at the foot of the LaSal Mountains, a town that came into prominence during the uranium exploration boom. Other accommodations are at Monticello and Blanding.

Moab. Zip 84532.

Apache. 166 S. 4th East St. Pool and playground. Senior citizen rate. 259-5727. M.

Best Western Green Well. 105 S. Main. Pool. 259-6151. M.

Landmark Friendship Inn. 168 N. Main. Pool; family rates. 259-6147. M.

Rustic Inn. 120 East 1st St. South. Pool; senior citizen rate. 259-6177.

Monticello. Zip 84535.

Canyonlands Motor Lodge-Friendship Inn. 197 N. Main. 587-2266. M.

Triangle 44 Motel. 164 E. Central. 587-2274. M.

Wayside Inn-Best Western. 197 E. Central. 587-2261. M.

Blanding. Zip 84511.

Best Western Gateway. Enroute to Glen Canyon National Recreation Area, with access to Natural Bridges and Hovenweep National Monuments. Under 12 free, senior citizen rate. Pool. 678-2278. M.

CAPITOL REEF NATIONAL PARK
Utah

Zip 84775. Area Code 801.

Besides the park campground, western style lodgings close at hand at Torrey and 38 miles east at Hanksville.

Torrey. Zip 84775.

Rim Rock Resort Ranch, 2 mi E of Torrey on UT 24. Two miles west of park boundary; with playground, picnic tables and dining room; facilities for trailers. Offers 4-wheel drive tours. 425-3843. M.

Hanksville. Zip 84734.

Poor Boy Motel. Pool. 564-3452. M.

Sunglow Motel (55 E. Main St., Bicknell, UT 84715), located on pleasant grounds. 425-3821. L to M.

CARLSBAD CAVERNS NATIONAL PARK
New Mexico

Zip 88220. Area Code 505.

Nearest facilities are at White's City, just outside the park, and at Carlsbad, 27 miles away (where you can visit Living Desert State Park, an unusual indoor/outdoor museum).

White's City. Zip 88268.

Best Western Cavern Inn. Virtually at the entrance to the national park, with heated pool, steambaths, playground. 785-2291. M.

Carlsbad. Zip 88220.

Best Western Motel Stevens. Pool. Family rates. 887-2851. M.

Carlsbad Inn. Pool. Family rates. 887-3541. M.

El Rancho Motel & Campgrounds. 885-3996. M.

Holiday Inn. Pool. Under 12 free; senior citizen rates. 887-2861. M.

Motel 6. Pool. 885-8807. L.

Five overnight private campgrounds with full facilities are located in Carlsbad.

CHANNEL ISLANDS NATIONAL PARK
California

Zip 93001. Area Code 805.

Smuggler's Cove Ranch. Bed down in a recently refurbished historic adobe at the east end of Santa Cruz Island. Solar panels provide electricity for hot water and showers. Bring your own bedding and food. Make reservations through Island Packers Co., 1867 Spinnaker Drive, Ventura, CA 93001 (642-1393).

Camping is available on Anacapa and Santa Barbara islands. Many park visitors stay on their own boats. For those taking the scheduled or chartered cruises to the islands, excellent accommodations in a wide range are located at Ventura, Santa Barbara and nearby communities.

CRATER LAKE NATIONAL PARK
Oregon

Zip 97604. Area Code 503.

Crater Lake Lodge. The concession-operated lodge and cabins at Rim Village offer a range of plain accommodations and dining (from cafeteria to coffee shop to dining room). Crater Lake Lodge is open only from mid-June to mid-September. Some rooms do not have bath. Reservations are strongly advised, especially for premium rooms ($2 extra) on the lake side. Ponderosa Cottages (with full bath) and Sleeping Cottages for 2 to 4 persons are open May to October, depending on snow conditions. (South and west entrances of the park are open all year; cross country ski rentals are available at the Lodge.) Some cottages are equipped with cold running water only and without private toilets. 594-2511. L to M.

Other facilities are located at Klamath Falls, from which daily bus service is offered to the park mid-June to mid-September, and other nearby communities.

Klamath Falls. Zip 97601.

Budget Host Inn, 11 Main St. Two-story motel with pool. 882-4494. L.

Cimarron, 3060 S. 6th St. Two-story motel with pool and several kitchen units. 882-4601. L to M.

Molatore's, 100 Main Street. Two-story motel with pool and dining room specializing in Italian and American cuisine. 882-4666. M.

Thunderbird, 3612 S. 6th St. Pool. 882-8864. M.

Fort Klamath Lodge, Box 428, Ft. Klamath, OR 97626. Youth hostel with motel rooms and dorm 22 miles from Crater Lake; on the shore of Wood River, known for fishing and rafting. 381-2234. L.

Prospect Hostel, 480 Mill Creek Drive, Prospect OR 97536. Located 40 miles from Crater Lake, this hostel has a unisex dormitory. It provided access to the wild Rogue River. 560-3795. L.

DENALI NATIONAL PARK
Alaska

Zip 99755. Area Code 907.

Denali National Park Hotel. Concession-operated facility adjacent to McKinley Park railroad station and Riley Creek Information Center provides hotel rooms late May to mid-September. 683-2215. (Year-round address and phone: Outdoor World, Ltd., 825 W. 8th Ave., Anchorage, AK 99501: 907/278-1122.) M to H.

Camp Denali. A wilderness retreat with tent cabins equipped for housekeeping and rustic chalet cabins with family-style meals in the dining room. Classic views of Denali above Wonder Lake. Sourdough Vacation packages include guided day hikes, canoeing, optional campouts. 683-2290 (winter, 683-2302). M to H.

At the edge of the park:

Harper Lodge. A large hotel (150 rooms) a mile from the park entrance, opened in

1987 by Princess Tours, with Jacuzzi-equipped deluxe rooms. 800/426-0442. H.

McKinley Chalets. Overlooking the Nenana River at the east boundary of the park. Suited for families. Managed by Denali National Park Hotel; reserve through same address and phone. H.

North Face Lodge. Reached by the park road to Wonder Lake and Kantishna, it offers wilderness stays of 1 and 2 days early June to early September. 683-2265. M to H.

Mount McKinley Village. Motel units and coffee shop 6 miles south of the park entrance at Mile 231 on the Parks Highway (Alaska Route 3). 683-2265. M.

McKinley Wilderness Lodge. Motel units, cabins, RV parking and dining room at Mile 224 on the Parks Highway, open mid-May to mid-September. 683-2277. M.

Other facilities are located in and near Cantwell and Healy. A rec vehicle campground in Healy offers hookups, groceries, showers, coin laundry.

EVERGLADES NATIONAL PARK
Florida
Zip 33030. Area Code 813.

Besides campgrounds at Long Pine Key and Flamingo, facilities in the park include the Flamingo Inn, operated as a concession by TW Services, Inc., Everglades Park Division, which also provides meals, charter fishing boats, sightseeing trips and bicycle rentals. The Inn includes motel-type rooms and housekeeping cottages suited for family use. 695-3101. M.

Motel accommodations are located at Homestead, 12 miles from the park entrance (46 miles from Flamingo), the Florida keys and resort communities of South Florida. Look into Florida's state parks—40 of them have camping facilities, and several have vacation cottages at reasonable rates, all located in attractive natural settings. Write for a copy of Florida State Parks Guide, Department of Natural Resources, 3900 Commonwealth Blvd., Tallahassee, FL 32303 (904/488-7326).

Homestead. Zip 33030.
Bel Air, 1202 N. Krome Ave. Under 12 free; family rates. 248-2277. L.
Coral Roc, 1100 N. Krome Ave. (Florida City, FL 33034). Pool, picnic tables. Some rooms with refrigerators. Under 12 free. 247-4014. M.
Best Western Motor Inn, 51 Homestead Blvd. Pool, playground. Rates for senior citizens. 245-1260. M.
Sea Glades, 1223 NE 1 Ave. (Florida City, FL 33034). Pool, playground. Senior citizen rates, family rates.

Islamorada. Zip 33036.
Cheeca Lodge, Box 527. A beachfront complex with lodge rooms and cottages, some with kitchens; pool, tennis, par 3 golf; dining room with ocean view. Under 18 free; family rates. 664-4651 and 800/327-2888. M to H.
Lime Tree Bay Resort, Box 839, Layton, Long Key, FL 33001. Facing the Gulf of Mexico below the Everglades, some rooms and cottages at this resort are kitchen-equipped; pool, lighted tennis, picnic tables and grills. 664-4740. L to M.

GATES OF THE ARCTIC NATIONAL PARK
Alaska
Zip 99707. Area Code 907.

Several private lodges (as well as excellent public campsites) are available throughout the park and adjacent preserve. These include:

Walker Lake Lodge, 930 9th Ave., Fairbanks, AK 99701. Rafting, sailing, sportfishing. 452-5417. M.

Wiseman Lodge, Box 10224, Fairbanks, AK 99701. Historic lodge, adjacent to North Slope Haul Road, offers backpacking, fishing, trail rides, natural history tours June to September. Private rooms, family-style meals. M.

GLACIER BAY NATIONAL PARK
Alaska
Zip 99826. Area Code 907.

Glacier Bay Lodge, Gustavus, AK 99826. The park concession, with modern rooms and meal service at Bartlett Cove, starting point of naturalist hikes and other programs. Tour packages assure reservations during popular, short season from mid-May to end of September. Dormitory rooms each accommodating up to eight persons (men and women separately) are available at lower rates. 697-3221. (Winter address: 1500 Metropolitan Park Bldg., Seattle, WA 98101; phone 206/624-8551). M to H.

Gustavus Inn, Gustavus, AK 99826. Family-run inn 12 miles from Bartlett Cove, with central bath, family-style meals; bikes available to guests. 697-3311. M.

GLACIER NATIONAL PARK,
Montana
Zip 59936. Area Code 406.

Extensive facilities are operated on concession by Glacier Park, Inc. These include lodging in mostly historic old structures at strategic locations, meals, camper supplies, boat rentals and launches, bus transportation, bicycle rentals. The address of Glacier Park, Inc. from May to September is

East Glacier Park, MT 59434. The reservations phone number is 226-5551. (During summer in Montana only call toll-free 1-800/332-9351.) From late September to mid-May the address is Greyhound Tower Station #5185, Phoenix, AZ 85077. (Phone 602/248-2600.)

On the east side of the park, lodgings include:

Many Glacier Hotel. Overlooking Swiftcurrent Lake in the Many Glacier region; a 5-story hotel (no elevator) with a variety of rooms and suites (including "family rooms" of two rooms with connecting bath). Services include coin laundry, barber and beauty shops. M to H.

Swiftcurrent Motor Inn and Cabins. A trail center for hikers, this complex ranges from motel rooms with full bath to cold water cabins without bath. L to M.

Rising Sun Motor Inn and Cabins. Near the St. Mary entrance, eastern gateway to Going-to-the-Sun Road. L to M.

Glacier Park Lodge. In a beautiful setting just outside the southeast corner of the park, reflects an earlier day. It rises 4 stories (without elevator) and includes picturesque lobby, swimming pool and 9-hole golf, as well as barber and beauty shops. M.

On the west side:
Lake McDonald Lodge. Built about 1914, is situated on the shore of Lake McDonald, just off the Going-to-the-Sun Road. The dining room, in rustic motif, has a choice view of the lake. Under 12 free. M.

Apgar Village Inn. Also overlooking Lake McDonald, provides motel rooms, some with kitchen units, and access to beach and swimming. Open summer only. 888-5484. M.

Strictly for hikers—Sperry and Granite Chalets are operated by another concessioner, Belton Chalets, Inc., Box 188, West Glacier, MT 59936. (Phone 888-5511.) Reservations are necessary. Lower rates for children 12 and under. L.

Lodgings of diverse types on the east side are located at East Glacier Park, Browning, St. Mary; on the west side at Apgar, West Glacier, Hungry Horse, Whitefish, Kalispell.

East Glacier Park. Zip 59434.
Jacobson's Cottages. A cluster of cabins, some with kitchen units; open summer only. 226-4351. L to M.
Mountain Pine. Summer only; family rates. 226-4403. M.
St. Mary's Lodge, St. Mary 59417. Motel units and cabins located along a rushing creek between East Glacier Park and Many Glacier; open summer only. 732-4431. M.

West Glacier. Zip 59936.
Glacier Highland Motel. Located on US 2 across from Amtrak at west entrance to the

national park. A 33-unit motel with jacuzzi, swim spa, cooking units, groceries, restaurant. Open summer only. 888-5427. M.

River Bend. Motel rooms and cottages (with kitchen) are open only during summer. West Glacier Restaurant here specializes in home-cooked meals. 888-5662. M.

High Adventure Guest Ranch. Rooms in lodge and cabins are enhanced by indoor pool, sauna and a variety of year-round activities from barbecues and scenic pack trips to cross country skiing. Family rates, ski plans. 387-5610. M to H.

Izaak Walton Inn, Essex, MT 59916. Unusual spot, classy without luxury, on US 2 southeast of West Glacier; early 20th-century railroad atmosphere. Popular for cross-country skiing. Access to hiking trails. 888-5700. L to M.

North Fork Hostel, Polebridge, MT 59928. This hostel embodies simplicity, with wood heaters and cooking range (and no electricity), complementing its natural setting between the national park and Flathead National Forest. Check at the Polebridge Store. L.

GRAND CANYON NATIONAL PARK
Arizona

Zip 86023. Area Code 602.

The South Rim is open year-round, while the higher and cooler North Rim is open approximately mid-May through early November, weather permitting. Consequently, facilities are much more abundant on the South Rim.

Grand Canyon National Park Lodges, the principal South Rim concessioner (phone 638-2401 for advance reservations and 638-2631 for same day reservations), offers varying overnight accommodations, including 795 rooms and 76 cabins. These are divided among the following:

El Tovar. A showpiece hotel of the national parks, built in 1905 and restored in the early 1980s, El Tovar has a lovely dining room overlooking the canyon. 638-2631. H.

Bright Angel Lodge. Well located in the park, it provides hotel rooms and cabins, some overlooking the canyon. Adjoining are Bright Angel Restaurant and the Arizona Room. 638-2401. M.

Yavapai Lodge. Opposite the park visitor center, this large facility has a cafeteria offering fast food service. M.

Kachina Lodge. Located next to El Tovar Hotel, on the canyon rim, has a variety of motel rooms and suites. Register at El Tovar. M.

Maswik Lodge. It offers more than 287 rooms; 37 cabins; and has a cafeteria. Under 8 free. 638-2401 (and 2631). L to M.

Moqui Lodge. At the park entrance on US 180 and Arizona 64. Casual dining; under 12 free. 638-2424. L to M.

Thunderbird Lodge. On the Village Loop Drive, next to Bright Angel Lodge. Register at Bright Angel Lodge. Under 8 free. 638-2401 (and 2631). M to H.

Other facilities in and close to the South Rim include the following (use same area code and zip):

Grand Canyon International Youth Hostel, Box 270. Converted from an old stone ranger dormitory, the hostel is somewhat primitive and for the young at heart. No smoking. 638-9018. L.

Quality Inn Red Feather, Box 520. A modern motel 1 mile south of the park entrance. 638-2673. M.

Grand Canyon Squire Inn Best Western, Box 130. It combines access to the park (two miles away) with resort activities — tennis, swimming, exercise room, pool and sauna — and Indian decor. 638-2681. M to H.

Seven Mile Lodge is a new modern motel located 1.5 miles from the park boundary and 7 miles from the canyon rim. 638-2291.

In the Inner Canyon:

Phantom Ranch. This small guest facility, alongside Bright Angel Creek, is reached by hiking or mules only. It consists of dormitories and cabins. Overnight packages are offered, but reservations through Grand Canyon National Park Lodges are essential.

At the North Rim:

Grand Canyon Lodge. Modest cabins and motel units on pine-shaded grounds provide magnificent canyon views. Dining room and cafeteria are part of the complex open summer only. For reservations, write TW Services, Inc., 451 N. Main, Cedar City, UT 84720 (801/586-7686).

Outside the park:

Kaibab Lodge. Less than 20 miles north of the North Rim in Kaibab National Forest, it offers motel rooms and rustic cottages. Address: North Rim Rural Route, Fredonia, AZ 86002. 638-2389. M.

GRAND TETON NATIONAL PARK
Wyoming

Zip 83012. Area Code 307.

Several choice accommodations are operated by concessioners in the park. (Some visitors, in fact, prefer to stay in the Tetons and make day trips to Yellowstone.)

The largest concessioner, Grand Teton Lodge Company (543-2811), provides not only lodging and meals, but guided bus tours, horse trips and float trips, and rec vehicle camping with full hookups. Its overnight accommodations are:

Jenny Lake Lodge. Log cabins of one and two rooms furnished in taste and sophistication, with patios facing Jenny Lake, are in great demand. So is seating at Sunday buffet dinner. H+.

Jackson Lake Lodge. Located in the center of activities, the large lodge consists of motel rooms, some with excellent views and some otherwise. The lobby is a well-known rendezvous, marked by picture windows facing the lake and the Tetons beyond. Facilities include dining room, coffee shop, picturesque bar, pool, beauty and barber shops. M to H.

Colter Bay Village, Distinctive log cabins, originals of pioneer settlers, have been assembled in one area and furnished with appropriate but modern facilities. Groceries and coin laundry are located in the village. L to M.

Colter Bay Tent Cabins. These combine log and canvas and are equipped with screen door and bunks, affording a touch of comfort to outdoors living. L.

Other lodging concessions in the park:

Signal Mountain Lodge. Lodgings, meals, groceries and marina services at this well-established family-operated lakefront lodge. Some units have private patios or balconies, some have kitchens. 543-2831. M.

Triangle X Guest Ranch. American Plan rates include cabin with shower bathroom, horseback riding, children's program, square dancing. Float trips are offered. 733-2183. M to H.

Flagg Ranch Village. On the Rockefeller Memorial Parkway, near the southern entrance to Yellowstone National Park, well-known Flagg Ranch has motel rooms and cabin units (with and without bath), grocery store, and rec vehicle camping with utilities. Activities include horse rides and float trips. 543-2861 and 733-8761; toll-free outside Wyoming, 800/443-2311. L to M.

Plus these on private land in or close to the park:

Dornan's Moose Enterprises, Box 39, Moose, WY 83012. Kitchen-equipped cabins and restaurant at convenient location on the Snake River near Jenny Lake. 733-2415. M.

Lost Creek Ranch, Box 95, Moose, WY 83012. A superlative resort with picture view of the mountains is designed around cabins, most with fireplace and private patio. Riding, swimming, tennis. 733-3435. H+.

Hatchet Motel, Box 318, Moran, WY 83013. On landscaped grounds, with restaurant and scenic view. 543-2413. M.

Fir Creek Ranch, Box 190, Moran, WY 83013.

A small family-run operation of 7 studio bedrooms with private baths. Riding is offered. Requires stay of 3 days or more, a week preferred. 543-2416. M.

Many other accommodations are in nearby Jackson and Teton Village and at Driggs, Idaho, on the west side of the Tetons. Two major seasons are summer and winter. In winter months deep snow usually makes for excellent skiing.

GREAT BASIN NATIONAL PARK
Nevada
Zip 89311. Area code 702.

The park has four campgrounds; no reservations. Baker, a small town, is next door in the desert.

Baker. Zip 89311.

Border Inn, Box 548. Small motel, popular in summer, so call ahead. 234-9982. M.

Silver Jack Motel, Baker Avenue. Tree-encircled, rustic character. 234-7323. M.

Ely. Zip 89301.

Ely, 70 miles west of the park, is the closest full-service town, with wide variety of motels and other facilities.

Copper Queen Motel, 701 Avenue I. Ask for a room in an older unit; wholly adequate, costs less, and you'll still have access to pool and all the rest. 289-4884. M.

Jailhouse Motel, Fifth and High. Have some fun in rooms called cells (the motel is on the site of the early-day jail). Dining room and menu are cellular too. 289-3033. M.

GREAT SMOKY MOUNTAINS NATIONAL PARK
North Carolina-Tennessee
Zip Code 37738. Area Code 615

Besides its campgrounds, simple overnight accommodations are provided in the park by a single concession:

LeConte Lodge, Box 350, Gatlinburg, TN 37738. Atop Mount LeConte, it is reached by foot or horse trail only; a favored outdoors rendezvous for years. It is open April through October. 436-4473. L.

On private land, at Elkmont, inside the park:

Wonderland Club Hotel, Gatlinburg, TN 37738. Formerly a private club, this facility of 27 rooms is open Memorial Day to November 1. 436-5490. M.

Accommodations in a wide range are plentiful around the park. Principal concentration on the Tennessee side is at Gatlinburg and Pigeon Forge.

Gatlinburg. Zip 37738.

Mountain View Hotel, Box 727. A venerable establishment in the heart of town includes modern motel addition, heated pool; serves excellent country food. Open

year-round. 436-4132. M.

River Edge Motor Lodge, 948 River Road. Rooms with balconies, heated pool. 436-9292. M.

River Terrace. This 2-story motel has rooms with patios or balconies, 2 pools; features golf, tennis privileges. 436-5161. M.

Rocky Waters Motor Inn, Box 229. At the edge of the Little Pigeon River, many of its rooms have balconies, some have kitchenettes; 2 pools. 436-7861. M.

Brookside Resort, Roaring Fork Rd. Motel and cottages, with pool and playground, are on attractive grounds, streamside. 436-5611. M.

Bell's Wa-Floy Retreat Hostel, Box 212, Rt. 3. For those who manage on their own; with swimming pool, volleyball, outdoor fireplace. Open April to October. L.

Wier Farm Home Hostel, RFD 15, Box 32, Pigeon Forge, TN 37863. Open April to November. 453-2033. L.

On the North Carolina side:

Bryson City. Zip 28713. Area Code 704.

Hemlock Inn, Drawer EE. Comfortable lodge in early American decor offers Modified American Plan (breakfast and dinner) late April through October. 488-2885. M.

Folkstone Lodge, Route 1, Box 310. This restored farmhouse on West Deep Creek Road has 5 guest rooms (with private bath) and mountain views. Country breakfast served; open June to October. 488-2730. M.

Nantahala Outdoor Center, Box 41. Hostel accommodations are furnished near the Appalachian Trail crossing of the Nantahala River. Seasonal activities include whitewater rafting, cross country skiing. 488-2175. L.

Holiday Inn, Cherokee, NC 28719. Indian-owned and operated, facilities include two pools, racquetball. Choice Indian crafts are on display. 497-9181. M.

Cataloochee Ranch, Box 500, Route 1, Maggie Valley, NC 28751. Distinctive, tastefully furnished lodge and cabins at 5,000 feet elevation operate on Modified American Plan mid-May to late October. Tennis, riding. 926-1401. M to H.

Fontana Village Resort, Fontana Dam, NC 28733. This unique family resort includes 250 housekeeping cottages of 1 to 3 bedrooms, 2 pools, par 3 golf, tennis, square dancing, crafts. Rent a boat and cross Fontana Lake to Hazel Creek or hike the Appalachian Trail to Hazel Creek for choice adventures in the national park. 498-2211. M.

GUADALUPE MOUNTAINS NATIONAL PARK
Texas
Zip 88220. Area Code 915.

Other than camping, there are no over-

night facilities in the park. The nearest are at White's City (35 miles northeast) and Carlsbad (55 miles northeast), both in New Mexico; these are listed under Carlsbad Caverns National Park. Nearest facilities in Texas are at Van Horn, 65 miles south.

Van Horn. Zip 79855. Area Code 915.

Best Western Inn of Van Horn. Pool; 9-hole golf privileges. 283-2410. L to M.

Holiday Inn. Pool; 9-hole golf privileges. Under 18 free. 283-2780. M.

Ranch. Some kitchen units. Pool. Family rates. 283-2225. L.

HALEAKALA NATIONAL PARK
Hawaii
Zip 96768. Area Code 808.

The sole accommodations in the park, other than campgrounds, are three cabins within the crater reached by trail. None is closer than 4 miles from the rim. These are equipped with bunks, cookstove, firewood, with maximum stay of two nights in each cabin. Because of their popularity and demand, a lottery for reservations is held the first day of each month. For details, write the Superintendent of the park, Box 369, Makawao, Maui, HI 96768. On Maui itself, you may phone park headquarters at 572-7749 or 572-9306.

Kula. Zip 96790.

The saying goes that "It's always cooler in Kula," center of Maui's vegetable and flower-growing, in the high valleys en route to the park. Two small chalet-hotels lie near each other at the 3,300 foot level, good bases for hiking and riding in Haleakala.

Kula Lodge. 878-1535. M.

Silversword Lodge. 878-1232. M.

Hana. Zip 96713.

"Heavenly Hana" has been a special place, at least till now, a little of the old Hawaii left over at the end of the road.

Hotel Hana Maui. One of Hawaii's finest, and lowest-keyed, hotels, with accommodations in cottages, patio-style dining, lush gardens, plus swimming, tennis, riding, 18-hole pitch-and-putt golf. No TV or air-conditioning. 248-8211. H to H+.

Hana Kai Resort Apartments. Two buildings on the water comprise this 20-unit condominium. Daily maid service, but no restaurant. 248-8435. M.

Wainanapanapa State Park. At the edge of Hana, the state park maintains kitchen-equipped rustic cabins sleeping 4 to 6. Reservations required well in advance. Write Division of State Parks, Box 1049, Wailuku, HI 96793. 244-4354. L to M.

HAWAII VOLCANOES NATIONAL PARK
Hawaii

Zip 96718. Area Code 808.

Volcano House. At the rim of Kilauea Crater and just across the road from the visitor center, this historic inn, a park concession, has rooms of varying quality (and price). Tour groups dominate the dining room at lunchtime, but at dinner it's all yours. 967-7321. M.

Namakani Paio Campground. Ten small unfurnished cabins are maintained by the park concessioner in a koa and eucalyptus forest 3 miles from park headquarters. Cabins accommodate 1 to 4 persons. 967-7321. L.

Outside the park, lodgings of varying size and quality are at visitor centers such as the Kona Coast and Hilo. Many are large, chain-operated. Others are locally owned, with access to the park and other points of interest. Hilo is the logical gateway, less than an hour by car from the park. If you're touring the island, however, bear these two places in mind:

Manago Hotel, Captain Cook, HI 96726. Family-run, friendly and old-style excellent cooking, it is near Kealakekua Bay and Pu'uhonua ō Honaunau National Historical Park (City of Refuge). 323-2642. L.

Shirakawa's Hotel and Motel, Naalehu, HI 96772. Midway between Kona and Hilo, the southernmost hotel in the country is set in a lush area 1,000 feet above sea level. New motel units apart from the main house have private baths; some have kitchenettes. 929-7462. L.

HOT SPRINGS NATIONAL PARK
Arkansas

Zip Code 71902. Area code 501.

Lodgings are provided by hotels, motels and resorts in Hot Springs and on the shores of nearby lakes, Catherine, Hamilton, Ouachita. Rates are higher during horserace season, early February to early April.

Hot Springs. Zip 71901.

Williams House, 420 Quapaw. This historic, well furnished inn, within walking distance of Bath House Row and park visitor center, includes full American breakfast in the rate. 624-4275. M.

Avanelle Motor Lodge, 1220 Central Ave. Located in the heart of town, some rooms have kitchenettes. Pool, lighted tennis. 321-1332. M.

Shorecrest, 230 Lakeland Dr. On Lake Hamilton, it provides kitchen-equipped cottages, marina, pool. 525-8113. M.

Buena Vista, Box 175, Rt. 3. Also on Lake Hamilton, cottages provide the lodgings, while marina, pool and tennis courts serve outdoors interests. 523-1321. M.

ISLE ROYALE NATIONAL PARK
Michigan

Zip 49931. Area code 906.

Rock Harbor Lodge. Lodge rooms and housekeeping cabins offer the only lodgings on the island (except for campgrounds). These are operated by National Park Concessions, Inc. (Box 405, Houghton, MI 49931 in summer; winter, Mammoth Cave, KY 42259), whose other services include marina, groceries, canoe and boat rentals, guided fishing trips. The attractive twin-unit housekeeping cabins are well suited for families. Bring food supplies with you for the cabins. Be sure to make reservations well in advance for the short season, June through Labor Day. 906/337-4993; winter, 502/773-2191. M.

Accommodations enroute to the park are available at Houghton and Copper Harbor, Michigan, and Grand Portage, Minnesota.

KATMAI NATIONAL PARK
Alaska

Zip 99613. Area code 907.

Two concession facilities in the park, operated by Katmailand, Inc., are open mid-June to early September, which makes reservations important. Package tours including air transportation and meals are a good bet. Consult a travel agent or Katmailand, Inc., 455 H Street, Anchorage, AK 99501 (phone: 907/277-4314 or 277-5149). The two lodges are:

Brooks River Lodge. The center of activities in the park, located at the mouth of the Brooks River. Starting point of daily tours to the Valley of Ten Thousand Smokes. M to H.

Grosvenor Camp. Located on a channel connecting Lake Coville and Lake Grosvenor, this fly-in lodge is favored by sportfishermen (after rainbow, arctic char, lake trout, northern pike, red salmon). It accommodates eight in rustic comfort. Rates include guide service, boat/motors. H.

KENAI FJORDS NATIONAL PARK
Alaska

Zip 99664. Area code 907.

Overnight lodgings are in and around Seward. Hotels, motels and RV campgrounds cover a wide range.

Seward. Zip 99664.

Breeze Inn Motel. At the small boat harbor, with views of Resurrection Bay and the Kenai Mountains. 224-5238. M.

Marina Motel. A small facility with rooms in the view of the bay; picnic area and tandem bikes available to guests without charge. 224-5518. M.

Murphy's Motel. Near Resurrection Bay and the small boat harbor. Deli-style restaurant. 224-5650. M.

New Seward Hotel. One block from downtown. In-room video. 224-5211. M.

Van Gilder Hotel. In the heart of Seward, this hospitable oldtimer is listed on the National Register of Historic Places. The restaurant (like virtually all of them here) specializes in seafood. 224-3079. M.

KOBUK VALLEY NATIONAL PARK
Alaska

Zip 99752. Area code 907.

The national park essentially is undeveloped, meant for wilderness camping. A few simple facilities are emerging in villages along the Kobuk River. Otherwise, the only accommodations offering convenience are at Kotzebue, Alaska's largest Eskimo village.

Nul-Luk-Vik Hotel, Kotzebue, AK 99752. Operated by the NANA regional native corporation, the hotel overlooks Kotzebue Sound on Arctic Bay. Though constructed as a modern facility, open year-round, service and upkeep are erratic. 907/442-3331. H.

LAKE CLARK NATIONAL PARK
Alaska

Zip 99513. Area code 206.

Several small lodges are located along the lakeshore on private land inside the park, close to the villages of Nondalton and Port Alsworth. These are reached by air taxi, most inexpensively from Iliamna. Lodges make available boats, fishing tackle, other outdoor gear.

Alaska's Wilderness Lodge, 7320 6th Ave., Tacoma, WA 98406. Features fly-out fishing (for salmon, rainbow trout, lake trout, char, grayling, Dolly Varden). Family rates. 206/564-6682. M to H.

Koksetna Camp, Box 69, Iliamna, AK 99606. Rustic, comfortable cabins and family-style meals match the wilderness setting. Bird and wildlife observation on the Chulitna River are featured. 907/345-1160; ask for radio-phone patch WHJ67. L to M.

Lakeside Lodge, Port Alsworth, AK 99653. Eight guests are accommodated in modern facilities. Guide service for sportfishing, backpacking, photography. M.

Van Valin's Island Lodge, Port Alsworth,

AK 99653. On the upper end of Lake Clark, log cabins and log lodge with modern facilities; features river float trips, fishing, flightseeing, photography. 907/345-1160 (or 345-1140). M.

Other accommodations are located at nearby Iliamna and on Lake Iliamna.

LASSEN VOLCANIC NATIONAL PARK
California
Zip 96063. Area code 916.

Drakesbad. A concession-operated facility of lodge and cabin rooms and bungalows, with thermally heated pool, serves as a good base for riding and pack trips. The concessioner also provides horses, camper store services, winter ski rentals. Address California Guest Services, Inc., Mineral CA 96063. 916/595-3306 summer; 916/529-1512 year-round.

Lassen Mineral Lodge, Box 160, Mineral, CA 96063. Motel complex (kitchenettes available) with pool, restaurant, general store, tennis, ski rentals. 916/595-4422. M.

Fire Mountain Lodge, Mill Creek, CA 96061. Mountain retreat 15 miles south and east of the park, with rooms in rustic lodge and cabins, some with kitchen. Springs furnish drinking water. 916/258-2938. M.

Childs Meadow Resort, Route 5, Box 3000, Mill Creek, CA 96961. Ringed by mountains nine miles from the park on California 36, it features cabins and motel units, some with kitchenettes; a haven for nordic skiers. 916/595-4411. M.

MAMMOTH CAVE NATIONAL PARK
Kentucky
Zip 42259. Area code 502.

National Park Concessions, Inc. operates the only lodgings in the park. These are:

Mammoth Cave Motel. This older facility of 108 rooms and nearby cottages is the center of activity. 758-2225. M.

Sunset Point Lodge. Consists of newer motel units. M.

Woodland cottages. Older units, economy-styled. L.

Many types of accommodations are in nearby communities of Cave City, Park City, Horse Cave.

Cave City. Zip 42127.

Quality Inn. Pool. 773-2181. M.

Oasis Motor Inn. Rooms with private patios or balconies. Pool. 773-2151. M.

Jolly's. Pool. Family rates. L.

Best Western Park Mammoth Resort, Park City, KY 42160. This resort-like inn on spacious grounds offers 18-hole golf, lighted tennis, hayrides, mini-train rides, indoor-outdoor pool. 749-4101. M to H.

Barren River Lake Lodge, Lucas, KY 42156. Located at Barren River State Park, it provides lodge rooms, kitchen-equipped cottages, tent and trailer sites. Pool, lighted tennis, 9-hole golf, swimming beach and fishing on reservoir lake. 646-2151. M.

MESA VERDE NATIONAL PARK
Colorado
Zip 81330. Area code 303.

Modern motel-type accommodations, expanded in 1983, are operated by a concessioner, the Mesa Verde Company, within the park. Other facilities are in the vicinity of Cortez, 10 miles west, and Durango, 38 miles east. The concessioner also operates grocery stores accessible to campgrounds. The concession motel is:

Far View Lodge (reservations address Box 277, Mancos, CO 81328). It is appropriately named considering the distant vistas of the Four Corners. Open mid-May to mid-October. Smaller rooms cost less. 533-7731. M.

Lake Mancos Guest Ranch, Box 218, Mancos, CO 81328. This distinct, rustic mountain resort has rooms and cabins with private patios (but no room phones). Pool, children's program. Open summer only. Weekly rates. 433-7900. M.

Saguache Hotel, Saguache, CO 81149. Each room is furnished differently but all in Victorian style at this renovated 19th century hotel. Some have bath, air conditioning. 655-2581. L to M.

Teller House Youth Hostel, Box 457, Silverton, CO 81433. Here's the chance to stay inexpensively in a famed old mining town. Hostelers won't find a kitchen, but the rate includes an American breakfast. 387-5423. L.

MOUNT RAINIER NATIONAL PARK
Washington
Zip 98304. Area code 206.

Concession-operated lodgings in the park are located at Longmire, near the Nisqually entrance, and at Paradise, at higher elevation. Outside the park, lodgings are located near Enumclaw and Buckley, 20 to 25 miles from the Carbon River entrance, and, on the east side, in the vicinity of White Pass and Packwood on Washington 123, near the southeast entrance. Concession operations are:

Paradise Inn. In a scenic alpine setting at 5,400 feet, Paradise Inn dates from 1916 (and is listed on the National Register of Historic Places; it was refurbished in 1981. Some rooms are with shared bath, and cost less. Open late May to mid-October. Make reservations for Paradise or National Park Inn with Mount Rainier Guest Services. Full-

service dining room, lounge, and snack bar. Star Route, Ashford, WA 98304. 569-2706. M to H.

National Park Inn. Adjacent to Hikers Information Center at Longmire, elevation 2,700 feet, the inn is scheduled to reopen for the winter 1988 season following major remodeling. The hotel was built in 1916 and is listed on the National Register of Historic Places.

Outside the park:

Mountain View Lodge, Box 525, Packwood, WA 98361. Located on wooded grounds 12 miles from Stevens Canyon entrance on the east side of the park, handy to Goat Rocks Wilderness in Gifford Pinchot National Forest. Pool, playground. 494-5555. L to M.

Crystal Mountain, Enumclaw 98022. Near the northeast boundary of the park, it was designed as a ski resort with a variety of accommodations. Now it provides tennis, riding, chairlift rides and access to fishing and hiking in summer, as well as skiing in winter. 663-2265. M to H.

King's, 1334 Roosevelt Way, Enumclaw, WA 98022. Rooms with private patios, some with kitchenettes. Heated pool. 825-1626. M.

Lodge Youth Hostel, Box 86, Ashford, WA 98304. A mere quarter-mile outside the Nisqually entrance, it is close to the trails, whether for summer hiking or winter skiing, snowshoeing. 569-2312. L.

NORTH CASCADES NATIONAL PARK
Washington
Zip 98284. Area code 206.

The following concessions provide lodgings in the national park complex:

Diablo Lake Resort, Rockport, WA 98283. A complex of housekeeping cottages of 1 to 3 bedrooms (completely furnished) also furnishes meals, groceries, boat rentals with and without motors. Call Newhalem 5578 through the operator. M.

North Cascades Lodge, Box 186, Chelan, WA 98816. Accessible via Chelan by float plane or by the Lady of the Lake tour boat. Lodge rooms vary in size and view (rates vary, too). Seven housekeeping units are completely furnished. Food service, groceries, boat rental. 509/682-4711. M.

Ross Lake Lodge, Rockport, WA 98283. Housekeeping units, sleeping 1 to 4 persons and completely furnished, are classed as: Modern Units, with shower, toilet, electric or propane cooking; Rustic Units, with wood burning stove, community sanitary facilities; and Modern Bunk Units, with shower, toilet, wood heat, propane cooking. Rental boats and canoes; transportation service provided from Seattle City Light Boat Dock. 206/397-7735 (Newhalem via Everett operator) L to M.

Two interesting facilities on private land at Stehekin, WA 98852 are:

Silver Bay Inn, unique B&B, well designed and furnished, with beautiful lakeshore setting, 509/662-0151. M.

Cascade Corrals, the Courtney Ranch. Simple tent-cabins with canvas roofs and kerosene lamps. The Courtneys also feature guided hiking and horse trips and winter cross-country skiing. 509/682-4677. M.

And at Chelan, outside the park:

Campbell's Lodge, Box 278, Chelan, WA 98816. Motel and cottage units with private patios overlook Lake Chelan. Seafood a specialty at the restaurant (with outdoor dining). Pool, sand beach. 509/682-2561. M.

Darnell's, Box 506, Chelan, WA 98816. This 2-story motel, with some kitchen units and private patios or balconies, has pool, 300-foot sand beach on Lake Chelan, tennis, rental boats and bicycles. 509/682-2015. M.

OLYMPIC NATIONAL PARK, Washington

Zip 98362. Area code 206.

The lodgings in the park are at these 4 concessions:

Kalaloch, Lodge, Star Route 1, Box 1100, Forks, WA 98331. Rooms at the Lodge, log cabins (some without cooking, eating utensils) and Sea Crest House motel vary in size and price. Services include meals, groceries. 206/962-2271. M.

Log Cabin Resort, 6540 East Beach Rd., Port Angeles, WA 98362. Lakeshore resort with housekeeping cabins (without cooking, eating utensils), RV sites with hookups, campground with central water supply and restrooms. Dining room, beach, boat dock on Lake Crescent. 206/928-3245. M.

Lake Crescent Lodge, HC62, Box 11, Port Angeles, WA 98362. Cottages and motel units, some with views of lake and mountains, are located 20 miles west of Port Angeles. Dining room, coffee shop, rowboat rental. 206/928-3211. M.

Sol Duc Hot Springs Resort, Box 2169, Port Angeles, WA 98362. This varied complex near the park campground includes modern furnished cabins, rustic woodstove-heated cabins, kitchenette motel units, unfurnished plain camping cabins, RV sites with hookups. It features hot mineral baths and warm mineral swimming pool (additional charge); Dining room, groceries and camping supplies. 206/327-3583. L to M.

Plus these others:

Red Lion Bayshore Inn, 221 N. Lincoln, Port Angeles, WA 98362. Rooms with private patios or balconies overlook the harbor. Pool. Nonsmoking area in dining room. 206/452-9215. M to H.

Uptown Motel, Port Angeles, WA 98362. Occupying a quiet location on a bluff overlooking downtown, some rooms are enhanced with a marine view. A few efficiencies. 206/457-9434. M.

Red Ranch Inn, 830 W. Washington, Sequim, WA 98382. Under 16 free, senior citizen rates. 206/683-4195. M.

Lake Quinault Lodge, Quinault, WA 98575. Beautifully sited in the rain forest of Olympic National Forest on the southwest border of the national park, it offers a chance to enjoy nature with creature comfort. Some rooms have fireplaces, balconies. Indoor pool. Dining room specializes in Northwest seafood, with expansive view of Lake Quinault. 206/288-2571. M to H.

Ft. Worden Youth Hostel, Ft. Worden State Park, Port Townsend, WA 98368. The hostel is 63 miles from the national park, in a historic Victorian port town, worth seeing in its own right. 206/385-0655. L.

PETRIFIED FOREST NATIONAL PARK
Arizona

Zip 86028. Area code 602.

A Fred Harvey lunchroom is located in the park. Coming from the West, motels are located at Holbrook, 19 miles from the park. If you're traveling north across the Navajo Reservation, facilities are at Ganado and Chinle.

Holbrook. Zip 86025.

Best Western Arizonian Inn, 2508 E. Navajo Blvd. Pool. 524-2611. M.

Motel 6, 2514 E. Navajo Blvd. Pool. 524-2666.

Arizona Rancho Motor Lodge, Box 698. Hostel. 524-6770. L.

Best Western Chieftain, Chambers, AZ 86502. 23 miles from the park. Pool. 688-2754. M.

REDWOOD NATIONAL PARK
California

Zip 95531. Area code 707.

Three state parks within the boundary of the national park offer a variety of camping experiences. Lodgings are principally located in Crescent City, northern gateway to the national park, and Eureka, 40 miles south of Orick, southern gateway to the national park. (Eureka is about 290 miles north of San Francisco).

Klamath. Zip 95548.

Requa Inn, 451 Requa Road. Country Inn at the edge of the park, freshly refurbished; overlooks Klamath River. 482-8205. M.

Crescent City. Zip 95531.

Crescent TraveLodge. Under 17 free. Senior citizen rates. 464-6106. M.

Northwoods Inn. Overlooks ocean harbor. 464-9771. M.

Pacific Motor Hotel. At north end of Crescent City. Senior citizen, family rates. 464-4141. M.

Town House. 464-4176. L.

Eureka. Zip 95501.

Best Western Thunderbird Lodge. Pool. Nonsmoking rooms. 443-2234. M.

Carson House Inn. One block from the famous Victorian Carson Mansion. Pool. Senior citizen rates. 443-1601. M.

Imperial 400. Pool. Senior citizen rates. 443-8041. L to M.

Eureka Inn. A classic 4-story building of 1922 in Tudor decor, with rooms remodeled; a national historic landmark. Pool, sauna. Under 16 free. 442-6441, or toll-free 800/862-4906. M.

Klamath Redwood Hostel. New facility in restored 19th-century home, at the mouth of Wilson Creek near the coast. Families accommodated in same room. 482-8265. L.

ROCKY MOUNTAIN NATIONAL PARK
Colorado

Zip 80517-8397. Area code 303.

Various services are furnished in the park—food, pack trips, mountaineering school and skiing—but accommodations were removed long ago in order to protect and restore wild nature. Principle tourist centers are Estes Park, at the east side of Trail Ridge Road; Grand Lake, the west entrance to the park; and Granby, south of the Grand Lake entrance.

Estes Park. Zip 80517.

Best Western Lake Estes Motor Inn. Some rooms with balconies. Pool, marina. 586-3386; toll-free 1-800/528-1234. M.

Fall River Motor Inn. Some rooms and cottages have private balconies or patios on the river, and some with refrigerators and fireplaces. Pool, lawn games. 586-4118 M.

Hobby Horse Motor Lodge. Heated pool, playground. Some rooms with saunas. 586-3336. M.

Aspen Lodge & Guest Ranch. At 9,000 feet, it features American Plan mid-June to late August (and is closed the rest of the year). Lodge rooms and bedroom cottage units. Heated pool, riding, square dancing. 586-4241. H.

Double JK Ranch. Rustic, informal American Plan resort open summer only. Some cabins have fireplaces, none have phones. Children's program, cookouts, hayrides. 586-3537. M.

Anderson's Wonder View Motel and Cottages. In a quiet location within view of

Long's Peak, it offers motel rooms and kitchen-equipped cottages with fireplaces, but no phones. Pool, playground, children's program. 586-4158. M.

H-Bar-G Ranch Hostel. This former dude ranch 3 miles from the park with superb view of the Front Range has tennis, volleyball, access to hiking trails. 586-4686. L.

Grand Lake. Zip 80447.

Driftwood Lodge. Overlooking Shadow Mountain Lake, some rooms are efficiencies. Pool, playground. 627-3654. M.

Western Riviera. A lakefront location, with picnic tables, playground and pleasant views. 627-3580. M.

Dougal's Mountain Inn. This hostel constructed of log in authentic style is 1 mile from the park entrance. 627-3385. L.

C Lazy U Ranch, Granby, CO 80446. This American Plan guest ranch is known for its friendly atmosphere and activities for all ages. Rooms in the lodge and cottages are attractively furnished, some with fireplace. Pool, tennis, children's program. Winter cross country skiing and sledding. Family rates; ski packages. 887-3344. H.

SEQUOIA AND KINGS CANYON NATIONAL PARKS
California

Zip 93262 (Sequoia); 93633 (Kings Canyon). Area code 209.

Accommodations in these twin parks are concession-operated by Sequoia Guest Services, Sequoia National Park, CA 93262. The reservations number is 561-3314. They consist of the following:

Giant Forest Lodge in Giant Forest Village. Open year-round facilities include motel with bath; cabin with bath; rustic room with bath; rustic semi-housekeeping with central bath. L to M.

Bearpaw Meadow Camp. Summer only. A chance to break away and yet have a little tent cabin comfort. Breakfast, dinner served family style and box lunches available. L.

Stony Creek Lodge. Motel unit, open mid-May to October. M.

Grant Grove Lodge. Open year-round, cottages and rooms here come with and without bath. Rustic semi-housekeeping canvas-topped cabins are heated by wood stove. Meal service, groceries. L to M.

Cedar Grove Lodge. Thirty miles east of Grant Grove, this motel unit is open mid-May to October. Fast food service, market, gas station, and bicycle rentals available. M.

Outside the park:

Three Rivers. Zip 93271.

Buckeye Tree Lodge, ½ mile from park entrance; small motel, friendly service on bank of Kaweah River. 561-4611. M.

Best Western Holiday Lodge. On the Kaweah River, with fishing, swimming, boating nearby. Heated pool. 561-4119 (and toll-free 1-800-528-1234). M.

Lazy J Ranch. On the Kaweah River. Pool, picnic tables. 561-4449. M.

River Inn. Overlooking the Kaweah River, 1 mile from Sequoia National Park entrance with scenic mountain views. Continental breakfast. 561-4367. M.

M Bar J Guest Ranch, Badger, CA 93603. Features trail riding into the park, square dancing, meals cooked with local foods. 209-337-2513. M.

SHENANDOAH NATIONAL PARK
Virginia

Zip 22835. Area code 703.

ARA Virginia Sky-Line Company operates the concession lodges, dining rooms, grocery and camper stores and coin laundries at key locations along the Skyline Drive. The address of this company is Box 727, Luray, VA 22835. (703/743-5100). Accommodations are:

Skyland Lodge and Cabins. A few miles below Thornton Gap entrance station (Route 211), season here runs from early April to early November. New units have the view of Shenandoah Valley from the ridgecrest; older units have the rustic feeling and cost less. L to M.

Big Meadows Lodge. About midway between Thornton Gap and Swift Run Gap entrance stations, it is handy to Byrd Visitor Center. Motel rooms with private balconies and a few cabins. Season runs Mar-Dec. M.

Lewis Mountain Cabins, southernmost accommodations, offers housekeeping cabins and tent cabins from May to late October. L.

Private campgrounds with facilities and hookups are located near all four park entrances.

Nearby accommodations are in Front Royal, Luray, New Market, Harrisonburg and Waynesboro. Charlottesville, Staunton and Lexington definitely are within easy driving range. Motels in various price ranges are plentiful. Resort-type lodgings include:

Shenandoah Countryside, Rt. 2, Box 377, Luray, VA 22835. Outstanding B&B accommodations with magnificent vistas, plush organic flower and veggie gardens, wood-fired sauna, and use of bicycles. 743-6434. M.

Boar's Head Inn, Charlottesville, VA 22905. Designed around an 1834 gristmill, rooms at this sophisticated resort have private patios, balconies. Facilities include pool, lighted tennis, golf privileges, jogging trail. 804/296-2181. H.

Graves Mountain Lodge, Syria, VA 82743. A family-owned resort that hails as a place "for people who enjoy good food and mountain beauty" and really does offer both. Activities include swimming, tennis, volleyball, and horseback riding, plus all the opportunities of the park. 703/923-4231. M.

Shenvalee Lodge & Motel, New Market, VA 22844. Located on 200 acres, most rooms have balconies with pleasant views. Pool, golf, tennis. Under 12 free; golf package plan. 703/740-3181. M.

Three family campgrounds, all with swimming, riding, hiking, other activities:

Masanutten Camp Forest. 7 miles southwest of Front Royal. 703/636-6061. M.

Montfair Family Resort. 4 miles north of Whitehall (east of Skyline Drive). 804/823-5202. M.

Shenandoah Acres. Off I-64, near Stuarts Draft. 703/337-1911. M.

THEODORE ROOSEVELT NATIONAL PARK
North Dakota

Zip 58645. Area code 701.

Rough Riders Hotel, Medora, ND 58645. The small hotel, where Theodore Roosevelt stayed, has been refurnished and open for business. It's one of a kind, almost part of the park itself; dining room specializes in Western country cooking, serving fresh walleye, trout, chopped buffalo steak. 623-4433. M.

Bad Lands Motel, Medora, ND 58645. Pool. 623-4422. M.

Dietz Motel, Medora, ND 58645. 623-4455. M.

Medora Motel, Medora, ND 58645. Pool. 623-4444. M.

Super 8, Watford City, ND 58854. 15 miles from the entrance to the North Unit of the park. 842-3686. L to M.

Dickinson has a number of motor hotels. This lively city is the site of Roughriders Days Celebration 4 days over July 4.

Best Western Prairie Winds Inn, Dickinson, ND 58601. Pool. Under 13 free; senior citizen rates 225-9123. M.

Ramada Inn, Dickinson, ND 58601. Indoor/outdoor pool. Under 18 free. 225-6791. M.

VIRGIN ISLANDS NATIONAL PARK
Virgin Islands

Zip 00801. Area code 809.

Cinnamon Bay Campground, Box 120 Cruz Bay, St. John, VI 00830. This park concession operates 40 modest beach cottages (with cots, bedding, linen, cooking utensils); 40 equipped tents, 10 bare tenting sites. All are in great demand, making reservations well in advance essential. Make reservations through Rockresorts, New York (see Caneel Bay, Inc., below), or by phoning direct: 809/776-6330 or 776-6111. L to M.

Caneel Bay Inc., Cruz Bay, St. John, VI 00830. Opened in 1956 by Laurance Rockefeller, Caneel Bay became one of the Caribbean's finest resorts. It is the largest guest facility on St. John. Expansion and various changes over the years have somewhat dulled the early image. Reservations during winter peak are sometimes hard to get; package plans in effect May 1 to November 1. Make reservations through a travel agency or Rockresorts, New York. 800/223-7637; 800/442-8198 (New York only); 212/586-4459 (New York City). H to H+.

Maho Bay Camps, 17 East 73rd Street, New York, NY 10021. The choicest place to stay and absorb the treasures of the national park. Attractive kitchen-equipped tent cottages are set in the woods overlooking the curved sand beach of Maho Bay, with access to community showers, toilets, camp store, moderately priced restaurant. 212/472-9453 (or toll-free: 800/392-9004). M.

Gallows Point, Box 58, Cruz Bay, St. John, VI 00830. A cluster of rustic furnished cottages on a hillside-with-view suited for carefree vacationing. M.

VOYAGEURS NATIONAL PARK
Minnesota
Zip 56649. Area code 218.

Two hotels operate as concessions in the park:

Kettle Falls Hotel, Box 1272, International Falls, MN 56649. One of the country's most unusual hostelries, it dates from 1913 when it was built to serve trappers, traders, fishermen, lumberjacks at the extreme east end of Rainy Lake. It is open mid-May through September, accessible by boat only. Still operated by the Williams family that purchased it in 1918 (for $1,000 and 4 barrels of whiskey), and still serving Rainy Lake walleye and wild rice. 218/374-3511 and (winter) 218/286-5685. L.

Whispering Pines Resort, Orr, MN 55771. Family housekeeping cabins, fully equipped (and boat furnished with each cabin), comprise this resort at the narrows between Kabetogama and Namakan Lakes. Accessible via the Ash River Trail to the central entrance of the park. 218/374-3321. M.

Resorts, many with family housekeeping cabins, adjoining the park are grouped at Crane Lake, Kabetogama Lake, Rainy Lake, with motels at International Falls. Resorts feature lake swimming, water ski-

ing, outfitting canoe trips, guided fishing, dropoffs by boat and plane.

Island View Lodge, International Falls, MN 56649. On Rainy Lake, it provides motel units and cabins, dining room overlooking the lake. 218/286-3511. M.

Thunderbird Lodge, Route 8, International Falls, MN 56649. Three-story lodge and cottages on Rainy Lake. Pool, tennis, 9-hole golf privileges. 218/286-3151. M.

Voyageur Park Lodge, Ray, MN 56669. On Lake Kabetogama, 25 miles southeast of International Falls (250 miles north of the Twin Cities), furnished cabins in a picturesque peninsula setting. 218/875-2131.

Nelson's, Crane Lake, MN 55725. Founded by the Nelson family in 1931 on spacious grounds fronting Crane Lake, it offers furnished housekeeping cabins and resort dining. 218/993-2295. M.

WIND CAVE NATIONAL PARK
South Dakota
Zip 57747. Area code 605.

Camping and concession-operated lunchroom are located in the park. Adjacent Custer State Park (Custer, SD 57730) offers camping, plus these three lodging facilities:

Blue Bell Lodge. Kitchen-equipped cottages, restaurant and store are open mid-May to early October. 605/255-4531. L to M.

State Game Lodge. Calvin Coolidge, once used by Calvin Coolidge as summer White House, it includes lodge rooms, furnished cabins, restaurant, playground open early May to late September. 605/255-4541. M.

Sylvan Lake. In a rugged Black Hills setting overlooking Sylvan Lake, it offers lodge rooms and cabins (some with fireplace), cafeteria, grocery June to Labor Day. 605/574-2561.

Best Western Inn by the River, Hot Springs, SD 57747. On the Southeast edge of the Black Hills, Hot Springs lies 12 miles south of the park. Pool. 605/745-4292. M.

El Rancho Court, Hot Springs, SD 57747. Bordering Fall River. Pool. 605/745-3130; toll-free 800/843-8313.

WRANGELL-ST. ELIAS NATIONAL PARK
Alaska
Zip 99588. Area code 907.

This huge, diverse park, still little known, is hardly the place to expect luxury or creature comfort, or to try to see in its entirety. There are several lodges, as well as campgrounds, most easily accessible by air taxi service to landing strips and lakes in the park. You can drive to accommodations at McCarthy, in the park interior, but the last 65

miles from Chitina is strictly for four-wheel-drive vehicles.

McCarthy Lodge, Glennallen, AK 99588. An historic facility near the old Kennecott copper mine is open May through September. Year-round phone (in Oregon) 503/485-0575. M.

Copper Lake Fish Camp, Gakona, AK 99586. Located on the shore of Copper Lake in the northern portion of the park, this lodge and cabins are reached via the 42-mile, four-wheel drive road from Slana to Nabesna, an abandoned mining town. Boats, motors available. 907/822-3316. M.

Tanada Lake Lodge, Box 258, Fairbanks, AK 99707. Rustic, modern lodge and cabins at lakeshore almost 3,000 feet elevation accommodates 12 guests from late June through September. Boats, motors provided for sportfishing, birding, nature photography. 907/452-1247. M.

Gakona Lodge, Gakona, AK 99586. An oldtime roadhouse listed in the National Register of Historic Places (it was built in 1905 overlooks the Gakona River on the Tok Cutoff (Alaska Highway 1). It lies near the Slana Road, within view of towering Mt. Sanford. 907/822-3482. M.

Standard accommodations are located on the Tok Cutoff, in Glennallen, and in Chitina enroute to McCarthy.

YELLOWSTONE NATIONAL PARK
Wyoming-Idaho-Montana
Zip 82190. Area code 307.

Accommodations are extensive along the Grand Loop in the park. Many date from an earlier day and earlier mode of travel. They are operated today as a concession by TW Services, Inc., Yellowstone National Park, Wyoming 82190. For reservations call 307/344-7311.

Accommodations come in 11 different classifications; price ranges are evident by the facilities. The following summary, or definition, of accommodations will help:

Deluxe room/bath: newest, modern rooms, fully equipped.

Superior rooms: similar to deluxe, but slightly smaller.

Luxury cabin: spacious, modern/contemporary furnishings, modern bath.

Room/bath: Standard hotel room, private bath.

Standard cabin: Rustic exterior, modern interior; Bath with shower, in some locations 2 cabins connecting.

One-room family cabin: Carpeting, curtains, half-bath, automatic heat. Showers nearby; bring your own towel.

Two-room family cabins: 2 rooms separated by half-bath; furnishings and shower same as one-room cabin.

Budget cabin: Automatic heat, hot and cold water. Showers nearby; bring your own towel.

Budget shelter: Automatic heat, hot and cold water; showers nearby. Bring sheets, blankets, pillow cases, pillows, towels.

Rough Rider Cabins: Cold water, wood-burning stove (presto logs provided). Showers nearby; bring your own towel.

Rustic shelter: Wood-burning stove (presto logs available but not provided). Showers nearby; bring towels and bedding.

These are spread over the following locations:

Mammoth Motor Inn, at the North Entrance. Rooms/bath; rooms without bath; standard cabins; budget cabins. L to M.

Roosevelt Lodge, in the Tower Falls area. Standard cabins; family cabins; Rough Rider cabins; rustic shelters. L.

Lake Yellowstone Hotel/Cabins. Oldest hotel in park (1891), undergoing major remodeling and upgrading. Summer reservations a must. Standard cabins; family cabins. M to H.

Lake Lodge Cabins. Luxury cabins; standard cabins. L to M.

Old Faithful Inn. Built early in the century, one of the first and finest examples of ''appropriate architecture'' with use of native materials; restored in 1981. Deluxe rooms; superior rooms; rooms with bath; rooms without bath. M to H.

Old Faithful Lodge. Standard cabins; family cabins; budget cabins; budget shelters. L.

Old Faithful Snowlodge. Standard cabins; family cabins; budget cabins; budget shelters. L.

Canyon Village, near the Grand Canyon of the Yellowstone River, a motel-type facility. Deluxe; standard. M.

Grant Village, the newest facility, nearest to the South Entrance. Superior rooms. M.

Accommodations are also available outside the park at Cooke City, Gardiner and West Yellowstone, Montana; along US 191, the Island Park section of Idaho; and Cody and Jackson, Wyoming. Some visitors use facilities in Grand Teton for touring both parks.

YOSEMITE NATIONAL PARK
California
Zip 95389. Area code 209.

The Yosemite Park & Curry Co., the park concessioner, maintains varied accommodations and services throughout Yosemite. The company address is: Yosemite National Park, CA 95389. The reservations phone number is 209/252-4848. Lodgings include the following:

Ahwahnee Hotel. The most celebrated (and luxurious) lodging in the park is a work of art of another day that has never gone out of style. Dinner reservations advisable year-round; dress code for dinner. Sunday brunch is a special treat. H.

Yosemite Lodge. Among the pines near the foot of Yosemite Falls, it ranges from lodge rooms with bath to family rooms, cabins with bath, cabins without bath. Ask for one of the older units. They're attractive, with character, and cost less. M to H.

Curry Village. Also a varied complex, it consists of hotel rooms, cabins with bath, cabins without bath, and more than 400 tent cabins. L to M.

Curry Housekeeping Camp. Along the Merced River, 300 tent cabins are rented unfurnished except for cots and stove. Bring or rent as much gear as needed. L.

Wawona Hotel. The oldest hotel in continuous service in the National Park system, lies 4 miles inside the South Entrance. The rambling gingerbread wooden structures date from 1879. Tennis, 9-hole golf, saddle trips. M.

Tuolumne Meadows and White Wolf Lodges. Cabins with bath and tent cabins offering uncrowded, pleasant experiences off the beaten path. L.

Muir Lodge, Midpines, CA 95345. 19 miles southwest of California 140 entrance, it offers pool, picnic tables, playground. 966-2468. L to M.

Narrow Guage Inn, Fish Camp, CA 95345. 4 miles from the South Entrance. Most rooms have balcony or porch with mountain views. Narrow-guage steam railroad rides are featured. Under 12 free. 683-7720. M.

Yosemite View Lodge, El Portal 95318. At California 140 entrance, with some rooms overlooking the Merced River rapids. 379-2681. M.

Cedar Lodge, El Portal, CA 95318. Motel units, restaurant, TV, pool, RV park. 379-2612. M.

ZION NATIONAL PARK
Utah
Zip 84767. Area code 801.

Inside the park:

Zion Lodge. Concession-operated by TW Services, Inc. (for reservations, 451 N. Main Street, Cedar City, UT 84720), it comprises motel, rustic cabins and dining room in the center of Zion Canyon (5 miles N from South park entrance). 586-7686. M.

Zion Lodge is open mid-May to mid-October. The park, however, is open all-year. Other accommodations are open year-round at Springdale, just outside the South entrance.

Springdale. Zip 84767.

Bumbleberry Inn. Pool. 772-3224. L to M.

Canyon Ranch Motel. Large shady lawn area, 3 kitchenettes. 772-3357. L.

Flanigan's Inn and Restaurant. Shaded natural setting. Pool. 772-3244. L to M.

Pioneer Village Lodge. Heated pool. Outdoor barbecue, dancing, Western show. 772-3233. L to M.

Zion House Bed & Breakfast. Home hospitality—and home-cooked breakfast. 772-3281. M.

Zion Park Motel. Pool; grocery. Family rates. 772-3902. L to M.

Camping:

Zion Canyon Campground. 772-3237.

Zion Village Motel and RV Park. 772-3427.

Subject Index

242

Geographical Index

Abbreviations

About the Author

Michael Frome has enjoyed a colorful and creative career as writer, activist and educator, which he continues to pursue with enthusiasm and unflagging energy. National parks (and the national forests also) are very much a part of his life. Michael has explored them in the United States and the rest of the world, often as camper, backpacker, canoer and horseman. He has been to the areas included in this guidebook over and over again, always learning new things about the parks.

Born in New York City, he served as a World War II navigator, flying to distant corners of the world. He has been a newspaper reporter, a successful travel writer, outdoorsman and eloquent conservationist. He has been called "the voice of the wilderness" and "the conscience of the national parks." Senator Gaylord Nelson of Wisconsin declared in Congress: "No writer in America has more persistently and effectively argued for the need of national ethics of environmental stewardship than Michael Frome."

He is now a member of the faculty of Huxley College of Environmental Studies at Western Washington University (Bellingham, Washington), where he is pioneering a program in environmental journalism and writing. He and his students utilize the resources of nearby national parks and national forests in the North Cascades and Olympics. Under Huxley College auspices, during 1988 Frome and his dean, Dr. John Miles, conducted successful seminars on the future of Glacier Bay National Park in Alaska and Virgin Islands National Park in the Virgin Islands. He has lectured at many colleges and universities. On a typical weekend, he spoke on Saturday in Seattle at a conference on Wilderness in Northwest National Parks, and on Sunday in Kansas City on Travel Ethics at the annual convention of the Society of American Travel Writers, of which he is a past president.

In 1986 he received the Marjorie Stoneman Douglas Award from the National Parks and Conservation Association for his many years of work on behalf of national parks. As a tribute to him, the University of Idaho, where he taught for four years, established the Michael Frome Scholarship for Excellence in Conservation Writing.

In addition to the *National Park Guide*, his books include *Promised Land—Adventures and Encounters in Wild America; The National Parks* and *America's Favorite National Parks; The Forest Service; Strangers in High Places—The Story of the Great Smoky Mountains;* and *Whose Woods These Are—The Story of the National Forests.* Early in 1989 his new book, *Conscience of a Conservationist,* will be published. He is now at work on a book about the future of the national parks and the National Park Service.

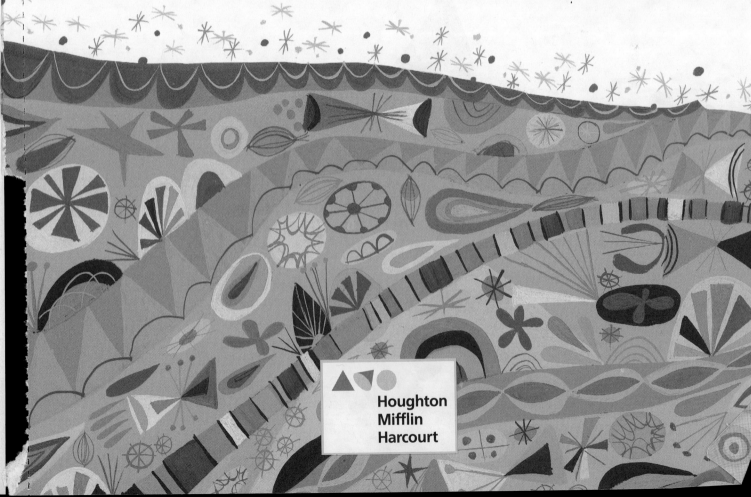

On Our Way to English®
Activity Book

Houghton Mifflin Harcourt

Contents

Contents

Contents

NAME _____

WHAT TO DO

If you can't think of a word . . .

point.

make a gesture.

draw a picture.

say it another way.

NAME _____

WAYS TO HELP

Be patient:

- with your words.
- with your expression.
- with your attitude.

Watch for cues:

- in actions.
- in gestures.
- in expressions.

Be encouraging by:

- asking questions.
- giving support.

Teamwork

WHAT TO DO

If you don't understand . . .

sit close to the teacher.

ask questions.

ask the speaker to slow down.

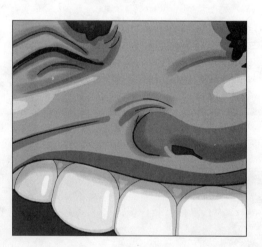

watch the speaker's mouth.

- This will help you understand.

- It will also help you with your pronunciation.

NAME _____

WAYS TO HELP

Act it out.

Lead the way.

Write it down.

Say it another way.

Be supportive.

Word Recognition

© HMH Supplemental Publishers Inc.

NAME _____

HIGH-FREQUENCY WORDS

ⓘ These are the most commonly used English words. Practice reading and spelling these words in order to become better readers and writers.

Unit 1	Unit 2	Unit 3	Unit 4
the	for	from	when
of	on	or	your
and	are	one	can
a	as	had	said
to	with	by	there
in	his	word	use
is	they	but	an
you	I	not	each
that	at	what	which
it	be	all	she
he	this	were	do
was	have	we	how

Unit 5	Unit 6	Unit 7	Unit 8
their	her	see	oil
if	would	number	sit
will	make	no	now
up	like	way	find
other	him	could	long
about	into	people	down
out	time	my	day
many	has	than	did
then	look	first	get
them	two	water	come
these	more	been	made
so	write	call	may
some	go	who	part

NAME —————————————————

MONITORING LISTENING CHECKLIST

	Unit 1	Unit 2	Unit 3
	Faces and Places	**Crafty Creatures**	**Then and Now**
1. What is the topic?			
2. I knew about the topic _____.	☐ already ☐ not at all	☐ already ☐ not at all	☐ already ☐ not at all
3. I knew _____ of the words.	☐ most ☐ some ☐ few	☐ most ☐ some ☐ few	☐ most ☐ some ☐ few
4. I followed _____ of my teacher's directions.	☐ most ☐ some ☐ none	☐ most ☐ some ☐ none	☐ most ☐ some ☐ none
5. I understood _____ sentences.	☐ most ☐ some ☐ few	☐ most ☐ some ☐ few	☐ most ☐ some ☐ few
6. When I didn't understand, I _____.	☐ asked for help ☐ said nothing	☐ asked for help ☐ said nothing	☐ asked for help ☐ said nothing

© HMH Supplemental Publishers Inc.

NAME _____

CHECKLIST

Word	I've never heard of it.	I've heard of it.	I know what it means.
affect	☐	☐	☐
symbol	☐	☐	☐
trail	☐	☐	☐
celebrate	☐	☐	☐
scale	☐	☐	☐
market	☐	☐	☐

Which word did you find most challenging?

_____

© HMH Supplemental Publishers Inc.

NAME

CHECKLIST

Word	I've never heard of it.	I've heard of it.	I know what it means.
farming	☐	☐	☐
fishing	☐	☐	☐
population	☐	☐	☐
continent	☐	☐	☐
compass rose	☐	☐	☐
common	☐	☐	☐

Which word did you find most interesting?

NAME _____

MONITORING SPEAKING CHECKLIST

	Unit 1 "Muddy Shoes"	Unit 2 "Luke's Bad Day"	Unit 3 "The Haunted Basement"
1. When I speak in class, I usually use ___.	☐ one or two words ☐ phrases ☐ complete sentences	☐ one or two words ☐ phrases ☐ complete sentences	☐ one or two words ☐ phrases ☐ complete sentences
2. I understand instructions and can repeat them in ___.	☐ one or two words ☐ phrases ☐ complete sentences	☐ one or two words ☐ phrases ☐ complete sentences	☐ one or two words ☐ phrases ☐ complete sentences
3. If asked about a story, I can identify ___.	☐ the characters ☐ the setting ☐ the conflict or problem	☐ the characters ☐ the setting ☐ the conflict or problem	☐ the characters ☐ the setting ☐ the conflict or problem
4. I can give my opinion or ideas about a story in ___.	☐ one or two words ☐ a sentence ☐ a discussion	☐ one or two words ☐ a sentence ☐ a discussion	☐ one or two words ☐ a sentence ☐ a discussion
5. I can tell my feelings about a story in ___.	☐ one or two words ☐ a sentence ☐ a discussion	☐ one or two words ☐ a sentence ☐ a discussion	☐ one or two words ☐ a sentence ☐ a discussion

NAME —————————————————————————

PERSONAL NARRATIVE RUBRIC

When you write a personal narrative, check it against this rubric.
Did you do everything you can to make it better?   Yes ☐   No ☐

Camping with the Bears		Dina's Model	Class Model	My Model
1.	It is told in the first person, using *I* or *we*.			
2.	It may use dialogue to make characters come alive.			
3.	The story reveals the characters through what they do and say.			
4.	The actions follow each other in a way that makes sense.			
5.	Words help explain the order.			
6.	It is clear **when** and **where** the story takes place.			
7.	The ending is good! It seems right for the story!			
8.	The grammar, spelling, and punctuation are correct.			
9.	Readers will like the story!			

Score
3. Excellent   2. Good   1. Needs work

NAME _____

PERSONAL NARRATIVE SEQUENCE ORGANIZER

1. Mom and Dad leave the campsite.

↓

2. Dina wakes up and finds her parents gone.

↓

3. Dina takes action (turns up radio, plays dead, sings loudly).

↓

4. When parents return, Dina is really upset.

↓

5. Mother explains the confusion.

NAME

CAPITALIZE PROPER NOUNS

> A proper noun begins with a capital letter.
>
> A proper noun is a particular person, place, thing, or idea. *My dog's name is Bing.*
>
> When a proper noun contains more than one word, only the important words are capitalized. *I live in the United States of America.*
>
> People's titles are capitalized, even when they are abbreviations. *That man is Mister Smith. I saw Dr. Clark.*
>
> An adjective that is formed from a proper noun is capitalized. *An American flag waved in the breeze.*

Rewrite each sentence. Capitalize the proper nouns.

1. jamie wrote to dr. eileen cruz.

   _____

2. The panda bear has a chinese name.

   _____

3. I can see venus through my telescope.

   _____

4. Watch out, katie!

   _____

5. The king of sweden has a crown.

   _____

© HMH Supplemental Publishers Inc.

NAME _____

EDITING FOR GRAMMAR, SPELLING, AND PUNCTUATION

See also pages 166 and 170.

> **i** A verb must agree with its subject.
> *I am tall. She is tall. We are best friends.*

> **i** A subject pronoun can take the place of a subject noun.
> *My aunt is an inventor. She builds robots.*
> *My aunt and uncle work hard. They build amazing things.*
> *My sister and I like robots. We like dogs, too.*

> **i** A proper noun begins with a capital letter.

Listen to your teacher. Compare the first draft of the practice paragraph to the edited draft.

First Draft

My mom and I visited the San Antonio Riverwalk. It (are) a path along the (san antonio river.) (He) flows through the middle of the city. We walked down some steps to the river. There (is) tiny white lights hanging in all the trees. At night, (it) twinkle. We looked in several shops. Then, we stopped at a Mexican restaurant. (They) ate and watched people walk by. We had a good time!

Edited Draft

My mom and I visited the San Antonio Riverwalk. It is a path along the San Antonio River. It flows through the middle of the city. We walked down some steps to the river. There are tiny white lights hanging in all the trees. At night, they twinkle. We looked in several shops. Then, we stopped at a Mexican restaurant. We ate and watched people walk by. We had a good time!

NAME —————————————————————————————

READER'S LOG: "HELLO!"

BEFORE READING: PAIR AND SHARE

1. My class talked about the

☐ title ☐ illustrations ☐ _____

2. I understood _____ of the discussion.

☐ most or all ☐ some ☐ little or none

DURING READING

3. What is the main idea of the three personal narratives?

_____

_____

_____

4. Is there anything in the story that you do not understand? Write about it here:

_____

_____

_____

AFTER READING: PAIR AND SHARE

6. Talk to your partner about anything in the story that you do not understand.

Now, my partner and I understand . . .

Me ☐ a lot better. ☐ a little better. ☐ no better.

My partner ☐ a lot better. ☐ a little better. ☐ no better.

NAME _____

MATCH IT UP

Write the letter of the definition that matches each word.

1. _____ celebrate

    A a path that people can follow

2. _____ scale

    B something that stands for something else

3. _____ affect

    C a feature on a map that tells distances on the map

4. _____ trail

    D a place where people buy and sell things

5. _____ market

    E to do things for a special event or day

6. _____ symbol

    F to make a difference to someone or something

NAME

WHICH WORD AM I?

Read the clues. Write the correct vocabulary word from the box to match each clue.

common	fishing	continent
farming	population	compass rose

1. I am the act of growing crops.

_____

2. I am one of the seven large land areas of the world.

_____

3. I am a sign that shows the directions north, south, east, and west on a map.

_____

4. I am the act of catching fish in the water.

_____

5. I am the number of people who live in a place.

_____

6. I am something that is seen often.

_____

NAME _____

A. What is a noun?

Read the sentences. Circle the letter of the answer that best completes the second sentence.

1. The word *girl* is a noun. This word names a _____.

   A person   C thing

   B place   D idea

2. The word *jar* is a noun. This word names a _____.

   A person   C thing

   B place   D animal

B. Subject Pronouns and *to be* verbs

Read the sentences. Circle the letter of the answer that best completes the second sentence.

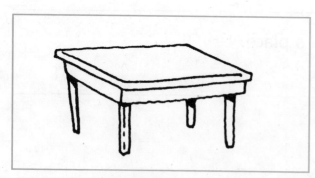 

3. This is my table. _____ is very old.

   A She   C He

   B They   D It

4. Look at the dots. _____ are black.

   A They   C She

   B It   D I

NAME —————————————————————————————

5. Do you see the queen?
She _____ mad at the duck.

   A are   **C** is

   B am   **D** be

6. The dad has two kids.
They _____ all very happy.

   A are   **C** is

   B am   **D** be

PAIR AND SHARE With your partner, discuss: What is your favorite animal?

Use this sentence frame:

I like _____ the best!

Use plural nouns in your answers. Here is an example: *I like cats the best!*

Check pages 159–161 if you need help.

Monitor Language: How's your grammar?

Listen to your partner. Were the plural nouns correct?

Yes, always	Sometimes	Never
☐	☐	☐

How were your plural nouns? Were they correct?

Yes, always	Sometimes	Never
☐	☐	☐

NAME _____

CLOSE READING OF THE TEXT

 Self-monitor your understanding as you read.

1. **Reread.** Start with the last sentence you understood. Then read on from that point.

2. **Take notes.** Write down the most important details. This can help you understand and remember what you read.

3. **Look up words you don't know.**

4. **Ask questions.** Then look for answers to your questions in the text, or you can ask someone.

Informative Text	Notes
A trail stretches fifty miles from Cusco. It leads to Machu Picchu. This city was built by the Incas over five hundred years ago. It sits about 8,000 feet above sea level, on a mountain in the Andes. The Incas used simple tools, but they were great builders. Somehow they carried giant stones to the top of the mountain. They cut the stones to fit together exactly. About 1,000 people lived in and around Machu Picchu. The population didn't stay very long. Less than a hundred years after the Incas built the city, they left. Nobody really knows why.	Underline anything you do not understand. Take notes. What are the most important ideas? _____ _____ _____ Tell what you reread or a question you asked. _____ _____

NAME ———————————————————————

READ WITH EXPRESSION

Read the poem aloud. Read with energy and strong emotion. Pause for punctuation marks such as commas and periods. Listen to your partner's reading. Then practice the passage a second time.

Note: One slash (/) indicates a short pause for a comma. Two slashes (//) indicates that you stop for a period or a question mark.

All I wanted was a carton of juice. //

But I got mixed up, / and asked

For a crate of oranges. //

Learning a new language isn't easy. //

People notice when I get it wrong. //

But they never seem to be around

When I get it right. //

They ask me, / "Where do you come from?" //

But they never bother to ask, /

"Where are you going?" //

NAME _____

CHECK YOUR UNDERSTANDING

A. Reread "Hello!" on **Student Edition** pages 26–35. Then read each sentence below. Circle the letter of the correct answer.

Wen

1. Wen was born in _____.

   A Lima

   B Los Angeles

   C São Paolo

   D Beijing

Wen

Pedro

Fernando

2. Now, Wen lives in the same city as _____.

   A both Fernando and Pedro

   B just Fernando

   C just Pedro

   D Machu Picchu

NAME _____

B. Read each sentence below. Circle the letter of the correct answer.

3. In Fernando's homeland, he _____.

   A helped his mother at the market

   B went to Cusco

   C spoke Portuguese

   D did a lot of fishing

4. Fernando and Pedro both _____.

   A come from the same country

   B spoke Spanish in their homeland

   C live in Los Angeles now

   D came to the United States as babies

C. Read each question below. Circle the letter of the correct answer.

5. Who tells the story of each child?

   A There is no way to know who tells each story.

   B The same person tells all the stories.

   C Each child tells his or her own story.

   D Pedro tells all the stories.

6. How do you know that Wen is happy in her new city?

   A She loves going to Chinese restaurants.

   B She says she is good at English.

   C She goes to the market with her mother.

   D She has made new friends.

NAME _____

A. Label

Write a word that names each picture. Use a word from the word box.

egg	hat	jam	mop
lip	sax	sack	duck	zip

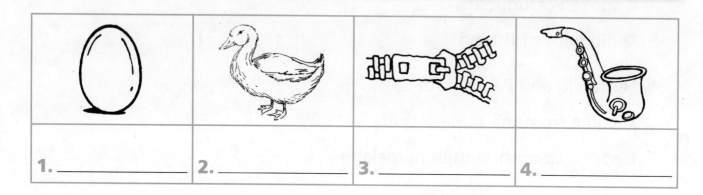

1. _____ 2. _____ 3. _____ 4. _____

B. Phonics

Read these words aloud. Use the phonics skills you have learned.

	A	B	C	D	E	F
5.	fan	Rex	it	not	up	no
6.	van	jet	quit	lot	sun	hi
7.	sat	egg	six	pop	fun	so
8.	has	yes	is	on	but	by
9.	mat	ten	zip	rock	cut	go
10.	gap	well	kill	sock	luck	my

C. High-Frequency Words

Read these words aloud.

11.	the	of	and	a	to	in
12.	is	you	that	it	he	was

© HMH Supplemental Publishers Inc.

NAME

D. Listen. Read. Check.

Your teacher will say a word. Mark the box next to the word.

13.	☐ me		☐ my		☐ hi
14.	☐ it		☐ hit		☐ at
15.	☐ fan		☐ fin		☐ fun
16.	☐ pit		☐ pet		☐ pot
17.	☐ sick		☐ sack		☐ sock
18.	☐ no		☐ not		☐ Nat
19.	☐ six		☐ sit		☐ sat
20.	☐ jet		☐ get		☐ Jed

E. Spelling

Your teacher will say a word. Write the word. Check your spelling.

21. _____   23. _____

22. _____   24. _____

NAME _____

CHECKLIST

Word	I've never heard of it.	I've heard of it.	I know what it means.
unique	☐	☐	☐
trait	☐	☐	☐
nature	☐	☐	☐
fish	☐	☐	☐
fin	☐	☐	☐
scales	☐	☐	☐

Which word did you find most challenging?

_____

© HMH Supplemental Publishers Inc.

NAME ——————————————————————————————

CHECKLIST

Word	I've never heard of it.	I've heard of it.	I know what it means.
bird	☐	☐	☐
bill	☐	☐	☐
cause	☐	☐	☐
describe	☐	☐	☐
mammal	☐	☐	☐
reptile	☐	☐	☐

Which word did you find most interesting?

_____

NAME _____

REPORT RUBRIC: Compare and Contrast

When you write a report with a compare/contrast structure,
check it against this rubric.

Did you do everything you can to make it better?   Yes ☐   No ☐

	Never Call a Spider an Insect	Kevin's Model	Class Model	My Model
1.	The facts are correct. (Should you check the information again?)			
2.	Identify what you are comparing and contrasting.			
3.	It is clear how the two topics are alike.			
4.	It is clear how the two topics are different.			
5.	There is a summary at the end of the report.			
6.	The grammar, spelling, and punctuation are correct.			
7.	Readers will find the report interesting.			

Score

3. Excellent   2. Good   1. Needs work

NAME ————————————————————————

REPORT ORGANIZER: TEXT STRUCTURE
Compare and Contrast

Body Part	Same or Different?	Explanation
Body parts?	Different	Spiders have two body parts. Insects have three.
Bones?	Same	Neither spiders nor insects have bones. Both have exoskeletons.
Eyes?	Same and Different	Spiders have eight pairs of eyes! Some insects have five eyes. Some have fewer. Some insects have compound eyes. Some have simple eyes. Some have both.
Legs?	Different	Spiders have 8 legs. Insects have 6 legs.
Antennae?	Different	Insects do. Spiders don't.
Body part for Smelling?	Different	Insects use their antennae to smell. Spiders smell through bristles in their legs.
Wings?	Different	Spiders never have wings. Many insects do have wings.
Foods?	Different	Spiders eat mostly insects. Insects eat all kinds of things, including paper, plastic, and lint!

NAME _____

END PUNCTUATION

 Every sentence needs punctuation at the end.

- **.** A statement tells or describes something. A statement ends with a period.
  The squirrel ran up the tree.

- **?** A question asks something. A question ends with a question mark.
  Do you want to go to the park?

- **!** An exclamation expresses excitement, the need to act, or a feeling. An exclamation ends with an exclamation point.
  I love walking in the park!

- **.** or **!** A command, or imperative, tells someone to do something. A command ends with a period or an exclamation point.
  Open your notebooks. Don't touch that wild animal!

Write the correct end punctuation for each sentence.

1. I'm excited about visiting the park _____

2. Where did you see the squirrel _____

3. The squirrel has a nest in the tree _____

4. What is the squirrel eating _____

5. Take a picture of the squirrel _____

6. Be quiet _____

7. You'll frighten the squirrel away _____

8. There it goes _____

NAME —————————————————————————————

EDITING FOR GRAMMAR, SPELLING, AND PUNCTUATION

See also pages 159 and 170.

 Some plural words end in –s. Some end in –es.

turtle and *turtles*   *fox* and *foxes*

 A verb must agree with its subject. Read these examples using forms of the verb *to be*.

I am here.	*I was here.*	*We are all here.*	*We were all here.*
You are here.	*You were here.*	*You are all here.*	*You were all here.*
She is here.	*She was here.*	*They are all here.*	*They were all here.*

 Every sentence ends with punctuation.

Listen to your teacher. Compare the first draft of the practice paragraph to the edited draft.

June 16

Something funny happened this evening. We sat outside after dinner. It were very dark. At first, it was quiet Then, something rustled in the bushs. Suddenly, there was a loud burping noise. Mom said it was a frog. It must have been as big as a dinner plate to make a noise that loud Soon, other frogs joined in. "They is all around us," I said. The quiet was gone.

June 16

Something funny happened this evening. We sat outside after dinner. It was very dark. At first, it was quiet. Then, something rustled in the bushes. Suddenly, there was a loud burping noise. Mom said it was a frog. It must have been as big as a dinner plate to make a noise that loud! Soon, other frogs joined in. "They are all around us," I said. The quiet was gone.

33

NAME _____

READER'S LOG: "HOW DO ANIMALS KNOW WHERE THEY ARE GOING?"

> ⓘ Active listeners take notes. Active readers do, too. Write only what you need to remember the most important information.

PAIR AND SHARE Reread the selection with your partner. Mark the boxes and take notes as you read. Add to your notes as you talk to your partner.

1. How difficult is the selection?

   ☐ very difficult   ☐ not too difficult   ☐ easy

2. What makes the selection difficult?

   ☐ the words   ☐ the information   ☐ everything!

3. List the most difficult words.

   _____

4. What did you do about the difficult words?

   ☐ We talked about them.   ☐ We looked at the pictures.

   ☐ We looked them up in a dictionary.   ☐ We asked our teacher.

5. How did you use the pictures? Did they help you?

   _____

6. Are there any sentences that you don't understand?

   Note the page number, and ask your teacher what they mean. _____

NAME ————————————————————————————————

UNSCRAMBLE THE WORDS

Unscramble each word to spell one of the words in the box. Write the word on the line under the scrambled word.

NATURE	FIN	UNIQUE
SCALES	FISH	TRAIT

1. ALCESS (what cover the bodies of some animals)

   _____

2. RITTA (something that makes one person different from another)

   _____

3. HIFS (an animal that lives in the water)

   _____

4. RETANU (everything that is not made by people)

   _____

5. NFI (part of a fish that helps it move)

   _____

6. EQUINU (not like anything else)

   _____

NAME _____

USE CLUES

Read each sentence. Use context clues to help you figure out the correct vocabulary word from the box to complete each sentence. Write the word on the line.

mammal	reptile	cause	describe	bird	bill

1. The feathers of a _____ can be many colors.

_____

2. When I _____ my brother, I say that he is very tall.

_____

3. Many people think a dolphin is a fish, but it is a _____.

_____

4. The bird grabbed the worm in its _____ and ate it whole.

_____

5. Jake thought the _____ would be slimy, but its skin was dry and rough.

_____

6. Too much rain will _____ the river to flood.

_____

NAME ————————————————————————

A. Subject Pronouns and *to be* Verbs

Circle the letter of the correct answer.

1. My sister and I work out.
   We _____ strong.

   A was   C is

   B are   D were

2. Please sing more, Marissa!
   _____ are a good singer!

   A He   C We

   B She   D You

3. Listen to me! Do what I say!
   I _____ the king.

   A is   C am

   B are   D will

4. This is my city!
   _____ is huge!

   A It   C We

   B She   D They

NAME _____

B. Combining Sentences

Write one new sentence that combines the information in the sentences above each picture.

The book is in my room.
The phone is in my room.

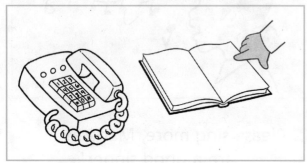

My dad cooks. My mom cooks.
I cook.

5. _____

_____

6. _____

_____

PAIR AND SHARE With your partner, discuss words you can use to describe yourselves. Use nouns and adjectives.

Use these sentence frames:

A. Nouns
I am a _____. (brother, boy, son)
You are a _____. (friend, student)

B. Adjectives
I am _____. (thin, tall, tired)
You are _____. (friendly, helpful)

Check page 164 to review adjectives. Make sure you use the correct verb form. See page 170 to review forms of *to be*.

Monitor Language: How's your grammar?

Listen to your partner. Were the nouns, adjectives, and verb forms correct?

Yes, always	Sometimes	Never
☐	☐	☐

How were your nouns, adjectives, and verb forms? Were they correct?

Yes, always	Sometimes	Never
☐	☐	☐

NAME —————————————————————————————————————

CLOSE READING OF THE TEXT

 Self-monitor your understanding as you read.

1. **Reread.** Start with the last sentence you understood. Then read on from that point.

2. **Take notes.** Write down the most important details. This can help you understand and remember what you read.

3. **Look up words you don't know.**

4. **Ask questions.** Then look for answers to your questions in the text, or you can ask someone.

Narrative Nonfiction	Notes
Huck is a honey badger. He lives in the grasslands in East Africa. Just like all honey badgers, Huck is tough. He is a fierce hunter. There are plenty of animals that Huck hunts. He is a snake killer. He can eat a five-foot snake in fifteen minutes. Scales and all! Huck also eats insects, reptiles, and small mammals. What he loves most of all, though, is honey. Honey isn't always that easy to find. That's why it's a good thing that Huck has a friend called Gus.	Underline anything you do not understand. Take notes. What are the most important ideas? _____ _____ _____ Tell what you reread or a question you asked. _____ _____ _____

NAME _____

READ FOR RATE

Read the following passage aloud. Have a partner time your reading for one minute. Then, fill in the chart at the bottom of the page with the number of words you read. Read the passage a second and third time. Try to increase the number of words you read accurately in a minute.

A spider web stretches between two objects. They may be	10
branches of a tree, or even the legs of a chair.	21
First, the spider spins a thin thread. The thread is carried by	33
the tiniest breeze. It makes a line between the two objects.	44
The spider makes threads from the center. Now you could	54
describe the web as looking like a bicycle wheel. Next, the	65
spider makes sticky threads in circles.	71
It's done, and the spider waits. An insect lands on the web.	83
It gets stuck. The spider rushes up! It bites! It wraps the insect	96
with more thread.	99
Dinner is served.	102

Number of Words Read		
First Reading	Second Reading	Third Reading

NAME ——————————————————————————————————

CHECK YOUR UNDERSTANDING

A. Reread "How Do Animals Know Where They are Going?" on **Student Edition** pages 72-77. Then read each sentence below. Circle the letter of the correct answer.

how animals find their way

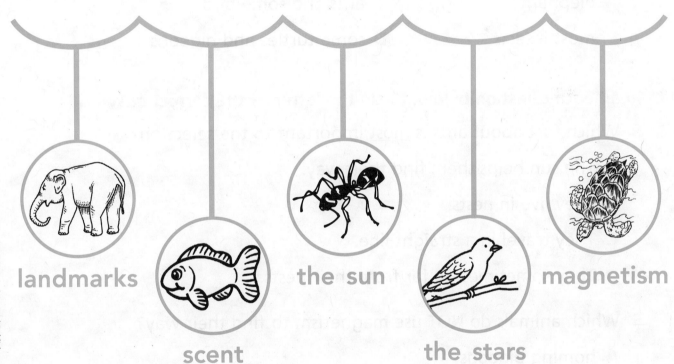

landmarks

scent

the sun

the stars

magnetism

1. Salmon find their way by using _____.

   A the sun   C landmarks

   B scent   D the stars

2. Animals that use landmarks include _____.

   A elephants   C ants

   B bees   D loggerhead turtles

NAME _____

B. Read each sentence below. Circle the letter of the correct answer.

3. One animal that travels by night is the _____ .

   A ant   C pigeon

   B indigo bunting   D elephant

4. The selection tells how _____ use magnetism.

   A elephants   C ants and some birds

   B most insects   D some turtles and pigeons

C. Read each question below. Circle the letter of the correct answer.

5. Which fact about ants is <u>most</u> important to the selection?

   A The sun helps them find their way.

   B They live in nests.

   C They travel in a straight line.

   D They sometimes go far from their nests.

6. Which animals do NOT use magnetism to find their way?

   A homing pigeons

   B salmon

   C loggerhead turtles

   D humans

NAME ——————————————————————————

A. Label

Write a word that names each picture. Use a word from the box.

bat	cub	boat	cube	ran	kit	rain	kite

1. _____	2. _____	3. _____	4. _____

B. Phonics

Read these words aloud. Use the phonics skills you have learned.

	A	B	C	D	E	F	G
5.	see	pane	kite	may	home	Eve	fume
6.	rain	tame	line	team	lone	Zeke	cube
7.	pay	safe	mile	coat	doze	Pete	tube
8.	toad	quake	pipe	keep	mole	beet	mute
9.	meat	tape	bite	pain	bone	peek	tune
10.	be	wade	hike	say	cope	feat	rude

C. High-Frequency Words

Read these words aloud.

11.	for	on	are	as	with	his
12.	they	I	at	be	this	have

NAME _____

D. Listen. Read. Check.

Your teacher will say a word. Mark the box next to the word.

13.	☐ quake	☐ cake	☐ quack
14.	☐ way	☐ wade	☐ wait
15.	☐ rain	☐ ray	☐ ran
16.	☐ cub	☐ cube	☐ cab
17.	☐ bit	☐ by	☐ bite
18.	☐ mutt	☐ mute	☐ muck
19.	☐ feed	☐ fed	☐ feet
20.	☐ pat	☐ pet	☐ Pete

E. Spelling

Your teacher will say a word. Write the word. Check your spelling.

21. _____   23. _____

22. _____   24. _____

NAME —————————————————————

CHECKLIST

Word	I've never heard of it.	I've heard of it.	I know what it means.
travel	☐	☐	☐
past	☐	☐	☐
present	☐	☐	☐
transportation	☐	☐	☐
railroad	☐	☐	☐
possible	☐	☐	☐

Which word did you find most challenging?

_____

NAME _____

CHECKLIST

Word	I've never heard of it.	I've heard of it.	I know what it means.
modern	☐	☐	☐
assembly line	☐	☐	☐
advanced	☐	☐	☐
century	☐	☐	☐
decade	☐	☐	☐
purpose	☐	☐	☐

Which word did you find most interesting?

_____

© HMH Supplemental Publishers Inc.

NAME _____

READING LONGER WORDS

 Reading Closed Syllables When a word or syllable has one vowel and ends in a consonant, the vowel usually stands for a *short* vowel sound.

 You can divide:

- between the words in a compound word.
- after a prefix, or before a suffix.
- between the consonants in a VCCV letter pattern.

A. Draw a slash (/) between the two words. Read the smaller words. Then read the compound word.

cannot	sunset	backpack

B. Draw a slash (/) between the two word parts. Read the word parts. Then read the compound word.

unlit	unpack	dismiss

C. In longer words, look for a VCCV letter pattern (a vowel plus two consonants plus another vowel).

upset	napkin	fabric

D. Use the strategies you have learned to divide the words. Read each part. Then read the whole word.

cactus	padlock	public

NAME _____

FRIENDLY LETTER RUBRIC

When you write a friendly letter, compare it to this rubric. Did you do all you can to make it better?   Yes ☐   No ☐

	Dear New Baby	Marco's Model	Class Model	My Model
1.	The letter is written in the first person, using *I* or *we*.			
2.	The letter has the date, a greeting, a body, and a closing.			
3.	The letter is written to communicate with a friend or relative.			
4.	The letter expresses the writer's thoughts and feelings.			
5.	The letter is readable and clearly written.			
6.	There are different kinds of sentences, and the sentences do not all start with the same word.			
7.	The grammar, spelling, and punctuation in the letter are correct.			

Score
3. Excellent   **2. Good**   **1. Needs work**

NAME

LETTER WRITING ORGANIZER

> Who will receive the letter? _____
>
> How would you describe the letter?
>
> ☐ Personal ☐ School ☐ Business

Check any that apply:	Circle examples:
☐ thank you	for a speech, a gift, help
☐ invitation	to a party, to speak, to join a club
☐ description	of a gift, new puppy, a storm
☐ news	game results, family news, a concert
☐ information	class trip, due date, request to parents, event
☐ excuse	dog ate my homework, illness, fell asleep
☐ events in sequence	first, second, then, finally

Explain in more detail.

_____

_____

_____

NAME _____

USE COMMAS IN A LIST

> ⓘ Commas tell a reader where to pause. We use commas to
> separate three or more items in a list.
>
> *Bicycles, roller skates, and skateboards have wheels.*
> *She got on her bike, pedaled hard, and flew down*
> *the street.*

Rewrite each sentence, using the correct punctuation.

1. Maria Tran and Luis went to the park.

_____

2. The park has trails a lake and rides.

_____

3. Children adults and pets walked on the trails.

_____

4. People swam fished and watched ducks at the lake.

_____

5. Tran carried a blanket a picnic basket and a book.

_____

6. Maria carried water cups and plates.

_____

7. Luis brought napkins forks and spoons.

_____

8. They ate sandwiches salad and fruit.

_____

NAME _____

EDITING FOR GRAMMAR, SPELLING, AND PUNCTUATION

See also pages 173 and 174.

 The present tense of a verb describes an action that is happening now. *The horses walk down the street.*

 The past tense of a verb describes action that happened in the past. *The horses walked down the street.*

 An adverb often describes a verb. It usually ends in *–ly*. Incorrect: *The drums beat loud.* Correct: *The drums beat loudly.*

Listen to your teacher. Compare the first draft of a friendly letter to the edited draft.

Dear Lydia,   September 5, 2011

    We had a terrible storm last night! I was at my cousin Sara's house. Lightning struck. A flash of light filled the room. Thunder (boom). I was terrified! The wind blew (fierce). It broke tree branches ∧ blew leaves ∧ and tore down signs. Then, the rain came. It drummed on the roof. It rattled the windows. Finally, the storm (pass). We hugged each other when it was over.

                                                    Your friend,
                                                    Amy

Dear Lydia,   September 5, 2011

    We had a terrible storm last night! I was at my cousin Sara's house. Lightning struck. A flash of light filled the room. Thunder boomed. I was terrified! The wind blew fiercely. It broke tree branches, blew leaves, and tore down signs. Then, the rain came. It drummed on the roof. It rattled the windows. Finally, the storm passed. We hugged each other when it was over.

                                                    Your friend,
                                                    Amy

© HMH Supplemental Publishers Inc.

NAME _____

READER'S LOG: "ANOTHER WAY TO GO"

BEFORE READING: PAIR AND SHARE

1. My class talked about the _____.

   ☐ title   ☐ illustrations   ☐ _____

2. I understood _____ of the discussion.

   ☐ most or all   ☐ some   ☐ little or none

DURING READING

3. How does a horseless carriage save the day?

   _____

   _____

   _____

4. Is there anything in the story that you do not understand? Write about it here:

   _____

   _____

   _____

AFTER READING: PAIR AND SHARE

5. Talk to your partner about anything that you did not understand.

   Now, my partner and I understand _____.

   Me   ☐ a lot better   ☐ a little better   ☐ no better

   My partner   ☐ a lot better   ☐ a little better   ☐ no better

NAME ——

WHICH WORD?

Write the vocabulary word from the box to complete each sentence.

present	railroad	travel
possible	past	transportation

1. When people ———, they go from place to place.

———

2. Something that happened long ago happened in the ———.

———

3. If something is ———, you can do it.

———

4. Railroads, cars, and airplanes are different kinds of ———.

———

5. Trains travel along the steel tracks of a ———.

———

6. Something that is happening in the ——— is happening now.

———

NAME _____

MATCH IT UP

Write the letter of the definition that matches each word.

1. ___ century   **A** part of a factory where work passes from one person to the next

2. ___ purpose   **B** ten years

3. ___ assembly line   **C** the reason that something exists

4. ___ decade   **D** something new and from the present

5. ___ advanced   **E** one hundred years

6. ___ modern   **F** greatly developed and using new ideas

NAME _____

A. Action Verbs: Present Tense

Circle the letter of the correct answer.

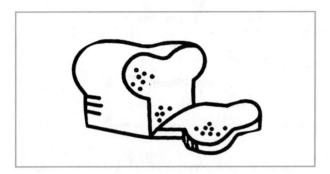

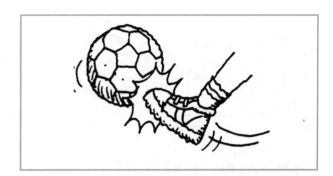

1. I like bread a lot. Juan _____ it a lot, too.

   A like   **C** liking

   B likes   **D** liked

2. Dan kicks the ball. Marta kicks the ball. We all _____ the ball.

   A kicks   **C** kick

   B licking   **D** were

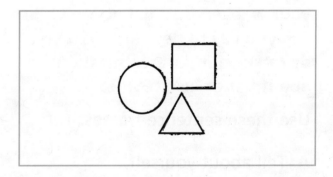

3. Look at the ducks! They _____ all the time.

   A quack   **C** quacking

   B quacks   **D** are

4. I see the shapes. Kim _____ the shapes too.

   A sees   **C** seeing

   B see   **D** is

NAME _____

B. Action Verbs: Past Tense

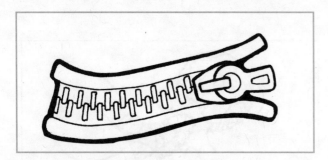

5. Last week, it was cold. I _____ up my coat to the top.

   A zip   C zipped

   B zipping   D zipper

6. Last week, we went to the zoo. Roberto _____ all day.

   A smiles   C smiling

   B smiled   D will smile

PAIR AND SHARE With your partner, discuss how you spend your weekends. What action verbs can you use to describe what you do? Ask your partner questions about her or his activities.

Use these sentence frames:

A. Tell about yourself.

   On the weekend, I usually _____. (run, play, study, sleep)

B. Tell about what a family member or friend does on weekends.

   On the weekend, my dad usually _____. (plays chess, watches TV, reads books)

Check page 173 to review action verbs. Make sure you use the correct verb form.

Monitor Language: How's your grammar?

Listen to your partner. Were the verb forms correct?

Yes, always	Sometimes	Never
☐	☐	☐

How were your verb forms? Were they correct?

Yes, always	Sometimes	Never
☐	☐	☐

NAME ———————————————————————

CLOSE READING OF THE TEXT

 Self-monitor your understanding as you read.

1. **Reread**. Start with the last sentence you understood. Then read on from that point.

2. **Take notes**. Write down the most important details. This can help you understand and remember what you read.

3. **Look up words you don't know.**

4. **Ask questions**. Then look for answers to your questions in the text, or you can ask someone.

Informative Text	Notes
Transportation changed in the twentieth century. In 1900, people depended on horses. Some cities had electric streetcars. Many buses were pulled by horses. People traveled by train between cities. In the country, there weren't many ways to get around. There were only 9,000 cars on the road. And there weren't very many roads! A lot happened in the first decade of the century. The airplane was invented. The first car that people could afford was made. Things were beginning to change.	Underline anything you do not understand. Take notes. What are the most important ideas? _____ _____ _____ Tell what you reread or a question you asked. _____ _____ _____

NAME _____

READ FOR ACCURACY

Work with a partner. Take turns reading the passage aloud. Try to speak clearly and pronounce each word correctly. Then review the passage together. Write the difficult words on the lines below. Practice saying the words aloud. Then read the passage a second time.

> You can be glad you didn't have to ride the first kind of bike. It had wooden wheels and iron tires. It was called "the boneshaker."
>
> Next came a bicycle with rubber tires. It was much more popular!
>
> Today's bicycles are light and fast. They have gears. This helps the rider get the most out of the bike.
>
> Bikes don't need any fuel. Riding a bike is kind to the planet, and good for your health.

_____   _____

_____   _____

_____   _____

_____   _____

_____   _____

NAME ———————————————————————————

CHECK YOUR UNDERSTANDING

A. Read the following questions about "The Transportation Century" on **Student Edition** pages 128–133. Circle the letter of the correct answer.

1900   1950   2000

first airplane   first space shuttle

1. People started flying in airplanes _____.

   A before 1900   C in 1950

   B before 1910   D after 1950

2. The space shuttle was invented _____.

   A before the airplane   C after 1950

   B before 1950   D after 2000

NAME _____

B. Read each sentence below. Circle the letter of the correct answer.

3. The twentieth century began in the year _____.

   A 2000   C 1920

   B 1900   D 1999

4. The first city buses were _____.

   A electric   C invented after the airplane

   B the same size as cars   D pulled by horses

C. Read each question below. Circle the letter of the correct answer.

5. How did transportation change from 1910 to 1950?

   A Millions more cars were on the road by 1950.

   B There were no more trains by 1950.

   C The space shuttle started flying between cities.

   D There were 9,000 cars in 1950.

6. What does the selection tell about jetpacks?

   A Jetpacks were a new invention in 2000.

   B Travelers get around by jetpack all the time now.

   C Travelers may use jetpacks someday.

   D People traveled to the moon and back with jetpacks.

NAME —————————————————————

A. Label

Write a word that names each picture. Use a word from the word box.

pad	page	ship	chip	bath	shapes
		cent	sell		

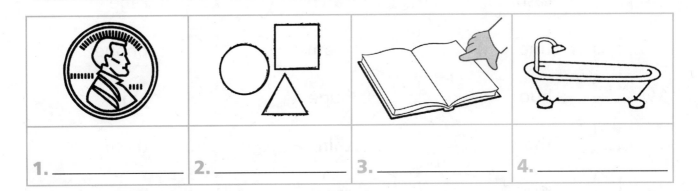

1. _____ 2. _____ 3. _____ 4. _____

B. Phonics

Read these words aloud. Use the phonics skills you have learned.

	A	B	C	D	E	F	G
5.	ship	sheet	path	thus	ace	game	gem
6.	chip	leash	thin	then	cage	coal	cell
7.	cash	wheel	math	that	mice	goal	gel
8.	rich	phone	with	them	huge	cope	cent
9.	rash	whee	thick	than	race	gain	gene
10.	catch	cheap	bath	this	wage	cone	cease

C. High-Frequency Words

Read these words aloud.

11.	from	or	one	had	by	word
12.	but	not	what	all	were	we

© HMH Supplemental Publishers Inc.

NAME _Ceci_

D. Listen. Read. Check.

Your teacher will say a word. Mark the box next to the word.

13.	☐ rash		☐ rich		☐ chip
14.	☐ cash		☐ catch		☐ cage
15.	☐ fine		☐ foam		☐ phone
16.	☐ hug		☐ huge		☐ jug
17.	☐ the		☐ thin		☐ them
18.	☐ rice		☐ race		☐ Russ
19.	☐ whip		☐ wipe		☐ hip
20.	☐ age		☐ jay		☐ gem

E. Spelling

Your teacher will say a word. Write the word. Check your spelling.

21. _____   23. _____

22. _____   24. _____

NAME ——————————————————————————————————————

MONITORING LISTENING CHECKLIST

> ⓘ Active listeners take notes. Don't try to write everything. Just note what you need in order to remember the most important information.

	Unit 4 Making Life Easier	Unit 5 Shoot for the Stars	Unit 6 Our Valuable Earth
1. What is the topic?			
2. The general meaning of the discussion was _____.			
3. I knew most of the words _____.	☐ already ☐ not at all	☐ very familiar ☐ unfamiliar	☐ very familiar ☐ unfamiliar
4. I understood the sentences _____.	☐ most of the time ☐ sometimes ☐ almost never	☐ most of the time ☐ sometimes ☐ almost never	☐ most of the time ☐ sometimes ☐ almost never
5. The main point of this topic is now _____.	☐ very clear ☐ a little clearer ☐ still confusing	☐ very clear ☐ a little clearer ☐ still confusing	☐ very clear ☐ a little clearer ☐ still confusing
6. My notes helped me understand the discussion _____.	☐ a lot ☐ a little ☐ not at all	☐ a lot ☐ a little ☐ not at all	☐ a lot ☐ a little ☐ not at all

NAME _Ceci_

CHECKLIST

Word	I've never heard of it.	I've heard of it.	I know what it means.
calculator	☐	☒	☐
monitor	☐	☒	☐
keyboard	☐	☒	☐
computer	☐	☒	☐
printer	☐	☒	☐
type	☐	☒	☐

Which word did you find most challenging?

The Monitor is the hard for me a litte.

NAME _Ceci_

CHECKLIST

Word	I've never heard of it.	I've heard of it.	I know what it means.
robot	☐	☑	☐
chore	☐	☑	☐
command	☐	☐	☑
plan	☐	☑	☐
report	☐	☑	☐
electricity	☐	☑	☐

Which word did you find most interesting?

The robot is the Interesting the most.

© HMH Supplemental Publishers Inc.

NAME _____

MONITORING SPEAKING CHECKLIST

	Unit 4	Unit 5	Unit 6
	"Lost Dog"	"Cooking Dinner"	"Pablo and Pedro"
1. I can describe the characters and setting in _____.	☐ one or two words ☐ phrases ☐ complete sentences	☐ one or two words ☐ phrases ☐ complete sentences	☐ one or two words ☐ phrases ☐ complete sentences
2. I can retell the story in _____.	☐ a complete way ☐ a sentence ☐ a word or two	☐ a complete way ☐ a sentence ☐ a word or two	☐ a complete way ☐ a sentence ☐ a word or two
3. I explain my opinion about the story and ideas in a way that others _____.	☐ often agree with ☐ understand ☐ do not understand	☐ often agree with ☐ understand ☐ do not understand	☐ often agree with ☐ understand ☐ do not understand
4. My speaking skills are _____.	☐ improving ☐ staying the same	☐ improving ☐ staying the same	☐ improving ☐ staying the same

NAME —————————————————

READING LONGER WORDS

Reading Open Syllables

When a word or syllable ends in a vowel, the vowel usually stands for a *long* vowel sound.

When you see a VCV letter pattern, first try dividing the word before the consonant. Read the word using a long vowel sound for the open syllable. (Example: p h o / t o) If the word doesn't sound quite right, try dividing after the consonant. Then read the word again, using a short vowel sound. (Example: p a n / i c)

A. Divide the word *before* the consonant in the VCV letter pattern. Read each syllable. Then read the whole word.

p h o t o	e g o	l o g o	p u p i l

B. Divide the word. Find the VCV letter pattern. Read each syllable. Then read the whole word.

b e g i n	r o b o t	c u b i c	m u s i c

C. Divide the word. Find the VCV letter pattern. Read each syllable. Then read the whole word.

p a n i c	c o m i c	r a p i d	r o b i n

D. Divide the word. Find the VCV letter pattern. Read each syllable. Then read the whole word.

s i r e n	r e c e s s	d e n i m	h u m i d
c o m e t	f i n i s h	o p e n	v i s i t

NAME _____

RUBRIC: PROCEDURAL TEXTS

When you write a procedural text, check it against this rubric.
Did you do everything you can to make it better?   Yes ☐ No ☐

	Getting Things Done	Li Yan's Model	Class Model	My Model
1.	A title describes the project or activity.			
2.	There is a list of necessary materials or tools.			
3.	Photos or illustrations may show the steps or final product.			
4.	Numbered steps tell how to do a task.			
5.	Each step is written clearly.			
6.	Words and numbers make the order of the steps clear.			
7.	The document is neat and easy to read.			
8.	The grammar, spelling, and punctuation are correct.			

Score

3. Excellent   **2. Good**   **1. Needs work**

NAME

ORGANIZER: PROCEDURAL TEXTS

Materials needed:

First,

Second,

Third,

Next,

Finally. . .

NAME _____

END PUNCTUATION

 **Every sentence needs punctuation at the end.**

- **.**   A statement tells something or describes something. A statement ends with a period.
My cat is called Buster.

- **?**   A question is a sentence that asks something. A question ends with a question mark.
Where do you live?

- **!**   An exclamation is a sentence full of excitement, urgency, or feeling. An exclamation ends with an exclamation point.
I am so happy!

- **.** or **!**   A command, or imperative, tells someone to do something. A command ends with a period or an exclamation point.
Stay away from that dog! Come to my house tomorrow.

Add the correct punctuation at the end of each sentence.

1. I need to write a letter to my aunt_____

2. How much does a stamp cost_____

3. Get the mail from the mailbox_____

4. Quick, the mail truck is coming_____

5. Find the zip code_____

6. A zip code helps the post office_____

7. I love colored envelopes_____

8. Let's be pen pals_____

NAME

EDITING FOR GRAMMAR, SPELLING, AND PUNCTUATION

See also pages 170–172.

A contraction is two words put together to make one word. An apostrophe takes the place of the missing letter or letters.

I am	⇒	I'm		you are	⇒	you're
she is	⇒	she's	he is ⇒ he's	it is	⇒	it's
we are	⇒	we're		they are	⇒	they're

A negative contraction combines a verb with the word *not*.

is not	⇒	isn't	are not	⇒	aren't
was not	⇒	wasn't	were not	⇒	weren't
does not	⇒	doesn't	will not	⇒	won't

Listen to your teacher. Compare the first draft of the practice paragraph to the edited draft.

Make Your Own Card

Have you ever made your own card It isnt hard. You need paper, scissors, glitter, magazines, glue, and markers. First, fold a piece of paper in half. Next, cut out some magazine pictures. Be sure to cut neat. Glue them to the front of the card. Add glitter. Then, write a message inside. Youre done!

Make Your Own Card

Have you ever made your own card? It isn't hard. You need paper, scissors, glitter, magazines, glue, and markers. First, fold a piece of paper in half. Next, cut out some magazine pictures. Be sure to cut neatly. Glue them to the front of the card. Add glitter. Then, write a message inside. You're done!

NAME _____

READER'S LOG: "ROBERT THE ROBOT"

BEFORE READING: PAIR AND SHARE

1. My class talked about
   ☐ titles.   ☐ illustrations.   ☐ _____

2. I understood _____ of the discussion.
   ☐ most or all   ☐ some   ☐ little or none

DURING READING

3. What are the major events in the story?

   _____

   _____

   _____

4. Is there anything in the story that you do not understand? Write it here:

   _____

   _____

   _____

AFTER READING: PAIR AND SHARE

5. Talk to your partner about anything that you did not understand.
   Now, my partner and I understand _____.
   Me   ☐ a lot better ☐ a little better ☐ no better
   My partner ☐ a lot better ☐ a little better ☐ no better

NAME ——————————————————————————————

USE CLUES

Read each sentence. Use context clues to help you figure out the correct vocabulary word from the box to complete each sentence. Write the word on the line.

monitor	computer	type	printer
keyboard	calculator		

1. A powerful _____ can do much more than emails and games.

   _____

2. I have a color _____ that makes beautiful copies of drawings that I make on the computer.

   _____

3. A _____ makes it easy for me to add a lot of numbers.

   _____

4. Maria opened the file and looked at it on the _____ of her computer.

   _____

5. Some people can _____ faster than they can write with a pencil or pen.

   _____

6. The _____ of my computer has keys to type letters and keys for commands.

   _____

NAME _____

UNSCRAMBLE THE WORDS

Unscramble each word to spell one of the words in the box. Write the word on the line under the scrambled word.

CHORE	PLAN	REPORT	ROBOT
	COMMAND	ELECTRICITY	

1. NAMDOCM (an order to do something)

_____

2. TREPOR (facts and ideas about a topic)

_____

3. BOORT (a machine that can help people work)

_____

4. HECOR (a job that needs to be done often)

_____

5. TETYLCRICEI (power that travels along wires)

_____

6. LANP (a drawing that shows how something is put together)

_____

NAME —————————————————————

Using Contractions with *to be* and *not*
Read each question. Circle the letter of the sentence that answers it.

1. Is that Dad's box?

  A Yes, it's his box.

  B Yes, they are.

  C Yes, we can.

2. Is that a drum?

  A Yes, it's a drum.

  B No, it isn't a drum.

  C It wasn't fun.

3. Are the kids pals?

  A No, it isn't.

  B He is a pal.

  C Yes, they're pals.

4. Are you kids all on the bus?

  A Yes, we're on it.

  B No, I'm not.

  C No, he isn't.

5. Is that a bell?

  A No, it isn't.

  B Yes, it's a bell.

  C You're a bell.

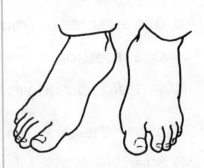

6. Were your feet sore?

  A Yes, they're feet.

  B No, I'm not.

  C Yes, they're sore.

NAME _____

7. Is it raining?

   A No, it isn't raining.

   B Yes, it's raining.

   C We're not wet.

8. Is that a fish?

   A No, I'm not.

   B Yes, it's a fish.

   C No, it isn't a fish.

PAIR AND SHARE With your partner, discuss what you did yesterday.

Use these sentence frames:

A. Ask a question.

What did you do yesterday?

B. Answer the question.

Yesterday, I _____. (cleaned my room, watched TV, finished my math)

Check page 174 to review the past tense forms of action verbs. Make sure you use the correct verb form.

Monitor Language: How's your grammar?

Listen to your partner. Were the past tense verb forms correct?

Yes, always	Sometimes	Never
☐	☐	☐

How were your verb forms? Were they correct?

Yes, always	Sometimes	Never
☐	☐	☐

NAME —————————————————————————

CLOSE READING OF THE TEXT

 Self-monitor your understanding as you read.

1. **Reread.** Start with the last sentence you understood. Then read on from that point.

2. **Take notes.** Write down the most important details. This can help you understand and remember what you read.

3. **Look up words you don't know.**

4. **Ask questions.** Then look for answers to your questions in the text, or you can ask someone.

Informative Text	Notes
Some people don't have good handwriting! Luckily, the typewriter was invented. The words are always neat. Also, people can type faster than they can write. Typewriters were used all around the world for about a hundred years. Then a machine that was faster and more useful took over. The world turned to the computer. A computer lets you correct your work as you write. If you're fixing a long report, you don't have to start all over again. There are commands on the keyboard for all sorts of helpful tasks.	Underline anything you do not understand. Take notes. What are the most important ideas? _____ _____ _____ Tell what you reread or a question you asked. _____ _____ _____

NAME _____

READ WITH EXPRESSION

Read aloud the following section. Read with energy and strong emotion. Pause for punctuation marks such as commas and periods. Listen to your partner's reading. Then practice the passage a second time.

Note: One slash (/) indicates a short pause for a comma. Two slashes (//) indicates that you stop for a period or a question mark.

Rosa opened her lunchbox. // As usual, / there was a cheese sandwich. // As usual, / her mother hadn't cut the sandwich in half. // So, / as usual, / Rosa would make a mess when she ate it. //

"Why won't Mom use a knife?" // Rosa said. // "Even cavemen used knives. // They made them by banging stones until some flaked off. // A sharp edge was left." //

"You can use this plastic knife," / said Elva. // "But it won't be much good for hunting a mammoth." //

NAME —————————————————

CHECK YOUR UNDERSTANDING

A. Reread "Robert the Robot" on **Student Edition** pages 164–173. Then read each sentence below. Circle the letter of the correct answer.

1. The father wanted a robot that ———.

   A did homework   **C** played ball

   B was a lot of fun   **D** did chores

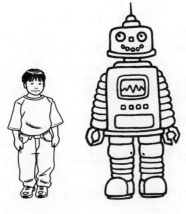

2. Robert the robot ———.

   A is smaller than a child   **C** is a machine

   B is a living thing   **D** looks like a person

NAME _____

B. Read each sentence below. Circle the letter of the correct answer.

3. The boy didn't like the robot at first because _____.

   A he wanted a different kind of robot

   B he didn't want a robot in the house at all

   C he wanted to buy computer games instead of a robot

   D the robot didn't follow Dad's commands

4. The first way the robot helped the boy was by _____.

   A doing one of his chores

   B driving him to school

   C making a really good dinner

   D making him scream

C. Read each question below. Circle the letter of the correct answer.

5. What caused the boy's feelings about the robot to change?

   A The robot showed that he could talk.

   B The robot liked to play games.

   C The robot turned out to be very helpful.

   D The robot did the boy's homework for him.

6. What is the one thing that Robert didn't understand?

   A He didn't understand how the stove worked.

   B He didn't understand the meaning of "lighten up."

   C He couldn't figure out how the car worked.

   D He couldn't figure out the answers to the boy's homework.

A. Label

Write a word that names each picture. Use a word from the word box.

| bank | back | king | kick | him | hand | hats | jets |

1. King	2. hand	3. bank	4. Jets

B. Phonics

Read these words aloud. Use the phonics skills you have learned.

	A	B	C	D	E	F	G
5.	skin	last	bank	toe	flip	baby	rapid
6.	stitch	mask	bang	tie	brain	logo	habit
7.	spoke	toast	sunk	foe	clap	total	timid
8.	snack	list	thing	dye	band	icon	valid
9.	smell	risk	rung	Joe	melt	veto	limit
10.	slide	gasp	think	woe	tree	minus	denim

C. High-Frequency Words

Read these words aloud.

11.	when	your	can	said	there	use
12.	an	each	which	she	do	how

NAME _____

D. Listen. Read. Check.

Your teacher will say a word. Mark the box next to the word.

13.	☐ laid	☐ lad	☐ lady
14.	☐ cave	☐ cabinet	☐ cabin
15.	☐ sell	☐ smell	☐ melts
16.	☐ ask	☐ ax	☐ sax
17.	☐ rink	☐ ring	☐ Rick
18.	☐ sank	☐ sang	☐ sand
19.	☐ time	☐ tide	☐ tie
20.	☐ toad	☐ toe	☐ to

E. Spelling

Your teacher will say a word. Write the word. Check your spelling.

21. _____   23. _____

22. _____   24. _____

NAME

CHECKLIST

Word	I've never heard of it.	I've heard of it.	I know what it means.
solar system	☐	☐	☐
planet	☐	☐	☐
orbit	☐	☐	☐
phase	☐	☐	☐
outer space	☐	☐	☐
astronaut	☐	☐	☐

Which word did you find most challenging?

NAME _____

CHECKLIST

Word	I've never heard of it.	I've heard of it.	I know what it means.
gravity	☐	☒	☐
train	☐	☒	☐
weightless	☐	☒	☐
crew	☐	☐	☒
experience	☐	☒	☐
space shuttle	☒	☐	☐

Which word did you find most interesting?

_____

NAME

READING LONGER WORDS

> **Reading Syllables with a VCe Letter Pattern**
>
> Read these words: *hope, bike, Pete, same, cube.* They all have a vowel + a consonant + silent e. Look for this letter pattern in longer words.

> **You can divide:**
>
> - between the words in a compound word.
> - after a prefix, or before a suffix.
> - between the consonants in a VCCV letter pattern.
> - before or after the consonant in a VCV letter pattern.

A. Divide the word. Circle the VCe letter pattern. Read each syllable. Then read the whole word.

erase	unite	locate
donate	refine	refuse

B. Divide the word. Circle the VCe letter pattern. Read each syllable. Then read the whole word.

inflate	dislike	mistake	exhale

C. Divide the word. Circle the VCe letter pattern. Read each syllable. Then read the whole word.

divide	decade	volume

D. Divide the word. Circle the VCe letter pattern. Read each syllable. Then read the whole word.

reptile	confuse	invite	escape
update	bedtime	online	inside

NAME _____

REPORT RUBRIC: Descriptive

When you write a report, check it against this rubric.
Did you do everything you can to make it better?   Yes ☐   No ☐

What's Up with Pluto?		Nela's Model	Class Model	My Model
1.	The facts are correct. (Should you check the information again?)			
2.	The topic of your report is clear.			
3.	Each paragraph describes one part of the main topic.			
4.	The organization helps the reader understand the information.			
5.	The grammar, spelling, and punctuation are correct.			
6.	Readers will find it interesting.			

Score

3. Excellent   2. Good   1. Needs work

NAME ————————————————————————————

REPORT ORGANIZER: TEXT STRUCTURE Descriptive

You have already analyzed an informational report in Unit 2. It was titled "Never Call a Spider an Insect." This report showed how spiders and insects are alike and different, so its organizer was based on a Compare/ Contrast structure.

In this unit, you will read another informational report, titled "What's Up with Pluto?" This report is organized to describe four different topics about Pluto. They are summarized below.

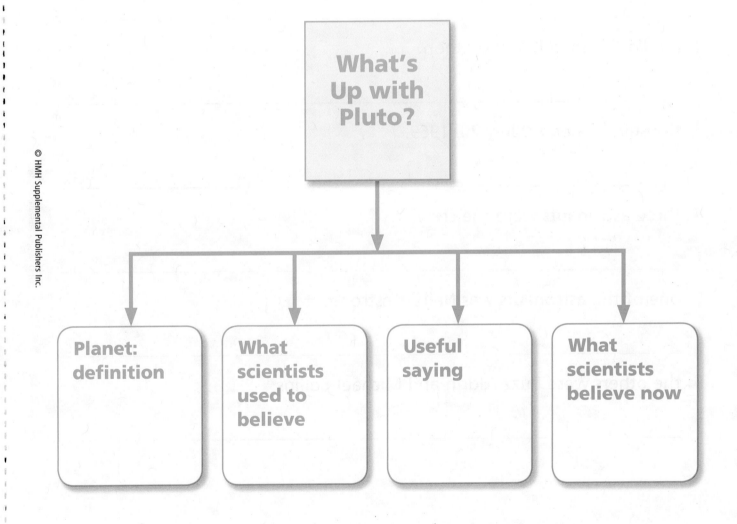

NAME _____

CAPITALIZE THE FIRST WORD OF A SENTENCE

> **i** Every sentence begins with a capital letter.
>
> Make sure you capitalize the first word of a sentence.
> *People have visited outer space.*
> *There are billions of stars.*

Write each sentence correctly.

1. today, our class studied space travel.

_____

2. *apollo 11* landed on the Moon.

_____

3. the ship landed on July 20, 1969.

_____

4. three astronauts were the crew.

_____

5. one of the astronauts was Neil Armstrong.

_____

6. the others were Buzz Aldrin and Michael Collins.

_____

NAME _____

EDITING FOR GRAMMAR, SPELLING, AND PUNCTUATION

See also pages 180 and 181.

A verb must agree with its subject.
I am here.   *She is here.*   *We are here.*

The present progressive form of a verb shows a continuing action. It uses *am, is,* or *are* and a verb that ends in *–ing*.
I am eating lunch.   *They are going away.*

The future tense of a verb shows action that will happen in the future. It uses the helping verb *will* plus the main verb.
Tomorrow we will visit my aunt.

Listen to your teacher. Compare the first draft of the practice paragraph to the edited draft.

First Draft

Long ago, people saw shapes in groups of stars. these shapes are called constellations. One constellation is called Orion. It look like a warrior. It has a club and a shield. It has a belt made of three stars. A sword hangs from the belt. Today, as people is looking at the night sky, they see the same constellations. people in the future will looked at the same constellations. The stars will shine for a very long time.

Edited Draft

Long ago, people saw shapes in groups of stars. These shapes are called constellations. One constellation is called Orion. It looks like a warrior. It has a club and a shield. It has a belt made of three stars. A sword hangs from the belt. Today, as people are looking at the night sky, they see the same constellations. People in the future will look at the same constellations. The stars will shine for a very long time.

NAME _____

READER'S LOG: "STARRING GRACE"

> ⓘ Active listeners take notes. Active readers do, too. Write only what you need to remember the important information.

PAIR AND SHARE Reread the selection with your partner. Mark the boxes and take notes as you read. Add to your notes as you talk to your partner.

1. How difficult is the selection?

   ☐ very difficult ☐ not too difficult ☐ easy

2. What makes the selection difficult?

   ☐ the words ☐ the information ☐ everything!

3. List the difficult words.

   _____

4. What did you do about those words?

   ☐ We talked about them. ☐ We looked them up in a dictionary.

   ☐ We looked at the pictures. ☐ We asked our teacher.

5. How did you use the photos? Did they help you?

6. Are there any sentences that you don't understand?
   Note the page number, and ask your teacher what they mean. _____

NAME —————————————————————————————

WHICH WORD?

Write the vocabulary word from the box to complete each sentence.

planet	phase	solar system	astronaut
	orbit	outer space	

1. The planets _____ the Sun.

_____

2. The Sun, the Moon, and the planets are in the _____.

_____

3. A person who travels in space is an _____.

_____

4. The planets and the stars are in _____.

_____

5. Each _____ of the Moon is a different shape.

_____

6. A _____ is a large object that moves around the Sun.

_____

NAME _____

MATCH IT UP

Write the letter of the definition that matches each word.

1. _____ weightless   A a team of people working together

2. _____ experience   B the force that pulls an object to Earth

3. _____ crew   C to practice to get better at something

4. _____ space shuttle   D a spacecraft that makes more than one trip

5. _____ gravity   E without having gravity pulling it down

6. _____ train   F to take part in an event

NAME

A. Asking Questions

Look at the picture. Which question best fits the picture?

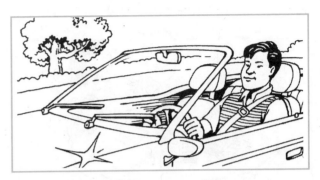

1. What is the best question?

   A Who are you?

   B What is the girl saying?

   C How much is it?

2. What is the best question?

   A Where is he going?

   B What is Mom doing?

   C Do you like cars?

B. Choosing the Verb Tense

Read the sentence. Which verb tense is used?

3. The girl is kicking the ball.

   A present tense

   B future tense

   C past tense

4. Yesterday, my brother helped me.

   A present tense

   B future tense

   C past tense

NAME _____

C. Present or Present Progressive Tense

Look at the picture. Read the sentences. Circle the letter of the BEST sentence to describe the picture.

6. Tell why you think the sentence you chose is best.

_____

_____

_____

_____

5. **A** They are talking about their plans.

    B They sometimes write stories.

PAIR AND SHARE Discuss what you do every day and what you are doing right now. Use these sentence frames:

A. Ask questions.

1. *What do you do every day?*
2. *What are you doing right now?*

B. Answer the questions.

1. *Every day, I _____.* (eat breakfast, read books, study math, talk to friends)
2. *Right now, I am _____.* (talking to you, doing my homework, sitting in class)

Check page 180 to review the simple present tense and the present progressive action verbs.

Monitor Language: How's your grammar?

Listen to your partner. Were the present and present progressive verb forms correct?

Yes, always	Sometimes	Never
☐	☐	☐

How were your verb tenses and forms? Were they correct?

Yes, always	Sometimes	Never
☐	☐	☐

NAME —————————————————————————————

CLOSE READING OF THE TEXT

 Self-monitor your understanding as you read.

1. **Reread.** Start with the last sentence you understood. Then read on from that point.

2. **Take notes.** Write down the most important details. This can help you understand and remember what you read.

3. **Look up words you don't know.**

4. **Ask questions.** Then look for answers to your questions in the text, or you can ask someone.

Informative Text	Notes
The closest object in outer space is the Moon. It's not easy to get there! In fact, only twelve people have ever been on the Moon. And nobody has been there since 1972. The rocket *Apollo 11* carried the first crew of astronauts to the Moon. As the first man stepped onto the Moon's surface, he said, "One small step for man. One giant leap for mankind."	Underline anything you do not understand. Take notes. What are the most important ideas? _____ _____ _____ Tell what you reread or a question you asked. _____ _____ _____

NAME _____

READ FOR RATE

Read aloud the following passage. Have a partner time your reading for one minute. Then, fill in the chart at the bottom of the page with the number of words you read. Read the passage a second and third time. Try to increase the number of words you read accurately in a minute.

The stars all look very much alike. Each one is a point of	13
light in the night sky. We can tell which star is which by the	27
patterns that the stars make in the sky.	35
The patterns of stars are called constellations. Long ago,	44
people gave them names. These were names of animals or of	55
people. Often, the characters were parts of stories.	63
The Great Bear is lowest in the sky in the fall. American	75
Indians said that it was because the bear was looking for a	87
place to sleep for the winter.	93

Number of Words Read		
First Reading	Second Reading	Third Reading

NAME _____

CHECK YOUR UNDERSTANDING

A. Reread "Traveling Through Space" on **Student Edition** pages 228–231. Then read each sentence below. Circle the letter of the correct answer.

1. Only _____ people have been on the Moon.

   A 3   **C** 200

   B 12   **D** 500

2. Astronauts in space _____.

   A float   **C** can run faster

   B glow   **D** become very heavy

NAME _____

CHECK YOUR UNDERSTANDING

B. Read each sentence below. Circle the letter of the correct answer.

3. Sometimes astronauts go on a spacewalk to _____.

   A get exercise

   B explore the area

   C make repairs or do an experiment

   D challenge themselves

4. The Voyager space probes fly _____.

   A on the Moon

   B under the water

   C to Mars

   D more than 10 billion miles from Earth

C. Read each question below. Circle the letter of the correct answer.

5. Why have people been to the Moon but not other planets?

   A The Moon is more familiar to people.

   B The Moon is closer than other planets, so it is easier to reach.

   C The other planets are more dangerous.

   D People cannot breathe on the other planets.

6. Why is *Curiosity* a good name for the probe on Mars?

   A Because curiosity is the reason people send probes to explore outer space.

   B Because the probe looks very strange and curious.

   C Because only curious people are interested in what is on Mars.

   D Because the things found on Mars are very curious.

NAME —————————————————————————

A. Label

Write a word that names each picture. Use a word from the word box.

bread	bed	con	hockey	hook
	coin	box	toll	

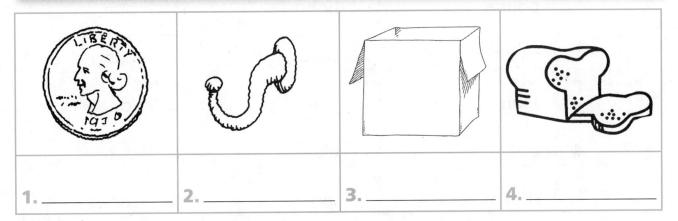

1. _____ 2. _____ 3. _____ 4. _____

B. Phonics

Read these words aloud. Use the phonics skills you have learned.

	A	B	C	D	E	F	G
5.	toy	stew	found	tea	book	moon	notebook
6.	soy	blue	house	sea	cook	troop	excite
7.	boy	chew	mouse	pea	rook	room	female
8.	coin	glue	loud	seat	took	cool	tadpole
9.	soil	few	out	bead	hook	proof	escape
10.	coil	true	about	treat	look	hoop	unmade

C. High-Frequency Words

Read these words aloud.

11.	their	if	will	up	other	about
12.	out	many	them	all	these	some

NAME _____

D. Listen. Read. Check.

Your teacher will say a word. Mark the box next to the word.

13.	☐ few	☐ food	☐ foot
14.	☐ pound	☐ pond	☐ pun
15.	☐ cheat	☐ chat	☐ Chet
16.	☐ Joan	☐ join	☐ joy
17.	☐ boo	☐ blue	☐ boot
18.	☐ choke	☐ shook	☐ shake
19.	☐ sun	☐ soon	☐ sound
20.	☐ joke	☐ go	☐ Joe

E. Spelling

Your teacher will say a word. Write the word. Check your spelling.

21. _____   23. _____

22. _____   24. _____

© HMH Supplemental Publishers Inc.

NAME ──────────────────────────────────

CHECKLIST

Word	I've never heard of it.	I've heard of it.	I know what it means.
natural resources	☐	☐	☐
energy	☐	☐	☐
oil	☐	☐	☐
pollute	☐	☐	☐
conserve	☐	☐	☐
careless	☐	☐	☐

Which word did you find most challenging?

───

© HMH Supplemental Publishers Inc.

NAME _____

CHECKLIST

Word	I've never heard of it.	I've heard of it.	I know what it means.
creek	☐	☐	☐
gallon	☐	☐	☐
recycle	☐	☐	☐
garbage	☐	☐	☐
chemical	☐	☐	☐
harm	☐	☐	☐

Which word did you find most interesting?

_____

NAME —————————————————————

READING LONGER WORDS

> ℹ️ Reading Vowel Pair Syllables
>
> Two vowel letters often stand for one sound.
> Examples: *keep, bead, goat, paid, sound*

> ℹ️ You can divide:
> • between the words in a compound word.
> • after a prefix, or before a suffix.
> • between the consonants in a VCCV letter pattern.
> • before or after the consonant in a VCV letter pattern.

A. Divide the word. Circle the vowel pair. Read each syllable.
Then read the whole word.

needed	loudly	weekly
wooden	braided	sleeping

B. Divide the word. Circle the vowel pair. Read each syllable.
Then read the whole word.

notebook	peanut	classroom	handrail
rowboat	textbook	cutout	bowtie

C. Divide the word. Read each syllable. Then read the whole word.

below	meadow	emu

D. Divide the word. Read each syllable. Then read the whole word.

elbow	mushroom	shampoo	explain
rowboat	window	rainbow	igloo

NAME _____

OPINION REPORT RUBRIC

When you write a report that states an opinion, check it against this rubric. Did you do all you can to make your position convincing? Yes ☐ No ☐

	Say "No!" to Plastic	Derek's Model	Class Model	My Model
1.	The title hints at the topic and the writer's opinion about it.			
2.	The writer's opinion is stated at the beginning of the report.			
3.	Facts and examples support the writer's opinion.			
4.	Facts and examples are important and convincing.			
5.	It is clear what the writer wants the reader to do.			
6.	The opinion report is neat and easy to read.			
7.	There are different kinds of sentences and they do not all start the same way.			
8.	The grammar, spelling, and punctuation are correct.			
9.	Readers will get involved with this opinion and take a stand!			

Score

3. Excellent   2. Good   1. Needs work

© HMH Supplemental Publishers Inc.

NAME —————————————————————————

OPINION REPORT ORGANIZER

The purpose of an opinion report is to convince the reader to agree with you and to take some kind of action. Follow these steps when you write your opinion.

1. Identify your topic. (You can hint at it in the title.)

2. State your opinion clearly in the introduction.

3. Identify facts that support your opinion.

4. Identify any possible argument against your opinion.

5. Tell readers what they should do. That's your call to action!

My topic: ——————————————————————

My opinion: ——————————————————————

————————————————————————————————

Facts that support my opinion:

- ————————————————————————————

- ————————————————————————————

- ————————————————————————————

Argument against my opinion: ————————————

Call to action: ————————————————————

————————————————————————————————

NAME _____

USING COMMAS IN SENTENCES

> ⓘ Commas tell a reader where to pause. There are several rules for using commas.
>
> Use commas to separate three or more items in a series. *Computers, cell phones, and calculators make life easier.*
>
> Use a comma to separate the parts of a compound sentence *Cell phones make keeping in touch easier, and calculators make math easier.*
>
> Use a comma after the words *yes* and *no* when they begin a sentence. *Yes, I love computers!*
>
> Use a comma to set off the name of a person you are speaking to. *Marie, please print a copy of your report.*

Write each sentence correctly. Use commas where needed.

1. Cars can carry one two or more people.

_____

2. Rita does your bike have gears?

_____

3. I will drive and Judy will ride her bike.

_____

4. I will research boats and bikes.

_____

5. No we can't stop now.

_____

NAME ——————————————————————————————

EDITING FOR GRAMMAR, SPELLING, AND PUNCTUATION

See also pages 175 and 177.

> The verb *make* is regular in the present tense. The verbs *go, do,* and *have* are irregular in the present tense.

I	make	go	do	have
You	make	go	do	have
He, she, it	makes	**goes**	**does**	**has**

> The verbs *go, do, have,* and *make* are irregular in the past tense.

Verb	go	do	have	make
Past Tense	went	did	had	made

> Form the possessive of most singular nouns by adding 's.
> *the dog's bone   my sister's car*

Listen to your teacher. Compare the first draft of the practice paragraph to the final draft.

Today, I made a peanut butter sandwich for lunch. My sister maked a turkey sandwich. We both started with bread, but the other parts were different. I haved grape jelly with peanut butter and my sisters sandwich had cheese and lettuce. Both were tasty and they both goed quick!

Today, I made a peanut butter sandwich for lunch. My sister made a turkey sandwich. We both started with bread, but the other parts were different. I had grape jelly with peanut butter, and my sister's sandwich had cheese and lettuce. Both were tasty, and they both went quickly!

NAME _____

READER'S LOG: "ALL THINGS ARE LINKED"

BEFORE READING: PAIR AND SHARE

1. My class talked about the _____.
   ☐ title   ☐ illustrations   ☐ _____

2. I understood _____ of the discussion.
   ☐ most or all   ☐ some   ☐ little or none

DURING READING

3. What do you think the Chief learned from the events of the story?

   _____

   _____

   _____

4. Is there anything in the story that you do not understand? Write about it here:

   _____

   _____

AFTER READING: PAIR AND SHARE

5. Talk to your partner about anything that you did not understand.

Now, my partner and I understand _____.

Me   ☐ a lot better ☐ a little better ☐ no better

My partner   ☐ a lot better ☐ a little better ☐ no better

NAME _____

USE CLUES

Read each sentence. Use context clues to help you figure out the correct vocabulary word from the box that completes each sentence. Write the word on the line.

energy	oil	natural resources	conserve	careless	pollute

1. My brother was very _____ and knocked a glass of water off the table.

   _____

2. The gas that cars use is made from _____.

   _____

3. The more people _____, the less healthy the Earth is.

   _____

4. Oil, air, water, and wood are _____ on Earth.

   _____

5. It takes _____ to run most of the machines in a house.

   _____

6. I turn off the lights so that I _____ electricity.

   _____

NAME _____

WHICH WORD AM I?

Read the clues. Write the correct vocabulary word from the box to match each clue.

chemical	recycle	gallon	garbage	creek	harm

1. I am the act of making sure that things can be used again.

_____

2. I am a material made by people.

_____

3. I am the act of hurting something.

_____

4. I am something that people do not want or need anymore.

_____

5. I am a small stream of water.

_____

6. I am used to measure liquids.

_____

NAME _____

A. Subject and Object Pronouns

Look at the picture. Read the sentence. Which word can replace the underlined words?

1. Anna kicks <u>the ball</u>!

   A she   **C** it

   B her   **D** them

2. <u>My parents</u> make the dinner.

   A Them   **C** It

   B They   **D** He

B. Combining Sentences

Which sentence **best** combines the information in the first two sentences?

3. Mr. Kim has a lot of books.
   I like his books.

   A I like Mr. Kim's books.

   B They are Mr. Kims books.

   C I like books.

4. The baby has toys.
   They are broken.

   A The babys toys are broken.

   B The baby's toys are broken.

   C Break the baby's toys.

NAME _____

C. Irregular Past-Tense Verbs

Choose the verb that best fits the sentence.

7. They sing very loud.
   Last week, they _____ in a concert.

   A sing   C is singing

   B sang   D will sing

8. My brother makes popcorn.
   Last week, he _____ a big mess!

   A make   C will make

   B makes   D made

PAIR AND SHARE With your partner, discuss what each of you or one other person owns.

Use these sentence frames:

A. Ask a question.

   Whose _____ is that? (book, pencil, pen, car)

B. Answer the question.

   That is _____. (Miguel's book, the teacher's desk, my mother's jacket)

Check page 177 to review how to say that someone owns something. Be sure to pronounce the 's.

Monitor Language: How's your grammar?

Listen to your partner. Was the correct possessive form used? Was the 's pronounced?

Yes, always	Sometimes	Never
☐	☐	☐

How were your possessive forms? Were they correct? Did you pronounce 's?

Yes, always	Sometimes	Never
☐	☐	☐

NAME _____

CLOSE READING OF THE TEXT

 Self-monitor your understanding as you read.

1. **Reread.** Start with the last sentence you understood. Then read on from that point.

2. **Take notes.** Write down the most important details. This can help you understand and remember what you read.

3. **Look up words you don't know.**

4. **Ask questions.** Then look for answers to your questions in the text, or you can ask someone.

Informative Text	Notes
A lot of things in your home use energy. The lights and the television use electricity. The heat and hot water use electricity or oil. We need to conserve oil. What about electricity? Most of the electricity in this country is made using coal. We need to conserve coal, too. So, don't waste electricity. Another resource you use at home is water. The water probably comes from a long way away. Making water clean uses energy. So, don't waste water. There's another reason not to waste. You save money!	Underline anything you do not understand. Take notes. What are the most important ideas? _____ _____ Tell what you reread or a question you asked. _____ _____

NAME _____

READ WITH EXPRESSION

Read the poem aloud. Read with energy and strong emotion. Pause for punctuation marks such as commas and periods. Listen to your partner's reading. Then practice the passage a second time.

Note: One slash (/) indicates a short pause for a comma or a dash. Two slashes (//) indicates that you stop for a period, question mark, or exclamation point.

> Look at that chimney— / all that smoke, /
> The air around is airless! //
> It's so bad all the trees will choke. //
> How can we be so careless? //
>
> Look at the mess dumped in the creek. //
> There's no point going fishing. //
> It's getting worse here, / week by week. //
> It won't be cured by wishing. //
>
> Look at the trash by the side of the road, /
> At the dead crops on the farm. //
> It hasn't rained or even snowed. //
> Someone pull the earth alarm! //

NAME

CHECK YOUR UNDERSTANDING

A. Reread "All Things are Linked" on **Student Edition** pages 256–261.
Then read each sentence below. Circle the letter of the correct answer.

1. At first, the Chief can't sleep because _____.

   A the mosquitoes are biting him

   B the frogs are making too much noise

   C the creek is overflowing

   D the people are protesting

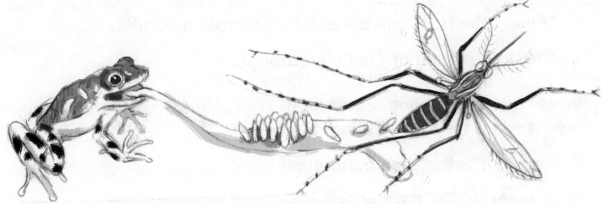

2. The important work the frogs were doing was _____.

   A eating mosquito eggs

   B keeping the Chief awake

   C linking everything together

   D providing food for the village

NAME _____

B. Read each sentence below. Circle the letter of the correct answer.

3. There are more mosquitoes now because _____.

   A the Chief has made them angry

   B the Chief notices them more than he did before

   C the villagers aren't able to kill them all

   D there are no frogs left to eat the mosquito eggs

4. The Chief's order to kill all the mosquitoes is _____.

   A difficult   C dangerous

   B impossible   D a joke

C. Read each question below. Circle the letter of the correct answer.

5. What phrase in the beginning of the story hints that the Chief will not get what he wants in the end?

   A "Frogs don't work," he said.

   B The Chief slept soundly that night.

   C "Killing the frogs was a mistake," she told the Chief.

   D They were afraid of the Chief, though.

6. Which of the following sentences BEST explains what Grandmother means when she says all things are linked?

   A Frogs are better than mosquitoes.

   B The world must have an equal amount of good and bad.

   C It is not smart to treat people—or things—badly.

   D You can't change one thing without affecting something else.

NAME ——————————————————————————————

A. Label

Write a word that names the picture. Use a word from the word box.

crow	cow	car	star	hook	foot	fur	core

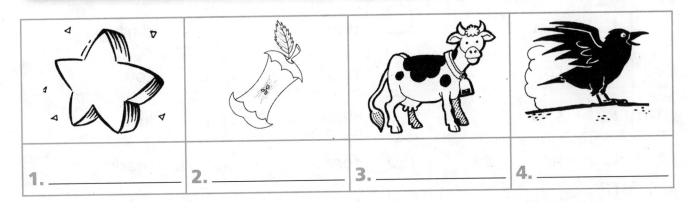

1. _____ 2. _____ 3. _____ 4. _____

B. Phonics

Read the words aloud. Use the phonics skills you have learned.

	A	B	C	D	E	F	G
5.	crow	cow	car	soar	bird	burn	railroad
6.	show	now	tar	more	fern	fir	dugout
7.	blow	wow	start	porch	word	herd	proceed
8.	grow	town	part	score	fur	stir	release
9.	low	owl	chart	for	sir	purr	repeat
10.	slow	how	lark	poor	turn	her	midweek

C. High-Frequency Words

Read these words aloud.

11.	her	would	make	like	him	into
12.	time	has	look	two	more	write

© HMH Supplemental Publishers Inc.

NAME _____

D. Listen. Read. Check.

Your teacher will say a word. Mark the box next to the word.

13.	☐ mark	☐ make	☐ mock
14.	☐ dirt	☐ date	☐ dart
15.	☐ crow	☐ row	☐ cow
16.	☐ sow	☐ slow	☐ low
17.	☐ sir	☐ sore	☐ shark
18.	☐ herd	☐ her	☐ hurt
19.	☐ park	☐ part	☐ par
20.	☐ sheer	☐ sharp	☐ chart

E. Spelling

Your teacher will say a word. Write the word. Check your spelling.

21. _____   23. _____

22. _____   24. _____

© HMH Supplemental Publishers Inc.

NAME ———————————————————————————————

MONITORING LISTENING CHECKLIST

	Unit 7	Unit 8	End of Book
	We the People	**In the Money**	
1. What is the topic?			
2. The general meaning of the discussion was _____.			
3. The words and sentences were mostly _____.	☐ clear ☐ confusing	☐ clear ☐ confusing	☐ clear ☐ confusing
4. Some of the important details include _____.			
5. I _____ ask for help when I don't understand.	☐ usually ☐ sometimes ☐ never	☐ usually ☐ sometimes ☐ never	☐ usually ☐ sometimes ☐ never
6. The way I understand discussions has _____.	☐ improved ☐ stayed the same	☐ improved ☐ stayed the same	☐ improved ☐ stayed the same

NAME _____

CHECKLIST

Word	I've never heard of it.	I've heard of it.	I know what it means.
citizen	☐	☐	☐
vote	☐	☐	☐
election	☐	☐	☐
campaign	☐	☐	☐
community	☐	☐	☐
responsible	☐	☐	☐

Which word did you find most challenging?

_____

NAME _____

CHECKLIST

Word	I've never heard of it.	I've heard of it.	I know what it means.
problem	☐	☐	☐
solution	☐	☐	☐
advice	☐	☐	☐
present	☐	☐	☐
speech	☐	☐	☐
city council	☐	☐	☐

Which word did you find most interesting?

_____

NAME _____

MONITORING SPEAKING CHECKLIST

	Unit 7	Unit 8	End of Book
	The Coat	Art Test	
1. I can retell the story by describing the ___.	☐ beginning ☐ middle ☐ end	☐ beginning ☐ middle ☐ end	☐ beginning ☐ middle ☐ end
2. I can support my opinions, ideas, and feelings about the story ___.	☐ all of the time ☐ often ☐ sometimes	☐ all of the time ☐ often ☐ sometimes	☐ all of the time ☐ often ☐ sometimes
3. I can describe and explain what I want to say ___.	☐ all of the time ☐ often ☐ sometimes	☐ all of the time ☐ often ☐ sometimes	☐ all of the time ☐ often ☐ sometimes
4. The way I can make myself understood has ___.	☐ improved ☐ stayed the same ☐ gotten worse	☐ improved ☐ stayed the same ☐ gotten worse	☐ improved ☐ stayed the same ☐ gotten worse
5. How do you explain your answer to #4, above?			

NAME ——————————————————————————

READING LONGER WORDS

 Reading Syllables with Vowel + *r*

When a vowel is followed by the letter *r*, the sound of the vowel sometimes changes.

Examples: *her, bird, girl, pearl, cart, cork*

 You can divide:

- between the words in a compound word
- after a prefix or before a suffix
- between the consonants in a VCCV letter pattern
- before or after the consonant in a VCV letter pattern

A. Divide the word. Read each syllable. Then read the whole word.

started	curling	artist	taller	worker

B. Divide the word. Read each syllable. Then read the whole word.

birthday	bluebird	homework
offshore	pitchfork	boxcar

C. Divide the word. Read each syllable. Then read the whole word.

diner	baker	tiger
liver	ever	cower

D. Divide the word. Read each syllable. Then read the whole word. Remember: Digraphs such as *ch*, *th*, and *sh* act as one letter.

concert	turnip	further	burger

NAME _____

NARRATIVE RUBRIC

When you write a story, check it against this rubric.

Did you do all you can to make it better?   Yes ☐   No ☐

The Truth About Aloha	Marissa's Model	Class Model	My Model
1. It is told in the third person, using proper nouns, *he, she,* or *they.*			
2. The plot and characters are believable.			
3. The story may use dialogue to make the characters come alive.			
4. The story reveals the characters through what they do and say.			
5. The actions follow each other in a way that makes sense.			
6. It is clear **where** and **when** the story takes place.			
7. The ending is good! It seems right for the story!			
8. The grammar, spelling, and punctuation are correct.			
9. Readers will like the story!			

Score

3. Excellent   **2. Good**   **1. Need work**

NAME

NARRATIVE SEQUENCE ORGANIZER

1. First, **Kevin gives an oral report about his ancestor.**

2. Then **the class applauds, but the teacher is critical.**

3. Later, **Kevin's father admits that the story is not true.**

4. At the end, **Kevin reveals the truth about Aloha to his class.**

© HMH Supplemental Publishers Inc.

NAME _____

USING QUOTATION MARKS FOR SPEECH

> ℹ️ Use quotation marks to show a speaker's exact words.
>
> Quotation marks go before and after a speaker's words. *"I like movies," said Ned.*
>
> Punctuation for a speaker's words goes inside the quotation marks. *"That's the best movie I've ever seen!" Anna said.*
>
> A comma separates a speaker's words from the rest of the sentence. *Ned said, "Meet me outside the theater."*
>
> A comma takes the place of a period inside quotation marks if it isn't the end of the whole sentence. *"I'll be there," Anna replied.*

Write each sentence correctly.

1. My friend said, Let's go to the park.

   _____

2. What about all this litter? I asked.

   _____

3. Let's take garbage bags my friend said.

   _____

4. Should we ask for help? I asked.

   _____

5. Yes, let's ask all our friends my friend said.

   _____

NAME —————————————————————

EDITING FOR GRAMMAR, SPELLING, AND PUNCTUATION

See also pages 177, 178, and 182.

To show possession of a singular noun, add *'s* to the word.
Bill's dog   *the dog's tail*

To show possession of a plural noun ending in *–s* or *–es*, add an apostrophe to the end of the word. *the dogs' collars*

To show possession of a plural noun that does not end in *–s* or *–es*, add *'s* to the word. *the men's coats*

In English, we use only one negative word in a sentence.

Incorrect: *She could not find nothing to read.*
Correct: *She could find nothing to read.*
Correct: *She could not find anything to read.*

Listen to your teacher. Compare the first draft of the practice paragraph to the edited draft.

Everyone should play a sport. Take a (doctors) advice. Exercise is good for (peoples) health. It helps build strong muscles. It also builds a strong heart and lungs. You might say, "I don't need to play (no) sport. I already exercise. But sports can also help in another way. Playing a sport can help you make friends. You can be part of a team. And you won't (never) run out of fun! So, play a sport today!

Everyone should play a sport. Take a doctor's advice. Exercise is good for people's health. It helps build strong muscles. It also builds a strong heart and lungs. You might say, "I don't need to play a sport. I already exercise." But sports can also help in another way. Playing a sport can help you make friends. You can be part of a team. And you won't ever run out of fun! So, play a sport today!

NAME _____

READER'S LOG: "COMMUNITY SERVICE GROUPS"

> ⓘ Active listeners take notes. Active readers do, too. Write only the most important information.

PAIR AND SHARE Reread the selection with your partner. Mark the boxes and take notes as you read. Add to your notes as you talk to your partner.

1. How difficult is the selection?

   ☐ very difficult   ☐ not too difficult   ☐ easy

2. What makes the selection difficult?

   ☐ the words   ☐ the information   ☐ everything!

3. List the most difficult words.

   _____

   _____

4. What did you do about the difficult words?

   ☐ We talked about them.   ☐ We looked at the pictures.

   ☐ We looked them up in a dictionary.   ☐ We asked our teacher.

5. How did you use the pictures? Did they help you?

   _____

   _____

6. Are there any sentences that you don't understand?

   Note the page number, and ask your teacher what they mean. _____

NAME ——————————————————

UNSCRAMBLE THE WORDS

Unscramble each word to spell one of the words in the box. Write the word on the line under the scrambled word.

COMMUNITY	ELECTION	RESPONSIBLE
CAMPAIGN	VOTE	CITIZEN

1. PIGAMANC (a plan that a person follows to try to win an election)

_____

2. SEBLIPNOSER (doing the right thing)

_____

3. ETVO (to make a choice)

_____

4. IMMYNUTOC (a group of people who live in the same area)

_____

5. NETZICI (a person who lives in a certain city or country)

_____

6. OCLEENIT (a method of choosing a leader by voting)

_____

NAME _____

WHICH WORD?

Write the vocabulary word from the box to complete each sentence.

solution	speech	city council	problem	present	advice

1. A _____ causes trouble.

   _____

2. When you _____ a report, you read it to others.

   _____

3. Giving good _____ can help someone solve a problem.

   _____

4. The answer to a problem is a _____.

   _____

5. The _____ makes decisions about the city.

   _____

6. A politician may tell ideas to the people in a _____.

   _____

NAME ————————————————————————————————

A. Using Negatives

Look at the picture. Read the question. Circle the correct answer.

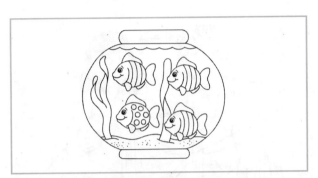

1. Are five goldfish in the bowl?

   A Yes, five goldfish are in the bowl.

   B No, five goldfish aren't in the bowl.

   C Yes, I see goldfish.

2. Is Lin in the house?

   A No, she isn't in the house.

   B Lin likes kites.

   C Nobody doesn't see nothing.

B. Plural Possessive Nouns

3. My two cousins own a cat. Is she cute?

   A No, my cat isn't cute.

   B Yes, my cousin's cat is cute.

   C Yes, my cousins' cat is cute.

4. Does this van belong to both of your parents?

   A No, it isn't my parents' van.

   B No, it isn't my parent's van.

   C Yes, I see my parents.

© HMH Supplemental Publishers Inc.

NAME _____

C. Combining Sentences

Read the two sentences. Which sentence best combines the meaning of the two sentences?

5. The dog runs. The cats just sit.

   A John has a cat and dog.

   B The dog runs, but the cats just sit.

   C Dogs can't sit.

6. The book belongs to Sari. It belongs to her sister, too.

   A The book is theirs.

   B They are sitting there.

   C They can read.

PAIR AND SHARE Ask questions that can be answered *yes* or *no*. Use contractions in your answer.

A. Ask questions. Examples:
Are you 15 years old?
Are you good at soccer?
Are you hungry?

B. Answer the questions.
No, I'm not 15 years old.
Yes, I'm good at soccer.
No, I'm not hungry.

Check pages 171–172 to review using contractions.

Monitor Language: How's your grammar?

Listen to your partner. Was the question answered? Was a contraction used correctly?

Yes, always	Sometimes	Never
☐	☐	☐

Did you answer the question and correctly use contractions?

Yes, always	Sometimes	Never
☐	☐	☐

CLOSE READING OF THE TEXT

Self-monitor your understanding as you read.

1. **Reread.** Start with the last sentences you understood. Then read on from that point.

2. **Take notes.** Write down the most important details. This can help you understand and remember what you read.

3. **Look up words you don't know.**

4. **Ask questions.** Then look for answers to your questions in the text, or you can ask someone.

Persuasive Essay	Notes
I'm angry! I'll tell you why I'm angry. You know Frank Picking? Well, forget Frank Picking. He thinks he should be mayor. Well, he should not. He doesn't deserve to be mayor. Frank Picking's campaign is a joke. His speeches are all lies. He will say anything you want to hear. Do you want a new park for the city? He will promise you a new park. But he won't keep his promise.	Underline anything you do not understand. Take notes. What are the most important ideas? _____ _____ _____ Tell what you reread or a question you asked. _____ _____ _____

NAME _____

READ FOR ACCURACY

Work with a partner. Take turns reading the passage aloud. Try to speak clearly and pronounce each word correctly. Then review the passage together. Write the difficult words on the lines below. Practice saying the words aloud. Then read the passage a second time.

> Lourdes was born in Cuba. Even so, she became a citizen of the United States. First, she had to live here for five years. She had to be able to read and write English.
>
> When Lourdes was eighteen years old, she took an exam. She showed that she understood the way the United States works. Then Lourdes saw a judge who decided she could be a citizen.
>
> Now Lourdes can vote in elections. And she does! She wants to have a say in how her city runs. She also votes in state elections and national elections.

_____   _____

_____   _____

_____   _____

_____   _____

_____   _____

NAME ————————————————————————————————

CHECK YOUR UNDERSTANDING

A. Reread "Community Service Groups" on **Student Edition** pages 302–307. Then read each sentence below. Circle the letter of the correct answer.

1. Kids can help their community by ———.

   A picking up litter

   B working as a firefighter

   C being a bully

   D driving a car safely

2. Kids can get help with ——— at Boys & Girls Clubs.

   A reading skills

   B farming

   C highway cleanup

   D environmental problems

NAME _____

B. Read each sentence below. Circle the letter of the correct answer.

3. An emergency is _____.

   A planned　　　　　　　　**C** not expected

   B welcomed　　　　　　　**D** useful

4. Joining a community service group means you will _____.

   A make money　　　　　　**C** travel to all 50 states

   B help out　　　　　　　　**D** campaign for office

C. Read each question below. Circle the letter of the correct answer.

5. Which sentence from the story tells about Earth Force?

   A They practice first aid.

   B They study farming and science.

   C Their slogan is "Do a good turn daily."

   D This group tells young people about the environment.

6. How are scouts and 4-H alike?

   A Members learn about farming.

   B Members learn first aid.

   C Members learn how to be leaders.

   D Both groups have the same number of members.

NAME _____

A. Label

Write a word that names the picture. Use a word from the word box.

chill	child	foal	fold	rid	car	fur	words

1. _____ 2. _____ 3. _____ 4. _____

B. Phonics

Read the words aloud. Use the phonics skills you have learned.

	A	B	C	D	E	F	G
5.	bore	fir	bind	sold	law	after	perfect
6.	soar	pure	kind	bold	saw	artist	thirsty
7.	core	word	find	cold	taught	dirty	garlic
8.	for	her	wild	hold	caught	disturb	fairway
9.	shore	shirt	child	fold	raw	forty	favor
10.	or	cure	mild	gold	paw	dirty	summer

C. High-Frequency Words

Read the words aloud.

11.	see	number	way	could	people	my
12.	than	first	water	been	call	who

© HMH Supplemental Publishers Inc.

NAME _____

D. Listen. Read. Check.

Your teacher will say a word. Mark the box next to the word.

13.	☐ mode	☐ mole	☐ mold
14.	☐ mine	☐ mind	☐ mint
15.	☐ rare	☐ roar	☐ row
16.	☐ pure	☐ peer	☐ pair
17.	☐ roll	☐ ram	☐ raw
18.	☐ tall	☐ talk	☐ told
19.	☐ bur	☐ bird	☐ bear
20.	☐ wild	☐ will	☐ wail

E. Spelling

Your teacher will say a word. Write the word. Check your spelling.

21. _____   23. _____

22. _____   24. _____

NAME

CHECKLIST

Word	I've never heard of it.	I've heard of it.	I know what it means.
price	☐	☐	☐
stand	☐	☐	☐
silver	☐	☐	☐
decide	☐	☐	☐
coin	☐	☐	☐
purchase	☐	☐	☐

Which word did you find most challenging?

_____

NAME _____

CHECKLIST

Word	I've never heard of it.	I've heard of it.	I know what it means.
fortune	☐	☐	☐
increase	☐	☐	☐
treasure	☐	☐	☐
bill	☐	☐	☐
foolish	☐	☐	☐
greed	☐	☐	☐

Which word did you find most interesting?

_____

NAME

READING LONGER WORDS

 You can divide:

- between the words in a compound word.
- after a prefix, or before a suffix.
- between the consonants in a VCCV letter pattern.
- before or after the consonant in a VCV letter pattern.

A. Divide the word. Read each syllable. Then read the whole word.

begin	robot	cubic	music
panic	comic	rapid	robin

B. Divide the word. Read each syllable. Then read the whole word.

reptile	confuse	invite	escape
update	bedtime	online	inside

C. Divide the word. Read each syllable. Then read the whole word.

turnip	target	concert	farther

D. Divide the word. Circle the vowel pair. Read each syllable. Then read the whole word.

elbow	mushroom	shampoo	explain
succeed	window	rainbow	igloo

NAME _____

POEM RUBRIC

When you write a poem, check it against this rubric.

Does your poem express personal feelings and ideas?   Yes ☐   No ☐

	What Would You Do with a Million Bucks?	Marianna's Model	Class Model	My Model
1.	The title gives a clue about the topic of the poem.			
2.	The topic is interesting and makes readers want to read the poem.			
3.	Descriptive words help readers see, hear, smell, taste, and touch the images described.			
4.	The lines in a poem often have a rhythm or pattern.			
5.	The words are chosen carefully so that every word counts.			
6.	A poem can help the reader view the topic, object, or idea in a new way.			
7.	In many poems, the first word in each line begins with a capital letter.			

Score

3. Excellent   **2. Good**   **1. Need work**

NAME ————————————————————————————————

WORD MAP

Poems use descriptive words to help readers picture what they read. A word map can help you think of words and phrases that describe the subject of a poem.

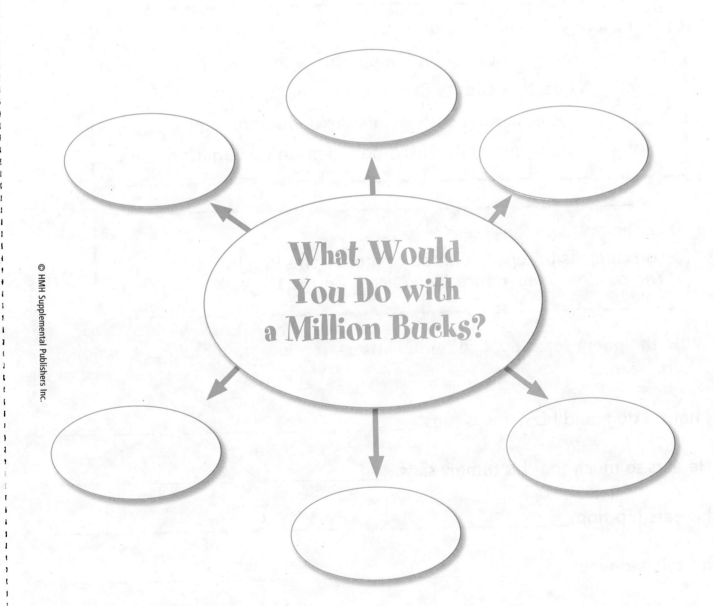

What Would You Do with a Million Bucks?

NAME _____

CAPITALIZATION AND PUNCTUATION REVIEW

> *(i)* A sentence always begins with a capital letter.
>
> All proper nouns begin with a capital letter.
>
> The first word in each line of a poem begins with a capital letter.

> *(i)* Every sentence ends with punctuation.
>
> - A statement ends with a period.
> **?** A question ends with a question mark.
> **!** An exclamation ends with an exclamation point.
> - or **!** A command ends with a period or an exclamation point.

> *(i)* Commas tell a reader where to pause.
>
> Use commas to separate three or more items in a list.
> *The children sang, danced, and acted on the stage.*

Write the poem correctly. Use capital letters, commas, and end punctuation where needed.

I have a dog, and his name is rags. _____

He eats so much that his tummy sags. _____

his ears flip-flop, _____

his tail wig-wags, _____

And when he walks, he goes zig-zag _____

NAME ————

EDITING FOR GRAMMAR, SPELLING, AND PUNCTUATION

See also pages 173 and 174.

 The present tense of a verb describes an action that is happening now.
The dogs bark.   *The cat walks.*

 The past tense of a verb describes action that happened in the past.
The dogs barked last night.   *The cat walked away.*

 An adverb describes a verb.
Incorrect: *The birds sing loud.*
Correct: *The birds sing loudly.*

Listen to your teacher. Compare the first draft of the poem to the edited draft.

First Draft

Slowly the sun went down,

slowly the shadows grew.

Quickly the folks in town

Got ready to eat their stew.

Now the moon shines bright,

Now the night is gray.

Now the people sleep light

And dreamed of the coming day.

Edited Draft

Slowly the sun went down,

Slowly the shadows grew.

Quickly the folks in town

Got ready to eat their stew.

Now the moon shines brightly,

Now the night is gray.

Now the people sleep lightly

And dream of the coming day.

NAME _____

READER'S LOG: "MONEY THROUGH THE AGES"

> ℹ️ Active listeners take notes. Active readers do, too. Write only what you need to remember the important information.

PAIR AND SHARE Reread the selection with your partner. Mark the boxes and take notes as you read. Add to your notes as you talk to your partner.

1. How difficult is the selection?

   ☐ very difficult   ☐ not too difficult   ☐ easy

2. What makes the selection difficult?

   ☐ the words   ☐ the information   ☐ everything!

3. List the most difficult words.

   _____

4. What did you do about the difficult words?

   ☐ We talked about them.   ☐ We looked at the pictures.

   ☐ We looked them up in a dictionary.   ☐ We asked our teacher.

5. How did you use the pictures? Did they help you?

   _____

6. Are there any sentences that you don't understand?

   Note the page number, and ask your teacher what they mean. _____

© HMH Supplemental Publishers Inc.

NAME

MATCH IT UP

Write the letter of the definition that matches each word.

1. _____ price

2. _____ silver

3. _____ purchase

4. _____ coin

5. _____ stand

6. _____ decide

A to buy something

B how much something costs

C a small store

D to think and then make a choice

E a shiny, gray metal

F a small piece of metal used as money

NAME _____

USE CLUES

Read each sentence. Use context clues to help you figure out the correct vocabulary word from the box to complete each sentence. Write the word on the line.

| treasure | bill | greed | fortune | foolish | increase |

1. It would be _____ to go hiking without any water.

_____

2. I had to pay with quarters, because I didn't have a dollar _____.

_____

3. We watched the number of his fans _____ as more people heard his song.

_____

4. The lucky woman discovered _____ hidden in a forgotten cave.

_____

5. I had the good _____ to meet the winner of the race.

_____

6. It was _____ that stopped him from sharing the money he found.

_____

NAME ——

A. Review

Look at the picture. Read the question. Write the correct answer.

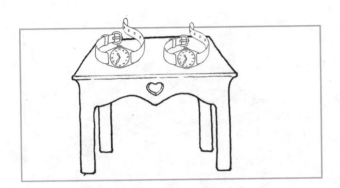

1. Is one watch on the table?

   A Yes, it is.

   B No, two watches are on the table.

   C Yes, I see two watches.

2. Ari wants to make cookies. What is she doing now?

   A She is mixing flour and milk.

   B She has lunch.

   C They mix flour and milk.

3. What is Dad doing?

   A They are riding in the car.

   B It is his car.

   C He is driving his car.

4. What game does Ella play?

   A She plays soccer.

   B They play soccer.

   C She play soccer.

NAME _____

B. Which sentence comes next?

Circle the letter of the BEST sentence to follow the sentence or sentences under each picture.

5. This house belongs to Mr. Brown.

   A It is his house.

   B It is her house.

   C It is my house.

6. Look at my dad's books. What if he puts more books on top?

   A They fell.

   B They fall.

   C They will fall.

PAIR AND SHARE With your partner, discuss something that is owned by more than one person.

Use this sentence frame:

A. Ask a question.

   Whose _____ *is that?* (house, car, bikes)

B. Answer the question.

   That is _____. (my parents' house, my brothers' bikes, my grandparents' car)

Check page 178 to review how to say that more than one person owns something. Be sure to pronounce the *s'*.

Monitor Language: How's your grammar?

Listen to your partner. Was the correct possessive form used? Was the *s'* pronounced?

Yes, always	Sometimes	Never
☐	☐	☐

NAME —————————————————————————

CLOSE READING OF THE TEXT

 Self-monitor your understanding as you read.

1. **Reread.** Start with the last sentence you understood. Then read on from that point.

2. **Take notes.** Write down the most important details. This can help you understand and remember what you read.

3. **Look up words you don't know.**

4. **Ask questions.** Then look for answers to your questions in the text, or you can ask someone.

Play	Notes
My first job was picking apples. I had to climb a ladder so that I could reach them. It was hard work, but I made money. I bought myself a new pair of shoes. Soon, it was winter. There were no apples left on the trees. I had to get another job. It was the busy holiday season. I worked in a bookstore. With the money I earned, I purchased a new shirt and a tie. The new year came. So did the snow. I worked clearing the roads. The job didn't last very long, but I earned money. I bought a nice pair of pants.	Underline anything you do not understand. Take notes. What are the most important ideas? _____ _____ _____ Tell what you reread or a question you asked. _____ _____ _____

NAME _____

READ FOR RATE

Read the passage aloud. Have a partner time your reading for one minute. Then, fill in the chart at the bottom of the page with the number of words you read. Read the passage a second and third time. Try to increase the number of words you read accurately in a minute.

Passage	Words
Pirates were driven by greed. They sailed the seas and stole	11
treasure from other ships. The pirate flag showed a skull and	22
bones.	23
When a pirate ship came near, other ships would try to get	35
away. They would be foolish to stay, unless they were ready	46
for a fierce fight. Pirates would show no mercy.	55
What did the pirates do with all their treasure? Sometimes	65
they buried it. Many people have dreamed of finding a	75
pirate's treasure map.	78
If the dream came true, it would be the chance of a lifetime.	91
If you had good fortune, there might be gold hidden	101
underground. It would be the best pay anyone ever got just	112
for digging!	114

Number of Words Read		
First Reading	Second Reading	Third Reading

NAME ——————————————————————————————

CHECK YOUR UNDERSTANDING

A. Reread "Money Through the Ages" on **Student Edition** pages 348–353. Then read each sentence below. Circle the letter of the correct answer.

about 10,000 years ago

about 2,500 years ago

about 1,000 years ago

1. A coin is money that is made of _____.

   A metal

   B shell

   C wampum

   D animal skins

2. The earliest form of money was _____.

   A government bills

   B gold

   C cattle

   D paper money

NAME _____

B. Read each sentence below. Circle the letter of the correct answer.

3. Before people used money, they _____.

   A used dollars

   B made paper

   C made gold into coins

   D traded one item for another

4. Salt is different from the first paper money because _____.

   A only salt could be traded for gold

   B you could use salt to keep food fresh

   C no one was ever paid with salt

   D paper money was heavier to carry around

C. Read each question below. Circle the letter of the correct answer.

5. Why would the value of grains increase if the crops didn't grow well?

   A When there is a lot of something, it is worth more.

   B People aren't willing to pay for crops that won't grow well.

   C If there is less grain available, people will pay more to get what they can.

   D People have to pay more to plant the crops again.

6. Which is NOT a reason to use paper money instead of cattle, grain, shells, or salt?

   A Paper money is lighter to carry.

   B Paper money cannot be burned or lost.

   C Paper money can't catch a disease and die.

   D Paper money can be made in different values.

NAME ——————————————————

A. Label

Write a word that names each picture. Use a word from the word box.

| write | child | lamb | castle | eight | chalk | hulk | walk |

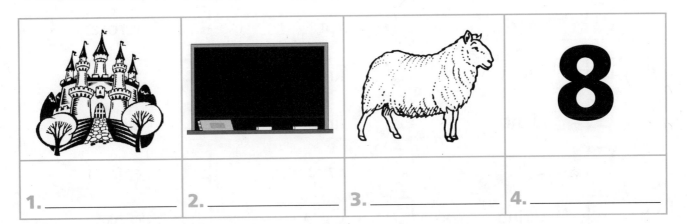

1. _____ 2. _____ 3. _____ 4. _____

B. Phonics

Read these words aloud. Use the phonics skills you have learned.

	A	B	C	D	E	F
5.	talk	high	write	path	photo	tiger
6.	chalk	sight	knit	half	cartoon	hatbox
7.	halt	light	knew	wrap	inside	upset
8.	walk	right	knife	wreck	pupil	supper
9.	salt	might	knee	wrong	raincoat	letter
10.	fault	fight	knock	sign	escape	seesaw

C. High-Frequency Words

Read these words aloud.

11.	am	its	now	find	long	down
12.	day	did	get	come	made	part

© HMH Supplemental Publishers Inc.

NAME _____

D. Listen. Read. Check.

Your teacher will say a word. Mark the box next to the word.

13.	☐ knit		☐ night		☐ nine
14.	☐ road		☐ rot		☐ wrote
15.	☐ night		☐ knife		☐ fine
16.	☐ climb		☐ limb		☐ climate
17.	☐ call		☐ cave		☐ calf
18.	☐ wring		☐ were		☐ rank
19.	☐ hate		☐ eat		☐ eight
20.	☐ shy		☐ sigh		☐ sing

E. Spelling

Write the hardest spelling list you can think of. Then test a friend.

21. _____ 23. _____

22. _____ 24. _____

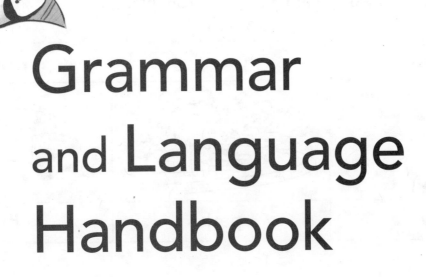

Grammar and Language Handbook

Grammar and Language Handbook

1 What is a noun?

A. A **noun** is a word that names a person, place, or thing.

person	place	thing

boy	park	bus

B. A **noun** can also name an animal.

cat	goat	goldfish
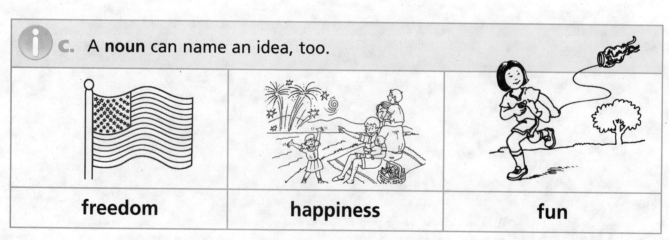		

C. A **noun** can name an idea, too.

freedom	happiness	fun

2 What are singular and plural nouns?

A. A **singular** noun names one person, place, thing, or animal. A **plural** noun names more than one.

To write the plural of many nouns, add -s to the singular noun.

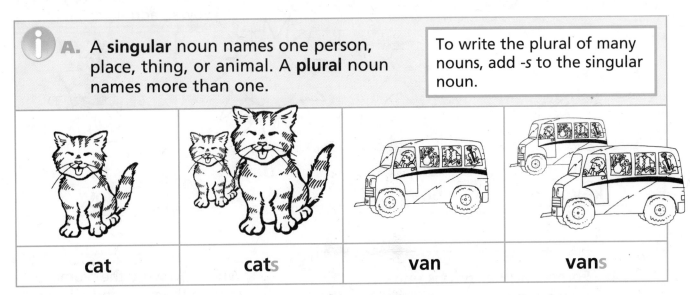

| cat | cats | van | vans |

B. Some **singular** nouns end in *x, ch, tch, sh, zz,* and *ss.*

To write the plural of nouns with these endings, add -es to the singular noun.

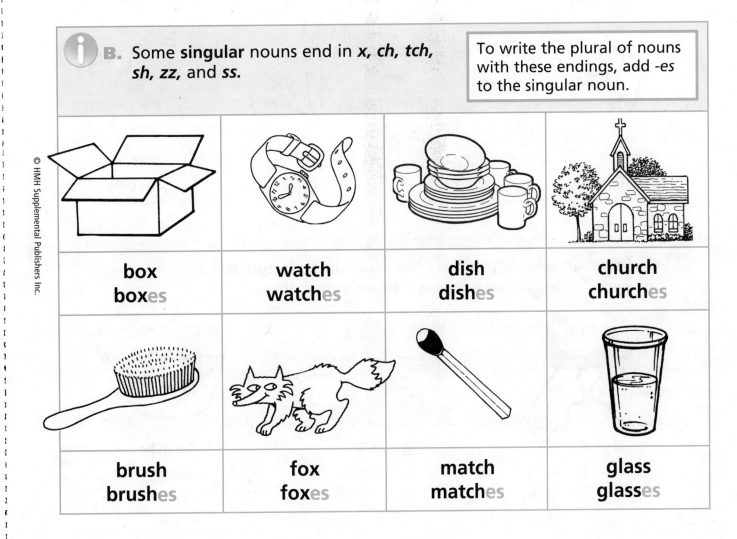

| box boxes | watch watches | dish dishes | church churches |
| brush brushes | fox foxes | match matches | glass glasses |

Grammar and Language Handbook

C. Some **singular** nouns end in **vowel + y.**

> If the letter before *y* is a vowel, add *-s* for plural.

| key | boy | day | toy |
| key**s** | boy**s** | day**s** | toy**s** |

D. Some **singular** nouns end in **consonant + y.**

> When you write the plural, change the *y* to *i* and add *-es.*

| pup**py** | ci**ty** | ba**by** | par**ty** |
| pupp**ies** | cit**ies** | bab**ies** | part**ies** |

E. Some singular nouns form the plural in an **irregular** way. These nouns change *oo* to *ee* in the plural.

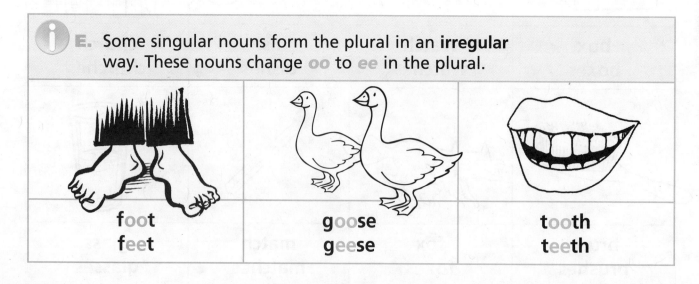

| foot | goose | tooth |
| feet | geese | teeth |

F. Some nouns are the same in the singular and the plural. They form the plural in an irregular way.

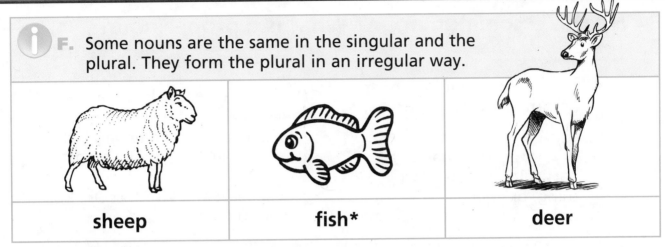

| sheep | fish* | deer |

* The plural of *fish* is sometimes written *fishes*. Both are correct.

G. These nouns name people. The spelling changes in the plural. They form the plural in an irregular way.

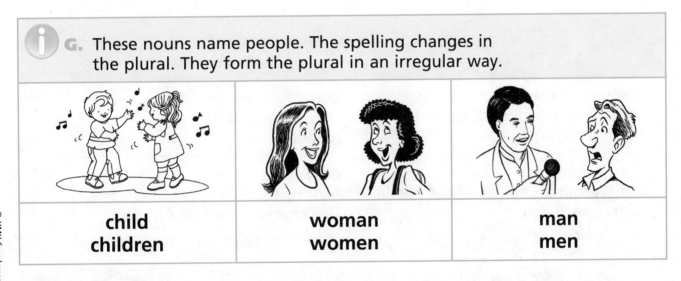

| child children | woman women | man men |

H. These nouns name animals. The spelling changes in the plural. They form the plural in an irregular way.

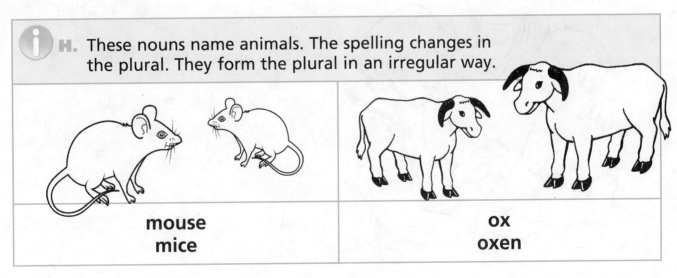

| mouse mice | ox oxen |

Grammar and Language Handbook

3 What is a common noun? What is a proper noun?

A. A **common** noun names any person, place, thing, or animal.

A **proper** noun names a particular person, place, thing, or animal.

Capitalize the **first letter** of the main words in a proper noun.

- Capitalize *the* and *of* only if they are the first words of a proper noun phrase.
- Capitalize **titles**, such as Dr., Ms., Mr., and Mrs.

persons	places
common nouns doctor, woman, mother, father, man, baby, girl	**common nouns** city, state, country, park, school
proper nouns Dr. Carolina Capella, Mrs. Capella, Carolina	**proper nouns** Austin, Texas, The United States of America

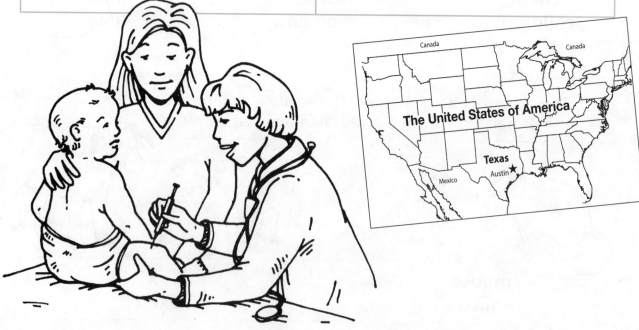

Common and proper nouns

things	animals
common nouns book TV show game	**common nouns** dog cat goat
proper nouns Write the names of your favorite shows or games. **?** _____ _____ _____	**proper nouns** names of pets Rufus

B. The words *day* and *month* are common nouns. Specific names of days and months are proper nouns.

Capitalize the days of the week and months of the year.

November

Sunday	Monday	Tuesday	Wednesday	Thursday	Friday	Saturday
			1	2	3	4
5	6	7	8	9	10	11
12	13	14	15	16	17	18
19	20	21	22	23	24	25
26	27	28	29	30		

Grammar and Language Handbook

4 What is an adjective?

An **adjective** is a word that describes a noun.

- Adjectives give information about nouns. When we read or listen to others speak, adjectives help us picture the nouns.

- When we speak or write, adjectives are words that help us describe what we see, hear, feel, taste, and smell.

huge, big, gray, mammal, male	small, tiny, little, gray, quick	young, spotted, orange and black, female, tall
 soft, fluffy, cute, white, young	 hard, blue, shiny, metallic	 slimy, brown, wiggly, shiny
 sweet, pretty, colorful, small	 salty, white and yellow, puffy, crunchy	 smelly, greasy!

5 What is a definite article?

There is one definite article in English. It is **the**.
Use **the** before any noun when you have only one thing in mind.

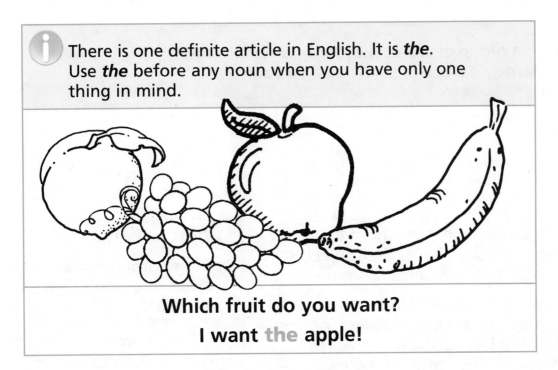

Which fruit do you want?

I want the apple!

6 What are the indefinite articles?

A. There are two indefinite articles: **a** and **an**.

"I want **an** apple!" means "I want **one** apple!"

"I want **a** pear!" means "I want **one** pear!"

You are not definite about which one you want.

B. Use **an** before a word that starts with a vowel.

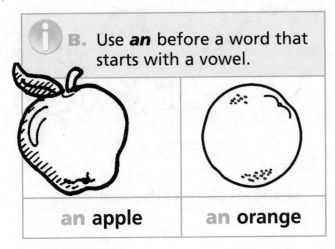

| an apple | an orange |

C. Use **a** before a word that starts with a consonant.

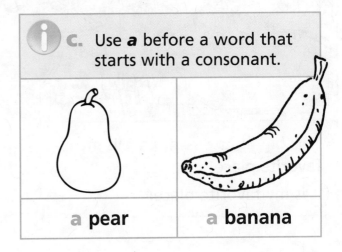

| a pear | a banana |

7 What is a sentence?

A **sentence** is a group of words that forms a complete thought. A sentence has two parts: a **subject** and a **predicate**.

8 What is the subject of a sentence?

A. The **subject** tells what or whom the sentence is mostly about. The subject can be a noun or a subject pronoun.

B. The **complete subject** includes all the words that tell about the subject. A complete subject can be many words or just one. In the sentences below, the complete subject is written in green type.

C. The **simple subject** of a sentence is a noun or a pronoun. In the sentences below, the simple subject is circled.

Subject Pronouns

D. These pronouns can be used as the subject of a sentence.

I	we
you	you
he, she, it	they

This big amusement (park) is my favorite place!

(It) is my favorite place.

My little (dog) chases all the kittens.

(She) chases all the kittens.

9 What is the predicate of a sentence?

A. The **predicate** of a sentence includes the main verb and other words that tell more about the verb. The predicate tells what the subject is, does, or feels.

B. The **complete predicate** includes the verb and other words that tell about the verb. In the sentences below, the complete predicate is written in green type.

C. The **simple predicate** is the verb or verb phrase. In the sentences below, the simple predicate is circled.

The girl (kicks) the ball hard.

The sad little boy (is sitting) on the floor.

Grammar and Language Handbook

10 What is a sentence fragment?

> ℹ️ A **fragment** is a group of words that *do not* form a complete thought! Something important is missing in a sentence fragment.

Read these sentence fragments. What questions do you have when you read them?

Fragment	Possible Questions
1. went to the mall 	Who did? Why? When?
2. the boy and girl with the rackets	What did they do? When? Where are they going?
3. rode the bike	Who? What? When? Why?

11 What are the four kinds of sentences?

	Kinds of Sentences	End Punctuation	Intonation
●	**Statement** (or, declarative)	I finished my homework. (ends with period)	Your voice should fall at the end of a statement.
?	**Question** (or, interrogative)	Did you finish your homework? (ends with a question mark)	Your voice should rise for a question.
!	**Exclamation** (or, exclamatory)	I did it! (ends with an exclamation mark)	Your voice should show excitement for an exclamation.
! or ●	**Command** (or, imperative)	Finish your homework now. (!) (ends with period or an exclamation mark)	When you make a command, your voice can vary, depending upon how strongly you feel. Ask your teacher to demonstrate.

Grammar and Language Handbook

12 What forms of the verb *to be* should I use?

A. Present Tense *to be* Use these verbs to tell about noun and pronoun subjects in the present time.

- Omar **is** tired.
- Those girls **are** good students.

I am	We are
You are	You are
He is She is It is	They are

B. Past Tense *to be* To tell about the subject of a sentence in the past, use the past tense of *to be*. There are only two verbs to remember!

- Omar **was** tired last night.
- Last year, the girls **were** good students.

I was	We were
You were	You were
He was She was It was	They were

C. Look at the arrows. Nouns and adjectives can follow forms of the verb *to be*. They always tell about the subject.

Present	Past
Omar is tired.	Omar was tired last night.
Those girls are good students.	The girls were good students last year.

© HMH Supplemental Publishers Inc.

13 What contractions are made with *am*, *is*, and *are*?

In English, there is a short, quick way to say some common phrases.

The short form is called a **contraction**.

Contractions can be made with pronoun subjects and present tense forms of the verb *to be*.

PAIR AND SHARE: Speaking

Practice with your partner.

Say the first sentence in each section.

Your partner will respond, using the contraction.

Change roles using the next sentence pairs.

Keep practicing!

A. I am an athlete.
I'm an athlete.

D. We are readers.
We're readers.

B. You are the best!
You're the best!

E. You are all great.
You're all great.

C. He is tall.   He's tall.
She is tall.   She's tall.
It is tall.   It's tall.

F. They are tall.
They're tall.

© HMH Supplemental Publishers Inc.

Grammar and Language Handbook

14 What contractions are made with *not*?

A. Contractions can be made with the word ***not***.
The word ***not*** makes a sentence negative.

PAIR AND SHARE: Speaking

Practice with your partner.
Say the first sentence in each section.
Your partner will respond, using the contraction.
Change roles using the next sentence pairs.
Keep practicing!

B. We can form contractions with
***not* + is** and with ***not* + are.**

He is not tall. → He isn't tall.	They are not tall. → They aren't tall.
She is not tall. → She isn't tall.	You are not tall. → You aren't tall.
It is not tall. → It isn't tall.	We are not tall. → We aren't tall.

C. Contractions can also be made with ***not* + was** and
with ***not* + were.**

I was not tall. → I wasn't tall.	We were not tall. → We weren't tall.
He was not tall. → He wasn't tall.	You were not tall. → You weren't tall.
She was not tall. → She wasn't tall.	They were not tall. → They weren't tall.
It was not tall. → It wasn't tall.	

15 What are action verbs?

A verb is the main word in the predicate of a sentence. An action verb tells what the subject **does**. The verb must agree with the subject. Present tense action verbs have two forms.

Agreement Rules for Present Tense Action Verbs

Rule 1 Add -s to most present tense action verbs if the subject is a singular noun or a singular subject pronoun: *he, she, it.*

Rule 2 Add -es to the present tense verb if it ends in -ch, -tch, -sh, -ss, -x, or -zz and the subject is a singular noun or a singular subject pronoun: *he, she, it.*

Four players run to the ball. Julio gets there first! He kicks the ball. His team wins.

The runners dash to the finish line. Marta catches up. She passes them all. She finishes first.

Grammar and Language Handbook

16 What is the correct form of regular action verbs in the past tense?

> In English, the same form is used for all regular past tense verbs.
>
> - When you write, add **-ed** to the verb to form the past tense.
>
> - When you speak, be sure to pronounce the **-ed** ending.

Singular Subject

I work**ed** last night.

John, you work**ed** last night.

The boy work**ed** last night.
The girl work**ed** last night.
The car work**ed** last night.
He, she, and it work**ed** last night.

Plural Subject

We work**ed** last night.

John and Darcy, you both work**ed** last night.

The students work**ed** last night.
The dogs work**ed** last night.
The cars work**ed** last night.
They work**ed** last night.

17 What are common irregular action verbs?

> **A.** The verbs **go, do,** and **have** are irregular in the present tense. They are called **irregular** because we don't **just** add **s** when the subject is a singular noun or **he, she, it.**

> **B.** The verbs **go, do,** and **have** are also irregular in the past tense. The same form is used for all subjects.

Present Tense			
Pronoun Subjects	Verb		
	go	do	have
I, You, We, They	go	do	have
He, She, It	goes	does	has

Past Tense	
to go	went
to do	did
to have	had

Verb *go*	Verb *do*	Verb *have*
We go home after school.	We do our homework.	We have a lot of books.
Kim goes home after school.	He does his homework on time.	The man has a lot of books.
Kim went home after school yesterday.	He did his homework on time last week.	The man had a lot of books before he moved.

Grammar and Language Handbook

A.
- **Nouns** that are **direct objects** are affected by the verb.

- To find the direct object in a sentence, say the verb. Then ask, *What?* or *Whom?*

B. **Direct object pronouns** can replace nouns in a sentence. When you replace a noun that is a direct object, use *them* if the noun is plural. If the noun is singular, use *him, her,* or *it.*

Singular	Plural
me	us
you	you
him, her, it	them

1. My friends feed the ducks.
Feed *what?* the ducks
The direct object is ducks.

2. My friends feed them.
The direct object is them.

3. The player kicks the ball.
Kicks *what?* the ball
The direct object is ball.

4. The player kicks it.
The direct object is it.

19 How do we show possession or ownership?

A. English has a special way to show that one person owns something. Use apostrophes!

This cat belongs to Sumi.

This cat is Sumi's.

This is Sumi's cat.

The car belongs to my dad.

The car is my dad's.

It is my dad's car.

B. **When you write,** here's how to show that one person owns something.

When you speak, be sure to pronounce the **s** that follows the apostrophe.

		Sumi	Dad
Step 1	Write the noun that names the person.	Sumi	Dad
Step 2	Write an **apostrophe s** after the noun.	Sumi's	Dad's
Step 3	Write what is owned.	Sumi's cat	Dad's car

C. Here's how to show that more than one person owns something.

The bike belongs to the boys.
This is the **boys'** bike.

These hoops belong to my sisters.
They are my **sisters'** hoops.

 D. **When you write,** here's how to show that more than one person owns something.

When you speak, be sure to pronounce the **s** ending of the plural noun.

Step 1	Write the noun phrase that names the persons who own something.	the two boys	my sisters
Step 2	Write an **apostrophe** after the plural noun.	the two **boys'**	my **sisters'**
Step 3	Write what is owned.	the two boys' **bike**	my sisters' **hoops**

© HMH Supplemental Publishers Inc.

E. You can replace possessive nouns with possessive pronouns.

- Some possessive pronouns come before the noun.
- Some possessive pronouns are not followed by a noun.

other possessive pronouns	
before a noun	**alone**
my bike	mine
your cat	yours
our car	ours

This is the **boys'** bike.
This is **their** bike.
The bike is **theirs**.

They are my **sisters'** hoops.
They are **their** hoops.
The hoops are **theirs**.

This is **Sumi's** cat.
This is **her** cat.
This cat is **hers**.

This is my **dad's** car.
This is **his** car.
This car is **his**.

Grammar and Language Handbook

20 How do we show that something is happening right now?

A. Here are two ways to talk about actions that are happening in the present tense.

B. Use the simple present tense when actions occur regularly or often.

C. To show that something is happening right now, use the correct form of *to be* + the *ing* form of the action verb.

Simple Present	Present Progressive
1. I read every day.	I am reading right now.*
2. The girls sing a lot.	The girls are singing right now.*
3. Celeste always studies math.	Celeste is studying math right now.*

*In these sentences, *am, are* and *is* are helping verbs.

© HMH Supplemental Publishers Inc.

21 How do we show that an action will happen in the future?

A. In English, there is an easy way to show that an action will happen in the future. The magic word is *will.* Just write *will* plus the main verb.

Present Tense	Future Tense
1. I am studying hard now.	I will go to a great college.
2. You are a good student now.	You will be a good doctor.
3. He is not watching television now.	He will watch tonight.

B. You can form a contraction with subject pronouns and *will.*

I will ⟶ I'll	We will ⟶ we'll	He will ⟶ he'll

C. To say that something will **not** happen in the future, you can use **will not** or **won't**.

Won't means the opposite of *will.* You can say either:

I *will not* go to bed or I *won't* go to bed.

© HMH Supplemental Publishers Inc.

181

Grammar and Language Handbook

22 What are negative words in English?

PAIR AND SHARE: Speaking
Study this page with your partner. Then close the book. See how many negative words you can list! Then practice saying a sentence, using just one negative word! Try some alternatives with the positive word list.

A. In formal English, use only one negative word in a sentence.

B. What are the negative words?

no	not	never	nobody	nothing	nowhere
isn't	wasn't	weren't	don't	doesn't	won't

C. If you already have one negative in a sentence, you can use *positive* words that are the opposite of the *negative* words.

negative words	never	nobody	nothing	nowhere
positive words	always	somebody anybody	something anything	somewhere anywhere

Not This	Try This
1. I never talk to nobody in class!	I never talk to anybody in class. I talk to nobody in class.
2. I didn't do nothing!	I didn't do anything. I did nothing.
3. I won't go nowhere today!	I won't go anywhere today. I will go nowhere today.

© HMH Supplemental Publishers Inc.

23 How can we make our sentences interesting?

> When you write, try making some sentences short.
> Make some sentences long. Change the way your
> sentences begin. There are many ways to vary
> your sentences.

Strategy 1. You can use the **connecting** word *and* to
combine different subjects when you write or speak.
Be sure to use a plural verb if the subject in the new
sentence is plural.

1. A watch is on the table.

2. A cell phone is on the table.

Write or say: A watch and a cell phone are on the table.

PAIR AND SHARE: Speaking

Find two objects in the same location
(under a desk, on the wall).
Say where one object is in a sentence.
Describe where the second object is.
Combine the sentences using *and*.
Use Strategy 1 as the model.

© HMH Supplemental Publishers Inc.

Strategy 2. When the subject in two sentences is the same, look for differences. If only one sentence has the word *not*, you may be able to combine sentences using the connecting word *but*.

PAIR AND SHARE: Speaking

Name one thing you like in a sentence.

Name one thing you don't like in another sentence.

Combine the sentences using *but*.

Use Strategy 2 as the model.

 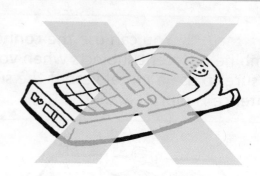

1. I like the watch.

2. I do not like the cell phone.

Write or say: I like the watch, but not the cell phone.

Strategy 3. Combine subjects that are different using a pronoun to replace the noun subjects.

1. My parents are good cooks.
(This is a simple subject.)

2. I am a good cook.
(This is a simple subject.)

Write or say: My parents and I are good cooks. (This is a compound subject.)
We are good cooks. (This is a simple subject.)

184

PAIR AND SHARE: Speaking

Think of two things you will not do.

Make a statement about one thing in a sentence.

Make another statement about the other.

Combine the sentences using *either or*, or *neither nor*.

Use Strategy 4 as the model.

Strategy 4. Use these pairs of conjunctions to combine sentences.

either or
neither nor

1. I will not scold my dog.

2. I will not scold my cat.

Write or say: I will not scold either my dog or my cat.
Or… I will scold neither my dog nor my cat.

Strategy 5. Some verb forms can be used as adjectives. Look for verb forms ending in *-ed* or *-ing*. See if there are ways to combine sentences using these verb forms.

Buzz! Buzz! Buzz!

1. The bees are buzzing.

2. The bees landed on a flower.

Write or say: The buzzing bees landed on a flower.

185

Grammar and Language Handbook

Strategy 6. Sometimes it is possible to combine sentences using one of these conjunctions.

after	before	because	when	until

When you combine two sentences using these conjunctions, you often need a comma to separate the two parts of the new sentence.

1. First I eat breakfast.

2. Then I get dressed.

Write or say: After eating breakfast, I get dressed.
Or... Before getting dressed, I eat breakfast.

PAIR AND SHARE: Speaking

Think of two things you do in a certain order.

Write a sentence about each one. (Use words such as *first, next,* and *then* to show the order.)

Combine the two sentences using conjunctions such as *after, before, because, when, until.*

Use Strategy 6 as the model.

Phonics
and Spelling
Handbook

Phonics and Spelling Handbook

Consonant Letters and Sounds

What is a Consonant?

A consonant is a letter and a speech sound. Consonant sounds are made when some part of the mouth blocks the air when you speak. Your lips, teeth, and tongue can block the air.

PAIR and SHARE: Phonics

Learn a key word that begins with each consonant letter. For example, the letter *f* stands for the sound at the beginning of *fish*.

Use the key word to remind you of the sound this letter stands for.

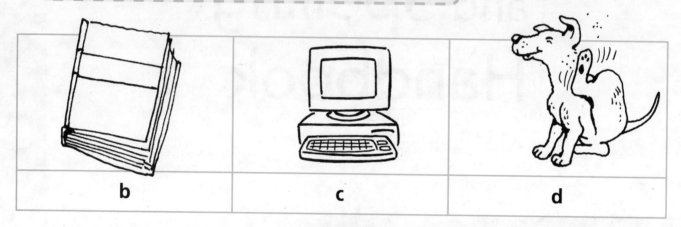

b

c

d

f

g

h

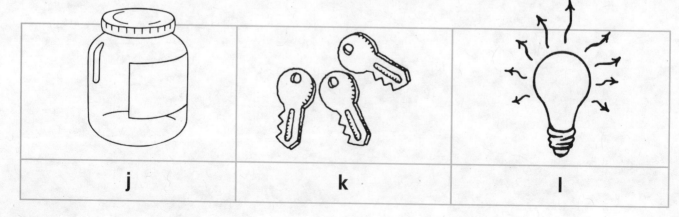

j

k

l

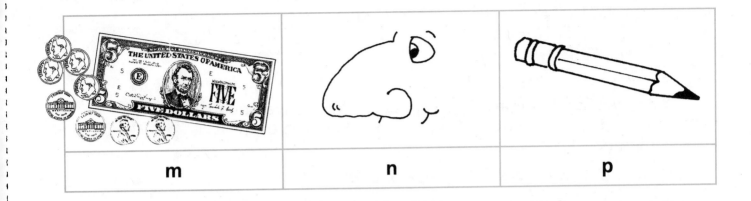

m	**n**	**p**

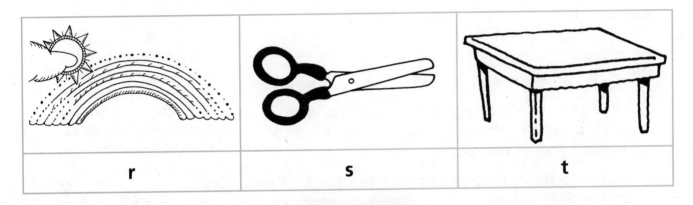

r	**s**	**t**

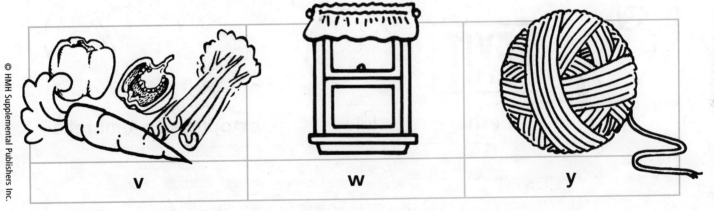

v	**w**	**y**

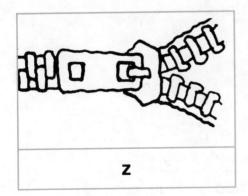

z

PAIR AND SHARE: Spelling

Say a new word aloud.

Match the first sounds in the new word and your key word.

Write the letter.

Phonics and Spelling Handbook

Vowel Letters and Sounds

A. What is a Vowel?

- A vowel is a letter and it is a speech sound. Vowel sounds are made when air is *not* blocked by some part of the mouth.

- There are five vowel letters: *a, e, i, o, u.*

- In English, all vowel letters stand for more than one sound.

B. How to Remember Short Vowel Sounds

PHONICS Learn a key word that starts with each short vowel sound. Use the key word to remind you of the sound.

Listen to the first sound as your teacher says each word.

PAIR and SHARE
Say, *"Short a"* (or e, i, o, u). Your partner will name the key word that begins with the sound. Then change roles.

apple	exit	igloo	octopus	umbrella

C. Letter Patterns in Words with Short Vowel Sounds

PHONICS Look at the word. Answer these questions:

1. Does the word have just one vowel letter?

2. Does the word end in a consonant letter?

If you can answer *yes*, the vowel letter probably stands for a short vowel sound.

Short a	Short e	Short i	Short o	Short u
an, man	Ed, bed	in, pin	on, mop	up, cup

Words with Short Vowels Sounds

PHONICS Reading

Read the slow way. Point to each letter. Say the sound.

Read the fast way. Say the whole word.

Circle a word if you have trouble reading it.

Ask your teacher for help if you need it.

Words with Short a

| c a n → can | b a g → bag | r a m → ram | v a n → van |

Words with Short e

| j e t → jet | h e n → hen | l e g → leg | w e t → wet |

Phonics and Spelling Handbook

Words with Short *i*

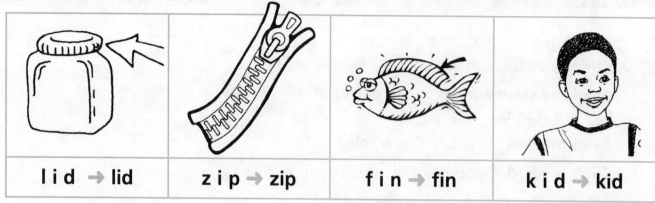

l i d → lid   z i p → zip   f i n → fin   k i d → kid

Words with Short *o*

d o t → dot   m o p → mop   p o t → pot   t o p → top

Words with Short *u*

s u n → sun   b u d → bud   s u m → sum   u p → up

PAIR AND SHARE: Spelling

Say the word aloud.

Say each sound as your partner writes each letter.

Change roles. It's your turn to write a word.

Circle hard words.

Special Consonants

A. The Letter *x*

The letter *x* stands for more than one sound.
Listen as your teacher reads these words.

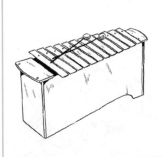	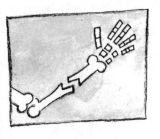		
xylophone	x-ray	six	exit

PAIR and SHARE: Phonics

Read each word.
Remember: The letter *x* stands for two sounds!
Listen to your partner read.
Circle hard words.

B. Where *x* Appears

The letter *x* appears most often at the end of a word or syllable.

Circle the *x* in these words. The letter *x* stands for two sounds: /k/ and /s/. Listen as your teacher reads the words.

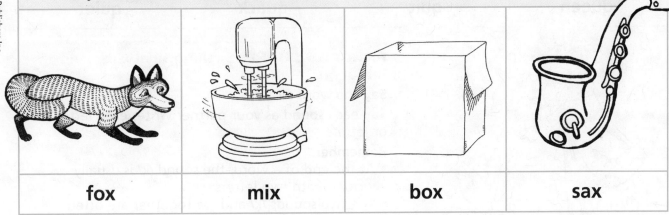

fox	mix	box	sax

193

Phonics and Spelling Handbook

 C. Letters *ck*

The letters *ck* stand for one sound. You will find them at the end of a word or syllable. Listen as your teacher reads the words.

PAIR and SHARE: Phonics
Underline *ck* and *qu* in each word.
Read each word.
Listen to your partner read.
Circle hard words.

duck

pack

sock

kick

 D. Letters *qu*

The letter *q* does not like to be alone! When you see a *q*, look for *u*! Together these letters stand for two sounds: /k/ + /w/. Listen as your teacher reads the words. Repeat.

| queen | quit | quack | quiet |

PAIR AND SHARE: Spelling final *x*, *ck*, and initial *qu*

Say the word aloud.
Say each sound as your partner writes each letter or letters.
Remember:
- At the end of a word, the sound /k/ is usually written with two letters: *ck*.
- The two sounds /k/ and /w/ together are often written with the letters *qu*.
- When you hear the sounds /k/ /s/ at the end of a word, they may be spelled with an *x*.

Change roles. It's your turn to write a word.
Circle hard words.

"QUIET, DUCK!" SAID THE QUEEN.

"QUIT QUACKING!"

194

E. Double Consonant Letters

Sometimes, words or syllables end in double consonants. The two letters always stand for one consonant sound.

			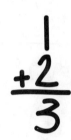
egg	**kiss**	**bell**	**add**

 F. Spelling Alert

Read the words above one more time. Many words ending in these sounds are spelled with a single consonant letter. Read the words below. Make sure you know whether the final consonant letter is doubled when you write the word.

l e g → leg	**b u s → bus**	**p a l → pal**	**d a d → dad**

Phonics and Spelling Handbook

Words with Long Vowel Sounds

A. PHONICS Do you know the name of each vowel letter? That is important information because long vowels say their own names. Your teacher will show you what that means.

Learn a key word that starts with each long vowel sound. Use the key word to remind you of the sound this letter stands for.

PAIR and SHARE
Say, "Long a" (or e, i, o, u). Your partner will name the key word that begins with the sound. Then change roles.

long *a* in *apron*	long *e* in *eat*	long *i* in *ice*	long *o* in *ocean*	Long *u* in *united*

B. Letter Pattern: consonant + vowel (as in *me, be, see*)

PHONICS When a vowel letter is at the end of a word or syllable, it usually has a *long* vowel sound. The letter *y* has the same sound as long *i* at the end of a word.

PAIR and SHARE. Read each word. Circle words that are difficult. Practice spelling the word.

Vowel Letters	Words with Long Vowel Sounds
e or ee	be he me we bee see Lee
i or y	hi by my
o	no so go

C. Irregular Words: *do* and *to*

These words *don't* have a long vowel sound! They are irregular. Listen as your teacher reads them.

© HMH Supplemental Publishers Inc.

Vowel Pairs with Long Vowel Sounds

 A. Vowel pairs: *ee* and *ea*

PHONICS The vowel letters *ee* stand for the long e sound. In most words, the two letters *ea* also stand for the long e *sound*. Circle the vowel pair in each word. Remember, the two vowel letters stand for one vowel sound. Listen as your teacher reads each word.

| beet | meal | peel |

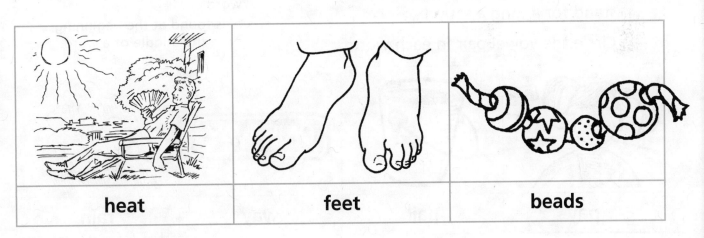

| heat | feet | beads |

Phonics and Spelling Handbook

Vowel Pairs with Long Vowel Sounds

 B. Vowel pair _oa_

PHONICS The vowel letters _oa_ stand for the long _o_ sound in most words. Underline the vowel pair in each word. Remember, the two vowel letters stand for one vowel sound. Listen as your teacher reads each word.

PAIR and SHARE: Reading

Read the word.
Listen to your partner read.
Circle hard words.

		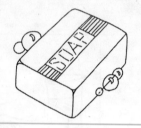	
boat	**toad**	**soap**	**oak**

 C. Vowel pairs _ai_ and _ay_

PHONICS The vowel pairs _ai_ and _ay_ stand for a long _a_ sound.

Circle the vowel pair in each word.

SPELLING NOTE:
- _ay_ is found at the end of a word.
- _ai_ is found at the beginning or in the middle of a word.

pay	**pail**	**way**	**rain**

PAIR and SHARE: Spelling

Long vowel sounds can be spelled in different ways. If you are not sure of the spelling of a word, look it up in a dictionary. Practice spelling the words on this page with your partner.

Long Vowel Letter Pattern: VCe

A. Letter pattern: vowel + consonant + e

PHONICS Look for this letter pattern:
Vowel + Consonant + e

1. The first vowel is long.

2. The final e is silent.

Listen as your teacher reads these words.

c a p e   p i n e   n o t e   c u b e   P e t e

SPELLING NOTE:

Words with long vowel sounds that end in a consonant can be spelled in several ways. Look up words with these patterns if you are unsure of the spelling.

long *a*	long *i*	long *o*	long *u*	long *e*
c a p e	p i n e	n o t e	c u b e	P e t e

B. READING STRATEGY

1. Does the word end in e? **Circle it.**

2. Does a consonant letter precede the final *e*? **Check.**

3. Does a vowel letter precede the consonant? **Underline it.**

4. Read the word:

- The first vowel is long.
- The final e is silent.

Phonics and Spelling Handbook

Long Vowel Letter Pattern: VCe

PAIR and SHARE:
Phonics
Use the reading strategy to read these words.

C. Long a spelled Vowel + Consonant + e

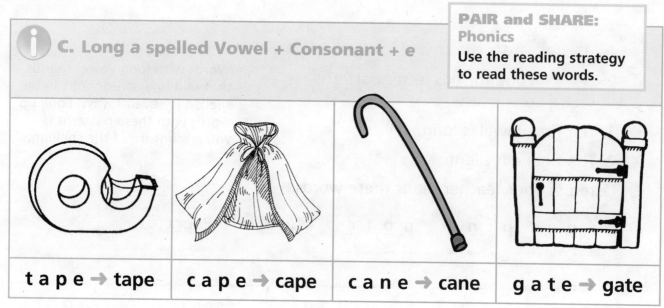

| t a p e → tape | c a p e → cape | c a n e → cane | g a t e → gate |

D. Long e spelled Vowel + Consonant + e

Most words with long e vowels with this letter pattern are people's names.

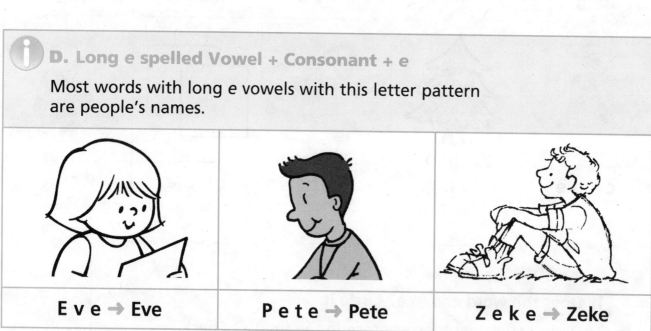

| E v e → Eve | P e t e → Pete | Z e k e → Zeke |

PAIR and SHARE: Spelling
Long vowel sounds can be spelled in different ways. If you are not sure of the spelling of a word, look it up in a dictionary. Practice spelling the words on this page with your partner.

E. Long *i* spelled Vowel + Consonant + *e*

| p i n e → pine | d i m e → dime | k i t e → kite | p i p e → pipe |

F. Long *o* spelled Vowel + Consonant + *e*

| b o n e → bone | c o n e → cone | n o t e → note | r o p e → rope |

G. Long *u* spelled Vowel + Consonant + *e*

SPELLING NOTE:
When you are writing a word with either of the two long *u* sounds plus a final consonant, use a VCe letter pattern.

The long *u* has two sounds: the sound you hear in *cube* and the sound you hear in *tube*.

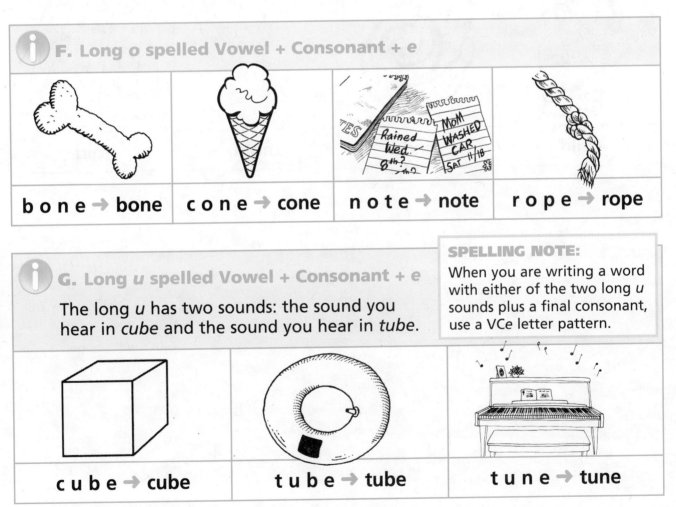

| c u b e → cube | t u b e → tube | t u n e → tune |

PAIR and SHARE: Spelling
Long vowel sounds can be spelled in different ways. If you are not sure of the spelling of a word, look it up in a dictionary. Practice spelling the words on this page with your partner.

Phonics and Spelling Handbook

Other Long Vowels

 Other Long Vowels

PHONICS and SPELLING When the letters *nd* and *ld* are preceded by *i* or *o*, the vowel has a long vowel sound. Examples are *wild, mild, cold, sold, told* and *mind, kind*, and *find*. Once you know the rule, these words are easy to spell.

PAIR and SHARE:
Phonics
1. **Circle** the vowel letter.
2. **Underline** *nd* or *ld*.
3. **Read** the word using a long vowel sound.
4. **Listen** to your partner read.
5. **Circle** hard words.

			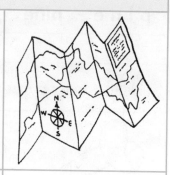
child	**rind**	**mold**	**fold**

Two Sounds of *c* and *g*

PAIR and SHARE: Phonics
1. **Circle** the letter *c* or *g*.
2. **Underline** the letter that follows *c* or *g*.
3. **Read** the word.
4. **Listen** to your partner read.
5. **Circle** hard words.

ℹ **PHONICS NOTES about *c* and *g***

Hard *c* and *g* The letter *c* stands for the sound at the beginning of *computer*. The letter *g* stands for the sound at the beginning of *gate*.

These sounds are called *hard c* and *hard g* sounds.

Soft *c* and *g* When the letters *c* and *g* are followed by *i*, *e*, or *y*, they usually stand for other sounds. Listen as your teacher reads the words below. The letters *c* and *g* are called *soft c* and *g* sounds in these words.

Soft C

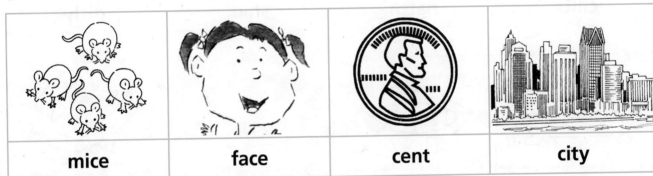

| mice | face | cent | city |

Soft G

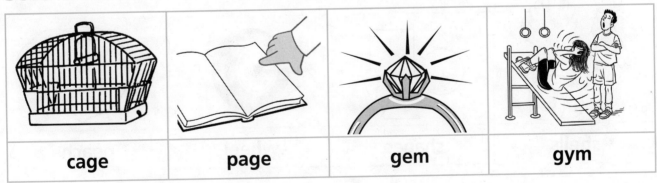

| cage | page | gem | gym |

PAIR and SHARE: Spelling

Be careful!
• Soft *c* as in *cent* can also be spelled with the letter *s*, as in *sent*.
• Soft *g* as in *gem* can also be spelled with the letter *j*, as in *jet*.
If you are unsure of the spelling, look up the word in a dictionary.

Phonics and Spelling Handbook

Consonant Digraphs and Trigraphs

A. Digraphs and Trigraphs *ch, tch, ph, sh, th,* and *wh*

PHONICS These consonant letters stand for just one sound.

PAIR and SHARE: Phonics
Underline the digraph or trigraph.
Read each word.
Listen to your partner read.
Circle hard words.

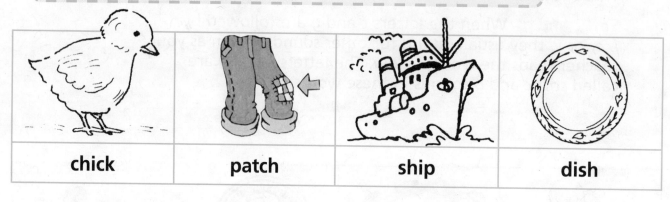

| chick | patch | ship | dish |

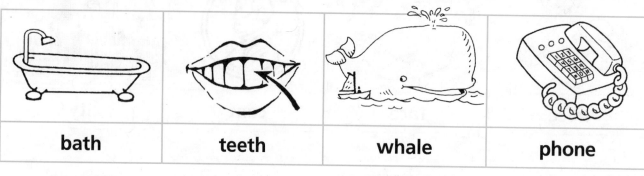

| bath | teeth | whale | phone |

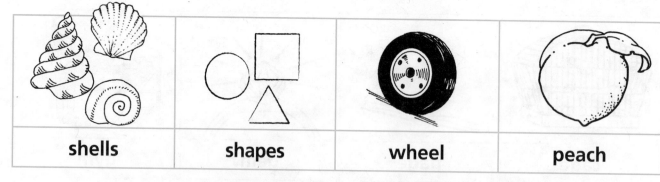

| shells | shapes | wheel | peach |

PAIR and SHARE: Spelling

The sound /ch/ is spelled in two ways: *ch* and *tch*. The spelling *tch* is found only at the end of a word, and *ch* is found at the beginning and end (as in *church*).

PHONICS Two other consonant pairs stand for one sound. Listen as your teacher reads the words below.

| wing | ring | sing | king |

| sink | tank | skunk | bank |

Phonics and Spelling Handbook

Other Vowel Pairs

 A. Vowel Pair *ea*

PHONICS The vowel pair *ea* usually stands for the long e sound as in *eat, beads,* and *heap.* This vowel pair also stands for two other sounds.

Listen as your teacher reads the words below.

PAIR and SHARE Circle the vowel pair in each word. Then read each word with your partner.

PAIR and SHARE: Reading

Words spelled with *ea* can be a challenge to read and spell. Ask your teacher for help or look up the word in the dictionary.

long *a*	short e	long e	short e long e
steak	bread	peak	Today, I read. Yesterday, I read.

long e	short e	long e	long *a*
heat	head	tea	break

B. Vowel pair *oo*

PHONICS The vowel pair *oo* stands for more than one sound. Listen as your teacher reads the words below.

PAIR and SHARE:
Reading
Underline the vowel pair.
Then read the word.
Listen to your partner read.
Circle hard words.

moon	**spoon**	**hoot**	**hoop**

book	**hook**	**cook**	**He took a rook.**

PAIR and SHARE: Spelling
Words with the vowel sound in *moon* can be spelled in other ways, as in *dune* and *due*. Look up words with this sound in the dictionary if you are unsure how to spell them.

Phonics and Spelling Handbook

Other Vowel Pairs

© HMH Supplemental Publishers Inc.

C. Vowel Pairs *ue* and *ew*

PHONICS Long *u* has two sounds: the sound we hear in *cube* and the sound we hear in *tube*. These long *u* sounds can also be spelled with the letters *ue* and *ew*. Listen as your teacher reads each word.

 **glue**	 **few**	 **blue**	 **new**

D. The Squawk Vowel

PHONICS That sounds like an odd name for a vowel! And this vowel is a bit odd! This sound can be spelled in a lot of ways. In fact, people often pronounce the word dog with this vowel sound.

alk	alt, aul, ault	all, oll	augh, ough	aw
balk	halt	ball	caught	paw
chalk	malt	call	taught	jaw
talk	salt	fall	bought	law
walk	Paul	mall	sought	raw
	Saul	doll	cough	saw
	fault			
	vault			

Diphthongs

PAIR and SHARE:
Reading

Listen as your teacher reads each word.

Circle the vowel pair.

Read the word. Listen to your partner read.

A. Sometimes, a vowel pair stands for two vowel sounds that glide into each other. This kind of vowel pair is called a **diphthong**.

B. *oi* and *oy*

PHONICS These letters stand for the same diphthong. Listen as your teacher reads these words.

SPELLING NOTE:
At the end of a word, this diphthong is spelled *oy*. At the beginning or middle of a word, it is spelled *oi*.

| oink | toy | soil | coin |

C. *ou*

The letters *ou* can stand for the vowel sounds in *you*, *youth*, and *your*. These letters often stand for a diphthong, as in the words below.

SPELLING NOTE:
The *ou* diphthong can also be spelled with the letters *ow*, as in *cow*. Look up words with this sound if you are unsure of the spelling.

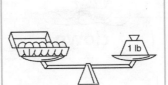

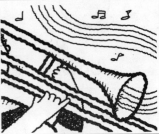

| hound | pound | ground | sound |

209

Phonics and Spelling Handbook

Diphthongs

 D. *ow*

PHONICS When the letter *w* is at the end of a word or syllable, it acts like a vowel. The letters *ow* are a vowel pair.

- These letters stand for the long vowel sound we hear in *crow*.

- They also stand for the diphthong we hear in *cow*.

There are no rules to use for pronouncing words spelled with *ow*.

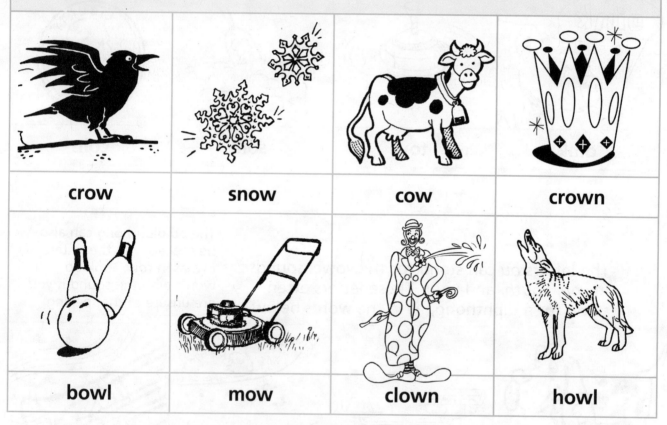

| crow | snow | cow | crown |
| bowl | mow | clown | howl |

Vowels + *r*

PAIR and SHARE:
Reading

Listen as your teacher reads each word.

Repeat the word.
Listen to your partner read.

A. Vowels + *r*

PHONICS When the letter *r* follows a vowel, it can change the usual sound of the vowel.

B. *a + r*

PHONICS When followed by *r*, or *r* + a consonant, the letter *a* has the same sound that it does in words such as *pa, ma,* and *watch.*
Read these words.

car	**star**	**yarn**

C. *or, oar, ore*

PHONICS In words spelled *or, oar,* and *ore,* the letter *r* changes the vowel sound. Read each word.

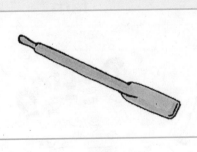		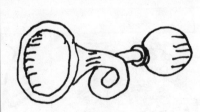
oar	**core**	**horn**

Phonics and Spelling Handbook

C. Exceptions

PHONICS In these words, you can hear the long vowel sound even though the letter *r* follows it.

steer

pair

fire

D. Vowels Combined with *r*

PHONICS AND SPELLING In these words, the vowel combines with the *r*. Listen as your teacher reads each word. The vowel + *r* stands for the same in all of these words, but the vowel letter can be *e*, *i*, *o*, or *u*. That makes spelling difficult!

bird

fir

fur

fern

herd

shirt

skirt

words

Silent Letters

> ℹ **Silent Letters**
>
> Some letters in English are silent. They can make reading *and* spelling difficult! Getting to know which letters are likely to be silent will help you. Look up words if you are unsure of the spelling or pronunciation. You can also search online for silent letters in English.

Silent Letters	Example Words				
b	numb	comb	lamb	climb	crumb
g	sign				
gh	eight	thought	straight	height	light	right
k	know	knew	knit	knock	knee	knife
l	calf	half	talk	walk	would	should
t	castle	fasten	whistle			
w	wrap	write	wrote	written	wreck	wrong

Phonics and Spelling Handbook

PHONOLOGY: CONSONANT BLENDS WITH /S/

> **A. Initial Blends with s**
>
> When a word begins with s + one or more consonant letters, be sure to pronounce all consonant sounds.

Practice with these words. Make a difference in how the words in each group sound.

sip, slip, skip	soup, stoop, sloop	sell, smell, spell
side, slide, snide	Sam, slam, scam	seep, steep, sleep
sub, snub, stub	sat, scat, slat	sop, stop, slop

> **B. Final Blends with s**
>
> When a word ends with s + one or more consonant letters, make sure you pronounce all of the consonant sounds. Say each consonant sound in the order it occurs in the word.

Practice with these words. Make a difference in how the words in each group sound.

lass, last, lasts	Tess, test, tests	less, lest, let's
mass, mast, masts	miss, mist, mists	Wes, west, wets
lap, laps, lapse	loss, lost, lots	Gus, gust, gusts

PHONOLOGY: CONSONANT BLENDS WITH /S/

C. Ask

When you say the word *ask,* pronounce it so that it sounds different from the word *ax.* The word *ask* rhymes with *task, mask,* and *bask.*

D. Word Sort

Which words have /sk/ sounds? Which words have /ks/ sounds? Write words in the first row that end in /sk/ sounds.

Write words in the second row that end in /ks/ sounds.

task	mask	tax
max	backs	ask
desk	oaks	risk

Row 1: /sk/ _____

Row 2: /ks/ _____

Practice reading these sentences. Pay close attention to how you pronounce the colored letters.

1. I have pins and tacks.
2. Did you wear that mask?
3. Did you ask me a question?
4. Can you move those desks?
5. He asked me politely!

Phonics and Spelling Handbook

PHONOLOGY: CONSONANT BLENDS WITH /S/

 E. Other Initial Blends

Some words begin with three consonants, as in *strong.* Some begin with one single consonant and a consonant digraph, as in *shrink.* Be sure to pronounce all consonants sounds in the order they occur in the word.

Practice with these words.

stream, scream	strap, scrap	stroll, scroll
shrimp, scrimp,	shrub, scrub	shriek, screech

 F. Other Final Blends

Make sure you pronounce all of the consonant sounds in a word. Say each consonant sound in the order it occurs.

Practice with these words. Make a difference in how the words in each group sound.

1.	rap, raps, rapt	pack, pact, packs	men, mend, mends
2.	an, and, hands	fine, find, finds	give, gift, gifts
3.	chip, chimp, chimps	pick, pink, ping	kick, kink, king
4.	putt, punt, punts	set, sent, sends	truck, trunk, trunks
5.	lit, lift, lifts	correct, corrected	land, lands, landing

© HMH Supplemental Publishers Inc.

Check Your Progress

LEARNING STRATEGIES

You are learning English in so many ways! Check the boxes to show how much progress you've made. Check all boxes that apply.

☐ I pronounce English words better than I did before.

☐ I can spell correctly.

☐ I use new words when I speak.

☐ I use new words in my writing.

☐ I use pictures, charts, graphs, and maps to help me understand words.

☐ When I see or hear an unfamiliar word or expression, I'm better at figuring out its meaning.

☐ I know much more about English grammar.

☐ I know how to speak to teachers and adults, and how to speak to my friends.

☐ I ask for help when I don't understand.

☐ I've gotten better at recognizing and correcting mistakes in my writing.

Check Your Progress

I'M LISTENING!

Check the boxes to show the ways you have become a better listener. Check all boxes that apply.

☐ I know which letters stand for sounds in words that I hear.

☐ I watch people's gestures and expressions to help me understand spoken English.

☐ I understand more of what I see and hear in newspapers and magazines, and on television, radio, and the Internet.

☐ I understand more of what people say about topics I already know.

☐ I understand more of what people say about topics I don't already know.

☐ I take notes to help me understand spoken English.

☐ I'm better at answering questions about stories and information that I hear.

☐ I understand more of my teacher's directions, and I can repeat them.

☐ When people speak, I understand faster and better than I did before.

Check Your Progress

SAY IT ALOUD

Check the boxes to show the ways you have become a better speaker. Check all boxes that apply.

☐ I know how to pronounce words better than I did before.

☐ I can describe people, places, and things better than I could before.

☐ I can use both simple and complex sentences when I speak.

☐ I use vocabulary words correctly when I speak.

☐ I can share information with my classmates when we work together.

☐ I know how to ask for help when I need it.

☐ I'm better at expressing ideas, opinions, and feelings.

☐ I can tell about events better than I could before.

☐ I'm better at retelling stories that I have read.

☐ I know how to speak to teachers and adults and how to speak to my friends.

Check Your Progress

READ IT!

Check the boxes to show the ways you have become a better reader.
Check all boxes that apply.

☐ I know how to read more words, including longer words.

☐ I recognize more high-frequency words than I did before.

☐ I understand more of the words that I see around me at school, at home, and in my town.

☐ I use pictures to help me understand what I read.

☐ I can use what I already know to understand new topics.

☐ I can use information from classroom discussions to help me understand reading selections.

☐ If I don't know a word, I can figure out the meaning by looking at nearby words and sentences.

☐ I can talk about and retell reading selections better than I could before.

☐ I ask for help from my classmates and teacher when I don't understand.

☐ I can take notes about reading selections.

☐ I can answer questions about reading selections.

☐ I read better, faster, and with greater understanding than I did before.

Check Your Progress

WRITE IT!

Check the boxes to show the ways you have become a better writer. Check all boxes that apply.

- ☐ I'm better at spelling high-frequency words than I was before.

- ☐ I use high-frequency words correctly in my writing.

- ☐ I'm better at using spelling rules to write new words.

- ☐ I use vocabulary words correctly in my writing.

- ☐ I use a variety of sentence types and lengths when I write.

- ☐ I'm better at applying grammar rules in my writing.

- ☐ I can edit my writing to correct mistakes and make it better.

- ☐ I can describe events in writing better than I could before.

- ☐ I'm better at giving information in writing.

- ☐ I'm better at expressing ideas in writing.

- ☐ I can write better and faster than I could before.

Index for Handbooks

Standardized
Test Practice

Standardized Test-Taking Tips

Cut out the tips below and use them with the Standardized Test Practice.

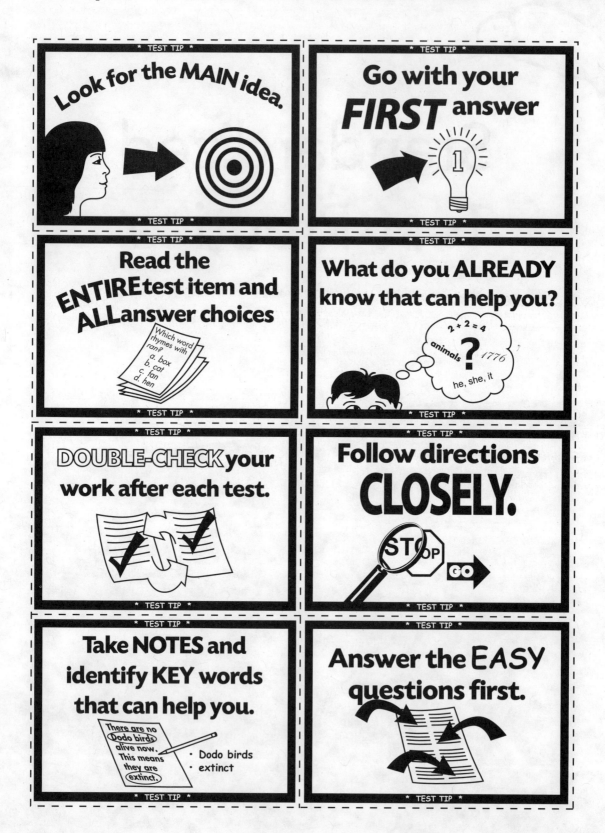

Practice Test 1

Read this selection. Then read each question and fill in the correct answer.

The Pine Needle

September Issue
Page 3

Serving the Students of
Lakeville Grade School

Getting Checked Out

by Diane Jones

1   Do you know why it is important to have a yearly health checkup? To find out, I interviewed Doctor Louise Winston. Her answers to my questions helped me understand why a checkup is important. Then she gave me a checkup.

2   "A yearly checkup helps me to know that all systems are go with each patient," Doctor Winston explained. "The checkup starts when my patient steps on the scale. Each patient should be weighed and measured at least once a year. That way, I keep track of how much my patient has grown."

3   Doctor Winston showed me a blood pressure machine. It has a cuff that goes around your arm. She wrapped the cuff around my arm. She squeezed a bulb at the end of the cuff to make it inflate. The cuff filled with air. It got tighter and tighter on my arm. This helped the doctor tell how well blood was sent to my heart. "Your blood pressure is fine," Doctor Winston said with a smile.

4   Next, she shined a light in my eyes. The tool she used looked like a small flashlight. "I use this to check your eyes," she said. After, I read an eye chart. The letters at the top were very big, but the lower letters got smaller and smaller. I read most of the letters, and Doctor Winston said that my eyesight was great.

5   After checking my eyes, she hit my knee with a tool that looked like a little rubber hammer. My leg jumped up!

6   "Good," Doctor Winston said. "That means your brain sent a message telling your leg to move."

Continued on next page

Getting Checked Out *continued*

7 Doctor Winston took out a wooden stick. She put the stick on my tongue.

8 "I'm holding your tongue down to make room to get a good look inside your throat," she said. "I can see that your tonsils look nice and healthy."

9 My favorite part of my checkup was when Doctor Winston let me use a special tool to listen to my heart. A stethoscope has earplugs attached to a long tube with a round part at the bottom. She put the earplugs in my ears and the round part on my chest. I heard a *boom da boom da boom.*

10 Then Doctor Winston listened. "Your heart is working just fine," she said. "Now, take a deep breath so I can listen to your lungs."

11 I took a big breath. "Your lungs sound really good," Doctor Winston said with a grin.

12 Finally, Doctor Winston asked me to stand up, bend over, and touch my toes. "I'm doing this to check your back and make sure that everything is straight and strong," she explained.

13 "You're in great shape," Doctor Winston said. "Your checkup is over. See you next year!"

14 It's good to know that everything is fine, but sometimes there is something that's not quite right. A yearly checkup can help the doctor find out if something needs more care. There's no easier way to stay healthy than by getting checked out every year.

© HMH Supplemental Publishers Inc.

1 In paragraph 1, which words help the reader know what <u>interviewed</u> means?
- *helped me understand*
- *Her answers to my questions*
- *she gave me a checkup*
- *a checkup is important*

TEKS 3.4B

2 Paragraph 3 is mostly about —
- how a stethoscope works
- the parts of a blood pressure cuff
- how a blood pressure machine works
- why it is important to have good blood pressure

GO ON

3   What is the title of this article?

○ *The Pine Needle*

○ *Keeping Healthy*

○ *Getting Checked Out*

○ *Diane Jones*

4   Which sentence from the story shows the reader why getting a yearly checkup is important?

○ *Her answers to my questions helped me understand why a checkup is important.*

○ *Each patient should be weighed and measured at least once a year.*

○ *A yearly checkup can help the doctor find out if something needs more care.*

○ *My favorite part of my checkup was when Doctor Winston let me use a special tool to listen to my heart.*

5   Why does Doctor Winston hit her patient's knee with a rubber hammer?

○ To check that the body receives messages from the brain

○ To find out if it hurts

○ To see if the patient's leg is strong

○ To be sure that the patient can feel the hammer

6   Use the chart below to answer the question.

What Happens	Why It Happens
The doctor uses a stick to hold the tongue down.	???

Which of the following belongs in the empty box?

○ To check the lungs

○ To make room to see inside the throat

○ To see the back teeth

○ To check that the patient can say "AHH" with the stick in her mouth

7   In paragraph 3, what does <u>inflate</u> mean?

○ Become tight

○ Fill with air

○ Cause pressure

○ Make blood flow

8   Which word from paragraph 1 means about the same as the word <u>understand</u>?

○ *important*

○ *questions*

○ *checkup*

○ *know*

GO ON

Read this selection. Then read each question and fill in the correct answer.

Spaghetti Sauce for Tommy

1   Tommy was shooting hoops in the backyard when he smelled Mom's special spaghetti sauce in the air. He put away his basketball and headed straight to the kitchen.

2   Mom was stirring a pot of red sauce with a wooden spoon. She dipped a piece of bread into the sauce and tasted it. Then she added other <u>ingredients</u> such as chopped peppers, garlic, and onion.

3   Mom dipped some bread in the sauce for Tommy. "Yum," he said. "Who taught you how to make such good sauce?"

4   "Grandma Angelina," Mom said. "When I was your age, I helped her in the kitchen."

5   "You know," Mom went on, "your Grandma came to America from a small Italian village. She and Grandpa had a farm near Granger, Texas. They worked very hard. They grew lots of vegetables, and their tomatoes were the best in the county."

6   "Grandma made spaghetti sauce from those tomatoes," Mom went on. "First, she'd drop tomatoes in a pot of boiling water for about a minute. Then she'd put them a bowl of ice water."

7   "Why did she make the tomatoes hot and then make them cold?" Tommy asked.

8   "So the tomato skin would slip off very easily," Mom answered. "You wouldn't like tomato skin in spaghetti sauce, would you?" Tommy shook his head. He couldn't talk because his mouth was full of bread!

9   "Grandma put the tomatoes in a large pot," Mom continued. "She'd <u>simmer</u> them on a low flame so that they'd cook very slowly. Then she'd add garlic, onion, spices, and sometimes a little bit of sugar."

GO ON →

© HMH Supplemental Publishers Inc.

10   "I stirred the sauce and listened to Grandma tell about her village in Italy," Mom continued.

11   "What stories did she tell you?" Tommy asked.

12   "Well, Grandma's village was high up on a mountain," Mom began. "School was in a town at the bottom of the mountain. Every day Grandma's father, your great-grandfather, took the village children down the mountain to school."

13   "Grandma said there was this pesky boy named Tonio who pulled her pigtails in school. She got so mad that she asked her father not to let him in the cart the next day."

14   "Then how did Tonio get to school?" Tommy asked.

15   "Well, he woke up very early the next morning," Mom said. "He walked all the way down the mountain to the school. He didn't pull Grandma's pigtails that day. He was asleep at his desk!"

16   "How did he get home?" Tommy asked.

17   "Grandma took pity on Tonio and asked her father to let him ride back in the cart."

18   "Grandma and Tony became good friends. When they grew up, they got married! That boy was your Grandpa Tony!"

19   "Then one day, your great-grandfather took Grandma and Grandpa down the mountain in the mule cart for the last time," Mom said. "He took them to the boat that brought them to America."

20   "Grandma said that her father handed her a note just before she got on the boat," Mom told Tommy. "It was a recipe for spaghetti sauce! And it was called *Tomasina's Sauce.*"

21   "Who was Tomasina?" Tommy asked.

© HMH Supplemental Publishers Inc.

GO ON

22   Mom squeezed Tommy and said, "Tomasina was your great-grandmother."

23   Tommy licked the spoon. "This sauce is just right," he said.

24   "That's because you are a great stirrer," Mom said. "We'll just call this *Tommy's Sauce!*"

25   "What would Grandma Angelina think about that?" asked Tommy.

26   Mom smiled, "She would say *molto bono*, which means 'very good' in Italian."

27   "Let's tell Grandma about *Tommy's Sauce*," Tommy said. "We can tell her that it's *molto bono!*"

28   Mom laughed and gave Tommy a great big hug. "You're *molto bono*," she said.

---

9   What does the word <u>simmer</u> mean in paragraph 9?

⭕ Put in a large pot
⭕ Cook slowly
⭕ Add garlic
⭕ Peel tomatoes

10   Tommy goes to his mom's kitchen because —

⭕ his mother asked him to stir the sauce
⭕ he wants to find out who taught Mom how to make the sauce
⭕ he wants to learn about his Grandma's village
⭕ he smells his mother's sauce cooking

GO ON ➡

11 Paragraph 12 is mostly about —

- ⬭ Grandma's village
- ⬭ Grandma's school
- ⬭ how village children got to school
- ⬭ Tommy's great-grandfather

12 What causes Mom to tell Tommy a story about Grandma's village?

- ⬭ Cooking with Tommy reminds Mom of the stories Grandma told as she cooked.
- ⬭ Tommy is curious about Grandma's village.
- ⬭ Mom wants Tommy to know how hard it was for Grandma to get to school.
- ⬭ Mom wants Tommy to know about his great-grandfather.

13 Which is the best summary of this story?

- ⬭ Tommy plays basketball and stirs spaghetti sauce.
- ⬭ Mom tells Tommy a story about how his grandparents first met.
- ⬭ Tommy helps his mother make sauce and learns about his family.
- ⬭ Tommy learns that the words *molto bono* mean "very good."

14 Which of these best describes how Tommy feels about his mother's sauce?

- ⬭ He thinks it is delicious.
- ⬭ He does not like it.
- ⬭ He doesn't want any.
- ⬭ He thinks it is too spicy.

15 In paragraph 2, which words help the reader know what <u>ingredients</u> means?

- ⬭ *Peppers, garlic, and onions*
- ⬭ *Dipped a piece of bread*
- ⬭ *Tasted the bread*
- ⬭ *A wooden spoon*

16 Look at the chart below.

Making Spaghetti Sauce

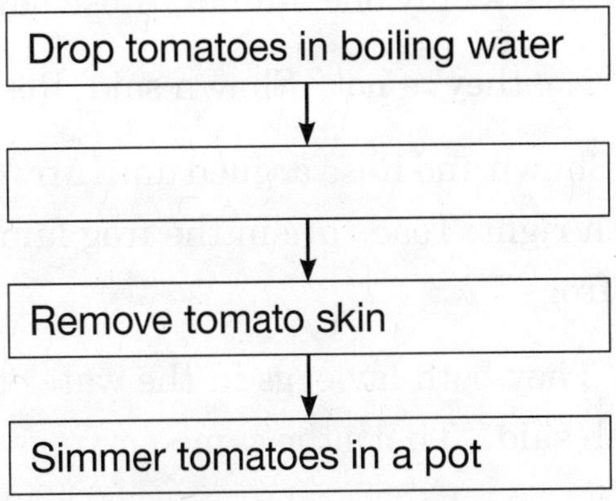

Drop tomatoes in boiling water

↓

↓

Remove tomato skin

↓

Simmer tomatoes in a pot

Which belongs in the empty box?

- ⬭ Add garlic
- ⬭ Put tomatoes in ice water
- ⬭ Stir the sauce
- ⬭ Put tomatoes in a large pot

GO ON ➡

> **Read this selection. Then read each question and fill in the correct answer.**

Frogs and Toads

1   "I have a surprise," Mr. Waters said to his third-grade class. "We're going to take a class trip to the Parkland Zoo."

2   The class started chattering noisily, asking one question after another. "When are we going?" "How long will we be there?" "Will we get lunch at the zoo?"

3   "Calm down, class," Mr. Waters laughed. "All the information about the trip is on a form for your parents. It also tells them that we've been learning about animals that can live in or out of the water. That explains why we'll be going to the <u>amphibian</u> house at the zoo. So, what kinds of animals are amphibians?"

4   "Salamanders are amphibians," Marcy answered.

5   "That's right," Mr. Waters said. "Who can name two more?"

6   "I can," Shawn said. "Frogs and toads are both amphibians."

7   "That's only one animal," Rosa said. "Toads are the same as frogs."

8   "No, they're not," Shawn said. Rosa disagreed, though.

9   Shawn and Rosa argued until Mr. Waters <u>interrupted</u> them to say, "You're both right. Toads *are* in the frog family, but they are not exactly the same as frogs."

10   "They both lay eggs in the water to hatch their baby tadpoles, though," Josh said. "That's the same for frogs and toads."

11   "That's right, Josh," Mr. Waters said. "Though frogs lay eggs in clusters, or lumps. Toads lay eggs in long lines like chains."

GO ON ➡

12   "Both frog and toad tadpoles breathe with gills," Maria added. "When they grow up, the tadpoles develop lungs to breathe air."

13   "I can tell you something different about frogs and toads," Ricardo said. "Someone told me that you can get warts from touching a toad."

14   "Some people think that, but it's not true. Toads have dry, warty skin, but you can't get warts from them." Mr. Waters continued, "Ricardo, how is a frog's skin different from a toad's skin?"

15   "Well," Ricardo began. "A frog's skin is smooth and slimy. I guess that's one difference between a frog and a toad."

16   "Here's another," Mr. Waters went on. "A frog has long legs so it can jump. Toads have short legs. They can only hop."

17   Lu Ann raised her hand. "My dad is reading me a story about a jumping frog contest," she said. "I guess there aren't any stories about jumping toad contests!" Lu Ann said.

18   "Now, here's one more difference that will surprise you," Mr. Waters said. "Frogs have teeth and toads don't."

19   "Yikes," Shawn and Rosa said at the same time. "You mean a frog could bite us?"

20   "I don't think so. They only have teeth in the top of their jaws," Mr. Waters said. "They also have long sticky tongues," he added. "They catch insects that way. Toads have sticky tongues, too."

21   "Here's another difference," Lu Ann said. "If you kiss a frog, it may turn into a prince! But who wants to kiss a frog?"

22   Everyone laughed, including Mr. Waters. "Now, let's get serious for a minute," he said. "I want you to think about what we learned today. Then, when we go to the amphibian house, you can pick out the frogs from the toads."

GO ON

17 The students in Mr. Waters's class will go to the zoo to —

◯ get lunch at the zoo

◯ see salamanders

◯ watch tadpoles grow

◯ visit the amphibian house

18 What is the main problem in the story?

◯ Rosa and Shawn have an argument.

◯ The students have to tell why they are going to visit the amphibian house.

◯ The students have to learn the difference between a frog and a toad.

◯ Touching toads causes warts.

19 Read the meanings below for the word raise.

raise ('r ā z) *verb* **1.** to lift, to move higher **2.** to help grow **3.** to take care of **4.** to collect, to earn

Which meaning best fits the way raised is used in paragraph 17?

◯ Meaning 1

◯ Meaning 2

◯ Meaning 3

◯ Meaning 4

20 In paragraph 3, what does amphibian mean?

◯ A form for parents

◯ A house at the zoo

◯ An animal that can live in or out of water

◯ Information about the trip to the zoo

21 This story was written mainly to —

◯ explain how frogs and toads are alike and different

◯ show that Mr. Waters is a good teacher

◯ explain how frogs and toads lay their eggs

◯ explain what an amphibian is

22 How do tadpoles breathe before they grow lungs?

◯ Only on the land

◯ With special tanks

◯ With gills

◯ With long legs

GO ON ➡

23 Look as the diagram about frogs and toads. Answer the question that follows.

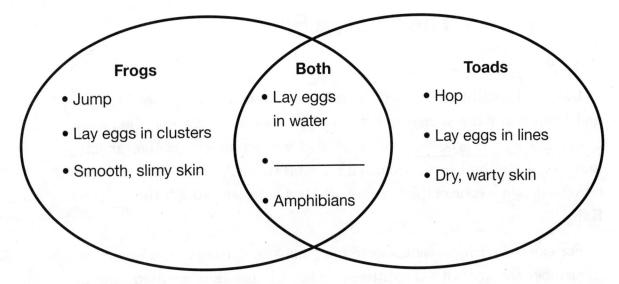

Which of the following goes in the blank?

⬭ Have short legs
⬭ Have teeth
⬭ Are in the frog family
⬭ Have long legs

24 Which of these **BEST** describes how the students feel about going to the zoo?

⬭ Amused
⬭ Afraid
⬭ Excited
⬭ Bored

25 What subject would you say that Mr. Waters class is studying in this selection?

⬭ Math
⬭ Science
⬭ Reading
⬭ Social Studies

26 In paragraph 9, the word <u>interrupted</u> means —

⬭ argued
⬭ stopped
⬭ laughed
⬭ yelled

GO ON

Read the two selections that follow.

The Garage Sale

Dear Judy,

1 I am so excited that you will be coming to visit us in two weeks. Dad and I can really use your help with our plans for a garage sale. Dad says the garage is so <u>overflowing</u> with stuff that we can hardly get the car into it anymore. He thinks we should sell the stuff we don't need. You and I can set up our own section of the garage sale. Maybe we can call it "Stuff Just for Kids."

2 For example, I have some electronic games that I never use anymore. Remember the one with the different colored lights that we used to play together years ago? You know, the lights would come on in a different <u>sequence</u> each time. Then we would have to push the colors to repeat in the same order. I'm going to sell it, unless you want it. I am also going to sell my old roller skates. Dad gave me a set of in-line skates last year!

3 Mom and Dad are going through their stuff, too. You wouldn't believe the junk they have. They even have records! I told them that no one uses records anymore. "Most everyone listens to CDs or MP3 players," I told them. They think that some people would love to have their old records. We'll see at the garage sale.

4 Do you have stuff to sell at our "Stuff Just for Kids" table? Bring it with you when your Mom drives you down. I bet you will be happy to get rid of things you don't use anymore.

5 We'll have to spend a day putting price tags on our stuff and helping Dad make signs telling about our sale. We'll also help him put up the signs around the neighborhood. Then we'll set up and spend the next day selling. It should be a lot of fun. We'll make some money, too!

Love,
Jill

GO ON

Kidding Around

A Magazine for 7- to 10-Year-Olds

September, 2009   Vol. 5. Issue 3

Money-Making Ideas for Kids

by Gia Treadwell

1   Is there a toy or game you'd like to buy? Perhaps you'd like to give a gift to a friend. Either way, you probably need to earn some money. Fortunately, there are lots of ways kids can earn money.

2   You can earn money right around your own house. Make a list of chores that you'd help out with and tell what you'd charge. For example, you can match socks on laundry day and charge a nickel a pair. Of course, you can't charge for chores you're already expected to do.

3   Assisting a neighbor is a good way to make extra money. First, make sure that your parents know the neighbor well and agree to your plan. If your neighbor has a pet, you can pet sit. That means you'll feed the pet and make sure it's okay while the neighbor is away. Don't take a job if you have to walk the pet though. Wait until you're older to do that.

4   When a neighbor goes away, you can also tend the garden. All you have to do is water the plants. If you live in an apartment building, you can pick up mail or newspapers. Put up a sign on your door to let neighbors know that you're available to do these jobs!

5   It just takes one good idea to get started making some extra nickels, dimes, and even dollars! Don't get carried away, though. Remember, you have to make time to do your homework, do your regular chores, play with your friends, and just relax.

GO ON

Use "The Garage Sale" (p. 115) to answer questions 27–31.

27 What is the main problem in this story?

⬭ There's too much stuff in Jill's garage.

⬭ Jill has too many stuffed animals.

⬭ Jill's dad does not want to sell anything.

⬭ No one listens to records anymore.

28 In paragraph 1, which words help the reader know what <u>overflowing</u> means?

⬭ *use your help*

⬭ *sell the stuff we don't need*

⬭ *can hardly get the car into it*

⬭ *coming to visit*

29 How can you tell that Jill and Judy have been friends for a long time?

⬭ They played together with an electric game a long time ago.

⬭ Jill's parents have records.

⬭ Judy is coming to visit Jill.

⬭ Jill and Judy will work together to make a "Stuff for Kids" table.

30 In paragraph 2, the word <u>sequence</u> means —

⬭ repeat in the same order

⬭ different colored lights

⬭ push the colors

⬭ the lights would come on

31 Use the chart below to answer the question.

What Happens	Why It Happens
Jill is going to sell her old roller skates.	???

Which of the following belongs in the empty box?

⬭ She got in-line skates last year.

⬭ Jill and Judy have the same shoe size.

⬭ Judy is going to try on Jill's skates.

⬭ No one will buy old records.

GO ON ▶

Use "Money-Making Ideas for Kids" (p. 116) to answer questions 32–34.

32 The author of this selection is trying to —

- ⬭ persuade the reader to think about saving money
- ⬭ inform the reader about ways to earn some extra money
- ⬭ entertain the reader with a story about pet-sitting
- ⬭ persuade the reader to water a neighbor's plants

33 In paragraph 3, the word <u>assisting</u> means —

- ⬭ avoiding
- ⬭ helping
- ⬭ calling
- ⬭ finding

34 What is the title of this article?

- ⬭ *Kidding Around Reporter*
- ⬭ *A Magazine for 7- to 10-Year-Olds*
- ⬭ *Gia Treadwell*
- ⬭ *Money-Making Ideas for Kids*

GO ON

Use "The Garage Sale" and "Money-Making Ideas for Kids" to answer
questions 35–36.

35 These selections are both mostly about —

◯ ways kids can earn extra money

◯ ways kids can help their neighbors

◯ ways kids can repair broken toys

◯ ways kids can work together to sort their toys

36 "Money-Making Ideas for Kids" is different from "The Garage Sale" because the article —

◯ tells how to decide what to sell and what to keep

◯ tells how to organize a garage sale

◯ suggests many different ways to earn extra money

◯ tells how a garage sale can help kids earn extra money

Practice Test 2

Read the writing prompt. Use your own paper to respond to the prompt.

> Write a composition about an animal that you would like to have as a pet.

The information below will remind you what to think about as you write.

REMEMBER—YOU SHOULD

❏ follow the steps to plan, draft, revise, and edit your writing

❏ write about an animal that you would like to have as a pet

❏ write a main idea sentence that names the animal and tells why you like it

❏ write detail sentences that tell about the animal so that the reader really understands why you chose that animal

❏ try to use correct spelling, capitalization, punctuation, grammar, and sentences

GO ON

> **Read the introduction and the passage that follows. Then read each question and fill in the correct answer.**

Mai read about Grandma Moses, a famous folk artist. Mai decided to write a report about her. Read the report. Think of how to make Mai's sentences better. Then answer the questions.

Grandma Moses

(1) Anna Robertson is beter known as the folk artist Grandma Moses. (2) Folk artists are artists who dont have any training.

(3) She was a painter. (4) She began painting as a hobby when she was about 75. (5) Her paintings tell stories of her simple life in hoosick falls, a small town in upstate New York. (6) She painted pictures of sleigh rides in the snow, farmhouses, and country holidays. (7) Her paintings were shown at county fairs and hung in store windows.

(8) An art collector named Louis Caldor visited Hoosick Falls on a trip through upstate New York. (9) He liked the paintings that he saw in a store window. (10) The storeowner told Caldor that the artist lived in a farm up the road. (11) Caldor went their and met Grandma Moses. (12) He liked the farm.

(13) Grandma Moses showed Caldor more paintings. (14) Grandma Moses became one of the most famous folk artists in America. (15) She is still famous today, although she died in 1961 at the age of 101.

© HMH Supplemental Publishers Inc.

---

1 What change, if any, should be made in sentence 1?

- ⬭ Change *folk artist* to **Folk Artist**
- ⬭ Change *known* to **know**
- ⬭ Change *beter* to **better**
- ⬭ Make no change

2 What change, if any, should be made in sentence 2?

- ⬭ Change *dont* to **do'nt**
- ⬭ Change *dont* to **don't**
- ⬭ Change *dont* to **do'not**
- ⬭ Make no change

GO ON ➡

3 What is the **BEST** way to combine sentences 3 and 4?

⬭ At 75, Grandma Moses began painting as a hobby.

⬭ She began painting at 75.

⬭ She began painting. She was 75.

⬭ She was 75, so she began painting.

4 What change, if any, should be made to sentence 5?

⬭ Change *hoosick falls* to **Hoosick falls**

⬭ Change *hoosick falls* to **hoosick Falls**

⬭ Change *hoosick falls* to **Hoosick Falls**

⬭ Make no change

5 What change, if any, should be made to sentence 11?

⬭ Change *their* to **there**

⬭ Change *met* to **meet**

⬭ Insert a comma before *and*

⬭ Make no change

6 Which sentence does **NOT** belong in this report?

⬭ Sentence 4

⬭ Sentence 8

⬭ Sentence 10

⬭ Sentence 12

7 Which sentence could **BEST** be added after sentence 13?

⬭ There were a lot of paintings to show.

⬭ He took them to his art gallery, and they were bought by museums.

⬭ No one wanted to buy the paintings.

⬭ Grandma Moses didn't like the gallery.

GO ON

> **Read the introduction and the passage that follows. Then read each question and fill in the correct answer.**

Jack wrote about his cat, Puff. He wants you to read his paper and help him improve it. As you read, think about suggestions you would give Jack. Then answer the questions.

My Cat Puff

(1) When Puff was a kitten, it looked like a puffball. (2) Thats how Puff got his name. (3) My brother said cats are too hard to care for. (4) My brother is wrong.

(5) I think cats are easyer to care for than dogs. (6) Cats don't need to be walked. (7) They indoor pets. (8) Cats need some care, though. (9) Their kitty litter needs to be kept clean. (10) I don't mind. (11) Their coats need brushing. (12) Their nails need cutting. (13) Puff loves when his coat is brushed, but not when his nails are cut.

(14) Some times Puff sleeps in my bed. (15) He cuddles up next to me and purrs in my ear loudly. (16) I don't mind, though, because his purring is like music to my ears. (17) Puff is the perfect pet or should I say "purrfect"?

---

8 What change, if any, should be made to sentence 1?

- ⬭ Change *it* to **its**
- ⬭ Change *Puff* to **puff**
- ⬭ Change *it* to **he**
- ⬭ Make no change

9 What change, if any, should be made to sentence 2?

- ⬭ Change *his* to **it's**
- ⬭ Change *Thats* to **That's**
- ⬭ Change *Puff* to **puff**
- ⬭ Make no change

GO ON ➡

10 What is the **BEST** way to combine sentences 3 and 4?

- ⬭ My brother said cats are hard to care for, so he's wrong.
- ⬭ My brother is wrong. Cats are hard to care for.
- ⬭ My brother said cats are too hard to care for, but he is wrong.
- ⬭ My brother said he is wrong.

11 What change, if any, should be made to sentence 5?

- ⬭ Change *easyer* to **easier**
- ⬭ Change *cats* to **cat**
- ⬭ Change *cats* to **cat's**
- ⬭ Make no change

12 Which sentence could **BEST** be added after sentence 9?

- ⬭ Bags of kitty litter are heavy.
- ⬭ Some kids hate cleaning litter.
- ⬭ The kitty litter box is plastic.
- ⬭ Kitty litter is like sand.

13 What is the **BEST** way to combine sentences 11 and 12?

- ⬭ Their coats need brushing and their nails need cutting.
- ⬭ Coats and nails need cutting.
- ⬭ Their coat needs brushing, because their nails need cutting.
- ⬭ Their coats need brushing although they need cutting.

14 Which of the following is not a complete sentence?

- ⬭ Sentence 4
- ⬭ Sentence 7
- ⬭ Sentence 13
- ⬭ Sentence 17

15 What change, if any, should be made to sentence 14?

- ⬭ Change *Puff* to **puff**
- ⬭ Change *sleeps* to **sleep**
- ⬭ Change *Some times* to **Sometimes**
- ⬭ Make no change.

16 What change, if any, should be made to sentence 15?

- ⬭ He cuddles up to me and purr in my ear loudly.
- ⬭ He cuddles up to me, and purrs in my ear loudly.
- ⬭ He cuddles up to me and purrs loudly in my ear.
- ⬭ Make no change

GO ON ▶

> **Read the introduction and the passage that follows. Then read each question and fill in the correct answer.**

Judy wrote a report on American schoolhouses of 200 years ago. Read her report. Think about how to make her sentences better. Then answer the questions.

A One-Room Schoolhouse

(1) About 200 years ago, most children in America went to a schoolhouse that had only one room. (2) Children from the first to the eighth grades were taught they're lessons in that one classroom. (3) Sum one-room schools had as many as 40 children. (4) Others had as few as six. (5) One teacher taught reading writing math history English and all other subjects.

(6) The teacher's desk was at the front of the room facing them. (7) The youngest children sat. (8) In the front of the room. (9) They wore old-fashioned clothes. (10) The oldest children sat in the back. (11) In some schools, the boys sat on one side of the room. (12) The girls sat on the other side of the room. (13) When the teacher called on a student, they stood up and answered the question. (14) The children who were in the same grade listened to the teacher's lesson. (15) The other children sat quietly reading their books or sat quietly writing their lessons while other children were reading their books.

(16) Would you like to be in a one-room schoolhouse. (17) As to me, I just don't know what I'd want. (18) We get along now, but who knows how wed feel after years and years in the same room?

---

17 What change, if any, should be made in sentence 2?

- ⬭ Change *classroom* to **class room**
- ⬭ Change *they're* to **there**
- ⬭ Change *they're* to **their**
- ⬭ Make no change

18 What change, if any, should be made in sentence 3?

- ⬭ Change *Sum* to **Some**
- ⬭ Change *children* to **childs**
- ⬭ Change *many* to **mini**
- ⬭ Make no change

GO ON ▶

19 What is the **BEST** way to revise sentence 5?

⬭ That one teacher taught reading. That teacher taught writing and math. That teacher taught English and all other subjects.

⬭ That one teacher taught reading, writing, math, history, English, and all other subjects.

⬭ That one teacher taught. Writing and math. English and all other subjects.

⬭ That one teacher taught reading, writing, math, history. And English and all other subjects.

20 The meaning of sentence 6 can be improved by changing **them** to —

⬭ each classroom
⬭ herself
⬭ the children
⬭ school

21 Which of the following is **NOT** a complete sentence?

⬭ Sentence 4
⬭ Sentence 5
⬭ Sentence 6
⬭ Sentence 8

22 Which sentence does **NOT** belong in this report?

⬭ Sentence 5
⬭ Sentence 6
⬭ Sentence 7
⬭ Sentence 9

23 What is the **BEST** way to combine sentences 11 and 12?

⬭ In some schools, the boys sat on one side of the room and the girls sat on the other side.

⬭ In some schools, the boys and girls sat on the side.

⬭ In some schools the boys sat on one side of the room so the girls sat on the other side of the room.

⬭ The boys sat on one side of the room the girls sat on one side of the room.

GO ON ➤

24 The meaning of sentence 13 can be improved by changing *they* to —

- ⬭ the teacher
- ⬭ that student
- ⬭ it
- ⬭ her

25 What is the **BEST** way to rewrite the ideas in sentence 15?

- ⬭ The other children sat quietly.
- ⬭ The other children were not reading or writing.
- ⬭ The other children sat quietly reading their books or writing their lessons.
- ⬭ The other children sat and read books.

26 What change, if any, should be made in sentence 16?

- ⬭ Change *me* to **I**
- ⬭ Change the period to a question mark
- ⬭ Change *would* to **wood**
- ⬭ Make no change

27 What change, if any, should be made in sentence 17?

- ⬭ Change *As to me* to **As for me**
- ⬭ Change *don't* to **do'nt**
- ⬭ Change *I'd* to **Id**
- ⬭ Make no change

28 What change, if any, should be made in sentence 18?

- ⬭ Change the question mark to a period
- ⬭ Delete the comma
- ⬭ Change *wed* to **we'd**
- ⬭ Make no change

STOP